Catastrophic Success

A VOLUME IN THE SERIES

Cornell Studies in Security Affairs

Edited by Robert J. Art, Alexander B. Downes, Kelly M. Greenhill,
Robert Jervis, Caitlin Talmadge, and Stephen M. Walt

Founding series editors: Robert J. Art and Robert Jervis

A list of titles in this series is available at cornellpress.cornell.edu.

Catastrophic Success

Why Foreign-Imposed Regime Change Goes Wrong

ALEXANDER B. DOWNES

Cornell University Press

Ithaca and London

First published 2021 by Cornell University Press

ISBN 978-1-5017-6114-0 (hardcover)
ISBN 978-1-5017-6116-4 (pdf)
ISBN 978-1-5017-6115-7 (epub)

Library of Congress Control Number: 2021944993

For Lisa, Connor, and Amelia

Contents

Figures and Tables

Tables

Acknowledgments

When it takes you a decade to write a book, a lot of "stuff happens," in the immortal words of former secretary of defense Donald Rumsfeld. Among other things, I have left one institution and moved to another; gotten divorced and remarried; and become a father to two amazing children. The danger, of course, is that with all that water under the bridge, you start to forget all those who helped you along the way. With that plea for forgiveness to anyone I have left out, here goes.

Behind the writing of every book there is a story. The seeds of this book were sown in March 2003 as I stood in the lobby of the Weatherhead Center for International Affairs at Harvard University, watching on television as US troops poured into Iraq. Being at the time immersed in research about targeting civilians in war, there was not much I could do other than think to myself, "this is a really bad idea." But as Iraq went up in flames and the Taliban made a resurgence in the mid-2000s, I returned to the subject and began thinking about why states pursue foreign-imposed regime change. I undertook my first serious research on the topic while on leave from Duke University as a postdoctoral fellow at the Belfer Center for Science and International Affairs at the Harvard Kennedy School in 2007–08, a highly congenial scholarly atmosphere. I thank Steve Miller, Sean Lynn-Jones, Steve Walt, and Susan Lynch for hosting me there.

The direction of the project changed radically after a lunch at the 2008 International Studies Association annual meetings in San Francisco with the inimitable John Mearsheimer. John proceeded to tell me that the causes of regime change were not interesting (presumably he changed his mind by the time Lindsey O'Rourke began her dissertation—which became the

ACKNOWLEDGMENTS

basis for her award-winning book in this series—on the causes of covert regime change). Rather, it was the *consequences* that were interesting, and furthermore—never one to come to lunch without an argument—he told me I should argue that regime change doesn't work. After I finished fuming at being informed that my big idea for a "second project" was a flop, I had to admit old John had a point. This is not to disparage all of the excellent work that has been done in the intervening years on why regime change occurs, much of which I draw on in this book. For me, however, understanding the fallout of such interventions was more urgent to understand. In March 2008, the surge in Iraq notwithstanding, recent US regime changes were not looking like winning propositions. Yet there were at least a handful of "successes" in the historical record (such as Germany and Japan after World War II). Why did some regime changes go horribly awry whereas others yielded stable, prosperous allies?

Colleagues at Duke who provided feedback on the project in its early stages include Peter Feaver, Chris Gelpi, Guillermo Trejo, and Erik Wibbels. I also want to thank Tanisha Fazal, then at Columbia University, for generously sharing her dataset on state death, which helped get my data collection efforts off the ground. While at Duke I benefited from participation in the Triangle Institute for Security Studies (TISS), a consortium of security scholars from multiple disciplines centered on Duke, the University of North Carolina at Chapel Hill, and North Carolina State University. I particularly appreciated my interactions with the group's historians, including Joe Caddell, Richard Kohn, Carolyn Pumphrey, and Alex Roland, who—although they mostly thought us political scientists and our theories were crazy—were nevertheless unfailingly cordial and supportive.

After moving to The George Washington University (GW) in 2011, I was surrounded by an extremely talented group of International Relations and security scholars with whom I was privileged to interact on a regular basis, including Michael Barnett, Mike Brown (who, as Dean of the Elliott School of International Affairs, helped recruit me to GW), Steve Biddle, Henry Farrell, Martha Finnemore, Charlie Glaser, Eric Grynaviski, Stephen Kaplan, Yon Lupu, Mike Mochizuki, Harris Mylonas, Henry Nau, Elizabeth Saunders, Joanna Spear, Rachel Stein, Caitlin Talmadge, and Paul Williams. I have learned a great deal from all of them and appreciate their collegiality and friendship.

Having composed much of the project as papers on the effect of regime change on this or that outcome, I faced the challenge of pulling this work together into a coherent manuscript. I dedicated an unexpected sabbatical year in 2017–18 to this task, as well as to performing much of the statistical analysis and researching and writing many of the book's case studies. With two small children at home, my "office" for much of this work was American University's Pence Law Library and the Cathedral Heights Starbucks on

Wisconsin Avenue, near my home in northwest Washington. I thank the staff and students at the library for tolerating my presence and the Starbucks staff for providing untold gallons of dark roast coffee.

In December 2018, I was extremely fortunate to have a day-long workshop on the draft manuscript hosted by the Institute for Security and Conflict Studies at GW and chaired by my colleague and friend Charlie Glaser. Although I may have absorbed perhaps 5 to 10 percent of what was said that day, I could revisit the collective wisdom shared by the participants thanks to copious notes taken by GW Political Science PhD students Danielle Gilbert and Stephen Rangazas. I can never sufficiently thank the scholars who convened that day for their invaluable advice: Hein Goemans, Matt Kocher, John Mearsheimer (on his birthday, no less), Lindsey O'Rourke, Jack Snyder, and Melissa Willard-Foster. I also thank my GW and DC-area colleagues who joined for all or part of the day, including Yon Lupu, Elizabeth Saunders, Todd Sechser, and Caitlin Talmadge. I did not always take your advice, but the manuscript improved immeasurably from your wise input.

I would like to thank the numerous individuals who read and commented on various parts of this book over the years, some of them multiple times: Robert Art, Mia Bloom, Jasen Castillo, Jon Caverley, Simon Collard-Wexler, Stephen David, Michael Desch, David Edelstein, Matthew Fuhrmann, Payam Ghalehdar, Charlie Glaser, Kelly Greenhill, J. Michael Greig, Stephen Kaplan, Michael T. Koch, Peter Krause, David Lake, Jeffrey Legro, Jason Lyall, Michael McKoy, Lindsey O'Rourke, John Owen, Stephen Rangazas, Patricia Sullivan, Melissa Willard-Foster, and Paul Williams. I am especially grateful to Lindsey O'Rourke for our fruitful collaboration over the years, which has greatly influenced my thinking on the effects of regime change. I thank my editor at Cornell University Press, Roger Haydon, for his kind encouragement and incisive comments at key points. The two anonymous reviewers for Cornell (one of whom revealed himself to be John Owen) also provided extensive constructive feedback, for which I am deeply indebted.

I am grateful to audiences at the following institutions where I presented parts of this book for their comments and reactions: Emory University; the University of South Carolina Political Science Department; the Lone Star National Security Forum; the Notre Dame International Security Program; Duke University's Security, Peace, and Conflict Workshop; the Program on Order, Conflict, and Violence and the MacMillan International Relations Seminar, both at Yale University; the Air Force Office of Scientific Research's "Effects to Influence Workshop," held at the College of William and Mary; the Institute for Security and Conflict Studies' Research in Progress Workshop and the Political Science Department's Comparative Politics Workshop, both at GW; American University's International Relations Workshop Colloquium; the Symposium on Political Violence at the University of Pittsburgh; the Seminar on Conflict and Political Violence at the Olympia Summer

Academy; the Bush School of Government and Public Service at Texas A&M University; and the Cato Institute. Thanks to all of you who kindly invited me to talk about my research on regime change.

This book would not have been possible without the help of numerous undergraduate and graduate student research assistants at Duke and GW. I thank the following for their contributions: Ditra Backup, Andrew Bell, Amber Diaz, Caitlin Gorback, Jamie Gordon, Alexander Gorin, Vanes Ibric, Daniel Jacobs, Michael Joseph, Daniel Krcmaric, Julia Macdonald, Michael Weaver, and Paul Zachary.

I was lucky to receive financial support from several institutions to support the research and writing of this book. I would like to thank Duke University's Arts and Sciences Committee on Faculty Research; the Smith Richardson Foundation (Junior Faculty Research Grant); and the Office of Naval Research (U.S. Navy Grant No. N00014–09–1–0557). In particular, I thank Mia Bloom for inviting me to participate in the ONR grant.

Portions of this book are based on my previously published work in the journal *International Security*. Parts of chapter 1 appeared in "Forced to Be Free: Why Foreign-Imposed Regime Change Rarely Leads to Democratization," *International Security* 37, no. 4 (Spring 2013): 90–131 (with Jonathan Monten). Portions of chapters 2 and 5 are derived from "You Can't Always Get What You Want: Why Foreign-Imposed Regime Change Seldom Improves Interstate Relations," *International Security* 41, no. 2 (Fall 2016): 43–89 (with Lindsey A. O'Rourke). I thank the journal's publisher, MIT Press, for permission to reproduce this material herein. I also thank several scholars who took the trouble to pen responses to these articles, including William G. Nomikos, Michael Poznansky, and Ruolin Su.

Finally, I owe an immense debt of gratitude to my family. My parents, Bryan and Sheri Downes, although on the opposite end of the country, continue to provide their love and support from a distance. My in-laws, Andy and Richard Danzig, are wonderful people—and not just because they live nearby and have a swimming pool! They are welcoming, kind, generous, and also amazing grandparents. My wife, Lisa Danzig, has been unfailingly supportive throughout the process of finishing this book, helping me to keep going and believing in me when I didn't even believe in myself. Writing a book is not an easy experience, and I would be lying if I said I was always a pleasure to deal with over the years it has taken me to complete these pages. Lisa, I cannot thank you enough for putting up with me. Finally, my children Connor and Amelia make it a joy to wake up every morning. Perhaps one day you will read this book and realize that's what Daddy was doing all that time!

Abbreviations

AFDL	Alliance des Forces Démocratiques pour la Libération du Congo-Zaïre
AFRC	Armed Forces Revolutionary Council (Sierra Leone)
AQI	Al Qaeda in Iraq
ARVN	Army of the Republic of Vietnam
CENTCOM	U.S. Central Command
CIA	Central Intelligence Agency
CINC	Composite Index of National Capabilities
COIN	counterinsurgency
COW	Correlates of War
CPA	Coalition Provisional Authority
DRC	Democratic Republic of Congo
ECOWAS	Economic Community of West African States
EFP	explosively formed penetrator
ELF	ethnolinguistic fractionalization
ENG	National Guerrilla Army (Spain)
FAC	Forces Armées Congolaises
FAR	Forces Armées Rwandaises
FATA	Federally Administered Tribal Areas
FIRC	foreign-imposed regime change
FRG	Federal Republic of Germany
GDR	German Democratic Republic
IR	international relations
IS	Islamic State
ISI	Inter-Services Intelligence (Pakistan)
IV	instrumental variables

JUI	Jamiat Ulema-e-Islam (Pakistan)
KUFNS	Kampuchea United Front for National Salvation
MAAG	Military Assistance Advisory Group
MACV	Military Assistance Command Vietnam
MCT	militarized compellent threat
MID	militarized interstate dispute
MR-13	Movimiento Revolucionario 13 de Noviembre (Revolutionary Movement of November 13, Guatemala)
MRC	Military Revolutionary Council (South Vietnam)
NATO	North Atlantic Treaty Organization
NLF	National Liberation Front (South Vietnam)
ORHA	Office of Reconstruction and Humanitarian Assistance
PA	principal-agent
PGT	Partido Guatemalteco de Trabajo (Guatemalan Communist Party)
RPA	Rwandan Patriotic Army
RPF	Rwandan Patriotic Front
RUF	Revolutionary United Front (Sierra Leone)
SAVAK	National Organization for Security and Intelligence (Iran)
SCIRI	Supreme Council for the Islamic Revolution in Iraq
SFA	security force assistance
SOF	Special Operations Forces
SOI	Sons of Iraq
UCDP	Uppsala Conflict Data Program
UFCO	United Fruit Company
UNGA	United Nations General Assembly
UNLA	Uganda National Liberation Army
UNSC	United Nations Security Council
USDS	United States Department of State
VC	Viet Cong (South Vietnam)
WMD	weapons of mass destruction

Introduction

Once upon a time, a large, modern army from a rich and powerful nation invaded Afghanistan, bent on overthrowing its recalcitrant leader and bringing a more accommodating ruler to power. After a brief and unequal fight, the targeted leader and his entourage fled the capital and escaped into exile. The commander of the victorious army soon installed a new leader friendly to his country's interests in Kabul and began contemplating a quick exit. But there was to be no happy ending to this fairy tale. The new ruler was not popular with his people, who resented the fact that he came to power—and remained in power—at the point of foreign bayonets and implemented policies that favored foreign interests. Soon outbreaks of rebellion spread across the country and the leader and his foreign backers were confronted with full-scale revolt. After years of failing to bring the insurgency under control, and suffering some embarrassing military defeats, political leaders in the foreign capital decided that they could not afford to fund an open-ended military commitment in a rugged country far away. After exacting a measure of revenge for previous defeats, the troops packed their equipment and withdrew, leaving the leader they had empowered to fend for himself against his domestic foes. He did not survive long. Shortly after the departure of his foreign patrons he was assassinated. A few months later he was replaced by the very same man who had been overthrown in the first place.

To contemporary readers, this story may sound eerily similar to the US experience following its invasion of Afghanistan in October 2001. That adventure began by ousting the theocratic Taliban regime, which refused to hand over Osama bin Laden and his crew of Al Qaeda militants who were responsible for the September 11 terrorist attacks in the United States. The toppling of the Taliban, however, was the sixth time an Afghan regime had been overthrown by foreign forces since 1839, putting Afghanistan second only to Honduras (eight cases) as the most frequent target of externally engineered changes of government over the last two hundred years.

Although the US intervention in Afghanistan at the time of writing appears to be winding down, the story above is based on the first foray by the

1

British into Afghanistan, from 1839 to 1842, when they overthrew Afghan Emir Dost Mohammad and replaced him with their own candidate, Shah Shuja ul-Mulk. In that campaign, according to one account, "fearing the growth of Russian influence over Dost Muhammad . . . the British attempted to replace him with a former emir more sympathetic to their desire to protect the northern approaches to India."[1] Aside from its outcome, this case shares many other features with recent regime changes, such as the US invasions of Afghanistan and Iraq. Like the US-led attack on Iraq in 2003, for example, this one had its threat inflators, such as Sir George de Lacy Evans, who described in his 1829 tract *On the Practicability of an Invasion of British India* how a Russian force of 60,000 men could somehow cross the Hindu Kush mountains, seize Herat, traverse the Khyber Pass, and threaten British India.[2] The British invasion of Afghanistan, also like the US-led attack on Iraq, was preceded by predictions of a quick and easy victory followed by an early withdrawal. In the Simla Manifesto announcing the British invasion, for instance, Lord Auckland, governor-general of India, foreshadowed Vice-President Dick Cheney's prediction that Iraqis would welcome US troops as liberators: "The Governor-General confidently hopes that the Shah will be speedily replaced on his throne by his own subjects and adherents; and once he shall be secured in power, and the independence and integrity of Afghanistan established, the British Army will be withdrawn."[3] And like the US-led invasion of Afghanistan, the British operation was plagued by policymakers' overconfidence and quick distraction by another war. As the historian William Dalrymple writes, "rather than concentrating on consolidating Shah Shuja's fragile rule in Afghanistan, and providing the resources needed to make the occupation viable and secure, Lord Auckland—like more recent invaders—instead took the premature view that the conquest was already complete and so allowed himself to be distracted by launching another war of aggression in a different theatre"—the Opium War in China.[4]

The practice of intervening in another country to remove its government and bring alternative leaders to power has come to be known as foreign-imposed regime change (FIRC).[5] The history of regime change is replete with stories like Afghanistan's. The British, for example, having seemingly learned nothing from their first Afghan debacle, invaded again in 1878 for the same reason (supposed Russian encroachment on Kabul), for the same purpose (to install a leader who would protect British interests), and with the same outcome (massive revolt after initial victory).[6] Similar fates befell regime-change efforts by France in Mexico in the 1860s; Guatemala in El Salvador and Honduras in the 1860s and 1870s; Brazil and Argentina in Paraguay in the 1870s; Chile in Peru in the 1880s; the United States in Haiti, the Dominican Republic, and Nicaragua in the 1910s and 1920s; Germany and Italy in the Balkans in the 1940s; the United States in South Vietnam in the 1960s; the Soviets in Afghanistan, Vietnam in Cambodia, and Tanzania in Uganda in the late 1970s and 1980s; Rwanda and Uganda in the Democratic Republic of Congo in the

1990s; and the United States in Afghanistan and Iraq in the early 2000s. In each of these cases, outside powers displaced one leader and empowered another (sometimes more than one) only for that leader to be overthrown by domestic opponents or for a civil war to break out. In some cases, the intervener's forces—if they remained in occupation of the target state—were drawn into combat with rebellious factions. In other cases, a further intervention or change of leader was required to try to stabilize the situation. And in still others, the intervener and target ended up in a militarized interstate dispute or a war. Why does regime change so frequently result in conflict—either inside the target state or between the intervener and the target?

Although the history of regime change is not solely of unmitigated disaster, successes are few and far between. In a few cases, externally imposed regimes survive and even thrive. The examples of Japan and West Germany after World War II are the shining success stories, but Panama made a successful and peaceful transition to democracy after the ouster of Manuel Noriega, as did tiny Grenada after the US invasion of 1983. The countries of Eastern and Central Europe during the Cold War achieved basic political and economic stability if not democracy and affluence after Soviet regime changes at the conclusion of World War II. Many small European monarchies managed to survive for decades after their overthrown rulers were restored to their thrones by the conservative powers Austria and Prussia in the nineteenth century. More recently, the shah of Iran remained in office for twenty-five years following the US-backed ouster of Mohammad Mossadegh in 1953. Other Cold War–era strongmen who gained power after foreign-assisted coups—such as Joseph Mobutu and Augusto Pinochet—survived nearly as long. Why does regime change sometimes result in peace and stability but other times lead to conflict and violence?

There is no single theory of why states undertake regime change in foreign countries.[7] Most existing explanations, however, have a common logic: states intervene to alter the preferences of other states and bring them into alignment with their own.[8] According to this logic, successful regime changes—by reducing the degree of preference divergence between states—ought to result in improved relations.[9] Interveners can thus use regime change to obtain accommodating and reliable allies or client states. As explained below, interveners can align a target's preferences with their own by installing like-minded individuals in power, remaking the political ideology and/or institutions of the target government, or both. As John Owen writes in his sweeping study of five hundred years of foreign regime promotion, "governments or rulers who use force to promote an ideology abroad nearly always believe it is in their interests to do so." Moreover, Owen claims they are usually correct: "When an intervention succeeds, the government that did the promotion is better off, the country it governs more secure."[10]

Although some readers may find it hard to believe in the wake of Afghanistan, Iraq, and Libya that regime change can "work," it has no shortage of contemporary backers. In the few academic studies of the effects of regime change, one finds that wars are less likely to recur when the winner imposes a new regime on the loser.[11] Other analysts support this view, arguing that "while Libya may be a recent stain on the U.S. record, the last century of 'regime change' as opponents of an internationalist policy label it, is one of amazing success."[12] Still others concede that recent US regime changes had undesirable outcomes but attribute these failings to misguided policy choices in particular cases rather than anything inherent in regime change itself.[13] With regard to Iraq, for example, this view, according to Michael MacDonald, maintains that "the taproot of failure was not the objective of regime change in Iraq, with whatever that entailed, but merely the [Bush] administration's inept efforts."[14] If done correctly, in other words, regime change can work. Finally, top former Trump administration officials such as Secretary of Defense James Mattis, Secretaries of State Rex Tillerson and Mike Pompeo, and National Security Advisor John Bolton have argued that regime change is the solution to Washington's problems with Iran.[15]

This book investigates the effects of regime change on relations between interveners and targets and on domestic conditions in the latter. To do so, it asks two principal questions. First, why does regime change, undertaken to improve relations between two states, so often go awry, failing to advance those relations and triggering further conflict—both inside the target of regime change and between the target and the intervener? Military intervention typically involves blood and treasure; are the costs of using force for regime change justified by the payoff afterward? Second, why do some regime change operations turn out better than others? Are there conditions under which regime change is more or less successful at producing good interstate relations and domestic peace and stability?

Although a variety of studies assess the effects of regime change in individual cases, and a few examine multiple cases carried out by the same country (typically the United States), there is no study that includes the universe of successful regime changes enacted by all countries in the world over an extended period of time.[16] Moreover, most existing studies focus only on cases in which regime change occurred, but do not compare instances of regime change to cases where it was absent, or where it was attempted but failed.[17] Doing so, however, is necessary to establish whether regime change actually *causes* domestic strife in targets and conflict between targets and interveners, or merely occurs where these outcomes were already more likely to happen.

The Argument

The argument of this book is that regime change that is undertaken to produce governments in target states whose preferences are aligned with those of interveners does not reliably do so. Instead, regime change often fails to

4

KEY TO CATASTROPHES AFTER REGIME CHANGE
1. Military disintegration
2. Competing principals (Intervening state vs domestic constituents)

INTRODUCTION

improve relations between interveners and targets: patron states and their protégés are no less likely than other pairs of states to come to blows after regime change, and patrons face great difficulty inducing protégé leaders to do their bidding. Moreover, leaders who come to power in foreign-imposed regime changes are more likely than other leaders to lose power violently, and states that experience regime change suffer from a heightened risk of civil strife over the ensuing decade. In short, regime change is an example of what might be termed a "catastrophic success": because it is so often carried out by stronger actors, regime change often achieves its short-term objective of overthrowing a targeted regime, but the longer-term consequences of this initial success are frequently disastrous.[18] Why does regime change produce these unwanted outcomes?

My theory explains these violent outcomes through two mechanisms. The first, which I label *military disintegration,* elaborates how regime change can produce immediate insurgency and civil war by fragmenting and dispersing the target's military forces. The second, the *problem of competing principals*, details how the mismatched preferences of imposed leaders' two masters—the intervening state and a leader's domestic audience—place leaders in a dilemma in which responding to the interests of one exacerbates the risk of conflict with the other, thereby increasing the likelihood of both patron-protégé conflict and internal conflict in the target.[19]

Framed slightly differently, regime change increases the likelihood of internal violence and external strife by undermining two key components of statehood, defined as a "human community that (successfully) claims the *monopoly of the legitimate use of physical force* within a given territory."[20] Military disintegration breaks the state's *monopoly on the use* of force, thereby increasing the likelihood of armed challenges (ironically by former members of the state's military). The problem of competing principals undermines the government's *legitimacy* in the eyes of its people by placing puppets at the helm of the state who are perceived to be in thrall to—and to cater to the interests of—a foreign power.

First, in cases of regime changes carried out by invasion, the resulting war may simply break the state's monopoly on the use of force by causing the target state's military to disintegrate. I define military disintegration as a situation in which the target state's army is defeated but, rather than surrendering, it breaks apart, allowing a significant fraction to melt away or escape to remote regions or across borders. In contrast to successful compellence, in which an intervener persuades a targeted leader to resign without having to use significant amounts of force, or military surrender, when the target state's military is defeated on the battlefield but remains cohesive and gives up in an orderly fashion, military disintegration is likely to spawn an insurgency launched by elements of the former regime. The reason for this increased risk of insurgency is that military disintegration provides both motive and opportunity for ousted leaders or factions to rebel. The motive is anger over an unceremonious and violent ouster; the opportunity is the existence of a residual armed force to pursue hostilities.[21] Even when the former leader is captured, killed, or otherwise unable to lead the resistance, military disintegration disperses thousands of armed men into the countryside who may be mobilized for further resistance by subordinates of the old leader or by entirely new leaders. Military disintegration often draws interveners into costly and protracted counterinsurgency campaigns to defend their newly installed protégés and their interests in the country, quagmires that may outweigh the benefit of changing the regime in the first place.[22] Military disintegration is thus the determinant of immediate insurgency and civil war after regime change. The US invasions of Afghanistan in 2001 and Iraq in 2003, for example, both resulted in military disintegration.

Second, the problem of competing principals explains how regime change, intended to align a target state's preferences with an intervener's by replacing leaders who refuse to implement an intervener's preferred policies with new ones who will, can end up reproducing the asymmetry of interests that prompted the intervener to resort to regime change in the first place. I argue that the key problem arises from the simple reality that no two states have identical interests. Interveners view regime change as a means to solve this problem—to remove leaders whose policies endanger the intervener's security or threaten its interests—and replace those leaders with different ones who will implement policies that are more congruent with the preferences of the intervener. The intervener—the "principal" in the language of principal-agent theory—tries to bring the interests of the two states into line by selecting a leader (an "agent") with compatible beliefs or policy priorities to its own.[23]

This attempt to align interveners' and targets' preferences by installing an agent who shares the intervener's preferences runs afoul of several problems that plague principal-agent relationships. First, principals are never completely informed about the quality and preferences of agents, which may lead them unwittingly to select an unqualified or otherwise undesirable agent—a problem known as *adverse selection*. Second, agents' interests are never fully consonant with those of principals, which creates incentives for agents to "shirk" (pursue their own interests at the expense of the principal's)—a problem known as *interest asymmetry*. Third, principals cannot fully observe agents' actions, which means that it is difficult for principals to detect when an agent is shirking—a problem known as *information asymmetry*.

In addition to these well-known difficulties of principal-agent relationships, foreign-imposed regime change suffers from another, less recognized, problem: the intervener is not the only principal trying to exercise control over the agent. Whether through voting or violence, all leaders are accountable to their domestic audiences, which may remove leaders who perform poorly or whose preferences diverge substantially from their own. A leader's domestic audience, in other words, constitutes a *second principal*.

A key claim of this book is that the preferences of these internal principals—although they may converge with those of external principals in rare circumstances—are typically at odds with the preferences of foreign interveners on at least some key issues. Each principal will try to induce the agent to take actions consistent with its preferences.[24]

Because foreign-imposed leaders are in effect agents of competing principals with divergent preferences, each of which can remove them from office, these leaders face a difficult dilemma. If, on the one hand, they maintain their commitment to uphold the intervener's directives—in effect ignoring their internal principal—they risk alienating domestic groups, which may seek to oust them, setting the stage for coups, rebellion, and civil war. This threat is very real. As this book shows, foreign-imposed leaders are overthrown or otherwise removed in a violent, "irregular" manner by domestic forces in nearly half of all cases. Similarly, one-third of all regime changes are followed by civil war within a decade. If, on the other hand, imposed leaders respond to the wishes of their internal principals—in effect breaking their prior commitments to their patrons—interveners may grow dissatisfied and attempt to push the leader out in favor of someone else more willing and able to deliver favorable policies. This dissatisfaction paves the way for another intervention or a militarized confrontation between intervener and target. At the very least, interveners will experience difficulty in persuading their protégés to enact policies that promote their interests.

In short, I argue that regime change simultaneously increases the risk of coups and civil conflict within the target state and increases the likelihood of interstate conflict between interveners and targets. The mechanism that generates the increased probability of both types of conflict is the asymmetry of interests between the leader's internal and external principals. The form that conflict takes in any particular case depends on whose interests an imposed leader is more responsive to, which in turn likely depends on which of the two principals poses the most immediate and credible threat to the leader's political (or physical) survival.

Despite the many disasters that have followed regime change, some regime changes turn out better than others. What explains this variation? I argue that regime changes vary in how acutely they activate the imposed leader's dilemma. As I elaborate in chapter 1, regime changes vary along two axes: whether they elevate a new leader to power or restore the immediately preceding leader, and whether or not they build new political institutions. Regime changes that empower new elites without building new institutions are known as *leadership regime changes*. Interventions that build new institutions in addition to installing new leaders are *institutional regime changes*. Regime changes that restore the previous government can do so by reinstating the prior leader, institutions, or both. In practice, regime changes that reempower the previous leader invariably restore the prior institutions as well, although the reverse is not always true.[25] Such cases are known as *restoration regime changes*.

Leadership regime changes replace one foreign leader with another without building new political institutions within the target state. (In fact, sometimes leadership regime changes deinstitutionalize target states, dismantling existing institutions without replacing them.) Elites installed during leadership regime changes face the problem of competing principals most severely. Because these leaders typically lack homegrown support, they are domestically unpopular and rely on their external patron to sustain their rule. Implementing the intervener's policies, however, alienates domestic constituencies. These leaders are thus likely to face strong internal pressures to break their commitment or else risk violent resistance, and hence face an elevated risk of civil war. Whether imposed leaders turn against the intervener on their own initiative or are displaced by other leaders who do so, leadership regime changes are also more likely to trigger intervener-target conflict.

Institutional regime changes seek to build new political institutions—either democratic or nondemocratic—in the target state in addition to replacing leaders.[26] I argue that *in the aggregate*, institutional regime changes neither increase nor decrease the likelihood of civil or intervener-target conflict but that this overall null finding conceals strong contradictory effects depending on whether the regime changes succeed or fail in building new institutions.

There are two distinct types of institutional regime change. The first variant aims to install repressive institutions, which increase the new leader's ability to survive in office by enhancing his capacity to crush domestic resistance. This repressive capacity enables him to carry out the intervener's policies without simultaneously raising the risk of removal at the hands of domestic forces, thereby ensuring harmonious relations. In effect, repressive institutional regime changes deactivate the problem of competing principals by eliminating the domestic principal's ability to express its preferences. The second variant of institutional regime change seeks to construct democratic institutions and promotes peaceful internal and external relations through different mechanisms.[27] Internally, the opportunities for political participation available to democratic citizens reduce the need for violence to effect domestic change, thereby lowering the likelihood of civil conflict. Democracies are also less likely than autocracies to experience coups, meaning that a democratic target backsliding into an autocracy is unlikely to provoke conflict with an intervener.[28] Finally, the ability of democracies to resolve their differences without violence additionally lowers the likelihood of interstate conflict.[29] Institutional regime changes that promote democracy, in other words, render the problem of competing principals less harmful because they remove incentives to use violence to resolve any disputes that may arise.

Common to both types of institutional regime change, however, is that interveners, in addition to promoting institutions, may promote ideologies as well. Shared ideology may further help interveners and targets avoid conflict after regime change.

Crucially, however, these mechanisms can exert their pacifying effects only if interveners *succeed* at building new institutions in targets. Failed institutional regime changes will tend to resemble leadership regime changes and will confront similarly escalated probabilities of the types of conflict explored in this book. What determines whether such regime changes succeed or fail at constructing institutions? I argue that conditions in target states conducive to stability and democratization, including high per capita income, ethnic homogeneity, and previous experience with democracy (in democracy-promoting regime changes) are the critical factors. Institutional regime changes carried out in countries where these conditions are present are more likely to succeed and reduce the likelihood of internal and intervener-target conflict.

Finally, restoration regime changes reinstate the government (leaders, institutions, or both) that most recently held power in the target state, assuming it has not been out of power for more than five years. I argue that restorations do not increase—and may actually decrease—the likelihood of internal and external conflict. At first glance this hypothesis may appear counterintuitive. Leaders who must be restored to office by an external power because they were overthrown by the domestic opposition, for example, must have been weak, unpopular, or both. Moreover, these leaders would seemingly be subject to the same dilemma of regime change that plagues other foreign-imposed leaders, pulled between the conflicting interests of an external patron and a domestic audience.

Two other factors about the context in which restoration regime changes occur, however, push in the opposite direction. One is the fact that many restorations return to office democratic regimes that were removed by foreign powers in prior regime changes, governments that were already accepted as popular and legitimate by their citizens and which had no conflicts of interest with the states that restored them.[30] A second is that successful restoration regime changes are akin to decisive victories in civil wars. Rebels in most such cases are heavily outgunned by interveners and are quickly crushed (nineteenth-century examples include Prussia in Baden and Saxony, and Austria in Tuscany and Modena), thereby removing the source of the conflicting interests that drives internal and external conflicts after regime changes. Because restorations sometimes reempower popular regimes and can eliminate the problem of competing principals, I hypothesize that such regime changes will not increase, and may possibly decrease, the likelihood of conflict inside targets and between targets and interveners.

Overview of the Evidence

My theory implies that *within* target states, foreign-imposed regime change ought to increase the likelihood of civil war and violent leader removal. *Between* interveners and targets, my theory implies that regime change increases the likelihood of interstate conflict. The theory further posits that two mechanisms—military disintegration and the problem of competing principals—explain these three forms of conflict. Finally, my theory holds that of the three types of regime change, leadership regime change is the most dangerous. The effect of institutional regime change should vary depending on factors internal to target states, and restoration regime change ought to be the most benign of the three types. I find ample evidence for these suppositions using statistical analysis of quantitative data and historical investigations of cases of regime change from the history of the past two hundred years.

In the first of three empirical chapters (chapter 3), I show that regime change substantially increases the likelihood that a target state experiences a civil war in the ensuing decade. I define civil war as an armed conflict inside a recognized state involving the government and one or more organized nonstate actors that causes at least one thousand combat deaths. Importantly, the term "government" refers to whoever is responsible for running the state, whether that is an indigenous actor or a foreign occupation authority, such as the United States in Iraq in 2003 and 2004 and Nazi Germany in many European states during World War II.[31] Internal rebellions against either type of government constitute civil wars.

I find that experiencing a regime change doubles the likelihood that a state suffers a civil war in the ensuing decade, and specifically that suffering a leadership regime change nearly triples the likelihood. Although other types of regime change have no significant effect on the probability of civil war, institutional regime change interacts with local conditions in interesting ways. Instances of regime change that promote new institutions in especially poor or ethnically heterogeneous locales increase the likelihood of civil war, whereas the same regime changes effected in wealthier or more homogeneous countries do not. Finally, contrary to previous research, I show that although civil war is more likely when regime change occurs simultaneously with defeat in an interstate war, the probability is not significantly greater than experiencing regime change alone.[32] This finding suggests that regime change is sufficient to bring about civil war on its own.[33]

In the qualitative section of chapter 3, I conduct numerous case studies to investigate the process through which regime change contributes to the outbreak of civil war.[34] The first three cases—insurgencies by the Khmer Rouge in Cambodia (1979–92), the Taliban in Afghanistan (2003 to present), and Sunni militants in Iraq (2003–11)—trace the military disintegration mechanism, whereby an army defeated in an interstate war disintegrates, flees to remote areas or across borders, and returns to wage a guerrilla insurgency against the new regime. I document the problem of competing principals, in which civil war is caused by the mismatched preferences of an imposed leader's foreign patron and domestic audience, in a further three cases: the First Afghan War (1839–42), Nicaragua's civil war in 1912, and the Guatemalan insurgency that followed the US-sponsored overthrow of Jacobo Árbenz in 1954.

In the second empirical chapter (chapter 4), I turn to the question of how long foreign-imposed leaders survive in office compared to other leaders. My theory implies that rulers brought to power in regime changes face an elevated risk of "irregular" removal from office, defined as taking place "in contravention of explicit rules and established conventions. . . . [It] is overwhelmingly the result of the threat or use of force as exemplified in coups, defeat in civil war, (popular) revolts and assassinations."[35] Elites empowered through regime changes should thus survive for shorter periods of time in office before suffering irregular removal compared to all leaders, and leaders that gain power specifically in leadership regime changes ought to survive for shorter durations than those installed in institutional and restoration regime changes.

This chapter uses competing risks hazard models to estimate the effects of different types of regime changes on leader tenure while recognizing that leaders may leave office in different ways (regular removal, irregular removal, or natural death). Consistent with my arguments, rulers installed in regime changes survive for significantly less time in office before experiencing irregular removal, which is another way of saying that they are more likely to be removed irregularly. Conversely, these leaders are less likely to lose office through regular procedures. Each of these relationships is most pronounced for leaders empowered in leadership regime changes. Institutional regime changes, by contrast, fail to exert a systematic effect on the likelihood of regular or irregular removal. Restoration regime changes, finally, although few in number, appear to inoculate imposed leaders against irregular removal.

The qualitative section of the chapter identifies six irregular ways that foreign-imposed leaders can lose office and provides examples—and two extended case studies—of each one. All six types are consistent with my argument that regime change is risky. Three of the six types, which together comprise a handful of cases, are not explained by the problem of competing principals: when regime change is merely a brief stop on the way to annexation (e.g., Estonia, Latvia, and Lithuania in 1940); when leaders installed by foreign occupiers are forced out because the occupier loses a larger interstate war (e.g., German regime changes in World War II); or when an intervener is forced to remove multiple consecutive leaders until it gets one who will carry out its wishes (e.g., the United States in Guatemala in 1954).

My causal mechanism, however, explains the remaining three types, which account for the majority of cases. First, interveners sometimes remove leaders they had previously put in power when those individuals—owing to domestic pushback—fail to act in ways that promote the intervener's interests. A good example of this is Chile's removal of two Peruvian presidents it helped bring to power during the War of the Pacific when these men refused to make concessions the Chileans appointed them to make. Second, interveners dissatisfied with a leader they empowered in some cases permit or encourage domestic actors to remove him. The example I explore in depth is Duong Van Minh in South Vietnam, the general who ousted Ngo Dinh Diem in a coup in late 1963 and was himself ousted a few months later. Third, imposed leaders are occasionally overthrown by domestic actors incensed by foreigners' heavy hand in determining the direction of the country. I examine in detail the case of Maximilian I, the French-installed emperor of Mexico, who suffered this fate in 1867. The chapter closes by considering why some imposed leaders, including Spain's Francisco Franco, Iran's Mohammad Reza Pahlavi, and communist leaders in Eastern Europe after World War II, were able to survive in office for extended periods.

In the third empirical chapter (chapter 5), I shift the focus to the effects of regime change on interstate relations between interveners and targets. I use two variables to proxy for the quality of these relations: the likelihood of intervener-target militarized interstate disputes (MIDs) following regime change and measures of the similarity of the two states' foreign policies. With regard to militarized conflict, I find that—unlike the previous two chapters—regime change does not increase the likelihood of such clashes but neither does it decrease it. Breaking regime change down by its three types, however, shows that leadership regime change increases the likelihood of armed conflict between interveners and targets; restoration cases reduce the likelihood of such conflict; and institutional regime change has no effect. Similarly, although regime change does not significantly reduce the closeness of intervener-target relations, leadership regime change increases the dissimilarity of the two states' foreign policies as measured by the overlap in their alliance systems. Other types of regime change have little systematic effect.

In this chapter, I conduct two detailed case studies to trace how the problem of competing principals can drive interveners and targets into conflict or push them apart in less violent ways. I first examine Rwanda's replacement of Zaire's Mobutu Sese Seko with Laurent Kabila in 1997. The Rwandans installed Kabila to crack down on Rwandan Hutu groups who were launching murderous incursions from Zaire into Rwanda. Kabila, however, came to be viewed internally as doing the Tutsis' bidding and had to break with Kigali or face internal revolt. Instead, he confronted another Rwandan attack aimed at unseating him. Second, I tell the remarkable story of Japan's assassination of outgoing Chinese president and Manchurian strongman Chang Tso-lin in 1928. Although it is debated whether Chang was still China's head of state when officers of Japan's Kwantung Army blew up his train car outside Mukden (I argue that he was), even if he was only the ruler of Manchuria (an autonomous province of China) at the time of his death this case perfectly highlights how regime change can backfire.

Why It Matters

The consequences of foreign-imposed regime change are not merely historical curiosities, but questions with real contemporary policy relevance. Before the September 11 terrorist attacks, the United States was already the most frequent perpetrator of regime change, having upended (alone or with allies) thirty-one leaders in countries as diverse as Nicaragua, Honduras, the Dominican Republic, Mexico, Haiti, Germany, Japan, Iran, Guatemala, South Vietnam, Chile, Grenada, and Panama. After 9/11, the George W. Bush administration dispatched US forces to take down two governments in a span of eighteen months. Although the difficulties encountered in Afghanistan and Iraq slowed momentum for further such interventions, regime change was much discussed during the Bush years in the context of several other troublesome states, including Iran, Syria, Venezuela, Libya, and North Korea.[36] Indeed, the Bush administration quickly recognized the junta that briefly overthrew Venezuelan president Hugo Chavez in April 2002; it was later revealed that administration officials had met with many of the putschists beforehand.[37] The US role in the ouster of Haitian president Jean-Bertrand Aristide in 2004 is also the subject of some controversy.[38]

The Iraq debacle and the election of Barack Obama temporarily put talk of regime change on the back burner, but civil wars in Libya and Syria resulting from the Arab Spring brought it back with a vengeance.[39] As violence raged in Libya in March 2011 and fears grew that Libyan president Muammar Qaddafi would carry out large-scale massacres to quell the rebellion, President Obama demanded that Qaddafi step down.[40] The United States, along with its NATO allies, later implemented an air campaign in support of Libyan rebels that helped drive Qaddafi from power and ended with his brutal murder in the streets of Sirte. A few months later, Obama made a similar demand of Syria's Bashar al-Assad, but this time declined to back it up with force, preferring instead to arm and train Syrian rebels covertly.[41] Donald Trump's tenure in the White House brought renewed calls for regime change in Iran, North Korea, and Venezuela.[42]

The current structure of the international system dictates that the question of regime change will remain on the table. The United States spends nearly as much on its military as the rest of the world combined, fields highly trained military personnel armed with the latest technology, and is able to project force virtually anywhere on the globe in a matter of hours. The dearth of restraints on US power makes it tempting for US policymakers to use that power. The enormous capabilities at Washington's disposal, however, are not matched by corresponding knowledge about the consequences of employing those capabilities for various ends. Upending the governments of weaker states is actually quite easy for a country as powerful as the United States; it is the aftermath that can pose serious problems. Apropos here is former deputy secretary of defense Paul Wolfowitz's testimony before Congress prior to the Iraq invasion in early 2003, in which he stated that it was "hard to conceive" that more troops would be required to stabilize Iraq after the removal of Saddam Hussein than would be needed to overthrow him in the first place.[43] Policymakers need to be aware that what may follow regime change can be worse than the costs of inflicting it.

Theoretically, this study contributes to a growing literature that seeks to evaluate the effects and effectiveness of different types of foreign intervention. Unsurprisingly, much of this literature is a product of the end of the Cold War, since the collapse of the Soviet Union has permitted the United Nations, the United States, and other actors far greater latitude to involve themselves in crises around the globe. In response to this interventionism, scholars have set about trying to understand the conditions under which various forms of intervention—such as military occupation, nation building, regime change, counterinsurgency, UN peacekeeping, and humanitarian aid—succeed or fail.[44] These studies aim not only to inform contemporary policy debates, but are also concerned with enduring questions about state formation, the sources of order in society, and the determinants of democratization.

This book also contributes temporally varying and international elements to literatures on civil conflict that have traditionally focused on static, domestic variables. The empirical literature on civil war onset, for example, has been dominated by studies that emphasize variables that are slow to change (population, gross domestic product, primary commodity exports) or that don't change at all (terrain).[45] This property of the literature has made it difficult for scholars to explain *when*—as opposed to *where*—civil wars will occur.[46] The occurrence of regime change, by contrast, is a time-varying factor and thus can help predict the timing of civil wars. Similarly, until recently leading scholarship on the causes of civil war neglected the effect of variables external to the state where civil war occurred.[47] Although it has long been recognized that third parties play an important role in causing, prolonging, and terminating civil wars, only in the past decade have scholars began to incorporate these outside influences in their models of civil war onset.[48] A similar story can be told about the causes of coups and other forms of irregular, violent removal of leaders.[49] My argument introduces a "third image" element—foreign removal of leaders—into the explanation of internal violence, which interacts with domestic conditions to shape outcomes.[50]

My inquiry into the effects of foreign-imposed regime change also informs recent studies of the efficacy of decapitation, targeted killing, and assassination. These studies are concerned with assessing the effects of strategies that kill leaders. Some examine whether removing political leaders—or preventing them from exercising control over their military forces in the field—helps win wars.[51] Others inquire into whether killing terrorist or insurgent leaders causes violent clandestine organizations to fragment or collapse, or at least reduce the number of attacks they are able to perpetrate.[52] Still other studies look at the effect of assassinations on domestic unrest and instability.[53] Foreign-imposed regime change is in a sense "the mother of all decapitations"; this study thus provides further insight into the value of trying to achieve objectives by starting at the top.

Methodology, Case Selection, and Selection Bias

Each of the book's empirical chapters contains a quantitative segment, where I estimate the effect of regime change on each of my outcome variables across a large number of cases, and a qualitative segment, where I study a small number of cases in great depth. The former is meant to establish correlations between regime change and civil war, irregular leader removal, and intervener-target relations. The latter is intended to evaluate whether the mechanisms identified by my theory—military disintegration and the problem of competing principals—explain why these conflicts occurred.

In each empirical chapter, the presentation of the statistical analysis is divided into two parts. In the main body of the chapters, I use simple descriptive statistics, figures, and graphs to summarize the quantitative results. To facilitate readability and accessibility for readers who are not quantitatively oriented, the details of the statistical analyses—including descriptions of datasets and variables, discussions of statistical methods, regression tables, and summaries of robustness tests—are relegated to appendixes that appear at the end of each chapter. Replication data and all supplemental materials referred to in the empirical chapters are available on the Harvard Dataverse at https://doi.org/10.7910/DVN/DFDODV.

The primary tool I use in the case studies is process tracing, a method for discerning whether a case unfolded according to the causal mechanism under investigation.[54] All theories spell out a chain of events that should take place in a given case. Process tracing follows this causal chain to determine if the evidence indicates that events occurred as the theory predicts. For example, the problem of competing principals suggests that when states undertake regime change, they impose individuals who they believe share their preferences and who will implement policies in line with those preferences. Executing such policies, however, generates resistance from an imposed leader's domestic constituency. These leaders will be caught between competing pressures from their internal and external principals. We ought to be able to observe these pressures as well as evidence that the leader grappled with them. When leaders continue to implement their foreign patrons' preferred policies, we should see evidence that anger or resentment over those policies drove domestic actors to take up arms against the leader. When leaders turn against their patrons, we ought to find evidence that the reason they did so was the threat to their political survival from domestic opponents. We should further observe that dissatisfaction or anger over their protégé's reversal is the reason why patrons attack or seek to remove these wayward protégés. In other words, the theory suggests numerous places to look for evidence; the theory receives support to the extent that it accurately describes the forces at work in the case and how leaders reacted to them.

CASE SELECTION

Several principles guided my choice of cases. First, I sought to include cases that covered the entire time frame of my study. Second, I chose cases that reflect the reality that regime change is a global phenomenon. As I demonstrate in chapter 1, after Europe, Latin American countries experienced the largest number of regime changes; I thus chose cases from Mexico, Nicaragua, and Guatemala. Other regions covered include South, Southeast, and East Asia, Africa, and the Middle East. Third, I sought variation in the identity and power of the intervener. The United States, of course, figures prominently in my cases, as do other major powers, including Britain, France, and Japan. Cases like these represent "typical" cases, instances in which interveners are dramatically more powerful than their targets. Regime change is not solely the preserve of great powers, however; minor powers also sometimes carry out regime change. I include cases in which Vietnam, Rwanda, and Uganda are interveners.[55]

Fourth, most of the cases I chose are correctly predicted by my theory—that is, cases in which civil war, irregular leader removal, or interstate conflict occurred after regime change. These "positive" cases allow me to demonstrate the causal logic of my theory in action. Moreover, most of these cases are instances of leadership regime change and thus, according to my theory, should be followed by conflict of some sort. As such, they are not highly demanding tests for the theory, but the absence of conflict in such cases would be stronger evidence against it. However, I also selected a number of negative cases—cases in which regime change was not followed by conflict. In chapter 4, I examine multiple cases in which imposed leaders survived for lengthy periods of time. In one set of cases, my theory predicts that no violence would occur (Soviet institutional regime changes in Eastern Europe following World War II), and thus these cases represent correct predictions.[56] Another case—Francisco Franco after the Spanish Civil War—is an outlier because my theory expects individuals who come to power in leadership regime changes to suffer irregular removal relatively quickly. Franco, however, ruled Spain for decades before dying a natural death. The shah of Iran, who also remained in power for an extended period after his restoration in a US-backed coup in 1953, is also an outlier because I hypothesize that restoration regime change should not exert much of an effect on leader survival.

Finally, I selected specific cases for a variety of reasons. I included the US regime changes in Afghanistan and Iraq, for example, because these are important recent cases—and particularly good examples of how regime change can go wrong. I selected Rwanda and Uganda's intervention in Zaire because it prompted Africa's most devastating war in modern times and one of the most disastrous conflicts since World War II. I chose two cases from Afghanistan because—even though they are separated by a century and a half—they allow me to hold many things constant and demonstrate both of my causal mechanisms in a single country. The US intervention in Guatemala permits me to test whether covert regime changes have consequences similar to overt ones. Lastly, I include Japan's 1928 regime change in China because it was followed by numerous militarized disputes. The case thus has a large effect on the statistical finding that leadership regime changes increase the likelihood of such disputes.

ADDRESSING SELECTION BIAS

Regime change is by no means a random event: states are chosen for regime change based on a set of factors that may be related to the outcomes I seek to explain in this book. In clinical trials, randomization ensures that receiving a treatment (often an experimental drug) is not correlated with another factor (e.g., age, ethnicity, or gender) that could explain the outcome (such as reduced symptoms or elimination of a disease). Randomization thus establishes that any effect associated with the treatment is in fact caused by the treatment and not something else. The problem is that international politics bears little resemblance to the controlled environment of clinical trials. Needless to say, interveners do not select targets for regime change on a randomized basis. It is thus possible that some factor that makes a state a likely target of regime change also increases the likelihood of observing one of the outcomes of interest in this study.

Specifically, this problem—known as selection bias—could manifest itself in my study in at least four ways. One danger is that states undertake regime change specifically to cause one of my outcomes of interest. It is possible, for example, that states carry out regime change to weaken rivals by fomenting chaos, such as setting off violent struggles for power or civil wars. The literature on the causes of regime change fails to corroborate this conjecture, however, and as I show throughout this book, there is little evidence to support it.[57]

Second, states that are selected for regime change may be systematically different from states that are not chosen in ways that make them either (1) prone to conflict with the intervener or (2) prone to internal conflict. If the former is true, a failure to observe a reduction in interstate conflict between the two states might stem from aspects of the relationship that predisposed them to fight, such as geographic proximity or an unresolved territorial dispute. If the latter is true, it is possible that interveners simply select targets for regime change that are at a higher risk of civil war. Perhaps these states are unusually poor or highly populous, for example, both factors known to increase the likelihood of civil conflict.

Third, the *type* of regime change that interveners choose to implement could be correlated with conditions that make conflict between the intervener and target—or conflict inside the target—likely. As I elaborate in chapter 2, leadership regime change—an intervention that removes and replaces a leader but does not build new political institutions—is the type of regime change that is most likely to lead to internal and external conflict. It is possible that, for some reason, interveners implement leadership regime changes in countries that are already at a high risk of civil war or conflict with the intervening state.

Finally, states in which regime change succeeds in displacing the target government could be systematically different from countries in which it fails. For example, one could easily imagine that regime change might succeed more often against poor and weak states than against rich and powerful ones. Again, the literature on civil war suggests that impoverished states are more prone to civil wars than wealthy states. Regime change may thus be likely to succeed in places that are predisposed to civil war, making it appear that regime change is correlated with the outbreak of such conflicts when in fact it is not.

Each of the empirical chapters takes steps to address these sources of selection bias. In general, I find that, on average, states that experience regime change are not much different from states that do not. States where regime change succeeds are also not much different from those that are targeted but where the operation fails. Furthermore, states that suffer different types of regime change are not much different from each other. In addition, I use a variety of methods that correct for selection bias, none of which is individually definitive but which collectively suggest that the effect of regime change is not spurious.

Plan of the Book

In chapter 1, I set the stage for what follows by laying out in detail my definition of foreign-imposed regime change. I provide a list of cases of regime change that took place between 1816 and 2011, identify the most frequent interveners and targets of regime change, and examine trends in regime change over time and across regions of the world. I then distinguish among three types of regime change—leadership, institutional, restoration—that I predict will have different effects on outcomes following regime change and summarize the frequency of these three types.

Chapter 2 turns to the core logic of my theory for why regime change produces counterproductive effects for interveners and in targets. In one mechanism, I assume that all deposed leaders would prefer to regain power but vary in their ability to do so. When regime change induces military disintegration, scattering armed soldiers across the countryside, deposed leaders (or their deputies) have both the motive and the opportunity to launch an insurgency. In the second mechanism, I argue that interveners wish to bring the preferences of the target state into alignment with their own by installing accommodating leaders. However, these leaders often run afoul of domestic opinion that disapproves of concessions to interveners. Forced to answer to two masters with divergent interests—both of whom can remove them from power—imposed leaders face an unappealing dilemma. Domestic pressure gives leaders incentives to renege on their commitments to interveners, which can increase the risk of another conflict with their foreign patron if they break the commitment and increase the risk of violent removal and civil war if they do not. I then differentiate among three different types of regime change that trigger this dilemma to varying degrees. The chapter closes by considering the question of why interveners fail to foresee that regime change will trigger the problems I outline.

The three empirical chapters of the book test my argument that regime change increases the likelihood of internal conflict in regime change targets and worsens relations between interveners and targets. I begin with the domestic consequences of regime change in the target and progress to how regime change affects patron-protégé relations. Chapter 3 shows that regime change increases the likelihood of civil war. Chapter 4 demonstrates that regime change heightens the risk that leaders are violently removed from office. Chapter 5 shows that regime change fails to reduce the likelihood of intervener-target militarized disputes and does not improve the quality of their relations with each other.

In the book's concluding chapter, I summarize my findings regarding the effects of regime change around the world over the course of two centuries. The evidence suggests that the poor track record of US regime changes in Afghanistan, Iraq, and Libya is far from anomalous: regime change increases the likelihood of several different types of conflict. I argue that in most cases, the United States (and any other would-be intervener) is better off not owning the problem. Regime change may appear to be a quick and easy solution, but over the longer term it turns out to be neither easy nor a solution. States are likely to be better off relying on other tools of influence in the majority of cases. These tools, such as negotiations, economic sanctions, and coercive diplomacy, may not be more effective but are likely to be less costly if they fail. Regime change should be reserved for truly exceptional cases and interveners should recognize that absent a (rare) set of promising preconditions, regime change may make things worse instead of better.

Defining Foreign-Imposed Regime Change

This chapter introduces the phenomenon that lies at the heart of this book: foreign-imposed regime change. I begin by laying out my definition of regime change, differentiating it from related concepts such as the imposition of regimes in new states emerging from colonialism (often referred to as imposed polities); military occupation; annexation; and state death. I discuss the three principal ways in which regime change is carried out: compellent threats demanding leader change; invasion; and overt or covert interventions in which external forces work with domestic factions located inside the target or in a nearby state. I provide a list of the 120 leaders who were removed in foreign-imposed regime changes from 1816 to 2008 and offer some basic descriptive statistics about the most common interveners and targets as well as the spatial and temporal distribution of regime changes.

Foreign-Imposed Regime Change: A Definition

Foreign-imposed regime change is the forcible or coerced removal of the effective, or de facto, leader of one state—which remains formally sovereign afterward—by the government of another state.[1] It should be immediately obvious that the word "regime" in the term "foreign-imposed regime change" is a misnomer. A political regime is rarely coterminous with an individual leader; it typically consists of a set of institutions through which the state is governed and an ideology, such as liberalism, monarchism, communism, or fascism. For example, the US "regime" consists not only of the president, but the rest of the executive branch, Congress, the courts, and the rules and procedures governing relations among those institutions as well as for how leaders are selected. Changing a president is not usually thought of as a change of regime, but rather as a change of leadership within the same regime.[2] Technically, therefore, the term regime change is inappropriate for the subject of this study, since the key factor identifying cases for inclusion is the forcible removal of the top political leader by an external actor. A more apt term would be "foreign-imposed leader removal" or "foreign-imposed leader change." In addition to being not very snappy acronyms, introducing a new term would be swimming against the tide of existing scholarship that applies the moniker of regime change to changes of leadership. In this book, I thus adopt the term regime change even though the minimum thing being changed is not the regime but rather the leader.

As should be evident from the focus on leaders, interveners need not promote new governing institutions in the target for a case to qualify as regime change. The degree to which interveners promote institutions in targets is a variable. Sometimes interveners take extensive measures to determine the governing arrangements that prevail after regime change, whereas in other cases they exert hardly any effort at all. As I explore below, these differences matter for the effects that regime change has on the likelihood of conflict both within target states and between interveners and targets.

Unlike interventions that change the "hardware" of a state either by annexing some or all of its territory or otherwise wrecking the state's power potential, changing the governing elites or institutions of a foreign state is akin to installing new software: the machine remains more or less the same, but the operating system is different. In other words, the power of the state targeted for regime change is redirected and put to different uses. This point is exemplified by Britain's demand for an end to "Prussian militarism" in Germany as a condition for ending World War I. Britain's policy did nothing to alter German capabilities. Rather, the idea was that these capabilities would be rendered less threatening if Germany were transformed into a democracy.[3] Just as those who adopt coercive strategies in wartime hope to achieve victory "on the cheap," states that employ regime change aim to neutralize threats and empower friendly governments without paying the costs of conquering and annexing the target or permanently garrisoning it.

Five specific elements of this definition merit elaboration.[4]

EFFECTIVE LEADER IS REMOVED

For a case to qualify as regime change, the individual removed through foreign intervention must be the actual, de facto, leader of the government, not a lower-ranking official, a ceremonial head of state that lacks any decision-making authority, or an individual considered to be the legal or de jure leader but who does not exercise actual power in the country. The *Archigos* project on leaders, which I rely on (with a few modifications) to make these determinations, refers to such individuals as "effective" leaders, "the person that de facto exercised power in a country."[5] In many cases, the head of state and leader of the government are one and the same person; this is true in presidential systems, for example. In parliamentary systems, by contrast, the head of state and head of government are separate offices held by different people, the former being a largely ceremonial post (as in the office of the president in Israel) whereas the latter wields the real decision-making authority. In constitutional monarchies, such as Britain, the role of head of state is filled by a hereditary monarch; the head of government is the prime minister, a member of Parliament who commands majority support in that chamber (typically the leader of the largest political party).[6] In some authoritarian systems, such as single-party regimes, there is no formal head of state; the leader of the government is often the leader of the dominant party.[7] To be considered an instance of regime change, however, an operation must remove the effective head of the target state's government.

REMOVAL, BUT NOT NECESSARILY REPLACEMENT, OF LEADERS

My definition requires only that an intervener remove the current leader from power, *not* that it also replace the deposed leader with someone else— although most interveners typically do both. In the modal case of regime change, the intervener not only wants to dispose of the current leader but it also has a preferred replacement it would like to install—an individual who is selected because he or she is viewed as friendlier to the intervener's interests than the current leader. According to Steven Hood, for example, when the Vietnamese invaded Cambodia on Christmas Day, 1978, their "intent was to strike a quick and fatal blow to the Khmer Rouge leadership . . . and place their man, Heng Samrin, at the head of a puppet government."[8] Yet this need not be true for a case to count as regime change. When British forces invaded Afghanistan for the second time—to depose Amir Sher Ali in 1878—they did not bring along a preselected replacement as they had in 1839.[9] After the initial target of regime change fled and placed his son, Yakub Khan, on the throne, British General Frederick Roberts deposed him but could not "find a puppet for the Afghan throne," which remained vacant for nine months.[10] The British eventually agreed to allow Abdur Rahman, a grandson of former Afghan emir Dost Mohammed, to take power. I code all three types of cases—foreign removal and immediate foreign replacement (Pol Pot to Heng Samrin in Cambodia), foreign removal and domestic replacement (Sher Ali to Yakub Khan in Afghanistan), and foreign removal and eventual foreign replacement (Yakub Khan to Abdur Rahman in Afghanistan)—as instances of foreign-imposed regime change.

This stipulation highlights the fact that the decision to depose a leader is separate from the decision to install a new leader.[11] Obviously the two decisions are closely linked and interveners typically make both before they act. Indeed, some scholars argue that the availability of a suitable replacement— in the form of a particular individual or at least a strong domestic political opposition—is a prerequisite for states to undertake regime change.[12] Yet interveners may not always make both decisions—or be able to implement both decisions—simultaneously for at least four reasons.

First, as discussed below, interveners sometimes use threats of military force to coerce targeted leaders to step down without a fight. In such cases, the intervener—not being present on the ground in the target state—may be unable to influence directly who succeeds the deposed leader.[13] Second, this condition is also true when leaders are assassinated or targeted by the airpower strategy known as decapitation.[14] When these methods are employed, the intervener cannot easily install a replacement leader because it lacks control over the target state.[15] Third, the need to act speedily in a crisis may preclude careful deliberation regarding a successor to the targeted leader. Consider, for example, that a mere twenty-six days passed between the 9/11 attacks and the US initiation of hostilities against Afghanistan on October 7. This condensed time frame meant that the Bush administration did not go to war with a preselected replacement for Taliban leader Mullah Omar.

Finally, regime changes that promote democracy may not be undertaken with the intention to empower a particular individual, and even if the intervener had a preferred candidate, he would still have to navigate the electoral process successfully to gain power. This is not to say that promoting democracy and obtaining a particular leader are incompatible objectives. Although foreign powers in these cases may not have intervened in support of a specific candidate, they often play a determining role in who eventually accedes to high office.[16] Despite going to war in 2001 without a predetermined candidate to govern Afghanistan, when a suitable individual—Hamid Karzai—emerged during the war, Washington was able to engineer his selection as interim leader, a status made official by elections in 2004. Similarly, some in the Bush administration aspired to replace Saddam Hussein with the exiled Iraqi politician Ahmed Chalabi, a favorite in neoconservative circles. When it became clear that placing Chalabi in office was not in the cards, however, the United States first took power into its own hands by installing Ambassador L. Paul Bremer as the head of a one-year US occupation, the Coalition Provisional Authority (CPA). US officials then pressured UN envoy Lakhdar Brahimi to select Ayad Allawi, another US favorite with close ties to the CIA, as interim prime minister. As the *New York Times* described Allawi's selection in May 2004, "Mr. Brahimi was presented with a 'fait accompli' after President Bush's envoy to Iraq, Robert D. Blackwill, 'railroaded' the [Iraqi] Governing Council into coalescing around him."[17] The United States—in the person of US ambassador Zalmay Khalilzad—also exerted decisive influence on the selection of Nouri al-Maliki as prime minister two years later.[18] In short, even interveners that topple a leader without a replacement lined up to step in may still be able to influence or even determine who is selected to lead the country as long as their military forces are present in the target or remain nearby. This is true no matter which type of regime the intervener promotes, including a democracy.

The potential drawback from the intervener's perspective of undertaking regime change without a clear successor at hand is that it risks ending up with a new leader who is unsympathetic to its needs and interests. One such case—the assassination of Manchurian warlord and outgoing Chinese president Chang Tso-lin by members of the Japanese Kwantung Army in 1928, examined in depth in chapter 5—illustrates how killing a foreign leader without the ability to choose a successor can backfire. The Japanese believed that Chang's death would produce chaos in Manchuria, providing a pretext for Japan to occupy the region, and additionally that Chang's son, Chang Hsüeh-liang, would be far more accommodating to Japan's interests than his father had been.[19] In actuality, the assassination did not produce anarchy in Manchuria; Chang Hsüeh-liang, who understood that the Japanese had killed his father, consolidated power and, rather than ally with the Japanese, quickly pledged allegiance to his father's successor in Beijing, Chiang Kai-shek.[20]

In sum, interveners need not both remove the current leader and determine his successor for a case to comprise foreign-imposed regime change; only the former is necessary. Although I argue that difficulties are likely to arise even when interveners choose replacements who are sympathetic to their interests owing to the problem of competing principals, it may be even more likely following regime changes in which they do not determine the successor leader. I investigate this possibility in the empirical section of the book.

TARGETS ARE INDEPENDENT STATES

Targets of regime change must be independent, sovereign states. I do not consider the imposition of regimes on newly independent states by departing colonial powers, for example, to constitute regime change. This criterion excludes cases such as US interventions in Cuba and the Philippines following the Spanish-American War of 1898 because these territories were Spanish colonial possessions. Although the United States did help generate new political systems in Cuba and the Philippines, these countries were not independent states prior to the war. More broadly, new governments that take power when a former colony becomes independent are excluded from the universe of regime changes. This stipulation distinguishes regime changes from "imposed polities," the vast majority of which consist of former colonies.[21]

TARGETS REMAIN (NOMINALLY) SOVEREIGN

Targets of regime change must retain at least nominal sovereignty after regime change occurs. Targets that are formally annexed by an intervener—such as Nazi Germany's incorporation of Austria, Czechoslovakia, and much of Poland (1938–39)—are excluded from the universe of regime change, as are states that are absorbed into empires, such as Britain's conquest of Sind

(1843) and Punjab (1846). This criterion rules out instances of what Tanisha Fazal terms "state death"—defined as "the formal loss of foreign policymaking power to another state"—when state death takes the form of annexation to another state or its empire.[22] The rulers and governing structures of states conquered and absorbed by other states are changed as a matter of course, but these changes are a by-product of conquest rather than an effort to establish a new regime in an independent state. Interveners may temporarily occupy and govern a state whose leader they have overthrown as long as the assumption of power is not intended to be permanent.[23] Examples include the US occupations of Haiti (1915–34) and the Dominican Republic (1916–24) and Germany's occupations of the Benelux countries in World War II.[24] Interveners may also install puppet regimes while garrisoning target countries with troops, as Nazi Germany did in Norway, Yugoslavia, and Greece. In some cases, the interval between regime change and formal annexation is brief: the Soviet Union ousted the leaders of Estonia, Latvia, and Lithuania in June 1940, and then annexed these countries in August. These states are coded as experiencing regime changes, and then exiting the international system two months later.

Finally, an external actor must be primarily responsible for deposing the targeted leader—or at least play a substantial role in his removal. This can occur in one of three ways. Interveners, for example, may employ threats of force to coerce a leader to relinquish power "without a military confrontation," as when Haitian junta leader General Raoul Cédras agreed to step down with the US 82nd Airborne Division poised to come ashore in October 1994.[25] For coercive threats against leaders to count as cases of regime change, an intervener must issue a verbal or written demand that the targeted leader step aside. Further, this demand needs to be accompanied by either an explicit threat to use force in case of noncompliance or an implicit threat of force communicated by the mobilization or movement of military forces.[26] The targeted leader must then resign in response to the threat.[27] For example, I code the ouster of Costa Rican president Federico Tinoco in 1919 as a regime change accomplished by a compellent threat because (1) President Woodrow Wilson refused to recognize Tinoco and demanded that he leave office; and (2) the United States dispatched warships to Costa Rican waters, after which Tinoco resigned and fled the country.[28] Additional cases include successful Soviet threats against the leaders of the Baltic states in 1940 and King Michael of Romania in 1945; and South Africa's 1994 threat to remove King Letsie III of Lesotho if he did not allow ousted prime minister Ntsu Mokhehle to resume office.[29]

In a second scenario, interveners attack a target with their own military forces to remove a leader, such as the United States did in late 1989 to apprehend Panamanian president Manuel Noriega. Other cases of direct invasions to topple and replace foreign leaders include the French campaign that felled Benito Juárez in 1863, Vietnam's blitzkrieg into Cambodia that ousted Pol Pot in 1979, and the US armored drive on Baghdad that ended Saddam Hussein's rule in Iraq a quarter-century later.[30]

In the final method of regime change, external forces work overtly or covertly with domestic actors in the target state to overthrow the target's regime. The extent to which the resulting change of regime in these cases is attributable to external versus domestic forces is sometimes ambiguous. For a change of government to qualify as a foreign-imposed regime change in these circumstances, I require evidence that (1) removing the target regime was an official (although not necessarily public, in the case of covert activities) objective of the foreign government, (2) agents of the foreign government were present in the target country and working toward regime change, and (3) the extent of the aid provided by foreign forces was of such importance that regime change would have been unlikely to succeed absent that support.

In the first variant of this strategy, a foreign state works in open collaboration with dissidents or rebels from the target state. In one of a half-dozen regime changes to afflict Honduras in the nineteenth century, for example, Honduran president Domingo Vásquez (a conservative) warned the new liberal leader of Nicaragua, José Santos Zelaya, in 1893 to stop harboring dissident Honduran liberals. Zelaya responded by allying with one such dissident—Policarpo Bonilla—and attempting to oust Vásquez. The combined forces of Nicaragua and the Honduran liberals eventually drove Vásquez from power and Bonilla was installed as president.[31] The Tanzanian invasion of Uganda in 1979 that drove Idi Amin from power followed a similar script. After a destructive incursion into Tanzania's Kagera Salient by Ugandan Army units in pursuit of rebellious troops, Tanzanian president Julius Nyerere decided to get rid of Amin once and for all. Although Tanzanian forces were joined in their attack by the recently formed Uganda National Liberation Army (UNLA), a rebel umbrella organization that included numerous anti-Amin exile groups based in Tanzania, the Tanzanian Army provided the bulk of the manpower and played the decisive role in defeating Amin and his Libyan allies.[32] Similarly, the United States worked in conjunction with troops of the Northern Alliance to defeat the Taliban and overthrow its leader, Mullah Omar, in Afghanistan in late 2001—an outcome that clearly would not have been possible absent US airpower.[33]

In the second variant of this strategy, interveners work behind the scenes to overthrow the targeted regime—employing their intelligence agencies or covert military force, or by providing critical financial or military aid to domestic actors. In Guatemala, for example, President Dwight D. Eisenhower formally authorized the overthrow of Jacobo Árbenz's government—in an operation dubbed PBSUCCESS—in August 1953. US government officials, chief among them Ambassador John Peurifoy, were present in Guatemala working to carry out the plot. Washington's chosen agent, Carlos Castillo Armas, stood no chance of overthrowing Árbenz without covertly provided US airpower, as well as the Guatemalan officer corps' belief that the United States would intervene directly if the army repelled Castillo Armas's ragtag invasion force.[34] I thus code this case as an instance of foreign-imposed regime change.

In Brazil a decade later, by contrast, the Brazilian army received no US aid when it toppled left-leaning President João Goulart in 1964. According to one account, President Lyndon Johnson was "prepared to take any action necessary to prevent a communist takeover" of such an enormous and strategically important country.[35] Brazilian military officers, however, took matters into their own hands, thereby obviating the need for US intervention. After the coup began, Johnson took steps to ensure it succeeded, such as ordering a US naval task force to head for Brazil and readying fuel, weapons, and ammunition to send to support the Brazilian military. "Johnson," writes the historian Michael Grow, "had been fully prepared to carry out a large-scale U.S. military intervention. . . . But in the end, Brazil's generals took care of the problem on their own."[36] Goulart fled the country before any US ships or supplies arrived. Because the United States contributed little to Goulart's ouster, I refrain from coding the Brazilian coup as a case of foreign-imposed regime change.[37]

The Universe of Cases

According to the criteria laid out in my definition, there were 120 cases of regime change involving 153 interveners between 1816 and 2008. These cases (plus two others that occurred after the end of the time period of my study) are listed in table 1.1.[38] The exact number of regime changes that appear in the analyses presented in later chapters, however, varies depending on the unit of analysis in each dataset. In my analysis of regime change as a cause of civil war in chapter 3, for example, in which the state-year is the unit of analysis, there are a total of 112 instances of regime change. The omitted cases consist of states that had multiple leaders removed in a single year: Peru (1881), Costa Rica (1919), Lithuania (1940), Guatemala (1954), the Dominican Republic (1961), Czechoslovakia (1968), and Cyprus (1974). In chapter 4, by contrast, where I examine the effects of being brought to power by foreign forces on the duration of leaders' tenure, the leader's time in office is the unit of analysis, and there are 109 cases of leaders entering office after foreign-imposed regime changes. Chapter 5, finally, which investigates the effect of regime change on intervener-target conflict, also contains 109 directed dyads with foreign-imposed regime change.[39]

Figures 1.1 and 1.2 show, respectively, the most frequent interveners and the most common targets of foreign-imposed regime change from 1816 to

Table 1.1 Successful cases of foreign-imposed regime change, 1816–2011

Target	Intervener(s)	Year	Leader removed	Type
Two Sicilies	Austria	1821	Revolutionaries	R
Spain	France	1823	Provisional Regency	R
Modena[†]	Austria	1831	Pellegrino Nobili	R
Parma[†]	Austria	1831	Conte Filippo Linati	R
Portugal	France, Spain, Britain	1834	Miguel I	R
Afghanistan[†]	Britain	1839	Dost Mohammed	L
Nicaragua[†]	El Salvador, Honduras	1845	Emiliano Madrid	L
Tuscany	Austria	1849	Francesco Domenico Guerrazzi	R
Saxony	Prussia	1849	Gustav Friedrich Held	R
Baden	Prussia	1849	Lorenz Peter Brentano	R
Roman Republic	France, Austria, Two Sicilies, Spain	1849	Triumvirate	R
Argentina	Brazil	1852	Juan Manuel de Rosas	L
Honduras[†]	Guatemala	1855	Trinidad Cabañas	L
Nicaragua[†]	Costa Rica, El Salvador, Guatemala, Honduras	1857	William Walker	L
Modena[†]	Piedmont, France	1859	Francesco V	L
Mexico	France	1863	Benito Juárez	L
Honduras[†]	Guatemala, Nicaragua	1863	José Francisco Montes	L
El Salvador[†]	Guatemala	1863	Gerardo Barrios	L
Paraguay	Brazil, Argentina	1869	Francisco Solano López	L
France	Prussia	1870	Napoleon III	L
El Salvador[†]	Honduras	1871	Francisco Dueñas	L
Honduras[†]	El Salvador, Guatemala	1872	José Maria Medina	L
Honduras[†]	El Salvador, Guatemala	1874	Celeo Arias	L
El Salvador	Guatemala	1876	Andres del Valle	L
Honduras[†]	Guatemala	1876	Ponciano Leiva	L
Afghanistan[†]	Britain	1879	Sher Ali	L
Afghanistan[†]	Britain	1879	Yakub Khan	L
Peru[†]	Chile	1881	Nicolás Piérola	L
Peru[†]	Chile	1881	Francisco Garcia Calderon	L
Peru	Chile	1882	Lizardo Montero	L
Guatemala	El Salvador	1885	Justo Rufino Barrios	L
Honduras[†]	Nicaragua	1894	Domingo Vasquez	L
Honduras	Nicaragua	1907	Manuel Bonilla	L
Korea	Japan	1907	Yi Hyong	L
Nicaragua	USA	1909	José Santos Zelaya	L
Nicaragua	USA	1910	José Madriz	I
Honduras	USA	1911	Miguel Davila	L
Dominican Republic	USA	1912	Eladio Victoria	I
Mexico	USA	1914	Victoriano Huerta	L
Belgium	Germany	1914	Charles, Baron de Broqueville	L
Dominican Republic	USA	1914	José Bordas Valdez	I
Haiti	USA	1915	Revolutionary Committee of Safety	L
Serbia[†]	Austria	1915	King Alexander	L
Albania	Italy	1916	Esat Pashe Toptani	L
Dominican Republic	USA	1916	Francisco Henriquez	I

Target	Intervener(s)	Year	Leader removed	Type
Montenegro[†]	Austria	1916	Nikola I	L
Greece	France, Britain	1917	King Constantine I	L
Belgium	France, Britain, USA	1918	Ludwig von Faulkenhausen	R
Latvia	Germany	1919	Karlis Ulmanis	L
Hungary	Romania	1919	Béla Kun	L
Costa Rica	USA	1919	Federico Tinoco Granados	I
Costa Rica	USA	1919	Juan Bautista Quiros	I
Mongolia	USSR	1925	Elbek-Dorzhi Rinchino	L
Nicaragua	USA	1926	Emiliano Chamorro	I
China	Japan	1928	Chang Tso-lin	L
Ethiopia	Italy	1936	Haile Selassie	L
Albania	Italy	1939	King Zog	L
Spain	Germany, Italy, Portugal	1939	José Miaja Menant	L
Norway	Germany	1940	Johan Nygaardsvold	L
Luxembourg	Germany	1940	Pierre Dupong	L
Netherlands	Germany	1940	Dirk Jan De Geer	L
Belgium	Germany	1940	Hubert Pierlot	L
Latvia	USSR	1940	Karlis Ulmanis	I
Lithuania	USSR	1940	Antanas Smetona	I
Lithuania	USSR	1940	Antanas Merkys	I
Estonia	USSR	1940	Konstantin Pats	I
Ethiopia	Britain	1941	King of Italy	R
Yugoslavia	Germany	1941	King Peter II	L
Greece	Germany	1941	Emmanouil Tsouderos	L
Iran	Britain, USSR	1941	Reza Pahlavi	L
Iraq	Britain	1941	Rashid Ali	R
Denmark	Germany	1943	Erik Scavenius	L
France	Britain, USA	1944	Pierre Laval	R
Belgium	Canada,[‡] Britain, USA	1944	Alexander von Falkenhausen	R
Luxembourg	USA	1944	Gustav Simon	R
Bulgaria	USSR	1944	Kyril, Prince of Preslav	I
Hungary	Germany	1944	Miklós Horthy	L
Romania	USSR	1945	King Michael	I
Hungary	USSR	1945	Ferenc Szálasi	I
Denmark	Britain, USA	1945	Werner Best	R
Netherlands	Canada,[‡] Britain, USA	1945	Arthur Seyss-Inquart	R
Norway	Britain, USA	1945	Vidkun Quisling	R
Germany	Britain, USA, USSR	1945	Admiral Karl Doenitz	I
Japan	USA	1945	Suzuki Kantaro	I
Czechoslovakia	USSR	1948	Edvard Beneš	I
Indonesia	Netherlands	1948	Sukarno	L
Iran	USA	1953	Mohammed Mossadegh	R
Guatemala	USA	1954	Jacobo Árbenz	L
Guatemala	USA	1954	Carlos Enrique Díaz	L
Guatemala	USA	1954	Elfegio Monzon	L
Hungary	USSR	1956	Imre Nagy	R
Congo[‡]	Belgium	1960	Patrice Lumumba	L
Dominican Republic	USA	1961	Rafael Trujillo	L
Dominican Republic	USA	1961	Rafael Leonidas Trujillo Jr.	L
South Vietnam	USA	1963	Ngo Dinh Diem	L

(continued)

Table 1.1 (continued)

Target	Intervener(s)	Year	Leader removed	Type
Gabon	France	1964	Jean-Hilaire Aubaume	R
Czechoslovakia	USSR	1968	Alexander Dubček	R
Czechoslovakia	USSR	1968	Ludvik Svoboda	R
Chile	USA	1973	Salvador Allende	L
Cyprus	Greece	1974	Archbishop Makarios III	L
Cyprus	Turkey	1974	Nikos Sampson	R
Cambodia	Vietnam	1979	Pol Pot	L
Uganda	Tanzania	1979	Idi Amin	L
Central African Republic	France	1979	Jean-Bedel Bokassa	L
Afghanistan	USSR	1979	Hafizullah Amin	L
Chad	USA	1982	Goukouni Oueddei	L
Grenada	USA	1983	Hudson Austin	I
Mongolia	USSR	1984	Yumzhagiin Tsedenbal	L
Afghanistan	USSR	1986	Babrak Karmal	L
Comoros	France	1989	Bob Denard	L
Panama	USA	1990	Manuel Noriega	I
Haiti	USA	1994	Raul Cedras	R
Lesotho	South Africa	1994	King Letsie III	R
Comoros	France	1995	Bob Denard	R
Zaire/DRC	Rwanda, Uganda	1997	Joseph Mobutu	L
Republic of Congo	Angola	1997	Pascal Lissouba	R
Sierra Leone	Ghana,‡ Guinea, Nigeria‡	1998	Jonny Koroma	R
Afghanistan*	USA	2001	Mullah Omar	I
Iraq*	Britain, USA	2003	Saddam Hussein	I
Central African Republic*	Chad	2003	Ange-Félix Patassé	L
Côte d'Ivoire*#	France	2011	Laurent Gbagbo	L
Libya*#	USA	2011	Muammar Qaddafi	I

† Denotes cases that are excluded from analyses in chapter 5 in which directed dyads are the unit of analysis because the Correlates of War does not consider the country in question to be a member of the interstate system at the time regime change occurred.

‡ Denotes cases omitted from the directed dyad analysis in chapter 5 because the dyad was not "politically relevant," i.e., the two states are not geographically contiguous and neither of them is a major power.

* Denotes cases omitted from the directed dyad analysis in chapter 5 because they occurred outside the time frame of the dataset (1816–2000).

# Denotes cases omitted from all statistical analyses because they occurred after 2008.

2008. With respect to interveners, it is unsurprising that great powers have overthrown the most foreign leaders.[40] The United States leads the way, having toppled thirty-three leaders, all in the space of less than one hundred years, beginning in 1909 with the ouster of Nicaragua's liberal leader José Santos Zelaya and concluding with the overthrow of Saddam Hussein in 2003.[41] Indeed, the United States alone accounts for more than one-quarter of all leaders removed by a foreign power and twice as many as each of its nearest competitors, Britain and the Soviet Union, each of which toppled sixteen leaders. Prussia/Germany and France also reach double digits with fourteen and eleven regime changes, respectively. Of course, the bulk of Germany's

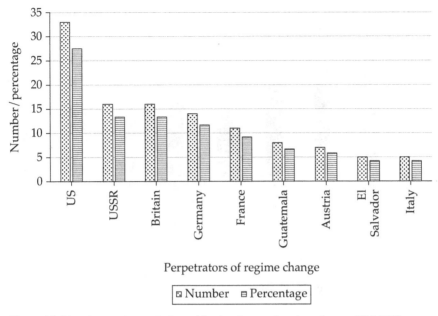

Figure 1.1. Most frequent perpetrators of foreign-imposed regime change, 1816–2008

regime changes occurred during World War II; neither the Federal Republic of Germany nor the German Democratic Republic during the Cold War, nor a reunited Germany since the end of the Cold War, carried out any regime changes. France, by contrast, was an active regime changer throughout the last two centuries, beginning in 1823 with the restoration of Ferdinand VII as king in Spain and continuing as recently as 1995 with its second regime change in the Comoros Islands.[42] Austria-Hungary and Italy round out the great powers on the list with seven and five regime changes, respectively.

Figure 1.1, however, also reveals some surprises that demonstrate that regime change is not only a game for great powers. Guatemala, the dominant power in Central America in the nineteenth century, is the sixth leading practitioner of regime change over the past two centuries, having overthrown eight foreign leaders. These eight cases were concentrated in the twenty-year period from 1855 to 1876. Each of Guatemala's neighbors other than Costa Rica—El Salvador, Honduras, and Nicaragua—suffered at least one regime change at Guatemalan hands. El Salvador, in addition to being a target of Guatemalan regime changes, also carried out five of its own. Strangely enough, in two of these cases El Salvador collaborated with none other than Guatemala to overthrow the leaders of other Central American Republics.[43] Other minor powers that have carried out at least one regime change include Brazil, Argentina, Honduras, Nicaragua, Vietnam, Tanzania, Romania, Greece, South Africa, Rwanda, Uganda, Angola, and Chad.

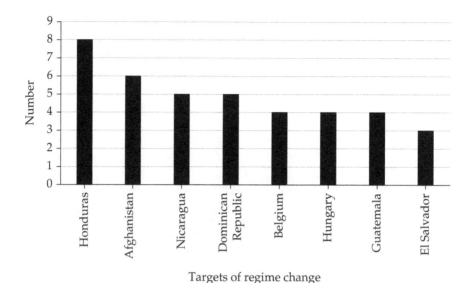

Targets of regime change

Figure 1.2. Most frequent targets of foreign-imposed regime change, 1816–2008

Figure 1.2 displays the most frequent targets of regime change in my data. Informed readers may have guessed that Afghanistan, the "graveyard of empires," would be the leading target of regime change, but that dubious honor belongs to Honduras, which has suffered eight changes of government inflicted by foreign forces. Counterintuitively, the United States was responsible for only one of these regime changes; the rest were inflicted by Honduras's Central American neighbors, particularly Guatemala, which (alone or in combination with others) overthrew five Honduran leaders. Afghanistan ranks second with six regime changes: three by Britain, two by the Soviet Union, and one by the United States. Nicaragua and the Dominican Republic each experienced five regime changes, the latter coming all at Washington's hands, whereas US threats or troops account for three of Nicaragua's regime changes. Belgium, Hungary, and Guatemala each had four leaders overthrown by foreign powers. Two of Belgium's are attributable to German invasions (1914 and 1940), whereas the other two are accounted for by the reversal of those German occupations and the restoration of previous democratic governments in 1918 and 1944, respectively. Romania, Germany, and the Soviet Union (twice) each overthrew Hungarian leaders, while Guatemala lost one leader to El Salvador in 1885 but three in rapid succession to the United States in 1954.

Figure 1.3 displays the distribution of regime changes over time. I divide the two centuries since 1816 into five periods: 1816–1849, 1850–1899, 1900–1945, 1946–1991, and 1992–2008.[44] Of all regime changes, 43 percent occurred in the first forty-five years of the twentieth century, an average of almost one

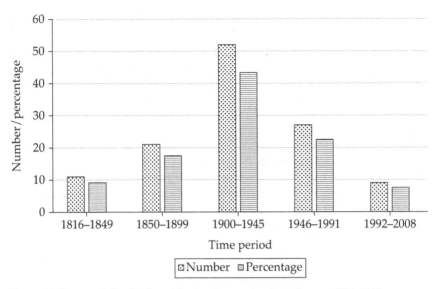

Figure 1.3. Temporal distribution of foreign-imposed regime changes, 1816–2008

per year. Twenty-seven of these cases (22.5 percent of all regime changes) took place during World War II, owing to Soviet and Axis expansion from 1939 to 1941; Allied reversal of Axis conquests in 1944 and 1945; and additional regime changes in Eastern Europe, as Stalin established Soviet satellite regimes at the end of the war.[45] By contrast, only six regime changes are directly attributable to World War I, although US regime changing interventions in Haiti (1915) and the Dominican Republic (1914, 1916), Romania's overthrow of Béla Kun's communist regime in Hungary (1919), and Germany's intervention in Latvia (1919) can arguably be linked to the war as well.[46]

The second most common era of regime change was the Cold War, with twenty-seven cases. Many of these regime changes were related in one way or another to the bipolar competition between the United States and the Soviet Union. Moscow, for example, intervened close to home in Hungary (1956) and Czechoslovakia (1968) to uphold communist orthodoxy in the sphere of influence it had created in Eastern Europe, and to preserve an endangered Marxist government in Afghanistan (1979) directly on its southern border. The United States, for its part, overthrew governments it viewed as "protocommunist" or susceptible to Soviet influence in its own backyard, such as Guatemala (1954), Chile (1973), and Grenada (1983). The United States also famously sponsored the failed Bay of Pigs invasion of Cuba by US-trained Cuban exiles in 1961, and targeted other supposedly left-leaning governments around the globe, including Iran (1953) and Congo (1960).[47] Washington even victimized its own ally, South Vietnamese president Ngo Dinh Diem, in 1963. Diem, contrary to the wishes of the Kennedy administration, refused to oust his unpopular brother (Ngo Dinh Nhu) from the regime and additionally appeared to be on the verge of negotiating a deal with North Vietnam that would neutralize South Vietnam.[48] In cases unrelated to the Soviet-American competition, France intervened in Gabon (1964), Central African Republic (1979), and the Comoros (1989), all former colonies; and minor powers such as Greece (1974), Turkey (1974), Vietnam (1979), and Tanzania (1979) all intervened to topple governments in neighboring countries.

Regime changes in Latin American dominated the second half of the nineteenth century, the period with the third-highest number of regime changes. Indeed, all but four of the twenty-one cases during this half-century occurred in Central or South America, and of the remaining seventeen, eleven involved El Salvador, Guatemala, Honduras, and Nicaragua.[49] This period also includes three other important cases. The first is the doomed French expedition (1862–67) in Mexico that removed Benito Juárez and installed Austrian Archduke Maximilian as emperor of Mexico until he was deposed and killed after his French benefactors withdrew.[50] The second is the overthrow of Paraguayan dictator Francisco Solano López by Brazil and Argentina during a six-year war (1864–70).[51] The third case consists of Chile's repeated attempts to find a Peruvian figurehead who would cede the territories Chile coveted to end the War of the Pacific (1879–83).[52]

In the first half of the nineteenth century, by contrast, the period with the second-fewest regime changes, the action was almost entirely in Europe and consisted for the most part of conservative monarchies intervening to reverse liberal revolutions in small states and minor principalities. Typical were the Austrian and Prussian interventions in Tuscany, Saxony, and Baden to put down the revolutions of 1848 and restore displaced monarchs to their thrones. The only regime changes outside of Europe at this time were Britain's first foray into Afghanistan in 1839 to oust Dost Mohammad and El Salvador's and Honduras's joint intervention that deposed Nicaraguan leader Emiliano Madrid in 1845.[53]

Finally, the post–Cold War era contains the fewest cases of regime change but is also the shortest period, with only sixteen years. Six of the nine cases (and eight of eleven if one includes Côte d'Ivoire and Libya in 2011) occurred in Africa, equaling the Cold War for the most regime changes on this continent and far surpassing it as a percentage of cases during the respective time periods. Most of these African interventions—including those in Lesotho (1994), the Comoros (1995), Republic of Congo (1997), and Sierra Leone (1998)—were implemented to restore recently ousted leaders to power. In the midst of the civil war in Sierra Leone, for example, democratically elected president Ahmed Tejan Kabbah was overthrown in a military coup in May 1997 and replaced by Major Jonny Paul Koroma. Koroma's junta, the Armed Forces Revolutionary Council (AFRC), invited the Revolutionary United Front (RUF), the principal rebel group known for its brutality against civilians, to join

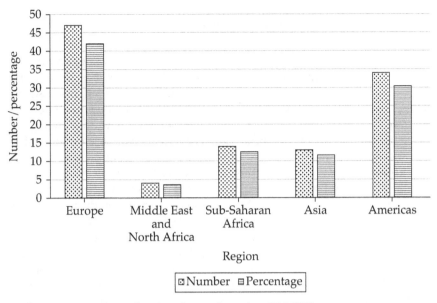

Figure 1.4. Foreign-imposed regime changes by region, 1816–2008

the government in Freetown. In February 1998, however, a Nigerian-led peacekeeping force operating under the banner of the Economic Community of West African States (ECOWAS) drove the AFRC/RUF junta from power and reinstated President Kabbah.[54] The other two African cases in the post–Cold War era include the joint Rwandan-Ugandan operation to replace Zaire's President Mobutu with Laurent Kabila in 1997, a case I discuss at length in chapter 5, and Chad's backing for General François Bozizé in his drive to overthrow Central African Republic president Ange-Félix Patassé in 2003.

Lastly, figure 1.4 highlights the distribution of regime changes by region of the world. Given the large number of cases associated with World War II, it is unsurprising that Europe has experienced the most regime changes of any region in the world (forty-seven). The frequent US interventions in its hemisphere combined with the numerous regime changes inflicted by Central American countries on each other ensure that the Americas are the second most regime-change-prone region on the globe with thirty-four cases. Sub-Saharan Africa and Asia place third and fourth with fourteen and thirteen regime changes, respectively. Perhaps most surprising is that the Middle East and North Africa have experienced so few regime changes (four). Indeed, Iran (1941 and 1953) and Iraq (1941 and 2003) are the only countries in the entire region to suffer regime changes, a remarkable fact given the large number of interstate wars, civil wars, coups, and revolutions that have taken place.[55]

A Typology of Foreign-Imposed Regime Change

With few exceptions, existing scholarship treats regime change as a homogeneous phenomenon.[56] I argue that this choice obscures important and consequential variation among different types of regime changes. At the most basic level, when contemplating regime change, all potential interveners face two choices. The first choice is whether to empower a new regime or restore an old one. If the former, interveners must choose between simply installing an individual or building a new set of supporting political institutions. I term the first of these choices *leadership regime change* and the second *institutional regime change*. If, on the other hand, an intervener desires to restore a prior regime, it has three options depending on the institutional structure of the target state. If the target was previously a monarchy or a dictatorship where governing authority is embodied in a single individual, then returning that individual is sufficient to restore the regime. If the target previously had a more elaborate set of institutions, such as democracy or single-party authoritarianism, restoring individuals may be less important than reviving institutions, although the two often go together. Interveners may thus choose to restore the prior institutions under the same leader as before or a different one. Either way, I refer to regime changes that return the prior ruler and/or set of institutions to power as *restoration regime changes*. Figure 1.5 illustrates my typology.

The combination of promoting a leader who was not the previous ruler of the country comprises what I call *leadership regime change*. In this category, interveners empower new elites but do little to develop target institutions, contenting themselves with replacing the leader and letting him

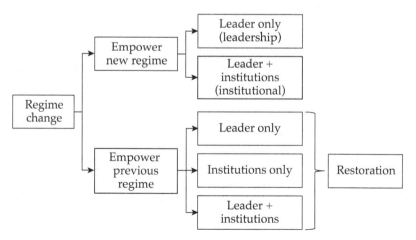

Figure 1.5. A typology of foreign-imposed regime change

establish whatever institutions he sees fit. Examples of leadership regime change include Britain's forays into Afghanistan (1839–42 and 1878–80), London's joint campaign with the Soviets to oust Iran's Reza Pahlavi (1941), and France's replacement of Jean-Bédel Bokassa with David Dacko in Central African Republic (1979).[57] Each of these interventions was concerned solely with *who* governed the target state, not *how* or through what means. In Afghanistan, Britain's primary grievance was that the leaders it sought to oust were cultivating closer relations with Russia. Enhanced Russian influence—or worse yet, Russian control over the country—threatened the northern approaches to India.[58] Two generations of British leaders thus sought to ensure that whoever ruled Afghanistan would maintain it as a bulwark against further Russian expansion in Central Asia. Similarly, Reza Pahlavi's tolerance of German influence in Iran endangered a crucial source of petroleum for the Allies as well as a vital supply line to the Soviet Union.[59] The joint Anglo-Soviet invasion sought merely to empower a ruler who appreciated the importance of Iran's place in the Allied camp. The French coup against Bokassa was triggered by his flirtation with Libya's Muammar Qaddafi as well as the self-styled "emperor's" implication in the deaths of over one hundred children killed by his government as it repressed student protests against compulsory school uniforms.[60] According to Brian Titley, however, for the French, "Getting rid of the emperor was only part of the task; it was equally important to choose his successor carefully. Such a critical detail could not be left to chance—or to democracy. The French were going to hand-pick the president of the restored republic and install him in power. Moreover, they were determined to select someone who, above all else, would best serve their interests."[61] As shown in figure 1.6, the sixty-five leadership regime changes over the past two centuries make it the most common type of regime change over that time period, accounting for 58 percent of the cases.

The second and most ambitious type of regime change—*institutional regime change*—combines empowering a new leader and promoting new institutions. There are two versions of institutional regime change. In one, democracies seek to establish democratic institutions in targets, as the United States did in West Germany and Japan after World War II, or more recently in Afghanistan and Iraq. In the other, interveners aim to set up single-party regimes in targets after intervention, as when the Soviets established communist regimes in Eastern Europe in the 1940s. It is important to note that institutional regime changes are coded based on the intentions and actions of the intervener, not on whether or not they succeeded in establishing consolidated democratic or single-party governments. The US regime change and occupation of the Dominican Republic in 1916, which sought but ultimately failed to promote democracy, is thus just as much of an institutional regime change as the successful establishment of consolidated democracies after US regime changes in Germany and Japan at the

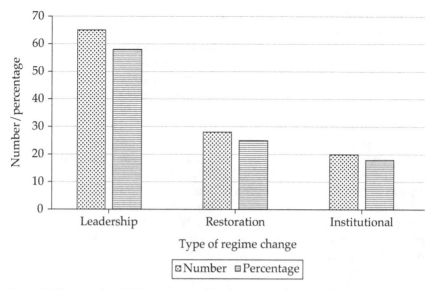

Figure 1.6. Frequencies of different types of foreign-imposed regime changes, 1816–2008. Because of rounding, these figures sum to 101 rather than 100.

conclusion of World War II. Twenty institutional regime changes took place from 1816 to 2008—18 percent of all regime changes.

The third type of regime change consists of what I call *restoration regime change*, which occurs when an intervener simply returns the leader or institutions to power that most recently governed a country before an interregnum of no more than five years caused by a coup, revolution, or foreign removal of a leader.[62] Indeed, when an intervener undertakes a restoration, there is typically little need to build institutions since the regime brought back to power reverts to the status quo that prevailed before it was dislodged. If, for example, the target country was previously a monarchy or dictatorship, the regime is typically synonymous with an individual; restoring that individual is sufficient to restore the regime. Several restorations of this kind occurred in Europe between 1820 and 1850, when conservative monarchies like Austria and Prussia intervened to reverse liberal revolutions and reinstall deposed kings in minor states in Italy and Germany. When the target previously possessed more elaborate institutions, such as in a democracy, restoration typically involves reinstating those institutions—and often the previous leader as well. Examples of this type include the Allied restorations of Western European democracies overthrown and occupied by Nazi Germany during World War II. In Belgium, for example, the Allied liberation of the country in 1944 reinstated Hubert Pierlot—the prime minister when World War II began and in exile during the German occupation. By contrast, in the Netherlands, the Dutch prime minister at the beginning of the war, Dirk Jan de Geer, lost power during the conflict, so the restoration of Dutch democracy in 1945 brought a different leader—Pieter Sjoerds Gerbrandy, the prime minister of the government in exile—to power.[63] I code each of these cases as restorations because their goal was not to impose a new leader or political order but to reestablish the status quo that existed prior to the German invasion. The twenty-eight restoration regime changes in my data compose 25 percent of the total cases.[64]

Foreign-imposed regime change consists of the removal of the effective leader of an independent state, which remains formally sovereign, by the government of another state by the threat or use of force. The most common method by which intervening states accomplish regime change is through the direct application of military force—typically an invasion by ground troops. States may also obtain the resignation of foreign leaders by threatening to use force or through overt or covert cooperation with individuals or groups that aspire to overthrow a sitting government. According to this definition, 120 individual leaders were removed in foreign-imposed regime changes from 1816 to 2008. In nearly 60 percent of these cases, interveners simply replaced the leader and did not bother with building political institutions in the target state. In just under 20 percent of the cases, interveners removed and replaced leaders and sought to implant institutions as well, whereas about 25 percent of regime changes consist of restoring a recently ousted ruler or set of institutions to power.

With these definitions in hand, in the next chapter I lay out my theory of why regime change so often goes wrong.

Theorizing the Effects of Foreign-Imposed Regime Change

This chapter lays out my theory of the effects of foreign-imposed regime change. I build directly on the argument touched on in the book's introduction that states undertake regime change to align a target's preferences with their own on an important issue. Interveners believe—and existing theories assume—that installing leaders who share their interests successfully aligns the two countries' preferences. My argument is that regime change fails to align preferences because imposed leaders—who value their own political survival once placed in power—must consider the interests of their domestic constituents, which are not isomorphic with the intervener's. Facing two principals with competing preferences and the ability to remove her from office places the leader in a difficult situation because policies that please one antagonize the other. In the language of principal-agent theory, imposed leaders face a *problem of competing principals*. Leaders who ignore their constituents and maintain their commitments to an external patron run the risk of forcible leader removal (e.g., assassinations, coups, and revolutions) and civil war. Leaders who follow the wishes of their domestic audience and renege on their external commitments run the risk of removal at the hands of—or provoking a conflict with—their foreign patrons.

Regime change can also break the state's monopoly on violence by inducing *military disintegration*, which can trigger immediate insurgency and civil war. This part of the theory assumes that all leaders ousted by regime change would like to regain power but vary in their ability to do so. The critical factors, according to this argument, are whether the leader escapes capture, exile, or death at the hands of the intervener and whether the intervention causes the target's military to collapse. Leaders that escape have the motive to fight their way back into power; when the army collapses and flees, this provides leaders with the opportunity—in the form of thousands of armed men on the loose—to launch an insurgency. Ironically, therefore, quick and decisive battlefield victories can create conditions favorable for insurgency. The military disintegration mechanism thus contends that what happens at

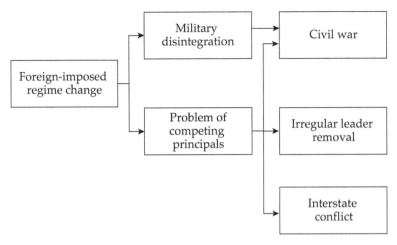

Figure 2.1. A diagram of the theory

the moment of regime change strongly influences whether violence unfolds in the immediate aftermath. Figure 2.1 illustrates these arguments.

The competing principals mechanism further differentiates among three types of regime change. *Leadership regime change* provokes the most serious dilemmas for imposed leaders and thus tends to have the most deleterious effects on intervener-target relations, imposed-leader survival, and the likelihood of civil strife. *Restoration regime change*, by contrast, tends to be stabilizing because it rehabilitates leaders and/or regimes that had at least some domestic legitimacy prior to their removal. It also destroys the domestic opposition, which ameliorates much of the interest asymmetry that drives post-regime-change internal and external conflict. *Institutional regime change*, finally, falls between leadership and restoration regime change depending on the target's suitability for building new (democratic or autocratic) institutions, which determines whether institutional regime changes succeed.

I begin the chapter, however, by briefly outlining *how* interstate disputes escalate to regime change, before reviewing the case for regime change—how regime change is supposed to work to generate amicable relations between interveners and targets—in the second section. Regime change optimists maintain that interveners can neutralize threats and create reliable allies by replacing hostile leaders with friendly ones, or—for democratic interveners—by democratizing the target's political institutions. The remainder of the chapter is devoted to laying out in detail the mechanisms of military disintegration and competing principals. I first explain why regime change often fails to deliver the hoped-for beneficial outcomes and then elaborate the conditions under which regime change is more likely to result in better or worse outcomes.

Paths to Regime Change: A Simple Model

I begin by sketching out a simple informal model of the paths to regime change.[1] The model assumes a dispute between two countries, State A and State B. The issue in dispute need not be over the leadership of one of the states; it can arise over any number of issues, including territory; ideology; the target's treatment of foreign businesses, its aspirations for nuclear weapons, or support for terrorism; or shifts in the balance of power.[2] The model is set in motion when State A (the challenger) decides to make a demand— formal or informal, public or private, with or without explicit consequences for refusing—of State B (the target).[3] State B can either choose to comply with A's demand, in which case the crisis ends with an outcome favorable to A, or it can refuse. If State B refuses, State A has three options. First, it can back down, in which case the crisis ends, and leaders in State A face the consequences, if any, of having issued an empty threat.[4] Second, State A can attack in pursuit of its original objectives, in which case (assuming that B resists) war ensues. Third, State A can decide to change its original objective and seek to remove the leadership of State B—a choice that does not necessarily imply an immediate overt attack.

Assume that State B rejects State A's demand and in response A chooses the second option above and attacks. In this case two scenarios are possible. In one, A and B fight and—depending on a number of factors—one prevails and imposes its preferred solution to the dispute that caused the war; or the two negotiate a settlement that reflects their updated assessments of the balance of power between them (based on the progress of the war to that point). Such a settlement may favor one or the other side (and thus be coded as a "win" for one and a "loss" for the other) or reflect a stalemate in which both sides achieve some but not all of their aims (often coded as "draws"). In a second scenario, however, depending on how the war unfolds, State A decides to expand its war objectives to include regime change. If this occurs, I assume that A imposes a change of leadership in B if it wins the war, but not if it loses or the war ends in a stalemate. An example of this kind of escalation was the US decision to eliminate the North Korean regime and unify Korea under Southern governance after the onset of the Korean War.[5]

Now let us consider what happens if State A, rather than attacking right away as in option two, chooses option three and decides to seek regime change. In this case, State A has multiple ways to proceed. It may issue a compellent threat demanding the replacement of State B's leaders or it may work overtly, covertly, or both to bring about the downfall of B's leaders. If A issues a compellent threat for regime change and B accepts, regime change occurs and the crisis ends. If B refuses, A again has three options: (1) it can back down, which ends the crisis; (2) it can attack and wage war—alone, in conjunction with other states, or together with forces from the target country opposed to the current leader—explicitly for regime change from the beginning; or (3) it can pursue regime change covertly. In either of these latter two eventualities, A's regime change efforts may fail, in which case the status quo prevails, or they can succeed, in which case regime change occurs.

The final step in the model involves the choice of which type of regime change to impose. Willard-Foster, for example, posits two types: partial regime change, in which only the target's leaders are replaced, and full regime change, in which both leaders and political institutions are replaced.[6] Which type of regime change the intervener carries out depends on which form of domestic opposition the intervener works with: the internal opposition, defined as a group that participates in the existing political system in the target state, or the external opposition, a group that resides outside the existing political system (and sometimes outside the target state). When an intervener collaborates with the internal opposition to bring about regime change, the result is usually a coup that replaces one leader with another. The advantage of partial regime change is that it is cheap, since insiders need little military support from the foreign power; the disadvantage is that it can result in a new leader who was close to the previous leader and thus may not align the two states' preferences. By contrast, if the intervener instead backs the external opposition, full regime change is typically the result. The downside of full regime change is that because external groups are weak, regime change requires more military participation from the intervener and is thus more costly. The upside is that because interveners have more control over who takes power and new institutions are put in place, full regime change is more likely to emplace a leader sympathetic to the intervener's interests and produce similar successor leaders.

In this book I propose a typology that partially overlaps with that of Willard-Foster.[7] I also argue that intervening states choose among two fundamental types of regime change, but I contend that the basic division is between cases where outsiders restore the preceding regime and those where they empower a new regime. In the former scenario, the previous set of institutions is restored and often the same leader as well. In the latter scenario, interveners choose between simply installing a new leader or empowering a leader *and* helping to create new political institutions. I argue that when restoration is not possible or appropriate, interveners typically opt for leadership regime change because it is cheaper and less time consuming than trying to build new institutions. Under certain circumstances, however, such as when the defeated target constituted a serious threat, interveners will invest in new institutions—but not at the expense of obtaining their preferred leader in the short term.

The paths to regime change outlined above dovetail nicely with the three ways that interveners enact regime change described in chapter 1: (1) as the result of successful compellent threats (e.g., Soviet threats against the Baltic states in 1940), (2) as the result of overt or covert efforts in cooperation with domestic forces in the target state (e.g., the United States and the Northern Alliance in Afghanistan, and the United States in Guatemala in 1954, respectively), and (3) as the result of wars launched specifically for regime change or wars launched for other reasons that escalate to regime change (e.g., Iraq in 2003, and the Western Allies in the two world wars, respectively).

One interesting point highlighted by the model is that many theories that ostensibly explain regime change actually explain the origins of disputes about other issues that may or may not escalate to regime change.[8] In most cases, the state undertaking compellence does not object to the target's leader per se, but objects to his policies. If the leader would simply change those policies, regime change would be unnecessary. Put differently, most existing theories do not explain why a challenger seeks to resolve a dispute with a target by overthrowing its leaders rather than employing some other means of influence, such as the threat or use of economic or military coercion.[9]

How Foreign-Imposed Regime Change Is Supposed to Work

Foreign-imposed regime change is motivated in almost all cases by the desire of an intervening state to alter the foreign policy preferences of a target state. Typically, the leader of the target state holds preferences that diverge significantly from the intervener's on an important policy issue and thus the intervener seeks to remove that leader and replace him with a more agreeable one. According to one of the few studies of the effects of overthrowing foreign governments, regime change enables an intervener to improve relations between it and a target by installing new leaders with similar policy preferences.[10] In theory, this alignment of interests should resolve disputes and enhance cooperation between the two states. In the best-case scenario, the newly installed regime becomes a reliable client state that promotes the intervener's interests at home and abroad.[11]

The logic of regime change optimism is simple: if the operation is successful, the newly installed regime and the intervener will have the same (or highly similar) interests, suggesting that the former will then act in the latter's interests without having to be bribed or coerced into doing so.[12] After regime change, disputes between the intervener and the target government are less likely to arise because the target state should of its own accord act in the intervener's interests. This logic suggests that, regardless of the specific source of disagreement during an interstate dispute, regime change should have a positive influence on intervener-target relations by changing the two states' relationship from one marred by conflicting interests to one characterized by mutual interests.[13]

There are two specific ways that regime change can "change the foreign policy preferences of the target country" to bring them into line with the intervener's preferences. The most obvious route is to eliminate trouble-some elites and promote ones who share the intervener's interests. According to Lo, Hashimoto, and Reiter, interveners can promote closer relations by "executing, imprisoning, or exiling militarist leaders and their supporters . . . and/or empowering or importing leaders with more compliant and/or peaceful foreign policy preferences."[14] Bruce Bueno de Mesquita and George Downs similarly argue that interveners are best able to achieve their goals by installing an "autocracy or a rigged election democracy in the target state."[15] Such regimes, they argue, are best able to deliver concessions since they need not cater to the preferences of the median voter to remain in power.

A deeper mechanism for achieving a congruence of interests is to "transform the political institutions of the target."[16] For a democracy, this would entail installing democratic institutions in a target or otherwise transforming its laws or constitution. Lo, Hashimoto, and Reiter, for example, argue that "democratization may be an institutional means of more permanently empowering actors with pacific preferences over actors with militarist preferences."[17] Interveners may further transform targets by forcing them to "hardwire pacifism into their constitutions or laws."[18] This mechanism is clearly different than simply installing leaders with similar preferences. It relies on the broader shared interest of democracies in avoiding conflict with one another and assumes that by empowering democracy abroad, a democratic intervener can foster peaceful relations with former adversaries in which disputes will be resolved by negotiation and compromise rather than force of arms. Installing democratic institutions may also help ensure that only leaders with preferences that are broadly compatible with the intervener's come to power. Forced democratization, however, is not inconsistent with a patron-client relationship: the intervener may make continued support for the new regime contingent on the target providing certain concessions, such as basing rights, alliance contributions, or other forms of security cooperation.

Whether regime change is achieved by installing particular friendly individuals in power in target states or by transforming their political institutions, it is supposed to result in stable, reliable allies disposed to protecting interveners' interests.

Four important assumptions underlie the optimistic perspective on regime change. First, the argument assumes that regime change can be implemented without fundamentally weakening the target state and provoking an immediate challenge to the intervener's and its protégé's authority. Although some regime changes have failed to incite a backlash in the target, the recent examples of Afghanistan, Iraq, and Libya ought to induce caution. Interveners, rather than departing and enjoying good relations with a new ally, may instead have to cope with an insurgency that threatens their control over the target.

Second, the optimist view of regime change assumes either a close alignment of interests between the intervening and target states or that the target population's interests are congruent with those of the installed leader, such that by doing what an intervener wants, the protégé does not endanger her own political survival. In the former variant, because all leaders are in some measure accountable to their own citizens—whether by voting or violence—and these citizens will presumably object if a leader's policies routinely prioritize foreign interests over their own, the interests of the two states *must* coincide for a divergence of interests (and the potential for conflict) to be avoided. Alternatively, if a state's interests are reducible to the interests of the leader of the state, then there would be no conflict by definition.

Third, the optimist perspective assumes that imposed leaders who survive any short-term backlash against regime change are able to maintain themselves in office in the medium to long term. This assumption might be reasonable: most imposed leaders are autocrats who could potentially repress any domestic opposition that might arise. If we loosen the assumption of congruent interests, however, and allow for the possibility of actors in the target state that oppose the imposed leader's policies, the argument starts to become tenuous. If we further acknowledge that many imposed leaders are exiles who ride to power at the point of foreign bayonets, the argument becomes even more shaky, since these leaders are likely to have little domestic legitimacy or support.

Finally, optimists assume that strategies of institutional transformation necessarily succeed. Existing research, however, does not support this assumption. Studies of nation building and other forms of forceful democracy promotion find that success is rare and further that it is heavily contingent on context. Democracy is much more likely to take root in societies where certain preconditions for democracy are present.[19] When democracy promotion fails, authoritarian rulers seize power who may or may not be friendly to the intervener. Either way, the deeper sources of convergence sought by interveners will be absent.[20]

Below I build on these points to develop an alternative understanding of regime change in which changing another state's preferences and behavior is not as simple as proponents suggest. One reason is that regime change sometimes triggers immediate resistance that can threaten an imposed leader's tenure even before it has begun. A second reason is that the key mechanism underlying the optimistic interpretation of regime change—that it empowers new leaders with similar policy preferences—neglects a number of problems that undermine principal-agent relations, such as adverse selection, information asymmetry, and interest asymmetry that can cause imposed leaders' behavior to diverge from interveners' expectations over time. Most importantly, however, regime change optimists ignore that an imposed leader's domestic constituents comprise a second principal, whose preferences differ from the intervener's and who can also remove the leader from power.

Because imposed leaders want to remain in office, they cannot ignore domestic opinion without risking defeat in the next election or, alternatively, a coup, revolution, or civil war. On the other hand, leaders who seek to appease domestic constituencies by defying the intervener risk angering their external principal and provoking interstate conflict with it. In short, these dynamics can recreate the interest asymmetry that caused the intervener to seek regime change in the first place. Regime change sets forces in motion that can threaten the survival of imposed leaders, increase the chances of civil war, and lead to conflict between interveners and targets.

Theory, Part I: Regime Change and Military Disintegration

This section and the next spell out my theory of why regime change can lead to negative consequences for target states and for intervener-target relations. The current section elaborates the first mechanism, military disintegration, which can quickly trigger insurgency in target states. The ensuing section details the problem of competing principals, which can increase the likelihood not only of insurgency, but also violent leader removal and intervener-target conflict. The first mechanism focuses on the process and immediate aftermath of regime change, whereas the second analyzes the patron-protégé (or principal-agent) relationship over time.

My theory implies that avoiding adverse consequences following regime change is a two-step process. First, interveners must successfully navigate the immediate aftermath of regime change when the target's military may disintegrate and violently resist the imposition of a new regime by waging an insurgency. Second, even if conflict does not erupt in this initial period, imposed leaders' preferences may diverge from the intervener's over time and provoke domestic unrest or conflict with it. In a handful of cases, including the recent cases of Afghanistan and Iraq, military disintegration triggers insurgency in the short term *and*, in the longer term, preference divergence stemming from the problem of competing principals contributes to difficult intervener-target relations. The military disintegration mechanism articulated in this section, however, focuses only on the relationship between regime change and insurgency or civil war. The problem of competing principals can cause not only civil war but also violent leader removal and intervener-target conflict.

ASSUMPTIONS

The military disintegration mechanism begins by assuming that leaders who are overthrown by foreign powers would prefer to have remained in office and would prefer to be restored to office. It is not overly difficult to understand why a leader who is thrown out of power would want to get it back. That national leaders desire to remain in office is one of the bedrock assumptions of modern political science.[21] Material and ideational factors undergird this assumption. Leaders—especially those who rule in an authoritarian manner—accrue significant material benefits from power. Once they assume office, moreover, authoritarian leaders' personal survival is often synonymous with their political survival, as losing power in such systems often means death. Leaders in all types of political systems may also have ideological agendas they wish to carry out, ranging from creating communist utopias or ethnically pure nation-states to reforming health care, social safety nets, the tax code, or campaign finance laws. Maintaining power may also satisfy personal desires for glory or fame. Whatever the particular reason, it is safe to assume that political leaders prefer to remain in power, are unhappy to be chased from office by foreign intervention, and are willing to go to some lengths to regain their former position.

Of course, not all ousted leaders have the ability to act on that preference. In the vast majority of cases they personally are captured, exiled, or killed, and their armed forces likewise are captured or surrender. This reality implies that the first set of factors analysts should consider when estimating the chance of resistance to regime change is whether the leader escapes or is neutralized during the intervention, and whether the ousted regime's military flees or surrenders.

WHY DEFEATS IN WAR ARE NOT ALL THE SAME

Whether interveners are able to neutralize the targeted leader and gain control of the target state's military is of critical importance for the likelihood that they will face civil war after regime change. However, I argue that neutralizing the military is the single most important factor. Leaders who manage to evade death or capture by the intervener's forces are powerless to resist their ouster without armed followers. If the army surrenders, the overthrown leader faces the difficult task of raising an entirely new force. Recruiting new fighters is especially onerous given that most ousted leaders must flee the country or go into hiding—particularly if the military capitulates. Because ousted leaders are generally much less of a threat if the military surrenders, I consider the military variable to be the dominant one.[22]

Previous studies, by contrast, have found that regime change increases the likelihood of civil war when it occurs simultaneously with defeat in an interstate war—no matter how it ends. Goran Peic and Dan Reiter, for example, claim that when regime change coincides with losing an interstate war, the combination can wreck the target state's industrial base, transportation network, and other infrastructure; cripple its military and other security forces; and oust experienced and capable officials.[23] The result of this destruction is that targets are gravely weakened, which provides opportunities for would-be rebels to challenge the state.

This argument has two important problems. First, there are clear exceptions to this purported relationship, since some of the most devastating defeats in recent history—those of Germany and Japan in World War II, for example—ended in regime changes but were not followed by civil war. Similarly, the overthrow (and killing) of Francisco Solano López by Brazilian forces toward the end of the War of the Triple Alliance in 1869 did not trigger a civil war in Paraguay even though it occurred near the conclusion of a six-year struggle in which Paraguay lost more than half of its population.[24] As I demonstrate in chapter 4, my data on regime change and the onset of civil war do not support the conclusion that losing an interstate war in combination with experiencing regime change significantly increases the chance of a civil war occurring afterward beyond experiencing regime change alone. It thus appears that there is no simple correlation between defeat in an interstate war, regime change, and subsequent civil wars. If anything, the cases cited above suggest that greater levels of destruction may *lessen* the chance of civil wars after regime change.

Second, the Peic and Reiter argument neglects the possibility that rebellions might be launched by the forces of order themselves, namely the armies of the recently deposed governments. Logically, the first concern of a state that is attempting to displace a foreign leader is the attitude of those who can forcibly resist change. That ability rests principally in the leader himself and the leader's military and security services. These are the most likely sources of immediate resistance, and thus interveners are concerned about neutralizing them if possible. For example, the United States successfully persuaded the Guatemalan Army not to resist Carlos Castillo Armas and his puny exile force in 1954—and indeed to topple President Jacobo Árbenz itself—by convincing Guatemalan officers that if they opposed Castillo Armas they would have to face a US invasion.[25] Sometimes the intervener goes so far as to work actively with the target's military in plotting a leader's demise, as the United States did in Iran (1953) and South Vietnam (1963). Leaders in each of these cases were either apprehended or killed.[26]

A TYPOLOGY OF REGIME CHANGE OUTCOMES

I divide regime changes into four types based on the extent to which they succeed in neutralizing the outgoing leader and the target state's military. This typology is shown in table 2.1. My argument is that the likelihood of violent resistance after regime change is highest in cases in which the military disintegrates and the leader escapes. Civil war is less likely, although still quite likely, when the military collapses and the leader is neutralized. By contrast, the likelihood that regime change is followed by insurgency is low when the military remains cohesive even if the leader escapes, and lowest when the military does not disintegrate and the leader is captured or killed.[27]

Table 2.1 Military disintegration and the likelihood of civil war

	Disposition of the army	
	Army disintegrates	Army remains intact
Disposition of the leader	Civil war most likely	Civil war unlikely
Leader escapes	Afghanistan (1839)	Nicaragua (1909)
	Mexico (1863)	Haiti (1915)
	Peru (1881)	Costa Rica (1919)
	Yugoslavia (1941)	Norway (1940)
	Greece (1941)	Luxembourg (1940)
	Cambodia (1979)	Belgium (1940)
	Uganda (1979)	Netherlands (1940)
	Afghanistan (2001)	Lithuania (1940)
	Iraq (2003)	Haiti (1994)
Leader neutralized	Civil war likely	Civil war least likely
	Iraq (2004–)	Paraguay (1869)
	Libya (2011)	Estonia (1940)
		Latvia (1940)
		Germany (1945)
		Japan (1945)
		Iran (1953)
		Guatemala (1954)
		South Vietnam (1963)
		Chile (1973)
		Panama (1990)

Military disintegration comprises situations in which the target state's army is defeated quickly but breaks apart, melts away, or a substantial portion of it escapes to a remote location or across an international border. The leader may also flee, but the key question is the disposition of the army. In cases of military disintegration, there is often no formal surrender ceremony where the defeated submit to the victors. Instead, substantial elements of the army elude capture and flee.

The US invasions of Afghanistan in 2001 and Iraq in 2003 were both cases of military disintegration. In Afghanistan, according to Ahmed Rashid, "The Taliban regime had been routed and driven from power, but it was still not possible to say it had been fully defeated. Between eight thousand and twelve thousand Taliban, or 20 percent of their total force, had been killed, with twice that number wounded and seven thousand taken prisoner. Those remaining fled to their home villages or to Pakistan."[28] Rashid estimates total Taliban strength before the war at 60,000, meaning that between 17,000 and 29,000 Taliban escaped.[29] The leader of the Taliban government, Mullah Mohammed Omar, also fled to Pakistan in a convoy of motorbikes. In Iraq, the United States actually ensured the disintegration of the army when Paul Bremer dissolved it along with the Ministry of the Interior, which included the police, other security services, and presidential security units, a total of over 700,000 people.[30] To be sure, much of the Iraqi Army had dis-integrated during the invasion, but Bremer's order prevented it from being reformed. Saddam Hussein initially eluded capture but spent his last months of freedom evading Coalition forces rather than directing the bud-ding insurgency. Afghanistan is thus an example of a case with the highest likelihood of insurgency after regime change. Iraq falls in the second high-est category (at the latest after Saddam's capture in December 2003) but demonstrates that the difference between these two types may not be large.

Civil war is much less likely when the target state's military remains co-hesive and either submits to the intervener or seizes power itself under threat of invasion or with the backing of the threatening power. The first scenario, in which the target's armed forces capitulate to an intervener, is demon-strated by military defeat and surrender. Military surrender occurs when the target's military is defeated on the battlefield but remains cohesive, sub-ject to higher command, and surrenders in a more or less orderly fashion. Examples of military surrender include the capitulations of Germany and Japan in 1945. German forces began surrendering to the Allies in the begin-ning of May, and General Alfred Jödl signed the formal document of sur-render on May 7. Only a handful of units continued fighting after May 8 when the cease-fire took effect, but these, too, soon gave up. The Allies dis-armed over five million German soldiers in the months after VE Day.[31] In Japan, Emperor Hirohito was able to convince the military high command to surrender following the Soviet invasion of Manchuria and the dropping of the second atomic bomb on Nagasaki.[32] A group of junior officers at-tempted a coup on the night of August 14, but it was quickly put down; the United States took roughly 4.3 million Japanese servicemen prisoner in the home islands.[33] Although not a case of foreign-imposed regime change, the French defeat by Germany in June 1940 provides another good example of a military surrender. Hit by the German blitzkrieg, much of the French Army lost cohesion, but French soldiers for the most part did not try to es-cape to fight again another day. Rather, they surrendered en masse: the Weh-rmacht took two million prisoners during and after the offensive.[34]

Regime changes accomplished by successful coercive diplomacy or com-pellent threats also tend not to induce military disintegration and are thus unlikely to trigger insurgency after a regime change. Regime change by compellence consists of instances in which an intervener persuades a tar-geted leader to resign through militarized threats rather than having to use significant amounts of force—and the state's military does not contest the change of regime.[35] This scenario played out between the Soviet Union and the Baltic republics (Latvia, Lithuania, and Estonia) in June 1940. Moscow delivered a similar ultimatum to each country demanding the establish-ment of governments capable of faithfully implementing the defense pacts Stalin had forced upon these countries the previous October—in other words, the installation of communist regimes.[36] Facing the might of the Red

Army, each state chose to acquiesce and was occupied by Soviet troops without a fight.[37] In other cases, such as Haiti in 1994, demands for leaders to step down coupled with threatening deployments of military force (and significant inducements, such as immunity from prosecution and a cushy exile) are sufficient to obtain a peaceful exit. Because there is no (or very limited) fighting, in cases of regime change by compellence, the target state's military is likely to remain cohesive and the ousted leader either is arrested or goes into exile. Either way, the likelihood of civil war owing to military disintegration is low after this type of regime change.

A third variety of regime change that is unlikely to trigger military disintegration consists of military takeovers, cases in which the target state's military, without being defeated in battle, assumes control over the state by forcing the sitting leader to abdicate either under threat from—or with the assistance of—the intervener. The key difference between a military takeover and successful compellence is that in the former the leader refuses to succumb in the face of the intervener's threats or hostility, and hence must be removed by force. Examples of military takeovers include the US-backed coups against Mohammad Mossadegh in Iran, Patrice Lumumba in Congo, and Salvador Allende in Chile. Although rare, military takeovers are almost by definition unlikely to result in military disintegration, and leaders removed by their own military (albeit at the behest of a foreign power) are highly likely to be arrested or killed.[38]

CAUSAL LOGIC

When an invader overthrows a foreign leader but the target state's military disintegrates, it is highly likely that further hostilities—in the form of an insurgency launched by the former leader or elements of the old regime—will occur in the short term, for two reasons. First, the former ruler (or ruling group) is motivated to rebel owing to his desire to return to power and has the ability to fight because he retains his capacity to use force. When the United States sought to oust Árbenz in Guatemala, he was unable to resist because the army acquiesced to implicit US threats and switched sides. In Cambodia after the Vietnamese invasion, by contrast, roughly 25,000 Khmer Rouge troops survived the assault and fled to remote areas in the western Cardamom Mountains and along the Thai border.[39] Pol Pot and the other leaders of the Khmer Rouge had both motive and opportunity to resist the Vietnamese and try to regain power.

Second, even when the former leader escapes but is unable to lead the resistance, as after the US attack on Iraq, or flees into exile, as in the German invasion of Yugoslavia in 1941, military disintegration lets loose thousands of armed men into the countryside who may be mobilized for further resistance by former subordinates of the ousted leader or by other elites. This indirect mechanism increases the likelihood of violent resistance by creating an aggrieved stock of armed manpower. This is exactly what Decree No. 2 of the Coalition Provisional Authority accomplished in Iraq. At a protest against the dissolution of the armed forces on June 18, 2003, one speaker said, "We will take up arms. . . . We are very well-trained soldiers and we are armed. We will start ambushes, bombings and even suicide bombings. We will not let the Americans rule us in such a humiliating way."[40] Thomas Ricks argues that combined with de-Baathification, eliminating the army "inadvertently gave the insurgency its biggest boost. . . . The de-Baathification order created a class of disenfranchised, threatened leaders. . . . The dissolution of the army gave them a manpower pool of tens of thousands of angry, unemployed soldiers."[41]

By contrast, when leaders get away into exile—either voluntarily or one step ahead of the invading forces—but the military is defeated or acquiesces in the change of regime, the leader lacks the capability to foment unrest in his native country and thus can do little to bring about resistance. Such was the case with Western European leaders who fled the Nazi invasion in 1940, including Dirk Jan de Geer (Netherlands), Hubert Pierlot (Belgium), Pierre Dupong (Luxembourg), and Johan Nygaardsvold (Norway). Leaders such as these, if they are to be restored to power, are entirely dependent on foreign powers to help them regain office. In the case of the Western European democracies, this strategy paid off when the Allies defeated Nazi Germany in 1945. Others, such as Lithuanian president Antanas Smetona, who fled into exile ahead of the invading Red Army in June 1940, were less fortunate.

The primary prediction that follows from this discussion is that violent civil conflict is likely to erupt shortly after regime change when the leader escapes and the military fractures, especially when the leader is able to join elements of his former military and lead them in attempting to reverse regime change. Nearly as dangerous, however, is the situation where the leader is neutralized but the military falls apart, leaving large numbers of former soldiers at large. When the leader escapes but the military does not disintegrate, the risk of rebellion in the immediate aftermath of regime change is low, and if both actors are neutralized, civil war is highly unlikely.

WHEN DO ARMIES DISINTEGRATE?

My argument posits that when target militaries disintegrate in the course of operations undertaken by interveners to overthrow their governments, regime change is likely to be followed by insurgency.[42] Although my argument takes disintegration as a given and theorizes its effects, it is worth pausing for a moment to consider the conditions under which militaries are more likely to disintegrate, and thus where regime change is likely to provoke immediate violent resistance. Fully explaining military disintegration is beyond the scope of this book, but it may be possible to identify a few factors that contribute to military collapse.[43]

The literature on military effectiveness suggests some plausible answers to this question. First, an army is more likely to fall apart when it faces an opponent who employs the modern system of force employment and it does not. The modern system, as elaborated by Stephen Biddle, is a bundle of interrelated techniques at the tactical level consisting of exploitation of cover and concealment, dispersion and independent small unit maneuver, coordination of suppressive fire with movement, and combined arms integration.[44] These tactical innovations allow attackers to survive the storm of steel that is the contemporary battlefield long enough to make meaningful gains on the ground and achieve breakthrough. Once in the open in the defender's rear, attackers can shift to less furtive, more mobile operations and exploit the gap created in the enemy's lines to disrupt and destroy the defender's command-and-control, communications, and logistics in an effort to induce disorientation and rapid collapse. Modern system offense at the operational level (i.e., exploitation) is identical to what others have called "blitzkrieg," as is the objective: to cause the adversary's collapse without having to defeat its forces in detail.[45]

Against a defender also employing the modern system, modern system attackers are able to make incremental gains but cannot achieve breakthrough, and modern system defenders are highly unlikely to disintegrate.[46] Similarly, defenders who employ a defense-in-depth or mobile defense strategy are less susceptible to being victimized by a blitzkrieg. When the defender does not employ the modern system, however, not even superior numbers or better technology can save it. Without proper exploitation of cover and concealment by defenders, greater numbers simply mean more targets for properly concealed attackers to kill. Further, better weapons in the hands of defenders are irrelevant if there are no targets to shoot at. Defenders who are unable or unwilling to implement the modern system are thus vulnerable to having their lines pierced by the enemy, much as the British experienced at German hands in Operation Michael in March 1918.[47] Blitzkrieg theorists would similarly argue that static and linear defenses—such as the French employed against the German Wehrmacht in May 1940—are more vulnerable to breakthrough.[48] We can thus hypothesize that defender disintegration is more likely to occur if an attacker employs the modern system and the defender does not, or an attacker employs a blitzkrieg strategy and the defender counters with a static or linear defense.

The case of Yugoslavia in 1941 provides a textbook example of blitzkrieg producing military disintegration. When the Wehrmacht attacked on April 6, 1941, writes Frank Littlefield, its progress was so swift that most Yugoslav troops and reserves never saw action: "As a result, most of them simply melted off into the mountains, often as complete units under their officers. The German advance was so rapid that the tanks left all these soldiers behind or bypassed them completely. By the time the German infantry could come up on foot, these troops had taken cover in the mountains."[49]

Because "there were so few roads usable by tanks," Littlefield notes that "vast stretches of country were untouched for weeks. This left the largest part of the Yugoslav army absolutely untouched." Although large numbers were eventually corralled and the Croatian contingents quickly surrendered, "Many units were still complete and thousands of individuals simply were untouched and wandered off into the mountains where they began to organize themselves in their traditional military role."[50] This explanation for military collapse appears to apply to several cases in table 2.1, including Greece in 1941; Cambodia in 1979; and Afghanistan and Iraq in 2001 and 2003, respectively.

Recent work on military effectiveness has sought to explain why some belligerents are willing and able to implement the modern system whereas others are not. One of the most compelling answers to date is that leaders who regard their own militaries as the greatest threat to their survival will take a number of steps—known as "coup-proofing"—to neuter these forces and render them unable to take advantage of modern system techniques.[51] Such leaders typically remove competent officers who might pose a threat and appoint incompetent loyalists (oftentimes family members or relatives) in their place, prevent their militaries from training, sever lines of communication among commanders and units, create highly loyal and well-armed parallel militaries, aggressively spy on officers with multiple intelligence agencies, and block access to foreign military expertise.[52] These steps are often highly effective at weeding out internal threats and prolonging the leader's rule, but they do so at the expense of reducing the military's ability to fight external enemies. Scholars have thus concluded that countries ruled by personalist dictators are likely to field the least effective armies for waging interstate war.[53] I thus conjecture that the armies of these regimes are most likely to collapse when facing an attacker whose objective is regime change. Prime examples include Uganda in 1979, Iraq in 2003, and Libya in 2011.

A different approach to explaining militaries' predisposition to collapse focuses less on an army's skill and more on its will to fight. One such argument identifies two factors that explain an army's ability to fight under adversity: society's level of cohesion, which is a function of the regime's ability to control the population, and the target military's cohesion, which is a function of its autonomy from civilian meddling.[54] Regimes that exert high levels of control over society purvey a collectivist ideology, such as nationalism, communism, or fascism, and pair it with strong coercive capabilities to silence dissent and enforce conformity. Militaries with a high degree of autonomy are able to engage in realistic training for warfighting, which forms strong bonds inside the organization and within small units, enables soldiers to improvise and innovate flexible solutions, and facilitates trust. Countries that combine these two characteristics, such as Nazi Germany and North Vietnam, fight with tenacity and do not disintegrate under pressure, whereas nations that lack these traits, like France in 1940 and Italy in both world wars, field armies that are prone to collapse.

A second argument along these lines contends that states that discriminate against or violently exclude a substantial fraction of their societies from access to power—such as Saddam Hussein's Iraq, Bashar al-Assad's Syria, and Laurent Kabila's Democratic Republic of Congo (DRC)—field militaries plagued by numerous weaknesses that make them prone to collapse.[55] The fundamental problem that leaders in these states confront is that they must rely on groups for military manpower that harbor serious grievances against them. Because such "noncore" groups pose a serious risk of deserting, defecting to the opponent, or turning their guns on their "core group" comrades during combat, states with high levels of what Jason Lyall calls "military inequality" must devise ways of organizing their forces to guard against these eventualities.[56] All of the available choices—such as "blending" core and noncore soldiers within units, allowing homogeneous noncore units but staffing them with core group officers, or employing blocking detachments to fire on reluctant troops or soldiers trying to flee the battlefield—either reduce the sophistication of a unit's tactics, increase casualties, or generate risks of mass indiscipline.[57] Hence, armies characterized by high degrees of military inequality perform poorly and lose cohesion in battle.

Finally, factors that facilitate escape also likely influence whether target militaries disintegrate under pressure. The availability of territorial sanctuary, either in a neighboring state or in rough terrain (mountains, jungles, dense forests) within the state, probably affects the decision to escape rather than stand and fight. Defeated Peruvian soldiers in 1881, for instance, were able to flee to the relative safety of the Andes, just as the remnants of the Cambodian Army retreated to the Thai border a century later.

In sum, the act of regime change under certain conditions causes military disintegration, which in turn increases the likelihood of an insurgency breaking out in the target country. Although military disintegration triggered by regime change can go on to harm intervener-target relations by displacing the imposed leader should the intervener withdraw, the more immediate problem for interveners is having to wage a second (counterinsurgency) war to protect the fruits of the first war (for regime change). Under these circumstances, the intervener is usually enjoined to maintain sizable military forces in the country to wage counterinsurgency (COIN). COIN campaigns following regime changes have tied down numerous interveners in costly and protracted military ventures that are hard to win. Examples include the Germans in Yugoslavia and Greece during World War II, the Soviets in Afghanistan, the Vietnamese in Cambodia, and the United States in Afghanistan and Iraq.

It is also worth noting that when post-regime-change insurgency brought about by military disintegration compels interveners to remain and fight a

COIN campaign, this makes interstate conflict between intervener and target impossible but can hardly be considered a success for regime change. Such cases, however, are coded in existing studies as instances of interstate "peace," thereby supporting the correlation between regime change and a reduced likelihood of intervener-target conflict.[58]

Theory, Part II: Regime Change and the Problem of Competing Principals

In this section, I argue that even if regime change does not trigger civil war immediately, over time it can still heighten the possibility of civil strife, threaten the survival of imposed leaders, and worsen relations between interveners and targets—even sometimes leading to armed conflict between them—because it confronts protégés with what I call the problem of competing principals. First, I explain how four simple assumptions combine to generate dynamics that undermine the optimistic model of regime change: interveners enact regime change in pursuit of their interests; interveners prefer to install leaders whose preferences are congruent with their own; internal and external imperatives dictate that no two states have the same interests; and imposed leaders aim to remain in office. Second, I explain how these assumptions yield a principal-agent problem with competing principals. Whereas the intervening state (the external principal) wants the new leader (the agent) to pursue policies that reflect its interests, once in power, the new leader is focused on ensuring his or her own political survival. This goal may be undermined by implementing the intervener's agenda owing to the presence of a second (internal) principal, the imposed leader's domestic audience, whose preferences fail to line up with those of the intervener. Foreign-imposed leaders therefore face a dilemma: the more they attempt to implement the intervener's preferred policies, the more likely they are to face resistance from domestic actors—and vice-versa. The result is that imposed leaders face a risk of provoking conflict no matter what they do: internal actors may seek to remove them by launching an insurgency or attempting a coup and external patrons may mount an overt or covert campaign to replace them.

Third, I argue that the problem of competing principals is more severe after some types of regime change than others. In particular, it is most likely to unfold following leadership regime changes. In these cases, imposed leaders are most dependent on interveners for aid, since these individuals tend to lack domestic support or legitimacy. The extensive reliance of these leaders on external patrons activates the competing principals problem most severely. In restoration regime changes, by contrast, interveners are able to reempower leaders with congruent preferences who also possess some legitimacy in the eyes of their own people. Institutional regime changes—when they succeed in establishing new institutions—circumvent the dilemma in different ways depending on whether they promote democratic or authoritarian, single-party, institutions. Both increase the likelihood of interstate peace by empowering leaders with similar ideologies. Democracies avert civil conflict by providing nonviolent outlets for voicing grievances, whereas single-party regimes avoid such strife by thoroughly penetrating society with a fearsome intelligence and repressive apparatus.

ASSUMPTIONS

The competing principals explanation for the effects of regime change relies on four assumptions. All four are reasonable, even intuitive, but together, they create a powerful dilemma for imposed leaders that can endanger their hold on power, spark rebellions, or bring them into conflict with their patrons. Here I unpack these four assumptions in some detail.

States Intervene for Self-Interested Reasons The first assumption is that states intervene to change foreign regimes for self-interested reasons. A wide variety of different motives can trigger disputes that sometimes provoke one state to try to change the regime of its adversary: the intervener's desire to protect the economic interests of its firms doing business in the target; ideological competition in general and democracy promotion in particular; competition between rivals to control buffer states between them; intervention by aspiring or actual regional hegemons to create or protect regional spheres of influence; domestic institutions in the intervener, which require installing a cooperative government in the target state to obtain their war aims; changes in the balance of power between the two states; the intervener's belief that the target leader is by disposition aggressive and certain to violate any agreement; or the presence of a strong domestic opposition in the target, which makes it difficult to coerce but easy to overthrow.[59] The common denominator among these arguments is that they explain the intervener's choice to overthrow the target government as a means to bring the two states' preferences into agreement on an important issue. Regime change supposedly accomplishes this objective by empowering a government that shares the intervener's interests.

It is extraordinarily rare for states to carry out regime change for altruistic reasons. One of the few potential cases in the last two hundred years was NATO's role in supporting Libyan rebels that toppled Muammar Qaddafi in 2011. Supporters of intervention cited Qaddafi's massacres of civilians early in the uprising, as well as his blood-curdling threats against the city of Benghazi, as evidence that intervention was needed to avert mass murder.[60] On March 17, 2011, the United Nations Security Council (UNSC) authorized the use of military force in Libya to protect civilians, yet from the very beginning there were signs that the intervention had broader goals. Only two weeks into the uprising, and two weeks before the UNSC authorized force,

President Barack Obama declared that Qaddafi needed to leave power immediately.[61] Once the immediate threat to Benghazi was relieved, according to intervention skeptic Alan Kuperman, "Rather than pursuing a cease-fire, NATO and its allies aided the rebels who rejected this peaceful path and who instead sought to overthrow Qaddafi."[62] The result was that the war continued for an additional seven months and resulted in many times more deaths than likely would have occurred had NATO not intervened.[63]

Although Kuperman has pointed out that fears of a bloodbath against civilians in Libya were vastly overstated, as were the estimates of those saved by intervention, it is nevertheless likely that the desire to protect the innocent was one motivation for NATO's intervention in Libya. The opportunity to get rid of Qaddafi once and for all, however, was also clearly present in the calculations of US and allied policymakers. While Qaddafi's support for international terrorism had largely abated after 9/11, as had his pursuit of a nuclear arsenal, the Libyan dictator had a long and reprehensible record, and his past actions likely influenced Western leaders in deciding on a policy of regime change, which, after all, was not necessary to fulfill the UNSC mandate to protect civilians. Even in this seemingly ideal case of humanitarian intervention, the intervening countries had strong ulterior motives to pursue regime change, and sought to choose successors to Qaddafi who would implement Western-style democracy.[64]

Interveners Install Leaders with Similar Preferences If states pursue regime change for self-interested reasons to align a target's preferences with their own, it follows that they would like to empower a regime in the target state that will ensure that the intervention will not have been carried out in vain—that is, a regime that will implement its preferred policies. When the British invaded Afghanistan over fears of increasing Russian influence in Kabul in 1839, for example, they naturally sought to install an Afghan leader who at a minimum would rebuff further Russian attempts to curry favor, and ideally would consent to a British protectorate over the country. Similarly, when the United States invaded Iraq in 2003 to prevent Saddam Hussein from acquiring nuclear weapons and potentially sharing them with terrorists, the least it hoped to achieve was a friendly regime in Baghdad that would assist in the fight against terrorism and not seek weapons of mass destruction.[65]

It seems intuitive that if states are willing to pay the costs—which can be substantial—of enacting regime change, they would want not only to achieve the immediate goal of overthrowing the target regime but also ensure that the intervention continues to yield benefits into the future. Indeed, David Lake notes the strong tendency for interveners to install leaders who favor their interests in cases of statebuilding. According to Lake, states that are "sufficiently motivated to bear the costs of building a state in some distant land are likely to have interests in the future policies of that country, and will therefore seek to promote leaders who share or are at least sympathetic to their interests and willing to implement their preferred policies."[66] Just as with regime change, Lake argues there are few altruists when it comes to statebuilding; states that are willing to pay the costs and take the time necessary to rebuild functioning state institutions in another country care about what policies that country pursues. To ensure their continued influence, therefore, interveners will take steps to make sure that the new leadership is sufficiently sympathetic to, and willing to protect, their interests.[67]

State Interests Are Not Congruent Existing studies of regime change assume either that the underlying interests of interveners and targets are roughly congruent or that they can be made so by imposing a leader in the target who shares the intervener's outlook.[68] I argue that neither of these assumptions is true. First, states' interests never completely overlap. Even close allies have major disagreements on important issues. In the post–Cold War era, for example, the United States and its NATO partners have diverged over how to approach the Bosnian conflict, how intensely to bomb Yugoslavia in 1999, whether or not to invade Iraq in 2003, how to deal with Iran's nuclear program, and how much the allies should contribute to the collective NATO defense burden.[69] Even during the Cold War, when the Western democracies had strong incentives to cooperate in the face of the common Soviet threat, intra-alliance controversies erupted during the Korean and Vietnam wars and the Suez Crisis; regarding whether certain US allies (West Germany, Japan, South Korea) should have an independent nuclear capability; and over the deployment of intermediate-range nuclear forces in Europe.

Given that the divergence of state interests can impede cooperation even among the staunchest of allies, this problem is generally much worse between adversaries, who may have fundamentally opposed preferences regarding the territorial status quo or any number of other matters. Clashes of interests are likely to be particularly severe when one state is contemplating regime change against another. In pursuing regime change, the intervener has decided that less violent forms of persuasion are unlikely to bring the target state in line with its preferences. Conversely, the choice of the target government to resist rather than acquiesce in the intervener's demands when the conflict first arose—thereby causing the dispute to escalate to the point of regime change—indicates that the target, too, perceived the interests at stake to be substantial, perhaps existential.[70]

The bottom line is that one cannot simply assume that the interests of any given intervener and target overlap to such an extent that a new leader imposed by one on the other will not confront some degree of preference divergence. This difference in interests raises the possibility that imposed leaders will face challenges to their rule if interveners prefer that their clients pursue policies that promote the intervener's interests in addition to—or at the expense of—the target state's own interests. There are, of course, exceptions to this rule, conditions that may cause the interests of interveners and targets to converge. David Edelstein, for example, argues that military occupations (some of which occur after regime change) can succeed if the occupier and the occupied face a common external threat.[71] This condition is rare, however, occurring in only seven of his cases (all of them coinciding with the end of World War II), two of which involved regime change: West Germany and Japan.[72] A shared external threat, however, could cause preferences to align and help the target population accept the necessity for regime change.

Second, states' interests are rarely those of individual leaders alone and therefore replacing them does not necessarily create alignment. Now that absolute monarchies are largely a thing of the past, personalist dictatorships may be the type of regime that most closely approximates the ideal of "l'état, c'est moi," but even in these regimes dictators have to go to radical and violent lengths to suppress alternative viewpoints in society.[73] When they succeed, as in Saddam's Iraq or Qaddafi's Libya, it may be possible to equate the interests of the state with those of the leader. Short of that extreme situation, however, individual leaders—although not unimportant—typically do not determine the interests of states. Jessica Weeks has shown, for example, that even in highly autocratic states like the Soviet Union, leaders such as Nikita Khrushchev did not wield anything like dictatorial authority, and indeed could be held accountable by other elites for perceived policy failures.[74] In democracies, leaders can exert important influence on the direction and details of states' foreign policies—within limits. Elizabeth Saunders, for example, documents the divergent approaches to the fight against communism in Vietnam taken by Presidents Dwight D. Eisenhower, John F. Kennedy, and Lyndon B. Johnson.[75] Yet despite their different tactics in this case, all three leaders agreed on a broad strategy of containing the Soviet Union from expanding its influence in Western Europe and East Asia.

Aside from the relative freedom that particular leaders have to determine state interests in different institutional environments, broader forces, such as geopolitics, ideology, and ethnicity can also play a powerful role in overriding individual-level variation among leaders. A well-known example was Britain's longstanding interest in preventing a single great power from consolidating control over the European continent, and particularly from controlling the European coast of the English Channel. As British foreign secretary Lord Palmerston put it in 1848, "We have no eternal allies, and we have no perpetual enemies. Our interests are eternal and perpetual, and those interests it is our duty to follow."[76] Similarly, it would be exceedingly difficult for any Pakistani leader to cede Kashmir to India, just as it has proven politically treacherous for Palestinian leaders to disavow the right of return for Palestinian refugees to their former homes now inside Israel. Individual leaders may vary somewhat in their particular approaches to these questions, but they tend to be herded by larger forces into pursuing similar overall policies.

Imposed Leaders Seek to Survive in Office The final assumption of my theory is that once put in power, imposed leaders intend to stay there. Once again, as discussed above, this is not a controversial assumption. All leaders are assumed to be reelection or office maintenance maximizers. In democracies, this means that politicians aim to provide public goods in order to win votes, since winning coalitions in democracies are too large to be bought off with private goods. In nondemocracies, because winning coalitions are much smaller, leaders use private goods (money, other perks, control over powerful or lucrative ministries or industries) to ensure that the individuals with the capability of removing them lack the motivation to do so.[77] Alternatively, autocrats can make sure they control sufficient military force to deter or defeat armed internal challenges to their rule.[78]

REGIME CHANGE AS A PRINCIPAL-AGENT PROBLEM

These four assumptions set up a classic principal-agent problem: the intervening state (the principal) installs a new leader (the agent) in the target state, but the interests of the two actors inevitably diverge to some extent and the principal has limited means to ensure that the agent follows the principal's demands rather than pursuing its own interests.[79] The irony of regime change is that the whole point of bringing a new leader to power in another state is to eliminate the interest asymmetry that is the cause of conflict between intervener and target in the first place, yet installing a new leader almost inevitably generates new interest asymmetries that can lead to further conflict.

The principal-agent (PA) framework applies to any situation in which one actor delegates a task, function, or authority to another. Delegation is attractive because it is a cost-saving device: in the words of Biddle, Macdonald, and Baker, it allows "principals to undertake manufacturing, home repair, regulation, legislation or national defense at less cost than doing it themselves."[80] Delegation is ubiquitous in economic and political life: homeowners delegate remodeling and maintenance to contractors; voters delegate governance to elected officials; Congress delegates regulation and enforcement of laws to federal agencies; civilian political leaders delegate the security of the nation to the military; and so on.

Although these examples are drawn mainly from the domestic context, PA relationships are also pervasive in international politics, where states delegate tasks to other states or nonstate actors, like international organizations or rebel groups. Rather than wage counterinsurgencies in other countries using their own military forces, for example, states sometimes delegate the task of fighting rebels to host governments by providing training, weapons, logistical support, and expertise—what is now called security force assistance (SFA).[81] States also sometimes deputize insurgent groups to destabilize other states rather than perform this task with their own troops.[82] States may also authorize international organizations to carry out certain functions, as ratifiers of the Nonproliferation Treaty have delegated the task of monitoring and verifying compliance with the nonproliferation regime to the International Atomic Energy Agency.[83]

Regime change is precisely this kind of strategy: by delegating governance of another state to an agent, regime change enables interveners to project their influence and advance their security and economic interests without having to pay the costs of occupying and running the country themselves.

Problems Inherent to PA Relationships Yet because they rely on delegation from one actor to another, all PA relationships are plagued to varying degrees by four problems that can lead to *agency loss*—the difference between what the principal wanted (or would have done had she done the job herself) and what the agent delivered. The first is known as *adverse selection*. Principals would prefer to obtain the services of the most qualified and reliable agents who will do the best job but may lack sufficient information to distinguish good agents from bad. While a principal "would like to attract highly qualified and motivated individuals," writes Terry Moe, "he cannot know any given applicant's true intelligence, aptitude, or work habits."[84] According to Forrest Maltzman, the principal's inability to differentiate among agents "is caused by prospective agents' tendency to present themselves, regardless of their true natures, in a manner that is consistent with the principal's preferences."[85] Indeed, concurs Peter Feaver, each agent "would like to be hired and so has an incentive to appear more diligent during the interview than he really is."[86] Principals, lacking sufficient information to differentiate among similar agents, may select one that is unsuitable for the task.

The second problem is *interest asymmetry*. Although the interests of principals and agents may overlap, they are far from congruent. In fact, the structure of the PA relationship guarantees that they diverge to some extent.[87] This is easiest to see in the realm of economic transactions. A homeowner, for example, would prefer that a contractor repair his roof skillfully, cheaply, and quickly (preferably before the next rain storm!), whereas the contractor has an interest in being paid well for doing the least amount of work. In politics, principals and agents typically have some interests in common, but diverge in other areas, or hold differing views on how to achieve their mutual interests. Civilian national security policymakers, for instance, want to maximize the security of the state against external threats. Military officers surely share this preference, but also have an interest in obtaining the greatest resources for their particular armed service, which may color their view of how best to obtain security for the state.[88]

The third problem inherent in the PA relationship is *information asymmetry*. Agents always have more information about their efforts and actions than do principals. A principal's imperfect ability to observe its agent's actions generates the fourth problem that typifies PA relationships: *moral hazard* or *shirking*, which consists of the agent's incentives to pursue its own interests rather than those of the principal. In simple economic examples, shirking may comprise simply doing nothing or only the minimum amount of work necessary to complete a task. In civil-military relations, shirking occurs when the military does what it wants rather than what civilians want.[89] In SFA, shirking occurs when recipient leaders use military aid for their own purposes—such as to line their pockets by selling weapons on the black market or to secure their rule by using aid as patronage, diverting money and equipment to their own supporters—rather than to create the professional and proficient military forces desired by aid providers.[90]

Principals are not without weapons with which to combat these problems but are unable to eliminate them completely. Principals, as already discussed, try to hire agents with similar preferences but, lacking complete information about agents, they make mistakes. Principals may also monitor agent behavior in an attempt to reduce the asymmetry of information that leads to shirking. Such efforts are costly, however, and reduce the savings and efficiency gains of contracting with an agent in the first place.[91] A third potential solution is to establish a system of rewards and punishments to incentivize the agent to pursue the principal's objectives and not its own. This approach, known as *conditionality*, "blends," in the words of Walter Ladwig, the provision of "positive benefits" when an agent takes favorable action "with threats to suspend or withhold assistance in the absence of client compliance."[92] Ladwig finds support for US conditionality in shaping agent behavior in the Philippines and El Salvador, but others argue that conditionality is very difficult to put into practice and is also subject to moral hazard, which may result in the agent shirking rather than working.[93]

PA Problems Applied to Regime Change Each of the four difficulties with PA relationships applies to regime change. In the case of adverse selection, elites from the target country who are willing and available to be put in power by a foreign invasion or coup may not be the best candidates to run the country—or truly share the preferences of interveners. Men like Carlos Castillo Armas, David Dacko, and Laurent Kabila had obvious limitations that undermined their abilities as leaders and statesmen. Castillo Armas, for example, was chosen by the United States to succeed Árbenz in Guatemala because he was strongly pro-American, anticommunist, a competent military officer, and perceived to be "malleable."[94] Others described him less charitably. "He didn't know what he was doing," remarked one CIA agent, "He was in way over his head." "They picked Castillo Armas," a former columnist for *Time* asserted, "because . . . he was a stupid man."[95] Once in office, Castillo Armas was described by the new US ambassador, Norman Armour, as "almost pathetic . . . he must literally be led by the hand step by step."[96] His administration was plagued by corruption, mismanagement of the economy, and incessant antigovernment plots and uprisings.[97] Similarly, the Central African Republic's Dacko, described in an obituary as a "well meaning, but ineffectual, African independence leader," was overthrown by his cousin, Jean-Bédel Bokassa, shortly after describing him as "too stupid to stage a coup."[98] In the same vein, the Marxist revolutionary Che Guevara depicted future Congolese leader Laurent Kabila in highly unflattering terms. Guevara, who traveled to the Congo with a small group of Cubans in 1965 to help Kabila's Simba rebellion, wrote of Kabila in his diary, "Nothing makes me think he is the man for the job. He lets the days pass without concerning himself with anything other than political squabbles, and all the signs are that he is too addicted to drink and women."[99]

Additionally, at the time that foreign powers decided to draft these men to serve as puppets, none of them lived in the country they hoped to rule, a trait they shared with Ahmad Chalabi, a popular choice within the Bush administration to lead Iraq after the overthrow of Saddam Hussein, whose family fled Iraq in 1958. As a result of their extended absences, these leaders lacked any solid base of support inside the country. Chalabi's political party, for example, received a whopping 30,000 votes out of 12 million cast in Iraq's first parliamentary elections in December 2005, amounting to 0.25 percent.[100] Lacking both qualifications and domestic support, men like these were far from ideal candidates to run a country.

Regime change, as already discussed, is also plagued by interest asymmetry. Interveners seek to install leaders who share their preferences and who will advance their interests once in office. Meanwhile, an agent's primary interest upon assuming power becomes survival in office, and following the principal's guidance may endanger that goal. Although the agent may have promised to implement the principal's preferred policies, political constraints can prevent him from doing so after assuming office. In retrospect, for example, it appears as though Kabila did not strongly share the preferences of his Rwandan and Ugandan backers, whose main objective was to end Zaire's provision of sanctuary and support to rebels opposed to their respective regimes. Kabila, however, was unable to prevent Hutu extremists from using Congolese territory as a base for launching attacks into Rwanda and soon made common cause with the enemies of his foreign backers when Kigali and Kampala turned against him.[101]

In other cases, the agent may be overthrown by domestic forces that object to the intervener's demands, which almost always brings a leader to power who is hostile to the intervener's agenda. Either way, the intervener is likely to experience significant difficulty obtaining compliance with its directives.

An asymmetry of interests between interveners and imposed leaders could also result from adverse selection. In this scenario, the agent is able to convince the principal that it shares the latter's interests when in fact it does not. Ultimately it is an empirical question which mechanism is responsible for interest asymmetry after a regime change, and both mechanisms could explain some portion of the cases. However, my argument is that the majority of interest misalignments are typically not the result of agents deliberately deceiving principals. Rather, they arise from the competing incentives that leaders face once in office.

Intervener-target relations following a regime change also suffer from information asymmetry and moral hazard. Leaders indigenous to the target country, for example, are likely to be better informed about the country's domestic politics, and in particular about the extent to which "working"—that is, implementing policies favorable to the intervener—will generate internal opposition to the leader's rule. This lack of information about the effects of its preferred policies may lead interveners to push their protégés to institute measures that endanger their political survival. Finally, moral hazard may also play a role. After regime change, leaders who expect their foreign patrons to back them unconditionally may be less attuned to domestic demands for more responsive governance, thereby heightening resentment against their leadership.

Of these four challenges to PA relationships, I argue that in the context of regime change, interest asymmetry is the crucial problem that leads to conflicts between interveners and targets, as well as within targets.

COMPETING PRINCIPALS AND THE EXACERBATION OF INTEREST ASYMMETRIES

The reason that interest asymmetry is the main source of difficulty in intervener-target relations following regime change is that interveners are not the only principals in this situation. Imposed leaders also face a second actor that tries to control their behavior: their domestic constituency.[102] This second principal also has the ability to remove the leader and its preferences almost always diverge—sometimes radically—from the intervener's. Because the target state's interests are not necessarily the same as its own, the intervener places a leader in power that shares its preferences to bridge the gap, thereby ensuring that the costs of intervention will be justified by policies in the target state that benefit the intervener. Once installed, however, externally imposed leaders want to remain in power, which means they cannot afford to ignore the preferences of the domestic principal since doing so can also jeopardize their rule. The fundamental dilemma, and the major dilemma for all regime changes, is that carrying out one principal's wishes is bound to conflict at least to some degree with the preferences of the other principal. The more that the imposed leader implements policies that promote the intervener's interests, the more likely it is that he provokes the ire of domestic actors, which increases the likelihood of coups and civil wars. By contrast, the more that the leader heeds the protests of his domestic audience, the more likely it is that the intervener will grow frustrated with its recalcitrant protégé and seek to oust him, thereby increasing the likelihood of hostilities between intervener and target.

Literature in international relations (IR) that studies the effects of multiple principals generally finds that agents become harder to control when they are subject to the authority of more than one principal. Two problems arise when multiple principals compete to control an agent. First, the agent can capitalize on differences in interests among principals and, in the words of Elke Krahmann, "can attempt to exploit disagreements among the principals in order to limit their control and pursue its own interests."[103] Idean Salehyan, David Siroky, and Reed Wood also note that agents with several masters are less dependent on each and can turn to others if one threatens or sanctions them.[104] According to Daniel Nielsen and Michael Tierney, the ability to play competing principals off against each other may allow agents to "more easily ignore threats and refuse to modify their behavior."[105] Second, the presence of multiple principals provides each the opportunity to free ride on the efforts of others in monitoring and controlling the agent. This collective-action problem among principals implies that control will be underprovided and the agent will have more slack with which to pursue its own interests.[106]

The examination of the problem of competing principals in this book, however, differs from existing treatments of the problem. In the regime change scenario I examine, two principals with different preferences compete to control an agent. What makes the situation unique is that the agent has been appointed by one of the principals, a foreign state, to rule another state inhabited by the second principal, the population of that state, with a mandate to implement policies in line with its preferences rather than local preferences. Given that both principals have tools with which to influence the agent to do its bidding—up to and including forcible removal from office—the greater the divergence in preferences between the two, the worse the dilemma that confronts the agent. Policies that favor one principal are bound to elicit threats, sanctions, or punishment from the other. Whichever principal is able to make the more credible threat to the leader's political (and often physical) survival is likely to prevail in this competition and win the leader's compliance. Failure, however, may spur the other principal into action. Faced with a nonresponsive agent, the spurned principal may seek to replace its wayward client.[107]

Given this setup, it is important to understand what might cause the preferences of the two principals to diverge. Above I argued that there are solid grounds—both domestic and geopolitical—for assuming divergent preferences across states. Here I investigate a more specific question: How do the policies enacted by the newly empowered agent—at the behest of the external principal, in line with its preferences—clash with the preferences or interests of the domestic principal? Although to this point, and in line with previous analyses, I have treated the domestic principal as a unitary actor, in reality it is what Nielsen and Tierney call a "collective principal"—that is, a principal "composed of more than one actor."[108] Any of these actors, affected adversely by an imposed agent's policies, can signal its disapproval through peaceful or violent means. The only requirement for such groups is that they be large or important enough to pose a real threat to the leader's survival.

Ethnic Groups In one type of case, regime change overturns the ethnic status hierarchy in a society, which can produce an asymmetry of interest between the two principals. A case that involves this kind of mechanism is Rwanda's installation of Laurent Kabila to rule Zaire in 1997.[109] To eradicate the threat posed by Hutu militants housed in refugee camps in eastern Zaire following the Rwandan genocide—who were receiving support from Zairian president Mobutu Sese Seko—Rwanda's Tutsi regime ordered an invasion in October 1996, ending Mobutu's three-decade-long rule.[110] To avoid a recurrence of this threat, the Rwandans empowered Kabila—whom they had selected to place a "Zairian face" on a rebellion that was largely a foreign invasion—in Mobutu's place. Kabila, however, struggled to consolidate control over the country because many Congolese viewed him as a Rwandan puppet. One of the key reasons Kabila was perceived as a tool of Kigali was the vastly enhanced role for Tutsis—of both Congolese and Rwandan extraction—in his regime. Although not himself a Tutsi, Kabila faced severe resentment and unrest from other groups over their perception of Tutsi dominance. Facing the prospect of domestic rebellion, Kabila turned on his Rwandan patrons, expelling all Rwandan troops in July 1998. In response, Rwanda launched a second invasion to overthrow its defiant protégé, sparking the Second Congo War (1998–2003).

The Military The attitude of the military can be pivotal in determining the survival of imposed leaders. Interveners in certain cases prod their agents to take steps that harm the interests of the military or that humiliate it in such a way that drives at least a portion of the officer corps to rebel.[111] This cause of interest divergence occurred in Guatemala when, several years after the US-backed coup that ousted Jacobo Árbenz, Washington persuaded Guatemalan president Miguel Ydígoras Fuentes to host Cuban exiles training to invade Cuba and overthrow Fidel Castro. Officers in the Guatemalan Army were angered and humiliated by this development.[112] Numerous scholars argue that this policy was a key cause of the MR-13 revolt, a three-day rebellion that began on November 13, 1960, in which one-third of the army participated.[113] Although the rebellion failed, the two most prominent leaders—army officers Marco Aurelio Yon Sosa and Luis Augusto Turcios Lima—went on to found a guerrilla movement that began operations in February 1962.

Political Parties Several US regime changes in the Caribbean basin in the early twentieth century were prompted by concerns that small countries in the region were growing susceptible to the influence of European great powers. Liberal Nicaraguan strongman José Santos Zelaya, for example, sought loans from European rather than American banks and repeatedly clashed with US businesses operating in his country. After the United States ousted Zelaya in 1909 and his Liberal successor, José Madriz, the following year, it negotiated the so-called Dawson Agreements with Nicaragua's new Conservative leaders, which specified that Nicaragua would receive a $15 million loan from American banks, guaranteed by US control over the country's customs collectorship. The terms of the Dawson Agreements provoked immediate Liberal outcry, and Liberals took to the streets to protest its terms. Moreover, prominent Liberals began plotting revolution, and were aided by the defection of Conservative minister of war Luis Mena. The ensuing civil war in 1912 triggered another US military intervention and cost the lives of 2,000 to 5,000 Nicaraguans.[114]

Economic Actors or Classes The repeated US interventions in the Dominican Republic between 1912 and 1916 imposed harsh and unpopular economic policies that contributed to resistance. In 1914, for example, the Wilson administration forced out President José Bordas Valdez, who was succeeded by Juan Isidro Jimenez. To enforce its demands, the United States sought to place two officials into the Dominican government to manage the country's finances. These officials would be nominated by Washington and could not be removed by the Dominicans. As historian Bruce Calder writes, in an excellent illustration of the dilemma of competing principals, "The terms of these demands . . . were such that no Dominican politician could have agreed to them and survived."[115] Jimenez did not, as he resigned in the face of unyielding US demands and open revolt at home. Eventually the US military took control in an occupation that would last from 1916 to 1924.

One of the notable results of the US occupation was the growth of the sugar industry, much of which was facilitated by the land registration law promulgated by the US military government in July 1920. Sugar companies were able to use their vast resources to file litigation under the new law and deprive peasants of their land, all according to the letter of the law. This growth of the sugar economy in turn deprived many Dominicans of their livelihood, especially in the southeast where sugar cultivation predominated, and triggered enormous social and economic dislocation for the Dominican people. Unsurprisingly, scholars attribute the onset of the insurgency in eastern Dominican Republic to these conditions. According to Calder's authoritative study of the US occupation, "after the negotiated surrender of guerrillas in 1922, military officials found a significant percentage to be men who had recently lost their land" and further that "the greatest number came from the sugar-growing heartland of the east."[116]

Geopolitical Concerns In addition to these internal reasons for asymmetric interests between internal and external principals, it is also possible that geopolitical factors could cause leaders of target states to refuse to heed adversaries' demands both before and after regime change. A weak state targeted for regime change, for example, may reject a stronger state's demand to relinquish some of its military capabilities or take other actions that would jeopardize its future security. Even if the two states can reach an agreement whereby the weaker state cedes some of its capabilities to avoid regime change, the stronger state would still have to commit not to renege on the agreement and exploit its opponent's weakened position.[117] Further complicating the target government's decision-making calculus, the intervening state may not be its only external security threat. Consequently, when a powerful state demands that the weaker state take an action that would substantially weaken it further—such as relinquishing nuclear weapons, surrendering territory, forgoing an alliance, or pursuing a less aggressive foreign policy—the target government is unlikely to comply.[118] This was the problem confronting Saddam Hussein prior to the 2003 Iraq War, as Neil MacFarquhar explains: "The fatal controversy over whether Iraq was still developing unconventional weapons stemmed in part from Mr. Hussein's desire to convince different audiences of different things. . . . He wanted the West to believe that he had abandoned the program, which he had. Yet he also wanted to instill fear in enemies like Iran and Israel, plus maintain the esteem of Arabs, by claiming that he possessed the weapons."[119]

The presence of other external threats may not only cause target states to resist interveners' demands prior to regime change but could also be the source of interest divergence afterwards. Experiencing regime change does not necessarily alter a target state's external security environment. As a result, states may confront the same security threats after regime change as they did before. If the intervener requires that the target reduce its military forces or relinquish strategic territory in ways that make it vulnerable to these sources of threat, the military, and possibly other domestic actors, might be expected to oppose such a demand. Imposed leaders who resist the external principal's demand risk punishment at its hands whereas leaders who comply risk resistance from domestic actors opposed to these concessions.

ALTERNATIVE SOURCES OF PREFERENCE DIVERGENCE

Other scholars—while not treating domestic interests as a competing principal—have offered competing sources of preference divergence after regime change. Here I discuss two of them: median voter theory and nationalism.

Median Voter Theory Although his work on the statebuilder's dilemma is quite consistent with the problem of competing principals I elaborate in this book, David Lake offers a different source of interest divergence. Lake posits that states will take on the onerous task of rebuilding other states only when they have strong interests at stake. For that reason, they will seek to install a loyal leader willing to implement policies that benefit their interests. Lake argues that this strategy goes awry when the statebuilder's "ideal point"—its preferred policy on any given issue—is far from the ideal point of the target population. When these preferences are similar, statebuilders can install a loyal leader without generating a backlash in the target state because the policies that the statebuilder asks its protégé to carry out are not much different from what she would have done anyway. By contrast, when the preferences of the median voter in the target are far removed from those of the statebuilder, empowering a loyal leader is sure to lead to trouble. Leaders in this situation will have no choice but to rule undemocratically because their ideal point is so far from their constituents' preferences. Such leaders will also direct aid from the statebuilder to their key supporters rather than to the population at large. Moreover, the statebuilder has little choice but to accept a corrupt, undemocratic ruler because the pool of individuals with preferences close to its own is so small that there are few alternatives. In sum, according to Lake, "the more loyal are the leaders, the less support they will receive at home, the more precarious their political positions will be, and the more often they will be challenged by domestic opponents. By emphasizing loyalty, the statebuilder increases the likelihood of getting favorable policies, but this comes at the cost of greater political instability and the risk that it will have to intervene again in the future."[120]

Lake's stylized representation emphasizes the divergence between the preferences of the statebuilder and the median voter in the target state. Although it is possible to ascertain the statebuilder's goals with some degree of accuracy, estimating the preferences of the median voter in targets of statebuilding is much more difficult. Lake, for example, uses a variety of indirect sources to deduce the preferences of the Kurds, Sunni Arabs, and Shiites in Iraq. The Kurds, for example, are said to be "warmly disposed toward the United States," although leaders in Washington opposed the single most important Kurdish objective: independence.[121] Sunni Arabs, by contrast, "deeply opposed the U.S. invasion and Washington's role in overturning the regime they previously dominated"; large majorities sanctioned attacks on US occupation forces.[122] The Shiite community, finally, was divided between "religious fundamentalists" loyal to Moktada al-Sadr and "presumably hostile to the United States from the outset," and moderates willing to work with Washington.[123] On the basis of this assessment, Lake offers the following summary: "Although evidence is indirect, it appears reasonable to conclude that the policy preferences of the United States and the average Iraqi were quite far apart before and immediately after the invasion."[124]

Lake's diagnosis may be correct, but it is hard to know. The Sunnis' hostile disposition toward the United States may have been counteracted by the more positive attitude of the Kurds (these two groups are roughly similar in size), leaving the attitude of the Shiite population as carrying the most weight in determining the overall view of the Iraqi electorate. Given that the Shiites stood to gain the most from the US invasion, it is not clear that the interests of this subset of the population would be so far from those of the United States.

Beyond the difficulty of determining how the median voter in foreign lands assesses her country's interests, Lake's model assumes that the view of the median voter is relevant. More likely to matter is the perspective of the median voter in the most disaffected community in the country, or the group whose interests are most adversely affected by regime change. The initial and primary threat to the survival of the Iraqi Shiite-dominated regime did not come from other Shiites, but rather from Sunni Arabs, who had seen their dominant position in Iraqi society overturned. Many were subsequently ousted from the government through de-Baathification, and others lost their role in the military when the Americans disbanded it. Because determining the preferences of a target country's median voter is so difficult, I focus directly on the preferences of particular societal groups.

Nationalism Others have argued, by contrast, that the simple fact that a leader is placed in power or maintained in power at the point of foreign bayonets is sufficient to taint his claim to rule and generate resistance because it violates the nationalist sentiments of the target country's population.[125] Nationalism is a doctrine that holds that the world can be divided into groups of people called nations and that nations should be self-governing.[126] Nations, which often have deep ties to particular pieces of territory, have distinctive cultures and—even though most members will never meet face to face—inspire a powerful sense of loyalty and unity. Crucially, nationalism prescribes that nations not only ought to be self-governing and free from external interference but that the ruler must be a member of the nation and represent its interests. External interference in the leadership selection process or direct imposition of a leader by a foreign power thus offends the nationalist beliefs of the population, sentiments that may be exacerbated if foreign forces remain in occupation of the state.

John Mearsheimer articulates both of these propositions in his book *The Great Delusion*. "Nationalism," he writes, "is all about self-determination, and people who live in a nation-state will want to shape their own politics without interference from an outside power. They will not want foreigners telling them how to conduct their lives, even if the intervening forces have noble intentions." Describing recent US interventions to promote democracy, Mearsheimer continues: "The problem is particularly acute when the United States invades another country, because the American military forces occupying that country inevitably end up tasked with the nation- and state-building necessary to produce a functioning liberal democracy. In the age of nationalism, however, occupation almost always breeds insurgency."[127]

Noted scholar of military occupations David Edelstein reaches a similar conclusion based on a broader study of occupations worldwide. "The greatest impediment to successful military occupation," he writes, "is the nationalism of the occupied population."[128] Unless there is a compelling reason for local populations to tolerate an occupation, such as the need to rebuild extensive wartime destruction or a perception of external threat shared by occupier and occupied, occupations will be plagued by internal resistance because foreign rule offends the nationalistic sentiments of local populations.[129]

There is no doubt that nationalism is a powerful force that shapes the modern world, yet there appears to be substantial variation in the degree to which even highly nationalistic populations resist external interference in their affairs. Few would dispute, for example, that France in 1940 was a nationalist country. French politicians and citizens, however, collaborated extensively with their Nazi occupiers after the country's defeat while resistance was limited and ineffective until late in the war.[130] Indeed, Matthew Kocher, Adria Lawrence, and Nuno Monteiro argue persuasively that although nationalists agree on goals, such as "the nation's right to self-determination and the odiousness of foreign occupation," nationalism "does not produce a consensus about what to do to defend these principles."[131] In other words, strategies of both collaboration and resistance can be compatible with nationalism. In line with this argument, Kocher, Lawrence, and Monteiro show that just as nationalism fueled resistance to the Germans, the collaboration of Vichy officials was motivated by the nationalist desire to preserve French sovereignty.[132] Moreover, in contrast to a nationalist account, which would predict uniform opposition to German occupation, these scholars find that the best predictor of the size of the resistance and the number of acts of sabotage in a region is the vote share of the leftist Popular Front in 1936. Collaboration was a predominantly right-wing phenomenon, and the right used it to further its domestic political purposes by marginalizing the formerly dominant leftist parties.[133]

Kocher, Lawrence, and Monteiro's conclusions from the French case are further buttressed by Lawrence's studies of resistance to French colonialism in North Africa, which demonstrate that nationalists often disagree on strategy, with some advocating nonviolent resistance and others—sometimes a small minority—calling for violence.[134] In Morocco, for example, a violent uprising began in 1952 that comprised both an urban terrorist element and a rural insurgency. Yet violence in this case was not an inevitable outcome. According to Lawrence, "For more than two decades, opposition to French rule in Morocco had been largely nonviolent. . . . Moroccan nationalists turned to violence only in the last years of colonial rule, and the violent period was far shorter than the nonviolent period."[135] The shift to violence was provoked by the French decapitation of the nonviolent Moroccan Istaqlal Party, which caused the nationalist movement to splinter and opened the way for more violent actors to emerge.[136]

Nationalism not only struggles to explain variation in resistance to foreign rule by different actors within countries, it also has trouble explaining variation across countries. A nationalist perspective, for example, cannot account for why violent resistance to German occupation beyond France during World War II was so much more pronounced and widespread in Eastern Europe (e.g., Yugoslavia and Greece) than in Western Europe (e.g., Belgium, the Netherlands, Denmark, and Norway). Although it is true that the Nazis took a far more ruthless approach to quelling resistance in Eastern rather than Western Europe, nationalism opposes the *principle* of foreign rule, and predicts resistance whether or not the occupier is highly coercive.

Finally, quantitative studies have produced mixed results on the effect of nationalism in motivating resistance to occupation. On the one hand, studies of suicide terrorism have consistently found that countries engaged in foreign occupations are more likely to be targeted for such attacks and experience them in greater numbers.[137] However, in the study most germane for my purposes, Simon Collard-Wexler examined all instances of military occupation from 1900 to 2010 to determine whether indicators of nationalism predicted greater violent resistance—measured as the number of fatalities suffered by the occupier's military forces.[138] Although nationalism is hard to measure, none of Collard-Wexler's proxies for the concept are associated with greater levels of resistance to occupation, and arguably the best of them—the literacy of the occupied population—significantly *reduces* occupier fatalities.[139]

Nationalism, in short, may generate resistance to regime change or occupation in some cases, but it may also induce the opposite response—collaboration. Moreover, the available evidence does not support the argument that nationalism is a powerful predictor of violent resistance.

IMPLICATIONS OF INTEREST DIVERGENCE

So far I have argued that implementing policies favorable to the intervener and defying the intervener can both be detrimental to an imposed leader's odds of surviving in office. The fundamental problem stems from the reality that imposed leaders must answer to two principals whose interests diverge to a greater or lesser extent. Contrary to the claims of Bueno de Mesquita and Downs, however, installing an autocrat does not solve this dilemma, but instead merely changes the accountability mechanism. Bueno de Mesquita and Downs are right that leaders in democracies are answerable to publics via regular elections, which can steer policy away from the intervener's preferences. But authoritarian leaders are also accountable; the means are just more violent. It is true that these leaders do not have to face elections. Instead, removing them requires the threat or use of force. While this can be dangerous, sometimes the institutions of authoritarian regimes permit it. In one type of civilian-led autocracy, for example, such as the Soviet Union under Nikita Khrushchev, leaders lack control over domestic intelligence agencies and repressive institutions, ensuring that other civilian elites can coordinate to remove them if warranted by poor performance.[140] Leaders are also vulnerable to removal in juntas, where military leaders are accountable to fellow officers. Only in personalist regimes are leaders able to insulate themselves from elite audiences, but that does not mean such leaders are safe. Even though they do their best to prevent coups, sometimes these plots succeed. Moreover, frustrated contingents of the military or society can also launch insurgencies to try to remove leaders whose policies they oppose.

The evidence in this book also demonstrates that imposed leaders respond to the danger of violent removal at the hands of their countrymen. Sometimes this risk causes leaders to break their commitment to the foreign principal, while in other cases they double down and gamble that they can defeat internal challenges with the help of the intervener. It is hard to predict ex ante which of these two options an embattled imposed leader will choose. It is likely that these leaders will seek to appease the challenge they perceive to represent the most dangerous and pressing threat to their rule. Since imposed leaders benefit personally from the intervener's support and largess, and expect that the patron will aid them against internal challengers, it is likely that they will lean toward standing by the external principal. It is thus possible that the relationship between regime change and irregular removal and civil war will be somewhat stronger than the link between regime change and intervener-target conflict, but the general prediction is that regime change ought to increase the risks of both.

MECHANISMS FOR AMELIORATING THE PRINCIPAL-AGENT PROBLEM

As mentioned earlier, principals are not helpless in the face of interest asymmetry and possess several tools to induce desired behavior by the agent. Here I review some of the traditional tools emphasized by PA theory before moving on to discuss more radical options.[141]

Incentivize Preferred Behavior One mechanism to reduce agent shirking is to monitor the agent's behavior and promise to reward compliance and punish disobedience with a strategy of conditionality. The ability to use these tools, however, depends on access to good information about the agent's behavior. Information on compliance can be hard to come by; even distinguishing between working and shirking may be tricky. The collapse of the Iraqi Army in 2014, for example, was easy to observe and signaled a clear failure of SFA. But the fact that SFA was failing was harder to observe before the army's spectacular collapse. On paper, units were fully manned, weapons were in good repair, salaries were being paid, and soldiers were being trained. What looked like working was only revealed to be shirking because of an exogenous shock—the invasion by the Islamic State (IS) from Syria.

Differentiating working from shirking is not always this hard—Ladwig, for example, analyzes a series of choices by the Salvadoran government that are easily identifiable—but in some cases it is difficult.[142] The Iraqi government, for instance, has cooperated militarily with the United States against Al Qaeda in Iraq (AQI) and IS, but also makes extensive use of Shiite militias armed and trained by Iran. Iran also provided weapons and training—including deadly explosively formed penetrators (EFPs)—to Shiite militias starting in 2005, some of which had ties to the regime.[143] These behaviors are hard to classify as working or shirking in a straightforward way. All of this is to say that information on agent compliance may not be available or definitive.

Assuming that a principal is able to monitor compliance, however, how can it incentivize agents to work rather than shirk? In the context of regime change, this is likely to be challenging. On the one hand, threats to punish the imposed leader by cutting or withdrawing support will lack credibility—an example of moral hazard at work. The fact that the intervener undertook regime change indicates that it had important interests at stake. Whatever the danger was may still exist, or new dangers may have developed since regime change took place. One reason the United States has found it so difficult to disengage from Afghanistan is the possibility that the condition that prompted US intervention in the first place—a safe haven for Al Qaeda in the country—may be reestablished if US forces withdraw and the Taliban wins the civil war.[144] Some clients may in fact develop an exaggerated sense of their importance, believing that the stakes dictate that the intervener could never abandon their regime. Arguably this was the case with the shah of Iran and South Vietnam's Ngo Dinh Diem, leaders who understood how much Washington valued their governments as bulwarks against communist expansion in their regions and believed that their patron had no alternative but to continue to support them.

Threats against a shirking leader are also likely to fail because these leaders may be shirking owing to countervailing domestic threats to their survival. Imposed leaders who face the risk of a coup or insurgency as a consequence of following the intervener's wishes are unlikely to respond to threats of punishment, since this would merely increase their vulnerability to domestic threats.[145] Promises of rewards to entice good behavior are also unlikely to be successful against leaders who shirk but do not face domestic threats, again owing to moral hazard. The same sense of entitlement that causes imposed leaders to believe patrons will never cut off aid is likely to cause leaders to believe that when push comes to shove, rewards will be forthcoming whether they work or shirk because their regimes are simply too important for the patron to let fail.

In short, traditional mechanisms for ameliorating the asymmetry of interests between principals and their agents are unlikely to successfully close the gap between the two actors.

Eliminate Interest Asymmetry If the preferences of internal and external principals could be made congruent, interest asymmetry would be drastically reduced and imposed leaders would not have to choose between alienating one of their masters. Unfortunately, existing scholarship suggests that such a congruence of interests is likely to occur only when both principals perceive a common external threat.[146] This mechanism, although rare, undoubtedly helps explain why the regime changes and occupations of West Germany and Japan were not met with much resistance. Yet because they are rare, and not something the intervener can control, shared external threats are not a viable solution to interest asymmetry.

Reduce the Consequences of Interest Asymmetry If interveners cannot fully eliminate preference divergence between themselves and target populations, perhaps they can render those differences less likely to result in serious conflict. This is essentially the mechanism posited by arguments that stress the promotion of shared ideologies or institutions.[147] Although promoting actors in other states with similar ideologies surely reduces preference divergence, interveners and targets are still bound to disagree on some issues. Actors who share a common ideology, such as liberalism, are more likely to trust each other and hence less likely to perceive these policy differences as threatening or warranting forceful action. Transforming target societies and remaking institutions is costly and time-consuming, however, and thus will be unattractive to most interveners most of the time. Even when interveners undertake efforts to promote their beliefs as part of regime change, such efforts fail as often as they succeed—and hence fail to align preferences or increase trust.

Eliminate the Agent If delegating the task of ruling a target state to an agent is so fraught with difficulties, why not simply dispense with the agent and rule the target directly by establishing a military occupation? This measure, however, generates problems of its own. In a full-scale military occupation, the intervener assumes responsibility for governing the target state, rather than appointing an agent.[148] In this arrangement, therefore, the intervener implements policies that favor itself directly, ensuring that any dissatisfaction with those policies by actors in the target state is aimed directly at the intervener rather than its local proxy. Post-regime-change occupations may thus breed resistance and draw interveners into protracted counterinsurgency operations to suppress that resistance. In support of this argument, Collard-Wexler finds that regime change is a powerful predictor of violent resistance to occupation.[149] Full-scale occupation also defeats the purpose of regime change, which from the principal's perspective is to delegate governance of the target state to an agent rather than pay the costs of running it.

Stationing troops in the target country without taking on governance functions, by contrast, is also expensive yet provides no guarantee that the intervener will be able to influence the agent's actions. The presence of large numbers of US troops in Iraq and Afghanistan, for example, has not provided US leaders with extensive leverage over the actions of leaders in those two countries. In Afghanistan, relations between the regime of Hamid Karzai and Washington deteriorated to such an extent that the Afghan president accused the United States of conspiring with the Taliban to convince Afghans that violence would increase if US troops left the country.[150] In Iraq, Nouri al-Maliki, the prime minister of Iraq from 2006 to 2014, declared that despite the United States' substantial troop commitment to his country and $60 billion in US support, "I'm a friend to the United States, but not America's man in Iraq."[151] Maliki was also believed to be complicit in widespread violence by Shiite death squads against Sunni civilians during the height of the sectarian civil war in Iraq in 2006.[152] Even with over one hundred thousand troops in Iraq, and with new reports of sectarian bloodletting coming in every day, a civilian adviser to the US Army recalled, "We'd go into his [Maliki's] office, we'd tell him about a massacre that had been carried out by his men. . . . And Maliki would just sit there and say, 'I'm sure they were terrorists.' We could never get him to act against the death squads."[153]

THE DIFFERENTIAL EFFECTS OF DIFFERENT TYPES OF REGIME CHANGES

In the previous subsections I laid out the general logic of regime change and how it exacerbates asymmetries of interests between interveners and domestic actors inside target states, which in turn increases the likelihood of conflict between the two states and inside the target. Upon closer inspection, however, regime changes are not all alike; in fact, they differ substantially in their ambition, and in the degree to which they trigger the dilemma described above. *Leadership regime changes* replace a country's sitting political leader but without meddling in its political institutions. *Institutional regime changes*, which are the most ambitious type, attempt a real change of regime, both replacing leaders and overhauling the target's political institutions—for instance, by transforming an autocracy into a democracy. *Restoration regime changes*, by contrast, are less ambitious, aiming merely to reinstate a previous leader and/or institutions in the target country that held sway prior to a coup, revolution, or external change of regime.

I argue that the type of regime change attempted by the intervener—leadership, institutional, or restoration—influences its subsequent relationship with the target state. Specifically, I argue that leadership regime changes increase the likelihood of conflict between the intervening and target state, and within the target state; institutional regime changes have a mixed effect that depends on conditions in targets; and restoration regime changes do not increase, and may decrease, the likelihoods of these two kinds of conflict.

Leadership Regime Change Leadership regime changes are likely to lead to civil and interstate conflict because they are most likely to confront leaders with the problem of competing principals. When interveners replace a foreign leader without building any supporting institutions to empower the new regime, the leaders are likely to remain heavily dependent on aid from the intervener to maintain power. Although such puppet leaders are thus more likely to adopt the intervener's interests initially, doing so tends to generate internal opposition, putting the leader's political survival in jeopardy. Furthermore, this kind of imposed leader often lacks a strong domestic base of support, making him especially vulnerable to domestic threats. Elites installed in leadership regime changes are thus subject to powerful pressures to cut ties with their foreign patrons, which may then cause interveners to seek to replace their protégés or trigger military conflict between interveners and targets.

Of the three types of regime change, leadership cases are also the most likely to cause civil war. Interveners prefer to install unencumbered strongmen because such leaders are able to provide strategic benefits. But such leaders also face the highest hurdles to establishing their authority and governing effectively. In some cases, these leaders are exiles who have not set foot in the country for years, even decades. Leaders like this often have little knowledge of the current political landscape, few domestic supporters, and little legitimacy, and may lack information about opponents or potential opponents. Their weakened militaries also lack the information to use force discriminately and may lash out wildly, breeding further resentment against the regime. Each of these factors is exacerbated when interveners temporarily govern the country or use their militaries to occupy the state. Interveners could assist local puppets in building repressive institutions capable of stifling domestic dissent, but doing so is costly and time-consuming. Rulers empowered by leadership regime change are thus most vulnerable to rebellion and civil war. For the same reason, leaders installed in leadership regime change are also more likely to be removed in a violent manner.

Institutional Regime Change Institutional regime changes exert little systematic effect on post-regime-change conflict, but this overall effect masks significant variation.

There are two types of institutional regime changes that mitigate the dilemma faced by foreign-imposed leaders in distinctly different ways. The first type increases the repressive capacity of the state by building a formidable internal security and intelligence apparatus. This variety of institutional regime change is unique to the Soviet Union. After World War II, Joseph Stalin established Soviet-style police states in the Eastern European satellites. The primary effect of these institutions—with their combination of extensive domestic intelligence capabilities and highly credible threats—was to stifle revolutionary impulses and enable local communist elites to follow Moscow's directives at relatively little risk to themselves. In other words, Stalin was able to empower elites that shared his preferences—these individuals shared the ideology of their Soviet backers and thus wanted their countries to have close relationships with Moscow—and these elites were able to implement Stalin's (and his successors') preferred policies without running a substantial risk of being overthrown by domestic opponents.[154] By reducing the ability of dissenting domestic audiences to express and act upon their grievances, the enhanced repressive apparatus suppresses the mechanism that produces asymmetric interests between interveners and target leaders.[155]

The second type of institutional regime change promotes democratic institutions. These democratizing institutional regime changes reduce the likelihood of conflict between interveners and targets. The logic, grounded in the notion of the democratic peace, holds that when a democratic intervener establishes democracy in a former rival, subsequent relations between the two states will be peaceful.[156] Democracies are thought not to fight each other because they have fundamentally similar interests and are able to resolve differences short of war.[157] Democratic interveners may thus choose to relinquish control over the particular leader who rules in the target in favor of installing a system that will produce leaders with interests generally compatible with their own.[158] Democratizing regime changes should also reduce the likelihood of civil war by enabling diverse constituencies to participate in the political process peacefully, thereby alleviating the need to take up arms to influence policy.

Although they promote symmetric interests with interveners and domestic harmony, democracy-promoting institutional regime changes often do not succeed. In a study of regime change and democratization in the twentieth century I carried out with Jonathan Monten, we found that only five of thirteen attempts to democratize a foreign government via regime change were successful: Japan (1945), West Germany (1945), Grenada (1983), Panama (1989), and Haiti (1994).[159] The cases where democratization was attempted after regime change but failed—the Dominican Republic (1912, 1914, 1916) and Nicaragua (1910, 1926), as well as the uncertain democratic trajectories of Afghanistan (2001) and Iraq (2003)—suggest that institutional regime changes are more likely to succeed in wealthy, homogeneous countries that have previous experience with democracy.[160] Democratizing regime changes in countries like these are likely to fail to establish democracy. If so, they revert to the dynamics of leadership regime changes and increase the likelihood of intervener-target conflict and conflict within the target.

Restoration Regime Change Regime changes that reinstall the previous leader and/or set of institutions in a country, such as Haiti's Jean-Bertrand Aristide in 1994 or Western European democracies after World War II, do not trigger the PA dynamics that are so harmful to intervener-target relations and domestic peace in the target to the same extent as leadership regime changes. Indeed, restoration regime changes have countervailing effects that at a minimum neutralize their impact on internal and external conflict, and perhaps even decrease the likelihood of such conflict.

On the one hand, it seems obvious that leaders who have been overthrown—and are thus in need of restoration—face significant domestic opposition that was sufficiently strong to eject them from power. A good example is Denis Sassou-Nguesso, who was stripped of his powers as president of the Republic of Congo in 1991, but eventually returned to office with Angolan assistance in 1997.[161] Moreover, the theory outlined above holds that states install leaders in foreign countries to further their own strategic interests. This is just as true if an intervener restores a previous leader to power as if it installs an entirely new leader. As a matter of logic, therefore, restoration regime changes may thus generate the same misaligned preferences that drive an asymmetry of interests in cases of leadership regime changes.

On the other hand, the circumstances in which restoration regime changes have been implemented historically work to reduce the asymmetry of interests between interveners and targets while also emplacing leaders with domestic legitimacy. Because these circumstances offset the conflict-inducing aspects just outlined, I expect that restoration regime changes will not increase—and may in fact decrease—the likelihood of violence inside target states or between interveners and targets.

First, in a large proportion of cases, the governments empowered by restoration regime changes previously enjoyed substantial domestic legitimacy and therefore were not viewed by their citizens as tools of foreign interests after being brought back to power. In these cases, regime change actually removes the key grievance that stoked resistance. In seven of the twenty-eight restorations, for instance, the intervener reinstalled leaders who had been ousted by foreign powers, not by their own populations. Six of these cases involved democracies removing German occupation regimes after the two world wars and restoring democratic governments.[162] In cases such as these, citizens were happy to see the reinstitution of their former governments.

Second, in almost all restorations, reinstalled leaders were previously aligned with the intervener—that is, the preexisting degree of interest asymmetry was low. Thus, these regime changes mark a return to an acceptable international status quo for both parties rather than an attempt to change state preferences by imposing entirely new leaders. Austria and Prussia, for example, shared monarchic principles of rule with leaders in the small countries where they intervened in the first half of the nineteenth century—for example, Sicily, Tuscany, Baden, and Saxony—to thwart republican revolutions and restore ousted monarchs to the throne. The United States and Britain similarly rehabilitated several democratic regimes in allied countries, such as Belgium, the Netherlands, Norway, and Denmark, that had been toppled by Nazi Germany during World War II. In the Soviet Union's Cold War restoration regime changes in Hungary (1956) and Czechoslovakia (1968), Moscow was formally allied with its Eastern European neighbors and had ideological confrères in each country committed to close relations with the Soviet Union. In these cases, the leaders being restored already shared the intervener's policy preferences—if they did not, the intervening state would not have reinstalled them.

Third, in many cases in which leaders were toppled by domestic rebellions rather than foreign powers, the rebels were extremely weak compared to the intervener and were largely destroyed as a result of the intervention. Restored leaders thus faced little resistance in reestablishing close ties with the intervener. In other words, the mechanism that promotes interest divergence between patrons and clients was largely disabled.

Nineteenth-century interventions by Austria and Prussia in Italian and German states, respectively, followed this pattern. Consider Austria's intervention in Sicily to restore King Ferdinand IV to his throne in 1821. According to historian Paul Schroeder, the primary reason Metternich sought to reverse the Sicilian revolution was the precedent it might set in Austria's Italian lands and beyond. As Schroeder writes about Metternich's motivation, "Above all, how could Metternich keep other princes from submitting to revolution and other peoples from rising in revolt if the bad example set by Ferdinand and the Neapolitans went uncorrected? . . . Therefore the revolution must be crushed. . . . The question was simply one of Austrian state interests."[163] To that end, Vienna sent an army of 60,000 men to quash the rebels, and kept troops in Naples until 1827. Later Austrian and Prussian interventions in 1831 and 1849 to reverse republican revolutions in minor Italian and German principalities were accomplished with little bloodshed against hopelessly outnumbered urban revolutionaries.[164]

More recently, French forces reversed in a matter of hours what was essentially a palace coup against Léon Mba in Gabon in 1964.[165] And French intervention in the Comoros in 1995 had to overcome only Bob Denard's band of two or three dozen mercenaries to restore President Said Mohamed Djohar.[166] Because the interveners in these cases were able to crush the rebels, restored leaders were *less* vulnerable to domestic dissent than they had been before. With their internal opposition dismantled, restored leaders are able to retain close ties with the intervener at relatively low risk to their political survival.

In sum, although the logic of restoration regime change suggests that it should lead to similar outcomes as leadership regime change, in practice a number of factors mitigate this tendency. I thus do not expect restoration regime changes to systematically increase the likelihood of conflict between interveners and targets or within targets. Indeed, it is possible that restorations reduce such conflicts.

The Puzzle of Regime Change

If I am right that regime change frequently leads to further turmoil in target states and conflictual relations between interveners and their protégés, the puzzle is why states continue to rely on regime change when it so often goes wrong. Regime change may be cheap in the short run given interveners' advantages in relative capabilities.[167] As I theorize and demonstrate in the remainder of this book, though, regime change often turns out to be quite costly in the long run owing to repeat interventions, counterinsurgency operations, state failure, and interstate conflict. To take two recent examples for which good estimates are available, US expenses in both Afghanistan and Iraq increased dramatically over time as insurgencies took off in those countries. In the former, the annual costs of the war for the first five years hovered around $20 billion. These costs began to increase rapidly in 2007, however, and finally peaked at $107 billion in 2011, more than a fivefold increase. US military fatalities also grew by a factor of ten from 49 in 2002, the first full year of the occupation, to 498 in 2010. Costs in Iraq escalated much faster from $51 billion in 2003 to $144 billion in 2008—a nearly threefold increase in five years. American combat deaths in Iraq also nearly doubled between 2003 and 2007.[168]

Why do strategic, forward-looking policymakers in intervening states fail to consider the possibility of resistance to regime change? Why have leaders not learned that regime change interventions are both risky and potentially very costly? In practice, a number of factors work to reinforce the perception that regime change will be less costly than compelling and enforcing a change of policy—and also help to explain why interveners often underestimate the costs of toppling foreign governments.[169]

First, interveners may lack intelligence on the target country or have biased intelligence. In some cases, interveners are unable to place their own agents on the ground and thus possess little or outdated knowledge about the regime's popularity, the strength and loyalties of the military, the attitudes of the population, and many other relevant factors. What is more, the intelligence that interveners do possess may be biased because it comes from the regime's domestic or exiled opposition. These actors have incentives to present a rosy scenario for interveners by systematically overstating the government's weakness and the public's support for regime change. Pressure to act quickly may also prevent interveners from gathering, compiling, and analyzing intelligence on the target. Even worse, interveners may consciously downplay or ignore any ominous information they do have in order to persuade the public that regime change will be cheap and easy.[170]

Second, past disasters—their own or those of others—are typically insufficient to deter future regime change efforts. As Willard-Foster observes, "previous failed attempts at regime change may simply prompt policymakers to adopt a different approach to regime change rather than to abandon it altogether."[171] Having observed the catastrophic aftermath of the Bush administration's invasion of Iraq, for example, President Barack Obama—rather than forswearing regime change—just opted to do it differently, using a light-footprint approach in Libya to avoid the blowback of a large US presence on the ground. While less costly in terms of American lives, the implosion of the Libyan state has proven disastrous for Libyans—and for American interests. Potential interveners are even less likely to learn from others' mistakes.

Third, interveners contemplating regime change tend to focus myopically on the immediate task at hand—the logistics and mechanics of overthrowing the target government—and neglect the details of how to govern once regime change occurs. On the one hand, this is understandable: there will not be a target country to govern unless regime change operations succeed. On the other hand, inattention to what comes after regime change can prove fatal—both for imposed leaders and for interveners' interests.

Fourth, interveners fail to appreciate the possibility of military disintegration and its deleterious effects after regime change—even when their military strategy for regime change relies on inducing confusion and collapse in the adversary's military. Quick and decisive victory, after all, is something that all military commanders and political leaders crave. What could be better than defeating the enemy in a few short fights with few casualties? When one's political objective is seizing a piece of territory from an adversary, such as in the 1991 Persian Gulf War, there are few downsides to pursuing the disintegration of its army. When the goal is to march on the enemy's capital, depose its leadership, empower a new regime, and physically control the country, however, as in the 2003 Iraq War, military disintegration is dangerous.

Finally, interveners do not understand the problem of competing principals. Some, for example, blithely assume that targets will welcome regime change and believe that targets share their interests. Because they are blind to the asymmetry of interests between themselves and the target, interveners fail to see that they jeopardize their protégé's political survival—and increase the likelihood that the protégé will push back or even turn against them—by pressuring the imposed leader to enact policies in line with their preferences. Interveners would be better off eschewing the imposition of their preferences after regime change. Imposing one's preferences, of course, is the whole point of regime change, and thus asking interveners to refrain from doing so is a nonstarter.

Given that institutional regime changes work out better than the leadership variety, it is natural to ask why interveners don't do more of the former and less of the latter. With the stipulation that the success of institutional regime changes relies heavily on conditions in target states, the answer is costs. Most regime changes, because they involve strong interveners and weak targets, are not of life-or-death importance for the former. Building institutions is costly and time-consuming; without a pressing security rationale for doing so, as existed for the United States and the Soviet Union at the conclusion of World War II, for example, interveners will tend to avoid paying these costs. Instead, they will rely on imposing an individual and hope that they can avoid downstream problems via careful agent selection. Unfortunately, the problem of competing principals tends to defeat strategies of minimizing interest asymmetry by selecting agents with congruent preferences. Most agents, moreover, are flawed, and agent selection is not always careful.

In this chapter I laid out my theory to answer the two questions posed in the introduction to this book: Why does regime change often fail to meet the expectations of interveners—triggering further conflict rather than peace and stability? And what explains why some regime changes turn out better than others? The answer to the first question focuses on military disintegration and the problem of competing principals. The military disintegration mechanism is primarily about how the act of regime change causes immediate civil war. Because all leaders prefer to remain in power and will seek to regain office after regime change if feasible, it behooves interveners to capture, exile, or kill the leaders they unseat. If deposed leaders manage to escape, however, they are powerless without access to armed followers. If the military surrenders or takes over in disciplined fashion, then the threat of immediate resistance is quelled. If the military falls apart, however, thousands of armed men on the loose provide the deposed leader (or a subordinate) with the raw material necessary to launch an insurgency.

The second mechanism focuses on how regime change can go wrong even if it does not provoke immediate resistance. The problem of competing principals explains how and why regime change fails to improve relations between interveners and targets—despite the fact that interveners install sympathetic leaders—and also endangers the survival of those leaders by inspiring domestic dissatisfaction with the new regime. This mechanism depicts regime change as a principal-agent problem, but one in which the agent, the imposed leader, faces two principals, the intervener and the domestic audience, both of which can remove her from office. Interveners empower leaders in the expectation that those leaders will favor their interests, but because states often do not have identical interests, carrying out the intervener's wishes may spark resistance by the domestic principal. Because imposed leaders wish to retain power, this asymmetry of interests puts them in a dilemma. Favoring the intervener's interests risks incurring the wrath of a leader's domestic principal, and vice versa. No matter what they choose, imposed leaders face an increased risk of removal from office, targets are more likely to suffer civil wars, and relations between interveners and targets are unlikely to improve.

To explain variations in outcomes following regime change—that is, why some regime changes foment conflict and violence whereas others promote stability and peaceful relations—I unpacked three different types of regime change: leadership, institutional, and restoration. The specific type of regime change an intervener implements determines the extent to which regime change activates the problem of competing principals. Leadership regime changes display all of the negative aspects of the dilemma most strongly, and thus I expect them to have detrimental effects on interstate relations and the domestic politics of the target. Institutional and restoration regime changes, however, counteract to varying degrees the conflict-inducing dynamics inherent in regime change. I thus do not expect these types of regime changes to worsen intervener-target relations or to cause violence in targets.

I now turn to testing these propositions empirically. In chapter 3, I assess the relationship between regime change and civil war in target states. Chapter 4 examines whether and how being brought to power by foreign hands affects the tenure of imposed leaders. Chapter 5 turns to the implications of regime change for intervener-target relations.

Foreign-Imposed Regime Change and Civil War

With this chapter I begin the task of empirically testing my theory of the consequences of foreign-imposed regime change. In this chapter and the next, I analyze the domestic consequences of regime change for the target state. The first domestic implication of my argument, examined in this chapter, is that targets of regime change should be more likely to descend into civil wars than other countries. The second domestic implication, investigated in chapter 4, is that foreign-imposed leaders ought to face a higher hazard of forcible removal from office than other leaders. The international implications of my argument, examined in chapter 5, are that regime change worsens relations between interveners and targets and increases the chances of conflict between them.

This chapter proceeds in four parts. First, I situate regime change in the literature on the causes of civil war. Second, I briefly recapitulate my arguments for how regime change can cause civil war and outline my specific hypotheses. Third, I present quantitative evidence from an analysis of a country-year dataset covering the years 1816 to 2008, which shows that outbreaks of civil conflict are significantly more likely in the years following regime change—particularly leadership regime change. Regime changes that simultaneously promote political institutions in addition to leaders have no overall effect on civil war onset but increase the risk in poor and ethnically diverse countries—that is, where institutional regime changes are likely to fail. Regime changes that restore previous leaders and/or governments to power, finally, slightly reduce the chances of civil war but this effect is not statistically significant. In this chapter and the two that follow, I summarize the quantitative results in graphical form in the body of the chapter while reserving the details for chapter appendixes. The final section of the chapter provides evidence from six historical cases that illustrates the two causal mechanisms connecting regime change and civil war.

The Literature on the Causes of Civil War

The literature on the causes of civil war historically has focused almost exclusively on domestic variables that vary slowly if at all. It has thus been much better at predicting *where* civil wars will occur than *when* they will occur. Foreign-imposed regime change introduces a dynamic external variable that helps explain both the location and timing of civil war.

DOMESTIC FOCUS

Most theories of civil war onset rely on domestic characteristics of countries to explain the outbreak of internal conflict. One well-known perspective, for example, champions grievances as the source of rebellion and emphasizes factors such as relative deprivation, various forms of inequality and discrimination, and resentment.[1] Observing that grievances are relatively common but large-scale violence is rare, a second group of economically minded scholars challenged the grievance-based consensus in the 1990s.[2] Some highlighted rebel "greed," arguing that civil wars occur where local conditions make it profitable for participants; others maintained that weak state capacity and rough terrain increase the likelihood of civil war by creating opportunities for insurgencies to challenge the state.[3] A third line of argument emphasizes the role of fear in causing civil war. This perspective maintains that the collapse of multiethnic states produces domestic anarchy, which can lead to civil war by causing security dilemmas between intermingled ethnic groups or commitment problems between majority and minority groups.[4]

Over time, scholarship on the causes of civil war began to recognize that state borders are not hermetically sealed and thus that external factors might mitigate or exacerbate the chances of civil wars breaking out. Research on external causes of civil war has taken a number of different directions.[5] Idean Salehyan, for example, argues that weak or hostile neighboring states that harbor or sponsor rebels increase the likelihood that a state will experience civil war.[6] Salehyan and Kristian Skrede Gleditsch find that influxes of refugees exacerbate the risk of civil conflict, as refugees can "change the ethnic composition of the host state; exacerbate economic competition; [and] bring with them arms, combatants, and ideologies that are conducive to violence."[7] Others explore the unintended consequences of interventions meant to protect civilians. Alan Kuperman, for instance, contends that external intervention to prevent atrocities in civil wars creates "moral hazard": by providing insurance against catastrophic outcomes, humanitarian intervention encourages risk-taking behavior by domestic groups, such as launching a rebellion or provoking a government crackdown.[8] Other scholars maintain that providing humanitarian aid in refugee crises can exacerbate conflict by feeding and sheltering militants and their supporters, inadvertently helping to fund militant groups, and providing legitimacy to combatants by allowing them to portray themselves as victims.[9]

Still other analysts argue that foreign military intervention triggers nationalist resistance by target populations. David Edelstein, for example, maintains that nationalism is the foremost obstacle to successful military occupation.[10] Similarly, John Mearsheimer argues that the power of nationalism has repeatedly frustrated American attempts at social engineering in foreign states by generating violent resistance.[11] And Robert Pape contends that foreign occupation spurs nationalist groups to turn to suicide terrorism to expel occupiers from their homelands.[12]

WHERE, NOT WHEN

The second distinguishing characteristic of the literature on the causes of civil war is its focus on relatively static factors, which helps it predict where civil wars will occur better than when they will occur. In one prominent example, James Fearon and David Laitin argue that insurgencies are more likely to develop in states with a weak capacity to control their territory. Of the factors their theory suggests as facilitating the outbreak of civil war, however, including low GDP per capita, large populations, rough terrain, noncontiguous territory, newly independent states, high petroleum exports, and political instability, almost all of them change slowly or—in the case of geography—not at all.[13] Another well-known model devised by Paul Collier and Anke Hoeffler relies on many of the same static factors as Fearon and Laitin's, but the ones it adds—economic growth, primary commodity exports as a percentage of GDP, male secondary school enrollment, and the size of the country's diaspora population—are similarly slow to change.[14]

The grievance literature is somewhat more dynamic but still relies to a large extent on factors that explain cross-national variation better than temporal variation. The newest grievance literature, for example, focuses on "horizontal inequalities," which are inequities between culturally defined groups rather than between individuals.[15] Intergroup economic inequality, however, which is the focus of some of this literature, is a slow-changing variable.[16] Similarly, in his tome on ethnic conflict, Donald Horowitz emphasizes legacies of colonialism that generate perceptions of "backward" versus "advanced" groups—perceptions that are essentially fixed.[17] Several studies that utilize the Minorities at Risk data also trace the outbreak of ethnic rebellion to a relatively unchanging factor: the degree to which groups are concentrated in space as opposed to dispersed or urban.[18] And although it is not persuasively linked to any particular grievance theory, numerous studies proxy grievance arguments with countries' levels of ethnic fractionalization, another slow-changing variable.[19]

Some grievance-based theories, however, rely on factors that vary to a greater extent than those discussed thus far. Exclusion of ethnic or cultural groups from access to political power, for example, another version of the horizontal inequality argument, could change as often as different leaders or regimes take office.[20] Roger Petersen's resentment argument also provides a clear trigger for when violence ought to occur: when a previously dominant group has been subordinated in the ethnic status hierarchy by a revolution or foreign intervention and has an opportunity to strike at the group that has been placed above it.[21] Fearon and Laitin's "sons of the soil" argument directs attention to situations in which an indigenous group perceives its local dominance threatened by an influx of economic migrants that the state, for various reasons, is unwilling to restrain.[22]

Other theories outside the grievance paradigm also emphasize variables that help explain the timing of civil war onset. Fear-based theories, mentioned above, maintain that ethnic civil conflicts are likely to erupt when multiethnic states fall apart.[23] Other scholars explain the outbreak of ethnic conflicts by arguing that leaders whose grip on power is threatened by co-ethnics may provoke conflict with other ethnic groups to consolidate their authority within their own group.[24] Adria Lawrence, in explaining why nationalist resistance to French colonial rule turned violent in some places but not others, argues that wars occurred only when French authorities decapitated moderate resistance groups, permitting radical figures more inclined to use violence to take over these movements.[25] Finally, Philip Roessler contends that leaders who fear a coup by a power-sharing partner may purge their rival from the capital, in effect accepting civil war at the periphery because it is less dangerous than a coup at the center.[26]

WHERE REGIME CHANGE FITS

Foreign-imposed regime change injects an external variable that can also explain when internal conflicts should occur into this domestically focused literature that struggles to explain the timing of conflict onset. As yet only a single study examines the link between regime change and civil war.[27] Goran Peic and Dan Reiter argue that regime change contributes to the outbreak of civil war through its effect on "state infrastructural power and political institutions."[28] These authors claim that regime change enacted concurrently with defeat in an interstate war often destroys "physical and human infrastructure," weakens state security forces, and removes competent government officials.[29] The cumulative effect of this damage is to undermine the state's capacity to deter and suppress rebellion, thereby encouraging potential insurgents to launch armed bids for power. Regime changes that alter political institutions can also trigger conflict because new institutions are viewed as lacking legitimacy or because "groups within society seek to shape political institutions to maximize their own power and advance their own interests."[30] Empirically, Peic and Reiter find support for these arguments using a dataset of regime change and civil war onset from

1920 to 2004: civil war is significantly more likely following regime changes that coincided with defeat in interstate wars or substantial changes in political institutions. Importantly, however, regime change in the absence of these two conditions does not have a systematic effect on civil war onset.

Peic and Reiter's study represents a major advance in our understanding of the relationship between externally sponsored leader change and internal conflict. I build on their work and aim to advance it in three ways. First, Peic and Reiter's state capacity story is questionable. It is unclear, for example, why regime change alone does not weaken the state sufficiently to open up opportunities for enterprising rebels to launch challenges. Furthermore, if defeat in war is needed in conjunction with regime change to precipitate civil war, one would surmise that the greater the extent of the defeat, the higher the likelihood of civil war. By 1945, however, Germany and Japan had experienced far more widespread and massive destruction than Afghanistan in 2001 or Iraq in 2003, yet civil wars broke out in the latter pair of countries rather than the former.

Second, regime changes don't simply create opportunities for would-be rebels to challenge the state, they generate ample grievances as well. Foreign interveners sometimes overturn long-established status hierarchies in societies, providing ample motivation for demoted groups to seek a return to power through violence. Foreigners also typically have specific preferences over who rules and how they rule that are at odds with the preferences of local populations. This mismatch can fuel resistance to externally imposed regimes.

Finally, a relatively small number of regime changes and civil wars underlie Peic and Reiter's results. Their dataset includes forty-two regime changes, but only six civil wars took place following those interventions, and two of them occurred in the same country (Indonesia).[31] Peic and Reiter nevertheless make ambitious claims based on this narrow empirical foundation, such as "interstate war and institutional change are both necessary though not sufficient conditions for an FIRC to cause civil war."[32] My study, by contrast, contains over one hundred instances of regime change, forty-two of which are followed by civil wars within ten years. The main reason for the discrepancy in the number of regime changes is the longer time frame of my study, but Peic and Reiter also use the *Archigos* dataset on leaders as their source for regime change.[33] This dataset—which I also use—is an excellent resource on leaders and leader tenure. In certain cases, however, I argue that cases coded by *Archigos* as irregular removal by domestic actors should be classified as cases of foreign-imposed regime change.[34]

Recapitulating the Argument

As outlined in detail in chapter 2, regime change causes civil war through two separate theoretical mechanisms. In the first, the intervention itself induces the target's military to collapse. In this mechanism, the intervener is a victim of its own success: it wins such a quick and crushing victory that the target army disintegrates. Although some elements may stand and fight, large numbers of soldiers flee, either taking shelter in remote areas or simply going home. Military disintegration creates conditions ripe for civil war because—compared to situations in which the military stays unified and surrenders in an orderly fashion—it litters the landscape with the raw material for insurgency. In some cases, as in Cambodia in 1979 or Afghanistan in 2001, the toppled leader escapes, rallies his surviving troops in a territorial sanctuary, and begins an insurgency to drive out the occupier or its puppet. In other cases, such as Peru in the 1880s, Yugoslavia and Greece in 1941, or Iraq in 2003, new figures emerge to lead the resistance. The key feature of military disintegration that facilitates rebellion is thus that it provides the critical component of insurgency—plentiful armed and trained manpower.

The second pathway from regime change to civil war is the problem of competing principals that foreign-imposed leaders face once they take power. The intervener (the external principal) expects the imposed leader (the agent) to implement policies that are consistent with its preferences. Doing so, however, may anger or inflict real injury on the leader's constituents—the domestic principal. Imposed leaders, many of whom were not resident in the country before regime change, often lack indigenous support and knowledge of the domestic political landscape. For these reasons, they tend to rely heavily on their external patrons and, in exchange, may be willing to implement policies that disproportionately benefit them. This favoritism of external interests can spur domestic actors to use violence to remove the imposed leader from power.

H3.1: *Foreign-imposed regime change increases the likelihood of civil war.*

THE DIVERGENT EFFECTS OF DIFFERENT TYPES OF REGIME CHANGE

Of the three types of regime change, *leadership regime change* is the most likely to cause civil war because leaders installed in this way are most vulnerable to the problem of competing principals. The defining characteristic of leadership regime change is that interveners empower a new ruler but do little to develop target institutions, contenting themselves with replacing the leader and letting domestic forces establish whatever institutions they see fit. Examples of leadership regime changes include Britain's forays into Afghanistan (1839–42 and 1878–80), London's joint campaign with the Soviets to oust Iran's Reza Shah (1941), and France's replacement of Jean-Bédel Bokassa with David Dacko in Central African Republic (1979). Interveners—even democratic ones—perceive dictatorial leaders as able to "deliver the goods" given the absence of institutional constraints on their actions.[35] Because these leaders frequently lack extensive bases of domestic support, they are more likely than leaders imposed in other ways to be heavily dependent on their foreign patrons and more likely to be responsive to their interests. These kinds of leaders are thus apt to generate the strongest domestic reaction because of their dependence on, and responsiveness to, foreign interests.

H3.2: *Leadership regime change increases the likelihood of civil war.*

In cases of *institutional regime change,* interveners attempt to establish new governing institutions in addition to empowering new leaders. There are two versions of institutional regime change. In one, democracies seek to establish democratic institutions in targets, as in West Germany and Japan after World War II, and in Afghanistan and Iraq more recently. In the other, interveners try to set up single-party regimes in targets after intervention, as when the Soviets established communist regimes in Eastern Europe in the 1940s. I argue that regime change is unlikely to lead to civil war when interveners *successfully* build repressive or representative institutions, which is likely to occur in countries that have preconditions for institutional development, including higher incomes and ethnic homogeneity. If institution building fails, as is probable in poor and diverse locales, civil war is more likely. Owing to these countervailing effects, I do not expect institutional regime change, on average, to increase the likelihood of civil war.

H3.3a: *Institutional regime change neither increases nor decreases the likelihood of civil war.*

H3.3b: *Institutional regime change increases the likelihood of civil war more in poor countries than in wealthy countries.*

H3.3c: *Institutional regime change increases the likelihood of civil war more in ethnically diverse countries than in homogeneous countries.*

Restoration regime change occurs when an intervener returns the leader or regime to power that previously governed the country (within the last five years) but was removed in a coup, revolution, or by an outside power. The goal of such restorations is not to impose a new leader or political order, but rather to restore the status quo ante. I argue that restoration regime changes do not increase the likelihood of civil war because the problem of competing principals is counteracted in these cases by several other factors specific to restorations. On the one hand, leaders that require restoration—unless they were driven from office by another foreign power—likely face a capable domestic opposition. These leaders, once restored, may be even more reliant on external support to sustain them in power than they were before they were ousted, thereby creating the same dilemma faced by leaders empowered in leadership regime changes. However, some restoration regime changes reinstate democratic leaders who were removed by another foreign power, which presumably reduces the risk of civil war. In other cases, the act of restoring the previous regime decimates the domestic opposition that was responsible for removing the leader, which increases his security once returned to office. Because of these countervailing effects, I expect that restoration regime change will not increase the likelihood of civil war.

H3.4: *Restoration regime change does not increase the likelihood of civil war.*

Finally, as noted above, previous studies find that regime change provokes civil war only in combination with a simultaneous defeat in an interstate war. Examples of defeats that coincided with regime change include Mexico in 1863, Belgium and the Netherlands in 1940, Germany and Japan in 1945, and contemporary Afghanistan and Iraq.

H3.5: *Foreign-imposed regime change inflicted concurrently with defeat in an interstate war increases the likelihood of civil war more than regime change or interstate war defeat independently.*

Statistical Results

Table 3.1 lists the forty-nine civil wars that broke out within ten years of a foreign-imposed regime change. The prevalence of leadership regime changes in table 3.1 is an early indication that regime changes that replace leaders but do not develop institutions are the type of regime change that is most likely to incite civil strife.

Figures 3.1 and 3.2 support this conjecture. Figure 3.1 shows the number of regime changes—and the number of each type of regime change— followed by at least one civil war within ten years (the left-most column in each pair), and the total number of civil wars that broke out within a decade of each type of regime change (on the right in each pair). Figure 3.2 shows the percentage of each type of regime change followed by civil war within a decade. According to figure 3.1, for example, a civil war broke out within ten years of thirty-six regime changes, which, as shown in figure 3.2, equates to 32 percent of all regime changes. Of the three types of regime change, thirty leadership regime changes (46 percent) were followed by civil war, as opposed to only four institutional regime changes (20 percent) and three restoration regime changes (11 percent). Fully 83 percent of regime changes after which a civil war occurred were leadership regime changes; such regime changes also account for 86 percent of the forty-nine civil wars that occurred within a decade of a regime change.[36] Given that the baseline probability of a country experiencing a civil war over the course of a decade is roughly 15 percent, figure 3.2 indicates—in line with my first two hypotheses—that regime change overall and leadership regime change in

Table 3.1 Cases of foreign-imposed regime change followed by civil wars

Country	Year of regime change	Type of regime change	Year of civil war onset	Description
Spain	1823	Restoration	1833	First Carlist War
Afghanistan	1839	Leadership	1840	Resistance to British occupation
Nicaragua	1845	Leadership	1854	Conservatives vs. Liberals
Argentina	1852	Leadership	1859	Federalists vs. Centralists
Argentina	1852	Leadership	1861	Federalists vs. Centralists
Mexico	1863	Leadership	1864	Resistance to French occupation
France	1870	Leadership	1871	Communards
Afghanistan	1879	Leadership	1879	Resistance to British occupation
Afghanistan	1879	Leadership	1886	Ghilzai Revolt
Afghanistan	1879	Leadership	1888	Uzbek Revolt
Peru	1881	Leadership	1882	Resistance to Chilean occupation
Peru	1881	Leadership	1884	Forces of Iglesias vs. forces of Caceres
Peru	1881	Leadership	1885	Atusparia Uprising
Korea	1905	Leadership	1907	Resistance to Japanese occupation
Nicaragua	1910	Institutional	1912	Liberals vs. Conservatives
Mexico	1914	Leadership	1914	Conventionists vs. Constitutionalists
Mexico	1914	Leadership	1923	De La Huerta Revolt
Haiti	1915	Leadership	1918	Caco revolt against US occupation
Hungary	1919	Leadership	1919	Reds vs. Whites
Nicaragua	1926	Institutional	1926	Sandino Rebellion
China	1928	Leadership	1928	Muslims
China	1928	Leadership	1929	Warlords
China	1928	Leadership	1930	Communists
China	1928	Leadership	1934	Fukien Revolt, 19th Route Army
Ethiopia	1936	Leadership	1937	Resistance to Italian occupation
Albania	1939	Leadership	1943	Resistance to German occupation
Greece	1941	Leadership	1941	Resistance to German occupation
Greece	1941	Leadership	1944	Communists
Yugoslavia	1941	Leadership	1941	Resistance to German occupation
Indonesia	1948	Leadership	1950	Moluccans
Indonesia	1948	Leadership	1953	Darul Islam
Indonesia	1948	Leadership	1956	Leftists
Guatemala	1954	Leadership	1963	Leftists
DRC	1960	Leadership	1960	Katanga
DRC	1960	Leadership	1963	Jeunesse Revolt
DRC	1960	Leadership	1964	Simba Revolt

(continued)

Table 3.1 (continued)

Country	Year of regime change	Type of regime change	Year of civil war onset	Description
Dominican Republic	1961	Leadership	1965	Leftists
Chile	1973	Leadership	1973	Military vs. Leftists
Cyprus*	1974	Leadership Restoration	1974	Turks vs. Greeks
Cambodia	1979	Leadership	1979	Khmer Rouge
Uganda	1979	Leadership	1980	National Resistance Army (Museveni)
Uganda	1979	Leadership	1986	Holy Spirit Movement
Chad	1982	Leadership	1989	Deby Coup
Afghanistan	1986	Leadership	1989	Mujahideen
DRC	1997	Leadership	1998	Mai Mai Rebellion; Rally for Congolese Democracy
Republic of Congo	1997	Restoration	1997	Cobra Militia
Republic of Congo	1997	Restoration	1998	Ninja and Cocoye Militias
Afghanistan	2001	Institutional	2003	Taliban
Iraq	2003	Institutional	2004	Former Baathists, Sunnis, AQI

* Cyprus experienced two regime changes in quick succession in 1974. The first was a leadership regime change supported by Greece and the second was a restoration carried out by Turkey. The civil war and Turkish intervention were triggered by the first regime change and terminated by the second one.

particular increases the likelihood of civil war. The former more than doubles the chance of civil war whereas the latter nearly triples it. Institutional and restoration regime change, by contrast, appear to have much smaller positive and negative effects, respectively, on the probability of civil war—in line with the expectations of H3.3a and 3.4.

Another way to assess the impact of regime change on civil war is to calculate the annual rate at which countries that experience regime change—and different types of regime change—suffer civil wars compared to countries that do not. Figure 3.3, for example, shows that the annual probability of civil war over the ensuing decade in a country that experienced regime change is 4.8 percent, whereas the probability for a country that suffered no regime change is 1.8 percent. States that experience regime change are thus nearly three times more likely to suffer a civil war each year over the following ten years than states that do not. The difference between the two estimates is significant in statistical terms, as indicated by the gap between the 95 percent confidence intervals in figure 3.3.

Breaking down regime changes by type yields results similar to those found in the previous figures. Leadership regime change, for instance,

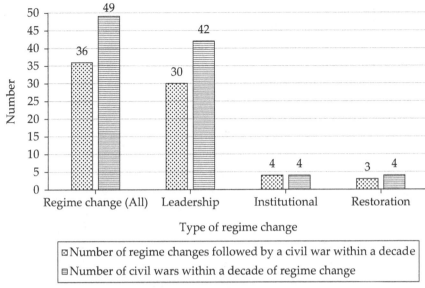

Figure 3.1. Number of foreign-imposed regime changes followed by civil war and number of civil wars following regime change within a decade. The numbers of civil wars after the different types of regime changes do not sum to the figures in the first set of columns (for all regime changes) because Cyprus experienced both a leadership and a restoration regime change in 1974 followed by a civil war.

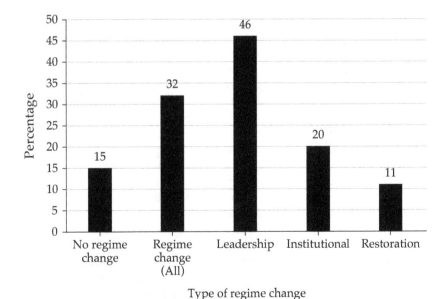

Figure 3.2. Proportion of foreign-imposed regime changes followed by civil war within a decade

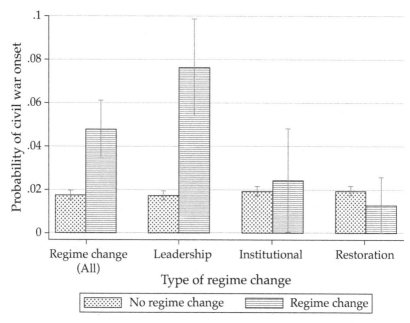

Figure 3.3. Annual probability of civil war onset in the decade after foreign-imposed regime change. Bars indicate probabilities; capped lines indicate 95 percent confidence intervals.

produces an annual probability of civil war of 7.8, which is about four and a half times greater than the rate for countries that do not suffer this type of regime change. By contrast, neither institutional nor restoration regime change exerts a discernable effect on the likelihood of civil war. Although institutional regime change increases the risk of civil war about one-quarter whereas restoration regime change reduces it by about a third, the overlapping confidence intervals for these effects in figure 3.3 indicate that they are not significantly different in a statistical sense.

Some readers might wonder whether the risk of civil war after regime change has increased or decreased over time. Upon examining this question, it appears that, if anything, the likelihood that regime change contributes to civil war has grown since the end of World War II. Through 1945, about 27 percent of all regime changes were followed by civil wars. During the Cold War and after, this figure increased perceptibly to 45 percent. Although the probability of civil war for each type of regime change jumped from before to after 1945, leadership regime change—which nearly doubled from 38 percent to 71 percent—grew the most in absolute probability. Institutional and restoration regime changes also exhibited substantial increases but at lower absolute levels of probability—from 15 to 29 percent for the former and from 6 to 20 percent for the latter—although caution is warranted given the small number of cases involved.

None of the results thus far has taken into account the effect that other variables might have on the likelihood of civil war. Figure 3.4 thus displays the marginal effects of regime change over the period from 1816 to 2008 calculated from probit regressions, discussed in the chapter appendix, that include a basic set of control variables.[37] The pattern of results is highly similar to that shown in figure 3.3. Regime changes considered together more than double the risk of civil war from 1.6 percent annually to 3.7 percent over the ensuing decade. States that experience leadership regime change have a 5.6 percent chance of civil war onset per year, a three-and-a-half-fold increase over countries that do not experience leadership regime change. Institutional regime change also increases the likelihood of internal conflict about 60 percent, but the overlapping confidence intervals for the two estimates in figure 3.4 indicate that this effect is not statistically significant. This is also true for restoration regime change, which reduces the risk of civil war about 10 percent.[38] These findings are consistent with my hypotheses on the effects of regime change in general (H3.1), leadership regime change (H3.2), institutional regime change (H3.3a), and restoration regime change (H3.4).

Before moving on to present evidence for my conditional hypotheses, recall from the definition of regime change in chapter 1 that although it invariably entails removing the current leader, interveners are not always

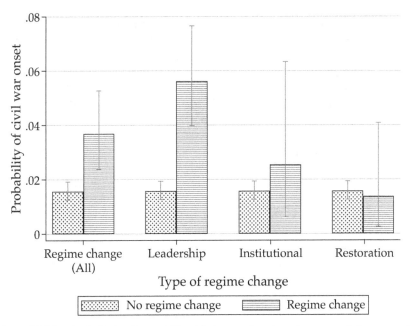

Figure 3.4. Marginal effects of types of foreign-imposed regime change on civil war onset controlling for the effects of other variables.

able to determine the successor leader. This may occur for a number of rea-sons, the most common being that regime change was achieved via coer-cive diplomacy or assassination, or the intervener intends to transform the target's institutions without empowering a particular individual. The fact that interveners sometimes do not exert control over who takes power after regime change, however, raises the possibility that leaders who gain office in cases like these will not share the intervener's preferences. Assuming that interveners choose strategically, when they have control over who takes power after regime change, they will empower individuals who are likely to share their views and who thus will implement acceptable policies. If this argument is correct, the cases in which interveners are unable to install such a leader should be the ones where preference divergences emerge and con-flicts are likely. In effect, this argument amounts to a claim that adverse se-lection explains the ill effects of regime change.

In the chapter appendix, I test for this possibility. I find that there is no dif-ference in the effect of regime changes in which interveners determine who succeeds to power and those where they do not on the likelihood of civil war in the category of leadership regime change, the variety that accounts for the positive effect of regime change on civil war.[39] It thus does not appear that ad-verse selection alone explains why regime change causes civil strife in targets.

CONDITIONAL EFFECTS OF REGIME CHANGE

The graphs depicted in figures 3.5 and 3.6 provide evidence on H3.3b and H3.3c, which maintain that civil war is more likely to occur after institu-tional regime changes in poor and heterogeneous locales because such regime changes are likely to fail in these conditions.[40]

Figure 3.5 shows the effect of institutional regime change on the likeli-hood of civil war as target states become more economically developed (proxied by the log of energy consumption). The solid line in each figure shows the marginal effect of regime change; dotted lines track the 95 percent confidence interval. If H3.3b is correct, the marginal effect of institutional regime change ought to decrease sharply from left to right.

This is in fact what we observe: at the lowest levels of economic develop-ment, institutional regime change increases the likelihood of civil war nearly 8 percent. This effect decreases quickly and becomes indistinguish-able from zero by the time the log of energy consumption reaches four and even becomes negative (although insignificant) at higher levels of wealth. This result resonates with the cases, as civil wars have broken out in impov-erished countries that the United States has attempted to democratize, in-cluding Nicaragua (twice) and Afghanistan (2001). It also makes sense given previous findings on regime change and democratization: attempts to democratize countries after regime change tend to fail in poor states, and this failure may in turn contribute to the outbreak of civil strife.[41]

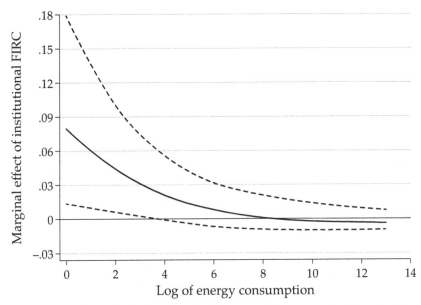

Figure 3.5. The effect of institutional regime change on civil war onset contingent on the target's level of economic development

Importantly, the negative effect of institutional regime change on the likelihood of civil war as countries grow wealthier shown in figure 3.5 is unique to this type of regime change. The effect of leadership regime change, for example, is significant at all levels of economic development and decreases by roughly 0.5 percent as development shifts from its lowest to highest observed value—producing a relatively flat line. The effect of leadership regime change is thus unaffected by changing levels of economic development. In contrast, the effect of restoration regime change on civil war increases over the range of economic development but is never significant.[42]

Figure 3.6 provides evidence on the proposition articulated in H3.3c that institutional regime change increases the likelihood of civil war more in ethnically diverse countries than in homogeneous ones. If this hypothesis is correct, the curve representing the effect of institutional regime change in figure 3.6 should bend sharply upward from left to right. Again, the data bear this out: at the lowest levels of ethnic diversity (measured on a scale of zero to one), as in a country such as the Netherlands, the effect of such interventions is essentially zero.[43] The effect becomes positive and grows as heterogeneity continues to increase, however. By the time ethnolinguistic fractionalization reaches 0.7, the highest value for a state that experienced institutional regime change, the probability of civil war exceeds 5 percent annually. It is significant only for states with diversity scores greater than 0.55. This result also tracks nicely with work on imposed democracy, which

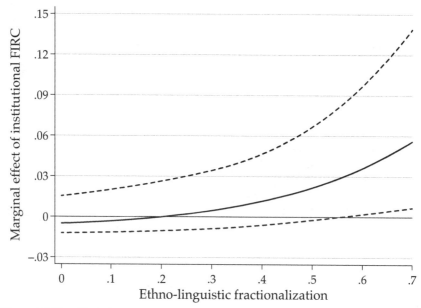

Figure 3.6. The effect of institutional regime change on civil war onset contingent on the target's level of ethnolinguistic fractionalization

finds that democracy is unlikely to take hold after military interventions when targets have high levels of ethnic heterogeneity.[44]

Other types of regime change evince the same increasing effect on civil war as states become more diverse. The effect of leadership regime change is less influenced by heterogeneity than its institutional counterpart: it is positive and significant at all values of ethnic diversity and increases only slightly as states grow decreasingly homogeneous. Restoration regime change evidences a stronger upward pattern of a similar magnitude to institutional regime change without the latter's statistical significance.[45]

Finally, figure 3.7 tests H3.5, which suggests that regime change is more likely to lead to civil war when inflicted concurrently with defeat in an interstate war. Figure 3.7 uses the combined regime change variable because this hypothesis is not contingent on the type of regime change implemented. The figure shows the probability of civil war when regime change and losing an interstate war are each zero (far left bar), when they are each one (far right), and when one or the other is one (middle two bars). In figure 3.7, the risk of civil war in states that lose a war but do not experience regime change is 2.8 percent, about 80 percent higher than in states that experience neither. The corresponding risk for states that undergo regime change but are not defeated in war is 3.9 percent, an increase

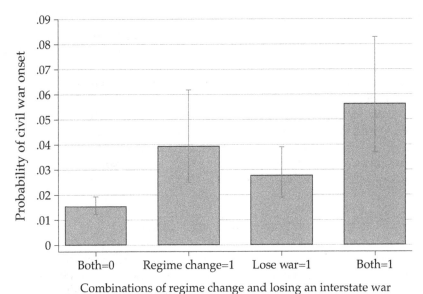

Combinations of regime change and losing an interstate war

Figure 3.7. The effect of foreign-imposed regime change on civil war onset contingent on target concurrently losing an interstate war

of 155 percent. The risk of civil war for states that experience regime change and defeat in war simultaneously is 5.6 percent, more than 2.6 times greater than a state that suffers neither event. Each of these three effects is significant. The difference between the effect of regime change by itself and the combination of regime change and defeat in an interstate war, however, is not significant.[46]

Thus, although suffering regime change while losing an interstate war significantly increases the likelihood of civil war beyond experiencing neither, losing a war and undergoing regime change does not appear to make civil war meaningfully more likely than experiencing regime change alone.[47] This finding fails to support H3.5—and the existing literature.[48] In contrast, it indirectly supports my argument that regime change enhances the probability of civil war in conjunction with only certain types of defeat in war, namely those that trigger military disintegration in the target.

In sum, the quantitative evidence supports my theory: foreign-imposed regime change increases the likelihood that civil war breaks out in target states over the ensuing ten years (H3.1). This overall finding is driven by the powerful positive effect of leadership regime change on civil war onset (H3.2). Institutional and restoration regime changes (H3.3a and H3.4), by contrast, on average neither increase nor decrease the probability of civil war. Hypothesis 3.3b, which proposes that institutional regime change has a larger effect in underdeveloped countries, is supported, as is H3.3c, which maintains that institutional regime change ought to have a more pronounced effect on civil war onset in ethnically diverse countries. Finally, in contradiction to H3.5, civil war is more likely when a target loses a war and suffers regime change simultaneously, but the effect is not significantly greater than undergoing regime change alone.

The chapter appendix contains the details of my statistical analysis, including variable descriptions, a discussion of methods, regression tables, robustness checks, and a battery of tests to detect possible selection bias. I encourage interested readers to explore those pages. Now, however, I turn to case studies to trace the causal mechanisms of my theory.

Regime Change, Military Disintegration, and Civil War

My theory posits two mechanisms through which regime change can contribute to the onset of civil war: military disintegration, which is the focus of this section, and the problem of competing principals, explored in the ensuing section. In the military disintegration logic, the act of changing the regime, which in this mechanism is typically achieved by a military invasion, precipitates the dissolution of the target's armed forces. For a variety of reasons, rather than standing and fighting, or surrendering in an organized fashion, the target's military shatters, scattering thousands of armed men across the country—often to remote locales untouched by the invaders or in the rear of the invading army. These individuals form the raw material for guerrilla resistance to the intervener and/or its local proxy. This situation is highly likely to lead to insurgency whether or not the deposed leader escapes and unites with elements of these forces. If the army remains a coherent body and surrenders in an organized fashion, however, this avenue to civil war is foreclosed. It is also likely foreclosed when the military—under threat from, or at the prompting of, the outside power—seizes power and ousts the leader without being defeated.

This section reviews three cases that illustrate the military disintegration mechanism: Cambodia after the Vietnamese invasion in 1978, Afghanistan after the US ouster of the Taliban in 2001, and Iraq following the US overthrow of Saddam Hussein in 2003. I selected these three cases because they are relatively recent and thus well documented. A number of earlier cases also provide good examples of military disintegration triggering insurgencies, including the French invasion of Mexico to overthrow Benito Juárez (1862–63); Chile's invasion of Peru in the War of the Pacific (1879–83), during which the Chileans ousted three Peruvian leaders; and the German conquest of Yugoslavia (1941), which sent King Peter II into exile.[49]

VIETNAM'S OUSTER OF POL POT AND
THE KHMER ROUGE IN CAMBODIA

Vietnam's overthrow of the Khmer Rouge regime in Cambodia consisted of an armored blitzkrieg that quickly penetrated Cambodian defenses, captured important bases in rear areas, and attacked the Cambodians from the rear. Khmer Rouge leaders facilitated the Vietnamese plan by forward-deploying their forces. Although the capital, Phnom Penh, was captured within days, Khmer Rouge leaders and forces were able to flee westward and gain sanctuary along the Thai border. Once there, they regrouped and launched an insurgency against the Vietnamese-backed regime of Heng Samrin. It is a textbook case of both leadership regime change and how military disintegration spawns guerrilla insurgency.

Origins and Conduct of Regime Change Vietnam's regime change in Cambodia, which commenced with an armored blitzkrieg on Christmas Day of 1978, had its origins in a territorial dispute between the two communist neighbors. Pol Pot's Khmer Rouge movement, having defeated Lon Nol's US-backed government in 1975, proceeded to implement a reign of terror in the country that ultimately resulted in the deaths of between 1.9 and 3.5 million Cambodians.[50] But the Khmer Rouge also pressed claims to Vietnamese territory.[51] These claims culminated in a series of brutal attacks on Vietnamese border villages in 1977 that inflicted hundreds of civilian deaths.[52] According to one assessment, "In two years, the Khmer Rouge destroyed twenty-five townships and ninety-six villages, and rendered 257,000 Vietnamese people homeless. One hundred thousand hectares of farmland had to be abandoned because of the fighting."[53]

In response, Hanoi launched an armored incursion into eastern Cambodia in December 1977 to clear the border areas, punish the Khmer Rouge, and deter further attacks.[54] Vietnamese troops withdrew a month later, but Hanoi's limited invasion did not resolve the problem, writes Edward O'Dowd: "Each time Vietnam withdrew its forces from an area it had cleared, Cambodian troops relentlessly filtered back. In January 1978, Cambodia still held portions of Vietnamese territory in the area of Ha Tien." "Vietnam," continues O'Dowd, "shifted now to a strategy of regime change. If it could eliminate Pol Pot and the Khmer Rouge and establish a friendly government in Phnom Penh, Vietnam reasoned that it could open the possibility of a negotiated resolution of the border problem."[55] This policy was formally adopted at a Central Committee meeting in February 1978. In short, consistent with the general logic of regime change, when Vietnam could not persuade or coerce the Khmer Rouge government to settle the border dispute, Hanoi sought to resolve the preference divergence between the two regimes by replacing Pol Pot with a leader whose preferences were more congruent with its own.

Initially, Vietnamese leaders preferred to accomplish regime change without an invasion. According to one account, "Hanoi apparently calculated that by a combination of internal mass uprising and external military pressure, the Kampuchean regime would collapse relatively rapidly."[56] Hanoi further worried that China would intervene if it launched a massive conventional attack.[57] However, by late autumn 1978, the international context had become more permissive: China, despite lavishing military aid on Pol Pot's regime, publicly declared that it would not send troops to defend its Cambodian protégé. Moreover, the Soviet-Vietnamese Treaty of Friendship and Cooperation was signed in early November, which provided Hanoi with further insurance against Chinese retribution. Indeed, Chang argues that it was the conclusion of this treaty "that gave the final green light for Hanoi to go ahead by removing whatever hesitation Vietnam might still have in executing her plans."[58]

To provide a fig leaf for its impending assault on Cambodia, Hanoi midwifed the birth of the Kampuchea United Front for National Salvation (KUFNS) in early December 1978, headed by a former Khmer Rouge division commander named Heng Samrin.[59] Later that month the Vietnamese launched their lightning invasion of Cambodia with fourteen divisions. A classic blitzkrieg, "The Vietnamese strategy," writes Elizabeth Becker, "was to bypass the established defense positions of the Khmer Rouge and move directly to the command posts, especially Phnom Penh."[60] The Khmer Rouge leadership hastened its own demise by deploying 30,000 troops along the border, where they were easily enveloped and destroyed by the advancing Vietnamese.[61] Phnom Penh, the Cambodian capital, fell on January 7, 1979. Vietnamese armored forces then continued up Highways 5 and 6 to Sisophon, 50 kilometers from the Thai border, which they captured on January 11. Fifty thousand Vietnamese troops then proceeded to attack Khmer Rouge base areas in western Cambodia in Battambang province.[62]

The Disintegration of Khmer Rouge Forces Initially, Pol Pot's forces tried to resist the Vietnamese invasion by fighting conventional set-piece battles. As Stephen Morris writes, however, "Against the numerically superior and much better-armed Vietnamese, this strategy was a recipe for military disaster. The Vietnamese forces annihilated entire units of the revolutionary army of Democratic Kampuchea, reducing the defending force to perhaps half of its preinvasion size."[63] Other accounts agree: "The Khmer Rouge troops fought fiercely, but they were completely outclassed by the Vietnamese" and their use of combined arms warfare.[64] Taken completely by surprise, Pol Pot and the Khmer Rouge leadership fled Phnom Penh ahead of the rapidly approaching Vietnamese. After the Vietnamese captured the Cambodian capital, a People's Revolutionary Council headed by Heng Samrin was proclaimed, which announced within a few days the founding of the People's Republic of Kampuchea. It is important to recognize that, as Michael Leifer writes, "The administration of Heng Samrin was brought into

Kampuchea in the saddle bags of the Vietnamese Army." Samrin's puppet government, Leifer continues, "began its political existence as little more than a list of names on an information sheet," completely dependent on Hanoi for its survival.[65]

In launching their blitzkrieg, Vietnamese leaders wanted to avoid getting bogged down in a quagmire in Cambodia. Like motorized invaders before and after them, however, Hanoi soon discovered that although rapid armored advances that bypass enemy troops may be good for seizing territory, they do not always result in firm territorial control. The German Wehrmacht, for example, discovered this in the wide-open spaces of the western Soviet Union, but should have been forewarned by its experience in Yugoslavia a few months earlier.[66] A similar fate befell the Vietnamese Army in Cambodia. Despite winning all the battles, quickly capturing the enemy's capital, and ousting the regime, the Vietnamese were unable to prevent roughly half of the Khmer Rouge army from slipping away to the Thai border where it regrouped to wage a decade-long insurgency against the Vietnamese occupation and its Cambodian puppets.[67] Khmer Rouge units, faced with conventional defeat, broke down into smaller groups and reverted to guerrilla warfare, thus confronting the Vietnamese with a whole new war. According to one early assessment, for example, following the capture of Phnom Penh, "The bulk of Pol Pot's forces dispersed into the countryside to conduct a protracted war. . . . By the end of February, the Vietnamese military presence was well entrenched but had failed to destroy the Pol Pot forces operating at platoon and company strength."[68] Steven Hood similarly notes, "Despite having captured most urban areas, including Phnom Penh, the Vietnamese military found that resistance in the hill areas of Cambodia was quite strong. The Khmer Rouge retreated to the highlands where it was able to regroup and forestall the Vietnamese drive."[69] After noting that the Khmer Rouge suffered serious casualties in the initial invasion, Stephen Morris contends that Cambodian strategy shifted: "Eventually the rump armed forces of Democratic Kampuchea broke up into smaller units and reverted to guerrilla warfare."[70]

Regeneration of the Khmer Rouge as a Guerrilla Force Following their initial defeat, thousands of Khmer Rouge fighters fled to the western Cardamom Mountains and north to the Thai border, where they regrouped, rearmed, and increased the size of their force.[71] Pol Pot's troops who arrived there were hardly in good shape. Chanda, for example, describes them as having been "reduced to starving, malaria-ridden ragtag bands . . . scattered and in disarray, out of touch with one another and even with their own commanders."[72] Analysts put their numbers at about 25,000, described as a "ragtag force . . . disorganized and scattered across the border in Thailand."[73] The regeneration of this force, however, did not take long: soon, analysts of the conflict estimated their strength at 35,000 or even 40,000 troops.[74] What factors facilitated the Khmer Rouge revival?

First, the political and military leadership of the group survived largely intact, including the preeminent leader, Pol Pot, which served to rally the troops and preserve their sense of mission. Second, the Khmer Rouge undoubtedly benefited from the territorial sanctuary afforded them by the mountainous terrain of western Cambodia and access to Thailand. As Michael Leifer puts it, "the continued porous quality of the extensive border with Thailand enabled the Khmer Rouge to avoid unnecessary confrontation and to have ready access to sanctuary and material supply."[75] Third, the rebel movement received lavish Chinese military aid. Not only did China attack Vietnam in February 1979 to punish it for invading Cambodia, Beijing began to send covert military supplies as well. As Chanda recounts, "a de facto alliance between Peking and Bangkok opened a 'Deng Xiaoping Trail' through Thailand. . . . Chinese ships delivered arms and ammunition to Sattahip and Klong Yai ports, from which the Thai army transported the materiel to Khmer Rouge camps . . . along the Thai-Cambodian border."[76] Aid also flowed from less likely sources. After the noncommunist Cambodian rebel groups were forced into a coalition with the Khmer Rouge by their outside backers, the movement jointly received $1.3 billion in assistance from China, the United States, Singapore, Malaysia, and Thailand over the course of the 1980s.[77]

Fourth, Pol Pot's forces benefited from humanitarian aid provided to Cambodians who had fled the fighting and were housed on both sides of the Thai border, providing a ready-made popular base for the Khmer Rouge. Initially, the Khmer Rouge had about 100,000 people under its control, but this number would grow owing to food shortages and famine inside Cambodia, which drove half a million more people to the Thai border in search of sustenance in late 1979 and early 1980.[78] The Khmer Rouge soon took control over the distribution of aid from humanitarian groups intended for displaced people in the camps inside Cambodia. "In 1980," writes Kelvin Rowley, "at least 80 percent of the material distributed there was commandeered by armed groups."[79] Unlike other groups, which sold much of this aid on the black market, the Khmer Rouge managed its distribution and thereby "built up a patron-client system and used this to rebuild their political and military apparatus."[80] Sophie Quinn-Judge argues that the "humanitarian operation saved many lives but also revived the Khmer Rouge troops."[81] In a precursor to what would happen in the Democratic Republic of Congo (DRC) following the Rwandan genocide, NGOs inadvertently supplied Khmer Rouge militants along with needy civilians.[82]

In short, the Vietnamese blitzkrieg quickly captured Phnom Penh and ousted Pol Pot, but because it precipitated the disintegration of Cambodian forces, it also proved unable to round up thousands of Khmer Rouge fighters. These combatants fled to remote western Cambodia and regrouped, taking advantage of territorial sanctuary and third parties—particularly Thailand and China—whose interests aligned with their own to launch another civil war.

REGIME CHANGE IN AFGHANISTAN IN 2001

The first two regime changes of the twenty-first century—the US invasions of Afghanistan and Iraq, both institutional regime changes—demonstrate that speedy military victories can lead to military collapse in the target, which in turn feeds the growth of insurgency. This section examines the disintegration of the Taliban in 2001 and its contribution to the outbreak of civil war.

Origins and Conduct of Regime Change Following the September 11, 2001, terrorist attacks, US intelligence quickly determined that Al Qaeda was responsible.[83] In his speech to Congress on September 20, President George W. Bush demanded that Afghan leader Mullah Omar—whose Taliban regime was harboring Osama bin Laden—hand over the Al Qaeda leader and his associates or face military intervention. Mullah Omar declined. This left the United States in an awkward position because the US military had no existing plans for launching an attack on Afghanistan.[84] Top officers and others were also reluctant to invade the country, which had earned its nickname "the graveyard of empires" by thwarting British and Soviet attempts to control it.[85] The CIA, however, briefed a "light footprint" approach to the president on September 13 that called for the insertion of small teams of CIA operators and Special Operations Forces (SOF) to work with the Northern Alliance—the umbrella resistance group that held a sliver of Afghan territory in the Panjshir Valley.[86] These teams both disbursed large amounts of cash to fortify support for the US cause and called in air strikes against Taliban ground forces in support of the Northern Alliance advance.

The first CIA team, led by Gary Schroen, landed in northern Afghanistan in late September; soon each of the major commanders of the Northern Alliance was accompanied by a US liaison team.[87] US airstrikes commenced on October 7, formally launching Operation Enduring Freedom. According to Ahmed Rashid, "Four weeks of bombing had weakened the Taliban and made them unable to resist a determined ground assault."[88] When the attack came, the Taliban rapidly gave way, fleeing Mazar-i-Sharif, which was captured by the Northern Alliance on November 9. As Rashid describes it, "As they fled in their four-by-four pickups, U.S. bombers targeted them from the air. The entire north became a shooting gallery, and over the next few days several thousand Taliban were killed."[89] On November 13, the Taliban evacuated Herat in western Afghanistan and the capital Kabul without a fight. Thousands of Taliban fighters were besieged in Kunduz, in the northeast, finally capitulating on November 24.[90] As many as 1,500 of these prisoners suffocated while being transported by General Rashid Dostum's Uzbek troops from Kunduz to Shiberghan in the war's worst mass killing.[91] After holding out for several weeks in Kandahar, the Taliban stronghold in southern Afghanistan, and attempting to kill Hamid Karzai, his soon-to-be designated successor, Mullah Omar sent Taliban defense minister Mullah Obaidullah to negotiate with Karzai on December 5—offering to surrender the city and asking that Taliban troops be allowed to return to their villages.[92] According to one account, Karzai and Obaidullah struck a bargain that would have permitted Mullah Omar to remain in Kandahar under the supervision of Karzai's governor, but Washington vetoed the deal. Karzai's handler from the US military "was directed to tell Karzai that such an arrangement with the Taliban was not in American interests."[93] Mullah Omar and his men soon abandoned Kandahar and retreated across the border to Pakistan.

"Hammer and Anvil" and Military Disintegration In one sense the US attack on Afghanistan was a smashing success. The Taliban regime was overthrown in less than two months with a few hundred CIA and SOF officers, heavy doses of US airpower that dropped 17,500 munitions, and about $70 million to bribe commanders on both sides.[94] US air power supported the Northern Alliance on the ground in a classic "hammer and anvil" strategy that obviated the need for large US ground forces.[95] Only a dozen Americans had died in the conflict by mid-December 2001, compared to roughly 10,000 Taliban (and foreign) fighters.[96] "The sheer alacrity with which United States and Northern Alliance forces overthrew the Taliban regime," writes RAND analyst Seth Jones, "was awe-inspiring."[97] In short, regime change was easy; as Hassan Abbas put it, "the Taliban government fell like a house of cards in a matter of days."[98]

There are two serious problems with this conclusion. First, regime change in Afghanistan was ancillary to US objectives, which were to apprehend or kill Al Qaeda's top leaders and disrupt or destroy the organization. Judged by these metrics, Enduring Freedom was at best a partial success. Osama bin Laden escaped from the battle of Tora Bora in December 2001, slipping away to Pakistan, where he was not tracked down and killed until nearly ten years later. Only two important Al Qaeda leaders were captured or killed in 2001: the group's chief of military operations, Mohammed Atef, who died in a missile strike in Kabul in November, and Ibn al-Sheikh al-Libi, who was captured as he tried to flee to Pakistan around the same time.[99] Other prominent Al Qaeda leaders, including Abu Zubaydah, Khalid al-Attash, Ramzi bin al-Shibh, and Khalid Sheikh Mohammed, the group's number three, were detained in Pakistan after the war was over in 2002 and 2003. Significant numbers of Al Qaeda foot soldiers escaped to Pakistan, settling in North and South Waziristan.[100] Al Qaeda responded to the weakening of its central organization by establishing franchises in numerous regions, such as Iraq, Yemen, Somalia, and the Maghreb.[101] Some of these franchises, like Al Qaeda in Iraq, became extremely deadly in their own right.

Second, although regime change in Afghanistan was achieved quickly and at minimal cost for the United States, Washington's preferred method of deploying hardly any US troops and relying on the Northern Alliance to do the bulk of the fighting on the ground ensured that large numbers of Taliban escaped to Pakistan, where they could regroup and live to fight another day. No US forces were ever inserted into the border regions to block Taliban and Al Qaeda fighters from escaping to Pakistan. Even at Tora Bora, where bin Laden was thought to be holed up, General Tommy Franks, head of US Central Command (CENTCOM), declined to put troops on the ground to block the exit, and only belatedly requested that the Pakistani Army do so.[102] Further, although sealing the border was one of the Bush administration's seven demands delivered to Pakistani president Pervez Musharraf in the days after 9/11, Pakistan not only failed to cooperate, it actively supported the Taliban even after the war began. The ISI continued to supply the Taliban with fuel and ammunition; Pakistani intelligence operatives and soldiers remained in Afghanistan supporting Taliban forces; and thousands of armed tribesmen crossed the border to fight with the Taliban.[103]

To be sure, sealing the Afghan-Pakistani border would have been a monumental task; Musharraf complained to US ambassador to Pakistan Wendy Chamberlin that it was "impossible," and a CIA officer, responding to President Bush's question before the battle of Tora Bora about whether the border could be sealed, replied: "No army on Earth can seal this."[104] The United States thus faced an uphill battle to stem the flow of Taliban and Al Qaeda operatives into Pakistan even had it deployed substantial ground forces to Afghanistan. But that the United States did not even try to block the exit, instead relying on local proxy forces to do the fighting and the Taliban's main supporter (Pakistan) to monitor the border, is puzzling. Coll speculates that Franks and others in the US military feared that inserting Americans in the border regions might stir up tribal unrest, and further that civilian policymakers like secretary of defense Donald Rumsfeld were opposed to repeating what they viewed as the Soviets' main mistake: putting large numbers of troops on the ground.[105] Whatever the reason, the result, as described by a former Pakistani general, Talat Masood, was predictable: "the Taliban were pushed into Pakistan" by the US attack "along with al Qaeda. And as there was no anvil, and there was only a hammer, and the border was porous, there were large numbers in Pakistan, and they filtered all over the place in Pakistan, wherever they found it more convenient to carry on their activities and to feel safe."[106] Jones agrees with this assessment, noting that "Taliban, al Qa'ida, and other militants simply slipped across the border into Pakistan, where they established new camps. Over the next several years, these groups recruited, rearmed, and plotted their return."[107]

The flight of the Taliban into Pakistan was further enabled by the US emphasis on pursuing only Al Qaeda members and foreign fighters and Washington's belief that the Taliban was a spent force. US officials, for example, pressed Pakistani president Pervez Musharraf much harder to apprehend and turn over Al Qaeda operatives than members of the Taliban. This emphasis was in turn reflected in the relative rates at which Pakistan captured Al Qaeda versus Taliban fighters. According to US figures, almost five hundred suspected members of Al Qaeda were detained in Pakistan.[108] By contrast, according to Carlotta Gall, "Only a single prominent Taliban official was arrested and handed over to the United States in the first years after 9/11: the Taliban ambassador to Pakistan, Mullah Abdul Salam Zaeef."[109] Far from detaining or arresting Taliban leaders, the ISI sheltered the Taliban's top commanders and allowed them to operate freely.[110] Rashid notes that this contrasting behavior was official policy: "To maintain its influence among the Taliban and Afghan Pashtuns, the ISI developed a two-track policy of protecting the Taliban while handing over al Qaeda Arabs and other non-Afghans to the United States."[111] This policy was confirmed by the former CIA station chief in Islamabad, Robert Grenier: "The ISI worked closely with us to capture key al Qa'ida leaders. . . . But they made it clear that they didn't care about targeting the Taliban."[112] Moreover, many on the US side believed that there was little need to pursue the Taliban after its catastrophic defeat. As one CIA officer involved quipped, "I don't think we thought much about them at all. . . . They were whipped." James Dobbins, at the time attempting to set up a post-Taliban government, similarly thought that the Taliban "had been so discredited by their performance in government and by the speed at which they had been displaced that they were not going to be a significant factor in Afghan politics."[113]

Sanctuary in Pakistan The ISI, however, had not given up on the Taliban, and welcomed them with open arms to Pakistan. As Rashid describes, "The Taliban did not just slip back across the border in the winter of 2001/2002; they arrived in droves, by bus, taxi, and tractor, on camels and horses, and on foot. As many as ten thousand fighters holed up in Kandahar with their weapons." These soldiers were greeted "at the border with blankets, fresh clothes, and envelopes full of money" by Pakistani extremist groups but also local government officials and officers of the ISI.[114] Evidence of Pakistani complicity in aiding and abetting the Taliban is overwhelming. Mullah Omar arrived in Quetta in the province of Baluchistan in early 2002 and was put up by the ISI in safe houses run by the provincial government, which was under the control of the party that initially spawned the Taliban back in 1994, the Jamiat Ulema-e-Islam (JUI). According to Rashid, "The full state machinery and facilities of the provisional governments were now available to the Taliban."[115] The Taliban was also active in the Federally Administered Tribal Areas (FATA), where former Taliban minister of tribal affairs Jalaluddin Haqqani set up shop in North Waziristan.[116] Al Qaeda militants in the FATA who had escaped Afghanistan provided the Taliban with training and weapons, and the ISI began funneling covert aid to the group as well. The Taliban's territorial sanctuaries in Pakistan, and the funding supplied by elements of the Pakistani state, were critical to the movement's revival.

The Taliban Revival The Taliban's resurgence was not long in coming. Already in December 2001, as their regime was crashing down, Taliban commanders met in Peshawar to plot their comeback.[117] Shortly after Mullah Omar arrived in Quetta, he appointed four commanders to organize the insurgency in Uruzgan, Helmand, Kandahar, and Zabul provinces. Within a year, the Taliban was back in southern Afghanistan, launching a new offensive in spring 2003. By 2005, the renewed Taliban insurgency had crossed the threshold of a high-intensity civil war (in excess of 1,000 deaths per year); total deaths in the conflict thus far exceed 100,000.[118] The Taliban's return was also facilitated by the small number of troops deployed in Afghanistan in the aftermath of regime change—8,000 US troops and 4,000 peacekeepers—and the related necessity of working with detested warlords.[119]

Finally, it is impossible to ignore the effect of preparations for the next regime change operation in Iraq on the outcome in Afghanistan. It is well known that top Bush administration officials, such as secretary of defense Donald Rumsfeld, his deputy Paul Wolfowitz, and even the president himself, believed that Saddam Hussein was linked to the 9/11 attacks, and that Rumsfeld and Wolfowitz immediately began pressing for an offensive against Iraq.[120] In late November, while the fight to oust the Taliban was still underway, Rumsfeld ordered CENTCOM commander General Tommy Franks to begin drafting a plan for invading Iraq.[121] Just as Lord Auckland did in 1839, Rumsfeld directed his attention to another theater, "ordering the campaign's commander to plan for a different war before he had completed the one at hand."[122] As preparations for Iraq heated up in 2002 and early 2003, CENTCOM removed intelligence assets, SOF teams, and naval forces from the Afghan theater and transferred them to the vicinity of Iraq, and the CIA closed several stations in Afghanistan as its expertise was also retasked to Iraq.[123] As former CIA analyst Bruce Riedel puts it, "the coalition and especially the United States took its eyes off the Afghan ball when the invasion of Iraq began. Afghanistan was then put on the back burner and given relatively little reconstruction assistance."[124] Riedel goes so far as to assert that "the Iraq war saved bin Laden and Mullah Omar."[125]

In sum, the combination of the Taliban's quick collapse, the absence of any ground force to block its retreat, and the availability of sanctuary and support across the border in Pakistan allowed Taliban commanders and substantial numbers of foot soldiers to escape and facilitated the Taliban's revival. Also relevant was the US emphasis on capturing Al Qaeda members while mostly ignoring the Taliban. Although US aircraft inflicted heavy casualties, killing about 10,000 of the Taliban's 50,000–60,000 fighters and wounding another 20,000, even subtracting the 7,000 Taliban taken prisoner and assuming that no wounded soldiers got away leaves a minimum of well over 10,000 men unaccounted for and possibly more than 20,000.[126] In reality, many of the wounded survived and either returned home or fled to

Pakistan. Despite their shellacking, therefore, Taliban leaders had plentiful manpower to draw on in their bid to retake control of Afghanistan.

CIVIL WAR IN IRAQ AFTER THE UNITED STATES INVASION

No survey of the potential for military disintegration to trigger civil war would be complete without consideration of the events that unfolded in Iraq after the US overthrow of Saddam Hussein in 2003. This section explores the preparations and planning for the invasion, as well as the conduct and aftermath of regime change. It demonstrates that the initial outbreak of insurgency in the country was triggered by the disintegration of the Sunni-dominated Iraqi Army and Sunnis' resentment at their reversal in status.[127]

Military disintegration in this case would later be supplemented by the problem of competing principals after the United States turned over power to an Iraqi government. This problem made it difficult for the United States to persuade Iraqi leaders, like Nouri al-Maliki, to adopt its preferred policies. I explore the impact of the problem of competing principals on US-Iraqi relations in chapter 5.

I classify Operation Iraqi Freedom as an institutional regime change because the United States—after invading Iraq without a serious plan for who would rule the country or how they would do it—eventually made serious efforts to promote democracy after toppling Saddam's Baathist, Sunni-dominated regime. Following weeks of chaos and looting by Iraqis with no political transition in sight, President Bush appointed Ambassador L. Paul "Jerry" Bremer III to lead the newly formed CPA. After Bremer gave way to Ayad Allawi in June 2004, elections for a constituent assembly empowered to write a new constitution were held in January 2005. The assembly chose Ibrahim al-Jaafari of the United Iraqi Alliance as the first elected prime minister of the new Iraq. Following the ratification of the constitution in October, parliamentary elections occurred in December. After lengthy deliberations, Nouri al-Maliki displaced his United Iraqi Alliance colleague Jaafari and was selected as prime minister.

The United States Breaks Iraq—without a Plan to Fix It It is still shocking nearly twenty years later that the United States government did not have a policy for a political transition in Iraq once Saddam Hussein was overthrown. As has been well documented, US preparations for a post-Saddam Iraq were in their infancy when the war began.[128] The Office of Reconstruction and Humanitarian Assistance (ORHA), led by retired general Jay Garner and responsible for what the military calls Phase IV (postwar operations), was established only two months before the invasion, was woefully understaffed, and lacked expertise on Iraq. ORHA was set up under the assumption that the transition to Iraqi rule would be rapid—Garner told subordinates that he expected to "reconstruct utilities, stand up ministries, appoint an interim government, write and ratify a constitution, hold elections," and hand over sovereignty to an Iraqi government within three months."[129] The US occupation would thus be short and US troops would be speedily withdrawn.[130] Events would soon upend these assumptions.

Different individuals and bureaucratic actors in Washington articulated different visions of regime change in Iraq. Many US government officials across the executive branch, for example, conceived of regime change as synonymous with decapitation—what this book calls leadership regime change.[131] National security advisor Condoleezza Rice, reflecting back after the war, perhaps put this view best: "The concept was that we would defeat the army, but the institutions would hold, everything from ministries to police forces. . . . You would be able to bring new leadership but that we were going to keep the body in place."[132] In the evocative words of Michael Mac-Donald, "decapitationists were content to stitch a new head onto the body of the old regime."[133] Unknowingly echoing the problem of competing principals, decapitationists hoped that a new strongman would be able to suppress domestic dissent and—by virtue of his domestic *un*popularity—have to rely heavily on US support and thus be responsive to US preferences.[134]

At first glance, the decapitationist view of regime change in Iraq appears to fit nicely with the widespread support among neoconservatives inside and outside the US government for installing Iraqi exile Ahmad Chalabi in power in Baghdad.[135] For example, shortly before the war began, under secretary of defense for policy (and neoconservative) Douglas Feith told ORHA head Jay Garner, "You know, Jay, when you get there [Iraq], we could just make Chalabi president."[136] Yet this view is incorrect. For neoconservatives, regime change in Iraq was always about democratization.[137] Neoconservatives supported Chalabi because they believed he could lead Iraq's transformation from a brutal dictatorship to a liberal democracy, US ally, and even a friend of Israel.[138] As Rajiv Chandrasekaran puts it, "the view was that Chalabi and his colleagues were going to lead the way in creating a secular, stable democracy."[139] Nor is it true that the Bush administration's emphasis on democratizing Iraq came about only in reaction to the failure of the decapitation model of regime change. In numerous speeches before the war, President George W. Bush articulated a liberal view of regime change that embraced the thoroughgoing democratization of Iraq. "Democracy," MacDonald notes, "was baked into the administration's sense of regime change from the outset."[140]

Unfortunately, nobody in the Bush administration seemed to have a clear idea of how to get from overthrowing Saddam to a democratic Iraq. Top US officials, including the president and vice-president, the secretary of defense, and the national security advisor, simply assumed that the United States would be welcomed as liberators, Iraqi institutions (including the military and police) would continue to exist, and Iraqis would embrace democracy of their own accord.[141] The Bush administration, writes David Lake, "assumed that inside the heart of every Iraqi was a 'small d' democrat yearning to be free. . . . The administration simply assumed that Iraqis would intuitively understand and immediately adopt democratic institutions."[142] Precisely how the transition to democracy would occur, however, was never made clear. According to one military participant in the postwar planning process, "There was no real plan. . . . The thought was, you didn't need it. The assumption was that everything would be fine after the war, that they'd be happy they got rid of Saddam."[143] Another explained that the administration "assumed that the dramatic ouster of Saddam would create a 'Wizard of Oz moment' in Iraq. . . . After the wicked dictator was deposed, throngs of cheering Iraqis would hail their liberators and go back to work under the tutelage of Garner's postwar organization."[144]

Confusion about how to proceed once Saddam was overthrown was rampant—even among those tasked with overseeing the political transition to Iraqi rule. The Pentagon and the vice-president's office, as shown, favored installing Chalabi. Many in the State Department, however, loathed Chalabi and thought the United States would need to occupy the country before handing over power to a representative group of Iraqis. Absent coordination or vision from the top (i.e., the president), each actor pushed its own agenda. This confusion was voiced by Garner, who later said "I never knew what our plans were. . . . But I did know that what I believed, and what the plans were, were probably two different things."[145] Garner eventually on his own authority threw his weight behind a plan to hand over power to a transitional government composed of a combination of exile leaders and "internals"—Iraqis who had remained in the country during Saddam's reign—but the exiles (Chalabi prominently among them) objected to sharing power.[146] This chaotic approach to the postwar period is perhaps best exemplified by Garner's statement to an assembly of prominent Iraqis he had convened on April 28 to discuss the future of the country. After much conversation, one Iraqi stood up and asked, "Who's in charge of our politics?" Garner replied, "You're in charge!"[147] With chaos erupting in Baghdad and the short transition strategy looking untenable, Washington shifted gears and prepared for a lengthier occupation.

Military Disintegration As Saddam's regime crumbled in the face of the US invasion, things quickly fell apart. First, the Iraqi military collapsed and disappeared. According to Lake, "as U.S. forces moved closer to Baghdad, the Iraqi military dissolved before their eyes."[148] The *Iraqi Perspectives Report*, for example, discusses the experience of the Republican Guard's Al-Nida Division, which disintegrated not from combat, but from the kinetic and psychological effects of coalition air strikes. According to the division's commanding officer, by the time the Al-Nida's 43rd Brigade was ordered to Baghdad on April 1, "the unit had simply ceased to exist as an organized combat unit." Overall, by the end of the war, "70 percent" of the division "'escaped' . . . between the air strikes and desertions only 1000–1500 soldiers remained out of more than 13,000."[149] One month later, General John Abi-zaid reported that "not a single Iraqi military unit remained intact."[150] As Chandrasekaran notes, "many members of the regular army changed into civilian clothes and went home."[151]

Second, when US Army and Marine units reached Baghdad and Saddam and his cronies fled, order collapsed, and anarchy ensued. US troops watched without instructions to intervene as Iraqis engaged in wholesale looting of government ministries. Computers, telephones, desks, chairs, filing cabinets, anything movable and of value was stolen; even the wiring inside the walls was torn out and removed. Entire ministry buildings were burned to the ground or left standing as empty, burned-out hulks. There was no electricity or running water, telephone service was intermittent, and of course there was no Iraqi police or military presence on the streets. In short, the situation resembled Hobbes's state of nature in which human nature, freed from the constraints of authority, showed itself in all its avariciousness—exacerbated by a dozen years of sanctions-enforced deprivation.[152] Needless to say, the United States was completely unprepared for this. "To Baghdad's residents," notes one analyst, "coalition forces appeared unable or unwilling to curtail the violence that swept across the city, encouraging the perception among would-be insurgents that the United States could not control the country. . . . The initial goodwill that greeted the liberation of Baghdad quickly turned into popular disenchantment with the occupation's failure to establish order, and into increased nationalist resentment of it."[153]

Resistance Begins Sunni resistance to the US occupation began almost as soon as the conventional war ended.[154] Resistance became concentrated in the "Sunni triangle" west of Baghdad that included the cities of Fallujah, Ramadi, and Samarra. At an antioccupation protest in Fallujah on April 28, US troops, believing they were under fire, shot and killed fifteen people, wounding another sixty-five.[155] By August, the insurgency was gaining momentum, signaled by two massive car bombings in Baghdad that destroyed the Jordanian embassy and UN headquarters, and a third that killed 125 Shiites in Najaf, including the leader of the Supreme Council for the Islamic Revolution in Iraq (SCIRI), Ayatollah Muhammad Baqir al-Hakim.[156] Four American contractors were murdered in Fallujah on March 31, 2004, and a Marine offensive to clear the town of insurgents in April was halted owing to concerns over collateral damage. Fallujah remained under insurgent control until a second Marine offensive in November expelled the militants but destroyed the city. In the meantime, Abu Musab al-Zarqawi's militant jihadist group Jama'at al-Tawhid wal Jihad had transformed into Al Qaeda in Iraq (AQI) and instigated brutal attacks on Shiites meant to touch off sectarian violence. In February 2006, AQI bombed the al-Askari Mosque in Samarra, one of the holiest shrines in Shia Islam, which set off a sectarian bloodbath of reprisal and counterreprisal. By the end of the year, more than 1,600 attacks were occurring every week, and 3,000 Iraqis were dying from the violence every month.[157]

The initial resistance to the US occupation was led by former Baathist officials and Sunni officers of the Iraqi Army. There is some evidence to suggest that Saddam Hussein understood that his army had little hope of opposing the US invasion and that he planned and organized for guerrilla resistance after a regime change.[158] Others, however, argue that Saddam established organizations like the Fedayeen Saddam and the Baath Party militia more to suppress Shiite and Kurdish uprisings that might follow a US attack—as had happened during the 1991 Persian Gulf War.[159] For supporters of this interpretation, "The force Saddam had established to conduct counterinsurgency against his internal foes had morphed into an insurgency all its own."[160] According to an assessment of the insurgency prepared in February 2004 for the new commander of US ground forces in Iraq, General Ricardo Sanchez, "when Saddam was toppled, there were 65,000 to 95,000 Special Republican Guard officers, Iraqi Intelligence Service officers, Fedayeen Saddam paramilitary forces, Baath Party militia, and the like who had gone to ground in and around Baghdad."[161] In other words, the overthrow of Saddam dispersed tens of thousands of these relatively specialized and loyal forces—to say nothing of Sunni officers and soldiers from the regular Iraqi Army—in the Baghdad area alone *before* Bremer's edicts ordering de-Baathification or the disestablishment of the military. George Packer agrees that the "insurgency's backbone—its organizers, financiers, suppliers—were officials of the Baath Party and the regime's many intelligence and security services."[162]

Kevin Petit's study of the Sunni resistance in three areas of Baghdad confirms that local armed groups were in many cases led by former Iraqi military officers. In Ghazaliyah, for example, the leader of the 1920 Revolutionary Brigade was a former Iraqi Air Force general. The leader of a second local group, Jayesh al-Rashideen, was a retired army artillery officer.[163] Similarly, in nearby Ameriyah, "the core of the groups" resisting the Americans, which formed immediately after Saddam's overthrow, "was made up of former Iraqi army officers and soldiers with fighting experience."[164] This includes Abu Abed, the man who led the defection of local Sunni militants from AQI in the summer of 2007 and subsequently commanded Ameriyah's Sons of Iraq (SOI) contingent, known as "The Knights between the Two Rivers."

The motivations of these men were the same as those of members and supporters of ousted regimes in other historical cases: anger and resentment at being dumped out of power and the desire to regain it. According to Michael Gordon and Bernard Trainor's account, "After more than fifty years of rule, the Sunnis were angry that they had been displaced from the top strata of Iraqi society and were fearful that they would be marginalized politically."[165] Packer similarly concludes that the "Sunni insurgency fed on the unhappiness of a minority group that had essentially run Iraq since its creation and foresaw a diminished role in the new order, especially after the abolition of the army and debaathification made the point clearer than it needed to be."[166] According to Petit's interviews with former Sunni militants, "the Resistance's goal was restoring the Sunni to a place of prominence in Iraqi society." "The Resistance, therefore," Petit continues, "was fighting a restorative insurgency, aimed at recovering their rule prior to the overthrow."[167]

In short, the lightning US invasion of Iraq precipitated the collapse and dispersion of the Iraqi Army and security services. These former officers and soldiers formed the base of armed groups that began resisting the US occupation almost immediately. Driven from power and seeing a group they viewed as inferior elevated above them, Sunnis fought to reclaim their previous position as rulers of Iraq.

Mistakes Were Made The United States made an astounding number of errors in preparing for, and conducting, the Iraq War. The most important mistake arguably was invading Iraq and overthrowing Saddam Hussein in the first place. The Bush administration's two most prominent reasons for launching the invasion—Saddam's supposed possession of weapons of mass destruction (WMD) and his ties to Al Qaeda—turned out to be false. As Michael MacDonald has observed, the justification for war rested on multiple "mights": Saddam might acquire WMD, he might form an alliance with Al Qaeda, and he might transfer the WMD he might acquire to Osama bin Laden's terrorist organization.[168] Given that the likelihood of each of these things was exceedingly low, Iraq represented little threat to the United States.

Having gone to war for far-fetched reasons, the administration then employed too few troops and failed to plan beyond the execution of regime change because of its aversion to nation building and the belief that Iraqis would spontaneously adopt democracy. When Baghdad devolved into anarchy, US officials, rather than providing security, declared that "stuff happens" and "freedom's untidy" while for months insisting that violence was the result of Baathist "dead-enders" rather than an Iraqi insurgency.[169] Once the administration belatedly realized that a quick political transition to Iraqi leadership was not possible, it implemented policies that were sure to stoke Sunni resentment and increase the likelihood of violent resistance, such as de-Baathification and the disestablishment of the Iraqi military. Finally, once US leaders admitted an insurgency was underway, they permitted the US military to fight it with the wrong doctrine, which was bound to increase rather than decrease resistance. There is plenty of blame to go around here: neoconservatives for promoting the war; Bush and Cheney for deciding on war; Rumsfeld for insisting on a small invasion force, refusing to plan for the aftermath of regime change, and denying that post-Saddam violence in Iraq was an actual insurgency; Colin Powell for helping to sell the war to the public; Bremer for implementing de-Baathification and disbanding the Iraqi military; the generals for failing to adopt counterinsurgency techniques earlier; the list goes on.

Many of these mistakes contributed to the civil war that would erupt in Iraq shortly after the United States deposed Saddam Hussein. Obviously, neglecting to plan for what came after regime change was deeply misguided and created a perception among Iraqis that the United States did not know what it was doing. It also prevented the US military from taking charge of public security from the outset. Sending too few troops, against the advice of those like army chief of staff General Eric Shinseki, who warned that it would take more troops to secure the peace than to win the war, made it impossible for US forces to secure the country and protect the Iraqi people. Extending de-Baathification beyond the 1,000 or so top officials down to the fourth tier of the party put several tens of thousands of Sunni professionals out of work, nullified their pensions, and destroyed their future prospects. "In a single stroke of the pen," writes the historian and former US Army officer Peter Mansoor, "Bremer had created the political basis for the Iraqi insurgency."[170] Washington's proconsul in Baghdad followed up this ill-considered move with another—disbanding the Iraqi security forces. According to Mansoor, "CPA Order Number 2 put out of work hundreds of thousands of armed young men, and even more critically, tens of thousands of officers—mostly Sunni—who were stripped of their rank and denied their livelihoods, their pensions, and any hope of a political future, and perhaps most importantly in Iraqi society, deprived of their honor. . . . In a second stroke of the pen, Bremer had created the military basis for the insurgency."[171] The overly aggressive and culturally insensitive way that some US military units interacted with the Iraqi population also generated resentment.[172]

Yet it would be a mistake to argue that the insurgency that emerged in Iraq could have been fully avoided if only the Bush administration had simply made better choices, such as sending more troops or carrying out a less extreme version of de-Baathification or not disbanding the Iraqi Army. Such arguments underestimate two factors. First, the disintegration of the Iraqi military and security services before any policy decisions were made about its fate virtually ensured that an insurgency of some kind would emerge by providing ample manpower to would-be resistance leaders. Second, such arguments neglect the reality that ousted groups almost always seek to regain power if they have the capability to do so. Pursuing what it believed to be US interests, the Bush administration—by removing Saddam and seeking to democratize Iraq—threatened Iraq's previously dominant Sunni Arab population with permanent disenfranchisement. Sunni Arabs represented a minority of perhaps 20 percent of Iraq's population. Shi'ites, by contrasted, made up 60 percent of the population. If people voted largely along sectarian lines, Sunni Arabs would lose power for good. Thus, the seeds of Sunni resistance were inherent in the kind of regime change that the Bush administration sought to impose in Iraq. This argument highlights how even regime changes that promote democratic institutions can help bring about civil war under certain conditions—in this case by threatening to disenfranchise an ethnoreligious group that had previously held power. Better policy choices may have lowered the intensity of the resulting insurgency but could not have avoided it entirely.

Epilogue The story of Iraq, of course, continued after the initial insurgency broke out. Once the United States handed power to an Iraqi government, the problem of competing principals emerged, an issue I examine in more detail in chapter 5. Iraq's Shiite leaders no longer owed their political survival primarily to the United States. Rather, they needed to placate Shiite voters, many of whom were terrified and outraged by AQI's sectarian onslaught. Ironically, the United States ended up allying with the non–Al Qaeda Sunni insurgents, who split from their domineering and doctrinaire partners in 2006 and 2007. This alliance was begrudgingly tolerated—but never fully accepted—by the Maliki administration. As US surge forces receded in 2008, the plan to incorporate the Sunni SOI militias into the government's security apparatus—and onto the government's payroll—never fully materialized. Only a fraction of the SOIs were ever accommodated and prominent Sunni militia leaders were arrested or fled into exile. After Washington helped Maliki retain office in the 2010 elections, he repaid the favor by insisting on conditions in negotiations for a status of forces agreement that the Obama administration could not accept. With the United States for the most part out of Iraq in 2011, Maliki pursued his Sunni enemies with renewed vigor, setting the stage for their embrace of ISIS in 2014.

My theory helps explain why Iraqi resistance—particularly Sunni resistance—to the US regime change in Iraq erupted in 2003. It highlights the disintegration of the target state's military as creating the conditions for insurgency by scattering large numbers of armed men around the country. Rather than heading for the mountains, jungles, or across the border, however, soldiers in Iraq—like many of the Taliban in Afghanistan—went home to their villages, towns, and cities, and waited to see what would unfold or in some cases joined resistance groups right away. Bremer's order disbanding the army exacerbated this situation but did not create it in the first place. Even had the CPA attempted to reconstitute the army, unknown thousands would likely have refused to go back and chosen to join the insurgency.

Regime Change, the Problem of Competing Principals, and Civil War

This section provides evidence on my theory's second causal mechanism that connects regime change to civil war—the conflicting incentives that imposed leaders face when trying to navigate the divergent preferences of domestic and foreign masters, known as the problem of competing principals.

121

Interveners bring new leaders to power in the expectation that these individuals share their preferences and will carry out policies that advance their interests. External patrons are not the only masters for imposed leaders, however; they must also take into account the wishes of a second principal— their domestic constituents, whether those constituents are other elites, the military, ethnic groups, economic or social classes, or the general public. Once in office, leaders can find themselves pulled in divergent directions. Interveners and constituents alike demand that leaders implement policies that benefit them, but only rarely will the same policy please both parties. Leaning too far in either direction, therefore, can incur the wrath of one principal or the other. In the scenario relevant to this chapter, imposed leaders that hew too closely to the desires of their foreign backers may spark rebellions by aggrieved domestic elements.

I begin with a case of leadership regime change: Britain's overthrow of Dost Mohammad in Afghanistan in 1839. The second case consists of a leadership regime change quickly followed by an institutional one by the United States in Nicaragua in 1909–10. Finally, I explore a covert leadership regime change: the US replacement of Jacobo Árbenz with Carlos Castillo Armas in Guatemala in 1954.

THE FIRST AFGHAN WAR, 1839–1842

In August 1839, Britain's Army of the Indus arrived in Kabul and ended the reign of Afghan emir Dost Mohammad Khan, replacing him with Shah Shuja ul-Mulk, a former king himself who had been deposed in 1809. Although this case involves the restoration of a previous ruler, according to my coding rules it is a leadership regime change because Shah Shuja was not the most recent leader of Afghanistan prior to Dost Mohammad. Indeed, thirty years had passed since Shuja had last sat on the Afghan throne. The history below clearly demonstrates the problem of competing principals that imposed leaders face, caught between dependence on their foreign backers and the preferences of domestic constituents, in this case tribal chiefs.

Origins and Conduct of Regime Change Britain's regime changes in Afghanistan in the nineteenth century were driven by the perceived need to protect India—the jewel in the crown of the British Empire—from Russian expansion in Central Asia. Afghanistan became a buffer state between Russia and British India, and the competition between the two empires to control the buffer, as argued by Fazal, created the conflict that led to the British invasion and regime change.[173] Following the defeat of Napoleon, Russia began expanding inexorably southward, defeating the Persian and Ottoman empires in a series of wars and annexing large swathes of territory in the Caucasus.[174] British leaders were stunned by the speed of the Russian advance and grew fearful of the threat it represented to British India. After reviewing the terms of the Treaty of Adrianople that ended the Russo-Turkish War in 1829, the British foreign secretary, Lord Aberdeen, wrote: "Russia holds the keys, both of the Persian and Turkish provinces; and whether she may be disposed to extend her conquests to the East or to the West, to Teheran or to Constantinople, no serious obstacle can arrest her progress."[175] Lord Ellenborough, newly appointed as the president of the East India Company's board of control and later governor-general of India (1842–44), believed that Russia's defeat of Persia the previous year would "practically place the resources of Persia at the disposal of the Court of St. Petersburgh," and thus argued that, "Our policy in Asia must follow one course only, to limit the power of Russia."[176]

These anxieties grew increasingly acute in the 1830s as Russia appeared to be gaining influence in Kabul. In 1837, the Russian envoy to Tehran, Count Ivan Simonitch, managed to persuade the Persian shah to lay siege to Herat, which at the time was ruled by Prince Kamran of Shah Shuja's Sadozai clan.[177] Dost Mohammad, of the Barakzai clan, ruled the remainder of Afghanistan minus Peshawar, which had been captured by the Sikhs, and Kandahar, which was ruled by his half-brothers. At around the same time as the Persians were moving to invest Herat, a Russian envoy, Ivan Vitkevitch, arrived in Kabul to negotiate with the Afghan leader on behalf of the tsar. A British agent, Alexander Burnes, was also in Kabul but was unable to persuade Lord Auckland, the governor-general of India, to offer more generous terms to secure an alliance with Dost Mohammad.[178] Facing the possibility of a Russo-Persian-Afghani alliance, Auckland recommended to London that Dost Mohammad be replaced by Shah Shuja, "who Auckland clearly believed would be more reasonable and do as he was told."[179] As Auckland wrote in a dispatch to London in August 1838, "The welfare of our possessions in the East requires that we should, in the present crisis of affairs, have a decidedly friendly power on our frontier."[180] British foreign secretary Lord Palmerston also favored an Afghan buffer, arguing that a "good Affghan [sic] state in connection with British India would make a better Barrier than Persia has been, because it would be more under our Controul."[181]

Even after the Persians called off the attack on Herat and the Russians withdrew both Simonitch and Vitkevitch, thereby disowning their proposed alliance with Dost Mohammad and removing the British casus belli, a 20,000-man British invasion force crossed the Indus in February 1839 to effect regime change in Afghanistan. The British took Kandahar without a fight in late April and seized the fortress of Ghazni in July. Meanwhile, a separate, smaller army advancing from Peshawar forced the Khyber Pass and took Jalalabad. With two British armies bearing down on Kabul, Dost Mohammad's supporters melted away, and the emir was forced to flee the city in early August heading north, first to Balkh, then on to Bokhara, where he and his son Akbar Khan were imprisoned. Shah Shuja marched victoriously into Kabul on August 7.

The British Debacle Shuja, unfortunately, was unable to enjoy his return to power for long. In August 1840 Dost Mohammad escaped from his dungeon in Bokhara and returned to northern Afghanistan to fight for his throne.[182] For several weeks, Dost Mohammad waged a successful guerrilla war, but unexpectedly surrendered to the British on November 4 and was sent into exile in Ludhiana, in British India.[183] Far from ending the uprising, however, resistance to Shuja's British-backed regime spread and intensified. "The reality," writes William Dalrymple in his comprehensive history of the conflict, "was that resistance was growing everywhere against the British, and only in Kabul itself was there still some support for the Anglo-Sadozai regime."[184]

The proverbial straw that broke the camel's back came when William Macnaghten, the British envoy in Kabul, reduced the subsidies paid by the crown to the tribes in autumn 1841, with the biggest reductions coming at the expense of the eastern Ghilzais. The Ghilzais, who maintained security in the mountain passes between Kabul and Jalalabad, promptly revolted and ambushed General Robert "Fighting Bob" Sale's brigade in the Khord Kabul pass east of the capital in October. The rebellion spread to Kabul on November 2 and soon British troops were besieged in their poorly sited cantonment. Unable to break out of their encirclement by the Afghans, who were buoyed by the return of Akbar Khan, Dost Mohammad's son, the British agreed to leave for Jalalabad. They marched directly into a trap, however, and were massacred almost to a man by sniping Afghans on the treacherous winter march through the mountain passes. Out of a force of 3,849 troops, 690 of whom were British regulars, exactly one British officer made it to Jalalabad.[185]

Although the British sent a new army—the so-called Army of Retribution—into Afghanistan to exact vengeance and restore British prestige, the new Tory government in London had already decided to abandon the disastrous Afghan adventure. After inflicting much suffering and ruin, and destroying Ghazni, Kabul, and Jalalabad, the Army of Retribution marched out of Afghanistan in October 1842. Shah Shuja had already been murdered by his own godson in April. He was succeeded by his son, Fatteh Jang, who was in turn ousted by Akbar Kahn, who made himself wazir. The Army of Retribution performed one last regime change, restoring Fatteh Jang to the Afghan throne. Upon learning that the British did not intend to stay, however, Fatteh Jang wisely abdicated, handing over power to his younger brother, Shahpur, who was overthrown by Akbar Khan after the British departed. The British, meanwhile, released Dost Mohammad, who returned home in December to reclaim the throne.

Shah Shuja's Dilemma Why did Britain's overthrow of Dost Mohammad and empowerment of Shah Shuja lead to such determined resistance? The most important reason was the perception by his fellow Afghans, created by British control over policy, that Shuja was nothing more than a puppet of foreigners. According to Dalrymple, "the biggest problem of all . . . was simply the growing taint to Shuja's reputation brought by his continued association with the infidel British and the spreading conviction that he was merely their puppet."[186] When the shah complained to Macnaghten about the growing scandal caused by liaisons between British officers and Afghan women, for example, Macnaghten ignored him. An Afghan history from the late nineteenth century comments as follows about this episode: "Until then it was still not generally known that when it came to affairs of state and matters affecting the army the Shah had no influence. Now the Barakzais went about revealing the way things really stood saying, 'The Shah is Shah in name only and has no hand in state matters.'"[187] Many analysts speak of a "double government," one where the shah served as a figurehead but "the British held the purse strings and the guns," and thus possessed the real power.[188] Historian Diana Preston, for example, argues that the "rebellion was also a sign of a wider dissatisfaction in Afghanistan with a 'double' system of government, in which an Afghan king ruled but only nominally and at the pleasure of foreign and infidel invaders who held his reins."[189] Similarly, John Waller asserts that "it was apparent to most Afghans that despite Shah Shuja's pretense of ruling, the British were in charge, and this rankled."[190] Shah Shuja understood that his subjects increasingly perceived him in this way, telling British official Alexander Burnes that it was difficult to convince anyone of his authority "when in the capital the troops are not my own and their movements take place without my knowledge." According to Burnes's summary of the conversation, "it was no wonder therefore that his subjects increasingly considered him a puppet ('a moolee,' or radish, was the word he used) & that he had no honour in his own country."[191]

The most important issue that contributed to the perception that Shah Shuja had no real power and that his British advisors were running the state—thereby generating anger and resentment that fueled rebellion—was the British policy of eliminating the feudal cavalry system in favor of creating a standing national army.[192] A central feature of this policy was to reduce the subsidies paid by the crown to the tribes. Creating military forces directly under the shah's control that could take on security functions in the country would permit the British to withdraw their forces and defray the burden on the treasury of occupying Afghanistan. Establishing such a force was clearly in British interests, as Macnaghten understood: "He knew," writes Preston, "that before the British could safely withdraw from Afghanistan, Shah Shuja had to be provided with troops more immediately available and more reliable and effective than feudal cavalry."[193] Establishing "an efficient Afghan national army for Shah Shuja," notes Dalrymple, would also "allow the [East India] Company to pull back its troops to India while leaving Shuja secure and able to defend himself."[194] Eliminating the tribal subsidies would also save money, and Macnaghten was under significant pressure to economize on expenditures as the Afghan occupation was proving far more expensive than anticipated.[195] British strategy in nineteenth-century Afghanistan thus closely resembled US strategy early in its occupation of twenty-first-century Iraq, which President George W. Bush summarized in the pithy phrase, "As the Iraqis stand up, we will stand down."[196]

The problem with this measure was that it not only contradicted the traditional Afghan way of raising military forces, it threatened to disrupt the entire existing social order of the country. In the Afghan system, the king essentially paid tribal leaders to provide security in their regions and to fight on his behalf if necessary. According to Thomas Barfield, "Half the state's revenue was devoted to such payments. . . . Local chiefs used such funds and land grants to maintain powerful patronage networks, not to fight wars." "What the British condemned as the corrosion of corruption," continues Barfield, "was unfortunately still the main glue that held the Afghan state in one piece."[197] The British idea of a standing army proposed to end this practice and eliminate a main source of income for the tribes. Moreover, eliminating the system of tribal levies also curbed Shah Shuja's ability to demand loyalty from his subjects. The situation is aptly summarized by Dalrymple:

> Shuja was all too aware that Macnaghten's strategy of diverting resources from the old tribal cavalry levies towards a professional standing infantry army removed his principal means of extending patronage to the chiefs. As far as the nobles were concerned, the Shah was duty-bound to give out money, land and estates to them in return for which they would provide cavalry. The system was certainly corrupt. . . . But it was nevertheless the glue that cemented the local and regional tribal leaders to the regime at the centre. By aiming to create a modern, drilled force at the expense of the chieftains, Macnaghten was taking away Shah Shuja's only real opportunity to reward his nobility for their support and undermining the power and wealth of his most important followers.[198]

Macnaghten nevertheless proceeded to trim the tribal subsidies by a quarter in 1840, and then again in autumn 1841, with the cuts each time most heavily affecting the Ghilzai tribe of eastern Afghanistan. To the tribes, it appeared as if they were about to lose not only a main source of income, but also their role in policing the country. "This was a very serious matter," writes Dalrymple. "By appearing to threaten the entire traditional order and to take away the income of the Afghan tribal leaders, Macnaghten succeeded in alienating many of the Shah's natural supporters who, until that point, had been quite happy to see the return of the Sadozais. It was certainly not a policy designed to endear Shah Shuja's rule to those who could do most to disrupt it."[199] Barfield concurs with this assessment: "Since it was the supply of feudal military units and the tax revenues granted to maintain them that sustained the Durrani elite, the threat to abolish the system undercut both their prosperity and political power."[200]

Although the issue of tribal subsidies as a cause of rebellion is mentioned in almost all histories of the period, a pair of other issues contributed to Afghan unrest. One was Macnaghten's insistence on removing the shah's chief minister (Nizam al-Daula), Mullah Shakur, whom he viewed as resistant to British preferences, and installing someone friendlier to British interests. According to Dalrymple, the new Nizam al-Daula, 'Uthman Khan, "did not get on with Shuja, and was entirely dependent on the British for his position," and thus "even the most pro-Sadozai nobles took this as final confirmation of all they suspected: that Shah Shuja was no longer in charge of his own government, and that the British were now holding all the reins of real power."[201]

A second issue that contributed to the perception among Afghans that Shuja was nothing but a British puppet was the way that British officers and men behaved with Afghan women.[202] One incident that is mentioned prominently in the Afghan sources is the rape of a girl by a drunken British soldier after the fall of Kandahar early in the campaign. Mohammad Husain Herati paraphrases the reaction of Afghans to this episode: "If, at the beginning of this foreign occupation, such an outrage to a girl of noble lineage can be countenanced . . . then no one's honour will be safe! It is becoming clear that His Majesty is a mere puppet and a king in name only!"[203] Later, after the conquest of Kabul, British officers married and carried on affairs with Afghan women from prominent families, and prostitution became rampant in response to the "needs" of the thousands of Indian sepoys and camp followers. One Afghan account refers to "this growing slight to Afghan honour" as "the biggest cause of the alienation of the Afghans from their new government."[204]

In each of these issues one can see the tension between what the British occupiers perceived as being in their interests and the preferences of the Afghans—particularly the tribal leaders who formed Shah Shuja's principal domestic constituency. As the British occupation officials exerted more and more control over Shuja, he was forced to acquiesce in policies that he did not agree with but which he felt powerless to stop. Yet Shah Shuja went along because he believed—rightly or wrongly—that he would be unable to maintain his position without British support. But the more he acquiesced in policies or situations that benefited the British but angered his own people, the more the latter viewed him as a puppet and grew resentful of British influence.

It is interesting to speculate whether Shah Shuja could have retained his office had he not been assassinated. Dalrymple argues that the rebellion that shook Afghanistan in 1841 was directly primarily at the hated British, not at Shuja. It was only his association with the British that was reviled, not Shuja himself.[205] If he had repudiated his British allies after their expulsion from

Kabul in January 1842 and had joined Akbar Khan in pushing them out of the country once and for all, Shuja might have persuaded enough Afghan tribal leaders to remain by his side to deny Akbar Kahn the throne.[206] It is much harder to believe, however, that he could have defeated Dost Mohammad upon his return to Afghanistan.

In 1839, British troops marched to Kabul to overthrow Dost Mohammad and impose Shah Shuja. The reason the British resorted to regime change in this case was their fear of Russian advances toward India and their belief that Dost Mohammad was contemplating an alliance with the tsar. What London needed was a reliable leader in Afghanistan who would oppose Russian inroads in South Asia. Once Shah Shuja was placed on the throne, the British forced him to accept policies that were in their interests—such as building a standing army—but which threatened the prerogatives of Shuja's key domestic constituency: Afghan tribal leaders. The unfortunate Shuja understood that this policy, and others pushed by his British patrons, were unpopular with the tribal chiefs, but he believed that British support was crucial to his ability to retain the throne. The threat that British policies represented to the tribes, and the belief among Shuja's followers that he was nothing but a British puppet, triggered the rebellion that led to Shuja's murder and Britain's exit from Afghanistan in 1842.

THE UNITED STATES AND NICARAGUA, 1909–1912

In 1909 and 1910, the United States forced two regime changes in Nicaragua, ultimately chasing the Liberal Party from power and installing Conservatives in their place. The terms that Washington imposed as the price for its support, however, rankled not only Liberals but some prominent Conservatives as well, resulting in a brief but violent civil war in 1912.

This case serves an important function in my research design because the United States ultimately imposed an institutional regime change in Nicaragua. Given that Nicaragua was extremely impoverished, my theory would expect an institutional regime change to fail to yield a successful democratic transition, which in turn could enhance the probability of civil war. Recall from figure 3.6 that the likelihood of civil war following an institutional regime change is highest when the target's level of economic development is at its lowest. According to the measure of development used in the statistical analysis—primary energy consumption—it would have been hard for Nicaragua to be any less developed in 1909: Nicaragua consumed no energy of this kind at all.[207] Nor did it produce any iron or steel, another indicator of the industrialization of an economy. And according to the Maddison Project Database, which tracks historical economic data, Nicaragua's GDP per capita was about 15 percent of that of the United States.[208] The chance of civil war in this case thus ought to be quite high.

Origins and Conduct of Regime Change In December 1909—in an example of leadership regime change—US military and diplomatic pressure secured the resignation of Nicaragua's Liberal president José Santos Zelaya. It was a strange turn of fate for a leader who had in earlier years earned the praise and admiration of US officials. The key event that reversed US attitudes toward Zelaya was President Theodore Roosevelt's decision to support the construction of the much-desired transisthmian canal through Panama rather than the previous front-runner, Nicaragua.[209] "During the years when it appeared the canal was going to be built across Nicaragua," writes Stephen Kinzer, "American officials got along well with President Zelaya. . . . After Congress chose the Panama route, this admiration quickly turned to disdain."[210] Washington's primary goal became security and stability in Central America, and Zelaya quickly emerged as the principal disturber of the peace in the region. The United States, for example, opposed Zelaya's bid to recreate a Central American federation as destabilizing.[211] Further, US officials, particularly President William Howard Taft's secretary of state Philander Knox, disapproved of Zelaya's efforts to borrow money from European banks to finance infrastructure projects.[212] According to historian John Findling, "The inability of many Latin American countries to repay these loans was an endemic problem in the hemisphere, and a serious one for the United States because of the threat of intervention on the part of disgruntled European creditors."[213] Knox, writes Kinzer, "understood perfectly well that by borrowing money from European rather than American banks, Zelaya was trying to make his country less dependent on the United States. This he could not abide."[214]

In 1909, the United States began to support Zelaya's Conservative opponents, who, led by General Juan José Estrada, launched a rebellion in October near the town of Bluefields on the country's eastern coast. Estrada was a Liberal who had been appointed to his position by Zelaya, but nevertheless switched sides. In the course of the conflict, government forces caught two US mercenaries fighting for the Conservatives, Lee Roy Cannon and Leonard Groce, laying mines in the San Juan River. Zelaya had the men executed, which caused the US government to break relations on December 1 and label Zelaya, in the words of Knox, "a blot on the history of Nicaragua."[215] The United States sent a force of US Marines and several naval vessels to intervene on behalf of Zelaya's Conservative opponents. Faced with this rebellion and apparent US determination to see him removed, Zelaya stepped down and fled to Mexico in mid-December. Zelaya's resignation constitutes the first regime change in this case.

Because Zelaya's ouster was accomplished by coercive diplomacy, however, and the Conservative rebels had not yet prevailed in the conflict against the government, the United States had little control over who succeeded the outgoing president in office. Zelaya handed over power to another Liberal,

José Madriz, who was also unacceptable both to the United States and to the rebels fighting to take control of the country. US intervention against Madriz was less subtle than against Zelaya. As government forces closed in on the rebels at Bluefields in May 1910, US Marines landed and, in the estimation of Yann Kerevel, "effectively blocked Madriz from taking Bluefields and crushing the rebellion." "It is clear," Kerevel continues, "that U.S. interference in this civil war prevented an end to the conflict."[216] According to Lester Langley and Thomas Schoonover, for example, the commander of the USS *Paducah*, anchored off Bluefields, "forbade any bombardment of Bluefields and declared the town 'off limits' to fighting."[217] Major Smedley Butler, who commanded the Marine contingent in the town, similarly forbade any firing by the Nicaraguan forces into Bluefields on the grounds that Americans might be injured. Madriz's forces could thus attack, but without using firearms.[218] The presence of the Marines helped turn the tide, as the rebels went on the offensive and defeated the government army in a series of battles. Madriz resigned on August 19, and Estrada assumed the presidency. This is the second regime change, which I code as institutional for reasons explained below.

Sources of the Problem of Competing Principals The agreement that the United States negotiated with Estrada and Nicaragua's most prominent Conservative leaders after their victory planted the seeds of the 1912 civil war. In October 1910, US envoy to Nicaragua Thomas Dawson negotiated the so-called Dawson Agreements with Estrada, Adolfo Díaz, Luis Mena, and Emiliano Chamorro. The first part of the accord stipulated that elections for a constituent assembly would be held that would subsequently elect Estrada as president and Díaz as vice-president.[219] This promotion of elections as a condition for US recognition is why I code the replacement of Madriz with Estrada as an institutional regime change. Another part of the agreement stated that Nicaragua would accept a sizable loan from the United States to stabilize its finances, guaranteed by US control over Nicaraguan customs receipts. Under the terms of the Knox-Castrillo treaty, negotiated in June 1911, the amount of the loan was set at $15 million. Contemporary Nicaraguan opponents of the loan pointed out that "it made little sense to contract an estimated $20 million loan when the public debt only amounted to $6 million."[220] In the words of one scholar, "the North American investors of Brown Brothers and J. and W. Seligman were loaning Nicaragua its own money and charging interest."[221] In the event, the US Senate rejected the treaty, so the US government arranged for smaller loans to Nicaragua in exchange for partial ownership of the national railway.[222]

The terms of the Dawson Agreements provoked immediate Liberal outcry, and Liberals took to the streets to protest its terms. Multiple demonstrations against the accords were held in Managua and León in early November, during which several people were killed and more wounded. Moreover, prominent Liberals began plotting revolution, first from Honduras and later from Costa Rica.[223] As Yann Kerevel writes, "The contents of the Dawson Agreements had put the Liberals into action."[224]

Meanwhile, the US-imposed regime was already beginning to crack as its Conservative members decided to expel Liberal president Estrada. Estrada attempted to head off the coup by having the principal plotter minister of war Luis Mena arrested, but US diplomats intervened and Estrada resigned.[225] He was replaced by Adolfo Díaz. But this was not the end of the intraregime plotting because key Conservative leaders—particularly Mena—secretly opposed surrendering control over the Nicaraguan government's main source of revenue to the Americans.[226] Even David Arellano, known as the "premier Yanquista" of Nicaragua and the foremost proponent of adopting the US political and economic model in Nicaragua, argued that "everybody knows that without control of public finances any form of rule is ridiculous in America. . . . It would be better to surrender our weapons than the customs and control of national revenue."[227] Mena—although he chose his words carefully—apparently agreed with these sentiments.

The Civil War On July 29, 1912, Mena, with six hundred men, rebelled against the Díaz government and inaugurated a civil war. Mena quickly fled to the Liberal stronghold of Masaya and joined forces with leading Liberals such as Benjamín Zeledón, with whom he shared command of the Allied Army. Responding to Díaz's pleas for intervention, US president William Howard Taft sent 2,300 Marines to rescue his protégé.[228] As in 1910, US troops quickly proved decisive: Mena, suffering from dysentery, unexpectedly surrendered on September 24, and Zeledón's forces were defeated shortly thereafter at Masaya and the Liberal general was killed. Between 2,000 and 5,000 Nicaraguans died in this short but violent civil war.[229]

Factors other than the US overthrow of Zelaya and Madriz certainly contributed to the outbreak of civil war in 1912. Michel Gobat, for example, highlights the ongoing drought that induced food shortages and hunger, as well as social conflict between traditional Nicaraguan elites and recent entrants to the upper class referred to as "parvenus."[230] Yet scholars agree that US intervention, and in particular the Dawson Agreements—negotiated to ensure "an exclusionary political order that served U.S. strategic interests"—was a primary cause of the civil war.[231] As Kerevel puts it, "U.S. actions increased political instability in the region by encouraging Liberal revolts in Nicaragua. These revolts forced the U.S. to station Marines in Nicaragua for decades to prop-up Conservative governments."[232] Similarly, Gobat, while conceding that "there is nothing inevitable about revolutions" nevertheless maintains that "if any intervention has made revolution inevitable . . . the Dawson Pact of 1910 came very close to doing so."[233]

THE UNITED STATES OUSTER OF JACOBO ÁRBENZ IN GUATEMALA

The Guatemalan case is in one sense challenging to explain because of the time that elapsed between the US-sponsored overthrow of Jacobo Árbenz in June 1954 and the initial organized armed rebellion against Guatemala's US-backed regime by part of the military in November 1960. This gap of more than six years raises difficulties for discerning the causal effect of regime change, especially compared to the close temporal connection between regime change and civil war in other cases. However, the evidence suggests that policies promulgated by the Guatemalan government—some of them, such as the hosting and training in Guatemala of a brigade of anti-Castro Cubans preparing for the Bay of Pigs invasion, explicitly at the behest of the United States—caused grievances that provoked the rebellion.

Origins of Regime Change The decision to remove Árbenz was undertaken primarily to defend US hegemony over the Americas and prevent the spread of communism—and Soviet influence—into the United States' sphere of influence. In 1944, the Guatemalan revolution ended the dictatorial rule of Jorge Ubico; Juan José Arévalo was sworn in as the country's first democratically elected president on March 15, 1945. A left-leaning professor who had spent most of the prior eighteen years in Argentina, Arévalo introduced a number of moderate reforms during his term, most notably the 1947 Labor Code, which established basic protections for workers, such as the right to unionize and strike.[234] The Labor Code, which, as Stephen Rabe points out, "granted Guatemala's workers some of the basic rights that U.S. workers achieved during the Progressive Era and the New Deal," provoked the ire of the Boston-based United Fruit Company (UFCO), employer of some 15,000 Guatemalans.[235] The company complained bitterly to the State Department that the measure was discriminatory. "It was United Fruit," writes historian Piero Gleijeses, "that first raised the specter of serious communist infiltration in Guatemala," but US government officials did not need much convincing. Soon the Truman administration viewed Guatemala as infested with communists and the CIA warned that "Arévalo's collaboration with communists . . . 'is a potential threat to U.S. security interests.'"[236]

Matters grew worse after Jacobo Árbenz was elected to succeed Arévalo in 1950. Árbenz's signature initiative was land reform. In 1950, 72 percent of Guatemala's land was owned by 2 percent of the country's landowners.[237] To reverse this extreme inequality, Árbenz introduced Decree 900, which allowed the Guatemalan government to expropriate all uncultivated land on estates larger than 672 acres, and land on estates between 224 and 672 acres that were less than two-thirds cultivated.[238] In light of later events, it is worth emphasizing that this measure was far from radical. Both Arévalo and Árbenz were inspired by the New Deal reforms of Franklin Delano Roosevelt, and placed in "the context of both Latin American and U.S. history," writes Rabe, "the labor and land reforms . . . were moderate and aimed at redressing Guatemala's centuries of socioeconomic injustice."[239] The US State Department found little to object to in the decree, noting that "of 341,191 private agricultural holdings only 1,710 would be affected," a mere 0.5 percent.[240] According to Richard Immerman, the US ambassador to Guatemala at the time, Edwin Jackson Kyle Jr., "emphatically upheld the code's benefits."[241]

By far the biggest loser of Decree 900, however, was UFCO, which lost 70 percent of its 550,000 acres to expropriation by February 1954.[242] The plight of UFCO again drew the US government's attention to the situation in Guatemala, but US officials hardly acted at the company's behest in targeting Árbenz for removal. Rather, officials focused on the communist threat.[243] Although American officials seem to have understood that "the communists were not in control of Guatemala"—it was hard to argue that Guatemala was a communist bastion when the Guatemalan Communist Party counted only five hundred members in 1952, a mere two hundred of whom were politically active—they worried about the future.[244] As the State Department's Bureau of Inter-American Affairs noted in a 1953 memo, "Communist strength grows, while opposition forces are disintegrating. . . . Ultimate Communist control of the country and elimination of American economic interests is the logical outcome, and unless the trend is reversed, is merely a question of time."[245]

Other evidence supports this interpretation. After his only meeting with Árbenz, a six-hour dinner in mid-December 1953, US ambassador John Peurifoy cabled Washington that "I came away definitely convinced that if President is not a Communist he will certainly do until one comes along."[246] Similarly, in a news conference shortly before the coup began, secretary of state John Foster Dulles told reporters, "If the United Fruit matter were settled, if they gave a gold piece for every banana, the problem would remain just as it is today as far as the presence of communist infiltration in Guatemala is concerned. That is the problem, not United Fruit."[247] Former Guatemalan communist leader José Manuel Fortuny agreed when he said years later, "They would have overthrown us even if we had grown no bananas."[248] In short, communism, not UFCO profits, motivated the US to move against Árbenz.

Communism in Guatemala, of course, was only a problem because of the US assumption that all communist movements around the globe were directed from Moscow. Communist control of Guatemala thus meant "a potential Soviet beachhead in the Western Hemisphere."[249] As Grow notes, however, inconveniently for the United States, "Evidence of a link between the PGT [Partido Guatemalteco de Trabajo, the Guatemalan Communist Party] and the Soviet Union proved frustratingly elusive."[250] Multiple intelligence reports before the intervention turned up nothing, and the most damaging evidence unearthed by a comprehensive investigation afterward (the CIA's Operation PBHISTORY), which examined half a million Guatemalan documents, consisted of "invoices totaling $22.95 that revealed the

PGT had purchased books from a Moscow bookstore."[251] Yet US policymakers did not need hard evidence of Soviet inroads to approve regime change. In a statement reminiscent of the Bush administration's attitude to evidence linking Saddam Hussein to Al Qaeda or the 9/11 attacks, secretary of state John Foster Dulles explained to a Brazilian interlocutor a month before the intervention, "it would be 'impossible to produce evidence clearly tying the Guatemalan Government to Moscow.'" Rather, the choice to intervene "'must be a political one and based on our deep conviction that such a tie must exist.'"[252]

Conduct and Aftermath of Regime Change Regime change by the United States in Guatemala was accomplished primarily through coercion rather than the use of force. The US's proxy, Carlos Castillo Armas, invaded Guatemala at the head of what one analyst described as a "motley group of 150 emigrés and mercenaries" in June 1954.[253] Dispatching this unimpressive lot should have been no problem for the 6,000-man Guatemalan Army, and the officers charged with crushing the rebellion pledged to President Árbenz to do just that. Yet with the exception of a minor battle at the town of Gualán, the army hardly fired a shot in defense of its country.[254] The reason is that the leading officers, according to one of their own, became "terrorized by the idea that the United States was looming behind Castillo Armas," and that by turning back his attack they would trigger a much larger US invasion.[255] Piero Gleijeses spells out the strategy: "From its inception, PBSUCCESS was based on one premise: only the Guatemalan army could overthrow Arbenz. . . . At no moment did PBSUCCESS assume that the exiles would be able to defeat the Guatemalan army. The purpose of the invasion . . . was to confront the Guatemalan officers with the stark choice: they could defeat the rebels and face the wrath of the United States, or they could turn against Arbenz and save themselves."[256] Thus, instead of confronting the invaders, the military—in the person of chief of the armed forces Colonel Carlos Enrique Díaz—demanded that Árbenz resign. Díaz took over as president at the head of a three-man junta, but was unacceptable to the pugnacious US ambassador John Peurifoy, who soon browbeat him into resigning. A second junta was formed, this time under the leadership of Colonel Elfego Monzón. The United States, however, was bent on seeing Castillo Armas take power, and Monzón was eventually persuaded to step down in favor of Castillo Armas on July 8.[257] Because Washington simply installed a strongman with no concern for building institutions around him, this case is a good example of a leadership regime change.

When Castillo Armas took power, he engaged in wholesale repression of Árbenz supporters and any suspected communists. Castillo Armas embarked on an immediate communist witch hunt in which thousands of people were detained and as many as 1,000 killed.[258] These mass arrests, according to the US State Department, were "inevitably made without careful investigation with result that many peasants with no ideas of Communism suddenly found themselves in jail."[259] Despite this description of indiscriminate arrests, however, careful planning went into the repression. Before the coup, the CIA compiled a list of people to be placed on the new junta's "disposal list."[260] In the months after the coup, the CIA helped its new protégé assemble a list of anyone affiliated with the Árbenz regime or associated with communism in any way, a database that eventually ran to 72,000 names.[261] Prisons were soon filled beyond capacity, causing "overcrowding, difficulties in food supply, and the resultant sanitary problems raised the danger of an epidemic."[262] Of the numerous *campesino* leaders arrested, it appeared that "few of them were in any sense indoctrinated Communists" and most were unable to distinguish photos of supposed communist leaders from Castillo Armas, the new president. When these wrongly arrested *campesinos* returned to work, it was "a fairly common practice for those so cleared and released to be evicted from the farms on which had worked."[263]

Castillo Armas also rolled back many Árbenz-era reforms that had benefited ordinary people at the expense of foreign (American) corporations. Castillo Armas quickly annulled Decree 900, and nearly all of the land expropriated under the law (99.6 percent) was returned to its previous owners.[264] Castillo Armas also ended literacy programs, which "were branded tools of Communist indoctrination," moved against organized labor by banning hundreds of unions, repealed legislation that taxed the profits of foreign corporations, and, under the Petroleum Code of 1955, granted extensive rights to foreign oil companies.[265]

Early Rumblings of Dissent Castillo Armas's brief time in office was turbulent, marked by corruption, scandal, protest (particularly student protest), and internal plotting.[266] The first armed challenge to his rule came only one month after he took power. On August 2, 100 of the 136 cadets at the military academy attacked Roosevelt Hospital, which at the time housed hundreds of Castillo Armas's armed supporters. Several cadets had been humiliated by the so-called *Liberacionistas* at a brothel the previous evening. The deeper cause of the outburst, however, was the humiliation felt by members of the army at having surrendered without a fight to a bunch of "swaggering youngsters" and the ridicule to which they were subjected both by Castillo Armas's men and the general population.[267] Tellingly, although no army units openly joined the fray in support of the cadets, neither did any come to the *Liberacionistas'* defense. The new president was saved largely through the vigorous intervention of US ambassador Peurifoy. According to historian Stephen Streeter, "If the ambassador had not been present to coerce the army into supporting the junta and then persuade Castillo Armas to remain in the capital, the government could well have been overthrown."[268] This was not an attempt by defeated Árbenz supporters to regain power; as Peurifoy put it, "anti-Communists were fighting anti-Communists."[269] Ultimately, the cadets (and the army) knuckled under, but resentment at their demeaned status simmered beneath the surface. Several dozen soldiers died in the one-day affair and as many as one hundred people were killed in total.[270]

Castillo Armas managed to hold on to power for three years, during which time he suppressed four coup attempts from the military, before an assassin's bullet ended his life on July 26, 1957.[271] After the results of a fraudulent election were annulled by a military junta that seized power, Miguel Ydígoras Fuentes—a former general who lost the 1950 election to Árbenz—was elected in 1958.[272] Ydígoras was not US policymakers' first choice to run Guatemala, but his strong anti-communist credentials made him acceptable to Washington.

Ydígoras's Dilemma Unfortunately, on multiple occasions the Eisenhower administration pressured Ydígoras to implement policies that benefited the United States strategically but undermined the Guatemalan leader domestically—the problem of competing principals in action. A good example is the issue of allowing communist exiles to return to Guatemala, a subject on which Ydígoras reversed himself repeatedly in the first two years of his rule. Washington opposed the repatriation of these exiles but allowing them to come home was a popular policy among Guatemalans. Knowing that US aid depended on a firm anticommunist stance but that his standing at home could benefit from taking a softer line, Ydígoras proceeded to perform policy backflips on the issue. First, he announced in Washington in February 1958 that communists would not be permitted to return while privately telling US officials some should be able to come home. Ydígoras then threatened to shoot exiles crossing illegally from Mexico but three months later invited exiles to apply for readmission. Then he flopped again in March 1959 when he accused a former conservative presidential candidate of organizing an exile invasion from Mexico. As Streeter observes, the most likely explanation for Ydígoras's frequent reversals on the exile question was "alternating pressures from the State Department and Guatemalan nationalists."[273] US officials estimated that the more conservative Ydígoras appeared, the less likely it would be that he would survive in office more than a year or two. "In their reasoning," Streeter comments, "U.S. officials did not consider that their own pressure on Ydígoras to follow pro-American policies, such as preventing the return of the exiles, could only enhance the general's conservative reputation," and thus harm his chances of political survival.[274]

Pressure to adhere to US strategic interests also helps explain the beginning of the MR-13 revolt. Roughly one-third of the Guatemalan Army participated in this three-day rebellion that began on November 13, 1960.[275] The officers who led this failed rebellion, Marco Aurelio Yon Sosa and Luis Augusto Turcios Lima—later organized another insurgency in February 1962.

The next month a second guerrilla organization was founded by former Árbenz administration official Carlos Paz Tejada, and the various insurgent factions merged into the Fuerzas Armadas Rebeldes (Rebel Armed Forces) in December. Although full-scale civil war is not coded as erupting in Guatemala until 1963, significant violence was underway already in 1962 when, according to one account, government forces "killed or jailed hundreds of students, labor leaders, peasants and professionals as well as ex-soldiers. They also decimated the fledgling rebel bands of Turcios and Yon Sosa and Carlos Paz Tejada."[276] The rebels rebounded, however, and the military (which had forced Ydígoras from power in 1963) responded with massive repression beginning in 1966, killing as many as 8,000 people (mostly civilians).[277] The civil war would continue (with a brief interruption in the 1970s) for thirty more years.

Causes of the Insurgency What caused a large faction of the army to try to overthrow the Ydígoras regime and then take to the hills and wage guerrilla warfare? One of the most prominent causes mentioned in histories of the period is resentment among military officers at the Guatemalan government's hosting—at Washington's behest—of Cuban exiles training to invade Cuba and overthrow Fidel Castro. In March 1960, President Eisenhower authorized the CIA to seek Castro's overthrow, and a CIA task force proposed training the exile force in Guatemala. The CIA station chief in Guatemala personally negotiated the basing deal with Ydígoras, who extracted unspecified concessions from the Americans in exchange for undertaking this risky project that was sure to generate controversy in Guatemala if discovered. It did not take long for reporters to uncover the operation, which became public knowledge in October 1960.

Officers in the Guatemalan Army reacted with anger and humiliation at this development. Streeter, for example, characterizes the MR-13 uprising as a "protest against the use of Guatemala as a staging ground for the US invasion of Cuba." According to Streeter, "The presence of the Cuban exile training camps in Guatemala offended military officers for two key reasons. To nationalists such as Turcios Lima, the 'puppet' Guatemalan government had permitted a 'shameful violation of our national sovereignty.' Other military officers, however, objected to the camps only because the Guatemalan military had not been consulted beforehand."[278] Schlesinger and Kinzer largely agree with Streeter's assessment of the causes of the MR-13 revolt: "Many officers, schooled in Guatemala's strong nationalist tradition, felt humiliated and angry at the alacrity with which Ydígoras was cooperating with the Americans. Many flatly opposed the use of Guatemalan soil to train foreign invaders, especially for purposes of attacking Castro, whom some officers admired as a nationalist."[279] Yon Sosa, one of MR-13's young leaders, stated that the Ydígoras regime "devoted itself to the defense of imperialism and large landowners," and maintained that "it was the movement's intention to prevent Guatemala's utilization as the base for aggression against Cuba, as planned by the U.S."[280]

No event as complex as civil war is ignited by a single factor. Studies of Guatemala highlight several other underlying causes of unrest. One important factor is the reversal of economic fortune suffered by the majority of the population during the counterrevolution: 92 percent experienced a decrease in per capita income during the 1950s and early 1960s. It is important to remember, however, that the initial rebellions in Guatemala were elite-driven affairs and centered in the military, so it is not clear how a mass-level cause like impoverishment would matter. Also mentioned are memories of the ten years of "spring" under Arévalo and Árbenz, and the high levels of repression under Castillo Armas and Ydígoras, which foreclosed opportunities to voice opposition.[281] But even studies that mention these factors highlight the Cuban exile issue.[282] According to Charles Brockett, the faction of the military that rebelled on November 13 held varied grievances, "including dismay that their country was being used as the staging area preparing for the U.S.-led counterrevolutionary Bay of Pigs invasion of Cuba that would occur in April 1961."[283]

In short, evidence suggests that the key event that initiated what would become the insurgency against US-backed right-wing regimes in Guatemala—the MR-13 revolt—was motivated by resentment over a policy adopted at the specific request of the United States. Ydígoras was not the specific leader brought to power by regime change in 1954, but he did represent a continuation of that regime and relied on the approval of the United States to remain in power. In pursuit of its own strategic interest in eliminating Castro's nascent socialist regime in Cuba, the Eisenhower administration jeopardized its Guatemalan client by asking him to host the Cuban brigade. As Streeter points out, Eisenhower administration officials were quick to point the finger at Castro as being responsible for the MR-13 revolt "because they did not want to admit that it was their own attempt to overthrow Castro that undermined the Guatemalan counterrevolution."[284]

This chapter has presented evidence in support of my argument that regime change causes civil war. Through a combination of quantitative analysis and multiple case studies, I demonstrated that there is not only a correlation between regime change, especially leadership regime change, and civil war, but that there is evidence of my two causal mechanisms— military disintegration and the problem of competing principals—in multiple historical cases. Indeed, military disintegration helps explain the onset of violent resistance after two of the United States' most recent regime changes, in Afghanistan (2001) and Iraq (2003).[285] Clashing external and internal interests, furthermore, contributed to civil war in cases as diverse as Afghanistan (1839–42), Nicaragua (1912), and Guatemala (1954–60).

For readers interested in the nuts and bolts of my statistical analysis, these are contained in the appendix that follows. In the next chapter, I turn to the question of whether—and for how long—leaders installed in different types of regime change survive in office.

Appendix to Chapter 3. A Statistical Analysis of Regime Change and Civil War

This appendix provides the details of the statistical analysis underlying the results that were summarized in the body of the chapter. It begins by defining my dependent variable (civil war), independent variables (types of regime change), and control variables. It then proceeds to present the results of my regression analysis, describes the results of a series of robustness tests, and explains how I deal with the possibility that selection bias affects my results.

DATA AND DEPENDENT VARIABLE

To test the relationship between foreign-imposed regime change and civil war, I compiled a dataset consisting of all country-years between 1816 and 2008. The dependent variable is the onset of a civil war, which I define as an armed conflict occurring inside the boundaries of a recognized state—one party to which is the government—that inflicts a minimum of 1,000 battle deaths over the course of the conflict.[286] Only a few sources provide data on internal armed conflicts before 1945; the two best known are the Correlates of War list (COW, v. 4.0) and Kristian Gleditsch's update of a previous version of that list.[287] Building on these datasets, I consulted additional data sources.[288] This survey revealed further civil conflicts, which I added if there was evidence that they surpassed the threshold of 1,000 battle deaths.[289]

Existing data collections are also not always well suited to my research question. The COW data, for example, code France's intervention in Mexico between 1862 and 1867 as an interstate war. French forces defeated the Mexican Army and overthrew the government of Benito Juárez in June 1863, installing Austrian Archduke Maximilian as the new emperor of Mexico the following year. The French regime change merely inspired further resistance by the Mexicans, who turned to guerrilla war to topple Maximilian and evict the occupiers. I thus code the interstate war as ending with the overthrow of Juárez and a new civil war beginning the next year. Similarly, the COW data code the 1918 Caco Revolt in Haiti during the US occupation as an extrasystemic (i.e., colonial or imperial) war, but Haiti was never colonized. I code wars against the governing authority—whether it is the national government or a foreign occupier—as civil wars as long as the country was not formally annexed to the intervener's metropole or colonial empire.[290]

The dependent variable is coded one for any year in which a civil war began and zero for all other years. According to my data, 315 civil wars began between 1816 and 2008.

INDEPENDENT VARIABLES

My primary independent variable consists of a dummy variable that indicates when a state experienced a foreign-imposed regime change, and three additional dummy variables signifying which type of regime change occurred. A case is coded as a restoration if one or both of the following conditions is true: (1) the individual placed in power by the intervention was the leader of the country immediately prior to the current leader but who was overthrown by a domestic rebellion or a foreign power within the previous five years; or (2) the intervention restores the institutions that governed the country immediately prior to the current set of institutions. Institutional regime changes consist of cases where the new leader was not the one who held power immediately prior to the current leader and the intervener attempts to build repressive or representative institutions. Specifically, I code cases as institutional regime changes if the intervener tries to engineer a transition to democracy, or if the intervener helps establish communist institutions. Leadership regime changes, finally, comprise cases where the leader installed was not the individual who held power immediately prior to the current leader and the intervener does not seek to establish new institutions.

To account for the fact that the effects of regime change continue to be felt over a period of time, states that experienced a regime change are coded one for the year in which it occurred and for the next ten years as well. This is consistent with the practice of other studies that attempt to measure the effects of intervention.[291] The actual relationship being tested, therefore, is the effect of a regime change occurring in the previous ten years on the likelihood of civil war. According to my data, 120 leaders were successfully overthrown by foreign powers between 1816 and 2008, a rate of more than one every two years. Because multiple leaders were removed in the same year in a few countries—such as Guatemala (1954) and Czechoslovakia (1968)—and the dataset is coded on an annual basis, 112 country-years with regime change appear in the dataset. Of these 112 country-years, 65 (58 percent) are leadership regime changes, 20 (18 percent) are institutional, and 28 (25 percent) are restoration.[292] Only one of these 112 cases (Montenegro, 1916) is dropped owing to missing data, meaning that 111 regime changes appear in the multivariate analysis.

CONTROL VARIABLES

I include many of the standard control variables used in studies of civil war onset. One of the best-documented empirical relationships in the study of civil war onset is the strong negative relationship between economic development and civil war. To proxy for economic development, I use the log of energy consumption from the COW National Material Capabilities dataset (v. 4.0).[293] By contrast, studies have found that larger populations are correlated with a greater chance of civil war. I thus include the log of each state's population, also taken from the COW National Material Capabilities dataset.[294] To capture rough terrain, I include the percentage of a country's surface area covered by mountains.[295] States that are very young are thought to be vulnerable to civil unrest because new governments are untested and may not have developed sufficient capacity to deter and defeat rebellions. Countries are coded as new states in their first two years of existence.[296] To proxy regime type, and to avoid the problems associated with using the Polity index in studies of civil war, I use a new dichotomous measure of democracy produced by Boix and colleagues.[297] I also include a dummy variable coded one if a state loses an interstate war.[298] Finally, I code whether a state had an ongoing civil war in the previous year.[299]

I also include several variables thought to influence the likelihood of civil war that are available only for limited time periods. For example, to measure ethnic heterogeneity, I include the ethnolinguistic fractionalization (ELF) index.[300] To capture ethnic exclusion and discrimination, I use two variables: the percentage of a country's population that consists of ethnic groups who are excluded from political power and the proportion who experience discrimination along ethnic lines.[301] The production of substantial quantities of petroleum has also been associated with an elevated risk of civil war.[302] I include two variables to assess the effect of oil. The first is a dummy variable taken from the work of Jeff Colgan, which is coded one if a "state's gross revenues from net oil exports . . . constitute at least 10 percent of annual GDP."[303] The second, developed by Michael Ross, is a state's per capita revenue from oil and gas production in a given year.[304] I also include a dummy variable indicating whether the target was a buffer state located between two other states involved in an enduring rivalry.[305] Finally, to deal with temporal dependence in the data, I include a variable that counts the number of years between outbreaks of civil war in each country plus three cubic splines.[306] Because the dependent variable is dichotomous, I use probit and logit models in my analysis.

RESULTS

Table 3.2 displays the results of nine probit models and two logit models in which the dependent variable is civil war onset. Models 1 and 2 include

Table 3.2 Probit estimates of foreign-imposed regime change and civil war onset

	1	2	3	4	5	6	7	8	9	10	11
	1816–2008	1816–2008	1816–2008	1816–2008	1920–2007	1946–2007	1946–2007	1946–2007	1960–2006	1816–2008 FE logit	1816–2008 FE logit
Regime change	0.362*** (0.084)	—	—	—	—	—	—	—	—	0.993*** (0.210)	—
Leadership regime change	—	0.555*** (0.081)	0.602*** (0.075)	0.573*** (0.082)	0.611*** (0.103)	0.681*** (0.132)	0.650*** (0.126)	0.665*** (0.128)	0.776*** (0.115)	—	1.274*** (0.233)
Institutional regime change	—	0.141 (0.234)	0.224 (0.216)	0.184 (0.232)	0.003 (0.217)	-0.034 (0.252)	0.008 (0.257)	-0.120 (0.257)	0.412* (0.197)	—	0.927 (0.583)
Restoration regime change	—	-0.138 (0.265)	-0.086 (0.259)	-0.135 (0.270)	0.008 (0.346)	0.153 (0.356)	0.147 (0.335)	0.051 (0.324)	0.424 (0.324)	—	-0.118 (0.554)
Economic development	-0.043*** (0.012)	-0.045*** (0.012)	-0.048*** (0.011)	-0.040*** (0.011)	-0.044** (0.013)	-0.045* (0.018)	-0.046** (0.018)	-0.067*** (0.018)	-0.061* (0.025)	-0.072* (0.029)	-0.083** (0.030)
Population	0.188*** (0.029)	0.191*** (0.030)	0.194*** (0.029)	0.193*** (0.028)	0.201*** (0.025)	0.188*** (0.032)	0.188*** (0.032)	0.224*** (0.029)	0.221*** (0.037)	-0.001 (0.153)	0.043 (0.156)
Mountainous terrain	0.128 (0.153)	0.091 (0.156)	0.092 (0.156)	0.144 (0.150)	-0.018 (0.162)	-0.055 (0.194)	-0.011 (0.189)	0.002 (0.196)	-0.063 (0.206)	2.940 (6.044)	3.368 (6.096)
New state	0.329* (0.192)	0.334† (0.195)	0.305 (0.195)	0.343† (0.194)	0.622** (0.205)	0.649** (0.235)	0.651** (0.233)	0.599** (0.223)	0.675** (0.253)	0.764* (0.374)	0.780* (0.374)
Democracy	-0.342*** (0.071)	-0.340*** (0.071)	-0.329*** (0.070)	-0.355*** (0.073)	-0.327*** (0.084)	-0.284** (0.083)	-0.260** (0.085)	-0.280** (0.089)	-0.296** (0.101)	-0.866** (0.263)	-0.863** (0.263)
Lose interstate war	0.221** (0.078)	0.209** (0.081)	—	0.226** (0.083)	0.352** (0.110)	0.277* (0.126)	0.302* (0.120)	0.301* (0.129)	0.423*** (0.121)	0.381* (0.184)	0.340* (0.186)
Ongoing civil war, $t-1$	-0.142 (0.090)	-0.161† (0.090)	-0.161† (0.092)	-0.184* (0.090)	-0.110 (0.120)	-0.143 (0.135)	-0.138 (0.132)	-0.125 (0.133)	-0.156 (0.141)	-0.673** (0.203)	-0.689** (0.204)
Interstate war involvement	—	—	0.230* (0.100)	—							

	(1)	(2)	(3)	(4)	(5)	(6)	(7)	(8)	(9)	(10)	(11)
Buffer state	–	–	–	–	–	–	–	–	–	–	–
Ethnic heterogeneity (ELF)	–	–	–0.271* (0.108)	0.217* (0.104)	–	–	–	–	–	–	–
Percent ethnic population discriminated against	–	–	–	–	0.586*** (0.154)	–	–	–	–	–	–
Percent ethnic population excluded from power	–	–	–	–	–	0.475*** (0.109)	–	–	–	–	–
Oil producer (Colgan)	–	–	–	–	–	–	0.354** (0.110)	–	–	–	–
Oil producer (Ross)	–	–	–	–	–	–	–	0.011 (0.019)	–	–	–
Constant	–3.251*** (0.274)	–3.273*** (0.279)	–3.270*** (0.274)	–3.292*** (0.266)	–3.678*** (0.255)	–3.532*** (0.312)	–3.627*** (0.317)	–3.759*** (0.276)	–3.673*** (0.322)		
N	14,909	14,909	14,909	14,909	9,863	7,686	7,686	8,694	6,806	9,540	9,540
Log pseudo-likelihood	–1333.315	–1326.030	–1325.877	–1320.378	–772.916	–610.553	–609.621	–621.887	–512.715	–1060.315	–1056.345
Wald Chi²	296.07***	369.69***	362.39***	431.05***	259.16***	172.00***	168.30***	182.70***	197.29***	112.17***	120.11***

Note: Robust standard errors clustered on country code in parentheses. Peace years and three cubic splines included in each model but not shown. None of these variables is ever significant. † p<0.10, * p<0.05, ** p<0.01, *** p<0.001.

the base set of control variables and cover the years from 1816 to 2008. Model 3 substitutes interstate war involvement for losing an interstate war, whereas model 4 inserts a dummy variable for buffer state status. Models 5 through 9 each add one variable that is available only for part of the twentieth century. Model 5 covers the period from 1920 to 2008; models 6 through 8 include the years 1946 to 2008; and model 9 runs from 1960 to 2006. Models 10 and 11, finally, rerun models 1 and 2 using a fixed effects logit estimator.

Model 1 in table 3.2 shows that the omnibus variable for regime change exerts a positive and significant ($p < 0.001$) effect on the probability of civil war onset. Model 2 demonstrates that the overall effect of regime change on civil war is driven by the large, positive effect of leadership regime change. Institutional and restoration regime changes, by contrast, exert no systematic effect on the outbreak of civil war. Wald tests confirm that although the coefficient for leadership regime change is significantly greater than those for institutional ($p = 0.086$) and restoration regime changes ($p = 0.01$), the coefficients for institutional and restoration cases are not significantly different from each other ($p = 0.43$). Model 3 substitutes interstate war involvement for losing an interstate war, finding the two variables to be of roughly the same magnitude and significance. Model 4 then inserts a dummy variable signifying buffer state status, which some have argued is an important determinant of regime change.[307] Buffer states, however, are less likely to experience civil wars.

The next five models include measures of ethnic diversity, discrimination, and oil production that are available for only the last half century or so. Model 5, which is confined to the years from 1920 to 2008, shows that the effect of leadership regime change strengthens when I control for ethnic diversity, which also increases the likelihood of internal conflict. Similarly, when I include measures of ethnic discrimination and exclusion in models 6 and 7, both of which are themselves strong predictors of civil violence, leadership regime change continues to have a powerful effect. The largest coefficient for leadership regime change is in model 9, which is limited to the most recent time period: 1960 to 2006. The effect of oil production, however, is inconclusive. The dummy variable in model 8 representing states that earn at least 10 percent of their GDP from oil exports is positive and significant, whereas the variable that measures per capita revenues from oil and gas production in model 9 is insignificant.[308]

Models 10 and 11 replicate models 1 and 2 but use fixed effects logit rather than the random effects probit estimator I have used thus far. Random effects models exploit variation between units (i.e., states), and thus estimate the effect of regime change on civil war compared to other states that did not experience regime change. Fixed effects models examine variation exclusively within rather than across subjects, and thus compare the effect of regime change on civil war to other years in the same state in which regime change did not occur. The large, positive, and statistically significant coefficient for regime change in model 10 indicates that countries are more likely to suffer civil war in the years after regime change than in other years. Model 11 confirms that of the three types of regime change, those that impose new leaders are the only ones that significantly increase the likelihood of civil war.

Figure 3.8 puts the substantive effect of regime change in perspective by showing the change in probability of civil war for all of the control variables, including those that are available only for limited time periods. The largest marginal effect is obtained by shifting the log of population from its twentieth to eightieth percentile, which increases the likelihood of civil war onset 2.3 percent. The next largest effect is for new states, which raise the risk of internal conflict 2 percent, although this effect is not significant at the 95 percent level of confidence. Colgan's measure of oil production increases the chance of civil war 1.5 percent, whereas moving from the twentieth to eightieth percentile on the log of energy consumption reduces the chance of civil war by the same amount. Recall from figure 3.4, however, that leadership regime change increases the probability of civil war more than 5 percent. Leadership regime change thus has the largest substantive effect on the risk of civil war onset of any of the variables in my analysis.

CONDITIONAL EFFECTS

Table 3.3 displays the regression results that produce the graphs in figures 3.6, 3.7, and 3.8. Recall that these figures tested the three conditional hypotheses, which maintain that the effect of institutional regime change on civil war would be mediated by the economic development and ethnic diversity of the target (H3.3b and H3.3c), and that the effect of regime change overall would be greater when inflicted simultaneously with defeat in an interstate war (H3.5). Model 12 includes an interaction between institutional regime change and economic development; model 13 includes an interaction between institutional regime change and ethnic fractionalization; and model 14 interacts regime change and defeat in interstate war. The significance of regression coefficients in interaction models, however, is a poor guide to judging the joint effect and statistical significance of the variables in question. What matters is whether the change in the likelihood of civil war caused by these three variables jointly is statistically significant.[309]

The appropriate way to assess interaction effects is to graph the joint marginal effect and associated 95 percent confidence interval over the observed range of the two independent variables. Because regime change is a dummy variable, figures 3.5 and 3.6 visualize the marginal effect of this variable across the range of energy consumption (logged) and ELF observed for institutional regime change—zero to 12.45 for the former and zero to 0.67 for the latter. Thus, these graphs are truncated short of the maximum values of energy consumption and ELF because extending the graph beyond

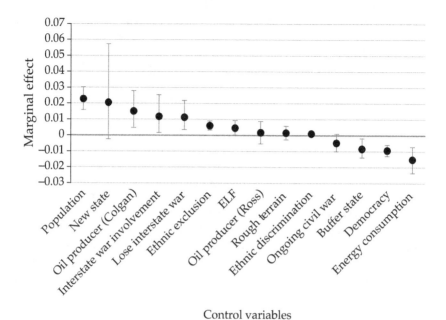

Control variables

Figure 3.8. Marginal effects of control variables on civil war onset

the observed values would result in extrapolations. The results of these graphs were discussed above, and hence I omit further discussion of them here—other than to note that that they support my hypotheses that the effect of institutional regime change on civil war depends on the target's level of economic development and ethnic diversity.

Assessing the joint effects of an interaction composed of two dummy variables, such as regime change and losing an interstate war, is simpler. All that is required is to report the predicted probabilities of civil war when both variables are zero and when both are one along with the 95 percent confidence interval for both estimates, as is done in figure 3.7. That figure went a step further by reporting predicted probabilities when each variable was one and the other was zero. This step is meant to determine whether the joint effect of regime change and losing a war is significantly different from suffering regime change or losing a war alone. As discussed previously, the results showed that although experiencing regime change and losing a war was significantly different from experiencing neither, the joint effect of the two variables was not differentiable from regime change alone, whereas it was distinguishable from just losing a war.

Robustness Tests In this section, I briefly summarize the results of nine robustness tests.[310] First, the results are not sensitive to the use of alterna-

Table 3.3 Probit estimates of foreign-imposed regime change and civil war onset: Interaction effects

	12	13	14
Regime change	–	–	0.383** (0.108)
Leadership regime change	0.553*** (0.081)	0.618*** (0.102)	–
Institutional regime change	0.623** (0.230)	−0.403 (0.372)	–
Restoration regime change	−0.138 (0.265)	0.011 (0.345)	–
Economic development	−0.043*** (0.012)	−0.045** (0.013)	−0.043*** (0.012)
Lose interstate war	0.222** (0.079)	0.341** (0.110)	0.238** (0.086)
Ethnic heterogeneity (ELF)	–	0.202† (0.104)	–
Institutional R.C. × economic development	−0.083* (0.037)	–	–
Institutional R.C. × ethnic heterogeneity	–	1.475* (0.609)	–
Regime change × lose interstate war	–	–	−0.059 (0.159)
Population	0.192*** (0.039)	0.201*** (0.025)	0.188*** (0.029)
Mountainous terrain	0.092 (0.156)	−0.038 (0.163)	0.127 (0.154)
New state	0.341† (0.195)	0.623** (0.205)	0.329† (0.193)
Democracy	−0.340*** (0.071)	−0.325*** (0.084)	−0.340*** (0.071)
Ongoing civil war, t–1	−0.167† (0.090)	−0.119 (0.122)	−0.142 (0.090)
Constant	−3.288*** (0.282)	−3.667*** (0.254)	−3.249*** (0.274)
N	14,909	9,863	14,909
Log pseudo-likelihood	−1324.547	−772.142	−1333.252
Wald Chi^2	389.10***	281.27***	295.31***

Note: Robust standard errors clustered on country code in parentheses. Peace years and three cubic splines included in each model but not shown. None of these variables is ever significant.
$^{\dagger} p < 0.10$, $^* p < 0.05$, $^{**} p < 0.01$, $^{***} p < 0.001$.

tive measures of certain independent variables, such as economic development and regime type.[311] Second, as already shown in table 3.2, the effect of leadership regime change on civil war remains at least as powerful after World War II (and after 1960) as it was in earlier times. Third, limiting the analysis to only those states that experienced regime change at some point in their history yields results highly similar to those shown in table 3.2. Fourth, given that civil war onset is a rare event (occurring in 2 percent of country-years), I reestimated the models in table 3.2 using rare events logit, but doing so had no effect on the results.[312] Fifth, the statistical significance of leadership regime change is not sensitive to alternative treatment durations, such as shortening it to five years or lengthening it by making the effect permanent.[313] Sixth, some might argue that coding whether a country had an ongoing civil war only in the year prior the year of observation underestimates the impact of previous or ongoing conflicts.[314] Yet coding this variable as one if a country had a civil war in any of the three years before the year of observation fails to yield a significant result, nor does it affect the significance or substantive effect of leadership regime change.[315]

Seventh, I took several steps to check for the effect of influential cases or groups of cases. For example, although several countries—Afghanistan, DRC, China, Indonesia, and Mexico—experienced at least three regime changes followed by civil wars, no single country is responsible for the result that leadership regime change increases the risk of civil strife. These same five countries plus five more (Peru, Argentina, Greece, Uganda, and Congo-Brazzaville) suffered multiple civil wars after the same regime change. To ensure that repeated conflicts do not inflate the results, I employ an alternative dependent variable coded one if a civil war occurred at any point during the ensuing ten years. Using this alternative measure does not attenuate the effect of leadership regime change.[316] The results are also robust to the exclusion of the six covert regime changes in my dataset and the numerous regime changes enacted by Germany and Italy during World War II.[317]

Eighth, there are fourteen cases in which leadership regime change and civil war occurred in the same year, raising the possibility of endogeneity or spuriousness. Recall that I include the year in which regime change occurred in coding for the effects of regime change on the argument that starting in the year following regime change would miss civil wars that start during the same year but after the change of regime. Indeed, my research indicates that in eight of fourteen cases, civil war onset followed regime change. In the other six cases—Hungary (1919), Nicaragua (1926), China (1928), DRC (1960), Chile (1973), and Congo-Brazzaville (1997)—civil war began before regime change occurred or was part of the process of overthrowing the regime.[318] Recoding these six cases to zero on civil war onset slightly reduces the coefficient of leadership regime change, but it remains highly significant ($B = 0.48$, $p < 0.001$). Omitting all fourteen civil wars that occurred in the same year as regime changes reduces the substantive effect but not the significance of leadership regime change ($B = 0.36$, $p < 0.001$). The effect of leadership regime change on civil war is thus not spurious or explained by endogeneity.

Finally, although I argue to the contrary, it is possible that regime changes in which an intervener both removes and replaces a targeted leader with a new protégé of its own choosing have different effects than regime changes in which an intervener does not control who comes to power after it removes an incumbent. To check for this possibility, I coded two new variables for each type of regime change: removal-only ($N = 17$) and removal-and-replacement ($N = 95$). The only type of removal-only regime change followed by civil war is leadership regime change. When inserted into my base model, the coefficients for both removal-only and removal-and-replacement leadership regime changes are significant, and although the former is slightly larger than the latter, the difference between the two is insignificant ($p = 0.30$). This test further validates the problem of competing principals by showing that even when interveners handpick new leaders, conflict can still emerge.

SELECTION BIAS

In this section, I review evidence using several methodological approaches that suggests that selection bias does not explain the results. As discussed briefly in the book's introduction, my analysis in this chapter is potentially vulnerable to three types of selection bias that could explain why states that experience regime change suffer from an elevated likelihood of civil war afterward: (1) targets of regime change are simply more prone to civil war than other states, (2) targets of leadership regime change are more prone to civil war than targets of other types of regime change, and (3) targets of regime changes that succeed are more prone to civil war than targets where regime change fails.

The first three analyses below—identifying confounding variables, matching, and instrumental variables—address the first type of selection bias, which holds that civil war is common after regime change not because of anything to do with regime change but rather because targets of civil war are simply more prone to such conflicts. The last two analyses address the second and third types of selection bias in turn, namely that targets of leadership regime change are more prone to civil war than targets of other types of regime change and targets of regime changes that succeed are more prone to civil war than targets where regime change fails.

Identifying Confounding Variables First, I conducted an analysis of the causes of foreign-imposed regime change to determine whether any of the variables that affect the likelihood of civil war also affect the likelihood that regime change occurs in the first place.[319] The findings of these two analyses combine to rule out several sources of selection bias. For example, economic underdevelopment increases the likelihood of civil war, but states that experience regime change are not less developed than other states.[320] Population also increases the probability of civil war, but states that suffer regime change are actually less populous than others. Oil production and ethnic diversity each elevate the risk of internal conflict, but neither is correlated with regime change. New states are more vulnerable to civil war but state age is uncorrelated with regime change. Buffer states and countries with ongoing civil wars are both more likely to experience regime change, but these factors each decrease the likelihood of civil war onset. Rough terrain is uncorrelated with regime change and civil war. Finally, political instability increases the risk of both regime change and civil war, but closer examination shows that instability is correlated only with restoration regime changes—which do not increase the likelihood of civil strife.

This process of elimination leaves only two variables that are correlated in the same direction with both regime change and civil war: interstate war involvement (positive) and democracy (negative). The size of any bias resulting from these two variables is likely to be modest. Democracy, for example, although it reduces the likelihood of leadership regime change, does so by the tiniest of margins: 0.06 percent.[321] Interstate war involvement has a much larger effect on leadership regime change—an increase of 1.8 percent. The matching procedure reported below creates a set of cases that have equal likelihood of occurring during an interstate war or being democratic in an attempt to eliminate any potential bias.

Matching Second, matching also suggests that the effect of regime change is not solely an artifact of states selecting targets that are vulnerable to civil war. Matching aims to adjust the sample to correct for the bias induced by nonrandom selection by identifying a set of control cases that on average is as close as possible to the treated cases along as many parameters as possible. In other words, matching techniques seek to approximate the experimental ideal by breaking any connection between the treatment and background factors.[322] The result, if done well, is a dataset in which the treated cases do not differ markedly from the control cases along as many other variables thought to influence the outcome as the analyst can measure. Any remaining difference in the dependent variable across the treated and control cases can thus be attributed to the treatment.[323]

Employing the *MatchIt* program, I used genetic matching to create four datasets, one each using the combined regime change variable, and each type of regime change, as the treatment.[324] To ensure that countries that experienced regime change were not matched to themselves in different years—a serious risk in time-series data—I dropped all country-years for these states other than the year(s) of regime change. I performed two matching runs for each treatment. In the first, I included the basic set of control variables as well as a set of five dummy variables representing the major regions of the world to assure that control cases were drawn from the same region as treated cases. In the second run, in addition to the basic controls and regional dummies I also included a dummy variable identifying buffer states, and I substituted a variable representing involvement in an interstate war for the variable capturing loss of an interstate war.

In both instances matching greatly improved the balance of the datasets: in the first run, using the basic controls and regional dummies, the difference in propensity scores between treated and control cases—the probability that a case receives the treatment conditional on its values on the covariates—shrank by 92 percent for all types of regime change combined, 87 percent for leadership, 89 percent for restoration, and just under 100 percent for institutional regime change.[325] In other words, differences in means between regime-change and non-regime-change cases on all matched variables were minor after matching. For leadership regime change, for example, matching improved balance by more than 50 percent—and often much more than 50 percent—for all variables with the exception of the dummy variable representing Asia, which worsened slightly.[326] For five variables the mean values of the treated and control cases after matching were exactly the same.

T-tests for difference of means performed on the matched datasets for each type of regime change show that nearly half of all leadership regime changes (47 percent) are followed by civil wars within ten years, compared to one-fifth (21 percent) of cases that avoid such intervention—a difference that is significant at better than the 99 percent level of confidence ($p = 0.0052$). Because matching is not perfect, however, I included the control variables along with each regime change variable in multivariate probit models.[327] The dependent variable is a dummy variable indicating whether a civil war began in the ensuing ten years. The marginal effects of each type of regime change (and 95 percent confidence intervals) are displayed in figure 3.9.

Here the effect of leadership regime change is even stronger: the probability of civil war following such a regime change is 48.1 percent, compared to 11.6 percent in cases where leadership regime change does not occur, more than a fourfold increase.[328] Restorations also have a positive effect on the likelihood of a civil conflict breaking out after matching but this effect is insignificant. The effect of institutional regime change cannot be estimated because matching produced no control cases that suffered a civil war to counter the four civil wars that followed this type of regime change (Nicaragua 1910 and 1926, Afghanistan 2001, and Iraq 2003). Although it might appear that institutional regime changes increase the likelihood of civil war, this appears to be true only in relatively impoverished and/or ethnically diverse societies.[329]

Matching, of course, cannot be performed on unobserved variables, and thus it is possible that an omitted variable correlated with both regime change and civil war exists that could render the relationship I have found between the two spurious. Although by definition I cannot measure such a variable, I performed a Rosenbaum Sensitivity Analysis to estimate how large such an unobserved effect would have to be to make the effect of leadership regime change invalid.[330] This test shows that, to paraphrase Luke Keele, to attribute the increased likelihood of civil war to some unobserved factor rather than to regime change, the unobserved factor would have to increase the risk of civil war between 2.5 and 3 times.[331] The only effect larger

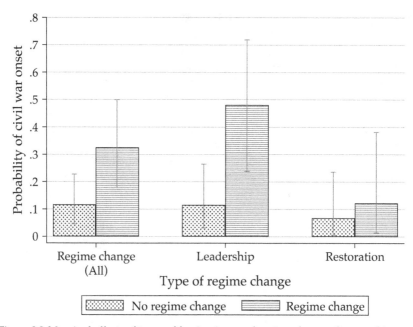

Figure 3.9. Marginal effects of types of foreign-imposed regime change after matching. Institutional regime change is omitted from the figure because there were no cases of civil war onset among the control cases, and thus the absence of institutional regime change perfectly predicted peace.

than this in my analysis (other than regime change itself) is produced by a very large increase in population size. The only other variables that generate effect sizes in this range include participating in or losing an interstate war. I thus conclude that it is unlikely that hidden bias owing to an unobserved confounder explains my results.

Instrumental Variables Another common way to correct for selection bias is to use instrumental variables (IV) analysis. The basic idea of IV analysis is to exploit variance in the independent variable that is not possibly caused by the dependent variable, and thus not vulnerable to the charge of spuriousness, to explain variation in the dependent variable. IV analysis is performed in two stages. The first stage estimates the effect of a group of variables—including at least one (the instrument) thought to be unrelated to the ultimate outcome—on the "endogenous regressor," and the second stage estimates the effect of the instrument plus control variables on the dependent variable of interest. In my application, the endogenous regressor is regime change, the ultimate outcome is civil war onset, and the challenge is to find a variable that explains regime change but not civil war to use as an instrument for regime change.[332]

I have been unable to identify a variable in the country-year format used in this chapter that is correlated with regime change but not with civil war. Because the dataset is not dyadic, it is impossible to include variables that measure aspects of the relationship *between* states that might explain regime change but not civil war and thus serve as useful instruments. Therefore, I built a directed-dyad dataset that includes measures of the relationship between pairs of states in addition to the same variables used so far to account for the characteristics of individual states.[333] I use two variables—State A's share of the dyad's total material capabilities and the distance between States A and B—as instruments for regime change. Using a two-stage least squares regression model, I find that each of these variables is not only strongly linked to the occurrence of foreign-imposed regime change (and leadership regime change) in the first stage, together they also significantly increase the likelihood of civil war when inserted as instruments for regime change in the second stage.[334] These results suggest that foreign-imposed regime change indeed exerts a causal effect on the outbreak of civil war and this effect is not merely a function of selection bias.

Leadership versus other Types of Regime Change The second type of selection bias that could taint my results is the possibility that civil war is more likely in states that are targeted specifically for leadership regime changes rather than institutional or restoration regime changes because the former are more predisposed to civil war than the latter. Among the 111 cases of regime change for which I have data, however, there is little evidence that leadership regime changes occur in poorer, more populous, less democratic, or newer states that have lost interstate wars. Table 3.4 summarizes several t-tests of these relationships; each line in the table

Table 3.4 T-tests of leadership versus institutional and restoration foreign-imposed regime changes and factors correlated with civil war

	Mean, leadership regime change	Mean, institutional and restoration regime change	P-value
Economic development	4.369	5.252	0.253
Population	7.919	8.140	0.483
New state	0.046	0.043	0.928
Percent mountainous	0.263	0.185	0.044
Democracy	0.138	0.149	0.877
Lose interstate war	0.477	0.340	0.151
Peace years	32.200	35.340	0.618

Note: N = 111, 65 leadership and 47 nonleadership regime changes. These numbers do not sum to 111 because Cyprus experienced a leadership and a nonleadership regime change in the same year (1974).

compares the mean value for leadership regime changes to those for institutional and restoration regime changes combined. In general, the differences between leadership and nonleadership regime changes are minor.
States that experience leadership regime changes, for example, are slightly
poorer, newer, less democratic, more mountainous, and more likely to
have lost an interstate war than states that are targeted for the other two
types of regime changes, but in only one case (percent mountainous terrain) is the difference statistically significant—and this variable is never
significant in my analyses. By contrast, targets of leadership regime change
are slightly less populous, but again the difference does not approach significance.

Successful versus Failed Regime Changes The final type of selection bias that
could affect my results is the possibility that cases in which regime change
succeeds are more predisposed to civil war than cases where it fails. Although this is a risk, if I can show that instances of success and failure are
indistinguishable in terms of background conditions, the fact that successful regime changes are positively associated with civil war whereas failures
are not would constitute powerful evidence that regime change has a causal
effect.[335]

To first establish that regime changes that succeed in overthrowing targeted governments increase the likelihood of civil war but failures do not,
I compiled two samples of attempted regime changes that failed and compared their effects on civil war onset to those of my collection of successful
regime changes. The first sample consists of thirty-three cases I encountered in my research where I was able to determine that one state was actively seeking to overthrow the leader of another state but was ultimately
unsuccessful. Examples include Britain and France versus Germany in
World War I; multiple countries that targeted the new Bolshevik regime in
Russia at the conclusion of the same war; Britain, France, and Israel hoping
to oust Egypt's Gamal Abdel Nasser in 1956; and Rwanda and Uganda
seeking to topple their wayward protégé Laurent Kabila in the DRC beginning in 1998.[336] The second sample, compiled by Lindsey O'Rourke, is composed of the portion of US covert regime changes during the Cold War that
failed.[337] Both sets of cases are coded one for ten years starting in the year
after the failed operation concluded. I inserted each of these variables into
models 1 and 2 from table 3.2.

Neither of the failed regime change variables is significant when included
with my omnibus regime change indicator, or with the three types of regime changes coded separately.[338] Moreover, the coefficients for successful and failed (overt and covert) regime changes, and for successful leadership regime change and both types of failed regime change, are significantly
different in all instances. Figure 3.10 demonstrates the differences between

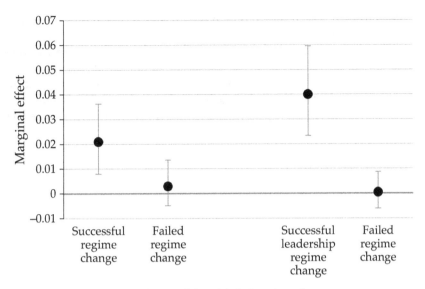

Successful and failed regime change

Figure 3.10. Marginal effects of successful versus failed foreign-imposed regime changes

Table 3.5 T-tests of successful versus failed foreign-imposed regime changes and factors correlated with civil war

	Mean, successful regime changes	Mean, failed regime changes	P-value
Economic development	4.737	5.397	0.428
Population	8.013	8.474	0.179
New state	0.045	0.031	0.740
Percent mountainous	0.230	0.221	0.813
Democracy	0.143	0.065	0.248
Lose interstate war	0.420	0.281	0.159
Peace years	33.518	31.625	0.785

Note: N = 143 or 144, 111 successful and 32 or 33 failed regime changes.

successful and failed regime changes graphically using my list of unsuccessful cases.

The final step is to show that countries where regime change succeeds are not obviously more prone to civil war than countries where regime change fails. Table 3.5 displays that evidence. In no instance are targets of successful regime change statistically more susceptible to civil war than targets where regime change failed.[339]

These findings constitute strong evidence against the allegation that regime change increases the likelihood of civil war because it is more likely to succeed in countries that are more prone to civil war than countries where it fails. Moreover, taken together, the finding that successful regime changes increase the likelihood of civil war but failed ones do not *and* the finding that countries where regime change succeeds are not more susceptible to civil war than countries where it fails constitutes powerful evidence that regime change exerts a causal effect on civil war.

Foreign-Imposed Regime Change and the Survival of Leaders

In this chapter, I turn to a second implication of my argument for domestic politics in targets of regime change: the fate of leaders brought to power at the point of foreign bayonets. I argue that regime change—and particularly regime change that simply substitutes one leader for another while paying little attention to supporting institutions—increases the likelihood that the leader so installed will be removed from power by force or the threat of force, what H. E. Goemans refers to as *irregular* methods. These leadership regime changes should also reduce the risk of *regular* removal, that is, departures from office that follow established rules and procedures for succession. I do not expect regime changes that also install governing institutions or restore leaders to power who previously held office to have much of an effect on the probability of regular or irregular removal.

Establishing that imposed leaders are vulnerable to irregular removal is crucial for validating the competing principals mechanism, which holds that rulers empowered through regime changes face competing incentives because they are beholden to multiple audiences. Leaders who favor the interests of the intervener that installed them run the risk of generating domestic dissent, such as protests, riots, coups, or insurgencies, which can imperil their tenure in office. Leaders who seek to placate their domestic audience at the expense of the intervener's interests, by contrast, run the risk that the intervener will meddle yet again and push them aside in favor of a more pliant ruler. For this theory to hold, it is crucial to show that regime change in fact endangers the survival of the individuals they install in office.

The evidence presented in this chapter supports my argument. Analyzing two different versions of the *Archigos* dataset on leaders, one in which the unit of analysis is the leader-year (i.e., one observation for each year a leader remains in office) and one in which it is the leader-spell (i.e., a single observation per leader), I consistently find that leaders who come to power after foreign-imposed regime change face a significantly higher risk of irregular removal and a lower risk of regular removal. This effect is most pronounced and significant for leaders empowered by leadership regime changes. The effect of institutional regime change tends to track that of leadership regime change for both types of removal, albeit at a lower level of significance, until 1945, after which no leader empowered via institutional regime change loses power irregularly. The effect of restoration regime change varies by unit of analysis: restorations drastically lower the hazard of irregular removal in the leader-year data but have no effect in the leader-spell data (except after 1960, when no restored leader loses power irregularly). Nor do restoration regime changes have any effect on the risk of regular removal (in either dataset).

I organize the case studies differently in this chapter than I did in chapter 3. Roughly half of all imposed leaders lose power in an irregular manner, yet the term "irregular removal" encapsulates a wide variety of coerced, forcible, or violent ways that leaders can lose office. I begin the qualitative section of the chapter by identifying the six distinct ways that imposed leaders have been pushed out of power irregularly. Three of these six modes of removal, which together encompass a small number of cases, are consistent with the broader proposition that installing leaders in foreign countries is a risky business but are not explained by my specific causal mechanism. The problem of competing principals, however, explains the remaining three types of cases. I discuss the first three types and provide examples of each. I then perform detailed case studies for two kinds of irregular removal: coups tolerated or encouraged by dissatisfied patrons against wayward protégés (the United States and Duong Van Minh in South Vietnam) and uprisings by dissatisfied domestic audiences against leaders strongly identified with foreign patrons (Emperor Maximilian of Mexico). I defer discussion of imposed leaders removed directly by their patrons to chapter 5. Finally, I examine a number of negative cases—cases in which imposed leaders managed to remain in power for lengthy periods—to identify factors that help protégés survive. I briefly examine the reigns of Francisco Franco (Spain), Mohammad Reza Pahlavi (Iran), and communist regimes established in Eastern Europe by the Soviet Union after World War II.

The chapter is laid out as follows. First, I review the existing literature on leader survival in IR. Second, I briefly reprise the theoretical argument presented in chapter 2 and lay out hypotheses relevant to the manner in which leaders are removed from office and how long they survive in power. Third, I review the key findings from the statistical analysis of leader survival that is presented in more detail in the chapter appendix. Readers interested in the nuts and bolts of the data and methods employed are encouraged to consult this appendix. Fourth, I present the case studies of how imposed leaders lose power irregularly, followed in a fifth section by a discussion of how some leaders beat the odds and managed to remain in power for extended periods. The final section concludes.

The Literature on Leader Survival in International Relations

The study of leaders in IR has undergone a renaissance since the end of the Cold War.[1] This section focuses specifically on the literature on leaders' political survival in office, including the effects on leader behavior of the threat of violent versus nonviolent removal and the factors that affect the risk of different forms of removal.

The systematic study of leader survival in IR owes much to the work of H. E. Goemans. In his pioneering study of war termination, *War and Punishment*, Goemans made a crucial innovation by differentiating among different ways that leaders could leave office and deducing the incentives that these modes of exit generated for leaders to continue or settle ongoing wars. Prior to Goemans's work, scholars focused exclusively on the role played by the *risk* of removal from office in shaping leader behavior. Proponents of democratic exceptionalism, for example, maintain that the increased likelihood of removal for policy failures, such as losing a war, discourages democratic leaders from initiating conflicts against other democracies, whose leaders are similarly motivated and will thus fight hard to avoid defeat.[2] These scholars likewise argue that leaders of democracies only start wars they believe they have a good chance of winning because defeat on the battlefield increases the risk of defeat at the ballot box.[3]

Goemans, by contrast, contends that *costs* of removal—as determined by the likelihood of punishment beyond removal from office—also exert a powerful effect on leader behavior. In his study of war termination, Goemans argues that leaders in what he calls semirepressive, moderately exclusionary regimes (also known as mixed regimes or oligarchies) are likely to be removed and punished whether they lose a war by a little or a lot.[4] In other words, leaders in these systems face both a high risk and high costs of removal. Leaders of highly repressive, highly exclusionary regimes (i.e., full autocracies) that lose wars on moderate terms can simply suppress any dissent with their powerful domestic security forces and thus face a low risk and low costs of removal. Elites in nonrepressive, nonexclusionary regimes (i.e., democracies) who accept a moderate defeat, by contrast, face the hardly daunting prospect of a comfortable retirement should they lose the ensuing election—that is, they face a high risk but low costs of removal.[5] In both of these regimes, leaders face a high prospect of removal *and* punishment only if they lose a war on catastrophic terms—and even then, punishment usually comes at the hands of the opposing state rather than their own people.

Leaders of mixed regimes, by contrast, do not possess sufficient coercive capabilities to suppress public discontent in the event of military defeat; rather, they rely on material gains from victory to compensate people for wartime sacrifices. If those benefits are not forthcoming, these leaders are likely not only to be overthrown but also imprisoned, exiled, or even killed. Importantly, leaders of mixed regimes are likely to be removed and punished whether they lose moderately or severely. They thus face powerful incentives to "gamble for resurrection" by adopting a risky military strategy that, if successful, will reverse the tide on the battlefield, but if unsuccessful could result in total defeat.[6] In support of this argument, Goemans finds that wars involving mixed regimes last significantly longer than wars involving only democracies or full autocracies. He also demonstrates how the leaders of oligarchic Germany in World War I consistently *increased* their war aims and adopted risky strategies, such as unrestricted submarine warfare, when they perceived the odds of victory as decreasing.

Goemans subsequently extended this work on how the postwar fate of leaders influences the manner in which they conduct ongoing wars to their choices to initiate wars in the first place. In line with his earlier work, Goemans (with coauthor Giacomo Chiozza) argues that leaders confronted with an elevated risk of forcible removal from office by domestic forces are more likely to initiate international conflict. Picking an external fight can increase a threatened leader's chances of survival because leaders can send the source of the threat off to war, thereby eliminating the problem. Winning the external conflict, furthermore, "can bring leaders the increased prestige, legitimacy, capabilities, and resources to either reverse the temporary shock . . . or increase the leader's chances against his domestic opponents."[7] By contrast, leaders who expect to be removed regularly have little to gain and much to lose by initiating international conflicts. "For such leaders," Chiozza and Goemans write, "Challenging and Victory may somewhat decrease their hazard of a regular removal from office, but Defeat significantly increases their hazard of an irregular removal from office. . . . For these leaders, then, international conflict constitutes a dangerous gamble."[8]

Of greatest relevance to this book, however, Chiozza and Goemans also reverse the causal arrow and analyze the effect of international conflict involvement and outcomes on leaders' hazard of being removed from office by regular or irregular means. The most striking finding is that defeat in crises or wars significantly increases the hazard of *irregular* removal from office but defeat either has no effect on—or even decreases—the hazard of *regular* removal. Prevailing in international crises or wars, by contrast, offers uncertain benefits: victory generally lowers the likelihood of both types of removal, but statistical significance is borderline. Leaders who initiate conflicts, however, face a lower hazard of regular and irregular removal while the conflict is ongoing.[9]

Goemans also tests the effects of numerous additional variables on the likelihood that a leader is ousted from office. I focus the remainder of my discussion on irregular removal because it is the central concern of this chapter.[10] Consistent with the findings of his earlier work, Goemans shows that leaders of mixed regimes face an elevated risk of forcible removal both in general and if they lose a war.[11] Leaders of parliamentary democracies, by contrast, are less vulnerable to irregular removal, whereas democratic presidents face neither an increased nor decreased likelihood of losing office by force. Economic variables, such as higher levels of GDP per capita, GDP growth, and greater trade openness decrease the hazard of irregular removal, as does having a larger population. As one might expect, leaders who gain office forcibly are much more likely to leave power the same way. The only other factor that has a significant (positive) effect on irregular removal is the number of times a leader has previously been in office. Civil war, state age, and being the target of an international conflict have no effect. I incorporate these variables in my analyses of leader survival below.

In this chapter I contribute to the literature on leader survival by further investigating whether how a leader comes to power affects her prospects for remaining in power. Can states replace troublesome foreign leaders with like-minded allies and expect their protégés to remain in office long enough in the face of domestic hostility to deliver meaningful benefits? Or does the necessity of responding to domestic actors cause imposed leaders to renege on their promises, in turn forcing patrons to seek yet another regime change?

Recapitulating the Argument

What predictions does my theory make for the manner in which foreign-imposed leaders will leave office? As detailed in chapter 2, regime change threatens the tenure of imposed leaders by placing them in an uncomfortable dilemma caused by the problem of competing principals.[12] Leaders put in office by external actors face two masters with incompatible preferences and hence pleasing one often displeases the other. On the one hand, interveners empower leaders who share their preferences and expect them to implement and pursue friendly policies. This external principal grows irritated if leaders are unable or unwilling to deliver. On the other hand, a leader's domestic constituents expect her to act in their best interests and grow angry or resentful if instead the leader caters to the intervener's demands or appears to be the puppet of foreign interests. The domestic side of the equation is made even more complex by the reality that multiple constituencies are present in any country, even in autocracies, and acting in the interests of a foreign power is likely to alienate at least one of them.[13] If the intervener eschews appointing an indigenous leader and instead chooses to rule the target directly through its own representative backed by a military occupation, thereby acting as both principal and agent, it simply makes itself the focus of the opposition. Whether an intervener enacts its preferences through a local agent or direct rule, the resentment generated among the population increases the likelihood of coups, assassinations, and other violent actions aimed at toppling the leader.

H4.1a: *Foreign-imposed regime change increases the hazard of irregular leader removal.*

H4.1b: *Foreign-imposed regime change decreases the hazard of regular leader removal.*

Regime changes that empower individual (usually autocratic) leaders without doing much to strengthen repressive or representative institutions in the country are the type most likely to generate resistance. Individuals brought to power through leadership regime changes typically lack domestic support (some are exiles who enter the country only during the regime change) and find themselves perched precariously in power. Rulers imposed in this way also may not have firm control over the military, an important source of threat to autocratic regimes. These leaders are also most dependent on their foreign backers for support, and thus are most likely to be viewed as puppets and stimulate opposition to their rule.

H4.2a: *Leadership regime change increases the hazard of irregular removal.*
H4.2b: *Leadership regime change decreases the hazard of regular removal.*

Institutional regime changes, by contrast, should have different effects on the likelihood of irregular removal depending on the context. Institutional regime changes that promote democracy and succeed—typically in targets with preconditions for democracy such as relatively advanced economies, homogeneous populations, or previous experience with democratic rule—ought to reduce the hazard of irregular removal since leaders in democracies overwhelmingly exit office in regular fashion. Institutional regime changes that promote democracy but fail—often in places with few preconditions for democracy—will result in autocracies that by definition will lack supporting democratic institutions, and thus ought to increase the probability of irregular removal. Institutional regime changes that promote socialist forms of government should decrease the hazard of irregular removal because these states develop such robust coercive institutions that coups and rebellions are exceedingly difficult to pull off. Because the effects of successful and failed institutional regime changes push in opposite directions, I hypothesize that these regime changes considered together will have little systematic effect one way or the other on the likelihood of forcible removal.

H4.3a: *Institutional regime changes neither increase nor decrease the hazard of irregular removal.*
H4.3b: *Institutional regime changes neither increase nor decrease the hazard of regular removal.*

Restoration regime changes should also have a mixed effect on the likelihood that leaders are removed from power by force. The fact that a restored leader needs to be restored—meaning that he was overthrown and required foreign intervention to regain power—suggests that significant domestic opposition exists. Moreover, whichever foreign state returns that leader to office has its own reasons for doing so, and it may pressure him to implement policies favorable to its interests. On the flip side, restored leaders have certain advantages, including intimate knowledge of the political terrain in the country and usually a sizable faction that supports their return. Empirically we know that many restorations involved bringing back popular democratic regimes after World War II in Europe. Owing to these countervailing effects, I do not expect restoration regime changes to systematically affect the survival of leaders.

> H4.4a: *Restoration regime changes neither increase nor decrease the hazard of irregular removal.*
>
> H4.4b: *Restoration regime changes neither increase nor decrease the hazard of regular removal.*

Statistical Results

This section presents the results of several analyses of the effect of foreign imposition on leader survival using data in which the unit of analysis is the leader-spell and the leader-year. As in previous chapters, I summarize the results graphically here while leaving the details of the analysis to the chapter appendix.

OVERVIEW OF THE DATA

To provide an overview of the data on leaders and regime change, table 4.1 lists the 109 leaders in the leader-spell dataset who entered office via foreign-imposed regime change from 1875 to 2004, the period covered by version 2.9 of the *Archigos* Data Set on Leaders.[14] Notice that this list is quite different from the list of leaders in chapter 1 who were *removed* from power via regime change. In this chapter I am concerned with the fate of leaders who come to power *after* their predecessor was removed by a foreign intervention. The intervener often—but not always—determines who takes office in this situation. After the US-aided assassination of Dominican strongman Rafael Trujillo in 1961, for example, the dictator's son Ramfis Trujillo quickly returned from Paris and (supported by his two uncles) assumed de facto control over the country with Joaquín Balaguer as a puppet president—hardly the hoped-for outcome in Washington. After a few months, President John F. Kennedy—in a second regime change—sent US naval vessels to Dominican waters and threatened an invasion to force the Trujillo family into exile in favor of Balaguer. Although the United States supported Balaguer, this was mainly because he was superior to a continuation of the Trujillo dictatorship rather than out of any particular affinity for him.[15]

Table 4.1 Foreign-imposed leaders and how they left office, 1875–2004

Country	Leader	Year of entry	Type of regime change	Mode of exit
Honduras	Leiva	1874	Leadership	Irregular
Honduras	Soto	1874	Leadership	Irregular
El Salvador	Zaldivar	1876	Leadership	Irregular
Transvaal*	Shepstone	1877	Leadership	Regular
Afghanistan	Jan	1879	Leadership	Regular
Afghanistan	Abdur Rahman Khan	1880	Leadership	Regular
Peru	Calderon	1881	Leadership	Irregular
Peru	Montero	1881	Leadership	Irregular
Peru	Iglesias	1882	Leadership	Irregular
Guatemala	Barillas	1885	Leadership	Regular
Vietnam*	Dong Khanh	1885	Leadership	Regular
Honduras	Bonilla	1894	Leadership	Regular
Orange Free State*	Milner	1902	Leadership	Regular
Transvaal*	Milner	1902	Leadership	Regular
Honduras	Davila	1907	Leadership	Irregular
Korea	Yi Ch'ok	1907	Leadership	Irregular
Nicaragua	Madriz	1909	Leadership	Irregular
Nicaragua	José Dolores Estrada	1910	Institutional	Irregular
Nicaragua	Juan José Estrada	1910	Institutional	Irregular
Honduras	Bertrand	1911	Leadership	Regular
Dominican Republic	Nouel y Bobadilla	1912	Institutional	Regular
Belgium	Von der Golt	1914	Leadership	Regular
Dominican Republic	Baez	1914	Institutional	Regular
Mexico	Carranza	1915	Leadership	Irregular
Albania	Von Kral	1916	Leadership	Irregular
Greece	Venizelos	1917	Leadership	Regular
Belgium	Cooreman	1918	Restoration	Regular
Costa Rica	Quiros Segura	1919	Institutional	Irregular
Costa Rica	Barquero	1919	Institutional	Regular
Hungary	Peidl	1919	Leadership	Irregular
Latvia	Borkovskis	1919	Leadership	Irregular
Latvia	Niedra	1919	Leadership	Irregular
Mongolia	Dambadorji	1925	Leadership	Regular
Nicaragua	Adolfo Díaz	1926	Institutional	Regular
China	Chiang Kai-shek	1928	Leadership	Irregular
Ethiopia	King of Italy	1936	Leadership	Irregular
China*	Wang Kemin	1937	Leadership	Regular
Austria*	Seyss-Inquart	1938	Leadership	Irregular
Albania	Verlaci	1939	Leadership	Regular
Spain	Franco	1939	Leadership	Natural death
Belgium	von Falkenhausen	1940	Leadership	Irregular
Estonia	Vares	1940	Institutional	Irregular
Latvia	Kirhensteins	1940	Institutional	Irregular
Lithuania	Merkys	1940	Leadership	Irregular
Lithuania	Paleckis	1940	Institutional	Irregular
Luxembourg	Simon	1940	Leadership	Irregular
Netherlands	Seyss-Inquart	1940	Leadership	Irregular
Norway	Quisling	1940	Leadership	Irregular
Ethiopia	Selassie	1941	Restoration	Irregular
Greece	Tsolakoglou	1941	Leadership	Regular
Iran	Mohammad Reza Pahlavi	1941	Leadership	Irregular
Iraq	Abdul-Ilah	1941	Restoration	Regular

Country	Leader	Year of entry	Type of regime change	Mode of exit
Yugoslavia	Nedić	1941	Leadership	Irregular
Denmark	Best	1943	Leadership	Irregular
Belgium	Pierlot	1944	Restoration	Regular
Bulgaria	Georgiev	1944	Institutional	Regular
France	De Gaulle	1944	Restoration	Regular
Hungary	Szálasi	1944	Leadership	Irregular
Denmark	Buhl	1945	Restoration	Regular
Hungary	Rákosi	1945	Institutional	Irregular
Japan	MacArthur	1945	Institutional	Regular
Luxembourg	Dupong	1945	Restoration	Regular
Norway	Nygaardsvold	1945	Restoration	Regular
Netherlands	Schermerhorn	1945	Restoration	Regular
Romania	Groza	1945	Institutional	Regular
East Germany	Pieck	1946	Institutional	Regular
Czechoslovakia	Gottwald	1948	Institutional	Regular
Indonesia	Beel	1948	Leadership	Irregular
Indonesia	Lovink	1949	Leadership	Regular
West Germany	Adenauer	1949	Institutional	Regular
Japan	Ridgway	1951	Institutional	Regular
Iran	Mohammad Reza Pahlavi	1953	Restoration	Irregular
Guatemala	Díaz	1954	Leadership	Irregular
Guatemala	Monzon	1954	Leadership	Irregular
Guatemala	Castillo Armas	1954	Leadership	Irregular
Hungary	Kadar	1956	Restoration	Regular
Democratic Republic of Congo	Mobutu	1960	Leadership	Regular
Dominican Republic	Ramfis Trujillo	1961	Leadership	Irregular
Dominican Republic	Balaguer	1961	Leadership	Irregular
Republic of Vietnam	Minh	1963	Leadership	Irregular
Gabon	Mba	1964	Restoration	Regular
Czechoslovakia	Svoboda	1968	Leadership	Irregular
Czechoslovakia	Husák	1968	Restoration	Regular
Chile	Pinochet	1973	Leadership	Regular
Cyprus	Sampson	1974	Leadership	Irregular
Cyprus	Klerides	1974	Restoration	Regular
Afghanistan	Karmal	1979	Leadership	Irregular
Cambodia	Samrin	1979	Leadership	Regular
Central African Republic	Dacko	1979	Leadership	Irregular
Uganda	Lule	1979	Leadership	Regular
Chad	Habré	1982	Leadership	Irregular
Mongolia	Batmonh	1984	Leadership	Regular
Afghanistan	Najibullah	1986	Leadership	Irregular
Comoros	Djohar	1989	Leadership	Irregular
Kuwait	Hussein	1990	Leadership	Irregular
Panama	Endara	1990	Institutional	Regular
Kuwait	As-Sabah	1991	Restoration	In office
Haiti	Aristide	1994	Restoration	Regular
Lesotho	Mokhehle	1994	Restoration	Regular
Comoros	El-Yachroutu	1995	Restoration	Regular
Democratic Republic of Congo	Kabila	1997	Leadership	Irregular
Republic of Congo	Sassou-Nguesso	1997	Restoration	In office

(continued)

Table 4.1 (continued)

Country	Leader	Year of entry	Type of regime change	Mode of exit
Sierra Leone	Kabbah	1998	Restoration	In office
Afghanistan	Karzai	2001	Institutional	In office
Central African Republic	Bozizé	2003	Leadership	In office
Iraq	Franks	2003	Institutional	Regular
Iraq	Garner	2003	Institutional	Regular
Iraq	Bremer	2003	Institutional	Regular
Iraq	Allawi	2003	Institutional	In office

* Denotes cases coded as regime changes in *Archigos* but not included in my list of regime changes because most of them occurred in countries that are not considered by the Correlates of war to be members of the international system. All but one consist of leadership regime changes followed by regular removal and thus cut against my argument. Excluding them would only strengthen the correlation between leadership regime change and irregular removal.

Figure 4.1 summarizes foreign-imposed leaders by the type of regime change that put them in power. Leadership regime changes were most common: sixty-five of the 109 leaders (60 percent) who entered office following a regime change did so after a leadership one. Twenty-four leaders (22 percent) came to power after institutional regime changes, whereas twenty leaders (18 percent) were restored to office after having been removed by internal or external forces. The distribution of regime changes in the leader-year data, which runs only from 1919 to 2004, is similar but—as shown in Figure 4.2—the dominance of leadership regime changes is less pronounced: forty of the seventy-eight foreign-installed leaders (51 percent) came to power after leadership regime changes, as opposed to sixteen (21 percent) following institutional and eighteen (23 percent) after restoration regime changes.

Figure 4.2 also contains suggestive evidence that leaders brought to power through different kinds of regime changes vary in how long they remain in power. Because foreign-imposed leaders are coded as such for the duration of their years in office, it is possible to compare the number of regime changes accounted for by a particular type with its proportion of total regime change leader-years. Leadership regime changes, although they comprise 51 percent of regime changes, account for only 44 percent of regime change years. Restoration regime changes, by contrast, constitute 39 percent of regime change years even though they comprise only 23 percent of regime changes. Leadership regime changes may thus result in shorter leader tenure whereas restorations lengthen time in office. Below I will unpack this association further by investigating the effect of different regime changes on regular versus irregular ways of leaving power.

FREQUENCY OF REGULAR AND IRREGULAR REMOVAL

One simple way to assess the effect of foreign imposition on leader fate is to examine the relative rates at which foreign-imposed leaders lose power in dif-

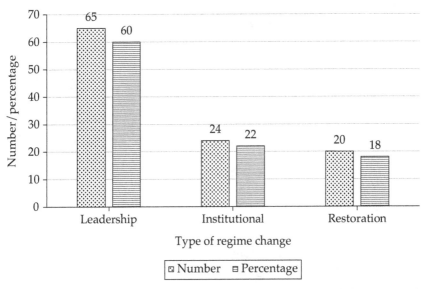

Figure 4.1. Number and percentage of foreign-imposed leaders, leader-spell data (1875–2004)

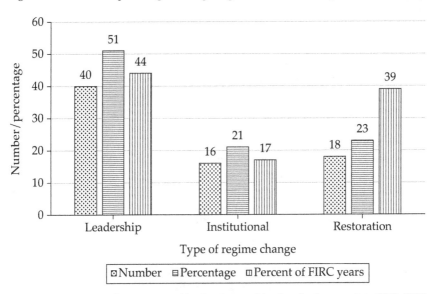

Figure 4.2. Number and percentage of foreign-imposed leaders, leader-year data (1919–2004)

ferent ways compared to other leaders—leaving aside how long it takes for those events to occur. Figure 4.3 shows the likelihood that leaders who gained power following a foreign-imposed regime change departed office by irregular versus regular means in the leader-spell data (95 percent confidence intervals for these estimates are indicated by the capped lines inside each bar). For the sake of brevity, I show results only for the leader-spell data since it covers

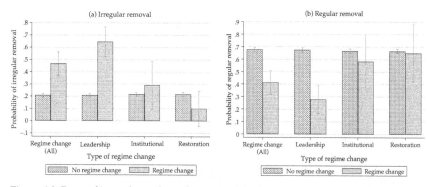

Figure 4.3. Rates of irregular and regular removal for foreign-imposed leaders (leader-spell data)

a longer time period and thus contains more foreign-imposed leaders; unless otherwise noted, results using the leader-year data are similar.[16]

Of the 103 leaders in the leader-spell data who entered office after a foreign-imposed regime change and who had lost power by 2004, nearly half of them (fifty-one) departed under irregular circumstances. As shown in the left-most pair of bars in figure 4.3(a), including the six leaders who remained in power in 2004, 47 percent of foreign-installed leaders exited office by forcible means, compared to 21 percent of leaders who came to power through domestic processes. Separating regime changes by type (and moving across figure 4.3(a) from left to right) reveals that nearly two-thirds of rulers who gained power via leadership regime changes ended up losing power in irregular fashion. The gap in rates of irregular removal is much smaller for leaders empowered in institutional regime changes—29 versus 22 percent—whereas leaders who are restored to office by outside powers are removed irregularly at less than half the rate of other leaders.[17] The differences in irregular removal are significant for all regime changes together and leadership regime changes but are not for institutional and restoration regime changes.[18]

Turning to regular removal, figure 4.3(b) shows the likelihood that foreign-imposed leaders in the leader-spell dataset leave office by regular rules and procedures. Unsurprisingly, given that regime change, and leadership regime change in particular, increases the risk of irregular removal, the combined regime change variable and leadership regime change each significantly reduce the likelihood that leaders lose office in nonviolent ways. Overall, 41 percent of foreign-imposed leaders are removed regularly, as opposed to 68 percent of other leaders. The figures for leadership regime change are 28 percent and 67 percent, respectively. Leaders who gain power via institutional and restoration regime changes, by contrast, are only marginally less likely to leave power regularly than leaders who take office via domestic processes. Neither difference is statistically significant.[19]

In short, this first look at the evidence supports my hypotheses for the overall effect of regime change (H4.1a and H4.1b), leadership regime change (H4.2a and 4.2b), institutional regime change (H4.3a and H4.3b), and partially supports them for restoration regime change (H4.4a and H4.4b).

TIME TO REGULAR AND IRREGULAR REMOVAL

A second way to assess the effect that foreign-imposed regime change has on the survival of leaders is to consider how long such leaders last in office before they are removed in different ways. Figure 4.4 presents simple comparisons of duration in office before irregular and regular removal for foreign-imposed leaders compared to other leaders using the leader-spell data. The results are broadly supportive of my argument.

Figure 4.4(a), for example, shows that foreign-imposed leaders on the whole survive in office over a year less than other leaders before being removed irregularly, a difference that is substantial if insignificant. Restricting the analysis solely to leadership regime changes reveals that the tenure of leaders who come to power in this way is cut short by forcible removal almost exactly two years earlier than for other leaders. This difference is both substantive and significant. The reduction in tenure by irregular removal is even greater—three years—for leaders empowered via institutional regime changes but the variance around this figure is also much broader, rendering the change insignificant. Restoration regime changes are not shown in figure 4.4(a) because the average time to irregular removal for the two restored leaders who lost office in this way—Ethiopia's Haile Selassie and Iran's Mohammad Reza Pahlavi—is over twenty-nine years, a duration that is hard to fit into the scale of the graph. Selassie, restored to power by British intervention in 1941, was overthrown in a military coup in 1974. The shah, returned to office by a U.S.-backed coup in 1953, lasted for more than

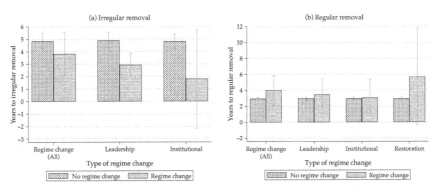

Figure 4.4. Years to irregular and regular removal for foreign-imposed leaders (leader-spell data)

twenty-five years before his ouster in Iran's Islamic Revolution. Restoration regime changes thus significantly increase time to irregular removal, but the small sample size ought to induce caution.

By contrast, regime change and all its subtypes increase leaders' time to regular removal. As indicated by the leftmost bar in figure 4.4(b), regime change increases the number of years leaders survive in office before experiencing a regular removal from three to four. This relationship is significant at the 90 percent level of confidence ($p < 0.08$). The only type of regime change that significantly lengthens leaders' tenure, however, is restoration regime change, which adds about two years and nine months to a ruler's time in power prior to regular removal.[20] Leadership and institutional regime change, although they extend the time that leaders survive until a regular removal by six months and one month, respectively, lack statistical significance.[21]

In sum, the results for time to irregular removal from office are largely consistent with my expectations. Regime change in general and leadership regime change decrease time to irregular removal (in line with H4.1a and H4.2a), restoration regime change increases it (consistent with H4.4a), and institutional regime change has no significant effect (supports H4.3a). Conversely, regime change—and restoration regime change in particular—increases the length of time that leaders enjoy in office prior to regular removal. These results support H4.1b but not H4.4b because I did not expect cases of restoration to increase time to regular removal. Although leadership regime change slightly lengthens leader tenure prior to regular removal, the effect is not significant (contradicts H4.2b). Finally, institutional regime change does not significantly change time to regular removal (supports H4.3b).

COMBINING LEADER TENURE AND TYPE OF REMOVAL

Looking at the probability of regular and irregular removal or average time in office until different forms of removal provides suggestive evidence of the effect of foreign-imposed regime change on leader survival. What is needed, however, is a method that combines the likelihood of removal with duration in office, specifically the probability that a leader will be removed from office in a particular way given that he has not been removed up to that time. A method is also needed that accounts for leaders who remain in power at the time the analysis ends. Survival models are appropriate for this situation, and I will use them below to conduct more sophisticated multivariate tests of the effect of regime change on the hazard of leader removal.[22] Before carrying out that analysis, however, this subsection compares the probability that leaders installed in different types of regime change survive in office before experiencing regular and irregular removal.

Figures 4.5 and 4.6 show Kaplan-Meier survivor functions that visually depict the effect of regime change on the hazard of irregular (figure 4.5) and regular (figure 4.6) leader removal. As above, these figures are derived from the leader-spell data as the figures produced by the leader-year data are similar.[23] Kaplan-Meier curves represent the probability that there are survivors following an event as a function of time. For example, in figure 4.5, the dotted line indicates the probability that foreign-imposed leaders remain in power without being removed irregularly over time. The solid line represents the probability that leaders who were not brought to power by foreign imposition remain in office without suffering irregular removal. The shaded area around each line shows the 95 percent confidence interval for each estimate.

Figure 4.5(a), for example, shows that the probability that foreign-imposed leaders are able to avoid irregular removal from office is strictly smaller than for leaders who come to power in other ways.[24] In figure 4.5(a), the curve for foreign-imposed leaders initially drops steeply. After one year, foreign-imposed leaders have a 75 percent chance of remaining in power. This probability drops steadily until it reaches 50 percent after five years, and 30 percent after ten years. After dropping to roughly 25 percent around the twelve-year mark, it remains there for roughly another fifteen years. The figure also indicates that the chances of survival for foreign-imposed leaders are significantly lower than they are for leaders who gain power in other ways for roughly twenty years after they take office.[25] Leaders who come to power in a foreign-imposed regime change are thus less likely to survive and more likely to suffer an irregular removal from office. This evidence supports H4.1a.

The results for leadership regime change, shown in figure 4.5(b), demonstrate that leaders who gain office through this type of regime change are the least likely to avoid irregular removal. The probability of survival for leaders empowered via leadership regime change is clearly and significantly lower than for other leaders. The trajectory for leadership regime change is similar to regime change as a whole for the first year, with a 75 percent chance of survival, but that for leadership cases drops faster and farther thereafter. By five years it is about 33 percent and at ten years it bottoms out around 10 percent, where it remains for another quarter century. Indeed, only three leaders empowered in leadership regime changes survive more than ten years in office: Abdur Rahman Khan of Afghanistan (1880–1901), Spain's Francisco Franco (1939–75), and Augusto Pinochet of Chile (1973–89). Rahman and Franco died of natural causes while in office, whereas Pinochet departed regularly as part of a transition to democracy. The evidence thus supports H4.2a.

The results for institutional regime change appear in figure 4.5(c) and support H4.3a. Leaders empowered in institutional regime changes are significantly less likely to survive in office than other leaders only for about the first two years. The probability of survival for these leaders quickly drops to about 75 percent, but after another slight decrease, remains flat for roughly ten years, during which time the likelihood of survival for other leaders actually drops below it. Just past the eleven-year mark, the survival probability for leaders brought to power via institutional regime change plunges to about

171

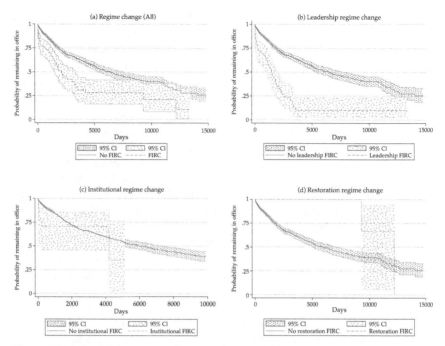

Figure 4.5. Kaplan-Meier survivor functions for types of foreign-imposed regime change and irregular removal from office (leader-spell data)

30 percent, where it remains until all leaders who obtained office in this way are gone. By this time, the only leaders still in office who gained power in this way are West Germany's Konrad Adenauer and Hungary's Mátyás Rákosi. The confidence interval for institutional regime change overlaps with that for other ways of gaining power for all leaders in office more than two years.

Figure 4.5(d) for restoration regime change and irregular removal appears exceedingly strange until one recalls that only two restored leaders lost power in irregular ways: Haile Selassie of Ethiopia and Mohammad Reza Pahlavi of Iran. Until the shah was overthrown in the twenty-sixth year after his return to power, the probability of survival for restored leaders was 100 percent, which is significantly greater than the corresponding probability for other leaders. Once the shah lost power, however, although the likelihood of survival for restored leaders still exceeds that for other leaders, the difference is no longer significant. This result contradicts H4.4a, which predicted that restoration regime change would have no effect on the likelihood of irregular removal. The small number of cases, of course, provides reason for caution.

Figure 4.6 turns to the effect of foreign imposition on the hazard of regular removal from office. The predictions here are that regime change as a whole (H4.1b), and leadership regime change in particular (H4.2b), ought to reduce the risk of regular removal, thereby extending imposed leaders' tenure in office prior to being ousted by regular rules and procedures. In figures 4.6a and 4.6b, therefore, the dotted lines representing the proportion of surviving leaders after regime change should be above the solid line, which signifies the surviving proportion of all other leaders. Institutional and restoration regime changes, by contrast, are not predicted to exert much effect on the hazard of regular removal (H4.3b and H4.4b).

The Kaplan-Meier survivor curves in figure 4.6(a) bear out the expectation from H4.1b that regime change reduces the hazard of regular removal. Initially the curves for foreign-imposed and non-foreign-imposed leaders are almost identical, but after about six months the two lines part ways with foreign-imposed leaders having a strictly higher probability of survival. For example, although the probability of survival for non-foreign-imposed leaders reaches 75 percent after slightly more than a year, it takes about eight more months for foreign-installed leaders to reach this figure. After five years, the probability of survival for foreign-imposed leaders still exceeds 50 percent, whereas that for other leaders is about 30 percent. At the ten-year mark, foreign-imposed leaders' chances of survival rest at 45 percent compared to less than 25 percent for other leaders. The difference in survival rates for foreign and non-foreign-imposed leaders is first significant after just over a year. The confidence intervals touch each other or overlap slightly with gaps of daylight in between out to four years in office; thereafter the difference is exclusively significant for the next twelve years until the two overlap for good between years sixteen and seventeen.[26] These results provide relatively strong support for H4.1b.

Figure 4.6(b) displays the survivor curves for leadership regime change. Here again the opposite relationship is evident than between leadership regime change and irregular removal: the hazard of regular removal is far smaller for leaders installed in leadership regime changes than for other leaders. The curves for the two types of leaders diverge almost immediately. Little more than a year passes before the likelihood that non-foreign-imposed leaders remain in power reaches 75 percent, a figure it takes leaders brought to power in leadership regime changes nearly three times as long to reach, by which time other leaders' chance of remaining in office is fast approaching 50 percent. The curves for the two groups diverge further by the five-year mark: the probability of survival for foreign-imposed leaders (about 67 percent) is roughly double that for other leaders (circa 33 percent). After ten years, this ratio remains and continues until no more individuals installed in leadership regime changes remain in office. This difference begins to be significant after about a year—sooner than for regime change as a whole—and remains so until between years sixteen and seventeen, the same time that regime change loses significance.[27] H4.2b thus also receives relatively strong support.

Figure 4.6(c) lends strong support to H4.3b, which maintains that institutional regime changes exert little influence on the hazard of regular removal

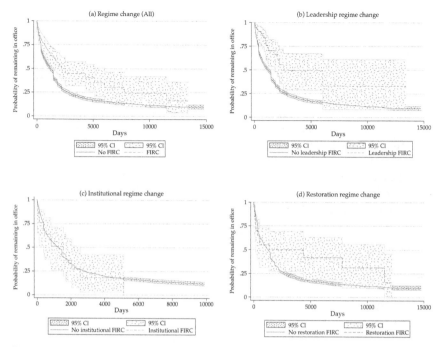

Figure 4.6. Kaplan-Meier survivor functions for foreign-imposed regime change and regular removal from office (leader-spell data)

from office. As shown in the figure, the two curves move in tandem with overlapping confidence intervals until the final leader that gained office via an institutional regime change, Konrad Adenauer, left power via regular procedures in 1963.[28]

Finally, although restoration regime changes reduce the hazard of regular removal, the curves in figure 4.6(d) show that this relationship is of dubious significance. Initially, restored leaders appear to be more likely to experience regular removal: the survival rate for these leaders is lower than for other leaders for about two and a half years. The two curves cross at just about 1,000 days, however, and thereafter restored leaders are always more likely to remain in office than nonrestored leaders, a difference that is significant from years eight to twelve, and again from approximately year fifteen to year twenty-one.[29] Overall, these results largely support H4.4b, which maintains that restoration regime change has no effect on the risk of regular removal.

OVERVIEW OF RESULTS OF COMPETING RISKS ANALYSIS

The quantitative analysis in this chapter employs survival models to estimate the effect of regime change on the hazard of leader removal from office controlling for other factors. These models (also known as duration or hazard models), which were originally developed in the context of medical research, evaluate the hazard that an event occurs—such as irregular removal from office—given that it has not occurred up to that time. Survival models are also able to handle the fact that some leaders never suffer any type of removal and thus remain in office at the end of the study period—in this case, 2004.

In assessing the hazard of irregular leader removal, however, there is an additional complication: leaders can lose power in multiple ways, including by regular procedures or natural death. These alternative means of losing office compete with irregular removal and must be accounted for in estimating the effect of foreign imposition on removal from office. For this reason, I employ a competing risks hazard model, where the competing risks are regular removal and natural death. By contrast, when I estimate the hazard of regular removal, the competing risks are irregular removal and natural death.

Although I defer detailed presentation of the results of these analyses to the chapter appendix, here I briefly summarize the main findings. Figures 4.7 and 4.8 show the substantive effect of regime change on the likelihood of irregular removal in the leader-spell and leader-year datasets without and with control variables, respectively. These effects are shown in the form of hazard ratios, which, unlike regression coefficients, are evaluated relative to one. Hazard ratios greater than one signal a higher likelihood that a leader is removed from office and thus a reduction in tenure. Hazard ratios between zero and one signal the opposite: a lower likelihood of removal and increased tenure. One nice feature of hazard ratios is that they are directly interpretable as substantive effects. A variable with a hazard ratio of 2, for example, doubles the likelihood of removal, whereas one with a hazard ratio of 0.5 halves the likelihood of removal.

In each figure, dots represent hazard ratios and capped lines show the 95 percent confidence interval. The effect of regime change on removal from office is significant when these bars do not cross the bolded line at 1 on the x-axis. In figure 4.7, for example, the first two dots indicate that regime change significantly increases the hazard of irregular leader removal in both the leader-year and leader-spell datasets by a factor of between two and three. The next two dots signify that leadership regime change results in a fourfold increase in the risk of irregular removal, an effect that is also significant. Institutional regime changes are also associated with a doubling of the hazard of irregular removal in both datasets but this effect falls short of statistical significance. Restored leaders, finally, have a lower hazard of irregular removal. This risk is almost zero for restored leaders in the leader-year dataset; the reduction in risk is still large (57 percent) for these leaders in the leader-spell data but fails to achieve significance. These findings, with the possible exception of restoration regime change, support my hypotheses regarding irregular removal.

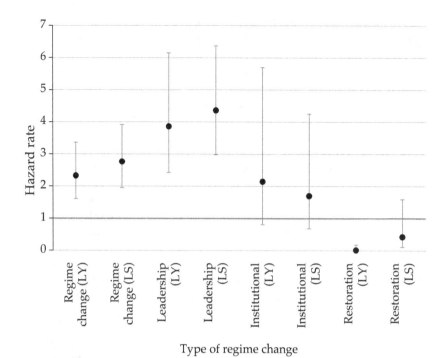

Figure 4.7. Hazard rates of irregular removal after foreign-imposed regime change, no control variables included. LY refers to the leader-year dataset; LS refers to the leader-spell dataset.

The basic pattern shown in figure 4.7 is repeated in figure 4.8, which shows the hazard ratios for regime change and irregular removal when the complete set of control variables from each dataset is included. The size of the effects is attenuated but—with the partial exception of regime change as a whole—not their significance levels. The combined regime change variable increases the hazard of irregular removal about 50 percent but just misses significance at the 95 percent level of confidence in the leader-year dataset.[30] Depending on the dataset, leadership regime change continues to increase the hazard of forcible leader removal by factor of two or more than three. Institutional regime change is insignificant in both datasets whereas restoration regime change lengthens tenure—significantly so in the leader-year data.

Figures 4.9 and 4.10 turn to the results for regular removal. When control variables are excluded, as in figure 4.9, regime change as a whole and leadership regime change each significantly reduce the hazard of regular removal from office in both datasets. All types of regime change taken together cut the risk of regular removal by a little more than half; leadership regime changes reduce this risk by 70 percent. These effects are in line with

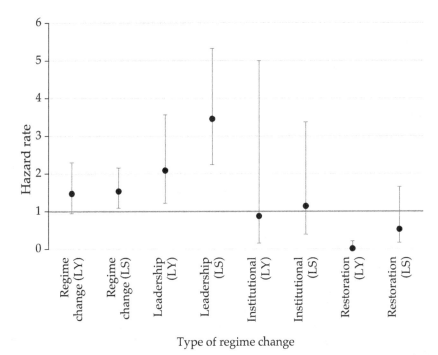

Figure 4.8. Hazard rates of irregular removal after foreign-imposed regime change, control variables included. LY refers to the leader-year dataset; LS refers to the leader-spell dataset.

H4.1b and H4.2b, respectively. Restoration regime changes, by contrast, have essentially no effect on the hazard of regular removal. Institutional regime changes, however, significantly increase the tenure of leaders prior to regular removal in the leader-year dataset, whereas the effect in the leader-spell data is insignificant.[31]

The difference between the effect of institutional regime change on regular leader survival in the two datasets disappears when control variables are added in figure 4.10, as this type of regime change is insignificant in both. Restorations also remain insignificant. Leadership regime changes, on the other hand, continue to reduce the hazard of regular leader removal in both datasets by nearly 70 percent. Regime change as a whole also reduces the risk of regular removal in both datasets, although this effect is significant only in the leader-spell data. The results thus provide solid support my hypotheses on the influence of regime change on regular removal.

CONDITIONAL EFFECTS

As in the analysis of civil war in chapter 3, there is some evidence to suggest that the effect of at least one type of regime change is conditional on

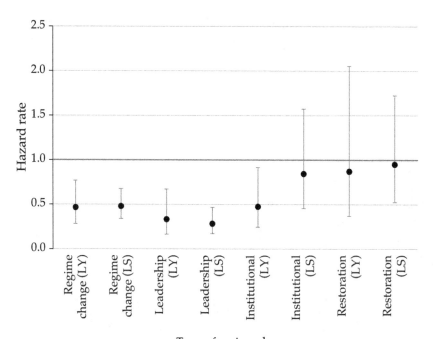

Figure 4.9. Hazard rates of regular removal after foreign-imposed regime change, no control variables included. LY refers to the leader-year dataset; LS refers to the leader-spell dataset.

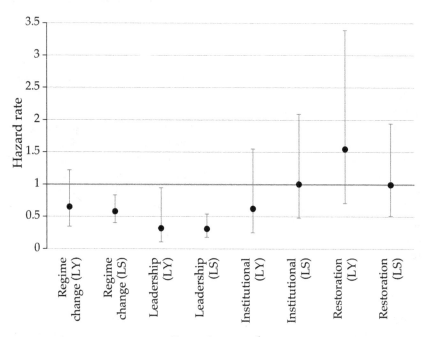

Figure 4.10. Hazard rates of regular removal after foreign-imposed regime change, control variables included. LY refers to the leader-year dataset; LS refers to the leader-spell dataset.

other factors, creating contradictory effects that wash out any overall impact. Institutional regime change, for example, appears to increase the likelihood of irregular removal in relatively underdeveloped states (e.g., the Dominican Republic and Nicaragua)—where I have argued such regime changes are likely to fail—but decreases it in more developed states (e.g., East and West Germany, Japan), where institutional makeovers are likely to succeed.[32] Imposed leaders are removed irregularly after 23 percent of institutional regime changes in the former but only 13 percent in the latter.[33] By contrast, 54 percent of leaders in underdeveloped states lost power regularly but all leaders in developed states left office via regular procedures, suggesting a more orderly process of political transition. These divergent effects hinging on development are lost at the aggregate level.

The effects of restoration regime change on irregular and regular removal also appear to be masked—for a different reason—in my statistical analysis. As noted above, only two out of twenty leaders imposed in regime changes of this kind were removed irregularly. This negative effect, however, tends to be significant in the leader-year dataset, with its larger number of observations, and insignificant in the leader-spell data, where there is only one observation per leader. On the flip side, of the remaining eighteen leaders installed in restoration regime changes, fifteen of them (83 percent) left power through regular, nonviolent procedures (the remaining three remained in office when the analysis ended). The positive effect of restorations on the likelihood of regular removal, however, is never significant; the reason is that two-thirds of all leaders lose power according to constitutional procedures. The difference between the fates of leaders restored to power and everybody else is simply not that great. Although these relationships fail to reach statistical significance owing to the small number of cases involved, they are nevertheless noteworthy and suggestive.

Overall, my hypotheses concerning the effect of regime change on the hazard of regular and irregular removal from office receive strong support from the two different datasets of leaders. Regime change as a whole and leadership regime change in particular increase the chance that leaders fall from power by force and lower the risk that they lose office through nonviolent, regular procedures. Institutional regime change has little effect on either type of removal, although there is some suggestive evidence that irregular removal is more likely to follow such regime changes in the same kinds of places that civil war was likely to occur after institutional impositions. Finally, there is some evidence that restoration regime changes reduce the hazard of irregular removal, but only two restored leaders lost power by force. More details on the statistical analysis underlying these results are available in the appendix, where I also provide evidence that suggests my results are not the product of selection bias. Next, however, I turn to cases of regime change and irregular removal.

The Many Irregular Ways that Foreign-Imposed Leaders Lose Power

In this section I turn my attention to instances of irregular leader removal following regime change to see how well my theory explains real-world cases. As the quantitative section of the chapter makes abundantly clear, foreign-imposed leaders face about a fifty-fifty chance of avoiding a forcible removal from office. Inspection of these cases reveals that the irregular removal of such leaders has numerous causes, some of which are consistent with my theory and some of which are not. The bigger picture that emerges from the historical record, however, is that overthrowing foreign leaders is a risky enterprise. Although it is tempting to try to do regime change "on the cheap" by simply swapping in one leader for another without investing in institutional development, this type of regime change is most likely to end badly for the leader in question. Putting in the time and money—and sometimes stationing sizable military forces in the target country for a lengthy period—to create representative or repressive institutions reduces imposed leaders' exposure to violent removal, but interveners are generally reluctant to do this and may make such an investment only when the stakes are high. Restoring previously overthrown leaders to power appears to be the sole type of regime change that reliably reduces the risk of forcible removal.

I organize the case studies according to the six main ways that foreign-imposed leaders lose power irregularly. Three of these six types are not predicted by my specific arguments but are largely consistent with my broader claims about the risks of regime change. In a few cases, for example, leaders are put in power temporarily by interveners as part of the process of annexing the target state. In cases like these, the installation of a leader is merely a temporary stop on the way to absorbing the target country. In several other cases, leaders placed in power by foreign occupiers are evicted from power when the occupiers are driven from the country, or a regime change carried out by one state triggers a counterintervention by another state that replaces the first imposed leader with a second one. Most of these cases involved countries occupied by Germany during World War II. The primary reason these leaders lost power was that Germany lost the war, but domestic resistance played a small role in countries like Yugoslavia and Greece. These cases are consistent with my argument in the broad sense that regime change is risky, and Yugoslavia and Greece support my theory about military disintegration leading to insurgency, but most of them do not exemplify either of my theoretical mechanisms. In a third group of cases, an intervener is forced to remove multiple leaders in rapid succession until it gets the one it believes will be most responsive to its interests.

The other three types of cases offer support for my argument about the problem of competing principals. First, interveners dissatisfied with the performance of their chosen proxy allow or encourage a coup against him by someone in the target country better suited to fill that role. In a second set of cases, the regime change is successful in the sense that the protégé faithfully implements policies friendly to the intervener, but in doing so runs afoul of domestic interests and triggers a coup or rebellion. Third, in some cases the intervener overthrows a leader it imposed who it initially believed would implement favorable policies but who over time failed to actualize the intervener's interests.

In each of these three types of cases, imposed leaders are victims of the problem of competing principals. In each scenario, the imposed leader runs afoul of either the intervener or his domestic audience for leaning too far toward one or the other. I defer discussion of cases of direct reintervention by dissatisfied patrons to remove recalcitrant protégés to chapter 5 since they fall into the category of postregime change intervener-target conflict. One case I explore in depth there is the experience of Rwanda and Uganda in Zaire, where the two countries ousted Mobutu Sese Seko in 1997 and replaced him with Laurent Kabila. The reason they sought to overthrow Mobutu was that he was providing safe haven for rebel groups to launch cross-border attacks into their respective territories. In Kabila, Rwanda and Uganda believed they had found a leader who would put a stop to this problem. Instead, Kabila found himself painted as a Tutsi puppet and under threat of violent overthrow by domestic opponents. This internal threat prompted him to break with his external patrons and ally with their enemies, most notoriously Rwandan Hutu extremists, many of whom had been complicit in the 1994 Rwandan genocide. In response, Kigali and Kampala initiated another war of regime change to depose Kabila. This time, however, numerous countries intervened to defend Kabila, leading to a protracted and deadly war of attrition that became known as Africa's World War. This conflict lasted for five years and was responsible for the deaths of millions of people. Kabila was eventually assassinated by his bodyguard in January 2001, an act allegedly masterminded by Rwanda.[34]

In the other two types of cases, domestic actors do the work of overthrowing the leader, in one instance in tacit cooperation with dissatisfied patrons, and, in the second instance, acting on their own interests against an imposed leader perceived to be too closely aligned with the intervener. I examine a case of each of these two types: the overthrow of Duong Van Minh in South Vietnam (1964) and Maximilian I of Mexico (1867).

In the final part of the chapter, I consider which factors help imposed leaders survive in office by looking at some outliers for my argument—cases where imposed leaders, such as Francisco Franco and Mohammad Reza Pahlavi, beat the odds and held onto the reins of power for decades.

Regime Change as a Prelude to Annexation

The first type of case in which foreign-imposed leaders are removed from office in an irregular manner consists of instances where leaders are installed as a placeholder whose primary job is to facilitate the target's annexation by the intervener. Occurring in only a handful of instances, these leaders are coded in *Archigos* as leaving office in an irregular manner when annexation occurs.

Regime change followed by annexation was the "Soviet method of conquest" in the Baltics following the signing of the Molotov-Ribbentrop Pact between Germany and the Soviet Union in 1939.[35] In autumn of that year, Stalin demanded—under threat of war—that Estonia, Latvia, and Lithuania sign mutual assistance pacts with the Soviet Union that permitted the Soviets to station Red Army troops on their soil. These tiny nations, faced with the overwhelming might of their powerful neighbor, had little choice but to comply.[36] In mid-June 1940, Moscow further demanded that these nations form pro-Soviet governments and submit to Soviet military occupation. The Soviet ultimatum to Estonia, for example, delivered on June 15, required that "a government be established in Estonia that would be capable and willing to warrant honest execution of the Soviet-Estonian mutual assistance pact."[37] The next day, the Soviets similarly demanded "the establishment of a new Latvian government and the free entry of Soviet troops into Latvia."[38] The three Baltic republics were quickly occupied by Red Army units and their leaders either fled or were arrested by the Soviets, who appointed new leaders to oversee elections in which communist victory was assured. In Estonia, Stalin sent Politburo member Andrei A. Zhdanov to direct the process. Zhdanov personally selected Johannes Vares as the new prime minister and all but one member of Vares's cabinet.[39] Elections in mid-July returned a communist-packed Chamber of Deputies, which immediately declared its intention to join the Soviet Union. Estonia became part of the USSR on August 6. The process proceeded nearly identically in Latvia and Lithuania.[40] The Soviet-appointed leaders of these countries thus lost power irregularly, but their removal was simply a by-product of the Soviet plan to first subordinate and then annex these nations. Irregular removals of imposed leaders like these are part of the process of annexation and thus not relevant to my theory.[41]

Foreign-Imposed Leaders Removed by Other Foreign Powers

A second way that foreign-imposed leaders are irregularly removed is when they are toppled not by the country that brought them to power, but by a different foreign state. The most common way this happens is that a leader who was imposed by foreign occupiers loses office when the occupiers are defeated and driven from the country.

This type of irregular removal was a frequent occurrence in German-occupied countries during World War II. The Germans did not have a uniform approach to governing conquered territories. Some countries, such as Poland and Czechoslovakia, were annexed and incorporated into the Third Reich.[42] Most of Hitler's other conquests in Europe, however, were governed either by German officials or German-backed puppet regimes. In Norway, unoccupied France, Greece, and part of Yugoslavia, the Germans chose to rule through local collaborators, the most famous of whom—Vidkun Quisling—became synonymous with the word traitor. In the Benelux countries, by contrast, Nazi officials ruled directly: Arthur Seyss-Inquart in the Netherlands; Alexander von Falkenhausen in Belgium; and Gustav Simon in Luxembourg. In Denmark, the Germans even allowed the country's democratic government to remain in power until August 1943, when it was dissolved in the midst of growing resistance. Denmark was placed under martial law and governed by SS officer Werner Best for the remainder of the war.

As Germany was progressively forced out of these conquered territories in 1944 and 1945, the leaders placed in office by the Third Reich also fell—for the most part irregularly—from power. In western Europe, Nazi administrators fled before the advancing Allied armies; these leaders are coded as being removed in (restoration) foreign-imposed regime changes.[43] In Norway, Quisling surrendered to his countrymen and was tried, convicted, and executed. In Yugoslavia, the German puppet Milan Nedić fled to Austria as the Wehrmacht withdrew in October 1944 but was arrested and returned to Belgrade by the British in 1946, where he committed suicide while in prison. The last of the three Greek collaborationist prime ministers—Ioannis Rallis—was tried and convicted for treason and died in prison.

A different twist on this story is provided by the experience of Hungary during World War II. Hungary, which was led by the fiercely anticommunist Miklós Horthy, was a revisionist power in the interwar period, and through its alliance with Nazi Germany it regained several territories it had forfeited after World War I. Hitler persuaded Horthy to send Hungarian troops to participate in the invasion of the Soviet Union, but after the destruction of the Hungarian Second Army at Stalingrad, Horthy began to consider seeking an armistice with the Allies. Sensing the growing recalcitrance of his ally, Hitler ordered the invasion and occupation of Hungary in March 1944. Horthy was forced to appoint a prime minister friendly to Germany and acquiesce in the deportation of Hungary's Jewish population. Horthy, however, secretly opened negotiations with the Soviets and on October 15 announced that an armistice had been concluded. Hitler responded by overthrowing Horthy in Operation Panzerfaust and installing Ferenc Szálasi, the head of the fascist Arrow Cross movement, as leader of Hungary. Szálasi's tenure would not last long, however, for the Red Army was already within one hundred miles of Budapest by late September, and reached the suburbs of the capital by early November. Szálasi fled the city on December 9 as the Soviet siege tightened; after the war he was captured in Germany and returned to Hungary, where he was convicted of treason and hanged on March 12, 1946.[44]

In other cases, a regime change enacted by one state provokes a counter-intervention and a second regime change by another state. Cyprus in 1974 provides a good example. Shortly after taking control of the Greek military junta in late 1973, General Dimitrios Ioannidis—a strong supporter of *enosis* (union) of Greece and Cyprus—decided to overthrow the Cypriot president, Archbishop Makarios.[45] Despite fears of Turkish intervention expressed by other members of the junta, on July 15, 1974, the Cypriot National Guard, led by officers from the Greek Army, instigated a coup that brought Nikos Sampson to power in a leadership regime change.[46] Sampson quickly "declared his intention of bringing the island into union with Greece."[47] The Turkish government perceived these events to represent an intolerable threat to the Turkish minority on the island. Turkish prime minister Bülent Ecevit ordered a Turkish invasion, which commenced on July 20. As a result of the invasion, Sampson resigned and was replaced in an acting capacity by Makarios's designated constitutional successor, the president of the Cypriot House of Representatives, Glafkos Klerides. Because Makarios subsequently returned to the island to serve out his term, I code the Turkish intervention as a restoration regime change. Days after this disastrous reversal, the Greek junta collapsed; Ioannidis was later arrested and imprisoned for his role in the 1967 military coup.

It is important to recognize, however, that coming to power during a military occupation does not necessarily imply that a leader will be removed by irregular means. Some countries under foreign occupation have multiple leaders who are appointed by the occupying country or who come to power through domestic processes, both of which are considered to be regular forms of removal. A good example of the former is the succession of US officials placed in charge of the occupation of Iraq in 2003 related in chapter 3. The head of US Central Command, General Tommy Franks, was initially responsible for administering Iraq after the fall of Saddam Hussein. After about two weeks, Franks was superseded by retired general Jay Garner, the head of the OHRA, the body created by the Pentagon tasked with overseeing a rapid handover of power to Iraqis. As Iraq sank into anarchy in the weeks following Saddam's overthrow, however, and it became clear that a quick transfer of authority was not a viable option, Garner was in turn replaced by Ambassador Paul Bremer in May 2003. Bremer became head of the CPA. A year later, Bremer departed after handing over power to Ayad Allawi, who had been selected by the Iraqi Governing Council to serve as interim prime minister. Although each of these leaders is coded as coming to power by foreign imposition in *Archigos*, all are coded as leaving office in a regular manner.

Occupied nations also sometimes have numerous leaders who enter and exit office by regular procedures. Greece, for example, had three collaborationist prime ministers who served during the Italo-German occupation. The first, General Georgios Tsolakoglou, volunteered for the post in April 1941 before Athens had even fallen. Eighteen months later, according to historian Mark Mazower, an "exhausted and disillusioned" Tsolakoglou was "allowed to leave" after making "several exorbitant demands as the price of his remaining in office."[48] His successor, the distinguished medical doctor Konstantinos Logothetopoulos, lasted six months before the Germans replaced his "floundering" government with one led by Ioannis Rallis.[49] Neither Tsolakoglou nor Logothetopoulos was forced from office by threats or violence, and thus I code their departures as regular. Similarly, in Albania after its conquest by Italy in 1939, a veritable parade of politicians followed Shefqet Bej Vërlaci into the prime minister's chair until the communist Enver Hoxha consolidated power after German withdrawal in 1944. Only the last of these leaders, Ibrahim Bej Biçakçiu, who lost office owing to the partisan victory, was removed in an irregular fashion.

Although the ouster of imposed leaders by foreign powers resulting from a lost war or a counterintervention is a real hazard for regime changers, it is not one emphasized by my theory, which focuses on the dilemma that imposed leaders find themselves in when they are asked to implement patron-friendly policies that are often unpopular with domestic audiences. It is, however, consistent with my broader argument that regime change is a risky enterprise.

Serial Regime Changes to Find an Acceptable Leader

The third way that foreign-imposed leaders are removed irregularly consists of instances in which interveners overthrow one leader only to see him replaced by an equally unacceptable successor, who is then also removed by the same intervener. Such cases are usually the result of compellence or covert action rather than invasion because in the two former approaches the intervener does not necessarily impose a successor, since its forces are not directly present in the country. I have already discussed one such case earlier in this chapter: the US-backed assassination of the Dominican dictator Rafael Trujillo. In early 1961, the CIA provided weapons to Dominican dissidents hoping to kill Trujillo. They succeeded on May 30 but failed to seize power; Ramfis Trujillo, the dictator's son, soon returned from Paris to take his father's place. It took a threat of invasion by John F. Kennedy in November to drive the Trujillos from power for good and bring about leadership more acceptable to Washington.[50] A second example is provided by the US ouster of Nicaraguan strongman José Santos Zelaya in 1909 discussed in chapter 3. Liberal Zelaya fled Nicaragua in the face of a US-backed Conservative rebellion, but was succeeded in office by another Liberal, José Madriz. This was not what Washington had in mind, and so US forces continued to support the rebellion until Madriz, too, was driven from office.

Forty-five years later, the United States similarly removed multiple Guatemalan leaders in quick succession. The primary target, as elaborated in chapter 3, was President Jacobo Árbenz, who was viewed by US officials as a communist sympathizer. The United States obtained Árbenz's ouster by supporting a small rebellion led by Carlos Castillo Armas but more importantly by convincing the officer corps of the Guatemalan Army that if the army defeated Armas, the United States might invade. Árbenz agreed to resign on June 27, 1954, but—much to the consternation of US ambassador John Peurifoy—Colonel Carlos Enrique Díaz, chief of the armed forces, took power at the head of a three-man military junta and promised to continue to resist Castillo Armas's invasion. According to historian Piero Gleijeses, however, "Díaz was doomed. The United States had not launched Castillo Armas's invasion in order to hand the presidency to a friend of Arbenz. Washington intended to impose its own man, a man with unblemished anticommunist credentials, a man who would not urge communist leaders to seek asylum, but who would destroy them."[51] US officials in Guatemala City moved immediately to oust Díaz, who was dragged from his bed in the middle of the night by two CIA officers and told that he would have to resign because he was "just not convenient for the requirements of American foreign policy."[52] Díaz resigned less than twenty-four hours later and was replaced by Colonel Elfego Monzón, a stronger anticommunist, at the head of a second junta. Monzón then traveled to San Salvador on July 2 for talks with Castillo Armas but he, too, was reluctant to hand over power. Peurifoy duly flew to the El Salvadoran capital to "crack some heads together," in the memorable words of secretary of state John Foster Dulles, and an agreement was forged that eased Monzón out of power.[53] On July 7, the United States got its man in Guatemala when Castillo Armas replaced Monzón as president.

A final case not explored thus far occurred in Costa Rica in 1919. After the onset of World War I, Costa Rica began to feel the grim economic effects of the loss of its principal coffee export market, Germany. Costa Rica's president, Alfredo González Flores, instituted a series of drastic measures to deal with the crisis but was overthrown by his minster of war Federico Tinoco Granados in January 1917. Unfortunately for Tinoco, US president Woodrow Wilson, upon assuming office, had proclaimed a policy of nonrecognition of regimes established by force in the region, to discourage such takeovers.[54] Wilson applied this policy to the Tinoco regime and maintained it despite the efforts of various US officials to persuade him of Tinoco's popularity and legitimacy. In response to growing domestic unrest, the assassination of his brother, as well as the US demand for his ouster, coupled with the arrival of a US warship in the Pacific port of Límon, Tinoco resigned and fled the country, handing over power to his vice-president, Juan Bautista Quirós Segura.[55] Wilson, however, was not placated by this move and demanded that Quirós also resign, a demand that was backed by the arrival of another US gunboat, the USS *Denver.* Quirós similarly complied, and after a brief interim period, new elections were held and Julio Acosta García was elected.[56] The Wilson administration eventually recognized the new government.[57]

Cases like these resemble regime changes perpetrated as a prelude to annexation discussed above in that they occur as part of the process of the intervener achieving its desired end state. The final objective is simply different: a friendly regime in an independent state rather than the annexation of that state. Yet these cases are congruent with my argument in the sense that the intervener targets these leaders because they are unable or unwilling to serve the intervener's interests. The intervener thus seeks their removal in search of a leader or regime who will.

Leaders Removed by Domestic Foes with the Intervener's Blessing: South Vietnam's Duong Van Minh

The fourth way that foreign-imposed leaders lose power irregularly occurs when interveners who are dissatisfied with their protégés and have knowledge of plots against them by domestic opponents allow those plots to go forward—or even encourage and support them. These leaders are victims of the problem of competing principals. Although they are removed by domestic actors, their sin was not that they favored domestic interests at the expense of the patron's. Rather, these leaders failed to implement their patron's preferred policies, prompting the patron to tolerate—and in some cases promote—domestic challenges to their protégé by individuals it perceived as more likely to follow directions. Examples include Cirilo Antonio Rivarola, Paraguay's first president after the disastrous War of the Triple Alliance (1864–70), ousted in an irregular parliamentary maneuver with the connivance of his Brazilian patrons in 1871; and David Dacko of the Central African Republic, abandoned by his French supporters and overthrown in a military coup in 1979.[58]

In this section, I chronicle in detail the problem of competing principals at work in the coup against Duong Van Minh, the South Vietnamese general who overthrew Ngo Dinh Diem with American support in November 1963—an instance of leadership regime change. Washington strongly backed Diem after he became president of the newly formed Republic of Vietnam, born out of the Geneva Accords that ended French rule in Indochina in 1954. The United States supported his regime against an insurgency first through the US Military Assistance Advisory Group (MAAG) and later via its successor, Military Assistance Command Vietnam (MACV). By 1963, however, relations between Diem and the US government had become so estranged that the Kennedy administration decided to back South Vietnamese officers seeking to remove Diem.

US officials did not know much about Minh's views but assumed that as a military man he would favor vigorously prosecuting the war against the Viet Cong (and North Vietnam). Indeed, Minh and his colleagues on the Military Revolutionary Council (MRC) initially pledged to continue many of Diem's initiatives, but it soon became clear that the preferences of the new leaders in Saigon diverged markedly from those of their American patrons in a number of areas. As a consequence of these disagreements, Washington quickly soured on its new protégés in Vietnam. When US officials in Saigon became aware of a new coup plot against the Minh regime, they did not report it to Minh or try to discourage it, and some may have abetted it. On January 30, 1964, a coup led by General Nguyen Khanh overthrew Minh and the MRC. After several more coups contributed to the chaos in South Vietnam, the United States ultimately decided to intervene in the war to save its client state.

ORIGINS AND CONDUCT OF REGIME CHANGE

The immediate cause of Diem's downfall was the Buddhist Crisis that began in May 1963. On May 7, Buddhists in Hue celebrated the birthday of the Buddha; one way they showed their devotion was to hang Buddhist flags. Unfortunately, a seldom-observed ordinance forbade the display of religious flags, which local officials were ordered to enforce despite the fact that Catholic flags had adorned the city just a week before to commemorate the installation of one of the president's brothers as archbishop.[59] In response to a Buddhist rally the day after the police removed the flags, police were called to the scene to disperse the protesters. In the melee that followed, at least seven people were killed. Accounts differ regarding how they died, but Diem refused to accept government responsibility (he blamed the deaths on a Viet Cong grenade), punish any officials, or compensate the victims' families.[60] The crisis escalated quickly and burst into international headlines when a Buddhist monk, Thich Quang Duc, burned himself alive in a busy Saigon intersection on June 11. The president's sister-in-law, Madame Nhu, provoked outrage by deriding Quang Duc's death as a "barbecue," telling one interviewer, "Let them burn, and we shall clap our hands."[61] The United States pressured Diem to meet the Buddhists' demands over the summer of 1963, going so far as to threaten to end American support for his regime, but although Diem made some superficial conciliatory gestures, he insisted that the Buddhist protests were a communist plot and continued to repress them.[62]

The event that precipitated a change in US policy toward Diem was the government's attack on Buddhist pagodas across South Vietnam in the early morning hours of August 21. At the recommendation of the South Vietnamese Army (the Army of the Republic of Vietnam, or ARVN), which wanted expanded authority to return several thousand Buddhist monks gathered in Saigon to the provinces, Diem had declared martial law the day before. Diem and his brother (and close adviser) Ngo Dinh Nhu decided to take advantage of the situation to suppress the Buddhist protest once and for all. Special forces under Nhu's authority, some dressed in army uniforms to implicate it in the violence, stormed pagodas across the country. Saigon's Xa Loi pagoda was ransacked and at least four hundred people were arrested.[63] The violence at Hue's Dieu De and Tu Dam pagodas—where monks and nuns resisted the attackers—was even worse.[64] More than 1,400 people were arrested.[65] According to one account, Diem understood that the Americans would be unhappy about his repressive actions but assumed that—although they might complain—US officials "would eventually recognize that there was no alternative to the present government in Saigon. They would continue to sponsor their Diem experiment. They always did."[66]

This time Diem was wrong. In South Vietnam, key generals were unhappy that Nhu had pinned the blame on the army for the pagoda raids and argued that it was imperative to get rid of the president's brother. General Le Van Kim, for example, told USAID official Rufus Phillips on August 23 that if the "US took [a] clear stand against [the] Nhus and in support of Army action to remove them from government, the Army (with the exception of Colonel Tung) would unite in support of such an action and would be able to carry it out."[67] Unfortunately, the generals also believed that it would be "practically impossible" to persuade Diem to part with the Nhus "because of the special positions they hold."[68] New US ambassador Henry Cabot Lodge, having only just arrived in Saigon, counseled against supporting a coup, which he thought at this point "would seem to be a shot in the dark."[69]

Anti-Diem officials in Washington, however, had decided that the time had come to act. On August 24, assistant secretary of state for Far Eastern affairs Roger Hilsman, with assistance from Averell Harriman and Michael Forrestal, drafted a memo for transmission to Ambassador Lodge that essentially endorsed a coup in Saigon: "US Government cannot tolerate [a] situation in which power lies in Nhu's hands. Diem must be given [a] chance to rid himself of Nhu and his coterie and replace them with [the] best military and political personalities available. If, in spite of all of your efforts, Diem remains obdurate and refuses, then we must face the possibility that Diem himself cannot be preserved." The cable went on to instruct Lodge to tell the generals that the "US would find it impossible to continue [to] support GVN [Government of Vietnam] militarily and economically" unless Nhu was removed.[70] Composed on a Saturday in August when the president and other key officials were away from Washington, this cable was condemned by some as "an egregious end run" by officials opposed to Diem.[71] Although the president himself signed off on the cable before it was sent to Saigon, it nevertheless became the subject of a bitter bureaucratic battle in Washington that unfolded over the last week of August.[72] Whether or not they supported a coup against Diem, however, all participants agreed that the Nhus had to be ousted from Diem's regime.[73] Lodge fully concurred with the cable and pushed back against opponents of a coup in Washington, replying a few days later, "We are launched on a course from which there is no respectable turning back: The overthrow of the Diem government."[74]

While the Kennedy administration debated whether to support a coup against Diem, the plotting in Saigon seemingly stopped at the end of August, cut off by ringleader General Duong Van Minh, who told his US contact that the generals were not ready. This was only a temporary pause, however, for the Kennedy administration began sending the kinds of signals the generals had been looking for to persuade them that Washington was serious about a change in leadership in Saigon.[75] In a television interview with Walter Cronkite on September 2, for example, the president opined that "I don't think that unless a greater effort is made by the government to win popular support that the war can be won out there." When asked if there was still time for the regime in Saigon to rally public support, Kennedy replied, in a clear reference to Nhu, "I do. With changes in policy *and perhaps with personnel* I think it can. If it doesn't make those changes, I would think that the chances of winning it would not be very good."[76] Kennedy then sent secretary of defense Robert McNamara and chairman of the Joint Chiefs of Staff General Maxwell Taylor to Vietnam. In their report, submitted on October 3, they argued that the "military campaign has made great progress and continues to progress" but they were not nearly so sanguine about the political situation.[77] The report recommended a series of steps to pressure the Diem government to improve, including continued suspension of the Commodity Import Program as well as cutting off funding to Nhu's Special Forces.[78]

These steps may have seemed moderate in Washington, but they reverberated strongly in Saigon. According to George Kahin, "Whether or not Kennedy's two senior military advisers realized it, the selective pressures they recommended, and which the president approved on October 5, persuaded the wavering generals that the United States was indeed encouraging them to act against Diem and Nhu."[79] The authors of the so-called Pentagon Papers concur: "While Diem's reaction to the tough new American policy was hostile, the senior South Vietnamese generals, predictably, interpreted the new policy as a green light for a coup. Plotting was reactivated almost immediately, if indeed it had ever been completely dormant."[80]

A number of scholars have argued that a crucial factor that reignited US interest in a coup in autumn 1963 was the possibility that Diem and Nhu would cut ties with the United States and negotiate an agreement with Hanoi.[81] US government sources reported that, faced with US pressure to reform, Nhu had reopened talks with the National Liberation Front (NLF) and North Vietnam. The State Department's Bureau of Intelligence and

Research, for example, reported in mid-September that Nhu had "claimed privately that should United States aid be cut he would seek help elsewhere. Should that fail, Nhu asserts he would negotiate a settlement with Hanoi."[82] The CIA's Chester Cooper reached a similar conclusion, as did the State Department's William Sullivan, who wrote to Roger Hilsman that Nhu would "'eject' the United States 'by a deal with North Vietnam when he feels he has adequate means to continue in power without its assistance.'"[83] Although it is plausible that Nhu's peace feelers to Hanoi were primarily a means of pressuring Washington to resume full support for his brother's regime, Fredrik Logevall argues that it was hard for U.S. officials to ignore the "possibility that Diem and Nhu might be abandoning the war effort altogether in favor of a negotiated settlement."[84] Given that US policymakers from Kennedy on down were "nearly unanimous" that the United States must remain in Vietnam, the prospect that the Ngo brothers might be pursuing a negotiated settlement between North and South that would force a US withdrawal weighed in favor of overthrowing them.[85]

While cables flew back and forth across the Pacific in late October between officials in Washington demanding the prerogative to call off a coup that appeared unlikely to succeed and Lodge's protestations from Saigon that it was too late to turn back, the generals struck.[86] Having finally gained the allegiance of General Ton That Dinh, the military governor of Saigon, the generals, led by Minh, executed a brief but violent coup on the night of November 1–2.[87] The only hitch was that Diem and Nhu escaped from the presidential palace before it was captured and had to be tracked down at a Catholic church in the Cholon district of Saigon. Although most of the coup leaders favored exiling the Ngo brothers, Diem and Nhu were murdered in an armored personnel carrier on the ride from their hideout to military headquarters, supposedly on the orders of Minh.[88]

A NEW REGIME DOESN'T SOLVE THE PROBLEM: INTEREST ASYMMETRY BETWEEN SAIGON AND WASHINGTON

When the new government was unveiled on November 5, Minh became head of a twelve-man military junta, the MRC. Initially there were high hopes for the regime, which seemed committed to democratic reform and, even better, appeared dedicated to prosecuting the war more effectively.[89] The MRC, according to Mark Moyar, promised that "military operations would be intensified and the strategic hamlets would be strengthened by implementing the modifications that the Americans advocated, such as a slower pace of expansion and reduced reliance on forced labor."[90] As Logevall writes, "U.S. officials assumed that because it comprised military men, the junta . . . would be implacably anti-communist and opposed to any form of compromise with the National Liberation Front (NLF) and Hanoi. They also assumed that the new government would provide a more aggressive military challenge to the Vietcong and accept a greater American direction of the fighting." "Very soon," Logevall continues, "it became clear that these American assumptions were mistaken."[91]

One immediate problem was that the military situation in South Vietnam—which numerous reports had previously described in optimistic terms—began to deteriorate rapidly under the MRC. Predictably, the Viet Cong reacted to the coup by stepping up its armed attacks, which reached record levels during the second week of November and remained at a high level throughout the month.[92] The Minh government's reaction was handicapped by the MRC's wholesale replacement of Diem-appointed officials at the province level and below.[93] It also emerged after the coup that the military situation beforehand was not nearly as rosy as it had previously appeared. Battlefield reports that had been ignored by McNamara and Taylor in the October 3 summary of their visit to South Vietnam showed a remarkable increase in VC military activity dating back to August. This "dramatic deterioration in the military situation," as Kaiser puts it, was confirmed later in October by a paper by the State Department's Bureau of Intelligence and Research.[94]

Another issue was that Minh appeared to possess little talent for governing. According to Stanley Karnow, for example, Minh "was a model of lethargy, lacking both the skill and the inclination to govern . . . he preferred to play tennis and tend to his orchids and exotic birds than to preside over tedious meetings and unravel bureaucratic tangles."[95] Michael Forrestal, one of the key figures in composing the cable that sealed Diem's fate in August 1963, later summarized Minh's most important qualifications for office as follows: he was "tall, a good tennis player, and spoke English." Former CIA Saigon station chief William Colby described Minh as having "a head of solid ivory," and the president of South Vietnam's National Assembly called Minh "naive, shallow, lazy, and empty-headed. He was principally interested in tennis as well as his orchid garden and aquarium."[96] In other words, the choice of Minh to govern after Diem's removal suffered from adverse selection.[97]

Even more serious, however, it quickly emerged that the Minh government had very different ideas about how to approach the war than did Washington. According to George Kahin, "Within less than two months after General Minh's group took power . . . senior Washington policymakers had become deeply disappointed at their unresponsiveness to U.S. prescriptions in the military field."[98] Five key areas of divergence—what my theory terms interest asymmetries or preference divergences—appeared. First, the junta advocated political rather than military solutions and resisted pressure from US officials to escalate its level of military activity. Minh and his colleagues believed that the NLF was mostly noncommunist and hence favored compromise and negotiations to peel away individuals and groups who had joined it because they opposed Diem.[99] Minh's prime minister, Nguyen Ngoc Tho, sought to persuade the NLF to enter a "government of reconciliation" and eventually to participate in elections.[100] The assumption that military men would favor military solutions was thus shown to be false.

Second, Minh refused to rebuild strategic hamlets that had been destroyed or overrun by the VC, and further planned to dismantle all strategic hamlets across South Vietnam.[101] "Minh officials," according to Logevall, "felt certain that the hamlets only exacerbated dissatisfaction in the countryside."[102] In their place, Kahin notes, the junta began to implement a new rural development plan that would "permit peasants to remain in their scattered homes" near their ancestral grave sites and under their own local leaders.[103] That the initial rollout of the government's plan in Long An province in January 1964 proved successful in reestablishing Saigon's control further "strengthened its conviction that the new approach should supersede the strategic hamlet system."[104]

Third, the Minh regime resisted US proposals to bomb North Vietnam. Shortly after Diem's death, secretary of defense Robert McNamara began advocating stronger military measures against the North and discussed a bombing campaign with Minh during his visit to Saigon in December.[105] The following month, in a preview of the Rolling Thunder campaign that would begin in 1965, the Pentagon, according to Kaiser, "approved a three-phase plan for pressure against North Vietnam" that "involved the infliction of 'increasing punishment upon North Vietnam . . . to create pressures, which may convince the North Vietnamese leadership, in its own self-interest, to desist from its aggressive policies.'"[106] According to Kahin, however, "Saigon leaders . . . quickly rebuffed these efforts."[107] Minh argued that aerial bombing of the North would kill innocent civilians and forfeit the South's claim to be fighting a just, defensive war. Bombing would also have little effect on the military situation in the South and cost the regime public support at home.[108]

Fourth, the junta vigorously opposed US efforts to increase the number of advisory personnel in ARVN units and US attempts to take greater control over military operations. The Minh government also requested that US military advisers, who under Diem were present down to the battalion level, not be permitted below the regimental level. The junta believed, according to Kahin, that the ubiquity of American advisers "would have serious adverse political consequences, robbing their government of legitimacy in the eyes of the population and undercutting its nationalist credentials. . . . Aware of the stigma of foreign dependency attached to the previous government, they wished to decrease the visibility of Americans."[109] The new regime similarly rejected a suggestion from US officials to place American advisers in South Vietnamese villages, arguing that doing so "would play into the hand of the VC and make the Vietnamese officials look like lackeys."[110]

Finally, US officials in Saigon and Washington worried that the Minh junta would conclude an agreement with the NLF for the neutralization of South Vietnam. Ever since the junta had taken power, reports had circulated that certain of its members were sympathetic to a neutralist solution.[111] Although Minh publicly denied it, his prime minister Tho later admitted, "We would have striven for a neutral government."[112] Support for a negotiated settlement and neutralization was at the same time growing both in the United States and around the globe. Prominent Democratic senators, including majority leader Mike Mansfield, for example, endorsed a political solution to the Vietnam problem in December.[113] French president Charles de Gaulle had already proposed reunification and neutralization as the best solution for Vietnam, and on November 30 Cambodian president Norodom Sihanouk, who also favored the neutralization of South Vietnam, proposed an international conference to consider the same status for Cambodia.

The United States government, however, as historians like Fredrik Logevall and David Kaiser have documented, was fundamentally opposed to a political solution in Vietnam. According to Logevall, the possibility that the Minh junta might have been entertaining negotiations and neutrality "struck fear into American officials. The notion of a negotiated settlement between the Saigon regime and the NLF or Hanoi was anathema to them, and they were determined to prevent it."[114] President Lyndon Baines Johnson, in Kaiser's words, "never seriously considered the alternatives of neutralization and withdrawal."[115] Nor was hostility to neutralization limited to LBJ, as evidenced by the vigorous attacks leveled against this option by administration figures like McGeorge Bundy, Walt Rostow, and Robert McNamara.[116]

To investigate the state of military and political affairs in South Vietnam, the new president sent McNamara on yet another fact-finding trip to Saigon in December 1963. McNamara's conclusions could not have been starker: "The situation is very disturbing. Current trends, unless reversed in the next 2–3 months, will lead to neutralization at best and more likely to a Communist-controlled state. The new government," McNamara continued, "is the greatest source of concern. It is indecisive and drifting." Newly installed province chiefs "are receiving little or no direction," and "military operations . . . are not being effectively directed because the generals are so preoccupied with essentially political affairs."[117] CIA director John McCone concurred with McNamara's assessment, writing in his own report that "there is no organized government in South Vietnam at this time. The Military Revolutionary Committee (MRC) is in control, but strong leadership and administrative procedures are lacking."[118] Ambassador Lodge expressed similar concerns around the same time: "I am disconcerted by an apparent lack of drive in conducting the war. The members of the junta give me splendid clear-cut answers and say all of the right things, yet nothing much seems to happen."[119] Unfortunately for Minh, Kahin notes that following these late December reports, "American disillusionment with the military policies and performance of Minh's government mounted. During

January [1964] it became even more evident that the military and political objectives of the Johnson administration differed more fundamentally from those of the Saigon regime than they had from Diem's."[120]

SOUTH VIETNAMESE DOMESTIC OPINION AND THE PROBLEM OF COMPETING PRINCIPALS

Why did Minh and his colleagues on the MRC have such divergent preferences on so many policies from their patrons in Washington? Although evidence on public attitudes in South Vietnam at the time is unsystematic and impressionistic, what is known strongly suggests that ordinary people were sick of the war and supported efforts to make peace. According to Logevall's account, for example, the idea of neutralism in South Vietnam had little to do with where the country stood in the global conflict between the American and Soviet camps. Rather it was "a less political and less coherent attitude springing from weariness of war and lengthy suffering at the hands of both sides."[121] The views of the British ambassador to Saigon support Logevall's assessment: "Intense and increasingly hopeless war-weariness certainly prevails among the great bulk of the peasantry, who ache to be free of the increasing demands made on them by both Government and the Viet Cong. . . . The peasants do not want Communism, but if the Government cannot protect them they will support the Communists."[122] "Neutralism," Logevall summarizes, "had gained significant appeal among many in the war-weary general population, among elements of the Buddhist leadership, and evidently among some in the Minh government."[123]

George Kahin provides further evidence of the pacific mood among the South Vietnamese peasantry in late 1963 as well as the role of adverse selection in producing preference divergence between Washington and its new protégé in Saigon. The Americans simply assumed that because Minh and colleagues were military men that they would favor military solutions. Yet, as Kahin writes, "The administration had been misled by its own wishful thinking, its scanty knowledge of the political views of Minh and his key lieutenants, and an inability to appreciate how profound and widespread was the desire for an end to the fighting among South Vietnamese."[124] Even though key policymakers in the Kennedy administration, including the president himself, backed Minh as the coup leader and presumably the head of South Vietnam's next government, they failed to ascertain his views on crucial matters such as whether he favored a negotiated or military settlement to the conflict.

Officials in the new Johnson administration were aware of neutralist sentiment in South Vietnam and greatly feared it. Johnson and his team, for example, understood that a "fundamental concern" in their relations with Saigon "was the antiwar pressure from within South Vietnam, which they feared might impel the new government toward an accommodation with the NLF."[125] Walt Rostow, for example, warned in a memo in January 1964 "of the rise in South Vietnam of a popular mood, spreading into the bureaucracy and the armed forces . . . that a neutralized South Vietnam is the only way out."[126] Neutralization, of course, would mean the end of the US military presence in South Vietnam, after which, according to Kahin, "no Saigon government could hope to resist popular pressures for an end to the fighting and negotiation of a compromise political settlement with the NLF."[127]

In short, Minh was in the grip of the problem of competing principals. His US patrons were pressuring him to take a number of steps—emphasizing military over political solutions to the conflict; rebuilding and expanding strategic hamlets; bombing North Vietnam; giving the Americans increased control over the war effort—that promised to be unpopular with the war-weary South Vietnamese public. In this instance, perhaps because Minh believed the Americans would not seek to replace him so quickly after sanctioning the overthrow of Diem, Minh resisted these pressures and chose a course he believed would resonate more with South Vietnamese and be more productive in ending the war. That course did not sit well with his American patrons.

ANOTHER COUP

On January 30, 1964, Minh was deposed in a bloodless coup by General Nguyen Khanh.[128] Khanh was resentful that he had not been better rewarded for his role in deposing Diem—he had been excluded from the MRC and transferred to command of I Corps in the far north along the border with North Vietnam—and thus had his own motives for opposing Minh's regime. Khanh began spreading rumors that certain "pro-French and pro-neutralist" members of the junta, including Generals Don, Kim, and Xuan, were plotting a coup and would declare South Vietnam a neutral state.[129] On January 28, Khanh made these allegations to his US military adviser, Colonel Jasper Wilson, who reported them to Harkins and Lodge. The next day Khanh met with both Harkins and Lodge in Saigon and proposed to launch a "preemptive" coup to foil the seizure of power by proneutralists that was supposedly in the offing.[130] None of the American officials objected, and Khanh executed his coup the following day.

Although it is clear that some US officials in South Vietnam were aware of an impending coup and did nothing to stop it, the existing evidence does not support the conclusion that the president or top officials in Washington authorized, supported, or were even aware of the coup. Because of the lack of evidence that Khanh's coup was US policy, I do not code it as a foreign-imposed regime change but rather as a domestic coup.

George Kahin makes the case for US responsibility most forcefully: "The principal Vietnamese actors on both sides of the confrontation—General

Khanh himself, as well as Generals Minh, Don, and Dinh, together with their prime minister, Tho—have testified that the United States was decisively involved in the coup of January 30, 1964, and all affirm that it would not have taken place without American backing."[131] To support his conclusion, Kahin cites the account of General Nguyen Van Chuan, a high-ranking coup plotter, who notes that Colonel Wilson was present in the coup-makers' headquarters during the putsch and phoned his superior officer, General Harkins, at regular intervals. Chuan further states that he "noticed the heavy involvement of the Harkins group" and "had the immediate feeling that this action was not being carried out independently" but rather "was directed by foreigners." Khanh himself later commented that "maybe in the coup of January 30, 1964, the U.S. Army had come to conclude that it too should have the capacity to bring about a coup."[132] Kahin further alleges that Harkins personally intervened to induce a critical South Vietnamese commander with armored units in Saigon, Colonel Duong Hieu Nghia, to switch sides.[133]

Kahin asserts that these US officers would not have acted without approval from Pentagon officials, such as Taylor or McNamara, but if such evidence exists, it has not surfaced. Policymakers in Washington reportedly were surprised: the Pentagon Papers note that the "Khanh coup of 30 January 1964 came as an almost complete surprise to the mission and to Washington."[134] Although the details are disputed, it is clear that the two top US officials in South Vietnam—Lodge and Harkins—were informed of the plot in advance yet made no move to alert Minh's government. As summarized by Kahin, "Whatever their varying depths of involvement, neither the military mission nor Lodge was willing to warn the South Vietnamese government to which they were accredited, and which they officially supported, of the plot to overthrow it."[135]

Unfortunately, the coup train did not stop with Minh's ouster: Khanh would be forced into exile a year after having seized power. These repeated coups were symptomatic of what Logevall calls the "fundamental problem" the United States faced in Vietnam, which was "finding a government committed to producing political stability in Saigon and to waging war against the Vietcong."[136] Indeed, as Logevall writes, "Kennedy, Johnson, and their advisers were convinced that a military solution was needed in Vietnam, and when the Diem and Minh regimes expressed doubts about such a solution, or at least appeared incapable of pursuing one effectively, the United States aided in their overthrow."[137] What Logevall thus terms the "fundamental problem" for the United States in South Vietnam was in fact the interest asymmetry between the two governments that is central to my theory when it came to how to oppose the Viet Cong.

Leaders Overthrown by Dissatisfied Domestic Actors: The Case of Maximilian, Emperor of Mexico

The fifth irregular way that leaders placed in power by external actors lose office—and the final one discussed in this chapter—is through coups or rebellions launched by dissatisfied domestic actors explicitly against the wishes of the foreign patron. In fact, what drives these revolts is resentment or anger over the patron's role in the target state and how the patron influences the imposed leader to implement policies favorable to it. Chapter 3 reviewed several cases where the problem of competing principals faced by foreign-imposed leaders triggered rebellions that threatened the survival of these leaders or resulted in their ouster, including Shah Shuja ul-Mulk in Afghanistan (1842), Juan José Estrada in Nicaragua (1910), and Carlos Castillo Armas in Guatemala (1957). An additional example is the case of Miguel Iglesias, the Peruvian general who stepped forward to sign a peace treaty on Chile's terms in 1883 to end the War of the Pacific (1879–84), who was overthrown by fellow Peruvians angered at his concessions only months after Chilean forces departed.[138]

This section focuses on a particularly powerful illustration of how a foreign-imposed leader too closely aligned with an intervener can fall victim to domestic opposition: France's intervention in Mexico during the 1860s. This doomed expedition ousted Liberal president Benito Juárez and placed Austrian Archduke Maximilian on the throne of the newly created Mexican Empire. Although French emperor Napoleon III's motives are disputed, he repeatedly denied any intention to impose a monarchy, or a particular monarch, on Mexico. Yet Napoleon did pursue regime change in Mexico, and his emissaries in the country, believing they were following his wishes, arranged for a hand-picked assembly of Mexicans to invite Maximilian to rule. In paving the way for Maximilian to assume the Mexican throne, however, French officials lost any chance they had of winning over Juárez's Liberal Party by appointing a regency dominated by Conservatives and Catholic clerics. Maximilian, although he actually favored liberal policies, such as freedom of religion and subjugation of church to state, thus faced an irreconcilable Liberal insurgency once he arrived in Mexico two years later. Unable to build an effective Mexican army, the new emperor was forced to rely on his French patrons to pacify the country. Napoleon, however, wanted the Mexican Empire to become self-sufficient so he could withdraw his forces and he grew impatient when this did not happen. Facing domestic and international pressure to quit Mexico, Napoleon ordered his troops home, hoping that his protégé would abdicate and leave with them. When he did not, Napoleon abandoned Maximilian and the Conservatives to face the Liberal challenge alone. Besieged in Querétaro in June 1867, Maximilian was betrayed to the Liberal army by one of his own officers, court-martialed, and executed.[139]

Put into the language of my theory, Maximilian's imposition was a leadership regime change. After engineering Maximilian's selection, France made no effort to build institutions in Mexico other than the army. Indeed, installing a monarchy is the opposite of building institutions.[140] Moreover, Maximilian's preferences diverged significantly from three critical actors. First, his interests clashed irreconcilably with the Liberal Party and regime he had displaced, whose leader, Juárez, sought to regain power. Maximilian actually had much in common ideologically with the Liberals but they were never going to accept a foreign-imposed monarchy—even a liberal one. Second, Maximilian's preferences diverged from those of the Conservative Party—the principal beneficiaries of his accession to the throne. His liberal beliefs and policies—and those of the French occupation regime that preceded him—deeply alienated the monarchy's strongest supporters. Third, Maximilian's preference for French troops to safeguard his regime diverged from that of his patron, Napoleon III, who refused to garrison Mexico permanently. The result was that Maximilian was unable to attract many Liberals to his cause and antagonized the Conservatives—and thus had to rely on the French Army for security. Napoleon, however, faced numerous pressures—not the least of which was a growing threat of US intervention once the American Civil War ended—to disengage. Once that happened, Maximilian was left to his fate.

This case shows the problem of competing principals in a different guise. Napoleon sought to regenerate Mexico by imposing an enlightened despotism led by a monarch who shared his liberal beliefs—particularly about the relationship between church and state. Maximilian was a faithful servant in this regard, which estranged him from Mexican Conservatives. Yet the very fact that he had accepted a throne handed to him by the force of French arms—which had overthrown a Liberal regime in the process—made him anathema to Mexican Liberals; he was indelibly associated with the French in their eyes. Should the French ever tire of supporting Maximilian, therefore, his only hope of survival would be to move towards the Conservatives and hope they could save him from the Liberal onslaught. This is in fact what happened—only the Conservatives were unable to defeat the Liberals and preserve the emperor.

IMMEDIATE CAUSES AND CONDUCT OF REGIME CHANGE

France's Mexican imbroglio began as a joint Anglo-French-Spanish effort—codified in the Convention of London of October 31, 1861—to recoup debts owed by the Mexican government by occupying the port of Veracruz and collecting customs receipts.[141] The primary objective of the agreement, according to historians Alfred and Kathryn Hanna, was to "coerce Mexico into paying long accumulated debts and claims covering the lives and property of citizens of the signatory powers."[142] Article 2 of the convention, moreover, specifically pledged the signatories "not to exercise in the internal affairs of Mexico any influence of a nature to prejudice the right of the Mexican nation to choose and to freely constitute the form of its Government."[143] Inserted at the insistence of the British government, this clause unfortunately could be interpreted to permit regime change as long as the Mexican people selected the new government. The signatories, although they agreed that a more stable regime in Mexico would be desirable, differed in their willingness to pursue this objective by force.[144]

To compel the Juárez government to comply with their demands, the three European powers sent 9,000 troops to Veracruz in December 1861 and January 1862.[145] Once landed in Mexico, however, the plenipotentiaries of the three powers immediately contradicted the convention by proclaiming that their "first duty" was to help the Mexicans establish a better government *before* obtaining settlement of debts.[146] "This was," historian Michele Cunningham observes, "a complete reversal of the priorities expressed in the Convention," and provoked dismay when news of it reached European capitals across the Atlantic.[147] Despite the European representatives' assertion that they wanted a capable government empowered in Mexico City, they disagreed about what kind of government that might be. Sir Charles Wyke and General Juan Prim, the British and Spanish commissioners, respectively, favored strengthening Juárez's existing government, whereas the French representative, Admiral Jean de la Gravière Jurien, believed that only a monarchy would suffice.[148] In reality, the British government wanted no part of any attempt at regime change in Mexico.[149] The Spanish government sympathized with the objective of establishing a monarchy, but its representative on the spot, General Prim, favored preserving the Juárez regime and refused to participate in any scheme to overthrow it.[150]

The European plenipotentiaries also disagreed on strategy and the validity of each other's claims against Mexico. Regarding strategy, Wyke and Prim favored negotiations with Juárez whereas Jurien—in line with his instructions from Napoleon—anticipated advancing into the Mexican interior, perhaps all the way to Mexico City, to "overthrow the Mexican government or to render more effectual the coercion exercised upon it by the seizure of its ports."[151] The British and Spanish representatives also found the French claims against Mexico, presented at an allied conference in January 1862 by French minister to Mexico Comte Alphonse Dubois de Saligny, to be highly inflated. France's allies objected specifically to the inclusion of certain loans contracted by Juárez's predecessor, Conservative General Miguel Miramón.[152] Commented Wyke, "That claim is inadmissible, the Mexican government will never accept it; before tolerating it, they will go to war, and the arms of England will never support such injustice."[153] At a final conference of allied negotiators on April 9, Jurien, following Napoleon's instructions, insisted on pressing France's claims, as presented by Saligny in January, and marching on Mexico City. As a result, the British and Spanish withdrew from the expedition, re-embarked their troops, and sailed for home.

French troops advanced inland in May 1862 headed for Mexico City to displace the Juárez government. After an initial defeat at Puebla on May 5 (the battle celebrated on the Cinco de Mayo holiday), French reinforcements arrived throughout the year and victories followed until French troops triumphantly entered the capital on June 10, 1863. Following Napoleon's blueprint, the French commander assembled a committee of thirty-five notable citizens, which appointed a three-member executive and then expanded to a constituent assembly of 250 members. This assembly, with no dissenting votes, offered the crown to Maximilian of Austria. After much agonizing, he eventually accepted, finally arriving with his wife Charlotte to assume power in June 1864.

DEEPER CAUSES OF REGIME CHANGE

Scholars have offered several deeper causes for why Napoleon sought regime change in Mexico. Perhaps the most popular view is that Napoleon was motivated by the desire to contain the southward expansion of the United States and prevent it from dominating the entirety of the Americas. Alfred and Kathryn Hanna, for example, conclude that "Napoleon III undertook to establish on the southern frontier of the United States a strong monarchy as a barrier against further U.S. expansion. He also proposed to convert the other Spanish American republics into monarchies similar to the Second Empire of France."[154] Consistent with this line of argument, Napoleon wrote to his third field commander in Mexico, General Elie Frédéric Forey, in July 1862, that while France desired a powerful United States, it had no interest in seeing that country dominate the entire New World. If, by contrast, "Mexico conquers its independence and maintains the integrity of its territory, if a stable government is constituted there by the arms of France, we shall have opposed an insuperable barrier to the encroachments of the United States."[155] The outbreak of the American Civil War, in this view, presented Napoleon with an opportunity to implement this plan.

A second argument is that Napoleon hoped that by nominating a member of the House of Habsburg to rule in Mexico, he could obtain concessions from Austria on other matters. Fenton Bresler, in a biography of Napoleon III, asserts that the French emperor supported Maximilian for the throne because, as the younger brother of the Austrian emperor, "he might be able to persuade Franz Joseph—on a quid pro quo basis—to hand over Venetia to the newly created Kingdom of Italy," an objective of Napoleon's left over from the War of Italian Unification a few years prior.[156]

Third, some scholars argue that Napoleon sought to ameliorate France's silver shortage by intervening in Mexico. Indeed, one dissertation on French intervention in Mexico is subtitled "A Quest for Silver."[157] According to this argument, the outbreak of the American Civil War had forced France to shift its source of cotton imports from the southern United States to India, where merchants preferred to be paid in silver. As M. M. McAllen describes, "When silver supplies became scant, cotton imports fell, and by 1861 unemployment soared." "To cure the French need for precious metals, especially silver," McAllen continues, "Mexico's mines, especially in Sonora, seemed a logical solution, further propelling Napoleon to the idea of its occupation, [and] installation of a monarchy."[158]

Finally, Napoleon believed that regime change in Mexico would be easy. Hanna and Hanna contend that Napoleon had been convinced by promonarchy Mexican exiles in Europe that "upon the landing of European troops, their compatriots would rise as one and support the establishment of a monarchy."[159] Evidence suggests that Napoleon discounted the need for public support in France for the Mexican adventure—and did not appoint highly capable military commanders—because he believed it would be accomplished with little effort.[160] His officers on the ground certainly thought that taking Mexico City presented little challenge. As one wrote to Paris as the French advanced inland in April 1862, "We are so superior to the Mexicans in race, in organization, in discipline, in morality, and in elevation of feeling, that I beg Your Excellency to be so good as to inform the emperor that, at the head of 6,000 soldiers, I am already master of Mexico."[161]

Whatever it was that motivated Napoleon to pursue regime change in Mexico when his allies would not, the case bears some resemblance to Willard-Foster's domestic opposition theory, with a couple of caveats. Willard-Foster argues that leaders who face powerful domestic oppositions are simultaneously hard to coerce and easy to overthrow, which leads coercers to calculate that regime change may be cheaper than coercion. When the opposition is strong, making concessions to the compeller is likely to endanger the leader's political survival because it signals weakness at home, which emboldens a leader's internal foes, who may launch a bid to overthrow her. Leaders facing this situation are thus likely to resist the compeller's demands. At the same time, the existence of a powerful opposition in the target state causes the compeller to believe that regime change will be cheap and easy, since alternative leaders exist who may be willing to exchange political concessions for its support in a bid for power. As Willard-Foster summarizes, "domestically weak leaders should be especially prone to FIRC. Their domestic vulnerability increases the stronger power's expected costs of obtaining a settlement with them, while simultaneously decreasing its expected costs of overthrowing them."[162]

As posited by Willard-Foster, the European powers perceived the absence of a strong government in Mexico as presenting a commitment problem. Given the constant regime turnover in Mexico, any treaty negotiated would not be worth the paper it was written on since the government that agreed to it could be overthrown at any time. As Palmerston told parliament in early

1862, "what Her Majesty's Government desire is, that there shall be established some form of Government in Mexico with which foreign nations may treat . . . some form of Government with which relations of peace and amity may be maintained with confidence in their continuance."[163] Also in line with Willard-Foster's theory, the presence of strong Conservative opponents made Juárez easier to overthrow. However, the domestic opponents that deterred him from making concessions were not Conservatives but rather extremists in his own Liberal Party.[164] Moreover, because Napoleon, as pointed out above, already believed that toppling Juárez with a small French force would be easy, it is doubtful that the Conservative presence exerted much additional leverage on his decision to pursue regime change.

THE MAXIMILIAN CONTROVERSY

One major disagreement in the historiography on the origins of regime change in this case is whether or not France's Napoleon III intended all along to overthrow Juárez and install a monarchy in Mexico under Maximilian or whether his subordinates on the ground misinterpreted or exceeded their instructions. Most scholars agree that imposing Maximilian was Napoleon's intention from the outset. Jasper Ridley's account, for example, maintains that the French emperor knew that "negotiations with Juárez about settling the foreign creditors' claims would almost certainly break down." If they didn't, Napoleon would simply have his representatives engineer a breakdown by making additional unreasonable demands. "Then," continues Ridley, "the French could persuade their British and Spanish allies to advance to Mexico City, overthrow Juárez, and install Maximilian as emperor."[165]

Michele Cunningham, however, points out that Napoleon's support for the establishment of a monarchy in Mexico was always conditional on whether that was the freely expressed desire of the Mexican people; only if they agreed did he support Maximilian of Austria for the throne.[166] In one of his most definitive statements on the subject, Napoleon wrote to General Comte Charles Latrille de Lorencez, his second military commander in Mexico, in June 1862: "It is contrary to my interests, my origin, and my principles, to impose any government on the Mexican people; let them choose, in complete freedom, the form that is the most suitable for them; I ask them only for sincerity in their foreign relations, and I desire only one thing, that is the happiness and independence of this beautiful country under a stable and legitimate government."[167] Napoleon wrote in a similar vein to Maximilian around the same time: "I have told my representatives that there was no question whatever of imposing any kind of government on the Mexicans, but only of supporting a monarchy if it found partisans in the country and a prospect of stability."[168]

Napoleon's many such proclamations, however, are at least partly contradicted by his efforts—even before the Convention of London was finalized—to recruit Maximilian for the job of Mexican emperor. The initiative to draft Maximilian came from Mexican exiles, one of whom—José Manuel Hidalgo—was a childhood friend of French empress Eugénie. Hidalgo pitched her and her husband on the idea of a Mexican monarchy as early as 1858.[169] Maximilian's name came up in a conversation between Napoleon, Eugénie, and Hidalgo in 1861, and in July other promonarchy Mexican exiles visited the Habsburg court in Vienna and Austria's minister in Paris, Prince Richard Metternich, to propose Maximilian as a candidate for the throne.[170] Although the Mexican exiles made the first approach in July 1861, the French emperor contacted the Habsburg court through his foreign minister, Count Édouard Thouvenel, to propose Maximilian as a candidate for the Mexican throne.[171] In early October, Austrian emperor Franz Josef, who had to approve before his younger brother could accept such an invitation, explained the situation to Maximilian, who was eager to agree.[172] Napoleon's movement to draft the Austrian archduke was thus well underway even as the French emperor disclaimed any intention of imposing a monarchy on Mexico.

Although British leaders understood Napoleon's policy at the time of the Convention of London to be support for monarchy (and Maximilian) conditional on the desires of the Mexican people, that policy may have been too nuanced for his subordinates to understand, for they clearly acted *as if* they believed French policy was to impose a monarchy headed by Maximilian in Mexico.[173] Lorencez, for example, wrote to the French minister of war in April 1862 that he hoped his slow progress in Mexico had not "discouraged" Maximilian "from accepting 'the crown that His Majesty wanted to put on his head.'"[174] Indeed, Cunningham argues that Napoleon's agents in Mexico—particularly Saligny—exceeded their mandate and repeatedly presented their master in Paris with *faits accomplis*. Saligny, who later said, "My only merit is to have correctly guessed the Emperor's intention to intervene in Mexico, and to have made the intervention necessary," sincerely believed that "the Emperor and his government were looking for a pretext for a military occupation of the country, and that he had done all he could to help realise that aim."[175] If true, Saligny's conduct highlights that principal-agent problems are not exclusive to relations between imposed leaders and their patrons, but also characterize relations between governments and their own diplomats.

This historiographical controversy is somewhat beside the point for my purposes because it concerns what *type* of regime might be installed in Mexico City after regime change, not whether regime change itself was or was not a good idea.[176] On the latter point it is clear that Napoleon believed regime change might be necessary to secure continued repayment of the debt he claimed was owed by Mexico to his country. In a letter to his minister in London, Comte Charles de Flahault, in early October 1861, for example, Napoleon wrote that "he believed that for Europe's sake, and for Mexico's, it was essential that the three powers be prepared to support whoever appeared capable of forming a stable government."[177] Holding this view, however, does not distinguish him from his British and Spanish allies, who understood that any agreement they reached on debt repayment with the Juárez regime would be meaningless if instability continued and Juárez was overthrown.[178]

Yet only Napoleon would order his generals to march to the Mexican capital and topple Juárez's government. Indeed, Napoleon was angered when he received word that his agents in Mexico were dickering with Juárez over terms of repayment in January 1862. According to Cunningham, Napoleon "believed that the question of reorganisation could only be usefully proposed and resolved after the City of Mexico or its environs had been occupied."[179] The French emperor backed the hard line taken by Jurien and Saligny, who in January had proposed sending Juárez an ultimatum demanding his government repay an inflated sum or face invasion.[180] On March 20, Napoleon, through Thouvenel, ordered his new military commander, General Lorencez, "to adhere, without any amendments, to Saligny's ultimatum of January 12, and to present it immediately to Juárez's government. . . . If Juárez did not accept the ultimatum, they were to start military operations at once and advance to Mexico City."[181] Napoleon would continue to aver, as he wrote in July, that his "aim is not to impose on the Mexicans a form of government they would not like," but whether he would depose the one they had was not in question.[182] And if they, of their own accord, decided for monarchy, the French would be happy to help—and recommend Maximilian for the job. In the end, Mexican Conservatives were only too happy to select the Austrian archduke, and thus I code the case as a leadership regime change.

THE LOGIC OF REGIME CHANGE

Once Napoleon decided on regime change in Mexico, he articulated the common logic espoused by regime changers everywhere—that leaders installed through regime change would serve as reliable promoters of the intervener's interests. In the letter to General Forey in which Napoleon laid out the procedures by which a new leader of Mexico was to be chosen, Napoleon opined: "As for the prince who may mount the Mexican throne . . . he will always be forced to act in the interests of France, not only by gratitude but especially because those of his new country will be in accordance with ours and he will not be able to sustain himself without our influence."[183] Similarly, Jack Dabbs argues that Napoleon "intended to set up a friendly government and gradually withdraw from direct political control as he withdrew his troops, leaving a friendly government. His further plan was that by the time direct French political and military influence began to withdraw, the government would be effective, independent, and friendly; that is, it would give preferential treatment to France."[184] Even Maximilian perceived Napoleon's intentions, commenting in early 1862 that "Napoleon's actions in the Mexican negotiations had convinced him 'of the evident desire of the Emperor of the French so to manage the affair that the future sovereign of Mexico will be quite unable to free himself of his tutelage.'"[185]

DOUBTS ABOUT THE WISDOM OF REGIME CHANGE

Even before it began, however, many observers expressed doubts about the feasibility of regime change in Mexico—especially a regime change that would establish a monarchy—concerns that only intensified as the campaign unfolded. Summarizing a conversation in which French foreign minister Thouvenel suggested that a monarchy in Mexico ruled by Maximilian would be in British interests, Lord Cowley, the British ambassador to France, wrote to his superiors in London that "he had told Thouvenel he thought the Emperor 'was preparing unnecessary difficulties for himself, for that if all I heard was true, the Emperor was quite deceived as to the state of public opinion in Mexico. . . . Any attempts to interfere with the free choice of the Mexicans themselves would, I was convinced, not succeed in the long run.'"[186] As British foreign minister Lord Russell responded the next day, "This attempt to set up a monarchy in Mexico will never do."[187] A month later, Russell wrote to his ambassador in Vienna that if "our estimate of the disorganization of Mexico is correct, the Archduke, if he were to assume the Crown, would have to rely wholly on the support of French troops," and further that "the idea of establishing a monarchy by foreign intervention was 'chimerical' as it would simply collapse as soon as foreign supporting troops were withdrawn."[188] Both Russell and Palmerston opposed such a venture on practical grounds. Spanish officials were no more sanguine about the prospects for monarchy in Mexico, with one remarking that "a Monarchy under a European prince, if not guaranteed by Europe, would not last a year."[189]

Once in Mexico, Allied representatives began to express doubts about the wisdom of regime change. For example, the British commissioner, Sir Charles Wyke, remarked in late December 1861 that it would be "difficult to subdue" the Mexican people given the "nature of the climate and the guerrilla habits of an armed people accustomed to war and strife for the last thirty years."[190] Wyke subsequently noted that he had "discovered no adherents to a monarchy in Mexico."[191] Similarly, the initial French military commander, Admiral Jurien, wrote in February 1862 that "they detest us here, only less than the Spaniards, that is all."[192] And the Spaniard Prim, in a letter to Napoleon the following month, warned him against regime change in Mexico: "It will be easy for Your Majesty to lead Prince Maximilian to the capital and to crown him King; but this King will find no support in the country, except from the Conservative leaders."[193]

Proponents of regime change, however, in terms that foreshadow those later used by supporters of the US invasion of Iraq in 2003, sought to convince skeptics that Mexicans would welcome French troops with open arms. Saligny, the principal culprit, told Jurien that the French were so adored that they could take Mexico City with a mere 500 men.[194] Just prior to the first battle of Puebla, Saligny sought to convince Jurien's successor Lorencez that "the inhabitants of the old and famous city of Puebla . . . would be waiting, flower laden, to greet their 'regenerators' and that priests would celebrate 'Te Deum.'"[195] Instead, the Juárist defenders inflicted a stunning defeat on the French that left close to five hundred French troops dead.[196] Afterward, according to Cunningham, Lorencez "soon came to the conclusion that there was little support for the French in Mexico." "Most Mexicans," Lorencez told Randon, "were liberal in their thinking and there was little support for a monarchy, which would only be achieved after years of occupation by the French."[197] Hanna and Hanna similarly conclude that "optimism gradually oozed away from Lorencez," who lamented to the French minister of war, "I continue to regret that I do not meet a single partisan of monarchy in Mexico."[198]

INTEREST ASYMMETRIES PRIOR TO MAXIMILIAN'S ARRIVAL

Once the French finally arrived in Mexico City in June 1863, it did not take long before things went downhill. Napoleon's instructions to Forey called for him to establish a provisional government to decide the future form of the Mexican regime but to retain real power in his own hands.[199] Forey, under the influence of Saligny and Mexican Conservatives, such as General Juan Almonte, who had served in the Conservative regime ousted by Juárez, named a thirty-five member junta dominated by Conservatives. The junta in turn chose three of its members to form a regency. The three men chosen—Almonte, General José Mariano Salas, and the Catholic archbishop Labastida—were all Conservatives, as were most of the other members of the 250-strong Assembly of Notables, which voted unanimously to offer the crown to Maximilian on July 10, 1863.

The problem with ruling through the Conservative Party was that its members—other than desiring a monarchy in Mexico—shared almost none of France's preferences. The French actually had much more in common ideologically with Juárez's Liberals than with the Conservatives they relied on to rule Mexico. Napoleon had told Forey, for example, to establish freedom of religion in Mexico and not allow a return to a situation in which Catholicism was the only permissible form of worship. Similarly, in one of the Liberals' most controversial laws, the Ley Lerdo, the government of Ignacio Comonfort, Juárez's predecessor as Mexican president, had confiscated church lands and sold them to private buyers. Forey was instructed not to reverse this legislation. Both of these preferences clashed with those of the regency. When priests began refusing to perform last rites for those who had purchased church property, Napoleon's new commander, General Achille Bazaine, stormed into a meeting of the regents with one hundred soldiers at his back and demanded that they sign a decree formally recognizing the sale of these lands. When Labastida refused, Bazaine sacked him from the regency, after which the archbishop excommunicated anyone working with the French. When Labastida threatened to refuse entry to Sunday mass to government officials and French soldiers, Bazaine in turn threatened to blast open the cathedral doors with cannon fire.[200] With these conflicts, the French alienated those who should have been their strongest supporters.

Even as Bazaine struggled to contain the clerical and Conservative revolt against France's liberal policies in Mexico City, the "apparent association of the French with the clergy" signaled by Forey's appointment of the Conservative regents and his orchestration of Maximilian's selection as emperor "created many difficulties for Bazaine and his army" with the Liberals, according to Cunningham.[201] In another example of the ideological mismatch at play in this case, a French general recounted the words of two French miners he encountered in northern Mexico. The men said that the Mexican Liberal leaders "consider France the source of progress and the light of civilisation; but they will never accept the reactionary and clerical government that you want to impose on them."[202] Mexican Conservatives, in other words, opposed the French for their liberal policies, and Mexican Liberals—even though they identified with French liberalism—opposed the French for what they perceived to be the occupiers' embrace of the Conservatives! Napoleon, in a misguided attempt to install a liberal monarchy in Mexico, overthrew the party that shared his values and empowered the one that did not—and alienated the French occupiers from both.

INTEREST ASYMMETRIES UNDER MAXIMILIAN

Once Maximilian was at last persuaded that the majority of the Mexican people desired that he rule Mexico, and once he had extracted Napoleon's promise to maintain French troops in Mexico until the empire could build its own army, he formally accepted the throne and sailed with his wife, Charlotte, for Mexico. The new monarchs arrived in Mexico City on June 12, 1864, a year after the French had entered the capital, but their installation in power unfortunately did not improve the outlook for the empire. The French never captured Juárez, and the former Mexican leader and his supporters retreated to Chihuahua in the north where they remained beyond the reach of French and imperial troops. At peak strength, French troops numbered fewer than 40,000, less than 10 percent of France's standing army at the time, to control a country more than three times the size of France.[203] Indeed, the situation unfolded much as one observer had predicted before the war: "Juarez had the advantage of being able to sustain himself and his supporters in some part of the huge country, which enemy forces would find impossible to occupy in its entirety. Juarez . . . would always be able to escape his enemies and wait for better times, and could feel secure in the support, direct or indirect, of his northern neighbours."[204] French forces under Bazaine racked up victory after victory, but victories did not translate into pacification or political support for the imperial project.[205] According to one account, "As French troops entered town after town, resistance went underground and the number of adherents multiplied." "Victories over Juaristas," this account continues, "did not end resistance to the regeneration program."[206]

Meanwhile, Maximilian alienated his own Conservative supporters by upholding Liberal religious policies, such as opposing efforts by the Catholic Church to reclaim property seized under Juárez and affirming freedom of worship.[207] The Mexican emperor refused to buckle in the face of a testy visit from the papal nuncio, Monsignor Meglia, who arrived in late 1864 with a list of demands including the restoration of church property and Catholicism as the exclusive religion of Mexico, among others.[208] In response, on December 27, Maximilian proclaimed that he would uphold Juárez's seizure of church property; over the ensuing weeks Maximilian also confirmed religious tolerance and decreed that no orders from Rome would be valid without his sanction.

The basic problem was that Maximilian's liberal beliefs were fundamentally at odds with the group (the Conservatives) that stood to benefit the most from his reign, which protested bitterly and grew increasingly disillusioned. But these liberal beliefs and policies, although they attracted a few moderate Liberals to his camp, could never persuade the bulk of the Liberals to accept him. Mexican Liberals were never going to accept a monarchy—particularly a foreign prince installed by a foreign power—no matter how liberal its policies.[209] In the short term, Maximilian turned to the French to support his rule, but over time circumstances would force him ever closer to the Conservatives owing to the Liberals' unbridgeable antipathy.

INTEREST ASYMMETRIES BETWEEN MAXIMILIAN AND NAPOLEON

Unfortunately, the preferences of the French and Mexican emperors were not fully aligned, either. The key difference concerned the nature and duration of French support for Maximilian's regime. In the Treaty of Miramar, Maximilian had managed to extract from his French patron a promise to garrison Mexico with 25,000 French troops until a capable Mexican army could be established, and further that 6,000–8,000 men of the Foreign Legion would remain for six to eight years after that. No sooner had Maximilian arrived in Mexico, however, than Napoleon wrote to Bazaine "emphasising the need to develop the indigenous army so the French could leave as soon as possible."[210] Over the balance of 1864 and into 1865, Napoleon became increasingly concerned over his protégé's lack of progress in establishing his government and his apparent belief that France would continue to underwrite the security of his empire indefinitely.[211]

The simple fact is that on the issue of defense, French and Mexican interests clashed. The Mexican Empire was broke, and Maximilian had promised to pay hundreds of millions of francs to Napoleon III in recompense for French expenses incurred while installing him in power.[212] Napoleon, by contrast, had no interest in permanently garrisoning Mexico and providing Maximilian with a French army. Contrary to Napoleon's earlier predictions, dependence on France did not breed compliance with French wishes. Symptomatic of the clash of interests was the inability of the French to build up a Mexican army to defend the empire when French troops went home. This failure, notes Dabbs, was attributable to multiple factors, including the "impoverishment of the Mexican treasury, the unpopularity of the cause, and the continual refusal of the Mexican authorities to introduce and enforce a regular system of recruitment."[213] A less recognized factor, however, was Maximilian's active resistance to French efforts to develop an indigenous army. In mid-1864, for example, Maximilian decided to discharge some of his troops and rely instead on French forces and local militia for defense. "While such a plan certainly would reduce the cost of government," notes Dabbs, "it directly opposed the purposes of Napoleon III."[214] Bazaine was able to talk the Mexican emperor out of implementing this measure—but only temporarily. In November, Maximilian, "as an economy measure . . . reduced the Mexican army to two regiments, thus discharging several thousand soldiers and officers."[215] According to McAllen, "the outcasts wasted no time in going over to the Liberals or guerrillas."[216]

Maximilian implemented other policies that clashed with the preferences of his French patrons. Once Maximilian took power, he declared a general amnesty and released all detainees—many of them men who had fought against the French—with sentences shorter than ten years. The emperor also regularly pardoned guerrillas convicted of killing French troops. The emperor subsequently ended the French blockade of the Mexican coast, which had prevented Juárez's forces from importing weapons and ammunition. Maximilian's government also resisted the insertion of French officers into its ranks to oversee finances and taxation, and the emperor appointed a council of state filled with men hostile to French interests.[217]

A number of factors explain Napoleon's increasing agitation and his desire to extricate himself from his Mexican commitment. First, Napoleon had underestimated the tenacity of Liberal resistance to his imperial project and overestimated Maximilian's capabilities as a ruler, both of which contributed to an unending war.[218] Second, the war was increasingly unpopular in France and the French legislature was unlikely to approve additional funds or troops.[219] Third, as the American Civil War wound down with a Union victory, the United States became more vocal in its support for Juárez and in its disapproval of the Mexican Empire and the French military presence. Washington began openly siding with Mexico's Liberals, supplying them with weapons and, in December 1865, demanding that the French evacuate Mexico or face sanctions.[220] Fourth, Napoleon could not ignore that a sizable fraction of his army was thousands of miles away when tensions were growing close to home—Prussia and Austria would fight for supremacy in Germany in 1866. On January 15, 1866, Napoleon informed his Mexican protégé that the French Army would be withdrawn by early the following year.[221]

THE FALL OF MAXIMILIAN

France's impending departure from Mexico drove Maximilian of necessity into the arms of the Conservatives—the only source of support and (limited) military power for his regime. According to McAllen, "Through the spring and summer of 1866, with support eroding, Maximilian knew he could not depend on the Conservatives and Clerical party with his current policies. Yet his open-minded, liberal ideals had done nothing to cement support with the Republicans."[222] So Maximilian finally embraced the Conservatives in the frail hope that they could save the empire. He brought more Conservatives into his cabinet and accepted the help of two men he had sent away to Europe—Generals Miramón and Marquez—owing to their proclerical fanaticism, all the while trying (with Bazaine's help) to build an imperial army. Maximilian also adopted more draconian measures to punish his enemies, most notably the "Black Decree" of October 1865, which mandated the death penalty for anyone caught carrying arms against the government—an edict that endeared him to Conservatives.[223]

As French troops pulled back from northern Mexico, Juárist forces moved in since there were not enough Mexican soldiers to hold the vacated territory. By the end of 1866, Maximilian held only a small island of territory extending from Querétaro in the north down to Mexico City and southeast to the coast at Veracruz. In October and November, Maximilian almost abdicated the throne but eventually decided to remain and submit to the will of the Mexican people as expressed in a national congress that would be convened to decide his fate.[224] When the last French troops departed Mexico City on February 5, 1867, Maximilian's army stood at nearly 30,000 men, but a pair of disastrous defeats soon reduced it to 22,000, compared to 60,000 in the Liberal army.[225] The emperor and his army advanced north to Querétaro but were quickly surrounded by converging republican columns. Captured trying to flee Querétaro on May 15, Maximilian was executed by firing squad a month later.[226] Juárez returned to Mexico City to resume the presidency.

In Mexico, France installed a monarch, Archduke Maximilian of Austria, who was opposed by the Liberal segment of the population and who alienated many of his Conservative supporters with his liberal policies, which were in line with those of his patron Napoleon. Although the French captured the capital and the major cities, Juárez and much of his army escaped and fled to the northern reaches of the country—a ready-made situation for insurgency, as shown in chapter 3. Although the irreconcilable hostility of the Liberals forced Maximilian to depend on the French Army for security, the preferences of patron and protégé diverged as Napoleon had no intention of maintaining a permanent military presence in Mexico. When the French announced their withdrawal, Maximilian joined forces with his ideological foes—the Conservatives—because they were the only constituency in the country that favored monarchy. As many predicted, the only way to sustain a European monarch in Mexico was with substantial European troops; once they departed, the emperor was doomed.

Negative Cases: Why Do Foreign-Imposed Leaders Survive?

The historical appraisal presented in this chapter demonstrates that foreign-imposed leaders—especially those installed in leadership regime changes—face a high risk of violent removal. This chapter has outlined six different pathways to irregular removal and provided evidence that the overthrow of foreign-imposed leaders was caused by the development of interest asymmetries between patrons and protégés, which in turn were driven by the problem of competing principals. Some leaders installed by outside powers, however, manage to postpone irregular removal for many years or avoid it altogether. This section investigates some of these negative cases to answer the following question: How do imposed leaders avoid forcible removal—either by increasing their time in office before suffering irregular removal (or natural death), or increasing the likelihood of experiencing regular removal?

At least three factors provide partial answers to this question. First, leaders who come to power in restoration regime changes are less likely to be removed by violence. Recall from the analysis earlier in the chapter that only two restored leaders (out of twenty) were removed irregularly between 1875 and 2004. In other words, 90 percent of leaders reempowered through restoration regime changes exited office in a regular manner. In the leader-year dataset, gaining power in a restoration regime change almost completely eliminated the risk of irregular removal; the reduction in risk in the leader-spell data was smaller but still substantial (almost 60 percent). The two restored leaders who did suffer forcible removals—Ethiopia's Haile Selassie and Iran's Mohammad Reza Pahlavi—remained in power after their restorations for an average of nearly thirty years. One reason for these findings is that more than a half-dozen of these restorations involved the reinstitution of democracy after an autocratic interregnum—usually owing to a foreign occupation—and democratic regime type drastically reduces the risk of irregular removal. Restoring democracy, of course, does not explain the lengthy tenures of autocrats like Selassie and the shah. For that, other explanations are needed.

Second, just as restoring democratic systems in previously democratic countries contributes to regular removal, successfully installing new democracies also enhances the prospects of nonviolent leader turnover. My dataset contains only three examples of democratic transformations—the Federal Republic of Germany, Japan, and Panama—but none of these countries has experienced an irregular removal since they became democracies.

A third factor that appears to lengthen the tenure of foreign-imposed leaders that come to power in autocratic settings is large-scale repression. Leaders that are able to develop an efficient repressive apparatus—often with the help of their foreign backers—and are unafraid to use it can typically extend their time in office. The effect of repression is consistent across types of regime change. Below I briefly trace how Spain's Francisco Franco, Iran's Mohammad Reza Pahlavi, and communist regimes in Eastern Europe used repression to avoid irregular removal.

FRANCISCO FRANCO, SPAIN, 1939–1975

One noteworthy example among leadership regime changes of a leader who was able to survive in office for decades is the reign of Francisco Franco in Spain. Franco's Nationalist forces prevailed in the bloody Spanish Civil War in 1939 and he retained office until he died in 1975—the longest tenure of any imposed leader in my data. Franco's victory is coded as a regime change owing to the substantial participation of Italian and German forces on the Nationalist side. Italy's contribution was massive: at its peak there were 50,000 Italians fighting in Spain under the guise of "volunteers." The Italian navy and air force also took part in the war, and Mussolini provided the Nationalists with large amounts of military equipment, including aircraft, tanks, and artillery pieces. Germany's contribution was numerically smaller—only about 5,000 men at any given time—but perhaps more important to the Nationalist war effort. Shortly after fighting erupted in July 1936, Hitler sent to Spain units of the Luftwaffe that came to be known as the Condor Legion. In effect, the Condor Legion became the Nationalist air force and provided effective air support, especially as the war went on.[227] Historians debate whether the Nationalists would have been able to win the war without this external assistance; it is impossible to know for sure, but Antony Beevor, for one, contends that "there can be no doubt that German and Italian forces greatly shortened the war in the nationalists' favour. To say that they won the war for Franco entirely would be going too far. The Condor Legion above all accelerated the conquest of the north. . . . But the truly devastating effectiveness of the Condor Legion came in countering the major republican offensives of 1937 and 1938, battles which were to break the back of the republican armed forces."[228]

The war was characterized from the outset by massive violence against civilians in rear areas. In regions controlled by the Republic, violence against ideological enemies, including the Roman Catholic clergy, erupted immediately; current estimates place the minimum number of victims of Republican violence at 37,843.[229] Nationalist violence also began as soon as the war broke out but continued after the Republic was vanquished, eventually consuming 150,000 victims—including 50,000 executions after the war was over.[230] The majority of these postwar killings were completed by the end of 1940, when the Francoist regime held a minimum of 280,000 prisoners in its jails.[231] Although the regime released most of these prisoners in the first half of the 1940s, its system of repression remained in place until Franco's death. This system consisted of military tribunals supplemented in 1963 by the Public Order Tribunal. The task of these institutions, according to Julius Ruiz, was to "ruthlessly eliminate clandestine anti-Francoist activity until the dictator's death in 1975."[232]

The regime's iron grip on the country made it exceedingly difficult for any armed opposition groups to survive. This viselike grip is exemplified by the regime's rapid defeat of the Valle de Aran operation, an invasion of northern Spain in October 1944 by 3,000 Spanish guerrillas who had fought with the French resistance against Nazi Germany. The guerrillas briefly occupied a few towns but were driven back across the border in a matter of days. Some fighters, however, remained in Spain and joined with existing armed bands to form the National Guerrilla Army (ENG), which consisted of eight units numbering a few thousand men.[233] To combat the guerrillas, Franco unleashed a ruthless campaign of terror that made the population suffer along with the rebels. Families of fighters were forbidden from working and the regime focused, according to one scholar, on "starving out the 'Reds'" by "forced clearance of cultivated land and crop burning."[234] Franco's forces also terrorized the guerrillas with paramilitaries that carried out large numbers of extrajudicial killings. By mid-1949, only two beleaguered units of the ENG remained; it officially gave up the struggle in 1952.[235] Approximately 4,000 people died in this relatively unknown civil war.[236]

THE SHAH OF IRAN, 1953–1979

The case of the shah of Iran provides a good example of the efficacy of repression in prolonging the survival of a leader restored to power. Mohammad Reza Pahlavi has the unique distinction of gaining office via foreign-imposed regime changes on two occasions: first, after the British and Soviets deposed his father, Reza Shah, in 1941; and second, when the CIA aided in the downfall of prime minister Mohammad Mossadegh in 1953. The *Archigos* project codes the shah's reign as effective leader of Iran being interrupted when he was forced by the Iranian parliament (the Majlis) to appoint a new prime minister in April 1951.[237] Mossadegh was thus the effective leader for more than two years until Operation Ajax resulted in his arrest and the reassertion of the shah's power.[238]

Immediately following the coup, the new regime—headed by the shah and his appointed prime minister, Fazlollah Zahedi—was in a tenuous political position.[239] The communist Tudeh Party remained popular among the middle and the industrial working class and also maintained significant support within the armed forces. The National Front—formerly the ruling coalition headed by Mossadegh—similarly had a strong base of support among the former two populations and formed the National Resistance Movement, which published two newspapers and organized antigovernment demonstrations and strikes.[240]

In order to discourage political dissent, Zahedi's new government made extensive use of blunt intimidation and punishment tactics such as jailing, torture, and killings in addition to subtler methods of intimidation. In the aftermath of the coup, six hundred Mossadegh loyalists in the officer corps were arrested and sixty were shot. Mossadegh's cabinet ministers and prominent supporters were also arrested, with some later released and others convicted of various offenses. Several student leaders at Tehran University were shot, and prominent supporters of Tudeh and the National Front (both of which were banned) were imprisoned or killed.[241] By the end of 1953, about 2,100 people had been arrested.[242]

Zahedi also began a crackdown on all opposition political forces immediately after the coup. About 3,000 government employees sympathetic to the Tudeh Party were dismissed, and some 1,800 royal officers were promoted as the armed forces were purged of members suspected of sympathies toward the opposition.[243] The majority of the arrests took place before the Eighteenth Majlis elections in January to March of 1954, which were rigged to cement the political control of Zahedi's government.[244] The National Resistance Movement was effectively shut down through the harsh government reaction, although it remained in existence into the 1960s.[245] Similarly, the Tudeh Party's membership had decreased by half by December 1953, and the arrest of 380 Tudeh Party members in July 1954 eliminated the party's power. In line with US anticommunist goals, the Tudeh Party was removed from Iran's political scene within five years, without much resistance.[246]

The force that would become the shah's principal instrument of repression—the feared security and intelligence service, SAVAK—had its origins in a US-organized and trained intelligence unit formed immediately after the coup.[247] SAVAK itself was officially established in 1957 under the tutelage of US and Israeli intelligence officers.[248] SAVAK employed about 2,000–2,400 operatives in the early 1960s and later grew to between 7,000 and 10,000 employees in the late 1970s (along with around 20,000–30,000 part-time informers and thugs).[249] The agency's initial goal was to extinguish the Tudeh Party but its operations expanded to include gathering intelligence regarding political developments within the country in order to neutralize the shah's opponents, such as the National Front and related parties, the Arab and Baluch minorities, the Kurds, and the clergy.[250] SAVAK also monitored politically active Iranian students abroad and infiltrated opposition groups. The agency gained legal authority to arrest and detain people indefinitely and became so notorious for the brutal beatings and torture it administered that by the 1970s, the head of Amnesty International commented, "No country in the world has a worse human rights record than Iran."[251]

In addition to forceful repression, the agency employed well-educated operatives who instilled a sense of fear by spreading word of the dangers of speaking out against the regime. A censorship office was created to monitor political dissent in academia, literature, journalism, peasant organizations, and labor unions.[252] SAVAK also created fake opposition groups to identify opposition elements and lure opponents into activities for which they could subsequently be arrested. This oversight served to weaken opposition political organizations and discourage Iranians from engaging in political activity.[253] Additionally, the security forces possessed extensive biographical files, which were used to screen members of the opposition seeking to obtain passports and government employment and which provided an incentive to abstain from opposition political activity.[254]

US policy in the immediate aftermath of the coup called for the stabilization of the shah's regime and the disintegration of Iran's communist forces, both of which necessitated money and violent repression. In addition to providing Zahedi with $1 million in the immediate aftermath of the coup, the Eisenhower administration provided his government with another $68 million over the next few weeks. US financial assistance to Iran over the ensuing decade totaled $1.2 billion.[255] The CIA in 1953 also provided intelligence on the Tudeh Party and (as noted above) trained Iran's nascent intelligence forces, offered financial resources to favorable candidates in the Eighteenth Majlis elections, and helped quash antiregime uprisings in September and November. In the early 1960s, the Kennedy administration's policy of joint reform and repression in combating communism provided the shah with American backing for violent responses to popular protests.[256] Only during the Johnson administration did the United States grow sufficiently confident of the shah's security in office to reduce its intelligence presence in Iran.

SOVIET INSTITUTIONAL REGIME CHANGES IN EASTERN EUROPE

Repression also plays a role in helping leaders imposed in institutional regime changes avoid forcible removal. The dearth of coups, revolutions, and civil wars in regimes established by the Soviet Union in Eastern Europe after World War II, for example, is striking. Not a single leader was removed in an irregular manner in Poland, East Germany, Romania, Bulgaria, or Czechoslovakia until the Soviets intervened to crush the Hungarian Revolution in 1956. In fact, the only national leader in these five countries who suffered irregular removal at the hands of his countrymen—as opposed to Soviet intervention—before 1989 was Poland's Władysław Gomułka in December 1970. Given that communism in these states was hardly popular and was imposed by forceful means, why was there so little armed resistance to these communist takeovers?

One of the incredible facts about the Sovietization of Eastern Europe is just how small the ranks of the communists initially were and how little popularity they had. In almost all cases, the men who would lead the communist revolutions in these countries were trained in Moscow; many of them had also spent the war years in Russia and only returned with the arrival of Soviet tanks.[257] Hungarian communist leaders, for example, including Hungary's future "little Stalin," Mátyás Rákosi, were flown into eastern Hungarian cities liberated by the Red Army in late 1944 and early 1945 aboard Soviet aircraft.[258] Anne Applebaum, in her excellent history of the period, refers to them as "Moscow communists."[259] Ironically, Stalin did not intend to impose communism in Eastern Europe immediately, believing that these societies first needed to experience bourgeois revolutions before fertile ground for socialism would exist. Indeed, in 1944, Stalin's foreign minister, Ivan Maiskii, predicted that communism would take three or four decades to take root Eastern Europe.[260] In the meantime, Stalin encouraged his communist protégés to participate in "popular front" governments with other parties of both the left and right.

Despite their small numbers—Hungarian communist party members numbered in the hundreds in 1945—the Moscow communists believed that the masses would respond to their message and thus agreed to hold elections in several countries. The reason was simple, according to Applebaum: "most of the parties in the region held elections soon after the war's end because they thought they would win."[261] In this belief, however, they were grievously mistaken. In country after country, voters went to the polls and—even in the face of propaganda, intimidation, and violence—decisively rejected communist parties. In Hungary, the communist party finished a distant third with 17 percent of the vote in November 1945, less than one-third of the tally of the noncommunist Independent Smallholders Party, which emerged victorious with 57 percent. In Poland, only 25 percent of the electorate voted in favor of a referendum supported by the communist government in June 1946. The communists also suffered defeat in the October 1946 elections in Berlin, winning just under 20 percent of the vote and finishing third behind the social democrats (49 percent) and the Christian democrats (22 percent). Only in Czechoslovakia did communists fare well at the polls, winning 38 percent of the vote and emerging as the largest party in parliament with 114 members.[262]

In the face of these electoral setbacks, the communists had to rely on their control over other crucial institutions to solidify their control in Eastern Europe. The principal institution they used was the secret police, as Applebaum explains:

> the Soviet Union did import certain key elements of the Soviet system into every nation occupied by the Red Army, from the very beginning. First and foremost, the Soviet NKVD in collaboration with local communist parties, immediately created a secret police force in its own image, often using people whom they had already trained in Moscow. Everywhere the Red Army went—even in Czechoslovakia, from which Soviet troops eventually withdrew—these newly minted secret policemen immediately began to use selective violence, carefully targeting their political enemies according to previously composed lists and criteria.[263]

Critically, these institutions were controlled by the communist party, not the state. "Everywhere in Eastern Europe," writes Applebaum, "their control over the secret police gave minority communist parties an outsized influence over political events. Through the selective use of terror, they could send clear messages to their opponents, and to the general public, about what kinds of behavior and what kinds of people were no longer acceptable in the new regime."[264] In Hungary, for example, the communists controlled both the interior ministry and the political police by late 1945, and the police—liberally sprinkled with Soviet advisers—reported directly to the party. In addition to deporting up to 200,000 Hungarians to the Soviet Union after the Red Army occupied the country, Soviet and Hungarian secret police jailed another 40,000 Hungarians between 1945 and 1949.[265] Control over these institutions—and the backing of the Soviet occupiers—allowed Rákosi to defy the victorious Smallholders in 1945. The Smallholders were forced by the Soviet commander in Hungary, Marshal Klement Voroshilov, to form a coalition government with the communists—showing where the real power lay in the country. Gradually the Smallholders were eliminated until the communists ruled alone by 1948.

In sum, leaders that attain power through foreign-imposed regime change can avoid irregular removal in multiple ways. Restored leaders and leaders of target states that successfully democratize are less likely to suffer forcible removal from office. In a more sinister vein, externally empowered regimes that administered heavy doses of repression have been able to extend their survival—in some cases for decades. In cases of leadership regime change, where interveners do little to establish political institutions, new leaders from the military—such as Franco and Chile's Augusto Pinochet—may have an advantage owing to their firm control over the key instrument of repression. In other cases, interveners help new regimes consolidate control and eliminate opposition both with their own military forces (e.g., the Soviets in Eastern Europe) and by helping to create new indigenous institutions of repression.

* * *

In this chapter I examined the effect of entry into office via foreign-imposed regime change on leaders' hazard of regular and irregular removal from office. I hypothesized that leaders brought to power in this way would be more likely to lose power by forcible means and less likely to exit through established rules and procedures. I further argued that these effects would be most pronounced for leaders empowered in leadership regime changes and less pronounced for those who attain office through institutional and restoration regime changes. The data analysis from two different datasets of leaders largely bears out these suppositions. In the qualitative section of the chapter, I further showed that most of the ways that foreign-imposed leaders are ousted irregularly comport with my arguments. Finally, I identified three mechanisms that reduce the likelihood of irregular removal: restoration regime changes, institutional regime changes that successfully democratize targets, and the development of powerful institutions of repression. The appendix below provides details, for those interested, on the quantitative analysis presented in the chapter. Next, however, I turn to the consequences of regime change for relations between intervening and target states.

Appendix to Chapter 4. A Competing Risks Hazard Analysis of Regime Change and Leader Survival

This appendix provides additional information on the statistical analysis that produced the results summarized in the body of the chapter. It is organized into three sections. First, I discuss the data used in the analysis and the research design employed to discern the effects of regime change on regular and irregular leader removal from office. Second, I present the main results from the competing risks hazard analysis. Third, I outline my efforts to address the possibility that selection bias explains my results.

DATA

To assess the effect of different types of regime change on leader survival, I use two versions of the *Archigos* data compiled by Goemans, Gleditsch, and Chiozza.[266] The two datasets differ in their dates of coverage and their units of analysis. The first dataset includes all leaders who held power from 1919 to 2004, with the unit of analysis being the leader-year.[267] In other words, there is an observation for every leader for each year he or she held office (e.g., Carter 1977, Carter 1978, etc.). One advantage of having the leader-year as the unit of analysis is that it allows for the inclusion of time-varying covariates, that is, control variables that vary over time, which permits a more accurate assessment of the effect of these variables on leader tenure. This version of the dataset also includes a large number of variables coded by Goemans that are relevant to leader removal, many of which are not included in my dataset. This combination of leader-year as the unit of analysis and numerous control variables provides the strongest test of regime change as a predictor of irregular leader removal. The disadvantage of this dataset is that it covers only a portion of the years for which data on leaders are now available.

The second version of *Archigos* that I analyze covers a longer time period (1875–2004) and thus includes more leaders than the leader-year dataset, but also has a different unit of analysis: the leader spell. In this dataset, there is only one observation per leader per time in office. Margaret Thatcher, for example, appears in the dataset once, her tenure as prime minister of Britain lasting from April 5, 1979, to November 28, 1990, a span of 4,226 days. Winston Churchill, by contrast, appears twice, serving from 1940 to 1945 and again from 1951 to 1955, whereas there are three entries for Stanley Baldwin (1923–24, 1924–29, and 1935–37). The obvious advantage of this version of the dataset is that it includes more than forty years of additional leaders over the leader-year version. Beyond method of entry into office, gender, and number of previous times in office, however, this version includes few control variables, and these variables do not vary over the course of the leader's tenure in office. I thus import control variables from my dataset into this one to conduct the leader-spell analysis.

METHOD

The dependent variable in this analysis is the amount of time a leader spends in office until he or she is removed by irregular or regular means. What I wish to estimate is the probability that a leader is forcibly removed from office given that he or she has survived in office up to that time, a quantity known as the hazard rate. Because estimating the hazard of removal from office involves analyzing the timing of an event, and the dataset includes right-censored observations—that is, leaders who remained in power at the end of the observation period (2004)—a special class of models, known as event history (or survival) models, is needed.[268]

Leaders, however, can leave power in more than one way; although some are overthrown in coups and revolutions, others depart according to normal procedures established by the state's constitution. Others die of natural causes while in office. Because there are multiple ways that leaders can leave office, I use a competing risks hazard model, which estimates the risk of one type of removal controlling for the fact that competing events—such as regular removal or death—may interfere with the ability to observe irregular removal.[269] In medical studies, where investigators often seek to estimate the effects of various factors on the risk of recurrence of some condition, such as cancer, recurrence is the outcome of interest and death is the competing risk. Both of these outcomes are different from subjects that drop out of the study and are thus lost to follow up. These subjects are treated as right-censored because they are still at risk of recurrence even though they are not observed. Subjects who experience a competing risk like death cannot suffer a recurrence, just as leaders who leave office in one way cannot simultaneously leave office in a different way. In my analyses, I estimate a leader's hazard of irregular (regular) removal controlling for the competing events of regular (irregular) removal and natural death.

In the leader-year dataset, I estimate a competing risks model with time-varying covariates. Leaders who are placed in power by a foreign country or who assume office after their predecessor was removed by a foreign power are coded as foreign-imposed leaders for the duration of their tenure in office. Each of these regime changes is also coded as either leadership, institutional, or restoration in nature according to the criteria adopted throughout this book. Each year a leader remains in office, her cumulative number of days in office is recorded, and variables are coded designating whether or not she experienced an irregular removal, regular removal, or natural death. These three indicators are combined into a variable called "failure type," where, for irregular removal, irregular leader exits are coded as 1, regular removal as 2, and natural death as 3. When regular removal is the event of interest, it is coded 1, irregular removal as 2, and natural death as 3. Leaders who remain in office in 2004—and thus are right-censored—are coded as 0. Like the Cox proportional hazards model, competing risk models assume that the effects of variables are the same over time. To check the validity of this assumption, regime change and its subtypes are interacted with the natural log of time to check for nonproportional hazards. In the analysis of irregular removal, restoration regime change shows evidence of nonproportional hazards and thus its interaction with time is included in the final models. When time to regular removal is the dependent variable, regime change as a whole, as well as institutional and restoration regime change, have nonproportional hazards. For the control variables, I follow Goemans, who checked for nonproportional hazards in his earlier article.[270]

In the leader-spell dataset, the data are a simple cross section and hence it is not possible to include time-varying covariates. Rather, leaders are coded as to whether or not they entered office via some form of regime change and the covariates are coded for the year the leader took power. The total number of days each leader held office is recorded, and the same failure variable records the leader's manner of leaving office.

CONTROL VARIABLES

Unfortunately, it is not possible to include the same set of control variables in both analyses. In his 2008 article that examined the effect of international crises and wars on the risk of regular versus irregular leader removal, Goemans used version 2.6 of the *Archigos* data, which at the time were complete for the years from 1919 to 2004.[271] For that article, Goemans compiled an extensive set of controls. In 2009, in version 2.9 of *Archigos*, the data were extended back to the mid-1870s. *Archigos* version 4.1, released in 2016, updated the data through 2015. The more recent and extensive versions of *Archigos* that are publicly available, however, do not include many control variables. For this reason, I adopt a compromise solution. To permit me to use Goemans's set of control variables, I use his leader-year dataset that covers the period from 1919 to 2004. To allow me to take advantage of the larger number of leaders available in updates of *Archigos*, I use the leader-spell version of *Archigos* 2.9 and import my own control variables. I do not use *Archigos* 4.1 because my dataset ends in 2008.

Table 4.2 lists the control variables in Goemans's leader-year dataset and in the leader-spell dataset.[272] Because the extensive set of control variables compiled by Goemans for use with the leader-year version of *Archigos* 2.6 is not available for the extended time period covered by the leader-spell data, I imported the control variables used in the other analyses in this book into the leader-spell dataset. A few variables, such as leader age, previous times in office, and method of entry appear in both datasets.[273] In a few additional cases, such as certain regime types (mixed regime, autocracy) and population, I created the same variables from the same or similar sources. Still other variables, like ongoing civil war and interstate war defeat, existed in my dataset but differ in the way they were coded. One other variable—primary energy consumption—is an oft-used substitute for GDP as a proxy for economic development.

Several other variables from the leader-year dataset that I am unable to incorporate do not fit well into the leader-spell format. The leader-year data, for example, contain nine variables related to the initiation or outcome of international crises or conflicts. It would be difficult to accommodate these variables into a setting where there is only one observation per leader. One could only code, for example, whether a leader initiated a conflict at some point during his tenure and assess the effect of that conflict initiation on his time in office. Finally, I am able to adjudicate the effect of several factors that Goemans could not, including mountainous terrain, state age, buffer status, oil production, and several measures of ethnic diversity and discrimination.

STATISTICAL RESULTS FOR IRREGULAR REMOVAL

Below I present the results of the competing risks hazard models for irregular and regular leader removal. In each section, I first discuss results generated by the leader-year dataset and then proceed to those from the leader-spell dataset. For reasons of space, I omit results for the control variables from the tables.[274]

Table 4.2 Variables in the leader-year and leader-spell datasets

Variable	Leader-year dataset	Leader-spell dataset
Democracy		✓
Parliamentary democracy	✓	
Presidential democracy	✓	
Mixed regime	✓	✓
Transitional regime	✓	
Autocracy	✓	✓
Civil war	✓	✓
GDP per capita	✓	
GDP growth	✓	
Energy consumption		✓
Trade openness	✓	
Change in trade openness	✓	
Population	✓	✓
Mountainous terrain		✓
New state		✓
Buffer state		✓
Ethnolinguistic fractionalization		✓
Percent of ethnic population suffering discrimination		✓
Percent of ethnic population excluded from power		✓
Oil producer		✓
Leader age	✓	✓
Times in office	✓	✓
Irregular entry into office	✓	✓
Crisis/war challenger	✓	
Crisis/war target	✓	
Crisis/war inheritor	✓	
Crisis victory	✓	
Crisis defeat	✓	
Crisis draw	✓	
War victory	✓	
War defeat	✓	✓
War draw	✓	

Table 4.3 presents results for the effect of foreign-imposed regime change on the hazard of irregular removal derived from the leader-year dataset. Cell entries are hazard ratios, with standard errors clustered on each state in parentheses. Unlike regression coefficients, hazard ratios are interpreted relative to 1 rather than zero. Hazard ratios greater than one imply that a variable increases the risk of irregular removal, thereby reducing the length of time a leader enjoys in office. Hazard ratios between zero and one mean that a variable reduces the risk of irregular removal and hence increases time in office. For each model, "number of observations" refers to the number of leader-years included; "number failed" is the number of leaders removed by irregular means, by either domestic or foreign actors; "number competing"

Table 4.3 Competing risks analysis of irregular removal from office, 1919–2004, leader-year data

	1	2	3	4	5	6	7	8
Foreign entry into office	2.328*** (0.438)	—	—	—	—	—	1.474† (0.332)	—
Leadership regime change	—	3.864*** (0.917)	5.157*** (1.290)	2.207** (0.528)	2.435** (0.723)	2.820*** (0.650)	—	2.086** (0.571)
Institutional regime change	—	2.145 (1.070)	3.650** (1.833)	1.760 (0.940)	0.523 (0.482)	2.653† (1.333)	—	0.875 (0.778)
Restoration regime change	—	0.013** (0.017)	0.016** (0.021)	0.011** (0.014)	0.015** (0.021)	0.008** (0.011)	—	0.009** (0.014)
Restoration regime change×ln(t)	—	1.001*** (0.000)	1.001*** (0.000)	1.001*** (0.000)	1.001*** (0.000)	1.001*** (0.000)	—	1.001*** (0.000)
Controls?	No	No	Yes~	Yes‡	Yes+	Yes#	Yes^	Yes^
Number of observations	10989	10989	10973	10989	9390	10989	9374	9374
Number failed	493	493	491	493	391	493	389	389
Number competing	1498	1498	1490	1498	1298	1498	1290	1290
Number censored	161	161	161	161	165	161	165	165
Log pseudo-likelihood	−3672.375	−3658.729	−3534.721	−3511.703	−2694.551	−3568.649	−2571.519	−2563.258
Wald Chi²	20.17***	56.50***	195.38***	131.12***	211.63***	307.27***	527.09***	627.10***

Note: Hazard ratios with standard errors in parentheses. † $p < 0.10$; * $p < 0.05$; ** $p < 0.01$; *** $p < 0.001$.

~ Irregular entry into office, leader age, times in office

‡ Four regime type variables

+ Five economic, trade, and population variables

Eleven civil and interstate crisis and conflict variables

^ All control variables included

refers to leaders who left office by regular procedures or died in office; and "number censored" refers to leaders still in office when the analysis ended in 2004.

Model 1 in table 4.3 includes only a dummy variable for all types of regime change combined. The hazard ratio of 2.328 implies that leaders brought to power by regime change are on average 2.328 times more likely to suffer irregular removal than leaders who obtain office in other ways. This effect is significant at the highest level ($p < 0.001$). This result strongly supports H4.1a. Model 2 breaks regime change into its three types. As predicted, the effect of leadership regime change is large, positive, and highly significant, nearly quadrupling the hazard of irregular removal. Leaders empowered in institutional regime changes are also more likely to experience forcible removal but this effect fails to obtain statistical significance. This pair of results is consistent with H4.2a and H4.3a. The result for restoration regime change reflects the finding from earlier in the chapter that restored leaders survive an extremely long time in office before suffering irregular removal. The hazard rate for restoration regime change is a mere 0.013, suggesting that restored leaders are 99 percent less likely to be removed by force than are other leaders. The interaction between restoration regime changes and time, however, is positive, which implies that the risk of irregular removal for these leaders grows—if very slowly—over time. While this result contradicts H4.4a, it is important to stress that only two leaders were removed irregularly following restoration regime changes.

Models 3–6 in table 4.3 each add a different group of control variables to the three types of regime change until all variables are combined in models 7 and 8. Across all of these specifications, leadership regime change is consistently significant, increasing the hazard of forcible removal by between a factor of two and three. The effect of restoration regime change is also consistent, reducing the hazard of irregular removal initially but increasing it over time. Institutional regime change, by contrast, achieves significance in only two of six models, and does not exert a systematic effect when all controls are included in model 7.[275]

Table 4.4 displays the results from my analysis of the hazard of irregular removal using the leader-spell data. Although many of the control variables in the table are different, the results for regime change are highly similar to those produced by the leader-year dataset. Model 9 in table 4.4 contains only my aggregated regime change variable. The hazard ratio of 2.767 indicates that leaders who are placed in power by foreign powers are nearly three times as likely as other leaders to be forcibly removed from office. Put another way, this result suggests that foreign-imposed leaders survive roughly one-third as long in office as non-foreign-imposed leaders before suffering an irregular removal. This result is highly statistically significant ($p < 0.001$). Splitting regime change up into its three types in model 10 reveals that, as in the leader-year data, leadership regime change is responsible for the increased hazard of

Table 4.4 Competing risks analysis of irregular removal from office, 1875–2004, leader-spell data

	9	10	11	12	13	14	15	16
					1946–2004	1946–2004	1946–2004	1960–2004
Foreign entry into office	2.767*** (0.491)	–	2.220*** (0.409)	–	–	–	–	–
Leadership regime change	–	4.362*** (0.843)	–	3.454*** (0.763)	3.250*** (1.064)	2.855** (1.099)	2.778** (1.075)	3.186** (1.120)
Institutional regime change	–	1.701 (0.795)	–	1.141 (0.630)	0.000*** (0.000)	0.000*** (0.000)	0.000*** (0.000)	0.000*** (0.000)
Restoration regime change	–	0.428 (0.288)	–	0.525 (0.307)	0.254 (0.237)	0.291 (0.283)	0.294 (0.285)	0.000*** (0.000)
Controls?	No	No	Yes	Yes	Yes‡	Yes+	Yes#	Yes^
Number of observations	3057	3057	2876	2876	1619	1551	1551	1261
Number failed	664	664	612	612	335	321	321	247
Number competing	2222	2222	2102	2102	1126	1081	1081	860
Number censored	171	171	162	162	158	149	149	154
Log pseudo-likelihood	–5187.274	–5175.348	–4483.560	–4476.474	–2215.241	–2109.850	–2109.468	–1572.833
Wald Chi^2	32.89***	61.98***	284.18***	292.60***	956.78***	875.26***	837.54***	3102.47***

Note: Hazard ratios with standard errors in parentheses. + $p < 0.10$; * $p < 0.05$; ** $p < 0.01$; *** $p < 0.001$.

‡ Adds ethnolinguistic fractionalization and a dummy variable for oil production.

+ Adds the proportion of ethnic population suffering discrimination.

Adds the proportion of ethnic population excluded from power.

^ Adds a continuous variable for oil production.

forcible removal faced by foreign-imposed leaders. Leadership regime change more than quadruples this risk. Although institutional regime change also increases the hazard of irregular removal about 70 percent, it is not statistically significant. Restorations reduce the hazard of forcible removal almost 60 percent but again do not achieve significance. This pattern of results supports my four hypotheses on irregular leader removal.

The effect of regime change as a whole, and leadership regime change, survives the inclusion of the full battery of control variables in models 11 and 12. The substantive effects are somewhat attenuated, but the former still more than doubles the hazard of irregular removal whereas the latter increases it three and a half times. Both variables remain significant at better than the 99.9 percent level of confidence. Models 13–16 include different proxies for ethnic heterogeneity and discrimination as well as oil production and thus are limited to the post-1945 period (post-1960 for model 16). Model 13, for example includes the ethnolinguistic fractionalization index as a measure of heterogeneity and Jeff Colgan's measure of whether a state produces substantial quantities of oil.[276] Neither of these factors significantly affects the hazard of irregular removal, and the impact of leadership regime change is largely unchanged. Models 14 and 15 introduce two measures of ethnic discrimination from the Ethnic Power Relations dataset: the proportion of the ethnic population in a state that experiences state-led discrimination (model 14), and the percentage of the ethnic population that is excluded from power (model 15). These variables each mildly increase the hazard of irregular removal but neither is significant. Their inclusion, however, does eat into the size and significance of the hazard rate for leadership regime change, which in these models is reduced below three but remains highly significant. Model 16, finally, includes Ross's measure of oil production, which is also unrelated to irregular removal.[277] The hazard rate for leadership regime change in this model rebounds above three.

Models 13–16 in table 4.4 reveal some interesting time trends in institutional and restoration regime changes. In these models, the hazard ratio for institutional regime change is zero and is highly significant. This is because no leader brought to power in an institutional regime change after 1945 has been deprived of office by force. This group of leaders includes communists installed by the Soviets after World War II in East Germany (Wilhelm Pieck) and Czechoslovakia (Klement Gottwald); and democratic leaders empowered by the United States in West Germany (Konrad Adenauer), Panama (Guillermo Endara), Afghanistan (Hamid Karzai), and Iraq (Ayad Allawi).[278] Similarly, the hazard ratio for restoration regime change in model 16 is zero because no leader restored to power in a regime change since 1960 has suffered forcible removal from office. For example, five African leaders were returned to office during this period; three subsequently left power regularly while two remained in office in 2004.[279] Jean-Bertrand Aristide of

Haiti, restored to power in 1994 by the United States, also falls into this category.

In sum, the results of the competing risks analysis for irregular removal strongly support my hypotheses. Regime change increases the likelihood of irregular removal in both the leader-year and the leader-spell datasets. Leadership regime change is the type that is responsible for the increased hazard of forcible removal for foreign-imposed leaders. It is significant at beyond the 99 percent level of confidence in every test. Institutional regime change is not significant in either dataset. Restoration regime change almost eliminates the likelihood of irregular removal in the leader-year dataset, but this result relies on only two leaders. After World War II, however, institutional regime change reduces the hazard of irregular removal, as does restoration regime change after 1960.

STATISTICAL RESULTS FOR REGULAR REMOVAL

Table 4.5 uses the leader-year dataset to estimate the effects of regime change on leaders' risk of removal from office by regular means, such as elections, hereditary succession, or other methods not involving coercion or force.[280] It repeats the sequence used in the analysis of irregular removal using the leader-year data.

Model 17 in table 4.5 demonstrates that regime change has the opposite effect on regular removal than it had on forcible exit from office. The hazard ratio for regime change in model 17 is 0.465, which indicates that regime change reduces the risk of regular removal by more than 50 percent. This finding supports H4.1b and is not especially surprising given that regime change increases the hazard of irregular removal. Model 17 also shows that the negative effect of regime change on regular removal diminishes over time, which conforms to the reduction in the difference in survival rates between foreign-imposed and nonforeign-imposed leaders observed in figure 4.11. The magnitude of the reduction is very slight—the hazard ratio for the interaction with time is only 1.00015—and takes a long time to manifest. The suppressive effect of regime change on the risk of regular removal remains when all control models are included (model 23) but it is smaller (a 35 percent reduction in the hazard rate) and no longer significant ($p = 0.18$). The loss of significance is likely attributable both to the addition of the large number of additional variables plus the contradictory effects of the different types of regime change.

The remaining models in table 4.5 show the effects of the three different types of regime change on the hazard that leaders experience a regular removal from power. The results confirm that, as expected, leadership regime change consistently lowers the hazard of regular removal. The magnitude of the reduction in risk ranges from 51 to 78 percent; when all controls are included (model 24) it is 68 percent. Institutional regime change also lowers

Table 4.5 Competing risks analysis of regular removal from office, 1919–2004, leader-year data

	17	18	19	20	21	22	23	24
Foreign entry into office	0.465** (0.120)	–	–	–	–	–	0.650 (0.209)	–
Foreign entry into office×ln(t)	1.000† (0.000)	–	–	–	–	–	1.000 (0.000)	–
Leadership regime change	–	0.332** (0.119)	0.302** (0.110)	0.489† (0.182)	0.225** (0.113)	0.367** (0.134)	–	0.319* (0.177)
Institutional regime change	–	0.473* (0.159)	0.402** (0.132)	0.579† (0.192)	0.755 (0.332)	0.445* (0.152)	–	0.623 (0.290)
Institutional regime change×ln(t)	–	1.000† (0.000)	1.000† (0.000)	1.000 (0.000)	1.000† (0.000)	1.000† (0.000)	–	1.000* (0.000)
Restoration regime change	–	0.872 (0.381)	0.835 (0.371)	1.016 (0.014)	1.066 (0.597)	0.880 (0.392)	–	1.547 (0.619)
Restoration regime Change×ln(t)	–	1.000* (0.000)	1.000 (0.000)	1.000** (0.000)	1.000 (0.000)	1.000† (0.000)	–	1.000 (0.000)
Controls?	No	No	Yes†	Yes‡	Yes†	Yes#	Yes^	Yes^
Number of observations	10989	10989	10973	10983	9390	10989	9374	9374
Number failed	1321	1321	1313	1319	1153	1321	1145	1145
Number competing	670	670	668	669	536	670	534	534
Number censored	161	161	161	161	165	161	165	165
Log pseudo-likelihood	–9509.129	–9503.062	–9360.461	–9260.434	–7945.710	–9480.151	–7724.686	–7719.357
Wald Chi²	9.27**	22.00***	109.04***	239.73***	138.06***	49.10***	406.63***	449.39***

Note: Hazard rates with standard errors in parentheses. † $p<0.10$; * $p<0.05$; ** $p<0.01$; *** $p<0.001$.

† Irregular entry into office, leader age, and times in office

‡ Four regime type variables

+ Five economic, trade, and population variables

Eleven civil and interstate crisis and conflict variables

^ All control variables included

the hazard of losing office by regular procedures. The size of this effect is smaller—ranging between 25 and 60 percent—and is less consistently significant than for leadership regime change. In model 24, which includes the full battery of controls, institutional interventions reduce the hazard of regular removal 38 percent but the effect is not significant. Like regime change overall, the effect of institutional regime change grows slightly less negative over time. Leaders who are restored to office by external powers are neither more nor less likely than other leaders to be removed regularly.

The results in table 4.6, which presents the findings for the hazard of regular removal from the leader-spell data, are similar to those in table 4.5. Regime change overall, and leadership regime change, reduce the risk of regular removal from office. The magnitude of the effect ranges from 42 to 52 percent for regime change and 61 to 72 percent for leadership regime change. Both variables are significant with and without controls. Institutional regime change has little systematic effect on regular removal until after 1960, when it increases the risk of losing office in this way. Restoration regime change, finally, is never significant in table 4.6.

Overall, the results for regular removal provide strong support for hypotheses 4.1b–4.4b. Regime change as a whole and leadership regime change decrease the hazard of regular removal. Institutional and restoration regime change have little effect on the likelihood of regular removal until after 1945 for the former and post-1960 for the latter.

As a robustness check, and to emulate the procedures used by Goemans, I reran all of the analyses above using the leader-year data after performing multiple imputation to fill in missing values. In the version of *Archigos* 2.6 that Goemans uses in his 2008 article, half a dozen control variables have missing data that results in the loss of about 1,600 cases in the full model. I use all of the other variables in the model to impute the missing values and generate five versions of the imputed dataset. I then analyze the five versions together and obtain the averaged coefficients. The results for both types of removal change little after imputation. For irregular removal, the only difference is that institutional regime change significantly increases the hazard of irregular removal, whereas in the previous analysis it had been insignificant. For regular removal, leadership regime change, although continuing to reduce the likelihood of this outcome, just misses the cutoff for statistical significance.[281]

SELECTION BIAS

This subsection evaluates the possibility that selection bias accounts for the effects on leader removal that I attribute to regime change. To reprise, three forms of selection bias might be at work that could explain the positive association between foreign-imposed regime change and irregular leader removal. For one, states targeted for regime change may simply be more

Table 4.6 Competing risks analysis of regular removal from office, 1875–2004, leader-spell data

	25	26	27	28	29	30	31	32
					1946–2004	1946–2004	1946–2004	1960–2004
Foreign entry into office	0.479***	–	0.580**	–	–	–	–	0.369*
	(0.084)		(0.108)					(0.160)
Leadership regime change	–	0.283***	–	0.311**	0.349**	0.393*	0.393*	0.369*
		(0.072)		(0.088)	(0.135)	(0.164)	(0.165)	(0.160)
Institutional regime change	–	0.845	–	1.004	1.630	2.854	2.867	5.981**
		(0.268)		(0.376)	(1.089)	(2.340)	(2.384)	(4.050)
Restoration regime change	–	0.950	–	0.997	0.979	0.819	0.803	1.060
		(0.289)		(0.339)	(0.357)	(0.304)	(0.299)	(0.452)
Controls?	No	No	Yes	Yes	Yes‡	Yes+	Yes#	Yes^
Number of observations	3057	3057	2876	2876	1619	1551	1551	1261
Number failed	2037	2037	1944	1944	1048	1005	1005	811
Number competing	849	849	770	770	413	397	397	296
Number censored	171	171	162	162	158	149	149	154
Log pseudo-likelihood	–15321.41	–15314.05	–14172.29	–14166.47	–6991.581	–6664.288	–6663.449	–5181.878
Wald Chi^2	17.42***	24.54***	277.55***	280.42***	305.90***	280.10***	284.13***	213.41***

Note: Hazard rates with standard errors in parentheses. $^+$ $p < 0.10$; * $p < 0.05$; ** $p < 0.01$; *** $p < 0.001$.

‡ Adds ethnolinguistic fractionalization and a dummy variable for oil production

$^+$ Adds the proportion of ethnic population suffering discrimination

Adds the proportion of ethnic population excluded from power

^ Adds a continuous variable for oil production

prone (for a variety of reasons) to violent processes of leader removal. Further, states targeted for leadership regime change in particular could also be more prone to irregular removal than targets of other types of regime change. Finally, targets of regime changes that succeed might be more prone to violent removal of leaders than targets where regime change fails.

Identifying Confounding Variables To address the first type of selection bias, I conducted an analysis of the causes of regime change (described briefly in the appendix to chapter 3) to determine whether there are variables that potentially cause both regime change and irregular leader removal. If a variable simultaneously increases or decreases the likelihood of regime change and irregular removal, then the effect of the former on the latter might be spurious. The results of that analysis reveal that only a handful of variables could be sources of bias.[282] Most consistently, democracies and states with large populations are both less likely to be targets of regime change and have a lower chance of irregular leader removal. Two additional variables—interstate war involvement and ongoing civil war—increase the chance of regime change but are only sometimes significant in my irregular removal analysis. It will be important to include these variables in the matching analysis described below. The remaining variables—the target's level of development, state age, ethnolinguistic fractionalization, rough terrain, and whether it is a buffer state or produces oil—are not sources of bias.

To address the second type of selection bias—that targets of leadership regime change are different than targets of other regime changes in ways that predispose them to irregular leader removal—I compare the mean values of cases where leadership regime changes are imposed versus cases where other types of regime changes occur. Table 4.7 reveals that the two categories differ along only a few dimensions. For example, targets of leadership regime change are less economically developed and less likely to be democratic than countries where institutional or restoration regime changes occur. Each of these conditions increases the propensity for violent leader removal. Targets of leadership regime change are also more mountainous than targets of other regime changes but rough terrain is unrelated to the likelihood of irregular removal. Countries where leadership regime changes occur, by contrast, are not significantly more populous or more likely to be a new or buffer state; be involved in or lose an interstate war; or have a civil war ongoing. Moreover, individuals installed in leadership regime changes have on average previously been in office fewer times than in other regime changes, which lowers their vulnerability to irregular removal.

Overall it seems unlikely that differences in economic development and democracy alone explain the divergences in the probability of violent leader removal after different types of regime change. The difference in the likelihood of being a democracy, for example, is not large (0.13); all targets of

Table 4.7 T-tests of leadership versus institutional and restoration foreign-imposed regime changes and factors correlated with irregular leader removal

	Mean, leadership regime change	Mean, institutional and restoration regime change	P-value
Economic development	5.319	6.895	0.039
Population	8.381	8.438	0.857
New state	0.065	0.023	0.322
Percent mountainous	0.261	0.165	0.020
Democracy	0.032	0.159	0.021
Interstate war involvement	0.419	0.295	0.196
Lose interstate war	0.306	0.182	0.150
Previous times in office	0.018	0.300	0.000
Buffer state	0.361	0.364	0.975
Ongoing civil war	0.306	0.182	0.150
Leader age	46.963	56.846	0.000

Note: N = 106, 62 leadership and 44 nonleadership regime changes.

regime change are highly unlikely to have a democratic regime type. Moreover, as already mentioned, the target's level of economic development does not increase the likelihood of regime change in the first place. Combined with the countervailing effect of leaders who have been in office fewer times, any bias is likely to be small.

Matching To further explore these two types of selection bias, I use genetic matching to create a set of control cases that is statistically indistinguishable from cases where (different types of) regime change occurred. To perform this analysis, and because the results from the two datasets were similar, I used the leader-spell dataset because it avoids the complications of implementing matching with time series data. To prevent leaders brought to power by regime changes from being matched to other leaders from the same state, I dropped all observations of leaders from states that experienced a regime change at any time other than the leader(s) installed in regime changes. The reason for doing this is that many of the variables used in the analysis are characteristics of states; it would introduce bias to match leaders from the same state if states are selecting leaders for regime change in part on these characteristics since leaders from the same state will have highly similar values on these variables.

I then created two datasets with different dependent variables: irregular removal compared to regular removal and natural death, and regular removal compared to irregular removal and natural death. Genetic matching in all cases produced improvements in balance between regime change and nonregime change cases of between 89 and 99 percent.[283] After matching, I performed both bivariate and multivariate (including all the controls

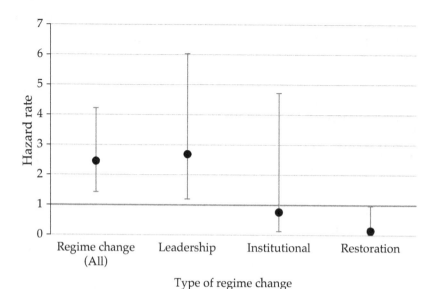

Figure 4.11. Postgenetic matching hazard rates of irregular removal after foreign-imposed regime change (leader-spell data). All control variables from the leader-spell analysis included.

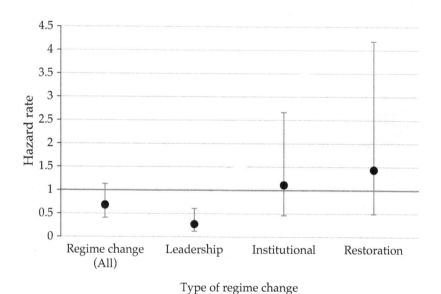

Figure 4.12. Postgenetic matching hazard rates of regular removal after foreign-imposed regime change (leader-spell data). All control variables from the leader-spell analysis included.

that were used for matching because matching is not perfect) competing risks hazard analyses for all types of regime change for regular and irregular removal. Figures 4.11 and 4.12 summarize the results of the multivariate analyses.

The results for both regular and irregular removal are strikingly similar to the results presented in the main body of the chapter. In particular, after matching, leadership regime change continues to make violent removal between two and three times more likely and regular removal about one quarter as likely—effects that are statistically significant.[284] Restoration regime changes also significantly reduce the likelihood of irregular removal by 85 percent. Importantly, all of the variables that I previously found to increase the likelihood of regime change are included in the matching procedure, as are the variables that differed across leadership and other types of regime change, which neutralizes their effects. Even after assembling a statistically indistinguishable set of control cases, I find that leadership regime change increases the likelihood of irregular removal whereas the other two types of regime change do not.

It is obviously not possible to measure and match on every possible variable that might affect how leaders are removed from office. My analysis, however, captures many of the important ones, including two that I previously found also affected the probability of regime change in addition to leader removal. Controlling for these potential sources of spuriousness, the relationships between regime change and different forms of removal from office identified above persist.

Finally, I cannot address the possibility that failed regime changes affect the political survival of imposed leaders because by definition no leader was imposed. This type of selection bias seems unlikely to affect the analysis in this chapter.

Foreign-Imposed Regime Change and Interstate Relations

This chapter examines how foreign-imposed regime change affects relations between interveners and targets.[1] In doing so, the chapter investigates whether interveners get what they want out of regime change. States turn to this tool to replace leaders with divergent preferences and bring to power more agreeable leaders who will act in accordance with the interveners' interests. In short, they wish to change the intentions of rival states by changing the leaders (and sometimes the institutions) of those states. Installing leaders who share their preferences allows interveners to eliminate the prior conflict and stabilizes relations going forward. In other words, interveners typically do not walk away after regime change; they care about who takes power in the target and often go to great lengths to ensure that individual is willing to accommodate their concerns.

Does regime change bring states into closer alignment and eliminate conflicts of interest between them? At the most basic level, if regime change works as its advocates predict, interveners and targets should be less likely than other dyads—and less likely than they were before regime change—to experience militarized conflict. One might also expect that measures of the quality of relations between interveners and targets—such as similarity of alliance portfolios or UN voting records—ought to improve. Moreover, interveners should be able to extract compliance with their interests or strategic priorities from targets. Put differently, in the patron-protégé relationship that results from regime change, the patron ought to get its way on issues it cares about most of the time.

In this chapter I explore these and other hypotheses in order to better understand how regime change affects relations between interveners and targets. My findings generally track with the propositions I have put forth throughout this book: on average, regime change—although it does not worsen relations between the two states involved—certainly does not improve them. Indeed, leadership regime changes can actually lead to an increased frequency of conflict, whereas institutional regime changes have no systematic effect and restoration regime changes reduce conflict occurrence. Nor is it the case that regime change of any type increases the closeness of relations between interveners and targets as measured by UN voting patterns. When quality of relations is proxied by similarity of alliance portfolios, only institutional regime change improves intervener-target relations whereas leadership regime change worsens them.

I complement these quantitative findings with three types of case studies. First, I trace how the dynamics of regime change can generate further conflict between interveners and targets. The military disintegration logic, as amply demonstrated in chapter 3, tends to result in wars of occupation that pit interveners against the remnants of the target's military, often supplemented by new recruits. In other words, in cases of military disintegration, interstate conflict between interveners and targets becomes impossible because the latter collapse and are occupied by the former. Any ensuing conflict almost by definition occurs inside the target state, pitting the intervener and its local allies against opponents of regime change. *Interstate* conflict between interveners and targets is thus produced by the problem of competing principals, in which imposed leaders—usually owing to domestic opposition—are unable or unwilling to implement policies favorable to interveners. I examine one particularly glaring example of this logic in action following Rwanda and Uganda's overthrow of Mobutu Sese Seko in Zaire.

Second, I show, in brief vignettes of several cases, that even when relations between interveners and targets do not devolve into open hostilities, they are often far from harmonious. In particular, interveners, despite having placed the new leader in office as well as holding a substantial advantage in power relative to the target, struggle to get their protégés to implement their preferences faithfully. In some cases, as discussed in chapter 4, this disconnect propels patrons to intervene a second time to empower a more pliant protégé. In other cases, patrons encourage domestic actors in the target state to do the job for them or simply stand aside when an impending coup promises to place a more pliable leader in power. In still other cases, although interveners clash repeatedly with their protégés, patrons are unwilling to overthrow the leaders they brought to power and simply accept (unhappily) their inability to control them. These three types of cases may not meet the threshold to be coded as militarized interstate disputes, but they nevertheless signify a serious conflict of interest between interveners and targets.

Third, I examine Japan's assassination of Manchurian strongman and outgoing Chinese president Chang Tso-lin because this case is followed by several militarized disputes and thus contributes disproportionately to the statistical finding that leadership regime change increases the likelihood of intervener-target armed conflict. Some have also argued that Chang Tso-lin's ouster is not a case of foreign-imposed regime change.[2] I argue that although the details of the case are unusual, there are solid grounds for coding it as a case of regime change. Moreover, the problem of competing principals helps explain why Chang's son and successor, Chang Hsüeh-liang, defied Japan and chose to throw in his lot with his father's adversary, Chiang Kai-shek's Nationalist regime.

This chapter is organized as follows. First, I briefly review how regime change is supposed to work to reduce conflict between states. Second, I recapitulate my theory and the hypotheses I will test.[3] Third, I summarize the results of my statistical analysis of the effects of regime change on intervener-target militarized conflict and multiple measures of interstate alignment. Fourth, I present qualitative evidence that demonstrates how the problem of competing principals can undermine relations between interveners and targets and even in some cases bring them to blows. After concluding the main part of the chapter, the appendix presents the details of the statistical analysis.

Recapitulating the Optimist Argument

States have a variety of options for persuading other states to change their behavior—and in particular to bring that behavior into line with their own preferences. One broad array of options involves the use of sticks: threatening to inflict some form of punishment on the target unless it changes its ways or actually inflicting punishment until the target yields and agrees to change its behavior. Tools that fall into this category include rhetorical coercion, such as exposing, naming, and shaming a target's unsavory or illegal behavior; the threat or infliction of economic pressure, such as cutting off economic aid or applying sanctions; coercive diplomacy, which entails military threats or limited uses of force; military coercion, such as bombing campaigns or naval blockades; and full-blown ground invasions to force targets to change their policies. A second broad category involves the provision of carrots—offering benefits or inducements of various kinds as an incentive to change behavior. This category also includes a wide variety of tools, such as economic or military aid; development assistance; preferential access to the persuader's domestic market; protection against third-party threats; and formal alliances.

Foreign-imposed regime change falls at the extreme end of the stick category. Rather than try to persuade an adversary to change its behavior, the intervener instead changes the leadership of the target state, installing someone it expects will yield the desired concessions or cease an objectionable policy. States have two options at their disposal if they adopt a policy of regime change: (1) empower a particular leader who has preferences similar to the intervener's in a leadership or restoration regime change, or (2) transform the institutions of the target to bring its preferences permanently into line with the intervener's in an institutional regime change. Leadership regime change focuses on installing authoritarian "puppets" who can implement friendly policies because they are not beholden to a domestic audience that can punish them for acting in ways contrary to its interests. Restoration regime change involves returning to power the previous leader whose preference were congruent with the intervener's. Institutional regime change features measures such as democratization or constitutional provisions that limit the target's military establishment or its ability to use force abroad.[4]

The optimistic view of regime change thus maintains that interveners can transform relations with a target for the better by (re)imposing leaders with preferences congruent with their own or by remaking a target's political institutions and thereby fundamentally altering the state's preferences. If this argument is correct, we would expect that relations between interveners and targets should improve after regime change (and relative to dyads in which no regime change occurred). For example, if regime change alters the preferences of target states to bring them into line with those of interveners, militarized conflicts and wars between them ought to be less likely after regime change than before. Likewise, measures of foreign policy similarity, such as alliance portfolios and UN voting records, should exhibit greater degrees of alignment in the wake of regime change.

One of the few available studies on the subject supports the optimist view. Lo, Hashimoto, and Reiter, examining the effectiveness of regime change as a war termination strategy, find that peace lasts significantly longer after wars in which the winner imposes regime change on the loser. The authors argue that by putting a friendly leader in charge—or overhauling a country's political institutions—an intervener changes the target's preferences and thereby reduces the likelihood of further conflict between them.[5] The conventional wisdom on the effect of regime change on intervener-target relations is captured by hypotheses 5.1a and 5.1b.

H5.1a: *Foreign-imposed regime change decreases the likelihood of militarized conflict between intervening and target states.*

H5.1b: *Foreign-imposed regime change results in closer relations between intervening and target states.*

The empirical basis for the optimistic view of regime change, however, is thin. To test whether regime change increases the duration of peace between former adversaries, Lo, Hashimoto, and Reiter expanded Page Fortna's dataset of interstate cease-fires—which covered the period from 1946 to 1998—to include all cease-fire agreements from 1914 to 2001.[6] This expansion entailed a significant research effort that nearly quadrupled the number of cease-fires in their study compared to Fortna's.[7] Yet, although the authors claim that their dataset has about three dozen regime changes, as shown in table 5.1, it actually contains only a dozen.[8] The remainder consist

Table 5.1 Cease-fires in interstate wars with foreign-imposed regime change, 1914–2001

Target	Intervener	Year	Outcomes
Ethiopia‡	Italy	1936	Occupation Insurgency Italian occupation regime overthrown Interstate war (1941) Regime change in Italy
Poland†	Germany, USSR	1939	Annexation
Belgium‡	Germany	1940	Occupation German occupation regime overthrown Interstate war (1944) Regime change in Germany
Netherlands‡	Germany	1940	Occupation German occupation regime overthrown Regime change in Germany
Norway‡	Germany	1940	Occupation German occupation regime overthrown Regime change in Germany
Yugoslavia‡	Germany	1941	Occupation Insurgency German puppet regime overthrown Regime change in Germany
Greece‡	Germany	1941	Occupation Insurgency German puppet regime overthrown Regime change in Germany
Germany, West	France, Britain, United States	1945 (1955)	Long-term occupation Peace
Germany, East	USSR	1945 (1954)	Long-term occupation Peace
Japan	United States	1945 (1952)	Long-term occupation Peace
Hungary	USSR	1945	Long-term occupation Interstate war (1956)
South Vietnam†	North Vietnam	1975	Annexation
Uganda	Tanzania	1979	Short-term occupation Peace
Afghanistan	United States	2001	Long-term occupation Insurgency

Source: Lo, Hashimoto, and Reiter 2008

† Indicates cases that are not instances of foreign-imposed regime change.

‡ Indicates cases in which interstate conflict was not possible because the target was occupied. Interstate conflict became possible only if the occupation ended before the end of World War II.

of "continuation dyads" created by (1) the division of Germany into East Germany (German Democratic Republic, GDR) and West Germany (Federal Republic of Germany, FRG) following World War II, and (2) the pairing of each of these German successor states during the postwar period with each state that suffered regime change at German hands during the war. This procedure creates a lot of regime change dyads (e.g., West Germany–Belgium, East Germany–Netherlands), but, unfortunately, they tell us nothing about the effects of regime change for two reasons.

First, every single government installed in a German regime change during World War II was ousted either by the Western Allies (restoration regime changes in Belgium, the Netherlands, Luxembourg, Denmark, and Norway) or by home-grown insurgent groups (Greece and Yugoslavia).[9] By 1945, in other words, none of the regimes put in place by Germany to carry out its preferred policies continued to exist. Second, the government in Berlin that installed those regimes was itself extinguished by its combined adversaries at the war's conclusion. In short, by the time World War II ended, neither the regimes that were emplaced by Germany nor the German regime that emplaced them survived. As this book has sought to demonstrate, however, regime change is a tool used by one government to bring to power in another state a leader or regime with compatible preferences. Once the leader or government brought to power in a regime change is replaced by a regime with completely different preferences *and* the regime that did the imposing is itself replaced by a wholly different regime, the logic of regime change simply no longer applies. There is no longer any "principal" that has installed an "agent" with similar preferences; both have been eliminated. Germany's regime change "victims" were essentially freed from the bonds of regime change by the overthrow of German occupation governments and the Nazi regime in Berlin. Dyads consisting of East Germany, West Germany, or Italy and their former regime change victims thus do not belong in a study of the effects of regime change on intervener-target relations.

Examination of the remaining cases in table 5.1 reveals that many of them have a common problem that lowers or eliminates their utility for estimating the effect of regime change on postwar intervener-target relations: the dependent variable—interstate war—was either impossible or highly unlikely to occur. This problem manifests in three ways. First, two cases—Germany's and Russia's division of Poland and North Vietnam's conquest of South Vietnam—should be omitted because they are not instances of regime change as defined by Lo, Hashimoto, and Reiter or in this book.[10] Rather, they are cases of annexation: Poland and South Vietnam were absorbed by their conquerors in 1939 and 1975, respectively. Obviously, it is not possible to fight an interstate war against a state that no longer exists.

Second, of the twelve actual regime changes in the study, interstate conflict could not occur in six of them—the five German cases during World War II plus Italy's regime change in Ethiopia—because the targets of regime change were occupied by the intervener and their armies were disbanded. Some members of the prewar militaries of these countries escaped and joined the Allied forces, but the countries themselves were controlled by the Germans or Italians, who in some instances governed them directly and in others through local proxies. Any hostilities that occurred during these occupations thus necessarily pitted Axis occupation forces against local insurgents.[11] As argued above, once these regime changes were reversed and the governments of Germany and Italy that imposed them were also removed, these cases are no longer relevant to a study of the effects of regime change.

In two of these cases, however, the Axis occupations ended before the larger war ended, opening up a window for possible interstate armed conflict between intervener and target. In May 1941, British and Ethiopian forces liberated Addis Ababa, ending the Italian occupation of Ethiopia and restoring the regime of Haile Selassie.[12] Three years later, in September 1944, Allied forces entered Brussels, expelling the German occupiers and reinstating Belgium's democratic government-in-exile. The COW Project codes Ethiopia as rejoining the war against its former occupier in January 1941 when Selassie and Ethiopian patriots invaded the country alongside the British.[13] Similarly, upon liberation, the Belgian government began recruiting volunteers to join the reestablished Belgian Army; 53,000 responded and Belgian battalions, partnered with the US Army, fought to the finish on the Western Front.[14] In other words, both cases in which regime changes were reversed while World War II continued resulted in war recurrence between interveners and targets.

Third, of the remaining half-dozen cases, all but one of the targets of regime change—Uganda (1979)—was subject to long-term and sometimes large-scale military occupation in the indefinite aftermath, which reduces the likelihood of *interstate* conflict between the regular armed forces of the two states (even as it permits antioccupation insurgency). Unlike Germany and Italy's World War II–era occupations, targets in these cases were allowed to develop and maintain their own armies, so interstate conflict between the two states was technically possible. The new West and East German states, for example, founded the Bundeswehr and the Nationale Volksarmee, respectively, in 1955 and 1956, and the United States, along with its NATO allies, has built and trained the Afghan National Army at great expense since 2002.[15] For their entire existence as separate states, however, the two German republics hosted hundreds of thousands of American or Soviet troops; even today, the United States maintains about 35,000 troops in a unified Germany. Japan hosted over 200,000 US troops in the early 1950s, a figure that declined until it reached roughly 50,000 in the 1970s, where it remains today. The presence of an occupier's military forces on the occupied country's soil helps deter any thoughts the protégé might have of reneging on its commitments to its patron.

The lone exception to the rule that large-scale occupations do not result in interstate wars between occupiers and occupied—the Soviet-Hungarian War of 1956—only highlights the unusual circumstances that must be in place for such a conflict to occur. This clash took place because a revolution chased Hungary's Stalinist, Soviet-aligned government from power and returned Imre Nagy to office—a reform-minded former prime minister who had been expelled from the Communist Party the previous year. Nagy soon pledged to transition Hungary to multiparty democracy and withdraw from the Warsaw Pact. In response to these events, Soviet Premier Nikita Khrushchev decided to crush the rebellion by augmenting the small Red Army occupation force and launching a full-fledged invasion with seventeen divisions. This attack involved direct hostilities between Soviet forces and the Hungarian Army, resulting in the conflict's classification as an interstate war.

In sum, two-thirds of the "regime changes" in Lo, Hashimoto, and Reiter's study are either irrelevant or not regime changes. Of the dozen actual regime changes, interstate conflict was impossible after most of the World War II cases because targets—occupied by Germany or Italy with their militaries dismantled—were incapable of resistance. Ethiopia and Belgium, however, were liberated before the war ended and thus interstate hostilities became possible. Both immediately attacked their former occupiers. In the six remaining cases, targets—though permitted to have militaries—were permanently garrisoned by interveners in five, thereby reducing the likelihood of interstate conflict between them. Only in the Ugandan case did the intervener fully withdraw. The bottom line is that interstate conflict between interveners and targets was possible after only eight cases of regime change in Lo, Hashimoto, and Reiter's study. War recurred in three of the eight (37.5 percent), and conflict in four of the other five was more likely to take an intrastate rather than an interstate form.

Recapitulating My Argument

My argument for why interstate relations between interveners and targets might not improve after regime change, and why regime change might not lead to a reduced likelihood of armed conflict, focuses primarily on the problem of competing principals. The reason, as noted above, is that in cases of military disintegration, interveners are almost invariably drawn into protracted occupations, meaning that any further conflict will very likely occur inside the target state and take the form of civil war. It follows that military disintegration after regime chance is unlikely to be the source of interstate conflict between interveners and targets. Such conflict in the wake of regime change is thus likely to be a function of the competing principals logic.

The problem of competing principals leads to different expectations than the optimistic picture sketched above about how relations between interveners and targets will unfold after regime change. As discussed throughout this book, interveners enact regime change to get rid of leaders whose preferences diverge from their own or who enact unfriendly or hostile policies. They install different leaders with congruent preferences who promise to implement policies friendly to the intervener's interests. Yet the story does not end there. Instead, replacing the leadership of another state creates a principal-agent problem with not one but two principals: the intervener and the leader's domestic constituency. Once they take power, foreign-imposed leaders endeavor to hold on to it. Because the interests of the intervening and target states are never fully congruent, however, serving the intervener's interests may clash with the wishes of a leader's domestic audience, which in turn could threaten her chances of political survival.[16] But responding with too much alacrity to domestic imperatives at the expense of the intervener's agenda risks angering the imposed leader's foreign patron, which can also endanger her survival by intervening again or supporting a coup.

Foreign-imposed leaders are thus often "damned if they do and damned if they don't." If they faithfully implement the intervener's preferred policies, they face possible removal by dissatisfied internal actors; if they diverge from the intervener's wishes, however, they increase the chance that the intervener will seek to remove them. Depending on how credible these domestic threats are compared to those of the intervener, the imposed leader may shift course and defy his patron, which may prompt the patron to ponder removing its protégé or supporting friendly actors in the target who will. This situation can lead to open conflict between the two states. As described in greater detail below, when the high visibility and influence of ethnic Tutsis (both Rwandan and Congolese) in his regime jeopardized newly installed Laurent Kabila's hold on power in the Democratic Republic of Congo (DRC), Kabila reacted by expelling his Rwandan backers and elevating members of his own ethnic group. In response, Rwanda and Uganda, which only the year before had put Kabila in power, invaded to drive him out. Less dramatically, patrons may be unable to induce compliance by their supposed client on issues they care about.

At a minimum, therefore, I expect that, on average, regime change should increase the likelihood of intervener-target conflict and worsen relations between them. This expectation leads to a second pair of hypotheses.

> H5.2a: *Foreign-imposed regime change increases the likelihood of militarized conflict between intervening and target states.*
>
> H5.2b: *Foreign-imposed regime change results in more distant relations between intervening and target states.*

Leadership regime changes are most likely to harm interstate relations because they frequently place leaders in a dilemma. When interveners replace a foreign leader without building any supporting institutions to empower the new regime, the leaders are likely to remain heavily dependent on aid from the intervener to maintain power. Although such puppet leaders are thus more likely to adopt the intervener's preferences initially, doing so tends to generate internal opposition, putting the leader's political survival in jeopardy. Furthermore, this kind of imposed leader often lacks a strong domestic base of support, making him especially vulnerable to domestic threats. Elites installed in leadership regime changes are thus subject to powerful pressures to cut ties with their foreign patrons, which may then trigger military conflict between interveners and targets or lead to poor relations between them.

My argument requires only the *threat* of irregular removal to generate pressure for a protégé to break with her patron. Of course, the protégé may actually be overthrown, which, as shown in chapter 4, is a common occurrence after leadership regime changes. Members of the opposition who seize power generally resent or despise the intervener for meddling in their nation's internal affairs, which in turn increases the likelihood of conflict between the two states. The overthrow of the shah of Iran is a prime example. In his analysis of the 1953 US-backed coup against Prime Minister Mohammad Mossadegh, historian Malcolm Byrne writes: "Because of its role in the coup, many Iranians came to identify Washington as the shah's all-powerful patron. . . . This virtually guaranteed that burgeoning hostility toward the shah would also be directed against the United States when the revolutionary Islamic regime came to power in 1979."[17] This possibility notwithstanding, in this chapter I focus on how interveners can end up in conflict with the leader they installed rather than different, hostile leaders who rise to power by ousting the intervener's protégé.

This discussion suggests hypotheses 5.3a and 5.3b.

H5.3a: *Leadership regime change increases the likelihood of militarized conflict between the intervening and target states.*

H5.3b: *Leadership regime change results in more distant relations between the intervening and target states.*

Institutional regime changes, I argue, are likely to have contrary effects on intervener-target relations depending on conditions in the target state, which determine whether institution-building succeeds or fails. Institutional regime changes that successfully promote democracy—an outcome that is likely to occur where promising preconditions for democratization exist, such as high incomes and ethnic homogeneity—ought to reduce the likelihood of armed conflict between the two states.[18] Similarly, the lone study that has examined the prevalence of conflict among different types of authoritarian regimes (i.e., single-party, military, personalist) finds that dyads that consist of single-party regimes are significantly less likely than mixed (democratic-autocratic) dyads to engage in militarized disputes.[19] Institutional regime changes, however, particularly those that promote democracy, frequently fail to result in consolidated democracy, mainly when they are attempted in poor countries with little experience of democracy and with heterogeneous populations. Failed institutional regime changes in effect resemble leadership regime changes and thus may worsen patron-protégé relations. I expect these countervailing effects to cancel each other out at the aggregate level.

> H5.4a: *Institutional regime change neither increases nor decreases the likelihood of militarized conflict between the intervening and target states.*
>
> H5.4b: *Institutional regime change results in neither closer nor more distant relations between the intervening and target states.*

As discussed throughout this book, restoration regime changes also likely have countervailing effects that work to negate any systematic effect on interstate relations. Leaders in need of restoring in many cases face an opposition that was sufficiently strong to chase them from power—and required foreign bayonets to overcome it. The continued presence of this opposition could endanger the restored leader's hold on power. Further, interveners—as after other types of regime change—presumably want the leader to implement policies favorable to them. This preference may put reimposed leaders at odds with domestic actors who could seek their overthrow.

On the other hand, restoration regime changes have effects that push in the opposite direction. First, in almost all restorations, reinstalled leaders were previously aligned with the intervener. Thus, these regime changes mark a return to an acceptable international status quo for both parties rather than an attempt to change state preferences by imposing entirely new leaders. Second, in nearly half of restoration regime changes, the regimes that were returned to power had not been overthrown by their own populations. Instead, they consisted of regimes with high levels of domestic legitimacy (many were democracies) that were toppled by foreign powers in a prior regime change. In these cases, restoration regime change *increased* the satisfaction of the domestic populations because they brought previously popular regimes back to power. Third, in many of the cases in which leaders were overthrown by their own constituents, regime change actually enhanced the security of the reimposed leader because the rebellion that removed the leader in the first place was very weak and was crushed by great-power intervention. These regime changes put leaders in a stronger position than they had been previously and thus enhanced their ability to maintain close relations with the intervener without imperiling their domestic standing.

Given these countervailing effects, I expect that restoration regime changes will not worsen intervener-target relations.

> H5.5a: *Restoration regime change neither increases nor decreases the likelihood of militarized conflict between the intervening and target states.*
>
> H5.5b: *Restoration regime change results in neither closer nor more distant relations between the intervening and target states.*

Finally, although I did not theorize the effects of failed attempts at regime change, or devote much attention to these effects in the previous empirical chapters, I expect regime changes that fail to unseat the target government will worsen intervener-target relations and increase the likelihood of conflict between them. In probing whether regime change increased the likelihood of civil war, for example, unsuccessful regime change attempts were of interest primarily as a counterfactual—to help ascertain whether regime change caused civil wars or was simply more likely to occur in places where civil war was already probable for other reasons. In this chapter, by contrast, failed regime changes have a direct impact on the intervener-target relationship and as such merit investigation.

It is not terribly surprising that unsuccessful regime change operations might increase the level of antagonism between the two states involved. Trying to overthrow the government of another state is hardly a sign of good relations, and the failed attempt—whether undertaken covertly or overtly—is likely to be discovered by the target, which is bound to increase tensions further.[20] Some failed regime changes occur during major wars, such as the Iran-Iraq War (1980–88) and the Korean War (1950–53), or not-so-major wars, such as the Suez War (1956) or the Israel-Lebanon War (1982). Others occur during failed pro-rebel interventions in civil wars, like the Allied intervention in the Russian Civil War (1918–22), or unsuccessful covert interventions, such as US efforts to unseat Indonesia's President Sukarno (1954–58). Oftentimes the countries involved have enduring hostile relationships, which are exacerbated by attempts at regime change. I thus hypothesize that unsuccessful regime changes of all types are likely to aggravate intervener-target relations.

H5.6a: *Failed attempts at foreign-imposed regime change increase the likelihood of militarized conflict between intervening and target states.*

H5.6b: *Failed attempts at foreign-imposed regime change result in more distant relations between intervening and target states.*

Statistical Results

This section summarizes results obtained from a dataset that consists of all interstate dyads (pairs of states) in the international system from 1816 to 2000, provided that they are geographically contiguous or one state in the dyad is a major power.[21] My analysis differs from existing studies in three ways. First, the sample of states in previous work includes only interstate war participants. As I have already shown, however, there are reasons to doubt the finding that wars that end in regime change are followed by longer-lasting peace. Even if it did, though, it is not clear that the effect of regime change in interstate wars would generalize to a broader context. Here I widen the lens by estimating the effect of regime change on relations between interveners and targets whether inflicted in peacetime or war.[22] Second, prior studies use war recurrence as the dependent variable. War is the most violent indicator of interstate relations, however. Interveners and targets could experience conflict-ridden relations after regime change without going to war. Including more sensitive indicators—such as militarized interstate disputes—expands the scope of the analysis regarding the effects of regime change on intervener-target relations. Third, existing studies do not differentiate among different types of regime changes that may have contradictory effects. In this study, I disaggregate regime change into leadership, institutional, and restoration types to provide a more nuanced analysis.

REGIME CHANGE AND MILITARIZED CONFLICT

Table 5.2 lists the thirty cases of militarized interstate disputes (MIDs) between interveners and targets that occurred within ten years of regime changes in my dataset. As displayed in figure 5.1, almost 90 percent of these MIDs took place in the aftermath of leadership regime changes. Only two MIDs occurred in the decade after an institutional regime change, both of which are accounted for by US reinterventions in the Dominican Republic during the Woodrow Wilson administration.[23] This result provides suggestive support for my argument that institutional regimes are likely to fail, and elevate the chance of intervener-target conflict, in places that lack the preconditions for stability and democracy: poor countries, heterogeneous societies, or countries without previous experience of democracy. None of the institutional regime changes carried out in targets with more promising conditions failed or sparked a MID between interveners and targets in the decade after regime change.[24] Finally, a single militarized conflict—between Spain and Portugal in 1840—followed a restoration regime change. Spain had participated in the ouster of the usurper Miguel I in 1834 and the reinstallation of Queen Maria II to the Portuguese throne.[25] Interestingly, in table 5.2, the vast majority of MIDs that occur after regime change (80 percent) were initiated by interveners, indicating that most post-regime-change conflicts—as posited by the problem of competing principals—stem from interveners' dissatisfaction with the behavior of their protégés.

It is worth noting that, as was the case with civil wars in chapter 3, certain regime changes are followed by multiple conflicts. Scholars have shown that interstate conflicts tend to cluster in space and are particularly likely between enduring rivals and states involved in territorial disputes.[26] One case that stands out in this regard in table 5.2 is Japan's regime change in China. After gaining a foothold on the Asian mainland in the Russo-Japanese War (1904–05), Japan steadily encroached on Manchuria and China south of the Great Wall in the 1920s and 1930s. In a particularly brazen move in 1928, officers of the Japanese Kwantung Army assassinated Chinese pres-

Table 5.2 Militarized interstate disputes between interveners and targets within ten years of a foreign-imposed regime change, 1816–2000

Intervener	Target	Year of MID
Leadership regime change		
United States (i)	Mexico	1915
United States (i)	Mexico	1916
United States	Mexico (i)	1918
United States (i)	Mexico	1919
United States (i)	Nicaragua	1910
Guatemala (i)	El Salvador	1885
Britain (i)	Greece	1922
Britain (i)	Iran	1946
Britain (i)	Iran	1951
France (i)	Greece	1922
Germany (i)	France	1871
Germany	France (i)	1871
Italy (i)	Albania	1918
Italy (i)	Albania	1920
Italy (i)	Albania	1952
Romania (i)	Hungary	1922
Russia (i)	Iran	1945
Russia	Iran (i)	1951
Russia (i)	Afghanistan	1993
Russia (i)	Afghanistan	1994
Rwanda	Democratic Republic of Congo (i)	1998
Japan (i)	China	1931
Japan (i)	China	1933
Japan	China (i)	1934
Japan (i)	China	1935
Japan	China (i)	1936
Japan (i)	China	1937
Institutional regime change		
United States (i)	Dominican Republic	1914
United States (i)	Dominican Republic	1916
Restoration regime change		
Spain (i)	Portugal	1840

Note: (i) indicates the country that initiated the dispute.

ident and Manchurian strongman Chang Tso-lin. Regime change, however, as discussed later in this chapter, backfired when the fallen leader's son, whom the Japanese expected to be a pliable puppet, defied them and allied with new Chinese president Chiang Kai-shek against Japan. There followed a series of escalating militarized incidents until full-scale war broke out in 1937. Given that this case accounts for a half-dozen militarized disputes, it is important both to ensure that it is an actual case of regime change and to check how much it affects the statistical results. I do the former in the case study section of the chapter; I do the latter in the chapter appendix.

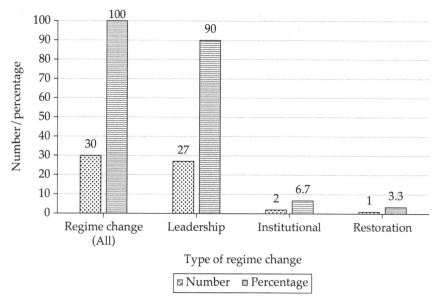

Figure 5.1. Number and percentage of militarized interstate disputes after foreign-imposed regime changes

Figure 5.2, which shows pairs of bars indicating the bivariate relationship between MIDs and different types of regime change, bears out the initial impression from table 5.2 and figure 5.1 that intervener-target conflict is most prevalent after leadership regime change. The bar on the right side of each pair shows the probability of MIDs between intervening and target states in each of the ten years following different types of regime change. The left side of each pair of bars shows the probability of a MID in dyads in which no regime change occurred. The capped lines indicate 95 percent confidence intervals for each estimate.

The bivariate evidence in figure 5.2 supports four of my five hypotheses regarding the effect of regime change on intervener-target conflict but fails to support the optimist hypothesis. Regime change, for example, as shown in the far-left pair of columns, increases the likelihood of a MID between interveners and targets by over 70 percent (contradicts H5.1a; supports H5.2a). This positive relationship is driven by leadership regime change, which (as shown in the middle pair of bars) boosts the probability of a militarized conflict three and a half times from 1.2 percent to 4.2 percent (supports H5.3a). Institutional regime change, in contrast, diminishes the chance of a MID by 40 percent, but the very broad confidence interval for the effect of institutional regime change indicates that it is insignificant (supports H5.4a). Restoration regime changes result in a dramatic and statistically significant 87 percent reduction in MID probability. This result contradicts H5.5a, which holds that the countervailing effects of restoration regime changes ought to

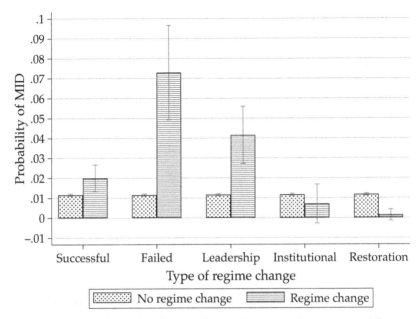

Figure 5.2. Bivariate relationships between foreign-imposed regime change and the probability of militarized interstate disputes

cancel each other out, producing no aggregate effect on the likelihood of militarized interstate disputes. Finally, consistent with H5.6a, failed regime changes result in a drastic sevenfold increase in the chance of armed conflict between interveners and their targets, supporting the argument that regime changes that misfire significantly worsen interstate relations.[27]

Figure 5.3 repeats figure 5.2 but this time shows the predicted probability of interstate disputes between interveners and targets in each of the ten years following different types of regime change generated by multivariate analyses that control for other factors associated with MID onset.[28] For example, the first pair of bars in figure 5.3 shows that the chance of a MID occurring after a successful regime change (all types aggregated together) is 0.0059 per year, whereas the chance of one occurring absent a regime change is 0.0062. The fully overlapping confidence intervals indicate that this minor difference is not statistically significant. In other words, one state inflicting regime change on another does not discernably increase or decrease the likelihood that the two states will experience a militarized conflict in the ensuing ten years. This result provides evidence against H5.1a, which maintains that regime change decreases the probability of intervener-target conflict, but it is also inconsistent with H5.2a, which argues that regime change increases the likelihood of such conflict.

The quantitative evidence supports my hypotheses about the effects of leadership and institutional types of regime change on the probability of

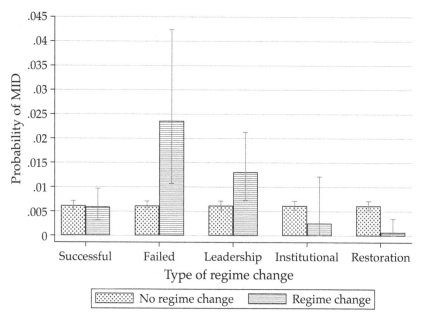

Figure 5.3. Predicted annual probabilities of militarized interstate disputes in the decade after foreign-imposed regime change

MIDs. Columns 3 and 4 in figure 5.3, for example, show that leadership regime change significantly increases the likelihood of a militarized conflict between the intervening and target states during the ten-year period following intervention.[29] Leadership regime changes more than double the likelihood of a MID, a result that supports H5.3a. In contrast, institutional regime change reduces the chances of a MID about 60 percent, but the uncertainty around this estimate is very broad (produced by a large standard error relative to the coefficient), and it lacks statistical significance (supports H5.4a). The effect of restoration regime change slashes the probability of conflict by almost 90 percent. This strong negative effect, contrary to H5.5a, is statistically significant, indicating that the conflict-dampening aspects of restoration regime changes outweigh the facets of these regime changes that exacerbate conflict. Finally, failed regime changes nearly quadruple the chances of militarized conflicts between interveners and targets (supports H5.6a).

In sum, my analysis of regime change and militarized interstate disputes from 1816 to 2000 indicates that leadership regime change significantly increases the likelihood of conflict between interveners and targets afterwards. Unexpectedly, however, restoration regime change significantly reduces the probability that interveners and targets fight in the ensuing decade. Only a single MID occurred within ten years of a restoration regime change—and that one happened almost two hundred years ago. Restorations thus appear to have a pacifying effect on intervener-target relations—just as they reduced the likelihood of irregular removal for imposed leaders and spawned relatively few civil wars. Institutional regime change, as predicted, has little effect on the likelihood of conflict following regime change. The strong negative effect of restoration regime change cancels out the positive effect of leadership regime change, rendering the overall relationship between regime change and intervener-target militarized disputes insignificant. Overall, the insignificant effect for the combined regime change variable highlights the importance of disaggregating regime change in its leadership, institutional, and restoration varieties. Otherwise, we would have missed the fact that two types of regime change significantly impact the likelihood of intervener-target conflict.

REGIME CHANGE AND INTERVENER-TARGET ALIGNMENT

The field of IR is not blessed with a plethora of good quantitative indicators of the closeness or quality of relations between states. In this section, I examine the effect of regime change on two of the best measures available: similarity of dyads' voting records in the UN General Assembly and similarity of two states' alliance portfolios.[30] Although acknowledging that the former is an imperfect proxy for political affinity, Bailey, Strezhnev, and Voeten write that "votes in the United Nations General Assembly (UNGA) have become the standard data source for constructing measures of state preferences, as they are comparable and observable actions taken by many countries at set points in time."[31] Indeed, according to Bailey, Strezhnev, and Voeten, "Scholars have used UN votes to measure foreign policy preferences virtually since the institution was established. . . . We found seventy-five articles published between 1998 and 2012 that used UN votes to construct measures of national preferences."[32] The disadvantage of using UN voting records as a measure of political affinity between nations is that these data exist only for the period after World War II. To offset this brief temporal coverage I also use data on the similarity of alliance portfolios, which exist for the entire period of my study.

While recognizing the limitations of these quantitative measures of interstate relations, analysis of these indicators yields results that are largely consistent with my theory of the effects of regime change on intervener-target relations. Beginning with votes in the UNGA, figure 5.4 shows that regime change essentially has no effect on the propensity of interveners and their targets to vote together in the ensuing decade.[33] The marginal effect of regime change is 0.0018, which over ten years amounts to an increase in voting similarity of 0.9 percent. This tiny effect is also insignificant, a result that does not support either H5.1b or H5.2b. Dividing regime change into its three types reveals that the effect of leadership regime changes is in the expected negative direction but fails to attain statistical significance. Institutional

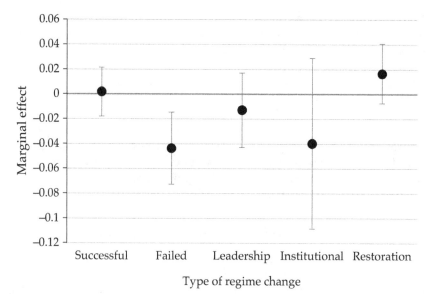

Figure 5.4. Marginal effect of foreign-imposed regime change on similarity of United Nations General Assembly voting

regime changes, by contrast, have a relatively large negative effect on political affinity but the broad confidence interval shows the uncertainty of this estimate. This category contains a very small number of cases so one ought to be cautious about reading too much into this result.[34] The effect of restoration regime changes, although positive, is also insignificant. Failed regime changes are the only type that exerts a significant effect: attempting and failing to overthrow a foreign government, unsurprisingly, worsens relations between interveners and targets. Collectively, these results contradict my expectation and that of regime change optimists (H5.1b and H5.2b) for the overall effect of regime change and support my hypotheses for institutional (H5.4b), restoration (H5.5b), and failed (H5.6b) regime changes. My expectation regarding the negative effect of leadership regime change on interstate relations (H5.3b) is only weakly supported.

As noted, the weakness of UN voting data is its relatively brief temporal coverage compared to the time period covered by my regime change data. Examining the degree to which two states share the same allies—although perhaps a weaker indicator of how good their relations are—partially offsets this drawback by covering the entire post-Napoleonic era.

Figure 5.5 summarizes the effects of regime change on the overlap between dyads' alliance portfolios.[35] The results here differ from those for UN voting patterns in three respects. First, institutional regime changes significantly increase the similarity of interveners' and targets' alliance portfolios. This makes sense because many of these cases consist of US and Soviet

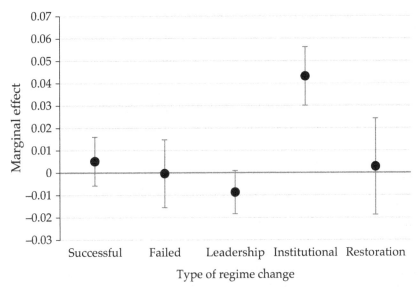

Figure 5.5. Marginal effect of foreign-imposed regime change on similarity of alliance portfolios

regime changes after World War II that successfully transformed targets into democratic or single-party regimes, respectively. These countries—West Germany and Japan for the United States; Hungary, Bulgaria, Romania, and Czechoslovakia for the Soviet Union—were absorbed into the interveners' alliance systems and should thus exhibit a high degree of similarity on the alliance portfolio variable. This result is consistent with my expectation that institutional regime changes ought to succeed in relatively advanced and homogeneous targets but contradicts my expectation that such regime changes ought to have no effect on intervener-target relations overall (H5.4b).[36]

Second, leadership regime changes reduce the overlap in the alliance systems of interveners and targets in the ensuing decade. This effect—although not especially large, reducing alliance similarity about 5.4 percent over the course of ten years—is significant at the 90 percent level of confidence.[37] This finding supports H5.3b. Finally, failed regime changes—in contrast to their strong negative effect on UN voting patterns—have no effect one way or the other on alliance portfolio similarity, contrary to H5.6b.

In sum, it seems reasonably clear that regime change in the aggregate has little effect on the quality of relations between interveners and targets. This finding supports the spirit if not the letter of my argument regarding the overall effect of regime change (H5.2b) and contradicts the perspective of the regime change optimists (H5.1b): regime change does not worsen interstate relations but clearly does not improve them either. Among types of regime change, none (except failed regime change attempts) exerts a systematic effect on UN voting patterns (supports H5.4b, H5.5b, and H5.6b). The effect of leadership regime change (H5.3b), although in the expected negative direction, falls short of significance. A short time period for analysis and missing data undermine this analysis. Effects are clearer for alliance portfolio similarity, where leadership regime change reduces dyadic affinity (supporting H5.3b), institutional regime change increases it (contradicting H5.4b), and restoration regime change has no effect (affirming H5.5b).

The overall tenor of my quantitative analysis of regime change and indicators of the closeness or quality of interstate relations contradicts the view that regime change on average changes intervener-target relations for the better. That said, my expectation that regime change worsens such relations is not supported, either. This null result, however, is not overly concerning because the effect of regime change is simply the aggregate of the effects of its three different subtypes. The negative effect of leadership regime change on intervener-target relations persists, as does the conditional (and, in the main, insignificant) effect of institutional regime change. For this set of dependent variables, however, the effect of leadership regime change is slightly weaker and that of restoration in the opposite direction is stronger than for the outcomes in the previous chapters. When combined, the two effects are offset. Still, the most common type of regime change reduces the quality of relations between interveners and targets.

This is not to say there are no success stories: West Germany and Japan stand out among institutional regime changes, and the United States was able to secure a fair amount of cooperation from Guatemala (leadership) and Iran (restoration)—although at the expense of contributing to civil war and mass killing in the former and a longer-term backlash in the latter. These successes, however, appear to be counterbalanced by cases like South Vietnam, Afghanistan, and Iraq, where interveners were unable to translate regime change into productive relations. In particular, leadership regime changes prove to be particularly prone to unhappy endings, whereas institutional and restoration regime changes produce highly varied outcomes depending on the circumstances. Successful institutional regime changes and the restoration of democratic regimes by democracies can transform interstate relations in positive ways. Institutional regime changes undertaken in targets with a low probability of democratization, by contrast, are unlikely to produce positive change. I now turn to qualitative evidence to trace how regime change can worsen relations between interveners and targets—or even bring them to blows.

Regime Change and War: Rwanda and Uganda in the Democratic Republic of Congo, 1996–1998

The remaining sections of the chapter turn to historical cases to explore the effect of regime change on intervener-target relations. In this section, I consider cases in which the problem of competing principals contributes to war between interveners and targets. The main focus of attention is how Rwanda and Uganda's installation of Laurent Kabila as president of Zaire (which he subsequently renamed the Democratic Republic of Congo) in 1997, rather than leading to peaceful relations, devolved into another war in little more than a year. In the next section, I turn to cases in which patrons, despite their overwhelming power advantages and sometimes provision of massive economic and military assistance to targets, are unable to persuade their protégés to conform to their wishes. I briefly revisit a number of cases discussed in chapters 3 and 4 in which interveners became so frustrated with their protégés that they pursued or acquiesced in the removal of a leader they had previously installed. I also show how the United States has frequently clashed with leaders it helped empower in Afghanistan and Iraq. In the final section, I consider the case of Japan's 1928 regime change in China, which exerts an outsized impact on the quantitative results owing to the numerous militarized disputes between the two countries that followed it.

Being overthrown by the same foreign power that put them in office in the first place is one of the six ways that foreign-imposed leaders can leave power irregularly discussed in chapter 4. My theory, based on the problem of competing principals, maintains that patrons will seek to oust their protégés when those leaders fail to perform in ways the intervener had hoped—that is, they fail to pursue policies in line with the patron's preferences or otherwise do not live up to its expectations. Instances of leaders who are attacked by their own patrons for failure to act in ways the patron would prefer are consistent with my theory, particularly if it can be shown that the reason the leader failed to promote the intervener's interests stemmed from domestic opposition to those policies. In some cases, these attacks escalate to full-scale interstate war.

In the remainder of this section, I explore how the problem of competing principals triggered a war between two intervening powers, Rwanda and Uganda, and the DRC, where they had only one year earlier installed a new leader, Laurent Kabila. Four factors guided my selection of this case. First, I chose a case of leadership regime change because it should demonstrate the problem of competing principals most clearly.[38] Second, I picked a case that was followed by militarized conflict to allow me to observe whether my proposed causal mechanism contributed decisively to the outbreak of the conflict. Third, despite the obvious policy relevance of recent regime changes carried out by the United States and its allies, I selected a case involving two minor powers to highlight the reality that regime change is a phenomenon not only of US foreign policy. Moreover, most recent US regime changes have resulted in military disintegration, prolonged occupations, and civil war, making it impossible to observe interstate conflict.

Fourth, the Rwandan and Ugandan regime change against Zaire—although initial appearances suggest otherwise—is a fairly typical case of a stronger intervener overthrowing a weaker target. According to traditional indices of power used in IR (and in the statistical analysis), Rwanda appears far weaker than its enormous neighbor. For example, Rwanda's share of global material capabilities in 1996 was roughly one-fifth that of Zaire's; in addition, Rwanda possessed about one-ninth of Zaire's population and one-eighty-ninth of its land area. By the time of Rwanda's invasion, however, the Rwandan Patriotic Army (RPA) and Zaire's army were roughly the same size, but the former was an experienced, battle-hardened force whereas the latter had by 1996 "been reduced to a mockery of itself."[39] This advantage is further accentuated when the capabilities of Rwanda's allies are taken into account. Both the Ugandan People's Defense Forces and the Angolan Armed Forces were much more capable than Kinshasa's military. In terms of actual military power, therefore, the Rwandan side possessed a considerable advantage over Zaire.

ORIGINS AND CONDUCT OF REGIME CHANGE

The origins of the Rwandan-led regime change in Zaire in 1997 lie in the Rwandan genocide. Beginning in April 1994, Hutu extremists organized the mass killing of between 500,000 and 800,000 Tutsis (and some moderate Hutu) to avert the implementation of a power-sharing agreement (the Arusha Accords) negotiated between the Hutu government of President Juvénal Habyarimana and the Tutsi rebel group, the Rwandan Patriotic Front (RPF). In response to the killings, the RPF attacked and eventually defeated the Rwandan Army (Forces Armées Rwandaises, or FAR), ending the genocide.[40] As they retreated, the FAR and allied Hutu militia, the Interahamwe, forced masses of Hutu civilians to flee alongside them. An enormous exodus from Rwanda took place in July and August 1994: roughly 2 million Hutu fled the country for neighboring states. Between 1.1 and 1.5 million of them ended up in North and South Kivu Provinces, in eastern Zaire, directly bordering Rwanda.[41]

Former members of the FAR and the Interahamwe quickly took control of the refugee camps and began to launch armed incursions back into Rwanda as early as October 1994.[42] Evidence of the complicity of Zairian president Mobutu and his government—a longstanding ally of the Habyarimana regime—in supporting these armed Hutu elements is overwhelming.[43] As Human Rights Watch concluded at the time, "Zairian forces close to president Mobutu Sese Seko have played a pivotal role in facilitating the re-emergence as a powerful military force of those directly implicated in the Rwandan genocide."[44] Unsurprisingly, the RPF regime perceived the presence of the ex-FAR and other Hutu militants in the camps in eastern Zaire as representing an intolerable threat to its security. Filip Reyntjens summarizes the view from Kigali: "The main reason why Uganda, Rwanda and—to a lesser extent—Burundi intervened in the Congo in the Autumn of 1996 was related to their security. . . . For Rwanda in particular, the presence of massive Hutu refugee camps, which housed hostile armed elements, close to the border constituted a major threat."[45]

Using the cover of an ethnic Tutsi rebellion in South Kivu that Rwanda itself had helped foment, the RPA invaded both North and South Kivu in October 1996.[46] Refugees fled in all directions, but many converged on the Mugunga camp outside Goma in North Kivu, which held approximately one million people by the time Tutsi forces assaulted it on November 13. Within days, hundreds of thousands of refugees began to cross back into Rwanda, while hundreds of thousands of others fled westward, deeper into Zaire.[47]

Only after the invasion was under way did Laurent Kabila emerge as the leader of the rebel forces. On October 18, the Alliance des Forces Démocratiques pour la Libération du Congo-Zaïre (Alliance of Democratic Forces for the Liberation of Congo-Zaire, AFDL) was formally created from a combination of four opposition groups, none of which had a strong presence in Zaire.[48] Kabila had nothing to do with the launching of the uprising or the Rwandan invasion; rather, he was appointed spokesman of the AFDL by the invaders to provide a "Zairian face" for the rebellion.[49] To counter Kinshasa's narrative that the war in the Kivus was the result of external aggression, "it was necessary," according to Reyntjens, "to exhibit leadership, the 'Zaireness' of which could not be challenged."[50] Gérard Prunier agrees that in the fall of 1996 Kabila "had just become the new local cover for the Rwandese attack on Zaire, in charge of making a foreign invasion look like a national rebellion."[51] It also helped that Kabila was not a Tutsi, which contributed to countering the impression of the rebels as Tutsi dominated.[52]

It is difficult to determine exactly when the Rwandan leadership—headed by RPF leader Paul Kagame—decided on regime change in Zaire. Some evidence suggests that it was an objective before the war began, and Kagame himself acknowledged in a 1997 interview that toppling Mobutu was one goal of the Rwandan invasion.[53] Other evidence, however, indicates that the goal developed during the war in response to events on the ground, particularly the ease and speed with which anti-Mobutu forces were able to advance.[54] Regardless of when the decision to remove Mobutu was made, it is clear that Rwanda—supported by Angola, Burundi, and Uganda—was the key driver of regime change in Zaire.[55] Rather than fight a final battle in the capital, Mobutu fled Kinshasa shortly before the victorious AFDL entered the city on May 17, 1997. Kabila was sworn in as president on May 29 and promptly renamed the country the Democratic Republic of Congo.

REGIME CHANGE IN KINSHASA: NO MAGIC BULLET

The removal of Mobutu and the installation of Kabila was a clear instance of a leadership regime change. The foreign powers that put Kabila in office made no attempt to build institutions to create support for the country's new leader. Reflecting Kabila's lack of a domestic political base, ten ministers in his new government were recently returned exiles.[56] Kabila also excluded anyone with ties to the Mobutu regime; almost all leaders of the domestic opposition fell into this category. Left largely to his own devices, Kabila floundered. "Kabila seems to have had only the vaguest notions of what he actually intended to do after overthrowing Mobutu," writes Prunier. "Everything seemed arbitrary," and the government was characterized by an "almost complete lack of institutionalization."[57] After a few months in power, Kabila banned all political parties and even purged the AFDL.[58] A new constitution issued on May 28, 1997, writes David Van Reybrouck, "essentially placed all power in the hands of the president."[59] The new government was highly authoritarian, repressive, centralized, and personalist, exhibiting many similarities to Mobutu's regime. As Thomas Turner observes, "The ouster of Mobutu created expectations of improvement but Kabila soon revealed himself to be a second Mobutu."[60]

Unfortunately for Rwanda, replacing Mobutu with "what looked like the perfect puppet regime" was insufficient to resolve the issues that led to the conflict in the first place, because the Rwandans could not induce their puppet to follow their instructions.[61] As noted above, Rwanda had intervened in Zaire to solve its security problem by destroying the refugee camps and eliminating the support base of the ex-FAR and other Hutu militants raiding western Rwanda. As a secondary goal, Kigali aimed to protect the Banyamulenge and other ethnic Tutsis in eastern Zaire from government depredations and attacks by other ethnic groups.

Rwanda's invasion of Zaire, however, failed to improve the security situation and worsened the position of the Banyamulenge by generating resentment against them among other Congolese ethnic groups. Although the RPA succeeded in disbanding the refugee camps in the Kivus, ex-FAR and Interahamwe militiamen soon resumed cross-border attacks into Rwanda.[62] Indeed, remnants of the ex-FAR and Interahamwe came together in late 1996 or early 1997 to form a new Hutu rebel group, the Armée pour la Libération du Rwanda (Army for the Liberation of Rwanda).[63] Hutu militants benefited from resentment of the Rwandan and Tutsi presence in Congo by non-Tutsi elements of the new Congolese Army (Forces Armées Congolaises, FAC), which allowed the armed Hutu groups to move freely, sometimes even accompanying them to the Rwandan border as they launched deadly raids.[64] In addition to cross-border attacks, between 10,000 and 15,000 Hutu fighters had filtered back into Rwanda with the returning refugees. One analyst concludes that, by the end of 1997, "These insurgents sparked the worst fighting the country had seen since the genocide."[65] "Clearly," concludes Emizet Kisangani, "the issues at stake under Mobutu were not solved during the takeover by Kabila, which presaged another conflict."[66]

The Rwandan presence in the DRC was also self-defeating because it generated powerful resentments among the non-Tutsi population against all Tutsis, regardless of whether they were Rwandan or Congolese.[67] According to Kisangani, "Many local authorities were killed in the Kivus by the Banyamulenge and Tutsi, and those who escaped the ethnic cleansing fled. These changes in leadership caused deep resentment when the Congolese saw people of Rwandan origin, whom they considered to be foreigners, claim supremacy in Congolese high offices."[68] Reyntjens concurs: "It is not surprising under these circumstances that the anti-Tutsi feelings rapidly became widespread."[69] Indeed, resentment of Tutsi domination and the perception of non-Tutsis in the Kivus that "they were under foreign occupation and their country was being run from Rwanda" sparked the Mai Mai rebellion in July 1997, which killed 3,000 people.[70]

KABILA'S DILEMMA

Kabila's main problem was that he lacked an independent power base.[71] As an exile who had come to power at the point of foreign bayonets, Kabila had to rely on Rwandan and Congolese Tutsis for support, placing him in a precarious dilemma: his dependence on outside backers was a domestic political liability that undercut his legitimacy and endangered his rule. At the same time, attempting to distance himself from Rwanda risked angering his sponsors in Kigali and raised the possibility that they would seek to replace him, as they had Mobutu.

Kabila's heavy reliance on foreign support to consolidate power in his early days as president of the DRC was obvious. Just as the Tutsis had dominated the AFDL, many foreign Tutsis occupied prominent roles in the new regime.[72] Most notable was the new chief of staff of the armed forces, James Kabarebe, who had previously been the commander of the Rwandan Republican Guard. Even Kabila's bodyguards were reputed to be Rwandans.[73] "Overall," concludes François Ngolet, "between October 1996 and January 1998 the Tutsi presence on Kabila's staff was overwhelming."[74]

There is also ample evidence that his fellow Congolese viewed Kabila as a Rwandan puppet. As Filip Reyntjens writes, "As soon as he [Kabila] assumed power, he was faced with a serious dilemma. Already during the rebellion, it was clear that his own military and political base was thin and that external forces . . . carried him to power. Although Kabila was initially well received . . . this dependency soon became a mortgage in terms of internal legitimacy. The continuing and highly visible presence of foreign troops and officers, particularly those of the RPA, raised accusations that Kabila was but a puppet of Rwanda and, to a lesser extent Uganda."[75] In polls taken in the summer and fall of 1997, a majority of Congolese agreed that Kabila was under the influence of foreigners and that Uganda and Rwanda were colonizing the Congo.[76] David Van Reybrouck summarizes Congolese sentiments: "As long as Kabila's court was filled with those hateful foreigners, he could forget about his authority being recognized."[77] The perception that Kabila was a Rwandan puppet also generated anti-Tutsi violence in addition to undermining his regime's legitimacy.

KABILA MAKES A CHOICE

Lacking domestic supporters and legitimacy, many foreign-imposed leaders have little alternative but to comply with the demands of their foreign sponsors, which is one reason why so many regime changes are followed by civil wars: disgruntled domestic groups resentful of external influence launch rebellions to displace the leader and terminate foreign meddling. As Prunier puts it in the Congolese context, "Did the local population agree to be ruled by a government in Kinshasa not really independent but largely in the hands of a foreign state, that is, Rwanda, which was highly suspected of harboring expansionist views?"[78] Kabila faced this situation in mid-1997 when Mai Mai militias sprang up and attacked ethnic Tutsis out of resentment of the latter's newfound prominence.[79] Indeed, the situation in the Kivus continued to deteriorate in late 1997 and early 1998, forcing Kabila to travel to Bukavu in January to give a speech in which he railed against the Mai Mai and defended the Banyamulenge. The speech, however, backfired: "Supporting them [the Banyamulenge] in that way," writes Prunier, "did more harm than good because Kabila looked like a puppet for the Kigali ventriloquists."[80]

To neutralize this local threat, Kabila sought to appease his domestic critics by reducing the influence of Tutsis in his government and distancing himself from Rwanda. Over the course of several months, Kabila shifted the balance of power inside his regime away from Tutsis and in favor of officials from his native region of Katanga.[81] According to Philip Roessler, "As Kabila maneuvered to give himself some breathing room, he used his power of appointment to move trusted individuals, including family members, to key positions."[82] For example, Kabila appointed his son deputy commander of the army, and North Katanga native Mwenze Kongolo interior minister and then justice minister. Kongolo's successor as interior minister was a childhood friend of Kabila's.[83] Kabila also purged influential Tutsis from his administration, most importantly Masasu Nindaga, a member of the RPF and one of the original founders of the AFDL.[84] The government then tried to increase its control over the Tutsis in the army by dispersing its Banyamulenge members across different units throughout the country.[85] "In effect," writes Kevin Dunn, "Kabila began creating a new cabinet and regional governments that ran counter to the team that put him in power."[86] Moves like these led Kabila's Rwandan backers to believe that their protégé was becoming unreliable and exerting too much independence.[87]

Even worse from the Rwandan perspective, according to multiple accounts, Kabila secretly carried out the ultimate betrayal, joining forces with Hutu militants operating out of the eastern DRC and launching attacks into

Rwanda. According to Roessler, "Kabila's men began providing supplies and logistical support to the *génocidaires* in the Kivus and Katanga (Kamina), at least from May 1998 onwards."[88] Similarly, Jason Stearns alleges that Kabila struck a deal with the ex-FAR to defend himself against an anticipated Rwandan move to unseat him.[89] When presented with evidence of his betrayal, Kabila refused to come clean.[90] In essence, the situation facing Kigali had come full circle: Rwanda had intervened in the DRC to supplant a leader (Mobutu) who was aiding and abetting its Hutu enemies and replaced him with a leader (Kabila) who was now aiding and abetting its enemies.

Given this turn of events, it was becoming increasingly clear in Kigali and Kampala that a change of leadership might be necessary. Little is known about the deliberations of the Rwandan and Ugandan governments in this period, but one source reports that "the intelligence chiefs of Angola, Rwanda, and Uganda held discussions regarding the desirability of finding an alternative leader for the DRC as early as January 1998."[91] Sources close to Kabila have reported that in May, DRC security forces detected a "very serious conspiracy" against the president among high-level Tutsis in the government that resulted in Kabila removing all Rwandans from his presidential guard.[92] Suspicious that Rwanda and its Congolese Tutsi allies were planning a coup, Kabila sacked James Kabarebe, the Rwandan officer serving as army chief of staff, and named his own brother-in-law, Célestine Kifwa, to the post. If the Rwandans had not been actively planning a putsch before, writes Roessler, "the RPF and their allies kicked into high gear their plotting to remove Kabila."[93] According to an account based on interviews with multiple participants, "Plan A was meant to be 'a swift strike'—in other words, a coup d'état . . . orchestrated by Rwanda's External Security Organization, with the help of Kampala, but implemented by disaffected Tutsi and non-Tutsi AFDL conspirators."[94] Kabila, however, aware of the plotting, preempted his patrons' plans to dislodge him from power by ordering the expulsion of all Rwandan soldiers from the DRC in late July.[95]

ANOTHER WAR FOR REGIME CHANGE

Kabila's removal of Kabarebe and his ejection of Rwandan troops from the DRC was the immediate cause of Rwanda's initiation of the Second Congo War to overthrow its wayward puppet in Kinshasa.[96] According to Turner, "'Africa's world war' began as a Rwandan attempt to overthrow Kabila." "The second war," Turner continues, "was the direct result of Laurent Kabila's expulsion of his Rwandan handlers."[97] Rwandan leaders were not about to accept the loss of influence in Kinshasa that Kabila's reforms implied, especially because they were facing the same security problems they had had in 1996, when they decided to overthrow Mobutu. In Kigali's calculations, a friendly, pliable leader in the DRC was required to help contain and eventually eliminate the Hutu militant threat to Rwanda's Tutsi population and to the RPF's continued rule.[98] As Georges Nzongola-Ntalaja puts it, "Since Kabila had not lived up to their expectations, Rwanda and Uganda were determined to find a new Congolese puppet."[99]

Rwanda's initial plan for removing Kabila consisted of a coup by Rwandan and Congolese Tutsi officers. When Kabila preempted this plot, a new plan emerged that was essentially a replay of the one used to oust Mobutu, with a twist: within days of the Rwandan invasion, a new Congolese rebel group—the Rassemblement Congolais pour la Démocratie (Rally for Congolese Democracy)—was cobbled together to put a "Congolese face" on what was essentially another foreign invasion. The members of this coalition, writes Prunier, "were a strange mix of former Mobutists . . . radical left-wingers . . . regional barons . . . UN and NGO figures . . . and well-known representatives of Rwandese interests." This "hodgepodge organization" was "so obviously incapable of military or even political autonomy that the whole thing looked more like an invasion than a genuine Congolese uprising."[100]

Where the new plan diverged sharply from the old one was that Kabarebe, in a bid to end the war quickly, hijacked three passenger jets and flew with several hundred Rwandan, Ugandan, and Congolese troops all the way across the DRC to Kitona on the country's Atlantic coast.[101] After seizing the air base and gathering FAC defectors and former Mobutuist soldiers along the way, Kabarebe headed for Kinshasa, which lay 250 miles to the east. Thwarted from seizing the capital by timely Zimbabwean and Angolan intervention, Kabarebe's force retreated and what remained of it was extracted by air.[102]

Kabarebe's "blitzkrieg" having failed, Rwanda's and Uganda's second war for regime change in three years devolved into a bloody and protracted stalemate.[103] Some of Rwanda's allies from the first war, including Angola and Zimbabwe, and a few newcomers—such as Chad, Libya, Namibia, and Sudan—intervened on Kabila's behalf.[104] Rwanda's renewed intervention also pushed nonstate militants both inside and outside the DRC—notably, the Mai Mai militias, ex-FAR, and Interahamwe—into Kabila's arms.[105] The conflict soon transformed into a war of plunder, as each belligerent exploited the Congolese territory it controlled. Kabila survived the immediate onslaught only to be assassinated by one of his bodyguards in 2001 in a move reputed to have been masterminded in Kigali; he was succeeded by his son, Joseph Kabila.[106] Although the interstate phase of the war officially ended in 2002, violence in eastern DRC has continued with an ever-changing constellation of actors.

In 1997, Rwanda and Uganda overthrew Zaire's Mobutu Sese Seko because of his support for rebel groups fighting against their governments. Kigali and Kampala installed Laurent Kabila in the belief that he would act according to their preferences and improve security in the eastern part of the country. What the interveners failed to anticipate, however, was the domestic opposition Kabila faced because of his close association with Rwanda and the increased influence of the Tutsis in the new DRC. Anti-Tutsi senti-ment endangered Kabila's rule; in response he moved to downgrade Tutsi/Rwandan influence, fill his government with loyalists, and even made com-mon cause with his patron's most hated and feared enemy, the Hutu ex-FAR and Interahamwe. Rwanda and Uganda began plotting to remove Kabila, but their protégé beat them to the punch, expelling his patrons' forces from the country.[107] This was the final straw: within days, Rwanda and Uganda launched a second invasion of the DRC, under the cover of a new rebel group they cobbled together to put a Congolese face on their attack.

The culprit in this case was the problem of competing principals. Kabila, empowered to implement the preferences of his external principals, found that playing this role endangered his political survival by angering his do-mestic principal. Ultimately, he perceived this domestic threat as most credi-ble and responded to it by distancing himself from his foreign patrons. My argument does not make a determinate prediction about which principal an imposed leader will choose to cross. The logic of leadership regime change holds that leaders brought to power in this way tend to lack domestic support and thus rely on interveners to keep them in office. But this very reality can produce compelling domestic threats that imposed leaders may seek to ap-pease by turning against their foreign friends. That was Kabila's choice in this case. The price was steep—interstate war against his patrons—but the benefit was that he secured his immediate survival. The price was far steeper for the Congolese people, millions of whom perished in the ensuing struggle.[108]

Regime Change and Patron Influence over Protégés

As amply demonstrated in earlier chapters, patrons often grow dissatisfied with their protégés when the latter—frequently owing to domestic opposition—resist implementing the former's agenda. This section briefly explores several cases—some of them detailed in previous chapters—to highlight the role of the problem of competing principals in causing proté-gés to refrain from bowing to patrons' wishes. In some of these cases, pa-trons responded by pursuing the removal of recalcitrant leaders they helped bring to power, whereas in others they simply tried to deal with the policy dispute as best they could.

DISSATISFIED PATRONS, ENDANGERED PROTÉGÉS

Peru During the War of the Pacific (1879–84), Chile removed three Peru-vian leaders. Peruvian president Nicolás Piérola fled following the decisive Peruvian defeat at Chorrillos and Miraflores in January 1881. His departure left the conquering Chileans with no one to negotiate with, much less some-one who would accept Chile's onerous territorial demands—the cession of the provinces of Tarapaca, Tacna, and Arica. The Chileans thus proceeded to create a new government: they had Francisco García Calderón elected by an assembly of leading citizens in February 1881. The Chileans now had a negotiating partner, but not a cooperative one, as García Calderón refused to make the desired territorial concessions. According to William Sater, "His obstinacy infuriated Chile's new president, Domingo Santa Maria. . . . When Garcia Calderón temporized, Chile's representative in Peru first confiscated his treasury, then disbanded his army, and finally arrested the now lame-duck president before sending him to a Chilean exile, not aboard a warship, but, for reasons of economy, on a squalid transport."[109] García Calderón named his vice-president, Lizardo Montero, as his successor in September, but Montero proved just as stubborn and suffered the same fate as his predecessor. Montero was ousted after General Miguel Iglesias, commander of the Army of the North, "issued a manifesto" in April 1882 "calling for peace with Chile on any terms available since victory for the allies [Peru and Bolivia] was clearly an impossibility."[110] The Chileans promptly installed Iglesias in power and negotiated the Treaty of Ancon, which ended the war on Chile's terms.

Why did both García Calderón and Montero resist making concessions to Chile? The reason was that not only did each of these men oppose handing over the contested provinces to Chile, relinquishing them was also extremely unpopular among Peruvians. The evidence for this is that no sooner had Iglesias ceded the territories to Chile, the forces that had fought tooth and nail to expel the Chilean occupiers and avoid these concessions, led by Colonel Andrés Cáceres, overthrew him.

Paraguay After Brazil and Argentina overthrew Francisco Solano López during the War of the Triple Alliance (1864–70), Brazil—the dominant party in the occupation of Paraguay—arranged to have Cirilo Antonio Rivarola elevated to the presidency. Brazilian emissaries believed Rivarola was the best candidate to safeguard their interests in Paraguay, but their commitment to him was purely instrumental: the Brazilians backed him only so long as Rivarola effectively promoted their interests. When Rivarola found himself pinched between doing Brazil's bidding and maintaining domestic support, Brazilian officials began to doubt his commitment and conspired with a new servant who promised to promote Brazil's agenda more faithfully—Juan Bautista Gill. Gill, with the knowledge and support of the Brazilian emissary in Asunción, engineered Rivarola's removal in December 1871.[111]

South Vietnam As described at length in chapter 4, the Kennedy administration decided for multiple reasons in the autumn of 1963 that South Vietnamese dictator Ngo Dinh Diem had to go. Washington placed its faith in a group of South Vietnamese generals led by Duong Van Minh to do the deed.

Although shocked by the brutality with which the generals carried out the task, Kennedy and many of his advisors believed that Minh and his fellow officers would pursue the war with greater determination and effectiveness than had Diem. The Americans were in for a rude surprise when Minh resisted their urging to escalate the war and instead sought to negotiate with the National Liberation Front, dismantled the strategic hamlets, resisted bombing North Vietnam, and opposed an increase in US military personnel and greater US influence over military operations. Minh and his colleagues perceived these measures to be popular in South Vietnam, but they directly contradicted American views on how the war should be waged. US officials thus at the very least failed to stop—and possibly encouraged—another coup by General Nguyen Khanh in January 1964 that toppled Minh.[112]

Central African Republic In 1979, France overthrew the flamboyant self-proclaimed emperor of the Central African Empire, Jean-Bédel Bokassa, replacing him with David Dacko. Dacko depended heavily on French troops and advisers once in office, but this dependence alienated his domestic constituents. Despite managing to eke out just over 50 percent of the vote in an election plagued by massive fraud, prior to which he had jailed his principal opponent for several months, Dacko was unable to control the "ethnic, political, and social strife [that] had engulfed the country since the restoration of the republic."[113] "It was widely felt," according to Peter Baxter, "that Dacko had been elected as a French puppet in an election engineered by the French to serve French interests."[114] Dacko lived in fear that Bokassa would launch a bid to return to power and he likewise fretted about the loyalties of the reformed army under General André Kolingba.[115] Rather than continue to deal with Dacko's paralysis, new French president François Mitterrand decided to wash his hands of his predecessor Valéry Giscard d'Estaing's wayward puppet, clearing the way for Kolingba to seize power on September 1, 1981.

Central American and Caribbean Cases Interveners may also seek to remove leaders that they inadvertently brought to power by ousting their predecessors in ways where they did not control who succeeded to office, such as through assassinations or covert operations in support of domestic factions. In 1909, for example, the United States coerced the resignation of Nicaragua's José Santos Zelaya only to see another Liberal, José Madriz, succeed to office. Madriz was also unacceptable to Washington, which intervened on behalf of Nicaraguan Conservatives to oust him.[116] A similar scenario played out in Costa Rica ten years later when the Wilson administration coerced the resignations of Federico Tinoco Granados and his equally unacceptable successor, Juan Bautista Quirós Segura.[117] In Guatemala, the United States removed two successors to Guatemalan president Jacobo Árbenz who were deemed surplus to requirements in a matter of a few weeks in 1954.[118] And after aiding and abetting the assassination of Dominican strongman Rafael

Trujillo in May 1961, the Kennedy administration had to threaten invasion to dislodge Trujillo's brothers and son from power.[119]

DEFIANT PROTÉGÉS, IMPOTENT PATRONS

The United States and Hamid Karzai in Afghanistan In chapter 3, I chronicled how the US overthrow of the Taliban regime caused insurgency in Afghanistan through the mechanism of military disintegration. As the military situation in the country devolved, so did Washington's relations with its hand-picked Afghan leader, Hamid Karzai. When the United States backed Karzai to become president of Afghanistan, it appeared that he shared the American vision for the country. According to one study of the evolution of US relations with Karzai, "He promised to introduce democratic elections, protect human rights, educate women, fight terrorism, strengthen civic institutions, and develop his country's private sector."[120] Over time, however, the relationship went downhill for reasons consistent with the problem of competing principals. US officials, for example, grew frustrated at the massive corruption that was consuming the lion's share of foreign aid and Karzai's inability to crack down on opium production or build effective security institutions.[121] On the Afghan side, as combat operations against the Taliban intensified and episodes of collateral damage from US air strikes became more common, ordinary Afghans began to turn against the Americans and the man they perceived to be America's puppet—Karzai. Emblematic of the pressures Karzai was subjected to, an Afghan official who investigated a 2008 US air attack that struck a wedding, killing forty-seven people, told Human Rights Watch: "The Afghan people cannot afford more civilian casualties. Therefore, we will demand that President Karzai talk with foreign forces to bring an end to such attacks."[122]

This crisis of domestic support for his regime caused Karzai to put distance between himself and his American allies. By 2007 the Afghan president was criticizing US military operations, denunciations that grew increasingly bitter over the years.[123] The incoming Obama administration increasingly viewed Karzai as an impediment to its plans for Afghanistan; relations plummeted further in 2009 when Karzai perceived US officials as working against his reelection. By his final year in office (2014), Karzai claimed that Washington was collaborating with the Taliban to preserve the US presence in Afghanistan.[124] Reflecting on the state of US-Afghan relations under Karzai in 2012, one European diplomat opined, "Never in history has any superpower spent so much money, sent so many troops to a country, and had so little influence over what its president says and does."[125]

The problem of competing principals contributed to the downward spiral in US relations with its Afghan protégé. Karzai clearly depended on US economic and military assistance to build a functioning state, fight the Taliban, and retain office. But his political survival also depended on the Afghan people, and he could not afford to let himself be tarred by their anger at the Americans over their conduct of the war. Karzai thus attacked his American patrons in increasingly strident terms until by the end of his term, all he could say was: "To the American people, give them my best wishes and my gratitude. To the U.S. government, give them my anger, my extreme anger."[126]

The United States and Nouri al-Maliki in Iraq The United States also struggled to induce its protégés in Iraq to implement policies in line with American preferences after it handed over power in 2004. As highlighted by the problem of competing principals, because those policies clashed with the imperatives of domestic political survival for Iraqi leaders, they were reluctant to implement them. Here I will focus on one issue in particular: the fate of the Sons of Iraq (SOI)—Sunni insurgents who defected from their alliance with Al Qaeda in Iraq (AQI) in 2006–07 to join with US troops in fighting against their former partners. The US-SOI alliance, which occurred as the US military surged additional forces into Iraq and stationed them inside Iraqi towns and cities, was highly successful at destroying AQI, drastically reducing the number of attacks and deaths in Baghdad and around the country.[127] The SOI program, however, was not popular with Iraq's Shiite-dominated government or army. Prime Minister Nouri al-Maliki, for example, "firmly believed the insurgents were volunteers who were plotting to overthrow his government and restore Sunni rule."[128] As one Iraqi brigade commander put it, "These people are like cancer, and we must remove them."[129]

In 2008, the United States began to draw down its surge forces and, in December, signed a status of forces agreement with the Iraqi government, which stipulated that all US troops would leave Iraq by December 2011. As part of the reduction in its forces, the US military turned control over the SOI program to the Iraqi government. As a result, US influence—and its ability to protect the SOI—began to wane, and Maliki's regime started to move against them.

First, although the government promised to absorb 20 percent of the SOI into the Iraqi security forces and find government or private sector jobs for the remainder, a year after the government took over the program, only about 5,000 of the roughly 100,000 SOI (5 percent) had joined the security forces.[130] According to a US officer stationed in Ghazaliyah at the time, by late summer 2008, "There were no police assignments in Ghazaliyah as promised. There were no more training classes. There was no more talk of transitioning to Police."[131] "The transition of the volunteers into the Iraqi security forces and civilian jobs," concurs Emma Sky, "had ground to a halt."[132] By 2010, 40 percent of the SOI had received some kind of government employment, but progress was slow and the quality of the jobs SOI were given did not always meet expectations—"mostly menial jobs like janitor or tea-server," according to Michael Gordon and Bernard Trainor.[133] According to news reports, Maliki was under significant pressure from his Shiite partners to "halt the hiring of Sons of Iraq members into police or military forces."[134]

Second, once the US military transferred responsibility for paying the SOI to the Iraqi government, irregularities immediately began.[135] Maliki's administration cut the SOI's salaries in October 2008 and then didn't pay them at all for the months of March and April the following year.[136]

Third, in 2008 and 2009, the Iraqi Army arrested large numbers of SOI leaders and rank and file.[137] One SOI commander from Diyala province reported in September 2008 that nearly forty SOI had been detained in his area; in Abu Ghraib fifty were arrested.[138] In March 2009 the army jailed the leader of the SOI in Ghazaliyah, Hussein Raad Ali, a former lieutenant colonel in the Iraqi Army under Saddam Hussein. Only about eighteen months earlier, Colonel Raad had been one of two SOI commanders flown by the Americans to Bahrain to meet President George W. Bush via videoconference.[139] Other Ghazaliyah SOI commanders were similarly detained.[140] An SOI leader from Fadhl was arrested around the same time as Raad and another from Ameriyah was imprisoned for four years on trumped-up charges.[141] According to Fawaz Gerges, "As long as US troops were in Iraq, the Sahwa [SOI] were protected and their actions were heralded as a triumph. . . . After the transfer of authority to the Iraqi government, many of their members were incriminated and placed under investigation, thus deepening the divide between local and national politics."[142] As an SOI leader in Diyala put it in December 2009, "The single biggest issue we SOI leaders are worried about is the arrest warrants, against which we have little protection. . . . The Americans used to protect us but now we have no one."[143] Maliki's persecution of his Sunni foes only escalated after US forces departed the country in December 2011, as he targeted top Sunni officials, including Vice President Tariq al-Hashimi, Finance Minister Rafi al-Issawi, and Deputy Prime Minister Saleh al-Mutlak.[144]

In short, there was a significant divergence of preferences between the United States and its Iraqi protégés on the question of the SOIs. Maliki and other Shia believed that the SOI were insurgents in waiting and that allowing them to join the military and police would be accepting a fifth column into the ranks. Although Maliki agreed to US requests that he integrate some SOI into the security forces, in reality he slow-rolled the process and targeted SOI leaders and men. He viewed the SOI as a threat to his political survival and accommodating US preferences on this point could also threaten his tenure by angering his Shia allies. The Sunni militiamen were thus caught between a rock and a hard place, targeted simultaneously by the government and the remnants of AQI, which assassinated them in droves.[145] The bitterness created by the unfulfilled promises to the SOI—and broader discrimination by the Maliki government against Sunnis—

contributed to their forging a new alliance with the Islamic State a few years later.[146]

In sum, after facilitating a change of regime in a target state, interveners often experience "buyer's remorse" as the leader they brought to power resists implementing favorable policies, fails to deliver on her promises, turns out to be just as unpalatable as her predecessor, or is simply a dud. Some of these conflicts—Peru, Paraguay, South Vietnam, Afghanistan, and Iraq—can be attributed to the problem of competing principals. Others can be chalked up to the intervener's lack of control over who succeeds to power. Whatever the cause, regime changers often end up in conflict with the leaders they helped gain office and either remove them directly or countenance their removal by domestic forces.

When Regime Change Backfires: Japan's Assassination of Chang Tso-lin

On June 4, 1928, officers of Japan's Kwantung Army, based in Manchuria, assassinated Chinese leader and Manchurian warlord Chang Tso-lin as he traveled by train from Beijing to his old home base of Mukden. Japan had long been a supporter of Chang Tso-lin but disapproved of his aspirations to rule China south of the Great Wall.[147] As Chiang Kai-shek's Nationalist armies closed in on Chang in Beijing in 1928, the Japanese government tried to coerce Chang to return to Manchuria by threatening to disarm his retreating forces if he lingered too long in the Chinese capital. Japanese prime minister Tanaka Giichi had not yet decided whether to overthrow Chang when Japanese officers took matters into their own hands. In an act that the Japanese government in Tokyo did not initiate but could not repudiate without signing its own death warrant, the Kwantung Army blew up Chang Tso-lin's train. They believed that Chang's son, Chang Hsüeh-liang, would be more deferential to Japanese interests in Manchuria and more compliant with Japanese directives. They could not have been more wrong. The assassination backfired when Chang the younger allied with his father's enemy, Chiang Kai-shek, against the Japanese.

The assassination of Chang Tso-lin played a particularly important role in the quantitative analysis of leadership regime change and militarized interstate disputes because no fewer than half a dozen clashes occurred between China and Japan in the ensuing decade—up to and including the onset of the Sino-Japanese War (1937–45). It is thus essential to ascertain whether the case is, in fact, an instance of regime change. In this section, I argue that the assassination of Chang Tso-lin, despite some interesting irregularities, qualifies as a case of regime change according to my definition. Because of the importance of the coding of this case, I delve into the details of Chang's status as leader of China and the structure of the Japanese regime, which allowed the Japanese military to take actions the civilian government could

271

not disavow. Although one should not attribute all of the militarized clashes between China and Japan to this successful yet failed regime change, the failure to install a compliant protégé in Manchuria meant that Japan had to rely on force to pursue its expansion on the Asian mainland.

CHANG TSO-LIN'S RISE TO POWER IN CHINA

Chang Tso-lin was a Manchurian warlord who eventually became the leader of China's internationally recognized government in 1927. By 1916, Chang had been named civil and military governor of Fengtian province (now known as Liaoning) by the authorities in Beijing. Chang quickly assumed control over the neighboring provinces of Heilongjiang and Jilin, such that within a year or two he controlled all of Manchuria outside those areas held by Japan. As Yoshihisa Matsusaka notes, "Chang Tso-lin's official title in 1920 was 'inspector-general of the Three Eastern Provinces,' a position that made him, in effect, an autonomous ruler in the region."[148] As another writer concludes, "Chang's personal control of the Northeast was complete. . . . His domain in Manchuria was, for all practical purposes, an autonomous state."[149] Chang thus became one of the most powerful men in all of China during the Warlord Era (1916–28).

Chang, however, was not content to rule Manchuria only; he had ambitions south of the Great Wall as well. At this time, North China was divided into three political-military factions: Chang's own Fengtian clique, based in Manchuria; the Anhui clique, led by Duan Qirui (Tuan Ch'i-jui); and the Zhili clique, whose leaders included Feng Guozhang (Feng Yü-hsiang), Cao Kun (Ts'ao K'un), and Wu Peifu (Wu P'ei-fu). These factions fought for control of the central government in Beijing, forming and re-forming alliances in the process. In 1920, for example, Chang joined with the Zhili clique to oust Duan Qirui as head of the Beijing regime.

The Japanese, who supported Chang's rule in Manchuria, discouraged his adventures in China. As James Sheridan puts it, "Japan would not help Chang pursue his ambitions in the central government; they wanted Chang to stay at home and attend to the peace and order of Manchuria, not become involved in matters that might produce war and disorder and thus threaten Japanese interests."[150] Chang was undeterred by Japanese opposition and continued to intrigue in Chinese politics. His alliance with the Zhili clique, however, as with many during the Warlord Era, was short-lived, as Chang's forces fought those of Wu Peifu in the First Zhili-Fengtian War in 1922. Chang lost this war badly, and he retreated with his troops to Manchuria where he declared the region's independence.

Chang licked his wounds over the next two years, rearmed and reorganized his forces, and was soon back inside the Great Wall in 1924, again fighting Wu Peifu and the Zhili clique for supremacy. This time the Fengtian troops were victorious when one of Wu's subordinates, Feng Guozhang, defected, seized Beijing, and ousted the government of Cao Kun.[151] Wu and the Zhili faction were defeated, and Duan Qirui was recalled to office. A further clash between Chang and Feng was brewing, however, and erupted in late 1925. Chang, now allied with his former adversary Wu Peifu, routed Feng's armies in early 1926 and the two of them became the de facto power brokers in Beijing.

For several weeks after Chang and Wu dispensed with Duan Qirui on April 20, 1926, "no national government existed in Peking" while the two warlords debated who should rule the country.[152] Eventually, in mid-1926 they inaugurated a series of regencies that nominally governed for about a year until Chang seized power. As Sheridan puts it, "In these circumstances, it was to everyone's relief that the man with real power finally stepped forward to assume formal responsibility for the government. Chang Tso-lin, on 17 June 1927 proclaimed himself grand marshal, or generalissimo, and organized a military government. Although a cabinet was created, including a prime minister, in essence the government was staffed with Chang's subordinates, and he ruled as a military dictator."[153]

It is not disputed that Chang Tso-lin became the leader of the internationally recognized government of China in June 1927.[154] On this point the general and country-specific sources are unanimous. Both of the leading historical encyclopedias of heads of state—Ross and Spuler's *Rulers and Governments of the World*, and Lentz's *Encyclopedia of Heads of States and Governments*— agree that Chang assumed the leadership of China in mid-June, as do the two leading online compilations of state leaders.[155] Gavan McCormack, author of one of the few English-language accounts of Chang Tso-lin's career, similarly dates his rise to dictatorial power in Beijing to June 18.[156] Contemporary media sources also confirm his position.[157]

Although it is clear that Chang Tso-lin attained the position of head of the Chinese government in Beijing, one might object that this government was merely one of a number of competing governments in China at the time and thus it is a mistake to regard Chang as a real head of state. This objection is difficult to sustain. It is true that China was territorially fragmented among numerous warlords during this period, yet multiple sources confirm that the regime in Beijing was regarded as the legitimate government of the country. According to Andrew Nathan, for example, "The death of Yuan Chih-k'ai in June 1916 ushered in the era of the warlords and yet throughout the ensuing decade or more of militarism, the Peking government remained the symbol of China's national sovereignty and hoped-for unity. In the absence of a dynasty, a dominant personality or a ruling party, the government at Peking still represented the idea of the state."[158] Nathan continues:

> To the end of its life, the Peking government held a claim to legitimacy which made it important even in a nation increasingly dominated by contending warlords. . . . A second reason for Peking's importance was foreign

recognition. Against all evidence of fragmentation, the foreign powers insisted that there was only one China and—as late as 1928—that its capital was Peking. . . . A third source of Peking's influence was financial. Taxes played but a small role in Peking's finances. . . . Far more significant was the financial consequence of foreign recognition: the ability to borrow.[159]

Jonathan Fenby, although he agrees that civilian government in Beijing was weak during the Warlord Era and plagued by frequent leadership turnover, maintains that the government there "retained an importance since the customs revenue went to the administration there that was also recognized by the foreign powers as the government of China."[160] Other studies note that Chiang Kai-shek "overthrew the internationally recognized government in Beijing" when he entered the city with his victorious Nationalist armies in June 1928.[161]

WAS CHANG TSO-LIN THE LEADER OF CHINA AT THE TIME OF HIS DEATH?

Even though it is clear that Chang Tso-lin became the leader of China in 1927, one could reasonably wonder whether he still held that position at the time of his death on June 4, 1928.[162] The crucial point that needs to be established is whether Chang Tso-lin officially abdicated power when he departed Beijing for Mukden on June 3, and thus whether he remained leader of China when his train was blown up the following day. It is surprisingly hard to obtain a clear answer to this question. Most sources simply note that Chang fled Beijing without mentioning anything about his official status. One prominent source, for example, describes Chang only as "Marshal" and never clarifies his official position, remarking only as follows: "Marshal Chang Tso-lin, facing defeat in China, grudgingly followed the advice [of the Japanese government] to withdraw to Manchuria and was enroute to his headquarters in Mukden when he was assassinated."[163]

The handful of sources that are more specific disagree. According to a *New York Times* article published on June 4, for example, "The five-barred emblem of the North China Republic was pulled down when Chang Tso-lin gave up his two years' dictatorship and left for Mukden early this morning."[164] Some scholarly accounts also imply that Chang formally gave up power before leaving the capital. According to C. Martin Wilbur's version, Chang called in the diplomatic corps on June 1 to notify them of his impending departure and "had already made arrangements to turn over governance of the city to a Peace Preservation Commission made up of Chinese elder statesmen, headed by Wang Shih-chen."[165] Wilbur also notes that the generalissimo "issued a farewell telegram to the Chinese people, expressing regret that he had not successfully concluded the anti-Red campaign, and announcing his return to Manchuria in order to spare further bloodshed."[166] Another account relates that "as the Northern Expedition forces approached Peking, Zhang [Chang] took leave of the diplomatic corps and assigned the security of Peking to the police force and a single Manchurian brigade."[167]

None of these sources definitely states that Chang Tso-lin formally abdicated. One says that he "gave up" his dictatorship; another notes that he delegated "governance" of Beijing to a commission; a third states that he assigned security duties to the police and a brigade of his army. Other sources, by contrast, assert that Chang did not renounce his position when he left for Mukden. Indeed, the same *New York Times* article that claims Chang "gave up" his position also reports that "Chang Tso-lin's farewell message, broadcast to all Provinces, hints at his possible return. He does not surrender his title of dictator but merely moves over to Manchuria to avoid further bloodshed and the possibility of further foreign entanglements."[168] This interpretation receives additional support from Keiji Furuya's biography of Chiang Kai-shek, which also discusses Chang's meeting with the foreign diplomatic envoys: "On June 1, in full military regalia, he [Chang] entertained the diplomatic corps at a farewell party. He announced that he had decided to withdraw his troops from within the Great Wall. The removal of his headquarters from Peking to Mukden, he said, did not detract an iota from his being a patriotic Chinese. 'I, Chang Tso-lin,' he proclaimed with considerable pride, 'will never sell China down the river, nor am I afraid to die.'"[169] Read literally, this recounting of events merely states that Chang intended to move his headquarters, and his statement about patriotism could be read as meaning that he did not intend to leave his position as leader of the republic. Further support derives from the fact that following Chang's death, his son, Chang Hsüeh-liang, continued to fly the Five Color Flag of the North China Republic in Mukden until December 28, 1928, when he formally pledged allegiance to the Kuomintang.[170] Finally, the two authoritative encyclopedias of world leaders each list Chang's rein as ending on or after June 4.[171] Both of these sources list Chiang Kai-shek as the next leader of China, noting that his tenure did not begin until October 10.[172]

Given the absence of clear evidence that Chang Tso-lin formally relinquished the office of dictator of China upon leaving Beijing, I follow the coding of the general encyclopedias and consider Chang Tso-lin to be the head of China's internationally recognized government until his death on June 4. Considering the historical ambiguity of what exactly happened in the last twenty-four hours of Chang's life and the absence of a successor regime during this period, I believe that this coding is appropriate. This assessment aligns with other political science datasets on leaders, including Cali Ellis, Michael Horowitz, and Allan Stam's *Leader Experience and Attribute Descriptions* (LEAD) dataset and H. E. Goemans, Kristian Skrede Gleditsch, and Giacomo Chiozza's *Archigos* dataset of state leaders.[173]

JAPAN'S ROLE IN THE DEATH OF CHANG TSO-LIN

A second reason that Chang Tso-lin's assassination may not be considered a regime change is that the killing was not initiated or approved by Japan's civilian leadership, and thus it was not Japanese policy. Rather, according to this view, it was the unsanctioned act of rogue officers within the Kwantung Army based in Manchuria. While it is true that Japanese military officials ordered Chang's assassination against the wishes of the Japanese Prime Minister, I argue that the details of the case justify its coding as a regime change.[174]

Chang's assassination arose out of a disagreement within Japanese official circles regarding whether to continue Japan's long-running policy of supporting Chang. The Kwantung Army was strongly in favor of disarming Chang and deposing him in favor of his son, Chang Hsüeh-liang, who they believed would be more responsive to Japan's demands. Prime Minister Tanaka Giichi, on the other hand, was more inclined to continue to support Chang Tso-lin as long as he could be made to see the error of his ways.[175] Numerous historical sources agree that the government of Premier Tanaka did not order the assassination.[176]

In an attempt to force Chang out of Beijing, Tanaka's envoy in Beijing presented Chang with an ultimatum on the night of May 17–18, 1928: retreat now and we will allow your forces to enter Manchuria unhindered, or wait to fall back until fighting comes to Beijing and be disarmed by the Kwantung Army.[177] The concern was that if the war spilled over into Manchuria, the Nationalists might be able to extend their control into the three northeast provinces, with negative repercussions for Japanese interests. Chang resisted this advice, however, and lingered on in Beijing until the beginning of June, although by May 19 he had made the decision to leave.[178] As a result of their disagreement over support for Chang, Tanaka did not issue the necessary orders for the Kwantung Army to deploy south so that it could be in a position to disarm Chang's retreating forces. Officers of the Kwantung Army felt that Tanaka's policy was not sufficiently aggressive and decided to take matters into their own hands. McCormack summarizes what happened next: "Muraoka Chōtarō, commander-in-chief of the Kwantung Army, made secret approaches to the commander of Japan's North China garrison army to have Chang Tso-lin assassinated before his return. When Muraoka's staff officer, Colonel Kōmoto Daisaku, learned of this, he thought he could do better by arranging the murder in the Northeast in such a way as to foment the immediate crisis that, it was hoped would allow a Japanese military takeover as a result."[179] In the early morning hours of June 4, explosives placed by engineers of Japan's Korea Army detonated under the car of the train in which Chang was riding; the generalissimo likely died from his wounds within a few hours, although his death was not formally announced until June 20.[180]

On the face of it, the basis for coding the assassination as an act of the Japanese state appears questionable. The procedures that characterized the Japanese government at the time, however, allowed the military to take actions that the cabinet could not stop beforehand or disavow afterward. The key issue, as Saburō Ienaga summarizes, was that "the military could topple cabinets by having an army or navy minister resign or prevent their formation by refusing to provide officers to serve in these positions. . . . Control over the appointment of service ministers gave the military the power of life or death over any cabinet."[181] The problem this created for Prime Minister Tanaka was that the perpetrators of the assassination could not be held responsible without the agreement of the military services.[182] Tanaka quickly suspected that the Kwantung Army was behind Chang's murder and set up a committee to investigate. Soon he possessed ample evidence that his suspicions were correct. Tanaka favored punishing the plotters, as did the young Emperor Hirohito. Tanaka, however, boxed himself in by promising the emperor that the perpetrators would be punished. War Minister Shirakawa Yoshinori, however, even though he knew that Kōmoto had carried out the crime, refused to go along, arguing that revealing Japan's involvement would damage the army's reputation and Japan's national interests. The dispute reached a head on June 27, 1929, when Shirakawa reported to Tanaka that the army leadership continued to deny any role in the killing. According to Edward Drea, "The prime minister upbraided Shirakawa, who stormed out in a rage, threatening to resign and bring down the government. Unwilling to self-destruct, the next day the cabinet endorsed the war minister's version of events."[183]

Tanaka not only lost this debate, he soon lost his job, and then his life. Tanaka reported to the emperor the next day that "there was no evidence that the Japanese Army or Japanese officers were involved in the incident and he recommended that only administrative measures (not court-martials) be taken in order to straighten out military behavior."[184] Having previously told the emperor that he would court martial Kōmoto and anybody else involved, Tanaka was caught. The emperor noticed the discrepancy in the prime minister's reports and immediately demanded that he resign. As Mayumi Itoh notes, "This was the first and only case in Japanese modern history in which the emperor's words caused the resignation of a prime minister and the resignation of a cabinet en masse."[185] Tanaka sunk into a deep depression and died a few months later.

In short, although it is true that officers of the Kwantung Army planned and executed the assassination of Chang Tso-lin without permission from—and against the wishes of—the Japanese prime minister, it still makes sense to code the assassination as an act of Japanese policy. The reason is that civilian governments could not renounce actions taken by the military without committing political suicide. If the cabinet had decided to acknowledge that Japanese officers had murdered Chang Tso-lin and tried to punish them, the ministers representing the military would have re-signed, thereby bringing down the government. Because the military would refuse to nominate ministers (who had to be active-duty officers) to serve in any cabinet that intended to implement such measures, Japanese policy was held hostage to the military's preferences. Tanaka learned this the hard way, having pledged to punish the guilty parties without checking first with the military. When he tried to save his premiership by reneging in front of the emperor, he was immediately forced to resign.

Moreover, although I have defended the decision to code Chang Tso-lin as the leader of China because China was a recognized state and Manchuria was not, if we relax the formal rules of recognition there are good grounds for considering Manchuria to be independent of China in the 1920s—and Chang Tso-lin was the undisputed ruler of Manchuria. Multiple accounts confirm that Manchuria under Chang was akin to an autonomous, or even a sovereign, state.[186] For example, Aron Shai writes that Manchuria, a "political entity . . . created almost from scratch, operated as a sovereign state and even made agreements with foreign countries such as Russia."[187] Thus, even if Chang is considered to be the leader of only Manchuria rather than China, there are still grounds for coding this case as, if not a formal regime change, then a de facto regime change—the overthrow of the ruler of a highly autonomous region, unrecognized state, or quasi-recognized state. Note that a "Japan-Manchuria" regime change in 1928 would still be followed by at least one militarized dispute—the 1931 Mukden Incident that resulted in the creation of the Japanese puppet state of Manchukuo on the territory of Manchuria.

JAPAN'S REGIME CHANGE BACKFIRES

Having established that it is appropriate to treat Chang Tso-lin's assassination as an instance of regime change, I demonstrate that his removal is a textbook example of the counterproductive effects of leadership regime change. The officer responsible for killing Chang Tso-lin, however, believed that regime change would facilitate the extension of Japanese control over Manchuria and bring to power a submissive leader ready to cooperate with Japan. According to one historian, Colonel Kōmoto, the principal plotter, believed that "the death of Chang Tso-lin would deprive Manchuria of its leader and plunge it into chaos. The Japanese army would then step in to restore order and occupy Manchuria."[188] Kōmoto also assumed that Chang's son and probable successor would be far more malleable than his father. In a speech at the Yamato Hotel in Dairen, Kōmoto had already made his views on the two men clear: "The malignant cancer today of Japan's Manchuria and Mongolia policy is Chang Tso-lin. If we get rid of him somehow, after that there will be no difficulty from appeasement with [sic] the youthful Chang Hsueh-liang."[189]

In the event, neither of these things came to pass. Understanding that the Japanese were his father's likely killers, Chang Hsüeh-liang was careful to refrain from any provocations that could give the Kwantung Army an excuse to swing into action.[190] Chaos did not result, calm soon prevailed, and no pretext emerged for Japanese forces to seize power.[191] Worse than this, however, was that the assassination was completely counterproductive from the point of view of Japanese interests, for it reduced rather than increased the chance of a friendly regime in Manchuria or a sympathetic government in Beijing. In fact, it pushed Chang Hsüeh-liang toward an alliance with Chiang Kai-shek's Kuomintang regime, which had no intention of allowing Japan to expand its control over Manchuria. After pledging his loyalty to the Kuomintang in late December 1928, Chang the younger was named commander of the Northeast Frontier Army and administrator of Manchuria; he later rose to become second in command of the Nationalist Army.[192]

This judgment is supported by every historical account available. Gavan McCormack, for example, writes that "Kōmoto's action was singularly counterproductive, since not only did it not lead to the resolution of any of the issues disputed between China and Japan . . . but it led very soon to the establishment of the Chang Hsueh-liang regime, which, by making its peace with Chiang Kai-shek's nationalist government at Nanking, realized the worst dreams of both Kōmoto and Japanese Premier Tanaka."[193] Marius Jansen comes to a similar conclusion: "This Japanese action thus removed Chiang Kai-shek's most important competitor for military unification in north China from the scene and replaced him with a son who was to show himself resentful of his father's murderers and later to cooperate with Kuomintang power."[194] Dick Wilson argues that assassinating Chang was another of Japan's "many miscalculations in China, because the Young Marshal proved more fiery and nationalistic than his father" and soon moved into the Nationalist camp.[195] In other words, as Donald Jordan writes, "When Chang Hsueh-liang seized the reins of power left by his father, he proved to be even less of a Japanese puppet than his father had been."[196] Saburō Ienaga similarly maintains that "the assassination of Chang backfired; the flames of Chinese resistance burned brighter. Chang Hsueh-liang pledged allegiance to the Nationalists and placed his forces under Chiang Kai-shek's banner and moved ahead with a plan to develop Manchuria without Japanese assistance."[197] Michael Barnhart's assessment concurs with the others: "Kōmoto's act ended any chance of an 'independent' regime in Manchuria friendly to Japan. Chang Hsueh-liang, the murdered warlord's son and successor, rapidly formed ties with the Kuomintang. By 1929 he had not only refused to allow the Japanese to build any railroads in Manchuria but also commenced construction of rival lines of his own. Army planners and railway officials feared that their entire interest and investment in Manchuria was in jeopardy."[198]

Many of these assessments focus on how, by increasing the likelihood that Chang Hsüeh-liang would throw in his lot with the Nationalists, the 1928 regime change failed to serve Japan's immediate interests in Manchuria. Indeed, some of the MIDs that occurred between 1928 and 1938 refer to Japanese attacks in Manchuria or other engagements with forces led by Chang Hsüeh-liang. These MIDs thus directly reflect the failure of the 1928 regime change to install a pliant leader willing to pursue Japan's interests in the region. The broader point, however, is that no matter who is considered to be Chang Tso-lin's successor—his son in Manchuria or Chiang Kai-shek in China—regime change removed a leader who at least sometimes acceded to Japan's wishes and replaced him with leaders determined to resist Japanese expansion on the mainland. This case is thus an unusually direct example of how regime change can empower hostile leaders opposed to the interests of the intervener.

THE PROBLEM OF COMPETING PRINCIPALS

It is clear that the assassination of Chang Tso-lin backfired: regime change did not provide a pretext for Japan to occupy Manchuria nor did it bring to power a leader who complied with its wishes. On the contrary, the man who replaced Chang—the murdered leader's son, Chang Hsüeh-liang—soon aligned with his father's enemy, Chiang Kai-shek, and resisted Japan's advances in Manchuria. A key unanswered question, however, is why Chang the younger was not frightened into submission and chose instead to join forces with Japan's enemies.

Part of the answer is surely Chang's anger at Japan for murdering his father. Part of the answer may also be his Chinese nationalism. But it appears that the problem of competing principals also contributed to the outcome. Despite Chang Hsüeh-liang's status as Chang Tso-lin's son, it was not a foregone conclusion that he would succeed his father. Nor was it a foregone conclusion that once he took power that he would ally with Beijing. Rather, Chang Hsüeh-liang faced competing pressures from Japan on the one hand, and pro-Nationalist domestic opinion on the other. To maintain his tenuous grip on power, Chang the younger had to balance these opposing pressures, only committing himself when one of them—the domestic one—grew strong enough to threaten his rule.

After Chang Tso-lin's assassination, there were numerous claimants to power other than the dead warlord's son, including Chang Tso-hsiang, the military governor of Kirin province (one of the three provinces that together made up Manchuria); Yang Yü'ting, Chang Tso-lin's chief of staff; and Tupan Chang, his brother-in-law.[199] Once Chang the younger was named commander-in-chief of the Three Eastern Provinces in early July 1928, rather than stampede into an alliance with Chiang Kai-shek in Beijing, Chang temporized owing to the fragility of his domestic position.

On the one hand, he could not ignore that Japan was keen to see him take power in Manchuria and, as Akira Iriye notes, "Japan was at this time the only reliable support on which he could count."[200] Yet on the other hand, two of his main competitors for power, Chang Tso-hsiang and Yang Yü'ting, were strongly in favor of joining with the Nationalists in opposition to the Japanese.[201] Chang was thus pulled in opposite directions by his international and domestic principals.

At first, Chang leaned in the direction of a Japanese alliance, even deciding, according to one account, to "follow a policy of friendship toward Japan."[202] Domestic imperatives, however, began to gain the upper hand. "Public sentiment," according to this account, "favored agreement between Mukden and the victorious Nationalists."[203] "Within the Three Eastern Provinces," agrees Iriye, "advocates of peace [with the Nationalists] grew steadily in strength and popularity, and memorials poured in from citizens of Manchuria, ardently requesting the raising of the Revolutionary flag."[204] In mid-July, Chang told a Japanese diplomat that given the strength of feeling in Manchuria in favor of a rapprochement with the Nationalists, "If he refused their demand . . . 'he would be in a very embarrassing position, and might perhaps be forced to resign.'"[205]

Just as it seemed that an agreement with the Chinese Nationalists was imminent, however, Japanese prime minister Tanaka warned the Manchurian that Japan "opposed the union of Manchuria with China proper, and that Japan would provide Chiang Hsueh-liang with advisers and other assistance if he would devote himself to the development of Manchuria—that is, if he would maintain Manchuria's autonomy."[206] In response, Chang temporized again; he suspended unification talks with the Nationalists and, in Iriye's words, "continued his policy of prevarication" and "talked softly to both the Japanese and to the Nationalists."[207] Given the competing pressures to which he was subjected, writes Iriye, "Chang's policy of waiting was . . . the only course he could follow in order to maintain his own position within the Three Eastern Provinces."[208]

Again, however, Chang perceived that the threat from his domestic opposition outweighed the threat from Japan. According to Iriye, in a meeting with the commander-in-chief of the Kwantung Army in mid-July, Chang lamented that "he could not resist a further rapprochement with the Nationalists unless he resorted to a coup d'état, which he might do with Japanese assistance." In early August, Chang further told the Japanese consul-general in Mukden that "he could not act against 'public opinion' in the matter of compromise with the Nationalists."[209] As Iriye describes, "Within Manchuria the influence of Yang Yü'ting and Chang Tso-hsiang," proponents of reaching an accommodation with the Nationalists, "was, if anything, growing; and it became imperative for Chang Hsüeh-liang to ally himself with the Nationalist government under Chiang Kai-shek."[210] The Nationalist leader, eager to add the Manchurian's formidable army to his side, offered attractive terms and the deal was consummated in late December. In the aftermath of this agreement and the anti-Japanese policies that Chang implemented in its wake, it "became increasingly clear" to the Japanese, writes Chang's biographer, "that Zhang [Chang] was actually their rival. He was not going to let them realize their plan to take over" Manchuria.[211] Japan would not have its Manchurian puppet after all; it would have to rely on threats, force, and war to continue its expansion into China.

Japan's regime change in China is an influential case in generating the finding that leadership regime change increases the chances of a militarized interstate dispute. Exploring this case in depth is thus warranted to validate that it is in fact a case of regime change and to verify that the problem of competing principals helps explain why regime change went so awry in this instance. I find that although the case is unusual in two respects—Chang Tso-lin's questionable status as the effective leader of China when he was assassinated and the lack of explicit authorization for the assassination by Japan's top political leaders—there are solid grounds for coding the case as a foreign-imposed regime change. Most sources agree that Chang remained the leader of China when his train was blown up en route to Mukden on June 4, 1928. Moreover, Japan's unique constitutional arrangement made the Japanese military the effective rulers of the country, since military officers could cause any government to fall from power if they disapproved of its policies. The Japanese cabinet thus had little choice but to acquiesce in the Kwantung Army's unilateral attack on Chang Tso-lin.

Contrary to the military's rosy predictions, however, Chang Tso-lin's son, Chang Hsüeh-liang, did not prove to be a weak Japanese puppet. In fact, he allied with Japan's enemy, the Nationalist government of Chiang Kai-shek. And the reason he did so was because of irresistible pressure from powerful domestic actors who could threaten his rule, as predicted by the problem of competing principals.

In this chapter I have explored the question of whether foreign-imposed regime change improves relations between interveners and targets going forward. My answer is that it generally does not. I argue that the problem of competing principals, just as it increases the chances of civil war and violent leader removal in the target, similarly decreases the chances that patrons and protégés will get along happily ever after. Promoting the intervener's policy agenda, by alienating domestic constituents, threatens the political survival of imposed leaders. Resisting that agenda, however, also threatens their political survival; the threat simply comes from the opposite direction. When leaders perceive the domestic threat to be most pressing, they will seek to placate it by defying their patron's demands. This can lead to contentious relations with the patron or a situation in which the patron, despite its advantage in relative power, is unable to persuade its protégé to pursue policies in line with its preferences. In extreme cases, patrons may attack their protégés or otherwise seek their removal.

I evaluated this argument quantitatively by analyzing the effect of regime change and its subtypes on several proxies for the quality of intervener-target relations, including the likelihood of militarized interstate disputes, similarity of voting in the UN General Assembly, and overlap in alliance portfolios. I found that while regime change overall has little effect on any of these outcomes, leadership regime change—the type of regime change most likely to activate the problem of competing principals—increases the likelihood of militarized disputes between patrons and protégés and reduces the similarity of their voting patterns in the UN and their alliance portfolios. Restoration regime changes surprisingly almost eliminate the probability that interveners and targets fight but has little effect on similarity of UN voting records or alliance portfolios. Institutional regime changes also enhance the similarity of alliances but otherwise have no significant effects.

I also showed the effect of regime change on intervener-target relations in real-world cases. Regime change regularly creates a problem of competing principals whereby protégés have domestic reasons to diverge from their foreign patron's wishes. When domestic incentives are sufficiently powerful, as in the DRC in 1998, patrons may launch a war to replace the protégé. More commonly, as in Paraguay, South Vietnam, and Central African Republic, patrons remove—or let somebody else remove—their erstwhile protégés without extensive violence. Less dramatically, as in Afghanistan, Iraq, and Manchuria, patrons are simply unable to get their way on important issues.

In this chapter I have not dwelled on any of the success stories of regime change, such as the transformations of West Germany and Japan from fascist warmongers to peaceful democracies—and reliable allies. It is important not to overlook such cases, but it is also important to keep them in perspective. First, it required six years of war and millions of Allied combat deaths to subdue these countries. The stakes involved in regime change hardly ever rise to the level at which interveners would be prepared to pay such costs. Second, Germany and Japan, although dominated by hostile ideologies, possessed many prerequisites for stability and democracy, including relatively high incomes per capita, industrial economies, sizable middle classes, homogeneous populations, and prior institutional development.

Third, although a number of factors—including US hegemony, joint democracy, and German and Japanese memories of the wartime suffering their societies had endured and inflicted on others—helped prevent disputes between these countries and the United States from becoming militarized, this does not mean disputes did not arise. West Germany, for example, pushed hard to acquire nuclear weapons in the 1950s and 1960s owing to fears of US abandonment in the face of the Soviet threat. Washington had to exert significant coercive pressure—and make credible deterrent promises—to shut these efforts down.[212] Similarly, US-Japan relations have experienced some rocky patches over the years concerning issues like Japan's nuclear status, the reversion of control over Okinawa to Japan, and the unpopularity of US bases on Okinawa.[213] Germany and Japan, of course, proved to be invaluable allies during the Cold War and beyond, and I do not mean to exaggerate the magnitude of the conflicts they experienced with Washington. Still, the relatively harmonious relationships the United States has experienced with these protégés appears to be the exception rather than the rule. All in all, regime change is far from the magic bullet it is often portrayed to be.

Appendix to Chapter 5. A Statistical Analysis of Regime Change and Interstate Relations

In this appendix I provide details on the statistical analysis that produced the results reported in the body of the chapter. I also report the results of a variety of robustness checks and a matching analysis intended to address potential selection bias.

DATASET

The dataset I use to estimate the effect of regime change on measures of intervener-target relations consists of all directed dyads in the international system from 1816 to 2000 provided that they are geographically contiguous or one of them is a major power—pairs of states known in the IR literature as "politically relevant dyads."[214] The problem with pairing all states with all other states over such a long time period is that it generates an enormous number of observations, most of which had little if any chance of experiencing a conflict or inflicting regime change on one another. It is extremely unlikely, for example, that Uruguay and Uganda in the 1980s, or Bolivia and Liberia in the 1880s, would have had the opportunity or willingness to engage in armed conflict with each other. The political relevance criteria recognize that states are far more likely to have conflicts of interest if they are geographically proximate or if one of them is a great power, and thus has the capability to project force outside its immediate neighborhood. Even with these restrictions, the dataset still includes many dyads in which conflict is highly unlikely, but it represents a significant improvement on a dataset that includes all dyads. Another way of understanding the difference is that the dyads excluded by the political relevance criteria have a near zero probability of experiencing a militarized conflict.[215] In politically relevant dyads, by contrast, this probability is significantly larger, if still small.

The unit of analysis in this dataset is the "directed dyad," which means that any given pair of states appears in the dataset twice each year: once as State A–State B and a second time as State B–State A. The main advantage of organizing the data in this way is that the dyadic setup includes information on both states in the dyad, and thus allows the analyst to include variables that measure the relationship between the two states, such as the balance of power or the distance between them. With regard to MIDs, directed dyads also allow the analyst to identify which side initiated the dispute. A third advantage related specifically to regime change is that directed dyads capture instances in which multiple states intervened together to effect regime change, which are counted only once in a state-year dataset.

The downside of the dyadic approach is that it entails the loss of about two dozen cases of regime change owing to the rules used by the COW Project to identify members of the international system.[216] Consider the case of Central America in the nineteenth century. Central America (excluding Panama, which was part of Colombia until 1903) achieved independence from Spain in 1821, and its component countries became independent states after the dissolution of the Central American Federation in 1839. Yet according to COW, Honduras, Nicaragua, and Costa Rica do not enter the international system until 1899, 1900, and 1920, respectively. Guatemala and El Salvador gain entry earlier—1868 and 1875, respectively—but still decades after they gained formal independence. The consequence of defining away Central American states is that it excludes a large number of regime changes. Central America was a hotbed of (leadership) regime change in the nineteenth century, experiencing a total of twelve successful cases (nineteen dyads) between 1845 and 1894. Ten of these twelve cases (and seventeen of nineteen dyads) are excluded owing to the COW rules for interstate system membership.[217] Many of these cases involved weak and impoverished states inflicting regime change on, and fighting wars against, equally weak and impoverished states.[218] Owing to the exclusion of these cases, the dyadic results may be biased toward finding that regime change is more likely when the intervener is more powerful than the target and may underestimate the effect of regime change (and especially leadership regime change) on militarized conflict.

DEPENDENT VARIABLES

My first dependent variable consists of whether the intervener or the target initiated a militarized interstate dispute against the other party.[219] The advantage of using the MID dataset is that it includes information on interstate conflicts below the level of war.[220] Specifically, states can exhibit one of five "hostility levels" in a militarized dispute: (1) no militarized action, (2) threat to use force, (3) display of force, (4) use of force, or (5) war.[221] I used a dummy variable that detects whether State A in a dyad initiated a militarized dispute of any severity (greater than 1) in a given year. In my dataset, there are 2,230 MID initiations.[222] Because the dependent variable is dichotomous, I employ probit regression with robust standard errors clustered by dyad on the assumption that events within dyads are not independent, but events across dyads are.[223]

To assess whether regime change brings targets into closer alignment with interveners, I use similarity (S) scores of two types. The first, developed by Erik Voeten and colleagues, measures the similarity of two states' UN General Assembly voting records (available after 1945).[224] The second represents the extent of overlap in dyads' alliance portfolios.[225] The former varies from –1 to 1, whereas the latter varies from –0.61 to 1. Because S scores are continuous variables whose values are strongly correlated over time, for these analyses I employ ordinary least squares (OLS) regression with a lagged dependent variable.

CONTROL VARIABLES

Possibly the most important variable that scholars have identified as contributing to the likelihood that two states will experience militarized conflict is geographic proximity. States that border each other simply have far more reasons to fight than countries separated by vast distances. This fact surely reflects both motive and opportunity. As Jessica Weeks puts it, "Geographically close countries are more likely to have disagreements (such as over the precise location of a border), and it is easier for a country to deploy its military forces against an immediate neighbor."[226]

Studies have taken two approaches to incorporate the effects of distance. The first is to use politically relevant dyads as I do in my analysis. Second, even when limiting the universe of cases to politically relevant dyads, studies of militarized disputes also include variables that capture the distance between two states and/or whether they are geographically contiguous. These variables are always highly significant: states that are closer to each other are more likely to fight.

Another important factor to account for in the study of conflict initiation is military capabilities. Powerful states are likely to have more expansive interests than less powerful countries and thus should be more likely to use force abroad. They also possess greater capabilities to do so. Similarly, the more powerful that State A is relative to State B within a dyad, the more likely State A ought to be to initiate force against State B. In contrast, states that have similar interests, as indicated by shared alliance ties or similar alliance portfolios, should be less likely to experience conflict. States that share extensive foreign policy interests with the leading state in the system should also be less likely to start conflicts owing to their relative satisfaction with the status quo. Further, dyads in which both sides are democracies ought to experience fewer conflicts than mixed dyads or pairs in which both states are autocracies. Finally, some studies also include levels of trade in a dyad on the theory that economic interdependence reduces the risk of conflict, while others incorporate regime instability to check whether governments experiencing turmoil are more likely to initiate, or be targeted for, conflict.

I include the following control variables identified by previous studies as affecting the likelihood of interstate conflict: The material capabilities of both states, measured as each state's share of total global capabilities, known as Composite Index of National Capabilities (CINC) scores; the share of total dyadic capabilities controlled by State A; the weighted global similarity (S) score for the two states; each state's similarity score with the system leader; the logged distance between the two states' capital cities; dummy variables indicating whether each state in the dyad is a democracy, as well as an interaction term to identify cases where both states are democratic; a dummy variable indicating membership in a joint alliance; and a variable that counts the number of years between MIDs, and three cubic splines, to control for temporal dependence.[227]

For the analysis of UNGA voting and alliance portfolio similarity, I include two additional variables. First, it is possible that states at similar levels of economic development could have similar interests and may be likely to vote in similar ways in the UNGA. I thus include a variable that records the log of the absolute value of the difference between State A and State B's energy consumption. Dyads with scores close to zero possess similar levels of development whereas in those with higher scores, State A or State B is more developed than its partner in the dyad. Second, one might expect that states with highly asymmetric military capabilities might have similar voting records because of the influence that the powerful wield over the weak. Similarly, states that are more powerful might be more defiant and less willing to go along with the preferences of others. I thus include the log of the absolute value of the difference between State A and State B's number of military personnel.

RESULTS: MILITARIZED INTERSTATE DISPUTES

The results of my core analysis of the effect of regime change on militarized interstate disputes are shown in the first four columns of table 5.3. Model 1 includes the variable for all types of regime change aggregated together, whereas model 2 disaggregates regime change into its three types. Models 3 and 4 repeat models 1 and 2 but use fixed effects rather than random effects, thereby controlling for unmeasured time-invariant factors unique to dyads that could influence the likelihood of militarized disputes. This procedure allows me to assess whether a militarized conflict within a dyad is more likely after a regime change compared to before. The cost of using fixed effects, however, is that all dyads that never experience a MID in their history are

Table 5.3 Probit models of foreign-imposed regime change and initiation of militarized interstate disputes, 1816–2000

	1	2	3	4	5	6	7	8	9	10	11	12
	Base model	Base model, types of regime change	Base model, FE	Base model, types of regime change, FE	Five-year treatment	Permanent treatment	Institutional regime change, alt. coding	Level 4 and 5 MIDs	Level 5 MIDs	Rare events logit	Cluster robust variance	China-Japan 1928 omitted
Regime change (all)	-0.027 (0.091)	—	-0.109 (0.195)	—	—	—	—	—	—	—	—	—
Leadership regime change	—	0.259** (0.100)	—	0.381† (0.211)	0.298** (0.103)	0.176** (0.066)	0.258** (0.099)	0.194 (0.129)	0.503** (0.206)	0.515* (0.217)	0.26† (0.15)	0.151† (0.091)
Institutional regime change	—	-0.484 (0.370)	—	-1.153 (0.754)	-0.307 (0.398)	-0.268† (0.145)	-0.373 (0.369)	-0.311 (0.379)	Dropped	-0.966 (0.985)	-0.48 (0.31)	-0.477 (0.369)
Restoration regime change	—	-0.898** (0.336)	—	-2.467* (1.016)	Dropped	-0.068 (0.121)	-0.897** (0.336)	Dropped	Dropped	-1.986** (0.985)	-0.88** (0.31)	-0.899** (0.336)
Capabilities, Side A	1.723*** (0.266)	1.750*** (0.266)	2.272** (0.820)	2.303** (0.820)	1.724*** (0.265)	1.742*** (0.267)	1.740*** (0.266)	1.507*** (0.286)	1.873*** (0.462)	4.093*** (0.643)	1.77*** (0.30)	1.752*** (0.266)
Capabilities, Side B	1.480*** (0.290)	1.487*** (0.291)	1.184 (1.022)	1.187 (1.023)	1.475*** (0.290)	1.497*** (0.292)	1.485*** (0.291)	1.586*** (0.307)	1.423** (0.509)	3.604*** (0.712)	1.51*** (0.50)	1.492*** (0.291)
Side A's proportion of dyadic capabilities	0.160** (0.054)	0.159** (0.054)	0.481 (0.367)	0.480 (0.367)	0.159** (0.054)	0.160** (0.054)	0.159** (0.054)	0.126* (0.057)	0.102 (0.105)	0.412** (0.135)	0.16** (0.06)	0.159** (0.054)
Dyadic S score	-0.117* (0.050)	-0.117* (0.050)	-0.606*** (0.122)	-0.600*** (0.122)	-0.118* (0.050)	-0.111* (0.050)	-0.117* (0.050)	-0.095† (0.055)	-0.001 (0.120)	-0.199† (0.120)	-0.10 (0.13)	-0.116* (0.050)
Side A's S score with system leader	-0.024 (0.071)	-0.031 (0.071)	-0.512** (0.164)	-0.523** (0.164)	-0.027 (0.071)	-0.034 (0.071)	-0.030 (0.071)	-0.080 (0.076)	0.193 (0.150)	-0.088 (0.178)	-0.03 (0.06)	-0.030 (0.071)

Side B's S score with system leader	0.055 (0.071)	0.052 (0.072)	0.309† (0.169)	0.302† (0.169)	0.051 (0.071)	0.048 (0.072)	0.052 (0.072)	0.002 (0.078)	0.188 (0.148)	0.036 (0.181)	0.05 (0.06)	0.053 (0.072)
Distance	-0.091*** (0.004)	-0.091*** (0.004)	-0.123*** (0.030)	-0.128*** (0.030)	-0.090*** (0.004)	-0.090*** (0.004)	-0.090*** (0.004)	-0.085*** (0.005)	-0.068*** (0.008)	-0.225*** (0.010)	-0.09*** (0.01)	-0.091*** (0.004)
Democracy, Side A	0.092* (0.038)	0.092* (0.038)	0.018 (0.100)	0.015 (0.100)	0.092* (0.038)	0.090* (0.039)	0.092* (0.038)	0.019 (0.043)	0.091 (0.076)	0.254** (0.094)	0.09 (0.08)	0.092* (0.038)
Democracy, Side B	0.144** (0.043)	0.143*** (0.043)	0.289** (0.093)	0.292** (0.093)	0.145*** (0.043)	0.141*** (0.043)	0.144** (0.043)	0.142** (0.048)	0.063 (0.102)	0.401*** (0.105)	0.14* (0.07)	0.143*** (0.043)
Joint democracy	-0.481*** (0.056)	-0.474*** (0.056)	-0.545*** (0.137)	-0.543*** (0.137)	-0.479*** (0.056)	-0.471*** (0.057)	-0.475*** (0.056)	-0.407*** (0.065)	-0.656*** (0.162)	-1.215*** (0.142)	-0.47*** (0.10)	-0.475*** (0.056)
Joint alliance	0.026 (0.040)	0.031 (0.040)	-0.072 (0.081)	-0.070 (0.082)	0.027 (0.040)	0.026 (0.041)	0.030 (0.040)	-0.004 (0.045)	-0.066 (0.083)	0.054 (0.100)	–	0.030 (0.040)
Constant	-1.489*** (0.069)	-1.487*** (0.070)	–	–	-1.488*** (0.069)	-1.492*** (0.069)	-1.487*** (0.069)	-1.523*** (0.077)	-2.718*** (0.140)	-2.606*** (0.166)	-1.49*** (0.15)	-1.489*** (0.069)
Wald Chi²/LR Chi²	1163.39***	1192.25***	426.67***	446.24***	1184.75***	1244.42***	1192.41***	975.00***	388.95***	–	–	1211.47***
Pseudo-R²	0.133	0.134	–	–	0.133	0.134	0.134	0.140	0.140	–	0.13	0.134
Log pseudo-likelihood	-9999.707	-9985.829	-6792.693	-6782.909	-9996.012	-9989.964	-9986.872	-7583.132	-1055.774	–	-9987.56	-9988.581

Note: N for all models is 180,498, with the exception of models 3 and 4 (fixed effects), where it is 55,233. † $p<0.10$; * $p<0.05$; ** $p<0.01$; *** $p<0.001$.

dropped from the analysis. In models 3 and 4, for example, nearly 70 percent of the cases in the dataset are omitted owing to absence of variation.

Model 1 shows that the effect of all types of regime change combined is negligible. Only when these types are broken out in model 2 do significant effects emerge: Leadership regime change increases the likelihood of intervener-target conflict by more than 100 percent, restoration regime change reduces the likelihood of conflict by 90 percent, while the effect of institutional regime change is negative, lowering MID probability 60 percent, but insignificant. The control variables perform mostly as expected: MIDs are more likely as the initiator and the target grow more powerful and when the initiator is more powerful than the target, and less likely when the two states are more closely aligned and farther apart geographically. Democracies are more likely both to initiate and to be the target of MIDs, but jointly democratic dyads are much less likely to engage each other in conflict. The similarity scores of each side with the system leader have no effect on the likelihood of interstate conflict. Finally, joint alliance membership is not significantly related to MID initiation.

Models 3 and 4 display the results produced using fixed effects logit, which are highly similar to those generated by the random effects estimator. Regime changes aggregated together (model 3) exert no significant effect on the likelihood of interstate conflict between interveners and targets. In model 4, by contrast, leadership regime change increases the likelihood of such conflicts ($p = 0.07$), restoration regime change reduces it ($p = 0.02$), while institutional regime change takes a negative sign but misses statistical significance ($p = 0.14$).

Robustness Tests Although these results provide support for my theoretical expectations, it is possible that they are sensitive to minor changes in variable coding, model specification, the type of model used, or other factors. To probe the stability of the findings, I subjected them to eight robustness tests, the results of which are shown in models 5–12 of table 5.3. First, I vary the length of the treatment effect of regime change. In model 5, for example, I shorten the treatment to five years, whereas in model 6 I and lengthen it to include all remaining years in the dyad. The only change in model 5 is that restoration regime change is dropped because there are no cases of intervener-target conflict within five years of such an intervention. In model 6, institutional regime change becomes marginally (negatively) significant whereas restoration regime change, while still negative, loses significance. Leadership regime change, by contrast, continues to increase the likelihood of militarized conflict significantly for the remaining life of the dyad.

Second, I recode institutional regime changes to include only cases in which interveners attempted to democratize targets, thereby excluding the Soviet regime changes in Eastern Europe at the conclusion of World War II. Model 7 shows that making this change has almost no effect on the coefficient and significance levels for any type of regime change. Institutional regime change in particular remains negative and insignificant.

Third, I employ more stringent versions of the dependent variable by excluding the two lowest levels of militarized disputes: threats and displays of force. Model 8 uses MIDs that escalated to the use of force (hostility levels 4 and 5) as the dependent variable; model 9 uses only those MIDs that resulted in war (hostility level 5). The two models show that although leadership regime change slips just below the 90 percent level of statistical significance for the two top levels of MIDs ($p=0.14$), when the dependent variable consists of MIDs that escalated to war, it is highly significant with a coefficient that is twice the size of the coefficient for when the dependent variable includes all MIDs (e.g., model 2). No level 4 or 5 MIDs occurred within ten years of a restoration regime change so this variable is dropped in models 8 and 9. The effect of institutional regime change remains insignificant for level 4 and 5 MIDs considered together (model 8) and is dropped from model 9.

Fifth, because militarized interstate disputes are a relatively rare event, in model 10 I reestimated the core model using rare events logit.[228] The pattern of results is unchanged.

Sixth, I implemented two types of methods—spatial lags and cluster robust variance estimation—to correct for potential nonindependence across (as opposed to within) dyads.[229] Model 11, for example, shows the results obtained from using Aranow, Samii, and Assenova's cluster robust variance technique. The results barely change. The same is true when spatial lags are included.[230]

Seventh, owing to the large number of MIDs that followed Japan's regime change in China in 1928, I tested the sensitivity of the results to omitting this case. In model 12, I recoded the variable for leadership regime change in this case to zero and reran model 2. The coefficient for leadership regime change shrinks by about one-third but retains statistical significance at the 90 percent level of confidence.[231] Although this case is influential in producing the finding that leadership regime change increases the likelihood of militarized disputes, excluding it does not eliminate the finding.

Selection Bias: Matching How likely is it that these results are explained by selection bias—countries choosing targets for intervention against which they may be predisposed to fight for other reasons? This subsection reports results obtained after performing genetic matching to check whether interveners select targets for different types of regime change against which they are already likely or unlikely to fight.[232] To create the matched datasets, I excluded non-regime-change years from dyads that experienced regime change to ensure that a dyad was not matched to itself in an earlier or later year or to other countries that suffered regime change. For example, in the dataset of leadership regime changes used for matching, all years for the Vietnam-Cambodia (and Cambodia-Vietnam) dyad other than 1979, the

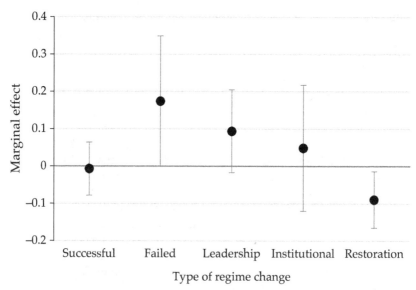

Figure 5.6. Marginal effect of foreign-imposed regime change on probability of militarized interstate disputes after genetic matching

year that regime change occurred, were dropped. Genetic matching produced a set of control cases that was statistically indistinguishable from cases that experienced different types of regime change; overall improvement in balance was upward of 98 percent in every case.

The dependent variable in this analysis is a dummy variable signifying whether a MID occurred at any point during the ten years after the year in which regime change occurred.

Figure 5.6 displays the treatment effects of different types of regime change after matching. As shown, aggregated successful regime changes exert a negligible effect on the probability of militarized disputes, whereas failed regime changes more than double the likelihood of MIDs. The effect of leadership regime change is somewhat diminished after matching but still increases the likelihood of a militarized dispute between interveners and targets from 0.15 to 0.25, a 60 percent increase that remains statistically significant at the 90 percent level of confidence.[233] The effect of restoration regime change also remains significant, as it reduces the likelihood of an intervener-target MID from 10 percent to 1 percent. Interestingly, after matching, the effect of institutional regime change increases the probability of a MID in the following decade. This 5 percent change, however, is also insignificant. In short, analysis performed after matching confirms the findings reported earlier for all types of regime change.

RESULTS: MEASURES OF DYADIC AFFINITY

Table 5.4 shows results from OLS regressions using similarity of UNGA voting between dyads as the dependent variable. More specifically, following Bailey, Strezhnev, and Voeten, I use the "dyadic affinity score" (S score) calculated using two category vote data, with yes votes (approval of a measure) assigned a value of 1 and no votes (disapproval) coded as 2.[234] Models 12 and 13 show random effects specifications whereas models 14 and 15 use fixed effects. As summarized in the main text of the chapter, the only significant effect is for regime changes that fail in model 12, which reduce dyadic affinity. Leadership and institutional regime changes also reduce dyadic voting similarity in model 13 but neither is significant. In the fixed effects models (14 and 15), none of the regime change types is significant.

Table 5.5 reruns the models in table 5.4 but this time using Signorino and Ritter's S score representing similarity in dyads' alliance portfolios. Again, as with UNGA voting, regime change has no general effect on the degree to which interveners' and targets' alliance commitments overlap (nor does failed regime change; see models 16 and 18). Dividing regime changes into types, however, begins to yield some interesting findings. Leadership regime changes, for example, significantly reduce this measure of dyadic affinity in both the random- and fixed-effects specifications (models 17 and 19). Institutional regime changes, by contrast, result in a greater degree of alliance portfolio similarity. Restoration regime changes, finally, have no effect in either model.

Selection Bias: Genetic Matching As with my analysis of militarized disputes, these findings may be the product of selection bias. It is possible that interveners select targets with which they may be predisposed to have bad relations or they may choose to implement a particular type of regime change in targets with which they anticipate having good or bad relations.

To investigate the extent to which these findings might be the product of selection bias, I performed two separate rounds of genetic matching, one using only the years after 1945 for UN voting and a second using the entire 1816–2000 time period for alliance portfolio similarity. I used all the same procedures here as I did previously, particularly matching on the year of regime change only and dropping all non-regime-change years for dyads that experienced regime change so as to prevent such dyads from being matched to themselves. As mentioned in the text, the small number of regime changes with no missing data in the post–World War II period ($N = 18$) posed a problem in using matching for UN voting patterns. The number of cases after matching is only thirty-six for all regime change types together, and twenty-two, eight, and six for leadership, restoration, and institutional, respectively. This helps explain the absence of significant effects for this dependent variable.

Table 5.4 Foreign-imposed regime change and voting similarity in the United Nations General Assembly, 1946–2000

	Random effects		Fixed effects	
	12	13	14	15
Successful regime change	0.002	–	0.003	–
	(0.010)		(0.012)	
Failed regime change	−0.044**	–	0.002	–
	(0.015)		(0.023)	
Leadership regime change	–	−0.013	–	0.011
		(0.015)		(0.019)
Institutional regime change	–	−0.040	–	−0.021
		(0.035)		(0.035)
Restoration regime change	–	0.017	–	−0.003
		(0.012)		(0.015)
Distance	−0.003***	−0.003***	0.003	0.003
	(0.000)	(0.000)	(0.003)	(0.003)
Capabilities, State A	−0.149***	−0.150***	0.733***	0.735***
	(0.002)	(0.002)	(0.038)	(0.038)
Capabilities, State B	−0.149***	−0.149***	0.734***	0.734***
	(0.002)	(0.002)	(0.038)	(0.038)
State A's share of dyad's total capabilities	−0.000	0.000	−0.000	−0.000
	(0.002)	(0.002)	(0.019)	(0.019)
Economic parity	−0.000	−0.000	0.012***	0.012***
	(0.000)	(0.000)	(0.001)	(0.001)
Military parity	−0.001	−0.001	−0.017***	−0.017***
	(0.000)	(0.000)	(0.001)	(0.001)
Democracy, State A	−0.051***	−0.051***	0.022***	0.022***
	(0.002)	(0.002)	(0.004)	(0.004)
Democracy, State B	−0.051***	−0.051***	0.022***	0.022***
	(0.002)	(0.002)	(0.004)	(0.004)
Joint democracy	0.072***	0.072***	0.008*	0.008*
	(0.003)	(0.004)	(0.004)	(0.004)
Joint alliance	0.006***	0.006***	0.031***	0.031***
	(0.002)	(0.002)	(0.004)	(0.004)
Lagged DV	0.881***	0.881***	0.710***	0.710***
	(0.003)	(0.003)	(0.002)	(0.002)
Constant	0.133***	0.133***	0.022	0.022
	(0.004)	(0.004)	(0.021)	(0.021)
N	92310	92310	92310	92310
F	334624.35***	333544.87***	8276.45***	7685.29***
R^2 within	0.540	0.540	0.548	0.548
R^2 between	0.980	0.980	0.947	0.947
R^2 overall	0.848	0.848	0.808	0.809

Standard errors in parentheses; * $p < 0.05$, ** $p < 0.01$, *** $p < 0.001$.

By contrast, eighty regime changes are included in the matching procedure for alliance portfolio similarity. The lowest number of total cases (treated plus control) after matching is twenty-eight (for institutional regime change), whereas both leadership and restoration have at least sixty. It is thus at least possible that significant effects could emerge from this

Table 5.5 Foreign-imposed regime change and similarity in alliance portfolios, 1816–2000

	Random effects		Fixed effects	
	16	17	18	19
Successful regime change	0.005	–	−0.000	–
	(0.006)		(0.004)	
Failed regime change	−0.000	–	0.002	–
	(0.008)		(0.007)	
Leadership regime change	–	−0.009[†]	–	−0.013*
		(0.005)		(0.006)
Institutional regime change	–	0.043***	–	0.021*
		(0.007)		(0.010)
Restoration regime change	–	0.003	–	0.002
		(0.011)		(0.006)
Distance	−0.002***	−0.002***	−0.003***	−0.003***
	(0.000)	(0.000)	(0.001)	(0.001)
Capabilities, State A	−0.115***	−0.116***	−0.241***	−0.242***
	(0.008)	(0.008)	(0.011)	(0.011)
Capabilities, State B	−0.114***	−0.114***	−0.241***	−0.241***
	(0.008)	(0.008)	(0.011)	(0.011)
State A's share of dyad's total capabilities	−0.000	0.000	−0.000	−0.000
	(0.001)	(0.001)	(0.005)	(0.005)
Economic parity	−0.000**	−0.000**	−0.004***	−0.004***
	(0.000)	(0.000)	(0.000)	(0.000)
Military parity	−0.002***	−0.002***	−0.001*	−0.001*
	(0.000)	(0.000)	(0.000)	(0.000)
Democracy, State A	−0.010***	−0.010***	0.008***	0.008***
	(0.001)	(0.001)	(0.001)	(0.001)
Democracy, State B	−0.010***	−0.010***	0.008***	0.008***
	(0.001)	(0.001)	(0.001)	(0.001)
Joint democracy	0.021***	0.021***	0.007***	0.007***
	(0.001)	(0.001)	(0.002)	(0.002)
Lagged DV	0.906***	0.906***	0.823***	0.823***
	(0.002)	(0.002)	(0.001)	(0.001)
Constant	0.092***	0.092***	0.171***	0.170***
	(0.002)	(0.002)	(0.005)	(0.005)
N	175582	175582	175582	175582
F	821964.11***	821723.67***	36940.26***	34100.96***
R^2 within	0.719	0.719	0.721	0.721
R^2 between	0.993	0.993	0.987	0.987
R^2 overall	0.898	0.898	0.896	0.896

Standard errors in parentheses; * $p < 0.05$, ** $p < 0.01$, *** $p < 0.001$.

analysis, and indeed that is the case. Matching for all four types of regime change produced major improvements in balance—at least 98 percent in each case.[235]

Figure 5.7 shows the effect of different types of regime change on similarity in UNGA voting after matching. None of the effects are statistically significant, which is not surprising given the small number of cases. The direction of the effects remains consistent with the exception of leadership regime change, which switches from weakly negative to weakly positive.

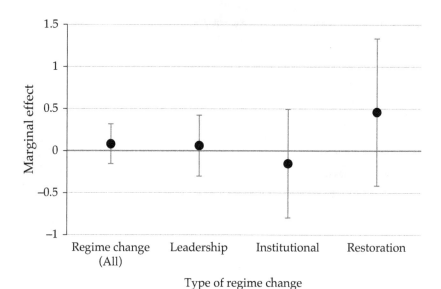

Figure 5.7. Marginal effect of foreign-imposed regime change on similarity of United Nations General Assembly voting after genetic matching

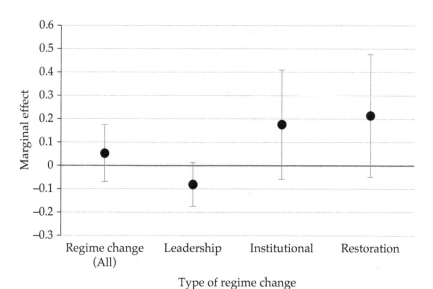

Figure 5.8. Marginal effect of foreign-imposed regime change on similarity of alliance portfolios after genetic matching

Given the very small sample sizes, however, it is hard to learn anything meaningful from the figure.

The results for alliance portfolio similarity after matching shown in figure 5.8 are more illuminating given the larger number of cases included ($N=80$). The most striking result in figure 5.8 is the persistence of the negative effect of leadership regime change on alliance similarity. On average, leadership regime change reduces intervener-target affinity by 0.08 points on a 2-point scale over the course of a decade, a reduction of 4.5 percent. This effect is significant at the 90 percent level of confidence. Institutional regime change continues to have a large positive effect on alliance similarity but this effect loses statistical significance after matching, indicating that the initial effect may have been driven by the characteristics of the states selected for this type of regime change or aspects of the relationship between the interveners and their targets. Finally, the opposite is true of restoration regime changes: Restorations strongly increase interstate affinity after matching, although the effect does not quite reach significance at the 90 percent level of confidence.

Conclusion

States have a variety of more or less violent tools at their disposal for changing the behavior of other states. At the low-violence end of the spectrum, states may express their displeasure using the tools of diplomacy, such as lodging formal diplomatic protests, withdrawing an ambassador from a foreign country, expelling foreign diplomats from its own, withholding recognition of a new leader or regime, or sponsoring resolutions of censure in the United Nations. Moving up the coercive ladder, states may impose economic sanctions, cutting off their economic relations with a target country in a bid to compel it to change its behavior.[1] Further up the forcefulness ladder is coercive diplomacy, defined by Robert Art as "the attempt to get a target . . . to change its objectionable behavior through either the threat to use force or the actual use of limited force."[2] At the high end of the violence scale, states may wage war—or use coercive violence in war—to compel adversaries to change undesirable policies or relinquish disputed territory.[3]

Each of these tools is a means of influencing the behavior of a foe but does not affect its preferences, which are assumed to remain fixed. France, after all, did not abjure its claim to Alsace and Lorraine just because Prussia defeated it in 1870; regaining the lost provinces remained an *idée fixe* in the French political imagination down to 1914. This is not to say that states' preferences never change, only that compellence is about altering behavior, not preferences. Regime change, by contrast, is about changing preferences. The logic is deceptively simple: if you can't persuade the existing leaders of a target state to do what you want, just change the leaders and put in ones who share your views. Taking this step aligns the target's preferences with those of the intervener, eliminates the conflict of interest, and promotes peaceful relations afterward.[4]

In reality, however, regime change rarely works as planned and often begets future conflict. The problem lies in the fact that two states rarely if ever have isomorphic interests. By placing a new leader in power in a foreign country, interveners create a double principal-agent problem—what I call in this book a *problem of competing principals*. Foreign interveners—the external principals—expect their agents to share their preferences and pursue policies congruent with those preferences. Yet once a leader is placed in power, she desires to remain in power and avoid suffering a sometimes violent and untimely demise. To maintain office, imposed leaders must consider the preferences not only of their external patrons but also those of an internal principal: their domestic constituency. Because the preferences of some segment of the leader's domestic constituency typically diverge from those of the intervener—and both principals can remove her from power—the leader faces a dilemma. By zealously implementing the external principal's agenda, imposed leaders risk angering their domestic audience, which may rebel or seek to remove them. But if imposed leaders cater to their domestic principal and resist carrying out the intervener's agenda, they risk angering their patron, which may also seek to oust them. Whichever choice an imposed leader makes, she faces a corresponding danger. For this reason, foreign-imposed regime change heightens the chances of both internal conflict in the target state—such as civil war and irregular leader removal—and external conflict between the intervener and the target.

Not all regime changes are alike, however. Some simply oust one leader and install another without building political institutions. Others are more ambitious and create new institutions in addition to empowering new leaders. Still others restore the prior leader and/or set of institutions that most recently governed the country. I argue that these different types of regime change have different effects depending on whether they exacerbate or attenuate the divergence of preferences between an imposed leaders' internal and external principals.

Leadership regime changes activate the problem of competing principals most acutely by imposing leaders with little domestic support and legitimacy. These leaders are most vulnerable to irregular removal and thus may lean heavily on—and hew closely to the preferences of—their external patron. Doing so, however, tends to generate internal dissatisfaction with the ruler and may spark armed resistance or the threat of a coup. Such leaders are "caught between a rock and a hard place." Depending on which party poses the most credible threat, the protégé will either remain loyal to his foreign master and face an elevated probability of civil war and irregular removal or turn on his patron and confront a higher likelihood of conflict with the patron.

Institutional regime changes—with the notable caveat that they succeed in creating new institutions—overcome preference divergences between internal and external principals in one of two ways. Institutional regime changes that construct authoritarian institutions enable imposed leaders to crush domestic foes. This ability allows them to implement policies aligned with their patron's preferences without having to worry much about internal dissent. Institutional regime changes that successfully promote democracy, by contrast, reduce conflict in a different way. For one, these regime changes do not necessarily reduce the divergence of preferences between an imposed leader's domestic principal and the foreign patron. For the patron, installing a democratic system in a target state reduces its influence over who succeeds to power in the target state. Over time, this may allow a preference divergence to reemerge but the shared norms or institutions of democracies help manage these disagreements without resort to force.[5] Internal conflict, moreover, can be accommodated through voice opportunities, such as elections, such that an imposed leaders' domestic opponents need not resort to violence to achieve policy change.

The catch for institutional regime changes is that institution building succeeds under only a narrow set of circumstances, namely when target countries have preconditions for strong institutions, such as being relatively wealthy or ethnically homogeneous.[6] When these factors are absent, as they are in poor or heterogeneous countries, institution building generally fails and these cases default to leadership regime changes with all of the problems those entail. In the aggregate, these contradictory effects cancel each other out, and thus I argue we ought not to observe a strong effect of institutional regime changes one way or the other on internal or external conflict. We should, however, observe the success stories among institutional regime changes where one or more preconditions for strong institutions and/or democracy are present and the failures where they are absent.

Restoration regime changes, finally, ought also to have mixed effects because under different circumstances they can either exacerbate or ameliorate the preference divergence between an imposed leader's internal and external patrons. On the one hand, restored leaders clearly have domestic enemies (or else they would not have been ejected from power) and interveners still expect them to implement their policy agendas. On the other hand, this type of regime change sometimes returns popular democratic regimes to power that were ousted by external forces, thereby eliminating any preference divergence between the regime and its internal constituency. In many such cases, furthermore, such as Allied restorations in Europe in 1944 and 1945, interveners lack strong preferences over the target's behavior other than that they return to the democratic fold. In other instances, restoration regime changes crush the domestic rebels responsible for expelling the leader in the first place. For these reasons, restoration regime changes in the aggregate should not make internal or external conflict more likely.

Of course, it is also possible that targets of regime change simply crumble before the problem of competing principals can take effect. When interveners implement regime change by invading the target, it sometimes triggers *military disintegration*, a situation in which the target military breaks apart and its members seek shelter in rough terrain or across an international border. When the target leader also escapes, military disintegration is particularly likely to lead to an immediate insurgency. Even when the deposed leader is captured, killed, or forced into exile, however, military disintegration creates the raw material for insurgency that can be exploited by other former regime officials or by entirely new leaders. When the military in the target state remains relatively cohesive and surrenders in an organized fashion, by contrast, insurgency is unlikely whether or not the former leader remains at large.

Summary of the Empirical Findings

In this book, I examined the effect of regime change—and different types of regime change—on the onset of civil wars; the likelihood that leaders are removed from office in a violent manner; and the quality or closeness of intervener-target relations. In chapter 3, I conducted a multivariate quantitative analysis of civil war onset. I found that regime change significantly increases the likelihood of civil war over the ensuing decade. Leadership regime change in particular increases the risk of civil war onset three and a half times compared to cases where no such regime change occurred, the largest effect of any variable in my analysis. Institutional regime changes aggravate the likelihood of civil war in places where this type of regime change is likely to fail: poor countries, such as Nicaragua and the Dominican Republic, and countries that are ethnically heterogeneous, like Afghanistan and Iraq. Where institutional regime changes succeed, by contrast, the likelihood of civil war is reduced. Restoration regime changes also tend to lower the probability of civil wars but this effect cannot reliably be distinguished from zero.

I followed up these statistical findings by tracing how military disintegration and the problem of competing principals contributed to the outbreak of civil wars in six cases from around the globe that span a period of more than 150 years. In Cambodia in the 1980s and Afghanistan and Iraq in the first decade of the twenty-first century, invasions in pursuit of regime change triggered militaries in these countries to fragment and break. The remnants fled to remote areas inside and outside their borders where they regrouped under their old leaders and renewed the fight to eject the intervener and retake power. Building on existing literature on military effectiveness, I offered some preliminary thoughts on the causes of military disintegration, but future work could further explore the determinants of this phenomenon and perhaps develop quantitative indicators to make the argument testable in a large-N study.[7] By contrast, civil wars in Afghanistan in the early 1840s, Nicaragua in 1912, and Guatemala in the 1960s were caused at least in part by the problem of competing principals. Imposed leaders in these cases found themselves caught between the wishes of their external patrons and their internal constituents. When they hewed too closely to the external patron, civil wars erupted as disgruntled segments of the elite, military, and population took up arms to topple the leader associated with the unpopular demands of the external power.

In chapter 4, I turned to a second implication of my theory for domestic outcomes in the target of regime change: violent leader removal. Analyzing two datasets with different units of analysis and temporal coverage, I consistently found that leaders brought to power in foreign-imposed regime changes face a greater hazard of irregular removal and a reduced hazard of regular removal. Leadership regime change again exhibited these effects most strongly: leaders who achieved office in this way were between two and four times more likely to suffer violent removal and about one-third as likely to experience nonviolent removal. The effects of institutional and restoration regime changes, by contrast, were more varied. Institutional regime changes had no significant effects in general on either type of removal, but no leader brought to power in this type of regime change was ousted irregularly after 1945. Leaders who are restored to power leave office regularly at about the same rate as other leaders but are less likely to lose office through violence. Only two leaders who came to power in restoration regime changes lost power irregularly.

Chapter 4 then laid out the various irregular ways that foreign-imposed leaders have been removed from office. Three of these forms of exit are idiosyncratic, although they support my broader contention that regime change is risky. In a few cases, regime change is merely a brief stop on the way to annexation. Leaders put in power while their country is in the process of being annexed by the intervener lose power irregularly, but this is not the result of the problem of competing principals. Another handful of foreign-imposed leaders are chased from power when the foreign occupiers that installed them are defeated in war. These cases consist exclusively of German occupations during World War II. And sometimes foreign interveners, such as Chile in Peru during the War of the Pacific (1879–83) or the United States in Guatemala (1954), are forced to remove multiple leaders consecutively until they obtain one who shares their preferences. The remaining three kinds of irregular removal, however, which comprise the bulk of the cases, are consistent with my argument. First, interveners that grow dissatisfied with the performance of their protégés acquiesce in, or encourage, their removal by domestic forces in the target state. Second, foreign-imposed leaders are occasionally overthrown by a coup or rebellion against the wishes of the foreign patron. Third, patrons sometimes intervene militarily a second time to try to remove wayward protégés. I defer discussion of this last form of irregular removal to chapter 5 since it involves interstate conflict between interveners and targets.

Chapter 4 presents extended case studies of the two most important of these mechanisms. First, I demonstrated how the United States, after greenlighting a coup against its longtime ally Ngo Dinh Diem, grew disappointed with the government of Duong Van Minh that succeeded Diem. Minh and his fellow generals in the ruling junta turned out to hold preferences regarding how the war should be conducted that were at odds with those of their US patrons. As a result, although Washington did not encourage another coup, US officials on the ground in Saigon with knowledge of coup plotting did nothing to stop it. Second, I showed how Emperor Maximilian of Mexico, a leader who was indelibly identified with his patron, Emperor Napoleon III of France, fell victim to the same Liberal regime the French ousted to place him on the Mexican throne. Despite holding preferences that were more congruent with the Liberals, who hated him, than the Conservatives, who supported him, and despite frequently finding himself at odds with the French, Maximilian could not overcome his association with his foreign patrons—or the fact that he had helped replace a republic with a monarchy.

Chapter 5 examined the international consequences of regime change, particularly the implications for a target's relations with the intervener. Regime change is undertaken to align preferences and improve relations between the two states involved. Does it? The answer is mostly no. Regime change in general does not lower the likelihood that interveners and targets experience militarized conflict afterward nor does it result in closer alignment as measured by similarity of UN General Assembly voting records or similarity of alliance portfolios. In fact, leadership regime change increases the chance that the two countries engage in hostilities and reduces the overlap in their alliances. Restoration regime changes, in contrast, reduce the likelihood that patrons and protégés experience another conflict but otherwise have little effect on the quality of their relations. Institutional regime changes have no effect on conflict propensity but have some positive effect on the closeness of relations. Failed regime changes, finally, increase both the likelihood of intervener-target conflict and the dissimilarity of how they vote in the UN.

Like chapter 4's discussion of irregular leader removal, chapter 5 also presented two in-depth case studies to illustrate how the problem of competing principals can contribute to armed conflict or worsened relations between interveners and targets. First, it examined a case—Rwanda and Uganda in the DRC—in which an imposed leader's domestic incentives pushed him to resist carrying out the interveners' agenda. Laurent Kabila was widely perceived inside Congo as a Rwandan puppet, a perception that generated opposition to his rule by non-Tutsis. To placate this opposition, Kabila sought to diversify his power base and lessen his dependence on his Rwandan allies. These moves in turn angered Kigali, which began plotting his overthrow. Kabila, however, preempted the Rwandan coup and expelled his erstwhile patrons from the country. Kabila's betrayal of his patrons resulted in a major war when the jilted Rwandans attacked and attempted to remove their wayward protégé.

Second, chapter 5 examined a case of regime change identified by the quantitative analysis as particularly influential—Japan's assassination of Chang Tso-lin in China in 1928. I determined that despite some atypical circumstances, the case was most appropriately coded as a foreign-imposed regime change, albeit one that promptly blew up in Japan's face when its new protégé, Chang Hsüeh-liang, defied its wishes and allied with its principal adversary. The reason he did so was because he feared the domestic consequences of a Japanese alliance.

The chapter also briefly reviewed a few cases that appeared in chapters 3 and 4, as well some new cases, to highlight the difficulty that patrons often have in getting their protégés to do their bidding. In many of these cases, including the US-led regime changes in Afghanistan and Iraq, the reason for the protégé's defiance lay in domestic opposition to the patron's desired policies.

Contributions to Scholarship

This book joins a growing body of literature that emphasizes the difficulties of governing or transforming foreign societies. Studies of military occupation, for example, have found that success is infrequent because it depends on factors that are rarely present, most notably a common threat perceived by both the occupier and the occupied that causes their preferences on the necessity of occupation to converge.[8] Scholars of nation building—the forcible democratization of a target country—have similarly found that success is rare and further that it depends on the same conditions in the target state highlighted in this book: high per capita income and ethnic homogeneity.[9] Literature on state building, defined by David Lake as efforts by outsiders to "create a state that is regarded as legitimate by the people over whom it exercises authority," has identified a dilemma similar to the one highlighted in this book for regime change: states that care enough to intervene and rebuild a failed state also care about the policies the target adopts afterward.[10] Statebuilders will thus support leaders whose preferences are compatible with their own. Because those preferences are rarely in tune with the preferences of the median voter in the target society, however, the regime will be regarded as illegitimate and its leaders will be forced to govern undemocratically. Scholars of imposed polities, defined as the imposition of new leaders and sometimes political institutions in new or existing states, have shown that unrest is rife in such countries.[11] More than one-third of the state-years in imposed polities recorded at least one episode of violent or nonviolent conflict; only 2 percent of such states suffered no domestic political challenges at all.[12] Finally, existing studies of foreign-imposed regime change have for the most part found that regime change has negative effects on conditions in target states and for intervener-target relations.[13]

This study contributes new theory, data, and detailed process tracing of historical cases to show that regime change is a perilous undertaking. Interveners cannot simply select a leader with compatible preferences, install him in power, and walk away expecting everything will turn out fine. Even leaders who shared their patron's preferences when they took office can be forced by domestic threats to their political survival to turn on their foreign sponsors or resist their policy demands. Alternatively, protégés may be overthrown or face insurgencies owing to domestic unhappiness with their propatron stance. Interveners—who already paid the costs of installing a new regime in the target—may see that investment jeopardized or face the prospect of having to sink further costs to defend their protégé.

Some might reply that because most of my cases are not true cases of _regime_ change but rather instances of leadership change, it is thus little wonder that I find few success stories. When states truly promote institutional change in targets, in contrast, they are able to transform target societies, gain reliable allies, and enhance their security.[14] I explained in the introduction that the equation of leader change with regime change in popular and scholarly discourse is well beyond reversing and thus I adopted a definition of regime change in this book that included leadership change. I have tried to respond to this objection by differentiating among types of regime change, and it is true that interveners obtain better results when they invest in building institutions—that is, when they implement institutional regime change. Although this result is noteworthy, there are three reasons for skepticism.

First, institutional regime changes lead to positive outcomes only when they succeed at establishing functioning governing institutions in target states. When these institutions fail to function as intended, the case (although still coded as an institutional regime change) essentially takes on the characteristics of a leadership regime change. Second, institution building does not succeed at random; success depends heavily on conditions in target states. Where these conditions exist, such as relatively high levels of wealth or low levels of ethnic heterogeneity, institutional transformation has a better chance of working as intended. Third, a small handful of cases accounts for the result that institutional regime change in the presence of promising domestic conditions can lower conflict. For democracy-promoting institutional regime changes, West Germany and Japan are essentially the only successes.[15] On the single-party regime side, there are more "successes"— Bulgaria, Czechoslovakia, Hungary, and Romania—but success in these cases derived from massive doses of repression, which is theoretically and empirically interesting but hard to prescribe as a strategy.

This book also contributes to specific literatures on the causes of civil war, the political survival of leaders, and interstate conflict. My argument contributes to the literature on civil war by bringing an identifiable triggering mechanism to a literature that often relies on static variables and hence has difficulty explaining _when_ civil wars are likely to occur. Although the military disintegration mechanism has much in common with opportunity explanations for civil war, the argument does not make sense without the underlying grievance on the part of the ousted leader and/or his group of supporters at being ousted from power. The problem of competing principals, on the other hand, clearly belongs in the grievance camp: the trigger for violence is resentment experienced by domestic groups at policies implemented by the leader at the intervener's behest.

This book also enhances our understanding of the conditions that affect the duration of leaders' tenure in office and the probability of irregular removal. Foreign imposition comprises a small but important fraction of the ways in which leaders come to power. Most leaders gain office according to the established rules and procedures in their country. About one-fifth as many seize power by force without foreign assistance; and one-fifth as many again, according to my data, were imposed by foreign powers.[16] Yet major wars—such as both World Wars, Korea, and the Iran-Iraq War—are sometimes waged at least in part to overthrow foreign leaders, and foreign-imposed regime change, as demonstrated in this book, has contributed to further conflicts as well as serious humanitarian disasters. My findings show that just as leaders who gain office through irregular methods are significantly more likely to leave power the same way, so are leaders placed in office by outside powers more likely than other leaders to be overthrown by force. Foreign-imposed leaders are not *more* likely to suffer this fate than leaders who obtain office violently without foreign help, but neither are they less likely to suffer irregular removal as regime change optimists would have it. I also demonstrate that the three types of regime change do not have uniform effects on leader survival. The overall finding reflects the strength of the effect of leadership regime change, but restoration regime change almost eliminates the chance of forceful removal from office.

Finally, this book adds to a growing body of evidence that states are unlikely to gain faithful protégés or reliable allies via regime change.[17] Although the quantitative results may be of marginal utility given the weakness of some of the proxies for intervener-target relations, I amply document how the problem of competing principals can lead to war between the two states—as well as the difficulties that patrons experience in their relations with their protégés even in the absence of violence between them.

Implications for Policy

What are the implications of the book's arguments for policy?

EASIER IS NOT EASIER

One implication that is worth underscoring is that regime change is likely to result in unfavorable outcomes where it is easy and better outcomes where it is hard. Regime change, as Melissa Willard-Foster points out, is often inflicted by great powers on minor powers, and the imbalance in capabilities between them makes deposing the leaders of these states easy.[18] Weak states, however, such as Haiti, the Dominican Republic, Nicaragua, Guatemala, Iran, Iraq, Afghanistan, and Libya, are just the kinds of places where regime change is likely to result in insurgency, civil war, or coups that can endanger or unseat imposed leaders. The risk of these unhappy events occurring can also generate pressure for imposed leaders to defy their patrons, leading at a minimum to patrons having difficulty getting their way and at maximum to repeated interventions and even war.

In stark contrast, regime changes ironically have been more successful where they were hard to implement. Germany and Japan, for example, successfully democratized after regime change and became close and valued allies of the United States. A major reason for this success was that these countries were relatively developed economically with a solid middle class; were quite homogeneous and thus had a strong sense of nationhood; and had previous experience with democratic or constitutional rule. Other factors also helped the populations of these countries see the necessity of regime change and occupation, such as the massive rebuilding required after they were pulverized in World War II and the threat to their security posed by the Soviet Union. The shared sense of external threat attenuated the preference divergence that so often emerges after regime change between external interveners and domestic constituencies in the target. In other words, multiple conditions were present, that are not present in most cases, that predisposed Germany and Japan to success. It goes without saying, however, that imposing regime change on great powers usually requires a major war. Countries in this category today might include Russia and China. No one is talking about regime change in these cases for the simple fact that carrying it out would require large wars against countries that possess formidable militaries and nuclear weapons.

The upshot of this discussion is that the United States, although it possesses the capability to change the regimes of many weaker countries, may not want to do so because regime change is likely to lead to trouble in just those cases. Many commentators on the Left and the Right, for example, lamented President Barack Obama's choice not to get more deeply involved in the early years of the Syrian Civil War and openly pursue regime change against the government of Bashar al-Assad.[19] It is possible that this could have worked: military aid to rebel groups significantly increases their likelihood of winning civil wars, especially when aid is provided early in the conflict before the government fully mobilizes.[20] This advantage only holds, however, if one's intervention does not attract counterintervention. Still, for the sake of argument, assume that aiding the moderate Sunni opposition in Syria resulted in Assad's defeat. Then what? The moderate opposition was not the only game in town, and it is likely that Assad's ouster would have been followed by a second civil war between moderate and extremist elements (such as Jabhat al-Nusra and IS) for control of Syria. To the extent that the United States had boots on the ground in Syria, it would have been pulled into such a conflict. Even if the Islamic extremists were defeated, would the United States be able to build a stable, democratic, prosperous, and inclusive Syria? Evidence from recent US experience in Afghanistan, Iraq, and Libya suggests otherwise. The lesson here is that the United States may not *want* to do the regime changes that it *can* do.

CLEAR-EYED THREAT ASSESSMENT

A second, related implication is that because the possible candidates for regime change are typically so weak, they are unlikely to constitute serious threats to the security of the United States, which in turn reduces the benefits of carrying out regime change. It is necessary to assess the risks in these cases in a clear-eyed fashion. Did the Tudeh Party in Iran, according to Maziar Behrooz, "with no plan, with no real base in the countryside, and with approximately five hundred army officers and between six and eight thousand members and supporters in Tehran," pose a real threat to launch a coup and impose communist rule in Iran in 1953?[21] As Behrooz comments, "None of the [CIA] reports" prior to the coup "seem to suggest that the Tudeh was viewed as an imminent danger in terms of its ability to topple the Mossadeq government."[22] Similarly, were Árbenz's liberal reforms in Guatemala—which he and his predecessor, Juan José Arévalo, based on President Franklin Delano Roosevelt's New Deal initiatives—and his collaboration with Guatemala's tiny communist party really such a threat that they merited overthrowing the country's government?[23]

Fast-forwarding to the twenty-first century, few would argue with the decision to topple Afghanistan's Taliban regime after it refused to hand over those responsible for the 9/11 attacks—although the Taliban was merely collateral damage in the hunt for Al Qaeda and Osama bin Laden.[24] But the justification for overthrowing Saddam Hussein was far flimsier, based on nonexistent weapons of mass destruction and imagined ties to Al Qaeda that in reality did not exist. Is a "1 percent" chance of catastrophe (which was actually much smaller than 1 percent) worth the real catastrophe that unfolded in Iraq after Saddam's overthrow?[25] Similarly, Muammar Qaddafi's Libya represented no threat at all to US security, particularly after Qaddafi cut ties to terrorists and abandoned his quest for nuclear weapons in 2003. The Arab Spring uprising in 2011 presented a mouth-watering opportunity to get rid of this troublemaker once and for all, but was eliminating an infinitesimal if annoying threat like Qaddafi worth the potential cost of a failed state in Libya—a country ruled by a personalist dictator for forty years with no institutions to speak of and no tradition of democracy?

The "benefits" of regime change in most of these cases, I argue, are very low because the threats they seek to counter are so minor. Because the benefits are so meager, the potential costs of regime change loom large.

IF ONLY WE HAD JUST DONE . . .

A third implication has to do with technique. The pervasive view in the United States—so pervasive, in fact, that Michael MacDonald calls it the "Elite Consensus"—is that regime change in Iraq could have succeeded, and fifteen years of war been avoided and tens if not hundreds of thousands of lives saved, if only . . . fill in the blank: the United States had properly planned (or planned at all) for the aftermath of regime change; if the Bush administration had sent more troops; if Donald Rumsfeld hadn't been secretary of defense; if Paul Bremer hadn't dissolved the Iraqi Army and purged hundreds of thousands of Baathist officials from the bureaucracy; if the Iraqis hadn't been so sectarian and chosen hatred and violence over peace; if the US military hadn't renounced counterinsurgency (COIN) after Vietnam and had had a proper COIN doctrine; or if President George W. Bush hadn't been so incompetent in handling the war.[26] This is in many ways a comforting view, but it is a misleading one. As MacDonald puts it, "The Elite Consensus proves that the Bush administration fouled up the occupation miserably. But its inference that incompetence was the decisive factor in American failures implied a prior, unacknowledged, and unwarranted assumption. It assumes that the United States would have succeeded if only Bush had not failed, that the taproot of failure was not the objective of regime change in Iraq, with whatever that entailed, but merely the administration's inept efforts."[27] "But while bad planning could ruin a potentially successful enterprise," MacDonald continues, "good planning was not sufficient to guarantee success. If the enterprise was misbegotten from its conception, then concentrating on the means is misleading and incomplete."[28]

Another supposed question of technique is the "light" versus "heavy" footprint debate. Critics of the US approach to regime change and occupation in Afghanistan argued that it was hamstrung by US reliance on airpower and small numbers of CIA operatives and Special Operations Forces; a reluctance to commit large numbers of ground troops to the occupation; and the retasking of US assets to the Middle East in preparation for Iraq, which further reduced the expertise and manpower available for Afghanistan.[29] After Iraq, however, the supposed lesson was that "going in heavy" with large numbers of troops was a mistake that contributed to anti-American sentiment in Iraq and elsewhere. This "lesson" was then applied to Libya in 2011, where (reminiscent of the initial Afghan operation) no traditional ground troops were deployed and airpower was the tool of choice to supplement indigenous ground power. But the disastrous results in these three cases are nearly indistinguishable, which suggests that the light versus heavy dichotomy is a false dichotomy: both can fail, they just fail in different ways.

My argument suggests that the downsides of regime change are built into the enterprise itself and cannot be fully avoided by doing it better or smarter or with more resources. The origins of regime change lie in clashes of interests between states; interveners carry out regime change to eliminate those conflicts of interest. The problem is that in most cases the differences in interests can't be eliminated, and the more that an intervener pressures its protégé to implement its preferred policies, the more likely it becomes that resistance will emerge among some domestic constituency in the target that will drive a wedge between patrons and protégés. One potential solution to this dilemma would be to ask the intervener to act in a disinterested, neutral fashion, but this is no solution at all. Asking interveners *not* to implement their preferences after regime change when the whole point of enacting regime change is to implement their preferences is a nonstarter. And don't forget that in a nontrivial number of cases, the target's military will simply disintegrate, laying the groundwork for an insurgency. Formally disbanding the Iraqi Army, for example, made a bad situation worse, but it was not the source of the problem, which stemmed from military disintegration. These problems are inherent to regime change and cannot be avoided.

RESTORING THE STATUS QUO, NOT CHANGING THE STATUS QUO

The foregoing discussion does provide some clues regarding the circumstances under which regime change might produce positive outcomes. The key is that the preference divergence between an imposed leader's two principals—the foreign intervener and the domestic audience—must be mitigated, eliminated, or rendered less dangerous. This can happen in three ways. First, the presence of a third party that threatens the security of both states, akin to how the looming shadow of Soviet power threatened both the United States and the countries it occupied after World War II (including West Germany, Japan, and South Korea), can ease interest asymmetries between them. Such common threats, however, are rare; there have been no instances since the 1940s. Second, regime changes that provide imposed leaders with the ability to repress domestic dissent—such as the imposition of Soviet-style police states in Eastern Europe after World War II or US assistance in establishing SAVAK following its restoration of the shah of Iran in 1953—permit these leaders to ignore the preferences of their domestic principals. Few democracies, however—at least in the current security environment—would be willing to facilitate these kinds of repressive institutions.[30]

Third, restoration regime changes that return popular leaders to power typically eliminate interest asymmetries, particularly when interveners previously enjoyed good relations with the leader who was deposed and lack strong preferences over the target's policies. This was arguably the case with Allied regime changes in Western Europe at the close of World War II. Such "defensive" regime changes, which restore an acceptable and conflict-free status quo, are more likely to succeed than "offensive" regime changes undertaken to alter the status quo. This does not mean that restorations will always succeed. Jean-Bertrand Aristide, for example, was popular with many Haitians but others remained hostile to him, and while his restoration in 1994 by the United States got rid of the military junta, it did not eliminate that opposition. Aristide faced a rebellion during his second term as president and was eventually forced from office in 2004. Yet restoration regime changes are still more likely to succeed than leadership or institutional regime changes.

Questions for Further Research

This book is far from the last word on the effects of foreign-imposed regime change. Indeed, a host of topics exist for further work. First, future research could be conducted to identify additional cases of regime change during the time period I have covered or in earlier eras, such as early modern Europe, the era of Italian city-states, ancient Greece, or the Chinese or Japanese warring states periods. Second, additional research should investigate the effects of regime change on outcomes beyond those included in this book, such as economic growth and development, mass violence and genocide, and terrorism. Third, more process tracing of case studies of regime change and civil war, irregular leader removal, and interstate relations ought to be conducted to further test the causal mechanisms I have outlined or to identify new ones. Fourth, scholars could apply more advanced statistical techniques to deal with the possibility that selection effects account for the findings reported in this book.

Stepping back, however, reveals several broader questions that deserve additional investigation. First, what are the causes of regime change? Why do states decide to overthrow the governments of other states rather than continue to bargain with them? Although this and other studies have identified an underlying logic to regime change—to replace unfriendly, uncooperative, or downright hostile leaders with others who share the intervener's preferences—few scholars have focused on the causes of regime change in particular, as distinct from related phenomena such as state death, unusually expansive war aims, forcible regime promotion, or forced democratization.[31] Work on covert regime change has uncovered several propositions that explain this form of intervention, such as maintaining regional hegemony, preventing the emergence of threats, or rolling back the influence of other states, and that deserve further testing.[32] Theories of overt regime change have zeroed in on commitment problems as a key cause, but changes in personnel are unsuited for solving such problems; the absence of enforcement mechanisms in the international system means that leaders can always renege on commitments made at one time when circumstances change.[33] Why don't leaders in states that implement regime change understand this fundamental mismatch between goals and strategies? Recent US regime changes exhibit no consideration of this problem—and indeed reveal almost a complete lack of planning for the aftermath of regime change. Existing theories also argue that the existence of alternative elites or a domestic opposition is a necessary condition for regime change, but this is questionable given the ease with which interveners have been able to come up with suitable puppets when the need arose.[34]

Second, how do states choose between different regime change options? Why do interveners opt for installing an authoritarian puppet in some cases whereas in other cases they choose to engage in institutional transformation? Institutional regime change, after all, is also more costly than simply imposing a new leader, so why not choose the cheaper option? Elizabeth Saunders suggests that leaders develop beliefs formed from prior experience regarding the efficacy of transformative strategies that explain why some leaders promote institutional change whereas others do not.[35] An examination of variation in US democracy promotion during military interventions suggests that Washington's choices may also respond to global power realities. The United States was less interested in liberalizing targets when it faced a peer competitor during the Cold War and more likely to do so when it did not—both before and after the Cold War.[36] Yet while democracy promotion and nation building have become Washington's default intervention strategy in the era since the Cold War, prior to World War II there was more variation in the US approach. The United States, for example, sometimes promoted democracy in one country (the Dominican Republic, 1916–24) but not in another (Haiti, 1915–34), and sometimes promoted democracy in the *same* country at one time but not another (Nicaragua in 1909 and 1910). The choice between installing leaders and promoting institutions thus merits further investigation.

Finally, why have states continued to employ regime change—particularly leadership regime change—despite its poor track record of success? Why, for example, after a century of US experience with regime change, did top officials in the George W. Bush administration believe that they could invade Iraq, depose Saddam Hussein, and get out within months with no occupation and no plan for leadership succession? I addressed this question briefly at the end of chapter 2. One answer is that interveners lack information about conditions in the target or have biased sources of information; they listen to those in the target country who have an interest in bringing about regime change, or to exiles with little knowledge of actual conditions in their homelands. Second, interveners are prone to disregard the hard-earned experience of others, confident that they are more skilled and will not make the same mistakes others have made. Third, interveners have a strong tendency to focus on the immediate task—how to overthrow the target regime—and neglect the more distant task—how to govern the target, select new leaders, or build new institutions. Fourth, interveners also fail to appreciate the possibility of military disintegration. Finally, interveners assume that elites and publics in foreign states share their preferences; states considering regime change thus fail to anticipate the problem of competing principals.

If Not Regime Change, Then What?

A natural response to my argument in this book is: If not regime change, then what? What are the alternatives to regime change and how effective are they? Placing regime change in the context of other means of influence and evaluating their relative effectiveness is outside the scope of this already expansive study. But the truth is that compellence is hard. Studies of economic sanctions, for example, find that sanctions obtain target compliance in as few as 4 percent of cases or as many as 38 percent.[37] The recent trend toward "smart sanctions"—measures that are aimed at specific economic sectors, institutions, or individuals in the target—unfortunately have not increased the success rate. One recent study found that smart sanctions succeeded only about 10 percent of the time.[38] Coercive diplomacy—the use of threats of force or limited force to obtain target compliance—also fails much more often than it succeeds.[39] Moreover, a growing body of scholarship argues that compellent threats from powerful states are especially prone to failure.[40] This meager success rate is an important reason why states—even (or especially) great powers—turn to regime change.[41] But to undertake regime change, as I have attempted to show in this book, is a high-risk strategy that is most likely to fail in the places where it is easiest to implement. It is also most likely to fail when done in the most cost-effective way, that is, by doing leadership change.

There are no easy answers. For the United States, given that prospective targets of regime change typically represent small threats—or even minor inconveniences—to US security, the benefits of regime change are unlikely to outweigh the costs in most cases. Even when regime change is unavoidable—as it arguably was in Afghanistan after 9/11—policymakers should understand that regime change is likely to backfire and should prepare a backup plan for containing the fallout.

Notes

Introduction

1. Kohn 1999, 5.

2. Evans 1829; Dalrymple 2013, 49. On threat inflation before the Iraq War, see Kaufmann 2004; Thrall and Cramer 2009. For selected examples from US policymakers, see Bush 2002; Cheney 2002; CNN 2002.

3. Auckland quoted in Evans 2002, 44. Cheney made his prediction on the NBC program *Meet the Press* a few days before the Iraq invasion commenced. For similar statements by other Bush administration officials, including secretary of defense Donald Rumsfeld and his deputy, Paul Wolfowitz, see Esterbrook 2002; Schmitt 2003; Fallows 2006, 81–84; Ricks 2006, 96–98, 109.

4. Dalrymple 2013, 197. On these problems following the US overthrow of the Taliban, see Rashid 2008, 64–65, 133–34; Abbas 2014, 89; Coll 2018, 135, 145. The British disaster in Afghanistan was not entirely unforeseen. Mountstuart Elphinstone, a British official with long experience in India, predicted that regime change in Afghanistan—although perhaps easy to accomplish initially—would be counterproductive and doomed to failure: "If you send 27,000 men up the Bolan Pass to Candahar (as we hear is intended) and can feed them, I have no doubt you will take Candahar and Cabul and set up Shuja." Elphinstone continued: "But for maintaining him in a poor, strong and remote country among a turbulent people like the Afghans, I own it seems to me to be hopeless. If you succeed I fear you will weaken your position against Russia. The Afghans were neutral and would have received your aid against invaders with gratitude—they will now be disaffected and glad to join any invader that will drive you out." Quoted in Dalrymple 2013, 126.

5. Political scientists tend to use the term foreign-imposed regime change to differentiate instances of foreign intervention to change governments from regime change carried out by domestic actors; popular and historical literature tends to simply use regime change. In this book, the term regime change refers to foreign-imposed regime change unless otherwise noted. For political science work on the subject, see Werner 1996; Lo, Hashimoto, and Reiter 2008; Downes 2011, 2018; Peic and Reiter 2011; Downes and Monten 2013; Downes and O'Rourke 2016; Zachary, Deloughery, and Downes 2017; O'Rourke 2018; Willard-Foster 2018; Denison 2020. For popular and historical treatments of regime change, see Kinzer 2006; Litwak 2007; Grow 2008; Sullivan 2008; Polk 2013; Gordon 2020.

6. On the striking similarity between the two cases, see Fletcher 1965, 141.

7. I count at least eight distinct causes of regime change in the literature: economic disputes (Schlesinger and Kinzer 1999; Kinzer 2006; Qureshi 2009), ideological promotion (Doyle 1983a, 1983b; Owen 2002, 2010), creation and maintenance of spheres of influence (Kinzer 2006; Grow 2008; O'Rourke 2018), competition over buffer states (Fazal 2007), shifts in the balance of power (Reiter 2009; Wolford, Reiter, and Carrubba 2011; Weisiger 2013), untrustworthy leaders in adversary states (Weisiger 2013), intervener regime type (Morrow et al. 2006), and a strong domestic opposition in the target (Willard-Foster 2018).

8. Lo, Hashimoto, and Reiter 2008; Downes and O'Rourke 2016; O'Rourke 2018.

9. Others argue that regime change improves intervener-target relations by removing leaders who cannot commit to enact an intervener's preferred policies and replacing them with leaders who can. For works that explain regime change via a commitment problem, see Bueno de Mesquita and Downs 2006; Morrow et al. 2006; Fazal 2007; Reiter 2009; Weisiger 2013; Willard-Foster 2018.

10. Owen 2010, 3.

11. Lo, Hashimoto, and Reiter 2008. This is particularly true if a victorious democracy transforms the loser into a democracy. For a contrary view, see Downes and O'Rourke 2016.

12. Pletka 2016.

13. See, for example, Khalilzad 2016; Pletka 2016; Jeffrey 2017.

14. MacDonald 2014, 85.

15. Bolton 2015; Perry 2016; Crowley 2017; Pelofsky 2017; Gordon 2018.

16. For a sampling of the case-specific literature, see Schmidt 1971; Sigmund 1977; Warren 1978; Calder 1984; Gleijeses 1991; Schlesinger and Kinzer 1999; Farcau 2000; Cunningham 2001; De Witte 2001; Kinzer 2003; Kornbluh 2003; Gobat 2005; Ricks 2006; Rashid 2008; Dalrymple 2013; MacDonald 2014. For studies that examine multiple cases of regime change by a single country, see Prados 1996; Kinzer 2006; Weiner 2007; Grow 2008; Sullivan 2008; Polk 2013; Gordon 2020. For studies of the causes of regime change that examine a large sample of cases, see O'Rourke 2018; Willard-Foster 2018. The former work also includes a chapter on the effects of US covert regime changes. See O'Rourke 2018, 73–96.

17. For exceptions, see O'Rourke 2018; Willard-Foster 2018.

18. On the use of the term catastrophic success in this context, see Gordon 2004; Kinzer 2006, 300.

19. In earlier work I referred to this problem as a Catch-22 (Downes and O'Rourke 2016). As described in Joseph Heller's famous novel, a Catch-22 is a situation in which one cannot escape a particular outcome whether one takes a certain action or its opposite (Heller 1961, 46). A foreign-imposed leader would face a Catch-22, for example, if his patron threatened to overthrow him if he did not suppress communists (failure to do so would demonstrate disloyalty) but also threatened to overthrow him if he suppressed communists (suppressing them would signal that the leader was reckless). In my theory, by contrast, leaders can avoid the ire of their external patrons by implementing their preferred policies. They may be punished by another party (such as their domestic constituents), but that is different than being punished by the same actor for taking an action or its opposite. I thank John Owen for clarifying this point.

20. Weber 2009, 78 (italics in original).

21. For a different argument that emphasizes opportunity as the cause of post-regime change civil wars, see Peic and Reiter 2011.

22. In the event that interveners decline to protect their protégés or withdraw without having defeated the insurgency, the protégé may be overthrown and relations between intervener and target could revert to the status quo before regime change.

23. Useful overviews of principal-agent theory in International Relations and Political Science more broadly include Moe 1984; Maltzman 1997, 10–13; Feaver 2003, 54–95; Miller 2005; Biddle, Macdonald, and Baker 2018; Berman et al. 2019.

24. Work in Security Studies that explicitly invokes multiple principals is rare; see Avant 1994 for an exception. The concept is common in American Politics, however; see, for example, Moe 1984, 1985; McCubbins, Noll, and Weingast 1987; Hammond and Knott 1996; Maltzman 1997; Shipan 2004.

25. Examples include the 1956 and 1968 Soviet interventions in Hungary and Czechoslovakia, which restored communist orthodoxy but under different leaders.

26. As one might guess, the promotion of democracy is carried out exclusively by democracies; the promotion of repressive institutions is carried out by single-party regimes, particularly the Soviet Union.

27. This variant assumes that the intervener is a democracy.

28. See Bermeo 2016; Thyne and Powell 2016.

29. Russett 1993. This view contradicts that of Bueno de Mesquita and Downs (2006), which argues that democracy brings policy more into line with voter preferences in the target state, which may or may not align with the intervener's preferences. To avoid the possibility that the target defies the intervener's wishes, which would be politically costly for the intervening state's leader, Bueno de Mesquita and Downs contend that democracies install autocracies when they engage in regime change.

30. Interveners in cases like these also may not have strong preferences over the target's policies and thus have little reason to pressure restored leaders to take actions contrary to the wishes of their domestic constituents.

31. The Nazis installed German (military or civilian) occupation administrators after regime change in some countries, such as Belgium and the Netherlands, but in others governed through local figureheads. Indeed, the term "Quisling" originated from the Nazi occupation of Norway, where Vidkun Quisling served as the collaborationist prime minister from 1942 to 1945. Similar arrangements prevailed in Greece and Yugoslavia. Denmark was self-governing until August 1943 when the Germans dissolved the Danish regime and ruled directly.

32. Peic and Reiter 2011.

33. It also supports my argument that not all interstate war defeats are the same. Only those that unleash military disintegration increase the likelihood of civil war.

34. I discuss the general logic of my case selection below.

35. Goemans 2008, 780.

36. Sanger 2003; Haass 2005; Litwak 2007.

37. Vulliamy 2002; Forero 2004. See also Avilés 2005; Clement 2005.

38. Farmer 2004.

39. Regime change still had its advocates, however, and not only among neoconservatives. See, for example, Haass 2010. Neoconservatives, of course, kept up the drumbeat for regime change in Iran and elsewhere during the Obama years. See Vlahos 2013; Heilbrunn 2015.

40. Landler 2011. See also Obama, Cameron, and Sarkozy 2011. On the motives of French president Nicolas Sarkozy, an early and ardent advocate of intervention in Libya, see Penney 2018. For an argument that fears of a humanitarian catastrophe were greatly exaggerated, see Kuperman 2013.

41. Obama's demand that Assad step aside was seconded by the leaders of Britain, France, and Germany. See Wilson and Warrick 2011. Unsurprisingly, neoconservatives pushed the president to intervene more decisively; Vlahos 2013.

42. On Iran, see Perry 2016; Crowley 2017; Gordon 2018. For a skeptical view, see Schramm and Tabatabai 2017; Downes and O'Rourke 2018. On North Korea, see Watkins 2017. On Venezuela, see Friedman 2019.

43. Quoted in Ricks 2006, 98.

44. On military occupation, see Quinlivan 1995; Edelstein 2004, 2008; Collard-Wexler 2013. On nation building, see Dobbins et al. 2003; Pei and Kasper 2003; Brownlee 2007. On foreign-imposed regimes, see Enterline and Greig 2005, 2008a, 2008b; Lo, Hashimoto, and Reiter 2008; Peic and Reiter 2011; Downes and Monten 2013; Downes and O'Rourke 2016; Zachary, Deloughery, and Downes 2017. On counterinsurgency, see Department of the Army 2006; Lyall and Wilson 2009; Friedman 2011; Hazelton 2017. On UN peacekeeping, see Doyle and Sambanis 2000, 2006; Fortna 2008; Gilligan and Sergenti 2008. On humanitarian aid, see Terry 2002; Lischer 2005; Kuperman 2008.

45. Fearon and Laitin 2003; Collier and Hoeffler 2004.

46. Lawrence 2010, 92–96.

47. Arguably, the two most prominent studies of civil war onset in the literature between them have at most a single variable—primary commodity exports as a percentage of GDP—that could plausibly be considered an international influence. See Fearon and Laitin 2003; Collier and Hoeffler 2004.

48. For example, see Lischer 2005; Salehyan and Gleditsch 2006; Kuperman 2008; Salehyan 2009.

49. See Londregan and Poole 1990.

50. On the three images, see Waltz 1959. My argument might also be termed "second image reversed." See Gourevitch 1978.

51. Pape 1996.

52. Jordan 2009, 2014, and 2019; Johnston 2012; Price 2012; Long 2014; Johnston and Sarbahi 2016.

53. Iqbal and Zorn 2008.

54. On process tracing, see Bennett and Checkel 2015; Beach and Pedersen 2019.

55. Even though these states are minor powers, they still greatly overshadowed their targets in terms of actual military capability.

56. I reference additional cases like these throughout the book, such as US institutional regime changes in Germany and Japan, and US restoration regime changes in Europe, both at the conclusion of World War II.

57. Of the eight causes of regime change in the literature, none of them argues that states inflict regime change merely to sow chaos in rivals.

1. Defining Foreign-Imposed Regime Change

1. Downes and Monten 2013, 109. See also Reisman 2004, 516.

2. Violent or coercive removal of a president, however, such as in a military coup, could entail a change of regime if it suspended or eliminated some or all of the state's governing institutions.

3. Jaffe 1985, 7–20.

4. Foreign interventions must result in a change in the effective leader of the target state to qualify as regime change. Interventions undertaken to support an existing regime, such as foreign regime maintenance (Sullivan and Koch 2009) or security force assistance (Ladwig 2016, 2017; Biddle, Macdonald, and Baker 2018; Karlin 2018; Berman and Lake 2019), are excluded.

5. Goemans, Gleditsch, and Chiozza 2009, 271. This criterion focuses attention on who controls the levers of power on the ground rather than in the abstract. For example, I count Germany's ouster of the Belgian government in 1940—and the Allied removal of the German occupation regime in 1944—as regime changes even though Belgium's legal government continued to exist in exile because the Germans under General Alexander von Falkenhausen ran the country. Similarly, I consider the 2011 UN-assisted removal of Laurent Gbagbo in Côte d'Ivoire to be regime change even though the UN Security Council had recognized Alassane Ouattara as the country's president because Gbagbo clung tenaciously to power in the capital, Abidjan.

6. Technically speaking, the British monarch is vested with key executive powers, but wields them only on the binding advice of the prime minister. In other parliamentary systems, the head of state post is truly symbolic and lacks any executive authority. In practice, the prime minister serves as the effective head of government in both cases.

7. Sometimes which office wields the crucial authority in a state can change over time. In Iran, for example, *Archigos* codes Mohammad Reza Pahlavi as the effective leader from the deposition of his father in 1941 to the appointment of Mohammad Mossadegh as prime minister in April 1951, likely because Mossadegh demanded (and received) special powers, including control over the military in 1952. After Mossadegh was ousted in a CIA-backed coup in 1953, *Archigos* once again deems the shah to be the effective leader of Iran. Thus, even though Mohammad Reza remained shah during Mossadagh's premiership, the powers

accumulated by the prime minister's office shifted who was judged to be the effective head of the government.

8. Hood 1992, 50.

9. In the former invasion, to depose Dost Mohammad, his chosen replacement, Shah Shuja, accompanied the invasion force.

10. Fletcher 1965, 135.

11. Haass 2005, 70.

12. O'Rourke 2018, 46–47; Willard-Foster 2018, 35–40.

13. In such cases, however, the intervener may just keep on trying until it gets an individual to its liking or obtains conditions—such as elections—that are likely to yield a government more in line with its preferences. This was the US strategy in Guatemala (1954) and Costa Rica (1919), respectively.

14. On decapitation, see Pape 1996.

15. Cases of assassination of leaders by foreign agents are rare. In the latest version (v.4.1) of the *Archigos* data on leaders (Goemans, Gleditsch, and Chiozza 2016), only one leader coded as exiting office in a foreign-imposed regime change was killed in the process or in the year after losing office. To date, no *state* leader has been killed in a decapitation strike. Decapitation, however, has been employed liberally and successfully (in the sense that targets of such strikes have been killed) against the leaders of violent non-state actors. For the debate on the effectiveness of decapitation against non-state actors, see Jordan 2009 and 2014; Johnston 2012; Price 2012; Long 2014; and Johnston and Sarbahi 2016.

16. Lake 2016, 131, 135.

17. Filkins 2004. Internal quotes are from an unnamed source "conversant with the negotiations."

18. See Gordon and Trainor 2012, 196–97; Filkins 2014; Lake 2016, 136–37.

19. Dull 1952, 455; Eto 1986, 113.

20. For a detailed description of the assassination, see Dull 1952. For judgments of its counterproductivity, see Jansen 1975, 306; Jordan 1976, 168; McCormack 1977, 248; Ienaga 1978, 59; Barnhart 1987, 31; Wilson 1991, 28; Dreyer 1995, 151. This inability to influence succession may be one reason why assassination and decapitation remain relatively rare despite increased technological capability by many states to carry out these policies.

21. To speak of the "imposition" of regimes in these cases, however, is often a serious overstatement, since departing colonial powers varied greatly in the degree to which they determined the nature of new indigenous regimes. On imposed polities and imposed democracies, see Enterline and Greig 2005, 2008a, 2008b.

22. Fazal 2007, 31–33.

23. Edelstein (2008, 3) argues that the intent to leave is part of what distinguishes an occupation from colonialism.

24. These countries were run by German officials but were not formally incorporated into the Third Reich.

25. Willard-Foster 2018, 59. She refers to these cases as "leader resignations."

26. This corresponds to Sechser's definition of a compellent threat (Sechser 2011, 380). On the use of compellent threats to remove foreign leaders, see Downes 2018.

27. If the targeted leader refuses to step down, interveners can always remove him via military force. This scenario would constitute a failed compellent threat but a successful case of regime change.

28. Munro 1964, 428, 440.

29. On the Baltic cases, see Raun 2001, 144–46; Smith 2002, 23–27; van Voren 2011, 24–26. On Romania, see Hitchins 1994, 514–15. On Lesotho, see Lundahl, McCarthy, and Petersson 2003, 28–29.

30. On France's foray into Mexico, see Cunningham 2001. On Vietnam's invasion of Cambodia, see Chanda 1986. On the US invasion of Iraq, see Gordon and Trainor 2006.

31. Scheina 2003, 258–59.

32. The UNLA appears to have numbered less than one thousand fighters in early 1979, most of them under the command of Colonel David Ojok (Avirgan and Honey 1982, 72–75). Ojok's

soldiers reportedly "played an active part in battles throughout the war," but Tanzania supplied multiple brigades and suffered far more combat deaths (Avirgan and Honey 1982, 75).

33. Biddle 2002. The Northern Alliance had been fighting the Taliban for years with little success until the US intervention.

34. Gleijeses 1991, 246, 338.

35. Grow 2008, 78.

36. Grow 2008, 79.

37. Note that this assessment diverges from that of O'Rourke (2018), who codes foreign assistance as instances of (covert) regime change whether or not the external aid was a decisive factor in the success of a coup. For additional details on how I code covert regime changes, and specifically for how I decide which of O'Rourke's twenty-five successful covert regime changes belong in my dataset, please see the online Supplementary Materials for chapter 1.

38. Although not apparent from the table, which lists only the leaders who were removed in foreign-imposed regime changes, two female leaders have come to power in this way. First, Duchess Maria Luigia was restored to the throne of Parma by Austrian troops following a brief revolution in 1831. Second, a coalition of France, Spain, and Britain restored Queen Maria II of Portugal in 1834 after she was overthrown by her uncle in 1828. I therefore use both male and female pronouns when referring to foreign imposed leaders in this book.

39. One would expect this number to more closely approximate the total number of leaders removed because the dyadic structure of the data counts each intervener-target dyad separately. Unfortunately, the Correlates of War (COW) data from which the dyadic dataset is built excludes many countries that COW does not consider states at the time they experienced regime change. I discuss this issue at greater length in chapter 5.

40. Willard-Foster 2018.

41. The United States also participated in the removal of Libya's Muammar Qaddafi in 2011 but this case falls outside the time frame of the study.

42. On each occasion, French troops removed the (French) mercenary Bob Denard after he briefly seized power. France also helped overthrow Côte d'Ivoire's Laurent Gbagbo in 2011 (Vaulerin, Despic-Popovic, and Hofnung 2011) and played a leading role in the coalition that ended Qaddafi's rule in Libya later that year. France, of course, overthrew numerous regimes during the French Revolutionary and Napoleonic Wars, but these cases precede the period under study.

43. Central America, as described in more detail in later chapters, was a hotbed of regime change in the nineteenth century owing to the sharp competition between Liberals and Conservatives in the region. See Chiozza and Goemans 2011, 117–94.

44. The nineteenth century I simply divide at its midpoint. I divide the twentieth century into the period of the two world wars, the Cold War, and the post–Cold War era.

45. Stalin, of course, maintained his grip on the Baltic republics, his main prizes from the Molotov-Ribbentrop Pact.

46. In the Caribbean, scholars argue that the United States was motivated to overthrow and occupy the countries of Hispaniola because the Wilson administration feared potential German intervention. On the Dominican Republic, see Calder 1984, xii; Fazal 2007, 141–43. On Haiti, see Schmidt 1971, 56, 60; Langley 1989, 71–72. On Latvia, see Purs 1998, 33.

47. The Bay of Pigs operation is coded as a failed attempt at regime change and thus does not appear in my dataset. However, I compile a sample of these failures to determine if they differ systematically from cases in which regime change succeeds. The United States also intervened in the Dominican Republic in 1965 to prevent former president Juan Bosch from returning to power. I do not code this intervention as a regime change. Although the military junta headed by Donald Reid Cabral was overthrown by Bosch supporters in the military, and rebel leader Rafael Molina Ureña was proclaimed provisional president by Bosch's Dominican Revolutionary Party, it is not clear that he ever established any effective control outside of the National Palace. Ureña's "government" was superseded within days by a succession of US-backed juntas. On this case, see Felten 1995. The US role in Mohammad Mossadegh's ouster is well known (see Wilber 1954; Kinzer 2003). In the Congo, a US attempt to assassinate Prime Minister Patrice Lumumba failed (Weiner 2007, 162–63) but the CIA supported Joseph Mobu-

tu's subsequent coup that removed Lumumba (Weissman 2014, 16). Belgium was ultimately responsible for his death (De Witte 2001).

48. Kahin 1987, 168–69; Logevall 1999, 48–51, 63–64.

49. Good sources on these cases include Scheina 2003 and Chiozza and Goemans 2011.

50. Dabbs 1963; Hanna and Hanna 1971; Cunningham 2001.

51. Warren 1978; Lewis 1993.

52. Farcau 2000; Sater 2007.

53. On the Nicaraguan case, see Chiozza and Goemans 2011, 152–53.

54. United Nations 2005; Cohen 2016, 99–100.

55. The removal of Qaddafi in 2011 slightly increases the total for this region. The dearth of regime change in the Middle East is not for lack of trying. Britain, France, and Israel launched the Suez War in 1956 intending to bring down Egyptian president Gamal Abdel Nasser (Kyle 1991, 148; Gorst and Johnman 1997, 68–69, 85; Shlaim 1997, 515). Israel escalated its war aims in the War of Attrition (1969–70) to include removing the Egyptian government and was on the verge of installing its Maronite Christian ally Bashir Gemayel in Lebanon in 1982 when Gemayel was assassinated (Bar-Siman-Tov 1980, 120–21; Merom 2003, 157). O'Rourke (2018, 109) counts four covert regime change attempts by the United States in the region during the Cold War: Syria (1955–57), Lebanon (1957–58), Iraq (1972–75), and South Yemen (1979–80). Only Lebanon is coded as a success. Others allege an additional US success in Iraq in 1963 (Cockburn and Cockburn 1999, 74; Lando 2007, 29; Weiner 2007, 140–41). For a history of US regime changes in the Middle East, see Gordon 2020.

56. An exception discussed below is Willard-Foster 2018.

57. Astute observers will note that Shah Shuja, Britain's replacement for Afghanistan's Dost Mohammad in 1839, was a former emir, having been toppled from the throne thirty years earlier. For a case to qualify as a restoration regime change, however, I require that the restored leader have been the most recent prior ruler and that no more than five years have passed since he was most recently in office. Shah Shuja qualifies on neither count.

58. Fletcher 1965, 141; Waller 1990, 121–22; Schroeder 1994, 758–59; Kohn 1999, 6; Phillips and Axelrod 2005, 1:16.

59. Gasiorowski 1991, 42–43.

60. Bokassa had mandated that all students wear the uniforms, which were produced by a company owned by his family. French president Valéry Giscard d'Estaing, who was friendly with Bokassa, was acutely embarrassed by his close association with the "Butcher of Bangui" (Titley 1997, 125). For more on this case, see chapter 4.

61. Titley 1997, 126. The French subsequently forced Dacko to hold elections, but more as a means of legitimating their intervention than to ensure that the will of the people was freely expressed, as "the campaign was anything but a showpiece of democracy in action" (158).

62. I invoke this five-year rule because longer intervals reduce the likelihood that restoration regime changes actually restore anything meaningful. Part of what makes restorations different from leadership regime changes is that the previous leader's network of supporters is still present in the country. The restored leader can draw upon this support to help stabilize her rule. I thus do not consider the return of Shah Shuja to the Afghan throne in 1839 after a thirty-year absence, for example, to constitute a restoration regime change.

63. Gerbrandy was quickly succeeded by Willem Schermerhorn in June 1945.

64. Although leadership regime change is the most common type overall, there is interesting variation over time. The period between the end of the Napoleonic Wars and the mid-nineteenth century was dominated by restoration regime changes as Europe's monarchies rolled back republican revolutions, whereas every single one of the regime changes that occurred in the second half of the century consisted of leadership regime changes. The predominance of leadership regime change continued during the era of the two world wars and the Cold War, with leadership cases accounting for just over half of the regime changes in the former period and two-thirds in the latter. The first half of the twentieth century was also the highwater mark for institutional regime changes: three-quarters of all such regime changes were implemented at this time. The relatively high number of restoration regime changes dur-

ing this period stems from the Allied ouster of Axis (mostly German) occupation regimes at the end of the two world wars. The number of restoration regime changes remained constant at six during and after the Cold War, but leadership regime changes plummeted from eighteen to one. Finally, only three institutional regime changes (11 percent of the regime changes during this epoch) were implemented during the Cold War; two of the nine regime changes (22 percent) from the end of the Cold War to 2008 were institutional in nature. Explaining variation in the type of regime change that states choose to implement is fodder for further research. For one argument, see Willard-Foster 2018, 52–64.

2. Theorizing the Effects of Foreign-Imposed Regime Change

1. For a formal model along similar lines, see Willard-Foster 2018, 254–60.

2. Some argue that states pursue regime change to establish or maintain territorial spheres of influence (Kinzer 2006; Grow 2008; O'Rourke 2018) or to gain control over buffer states (Fazal 2007). Others view the promotion of ideologies as a cause of regime change (Owen 2002, 2010; Doyle 1983a, 1983b). Some maintain that regime change is undertaken at the behest of a state's national firms doing business in the target or to secure important resources (Schlesinger and Kinzer 1999; Kinzer 2006; Qureshi 2009). On shifts in the balance of power, see Reiter 2009; Wolford, Reiter, and Carrubba 2011; Weisiger 2013. For a critical summary of these and other causes of regime change, see Downes 2020.

3. Obviously, if State A never makes a demand, no crisis occurs.

4. Whether State A's leaders face audience costs for backing down, and how severe those costs are, may depend on whether the threat was public or private, whether the political opposition in State A supported or opposed the threat, whether State A postulated specific or vague consequences for failing to comply, or State A's regime type. For a sampling of the debate on audience costs, see Fearon 1994; Schultz 1998; Tomz 2007; Weeks 2008; Snyder and Borghard 2011; Trachtenberg 2011; and Downes and Sechser 2012.

5. Labs 1997, 34–39.

6. Willard-Foster 2018, 7–8, 52–64.

7. Willard-Foster 2018.

8. Willard-Foster 2018, 7, 11.

9. The exception is Willard-Foster (2018), which argues that states opt for regime change when domestic opposition in the target lowers the cost of doing so.

10. Lo, Hashimoto, and Reiter 2008.

11. Other studies that articulate a version of this logic include Bueno de Mesquita and Downs 2006; Reiter 2009; Downes and O'Rourke 2016; O'Rourke 2018. A few quantitative studies have found economic benefits of regime change. See Dube, Kaplan, and Naidu 2011; Berger et al. 2013. For a contrasting view, see Zachary, Deloughery, and Downes 2017.

12. Lo, Hashimoto, and Reiter 2008, 719; Reiter 2009, 26–27; O'Rourke 2018, 42–44. Appointing like-minded agents is a classic means of reducing preference divergence; see Maltzman 1997, 12, 15. An alternative way to frame regime change is as a means of solving a commitment problem. See, for example, Bueno de Mesquita and Downs 2006; Morrow et al. 2006; Fazal 2007; Reiter 2009; Weisiger 2013; Willard-Foster 2018. Commitment problems occur in anarchic systems because there is nothing to prevent states from repudiating agreements made today if conditions change tomorrow that make it advantageous to do so. According to this view, regime change eliminates commitment problems by overthrowing leaders who cannot commit to implement policies preferred by an intervener and replacing them with leaders who can. Regime change, however, cannot truly *solve* commitment problems because it does not establish any third-party enforcement mechanism. Rather, regime change reduces the *risks* presented by commitment problems. By installing a government with similar preferences to the intervener's, regime change reduces (but does not eliminate) the target's disposition to defect.

13. For more on how misaligned preferences can lead to conflict, see Axelrod 1967; Axelrod and Keohane 1985; Kim and Morrow 1992; Lemke and Werner 1996; Joseph 2018. O'Rourke

(2018, 42–43) also argues that regime change reduces conflict by reducing uncertainty about intentions.

14. Lo, Hashimoto, and Reiter 2008, 719.

15. Bueno de Mesquita and Downs 2006, 632.

16. Lo, Hashimoto, and Reiter 2008, 719.

17. Lo, Hashimoto, and Reiter 2008, 720.

18. Lo, Hashimoto, and Reiter 2008, 719.

19. Pei and Kasper 2003; Bellin 2004–05; Brownlee 2007; Downes and Monten 2013.

20. Moreover, there is a potential tension between promoting democracy after regime change and the reality that interveners overturn target governments for self-interested reasons. For a democratic intervener, establishing democracy in the target reduces the likelihood that the two states will fight again, but it may not necessarily increase the likelihood of policy convergence. Democratic leaders must respond to the will of the people, and public preferences in the target will on at least some issues not be congruent with the intervener's preferences. Such disagreements may be more common between states at very different levels of economic development, whereas interveners and targets that are both highly developed may have common preferences in more areas. So, while conflicts of interest between interveners and targets may not turn violent when a democratic intervener promotes democracy in a target, promoting democracy may not minimize the likelihood that disagreements will arise in the first place. Depending on how highly the intervener values target cooperation, therefore, it may choose not to democratize the target—or it may promote democratization but still influence which leader ultimately takes power. This has arguably been US strategy in many of its democracy-promoting regime changes, including the recent cases of Afghanistan and Iraq. On the use of this strategy in Iraq, see Lake 2016.

21. Bueno de Mesquita et al. 2003.

22. In practice, when the military disintegrates, leaders are also very likely to escape. There are cases, however, of leaders escaping when the military surrenders.

23. Peic and Reiter 2011, 453.

24. Leuchars 2002, 233.

25. According to the US Army attaché in Guatemala at the time, "The Guatemalan officers were definitely afraid of the possibility of U.S. intervention against Arbenz and with good reason. That fear was the stabilizing influence that kept them from coming to Arbenz's support when the chips were down." Quoted in Gleijeses 1991, 338.

26. Árbenz was exiled, Mohammad Mossadegh was put on trial and sentenced to house arrest, and Ngo Dinh Diem was assassinated.

27. As I explain in the next section, however, this does not mean that civil wars do not occur after these kinds of cases. If they happen, they usually break out for the reasons laid out in the competing principals mechanism.

28. Rashid 2008, 96.

29. Rashid 2008, 80. It is impossible to estimate how many of the roughly 15,000 foreign fighters got away, although 600 to 800 Al Qaeda fighters escaped via Tora Bora (98). On numbers of foreign fighters, see 80–81.

30. Ricks 2006, 162.

31. McCreedy 2001, 735. Admiral Karl Doenitz, the acting head of state following Hitler's suicide, was arrested by US forces on May 23.

32. Frank 1999, 314–15; Hasegawa 2005, 238–40.

33. Cook and Cook 1992, 403. Overall, the Allies took 7.2 million Japanese prisoners. Weinberg 1994, 892.

34. On this case, see Bloch 1968; Posen 1984; May 2000; Castillo 2014.

35. For an analysis of this type of regime change, see Downes 2018.

36. See, for example, Raun 2001, 144.

37. See, for example, Šneidere 2005, 45.

38. This is not to say disintegration is impossible; it would likely be a result of splits within the military over who ought to rule or which branch should hold the dominant position in a junta.

39. Leifer 1980, 35; Gordon 1986, 73. The Khmer Rouge benefited from territorial sanctuary in Thailand as well as ready access to resupply thanks to their Chinese allies. Becker 1998, 435–36, 449, 458.

40. Tahseen Ali Hussein, quoted in Ricks 2006, 164.

41. Ricks 2006, 191.

42. On the general question of military cohesion under adverse conditions, see Castillo 2014.

43. There are many reasons why armed forces collapse in wartime, and it is impossible to foresee all of the circumstances under which this might occur. Beyond the arguments discussed below, poor leadership (Murray and Millett 2001, 63–90), bad strategy (Alexander 1974), competition for power between political and military elites and a divergence of preferences between them (Brooks 2008), bad luck, poor weather, and random chance (Clausewitz 1976) can each produce battlefield collapse.

44. Biddle 2004, 35–38.

45. Mearsheimer 1983; Biddle 2004, 40–42.

46. Biddle 2004, 52–77.

47. Biddle 2004, 82–83.

48. Mearsheimer 1983.

49. Littlefield 1988, 129.

50. Littlefield 1988, 130.

51. Biddle and Zirkle 1996; Quinlivan 1999.

52. Biddle and Zirkle 1996, 173–74, 178–83; Quinlivan 1999, 134–55; Talmadge 2015, 15–18.

53. Biddle and Zirkle 1996; Quinlivan 1999; Weeks 2014; Narang and Talmadge 2017. For a qualification of this argument, which maintains that personalist dictators will allow their armies to develop expertise in conventional warfighting under certain conditions, see Talmadge 2015.

54. Castillo 2014, 28–36.

55. Lyall 2020.

56. Military inequality, according to Lyall (2020, 49), is a function of "the share of soldiers [in an army] represented by each ethnic group, and their prewar treatment by the state," which ranges from "inclusion" to "collective discrimination" to "collective repression."

57. On the options for dealing with noncore groups and their plusses and minuses, see Lyall 2020, 62–76.

58. Lo, Hashimoto, and Reiter 2008. For more on this point, see chapter 5.

59. On economic motives for regime change, see Kinzer 2006; Sullivan 2008; and Qureshi 2009. On ideological competition and democracy, see Owen 2002, 2010; Doyle 1983a, 1983b. On buffer states, see Fazal 2007. On regional hegemony and spheres of influence, see Kinzer 2006; Grow 2008; and O'Rourke 2018. On the intervener's domestic institutions, see Morrow et al. 2006. On changes in the balance of power, see Weisiger 2013. On aggressive leaders, see Reiter 2009; Weisiger 2013. On domestic opposition in the target, see Willard-Foster 2018.

60. Obama, Cameron, and Sarkozy 2011.

61. Landler 2011. Secretary of State Hillary Clinton made the same declaration even earlier. See Quinn 2011.

62. Kuperman 2013, 114.

63. Kuperman 2013, 123.

64. Becker and Shane 2016. Some have suggested even more venal motives for intervention in Libya. According to reports, French president Nicolas Sarkozy accepted large illegal contributions from Qaddafi to fund his 2007 campaign. Sarkozy thus pushed hard for war against Libya in 2011 to shift the narrative to "one that distanced himself from the regime and any questions about his former proximity to Gaddafi." Penney 2018. Sarkozy was recently charged with conspiracy over the Qaddafi contributions. Middle East Eye 2020. Syria is another case in which altruistic motives for regime change may have been present. If so, however, these motives must not have been strong, since the Obama administration's covert efforts at regime change via arming and training the moderate Syrian opposition were feeble. Nor were humanitarian motives the only ones for acting. On regime change in Syria as a means to enhancing Israeli security by weakening Iran, see Rubin 2012.

65. US ambitions of course went well beyond this baseline, including the hope that democratizing Iraq would spark a wave of liberalization across the Middle East.

66. Lake 2016, 1–2.

67. For Bueno de Mesquita and Downs (2006), the intervener's desire to harvest the fruits of its intervention is why all interveners—including democratic ones—bring autocrats to power. Because autocratic leaders are unaccountable to the mass public, they are able to make the desired concessions without jeopardizing their political survival. However, this is true only if one assumes that the sole way leaders lose office is through elections. Below I argue that making concessions to interveners can in fact endanger the survival of autocratic leaders.

68. Lo, Hashimoto, and Reiter 2008.

69. In many cases, states are able to cooperate in areas where their interests overlap, such as when facing a common threat, but this cooperation disintegrates when the threat disappears (e.g., the collapse of the Anglo-American alliance with the Soviet Union against Nazi Germany after World War II). Moreover, even seemingly unified alliances—such as the Arab alliance against Israel in 1948—can crumble in the face of adversity. See Shlaim 1988; Morris 1999, 218–22.

70. Haun 2015; Willard-Foster 2018. I believe the assumption that states' interests are not isomorphic is uncontroversial, and it is not difficult to think of many reasons why this should be the case. One set of reasons is geopolitical, including competition for relative power or status, incompatible claims to territory, competition for access to resources, or differing motives (greed versus security). Even fish can be a source of conflict: Britain and Iceland twice experienced crises in the 1970s over cod fishing rights in Icelandic waters. Other sources of conflicting interests include clashing domestic ideologies, divergent regime types, ethnic or religious differences, migration and refugee flows, trade disputes, and historical grievances over past injustices.

71. Edelstein 2004, 2008. Edelstein also notes that occupations are less likely to meet with resistance when they are perceived to be necessary (mainly owing to massive wartime destruction) and the occupier credibly commits to leave.

72. Technically, the US occupation of the Ryukyu Islands also coincided with regime change, but these islands were part of Japan so the cases are not independent.

73. On the techniques that these rulers use to ensure conformity with their beliefs and guard against overthrow, see Biddle and Zirkle 1996; Quinlivan 1999; Greitens 2016.

74. Weeks 2008, 2014.

75. Saunders 2011.

76. Palmerston 1848.

77. Bueno de Mesquita et al. 1999, 2003.

78. This mechanism corresponds roughly to personalist regimes. See Weeks 2014. Personalist rulers often rely on familial, tribal, or ethnic ties to maintain control over key coercive institutions. On how guarding against coups can cause leaders to trigger civil wars, see Roessler 2016.

79. For applications of principal-agent theory in security studies, see Downs and Rocke 1994; Feaver 2003; Byman and Kreps 2010; Salehyan 2010; Mitchell, Carey, and Butler 2014; Ladwig 2016, 2017; Biddle, Macdonald, and Baker 2018; Berman and Lake 2019.

80. Biddle, Macdonald, and Baker 2018, 96.

81. Department of the Army 2006; Ladwig 2016, 2017; Hazelton 2017; Biddle, Macdonald, and Baker 2018; and Berman and Lake 2019.

82. Salehyan 2010.

83. On delegation by states to international organizations, see Hawkins et al. 2006.

84. Moe 1984, 754.

85. Maltzman 1997, 12.

86. Feaver 2003, 55.

87. Miller 2005, 205.

88. It could also be the case that officers simply disagree with civilians on strategy irrespective of where in the military bureaucracy they "sit." Feaver (2003, 60, 65) also emphasizes that disagreements between civilians and soldiers, at least in the American context, are over means rather than ends.

89. Feaver 2003, 60.

90. Biddle, Macdonald, and Baker 2018, 101.

91. Moreover, in the context of SFA, Ladwig (2017, 70–71) finds that indicators of more intensive monitoring are not associated with improved proxy compliance.

92. Ladwig 2017, 76.

93. Biddle, Macdonald, and Baker (2018) contend that for conditionality to work, principals must be able to make credible promises of reward for working and credible threats of punishment for shirking. The more credible are these promises and threats, however, the more likely they are to give rise to a different form of moral hazard. When agents are convinced of their indispensability to the principal's interests, they are unlikely to believe threats to withhold or cut off aid and are thus likely to shirk. Credible promises of rewards for working, in other words, can induce moral hazard on the part of the agent. Conversely, Biddle, Macdonald, and Baker write that "the more forcefully the US threatens an ally with aid withdrawal in the event of shirking, the more a rational ally will doubt the US promise to follow through with its commitment if the ally works" (102). Credible threats for shirking can thus induce moral hazard on the part of the principal. In other words, the use of carrots and sticks to try to incentivize agents to work can have the perverse consequence of inducing shirking instead.

94. Schlesinger and Kinzer 1999, 122. See also Gleijeses 1991, 250, 382

95. Quoted in Schlesinger and Kinzer 1999, 122.

96. Quoted in Streeter 2000, 57.

97. Schlesinger and Kinzer 1999, 233–35.

98. Meldrum 2003.

99. Quoted in *The Economist* 2001.

100. Chan 2015.

101. For more on this case, see chapter 5.

102. The domestic principal in this case, unlike typical principals in PA theory, did not delegate the task of governance to the agent because the agent was appointed by an outside power. Nevertheless, domestic principals try to exercise control over foreign-imposed leaders just as other principals do.

103. Krahmann 2016, 1414.

104. Salehyan, Siroky, and Wood 2014, 643.

105. Nielsen and Tierney 2003, 249.

106. Gailmard 2009; Salehyan, Siroky, and Wood 2014, 643; Krahmann 2016, 1414–15.

107. Berman et al. 2019, 16–18.

108. Nielsen and Tierney 2003, 247. For previous, similar analyses that treat domestic audiences as unitary actors, see Lake 2016.

109. The country was subsequently renamed the Democratic Republic of Congo.

110. Uganda was also involved, and for similar reasons: Mobutu's support and sheltering of militant groups opposed to Yoweri Museveni's rule in Kampala.

111. This type of interest divergence is induced by the intervener; it does not predate regime change.

112. Lafeber 1984, 165; Jonas 1991, 66; Schirmer 1998, 15; Recovery of Historical Memory Project 1999, 190; Schlesinger and Kinzer 1999, 238–41; Streeter 2000, 222–24; Brockett 2005, 99.

113. MR-13 stands for Movimiento Revolucionario 13 de Noviembre (Revolutionary movement of November 13). The official casualty figures for the three days of fighting amount to thirteen dead and sixty wounded. Streeter 2000, 230.

114. Gobat 2005, 120.

115. Calder 1984, 7.

116. Calder 1984, 120.

117. Wolford, Reiter, and Carrubba 2011.

118. Downes and O'Rourke 2016, 54–55; O'Rourke 2018, 45.

119. MacFarquhar 2006. See also Lake 2010–11.

120. Lake 2016, 78.

121. Lake 2016, 133.

122. Lake 2016, 134.

123. Lake 2016, 134.

124. Lake 2016, 134.

125. Pape 2003, 2005; Mearsheimer 2018.
126. Gellner 1983, 1.
127. Mearsheimer 2018, 142, 169.
128. Edelstein 2008, 10.
129. Edelstein 2004, 50–51. On nationalist reactions to foreign occupation, see also Pape 2005.
130. Kocher, Lawrence, and Monteiro 2018.
131. Kocher, Lawrence, and Monteiro 2018, 124.
132. Kocher, Lawrence, and Monteiro 2018, 130–33.
133. On these points, see Kocher, Lawrence, and Monteiro 2018, 144–46.
134. Lawrence 2010, 2013.
135. Lawrence 2010, 104.
136. Lawrence 2010, 105–8.
137. Piazza 2008; Collard-Wexler, Pischedda, and Smith 2014.
138. Collard-Wexler 2013.
139. Collard-Wexler 2013, 16–18.
140. Jessica Weeks terms such regimes "machines." On the types of authoritarian regimes discussed in this paragraph, see Weeks 2014, 14–36.
141. I omit discussion of the most obvious method of avoiding interest asymmetry— selecting an agent with similar preferences—because I have already explained how adverse selection and competing principals can defeat that solution.
142. Ladwig 2016.
143. Gordon and Lehren 2010; deGrandpre and Tilghman 2015.
144. The Taliban need not win the war for an Al Qaeda safe haven to be reestablished; it merely needs to deny the Afghan government control over substantial amounts of territory.
145. Ironically, patrons would need to offer rewards for bad behavior (i.e., shirking) to deal with a leader in this situation—which they would obviously never do. Even these inducements could fail, however, because they would provide more evidence to the leader's domestic opponents that he is in the patron's pocket.
146. Edelstein 2004, 2008.
147. Doyle 1983a, 1983b; Owen 2002, 2010.
148. More accurately, the occupier delegates authority to one of its own officials rather than an agent native to the occupied country. Prominent definitions of occupation stress that it involves military forces to control all or part of another state's territory in which the occupier exercises coercive authority (Edelstein 2004, 52; Collard-Wexler 2013, 2–3). Occupations can thus govern a target state's entire territory or only some fraction of it. Edelstein also emphasizes that occupations must be intended to be temporary.
149. Collard-Wexler 2013, 15.
150. Rubin and Shanker 2013. For more on the turbulent relationship between Washington and Karzai, see Downes and O'Rourke 2019.
151. Taylor 2014.
152. Ollivant 2011, 4–5.
153. Quoted in Filkins 2014.
154. On shared values among Marxist regimes as a source of peace, see Peceny, Beer, and Sanchez-Terry 2002, 19–20.
155. Leaders in these cases are able to deter domestic opponents with the threat of overwhelming punishment. Although moderate amounts of coercion may provoke a backlash, overwhelming repression can obtain compliance through sheer terror. See Liberman 1996. This is not to say that repression is foolproof. Leaders in highly oppressive systems may lose their will to engage in wholesale repression, in which case domestic unrest may threaten the regime's survival. When this occurred in Hungary in 1956 and Czechoslovakia in 1968, the Soviets were forced to intervene to restore communist orthodoxy.
156. See, for example, Russett 1993.
157. Dixon 1994; Farber and Gowa 1997.
158. Willard-Foster 2018, 52. A countervailing logic, however, suggests that by making imposed leaders more responsive to their publics, installing democratic forms of government

makes such leaders less responsive to interveners. If such leaders align themselves too closely with the intervener, voters may replace them with elites more oriented to their own needs and desires, which could produce disagreement—if not open conflict—between the two states. Bueno de Mesquita and Downs 2006.

159. Haiti, however, reverted to autocracy in 1999. A sixth case, Costa Rica in 1919, resulted in democracy. Because the country was already a democracy before regime change, it does not constitute a case of democratic transition.

160. Downes and Monten 2013, 122–28.

161. Clark 1998.

162. The lone case that did not restore a democracy was Britain's restoration of Haile Selassie in Ethiopia in 1941.

163. Schroeder 1962, 42–43. See also Schroeder 1994, 613

164. On Austria's interventions in Modena and Parma in 1831, see Schroeder 1994, 692. On Prussia's interventions in Baden and Saxony in 1849, see, respectively, Valentin 1965, 402; and Showalter 2004, 41. See also Leurdijk 1986, 241–42.

165. Giniger 1964.

166. One report states that Denard's force numbered only thirty-three individuals. See Simons 1995.

167. Indeed, given that regime changes typically start as attempts by powerful states to compel weak targets to change their behavior, Willard-Foster (2018) argues that the puzzle of regime change is why weak states resist and risk a regime change attempt. I argue elsewhere (Downes 2020) that this puzzle is less compelling than it appears because weak targets have a host of reasons for refusing to comply with demands from powerful states.

168. Data on the financial costs of the two wars is from Belasco 2014, 14–16. Direct costs for both wars combined through 2014 came to $1.6 trillion. Data on US fatalities are from Iraq Coalition Casualty Count 2020.

169. For a good summary, see Willard-Foster 2018, 66–70. Information problems also hinder principals' abilities to monitor agents *after* regime change. This problem makes it difficult for principals to grasp the domestic pressures their agents face, which in turn hinders their ability to craft carrots and sticks to incentivize agents to follow their preferred policies.

170. On this possibility, see Lake 2010–11, 33.

171. Willard-Foster 2018, 69.

3. Foreign-Imposed Regime Change and Civil War

1. Davies 1962; Russett 1964; Gurr 1970, 1993, 2000; Scott 1976; Horowitz 1985, 141–84; Muller 1985; Muller and Seligson 1987; Petersen 2002; Boix 2008; Stewart 2008; Cederman, Wimmer, and Min 2010; Cederman, Weidmann, and Gleditsch 2011; Cederman, Gleditsch, and Buhaug 2013.

2. The debate over motivations (such as grievances) versus opportunities in leading to violence predated the 1990s, however. Resource mobilization theory, for example, arose in response to early work on grievances. See Snyder and Tilly 1972; Tilly 1978; McAdam 1992.

3. On greed, see Collier and Hoeffler 1998, 2004; Collier 2000; Ross 2004, 2006, 2012. On opportunity, see Fearon and Laitin 2003; Collier, Hoeffler, and Rohner 2009.

4. Posen 1993; Kaufmann 1996; Fearon 1998.

5. Related work examines the effect of external intervention at the conclusion of civil conflicts on the likelihood of war recurrence, finding that such intervention (by states or the UN) reduces the likelihood that civil wars recur and increases the duration of peace. See Walter 1997, 2002; Doyle and Sambanis 2006; Fortna 2008; Gilligan and Sergenti 2008.

6. Salehyan 2009.

7. Salehyan and Gleditsch 2006, 338.

8. Kuperman 2008.

9. Terry 2002; Lischer 2005.

10. Edelstein 2008, 11. See also Liberman 1996.

11. Mearsheimer 2018, 142, 164–71.

12. Pape 2003. See also Piazza 2008; Collard-Wexler, Pischedda, and Smith 2014. Other studies, by contrast, find that resistance to occupation is far from automatic. See Lawrence 2010, 2013; Collard-Wexler 2013; Kocher, Lawrence, and Monteiro 2018. And some find that resistance to occupation is muted when occupiers devolve powers of self-governance to occupied populations or commit to treat the population benevolently and depart promptly. See Edelstein 2008, 14; Hechter, Matesan, and Hale 2009, 44; Collard-Wexler 2013; Ferwerda and Miller 2014 (but see Kocher and Monteiro 2016).

13. Fearon and Laitin 2003, 79–82. The principal exception is political instability but this is not one of their central variables.

14. Collier and Hoeffler 2004, 565–70.

15. Stewart 2008.

16. Recent studies use income inequality across groups as a proxy for economic inequality. See Cederman, Weidmann, and Gleditsch 2011; Cederman, Gleditsch, and Buhaug 2013. Older studies proxied economic imbalances as inequality in land distribution, a measure that also changes slowly. See Davies 1962; Russett 1964; Scott 1976.

17. Horowitz 1985.

18. Gurr 1993, 2000; Toft 2003.

19. Fearon and Laitin 2003; Collier and Hoeffler 2004.

20. Cederman, Weidmann, and Gleditsch 2011; Cederman, Gleditsch, and Buhaug 2013.

21. Petersen 2002.

22. Fearon and Laitin 2011.

23. Different fear-based arguments highlight different causal mechanisms. Security dilemma arguments depend on ethnic intermingling (e.g., Posen 1993; Kaufmann 1996) whereas commitment theories emphasize changes in the balance of power between ethnic majorities and minorities (e.g., Fearon 1998). Each of these arguments is obviously of limited applicability.

24. Gagnon 1994–95; Brown 1996.

25. Lawrence 2010.

26. Roessler 2016.

27. Peic and Reiter 2011. For closely related work on civil unrest in imposed polities, see Enterline and Greig 2008a.

28. Peic and Reiter 2011, 453.

29. Peic and Reiter 2011, 453.

30. Peic and Reiter 2011, 459.

31. Peic and Reiter 2011, 462, 465.

32. Peic and Reiter 2011, 468.

33. Goemans, Gleditsch, and Chiozza 2009.

34. For a list, see the Supplemental Materials for chapter 4.

35. Bueno de Mesquita and Downs 2006.

36. Ten years is a relatively long period of time. It is unclear, for example, to what extent Britain's 1879 regime change in Afghanistan is responsible for the Ghilzai and Uzbek Revolts that followed seven and nine years later, respectively. This is not to say that regime change cannot cause such temporally distant conflicts. I argue below that the civil war in Guatemala, which did not formally begin until nine years after regime change, is one such case. The vast majority of civil wars that follow regime changes, however, break out within five years: in thirty of the thirty-six regime changes followed by civil war within a decade (83 percent), the conflict began within five years of regime change (and 84 percent broke out after leadership regime changes).

37. These results are shown in table 3.2 in the appendix. Controls included are primary energy consumption (logged), population (logged), percentage of mountainous terrain, time since the previous civil war (and three cubic splines), and dummy variables indicating new states (in their first two years of existence), democracies, states that lost an interstate war in the previous ten years, and states with an ongoing civil war in the year prior to the year of observation.

38. As shown in the chapter appendix, these results are quite robust and survive a variety of tests to correct for potential selection bias.

39. See the chapter appendix section on robustness tests for further details.

40. See table 3.3 in the appendix for the models that form the basis of these graphs. For these analyses, other variables are held constant at their means or modes.

41. Downes and Monten 2013.

42. This odd effect is likely explained by the large number of restorations that occurred in European microstates in the first half of the nineteenth century, most of which consumed hardly any energy and none of which was followed by civil war. These results are available in the online Supplemental Materials for chapter 3.

43. The effect is slightly negative but insignificant.

44. Bellin 2004–05; Enterline and Greig 2008b; Downes and Monten 2013.

45. For these results, see the online Supplemental Materials.

46. The change in probability is 1.7 percent, but the 95 percent confidence interval includes zero, indicating an insignificant effect. By contrast, the change in probability that results from shifting regime change and the interaction term from zero to one while holding defeat in war constant at one is 2.9 percent, and the confidence interval is strictly positive.

47. This result holds if each type of regime change is analyzed separately.

48. Peic and Reiter 2011.

49. I discuss the Peruvian case briefly in chapters 4 and 5 and explore the Mexican case at length in chapter 4. Peru actually suffered three civil wars in succession following its defeat by Chile: one against the Chilean occupiers triggered by military disintegration; a second between Peruvian factions in favor of and opposed to collaborating with the occupiers caused by the problem of competing principals; and a third, the Atusparia Revolt of 1885, that was unrelated to regime change.

50. Harff 2003, 60.

51. For an overview of the border conflict, see Heder 1981.

52. On these incursions and civilian casualties inflicted, see Chanda 1986, 87, 193; Evans and Rowley 1990, 104–7; S. J. Morris 1999, 266n35.

53. Evans and Rowley 1990, 107.

54. Chanda 1986, 206; S. J. Morris 1999, 102.

55. O'Dowd 2007, 37.

56. Chang 1985, 73. The Khmer Rouge renamed the country Democratic Kampuchea after the movement seized power in 1975.

57. Chang 1985, 72.

58. Chang 1985, 75–76.

59. Samrin was among those who fled the fierce purges that followed the Eastern Zone of Cambodia's failure to repel the Vietnamese incursion in December 1977. Chanda refers to this episode as "the goriest chapter in the blood-soaked history of Democratic Kampuchea," and estimates that at least 100,000 people were killed (Chanda 1986, 253, 254). See also Nguyen-Vo 1992, 102–4.

60. Becker 1998, 432.

61. Etcheson 1984, 196; Chanda 1986, 342.

62. O'Dowd (2007, 90) reports that "by mid-May, 15,000 of the 30,000 Khmer Rouge troops in the area had been killed, wounded, or captured."

63. S. J. Morris 1999, 220.

64. Becker 1998, 432.

65. Leifer 1980, 38.

66. On the German experience with partisans in the Soviet Union, see Cooper 1979. On the German invasion of Yugoslavia, see Littlefield 1988.

67. Conboy 2013, 129.

68. Leifer 1980, 34.

69. Hood 1992, 50.

70. S. J. Morris 1999, 220.

71. Leifer 1980, 35; S. J. Morris 1999, 220.

72. Chanda 1986, 382.

73. Gordon 1986, 73.

74. Chanda 1986, 382

75. Leifer 1981, 94.

76. Chanda 1986, 381; Rungswasdisab 2004, 90; Rowley 2006, 194; Conboy 2013, 130–31. Chanda (1986, 381–82) credits this aid with rejuvenating the Khmer Rouge.

77. Richardson 2000.

78. van der Kroef 1983, 26–27. Quinn-Judge (2006, 215) puts the number of Cambodians living in this "rival Cambodia" at one million.

79. Rowley 2006, 193.

80. Rowley 2006, 193.

81. Quinn-Judge 2006, 215.

82. Terry 2002; Lischer 2005.

83. According to Steve Coll's account, CIA director George Tenet informed President Bush on the afternoon of 9/11 that Al Qaeda had carried out the attacks. Coll 2018, 40.

84. Bergen 2011, 54–55.

85. On skepticism about military options in Afghanistan, see Mearsheimer 2001. On Afghanistan as the graveyard of empires, see Jones 2009; Isby 2010.

86. Jones 2009, 89–90; Bergen 2011, 55. The Northern Alliance had been led by Ahmed Shah Massoud until his assassination by Al Qaeda two days before 9/11. Massoud had brokered a united front with other Afghan warlords that included Tajiks, Uzbeks, Hazaras, and some Pashtuns.

87. Bergen (2011, 59) estimates that there were 110 CIA officers and 300 SOF in Afghanistan during the war.

88. Rashid 2008, 81.

89. Rashid 2008, 82.

90. In what became known as the "Great Escape," the United States allowed as many as 2,000 Pakistanis to be flown out of Kunduz in the days before the city fell. These men were Inter-Services Intelligence (ISI) officers and members of the Frontier Corps who had remained in Afghanistan to fight alongside the Taliban. Rashid 2008, 91–94; Gall 2014, 8.

91. Abbas 2014, 77.

92. On November 18, Omar sent 1,000 Taliban to attack Karzai in Tarin Kot, in Uruzgan province. The attack was repelled by US air strikes. Rashid 2008, 95; Gall 2014, 31, 33–34.

93. Fairweather 2014, 44.

94. The figure for bombs dropped is from October 7 to December 23, 2001; see Lambeth 2005, 247–48. If missiles and other munitions are counted, the total rises to 22,434. Lambeth 2005, 249. The figure for bribes is from Woodward 2002, 317.

95. On the hammer and anvil strategy, see Pape 2004; Pape, Ruby, and Bauer 2015.

96. Coll 2018, 110–11. On Taliban casualties, see also Rashid 2008, 96.

97. Jones 2009, 108.

98. Abbas 2014, 76.

99. Al-Libi was turned over to Egyptian intelligence in January 2002, where he made claims about Iraqi training of Al Qaeda in chemical weapons that were later cited by Secretary of State Colin Powell in his speech to the UN Security Council. Al-Libi later recanted these claims. Jehl 2005; Finn 2009.

100. Gall 2014, 81. Rashid (2008, 98) estimates that between 600 and 800 Arab fighters escaped at Tora Bora alone.

101. Mendelsohn 2016.

102. Rashid 2008, 99; Coll 2018, 104–9. The Pakistanis were unable to move many troops to the area, and thus blocked only a few routes into Pakistan. Coll 2018, 107–8.

103. Rashid 2008, 77–78.

104. Coll 2018, 55, 103. Even had the Pakistanis been interested in combating the Taliban, the crisis with India that followed the attack on the Indian parliament building by the Kashmiri militant groups Lashkar-e-Taiba and Jaish-e-Mohammed led the Pakistanis to redeploy the army to the Indian border and away from the tribal areas. Abbas 2014, 104.

105. Coll 2018, 105–6. See also Bergen 2011, 80–81.

106. Quoted in Gall 2014, 62–63.

107. Jones 2009, 100–101. See also Riedel 2008, 83.

108. Rashid 2008, 225.

109. Gall 2014, 63.

110. Rashid 2008, 221.

111. Rashid 2008, 221.

112. Quoted in Jones 2009, 101.

113. Both quoted in Coll 2018, 102. This belief helps explain why no effort was made to engage the Taliban in the negotiations for a new government or even to discuss surrender terms.

114. Rashid 2008, 240.

115. Rashid 2008, 243.

116. The ISI also arranged the return of Gulbuddin Hikmetyar, its favorite mujahideen commander, from exile in Iran to Peshawar. Hikmetyar was not a member of the Taliban, but allied with the group. Rashid 2008, 244; Jones 2009, 101–2.

117. Gall 2014, 21.

118. On Afghanistan as a high-intensity conflict, see Harbom, Högbladh, and Wallensteen 2006. On total deaths in Afghanistan, see Crawford 2016.

119. Jones 2009, 115, 129–31.

120. Woodward 2002, 49, 83–85; Clarke 2004, 30–32; Bergen 2011, 52–56.

121. Franks 2004, 315. Rumsfeld asked for military options for Iraq as early as September 17. Bergen 2011, 56.

122. Coll 2018, 102. Abbas (2014, 89) calls the Iraq campaign a "fatal distraction" for Washington "at a time when the Afghanistan project needed their undivided attention."

123. Rashid 2008, 133–34.

124. Riedel 2008, 82. Only $1 billion was appropriated in 2002 and 2003 for Afghan reconstruction (82).

125. Riedel 2008, 83.

126. For Taliban casualties, see Abbas 2014, 77.

127. Standard works on the causes and conduct of the war include Woodward 2002; Packer 2005; Fallows 2006; Gordon and Trainor 2006; Ricks 2006; MacDonald 2014.

128. Fallows 2006, 43–106; Gordon and Trainor 2006, 138–63; Ricks 2006, 78–81, 101–11; Bensahel et al. 2008; Ferguson 2008, 24–70.

129. Packer 2005, 133. The short timeline reflected the views of secretary of defense Donald Rumsfeld—who was skeptical that Iraq could be democratized and was hostile to nation building—in large part because the Pentagon had been put in charge of postwar planning.

130. The Pentagon expected the US presence to be about 30,000 to 40,000 troops by fall 2003. Bensahel et al. 2008, xx.

131. MacDonald 2014, 60.

132. Quoted in Gordon 2004.

133. MacDonald 2014, 60.

134. MacDonald 2014, 62–63.

135. On the preference in the Pentagon for Chalabi to lead a liberated Iraq, see Packer 2005, 115; Phillips 2005, 7–8, 67–68; Chandrasekaran 2006, 29–30, 32–33, 37; Ricks 2006, 124.

136. Quoted in Ricks 2006, 104. Pentagon officials also arranged to have Chalabi and several hundred fighters flown into southern Iraq after the war began, according to George Packer (2005, 141), "to give Chalabi a head start in the race to power." See also Gordon and Trainor 2006, 315–17.

137. Packer 2005, 74–75. MacDonald, however, argues that the neoconservative view was about more than just democratization; what was required was a fundamental remaking of Iraqi culture and society. See MacDonald 2014, 106–10.

138. Packer 2005, 78. Further, they believed that democratization in Iraq could spur democratization of the entire Middle East.

139. Chandrasekaran 2006, 33.

140. MacDonald 2014, 92.

141. According to MacDonald (2014, 58–59), these were sincere beliefs, not mere rhetoric.

142. Lake 2016, 108.

143. Lieutenant General Joseph Kellogg Jr., quoted in Ricks 2006, 109–10.

144. General Carl Strock, quoted in Gordon and Trainor 2006, 463.

145. Chandrasekaran 2006, 52.

146. Packer 2005, 140; Chandrasekaran 2006, 51–53.

147. Packer 2005, 144. Rumsfeld had already informed Garner on April 24 that he was being replaced by Bremer.

148. Lake 2016, 110.

149. Woods 2006, 129.

150. Chandrasekaran 2006, 75.

151. Chandrasekaran 2006, 74.

152. Hobbes (1651) 1982. I purposefully echo Thucydides's portrayal of the civil war in Corcyra (Thucydides 1954).

153. Dodge 2006, 214–15.

154. I focus here on Sunni resistance, but the Shiite militia of Moktada al-Sadr—Jaish al-Mahdi—also fought against the US occupiers in the summer of 2003 in Baghdad and the cities of southern Iraq.

155. Hashim 2006, 23.

156. Napoleoni 2005, 157; Ricks 2006, 215–16.

157. Petraeus 2007. Commentary at the time warned that Iraq was on the verge of "full-scale civil war," but in reality civil war had been underway in the country since 2003. These warnings were likely based on a flawed understanding of civil war that conceives of it as possible only between indigenous actors in a country. But as Nicholas Sambanis pointed out in the *New York Times* in the summer of 2006, civil war is organized violence by domestic actors against the government—whether or not that government is run or supported by a third party. Violent resistance to the US occupation thus also qualifies as civil war. Sambanis 2006.

158. See Packer 2005, 298–99; Ricks 2006, 190.

159. Gordon and Trainor 2012, 20–21.

160. Gordon and Trainor 2012, 21.

161. "Sunni Arab Resistance: The Politics of the Gun," cited in Gordon and Trainor 2012, 21.

162. Packer 2005, 318.

163. Petit 2020, 113–14. It is noteworthy that all three men hired in 2007 by the US military commander in Ghazaliyah to lead the "Ghazaliyah Guardians," as the local Sons of Iraq were called, were former Iraqi Army officers. Petit 2020, 153–54.

164. Petit 2020, 192.

165. Gordon and Trainor 2012, 23.

166. Packer 2005, 308.

167. Petit 2020, 129.

168. MacDonald 2014, 33–34. On why even a one percent chance of these things happening was too much, see Suskind 2006.

169. Rumsfeld, quoted in Packer 2005, 300; Ricks 2006, 136.

170. Mansoor 2013, 8.

171. Mansoor 2013, 9. On the furious reaction to the order disbanding the Iraqi Army, see Gordon and Trainor 2006, 484; Ricks 2006, 164. It is important to note that neither of these decisions was made unilaterally by Bremer. Both were cleared with his superiors in Washington.

172. Breaking into houses and searching female family members without the male head of household present are good examples, as were the large-scale detention of Sunni men of fighting age and the ill-treatment of detainees in US facilities, such as Abu Ghraib.

173. Fazal 2007.

174. Russia fought Persia from 1804 to 1813 and again from 1826 to 1828. The Russo-Turkish wars of this period were fought from 1806 to 1812 and 1827 to 1828.

175. Quoted in Norris 1967, 28.

176. Quoted in Norris 1967, 22; quoted in Dalrymple 2013, 47.

177. On Russian influence in Tehran, see Durand (1879) 2000, 26–27. Indeed, Sir Henry Ellis, Britain's envoy to Persia, "brought himself to regard Persia, under Russian influence, 'as no longer an outwork for the defence of India, but as the first parallel from whence the attack may be commenced or threatened'" (Durand [1879] 2000, 29).

178. The key issue preventing an alliance was Dost Mohammad's claim to Peshawar, the Afghan winter capital, which had been conquered by Britain's ally Ranjit Singh, maharaja of the Sikh Empire. J. J. Roberts 2003, 5. Auckland was also heavily influenced by his advisers, including Claude Wade, who viewed Dost Mohammad unfavorably and supported putting Shah Shuja in power. Durand (1879) 2000, 33, 43.

179. Dalrymple 2013, 118.

180. Quoted in Norris 1967, 201.

181. Quoted in Norris 1967, 209.

182. The first signs of unrest actually occurred in May when a Ghilzai force of 2,000 attacked a British column on the road to Ghazni. Johnson 2011, 59.

183. For an explanation of why Dost Mohammad capitulated, see Barfield 2010, 115–16.

184. Dalrymple 2013, 236.

185. Roughly 12,000 camp followers also died. Clodfelter 2008, 248. This figure probably overstates the casualties, as Dalrymple notes that when the British Army of Retribution reached Kabul in October 1842, it found up to 2,000 sepoys and camp followers who had survived. Dalrymple 2013, 407.

186. Dalrymple 2013, 210.

187. Quoted in Dalrymple 2013, 202.

188. Dupree 1973, 381.

189. Preston 2012, 125.

190. Waller 1990, 183.

191. Quoted in Dalrymple 2013, 212.

192. Waller 1990, 194–95; Durand (1879) 2000, 208–9; Barfield 2010, 118–20; Johnson 2011, 57; Preston 2012, 125; Dalrymple 2013, 204–6.

193. Preston 2012, 126.

194. Dalrymple 2013, 203.

195. Durand (1879) 2000, 328; Barfield 2010, 121; Preston 2012, 132; Dalrymple 2013, 203, 246. Indeed, the need to economize on expenses—and the diversion of attention and resources to China and the Opium War—played a central role in Macnaghten's decision to cut the Ghilzai subsidies in autumn 1841. On the China diversion, see Dalrymple 2013, 197–98.

196. Bush 2005.

197. Barfield 2010, 119. See also Johnson 2011, 57.

198. Dalrymple 2013, 204.

199. Dalrymple 2013, 205.

200. Barfield 2010, 119–20. See also Durand (1879) 2000, 208. In this sense, as Johnson (2011, 63) notes, the Afghan "resistance to the foreigners and even to Shah Shuja was conservative rather than revolutionary. The emphasis of the rebel leaders was on preserving the status quo and the 'old order.'"

201. Dalrymple 2013, 244.

202. Dupree 1973, 384–85; Preston 2012, 105–6.

203. Quoted in Dalrymple 2013, 156.

204. This is the assessment of Fayz Mohammad, author of *Siraj ul-Tawarikh* (The lamp of histories), published in 1913. See Dalrymple 2013, 202. The British committed their share of "unforced errors," too, such as choosing a vulnerable site to construct their main base in Kabul, sending poorly suited administrators and military commanders to oversee the occupation, and reacting too slowly as rebellion spread in October and November 1841.

205. Dalrymple 2013, 378.

206. Johnson (2011, 75–84) provides a good discussion of the divisions within the Afghan camp in 1842. The rebellion, as he shows, was far from unified, with several leaders competing for power and influence.

207. The Correlates of War National Material Capabilities Dataset defines primary energy consumption as energy derived from coal, petroleum, electricity, or natural gas. It is intended to gauge the size of a country's manufacturing and industrial base. See Correlates of War Project 2017, 57–58.

208. Maddison Project Database 2018. This comparison uses data from 1920, the first year for which figures are available for Nicaragua.

209. The United States sent gunboats to support an uprising in Panama, which in 1903 was a province of Colombia, prevented Colombian authorities from putting down the rebellion, and quickly recognized the sovereignty of Panama.

210. Kinzer 2006, 60.

211. After his fellow presidents balked at the idea, Zelaya began to support Liberal factions in other Central American countries and succeeded in overthrowing the Conservative government of Manuel Bonilla in Honduras during the Fourth Central American War of 1907.

212. In 1909, for example, Zelaya secured two loans in the amount of £1.25 million from the Ethelburga syndicate, based in Britain. Findling 1987, 58.

213. Findling 1987, 58. Indeed, this was the main reason President Theodore Roosevelt proclaimed the "Roosevelt Corollary" to the Monroe Doctrine, which stated that the United States maintained the right to intervene in any country in the hemisphere to keep order and preempt potential European intervention.

214. Kinzer 2006, 65.

215. Quoted in Langley and Schoonover 1995, 90.

216. Kerevel 2006, 23, 24. See also Langley and Schoonover 1995, 106.

217. Langley and Schoonover 1995, 106.

218. Clark 2001, xxiii.

219. Kerevel 2006, 32. The accords also required that the next president be a Conservative.

220. Quoted in Kerevel 2006, 33.

221. Harrison 1995, 58.

222. Gobat 2005, 81–82.

223. On demonstrations and coup-plotting, see Kerevel 2006, 31.

224. Kerevel 2006, 31.

225. Harrison (1995, 58) quotes a State Department memorandum suggesting that Estrada resigned "thinking he no longer had the support of the United States." Most accounts, however, do not attribute responsibility for Estrada's resignation to the United States.

226. Gobat 2005, 83.

227. Quoted in Gobat 2005, 84.

228. Clark 2001, 5.

229. Gobat 2005, 120. See also Lafeber 1984, 50; Healy 1988, 159.

230. Gobat 2005, 88–98.

231. Gobat 2005, 75.

232. Kerevel 2006, 35.

233. Gobat 2005, 99.

234. Gleijeses 1991, 41.

235. Rabe 2016, 39.

236. Gleijeses 1991, 99; Grow 2008, 13. State Department reports in 1950 were filled with warnings about the communist threat, which Grow concludes "U.S. officials grossly exaggerated."

237. Rabe 2016, 39.

238. Gleijeses 1991, 150.

239. Rabe 2016, 56. On Arévalo's reverence for FDR, see Grow 2008, 6.

240. Office of Intelligence Research, "Agrarian Reform in Guatemala," March 5, 1953, quoted in Gleijeses 1991, 152. The problem was that those 1,710 estates controlled more than half of the country's private land holdings.

241. Immerman 1982, 54.

242. Schlesinger and Kinzer 1999, 76.

243. Grow 2008, 15–17.

244. Gleijeses 1991, 365. On communist party membership in Guatemala, see Rabe 2016, 38. These small numbers did not stop US officials from assuming that Guatemala was under the influence of the global communist movement led by the Soviet Union. See Immerman 1982, 101–5; Rabe 2016, 39.

245. Quoted in Cullather 2006, 35.
246. Quoted in Rabe 2016, 46.
247. Quoted in Immerman 1982, 82.
248. Quoted in Gleijeses 1991, 366. It is also worth noting that as soon as Árbenz was toppled, the Justice Department filed an antitrust suit against UFCO, which "had a major impact on breaking up the firm's banana business and ending its role in Guatemala." See Schlesinger and Kinzer 1999, 221; Zachary, Deloughery, and Downes 2017, 774–75.
249. Prados 2006, 108, quoted in Grow 2008, 17.
250. Grow 2008, 17.
251. Rabe 2016, 45.
252. Quoted in Rabe 2016, 47–48.
253. Schirmer 1998, 14.
254. At Gualán, a thirty-man detachment defeated a larger rebel force on June 20. Gleijeses 1991, 326.
255. A Guatemalan officer quoted in Gleijeses 1991, 338. See also Grow 2008, 1; Rabe 2016, 50.
256. Gleijeses 1991, 246.
257. On these events, see Schlesinger and Kinzer 1999, 194–98, 205–15.
258. Schirmer 1998, 14; Streeter 2000, 31. Others put the death toll much higher, at between 3,000 and 5,000. See Grandin 2004, 66. Jonas (1991, 41) estimates that 9,000 were imprisoned, whereas the Guatemalan Human Rights Office estimates 12,000 (Recovery of Historical Memory Project 1999, 189). US government documents report a lower figure of 4,000. USDS 1954a.
259. USDS 1954a.
260. CIA memorandum dated March 31, 1954, reproduced in Cullather 2006, 141–42.
261. Schlesinger and Kinzer 1999, 221.
262. USDS 1954a.
263. USDS 1954b.
264. Jonas 1991, 42.
265. Jonas 1991, 42.
266. Schlesinger and Kinzer 1999, 233–35.
267. Gleijeses 1991, 359.
268. Streeter 2000, 43.
269. Quoted in Gleijeses 1991, 358.
270. Gleijeses 1991, 360; Streeter 2000, 42. This death toll would qualify the fighting as a low-intensity civil war according to the Uppsala Conflict Data Program (UCDP), which uses a threshold of twenty-five battle deaths for identifying such conflicts. UCDP already codes Castillo Armas's invasion as a civil war in 1954.
271. The assassin—one of the president's bodyguards—committed suicide immediately after killing Castillo Armas and no one has ever determined with certainty why he did it or who he was working for.
272. Because no candidate won a majority, Congress voted forty to eighteen in favor of Ydígoras. The CIA bribed several congressmen to vote for him. Ydígoras also fixed the 1959 congressional elections. See Streeter 2000, 75 and 91, respectively.
273. Streeter 2000, 85.
274. Streeter 2000, 85.
275. The official casualty figures for the three days of fighting amount to thirteen dead and sixty wounded. Streeter 2000, 230.
276. Schlesinger and Kinzer 1999, 242. For evidence of significant violence before 1966, see Wickham-Crowley 1990, 209–10.
277. Jonas 1991, 68.
278. Streeter 2000, 222, 223–24. One Guatemalan navy officer attributed the rebellion to resentment that some officers were being paid high salaries to train the Cubans, especially when other officers had not been paid their regular (low) salaries for two months. See Schirmer 1998, 15.
279. Schlesinger and Kinzer 1999, 238.
280. Quoted in Schlesinger and Kinzer 1999, 240.
281. See Jonas 1991, 64–66.

282. Jonas 1991, 66; Schirmer 1998, 15.

283. Brockett 2005, 99. See also Lafeber 1984, 165; Recovery of Historical Memory Project 1999, 190; Rabe 2016, 56.

284. Streeter 2000, 216.

285. It also explains civil war in Libya after the US-backed ouster of Muammar Qaddafi.

286. Fearon and Laitin 2003, 76.

287. Sarkees and Wayman 2010; Gleditsch 2004.

288. Kohn 1999; Sambanis 2004; Clodfelter 2008.

289. A documented list of civil wars in the author's dataset is available in the Supplemental Materials.

290. Cases of resistance to German occupation during World War II thus count as civil wars.

291. Bueno de Mesquita and Downs 2006. Peic and Reiter (2011) use a five-year lag.

292. These figures sum to 113 because one country (Cyprus) had two regime changes of different types in the same year (1974). Counting regime change years by type thus yields 113 whereas counting by whether a country had any type of regime change in a given year yields 112.

293. Sarkees and Wayman 2010.

294. Missing values are filled in (where available) using data from Banks and Wilson 2020.

295. Fearon and Laitin 2003.

296. Fearon and Laitin 2003.

297. On problems with using Polity, see Vreeland 2008. On my measure of democracy, see Boix, Miller, and Rosato 2012.

298. Because this effect, like that of regime change, may be prolonged, I code this variable as lasting for ten years. In robustness checks I substitute the target state's involvement in an ongoing interstate war.

299. In robustness tests, I check the effect of having a civil war ongoing in any of the three years prior to the current year.

300. Roeder 2001. I have "stretched" these data, which were coded in 1961 and 1985, to cover the period from 1920 to 2008, as do Peic and Reiter (2011).

301. These two measures are drawn from the Ethnic Power Relations country-level dataset (Wimmer, Cederman, and Min 2009) and cover the years from 1946 to 2008.

302. Fearon and Laitin 2003; Ross 2004, 2006, and 2012.

303. Colgan 2010, 676.

304. Ross 2012, 16.

305. Fazal 2007.

306. Beck, Katz, and Tucker 1998.

307. Fazal 2007.

308. Although this result contradicts Ross's general hypothesis, he argues that oil should increase the probability of civil war beginning only in the 1980s after most states nationalized their oil industries. Ross 2012, 6–8, 37–39, 153.

309. Braumoeller 2004; Brambor, Clark, and Golder 2006.

310. Detailed results for these tests are available in the Supplemental Materials.

311. Results are stable when historical GDP data (from Boix 2008) or alternative indicators from the Correlates of War project (sum of iron and steel production, CINC score) are used to proxy economic development, and when Vanhanen's (2000) Polyarchy measure is substituted for my dichotomous measure of democracy.

312. King and Zeng 2001.

313. Lo, Hashimoto, and Reiter 2008. The substantive effect of leadership regime change is larger with a five-year treatment effect and smaller when the treatment effect is permanent, but statistical significance is unaffected.

314. Fearon and Laitin (2003, 84) use this version of the ongoing civil war variable and find it has a negative and significant effect on the outbreak of a new civil war. Sambanis (2004, 847), however, shows that this effect is not robust across different civil war datasets. Others (e.g., Collier and Hoeffler 2004, 569) argue that time since the previous civil war is a better proxy of the effect of recent conflicts, but this variable, too, has been found not to be robust (Hegre and Sambanis 2006, 524–25).

315. Moreover, the variable that counts the years since the last outbreak of civil conflict is never significant in my models, nor are any of its cubic splines.

316. In this analysis, regime change is coded one in the year that it occurred; the dependent variable is coded one if a civil war occurred in that year or any of the following ten years.

317. The six covert regime changes are Iran 1953, Guatemala 1954, DRC 1960, South Vietnam 1963, Chile 1973, and Chad 1982.

318. In Nicaragua and Congo-Brazzaville, the eruption of civil wars caused external powers (the United States and Angola, respectively) to intervene and force regime change. In Hungary, civil war between Reds and Whites occurred simultaneously with Romanian intervention, whereas in Chile, a brief civil war occurred when a US-backed military coup ousted Salvador Allende. In DRC, the secession of Katanga was aided and abetted by the same external power (Belgium) responsible for removing Patrice Lumumba. The Muslim rebellion in Gansu province in China was unrelated to the Japanese assassination of Chang Tso-Lin later that year.

319. This is the method employed in Fortna (2004, 2008, 2015) to check for selection effects. Details of this analysis may be found in the Supplemental Materials.

320. Dyadic analysis shows that, compared to interveners, targets of regime change are less developed and powerful, but monadic analysis demonstrates that targets are not less wealthy or powerful than all other states.

321. Results are available in the Supplemental Materials.

322. Users can specify how many control cases are selected per treatment case.

323. On matching, see Ho et al. 2007; Diamond and Sekhon 2013. To yield unbiased estimates, matching must be performed using only variables that precede the treatment. Including factors that follow the treatment temporally would introduce posttreatment bias, that is, controlling for something that may be a consequence of the treatment rather than a cause. For recent applications of matching in security studies, see Gilligan and Sergenti 2008; Lyall 2009, 2010; Downes and Monten 2013; and Downes and O'Rourke 2016. For a critique of using matching to address selection bias, see Miller n.d.

324. On *MatchIt*, see Ho et al. 2007.

325. Balance was comparable or better—with the exception of restoration regime change—in the second run of matching that included buffer states and used interstate war involvement rather than loss in an interstate war. These results are available in the Supplemental Materials.

326. The absolute difference between regime change and non-regime-change cases on this variable grew from 0.0192 to 0.0312.

327. Bivariate results, however, are similar. Some variables had to be excluded from the institutional and restoration regime change models owing to the small number of cases. Detailed results are available in the Supplemental Materials.

328. Other variables are held constant at the mean or modal values.

329. The second run of matching that included variables for buffer states and interstate war involvement produced one control case with a civil war, which was sufficient to render the bivariate relationship between institutional regime change and civil war insignificant.

330. I ran this analysis using the *rbounds* package in R, a statistical software program. Because *rbounds* is not compatible with *MatchIt*, genetic matching for this analysis was performed using the *Matching* program (Sekhon 2011).

331. Keele 2010, 10. Specifically, the upper bound of the 95 percent confidence interval for the effect of leadership regime change crosses 0.05 between 2.5 and 2.6, and exceeds 0.10 between 3.0 and 3.1. These results are available in the Supplemental Materials.

332. Instrumental variables must satisfy two conditions to be considered valid. The first is known as the identification restriction: the instrument must be sufficiently correlated with the independent variable to enable an estimate of its effect on the dependent variable with any degree of accuracy. The second is the exclusion restriction: the instrument must be a cause of the independent variable only, not the dependent variable. In other words, to be valid, an instrument cannot cause both the independent and dependent variables. In many situations, however, such an exogenous variable may not exist, and some analysts doubt the ability of a single set of equations to capture what is in reality often a complicated, multistep selection

procedure. On these points, see, respectively, Fortna 2008, 115; and Gilligan and Sergenti 2008, 90–91.

333. The significant complication this procedure introduces is that each civil war State B experiences in a given year appears in every dyad of which State B is a member in that year. For example, the Ugandan civil war that began in 1980 appears in all ten dyads (with the United States, Britain, France, Russia, DRC, Kenya, Tanzania, Rwanda, Sudan, and China) in which Uganda is State B in 1980. In other words, a model intended to predict the onset of civil war in Uganda in 1980 would predict the same civil war ten times. This problem will reduce the standard errors of the control variables but should not affect the regime change estimates because regime change occurs in only one of those dyads.

334. These results are available in the Supplemental Materials.

335. In the language of design-based inference, it would help "identify" the effect of regime change on civil war.

336. The full list is available in the Supplemental Materials.

337. O'Rourke 2018, 103, 109, and 117.

338. These results are available in the Supplemental Materials.

339. Successful regime changes occur in poorer countries that are more likely to have been defeated in interstate wars than failed covert regime changes. Yet the former take place more often in smaller and more democratic countries than the latter. Since these pairs of variables have opposite implications for the likelihood of civil war, it is unlikely that there is any overall bias.

4. Foreign-Imposed Regime Change and the Survival of Leaders

1. Scholars have generally deemphasized attributes that do not vary across individuals (such as human nature or cognitive biases) and embraced attributes that do, including leaders' foreign policy beliefs (Saunders 2011); attitudes toward risk (Levy 1992; Farnham 1995; McDermott 1998; Taliaferro 2004); identities (Bayram 2017; Herrmann 2017); gender (Caprioli 2000; Hudson et al. 2012; Horowitz, Stam, and Ellis 2015, 158–77); and various aspects of leaders' backgrounds, like education (Gift and Krcmaric 2017), foreign policy experience (Saunders 2017), military service (Betts 1977; Feaver and Gelpi 2002; Weeks 2014; Horowitz and Stam 2014), and rebel or revolutionary experience (Colgan 2010 and 2013; Fuhrmann and Horowitz 2015).

2. Bueno de Mesquita et al. 1999 and 2003.

3. Reiter and Stam 1998 and 2002; Bueno de Mesquita et al. 1999. Victory in war, unfortunately, does not necessarily translate into reelection, as President George H.W. Bush discovered to his chagrin in 1992.

4. Goemans 2000.

5. To avoid the possibility of removal and punishment at the hands of the adversary, democratic leaders have incentives to settle wars on moderately losing terms and to accept removal from office by the electorate as the lesser of two evils.

6. Goemans (2000, 45) refers to such strategies as "high variance"—they increase the likelihood of both total victory and catastrophic defeat.

7. Chiozza and Goemans 2011, 25.

8. Chiozza and Goemans 2011, 34.

9. Chiozza and Goemans 2011, 62–68.

10. All references, unless otherwise noted, are to Goemans 2008, 782.

11. See also Chiozza and Goemans 2011, 70. Contrary to the argument of his earlier work, however, Goemans finds that leaders of all regimes—not just mixed regimes—are more likely to be removed irregularly in the event that they lose a war (70).

12. Regime change also sometimes causes the security forces in the target state to disintegrate. Military disintegration, as documented in chapter 2, is highly conducive to the onset of armed resistance to the new regime, which in turn could elevate the new leader's risk of irregular removal. One of the cases I examine later in the chapter—Maximilian's tenure in Mexico—is a case of military disintegration. For the sake of simplicity, however, and to avoid turning one of my dependent variables (civil war) into an independent variable that explains another of my

dependent variables (leader survival), this chapter explicitly brackets the potential indirect effect of regime change on leader survival via military disintegration and civil war to focus on the direct effect of the problem of competing principals.

13. Lake 2016.

14. In some instances, my coding of whether a leader entered office in a foreign-imposed regime change diverges from that of *Archigos*. A list of such cases is available in the Supplemental Materials.

15. Balaguer's stint in office was also brief: he resigned on January 16, 1962, after about two months in power.

16. Figures derived from the leader-year data are available in the online Supplemental Materials.

17. Only two leaders put in power via restoration regime changes lost power irregularly, however.

18. The only difference between the leader-spell and leader-year data is that the reduction in the likelihood of irregular removal after restoration regime changes is significant in the latter but not in the former. As noted, however, this relationship is based on very small numbers.

19. Again, the only difference in the leader-spell data is that leaders empowered in restoration regime changes are less likely to leave office by regular means (although statistical significance is marginal).

20. One might wonder how the effect of restoration regime change could be significant when the confidence interval for its effect completely overlaps the effect of not having experienced a restoration. In the leader-spell data, the mean difference between the two effects is 998 days with a confidence interval of 216 to 1,780 days and a t-statistic of 2.50. Similarly, in the leader-year data, the mean difference is 1,141 days with a confidence interval of 182 to 1,824 days and a t-statistic of 2.40.

21. Results using the leader-year data for time to regular removal from office, available in the Supplemental Materials, are similar if more discernible. Although the differences in tenure between foreign-imposed and other leaders are larger, the combined regime change indicator and restoration regime change are the only two that are significant.

22. Box-Steffensmeier and Jones 2004.

23. These figures are available in the Supplemental Materials.

24. The difference between the two groups is larger and more significant in the leader-spell data than in the leader-year data, but the trend is the same.

25. The confidence intervals overlap much more in the leader-year data, which is not surprising given the shorter time period and smaller number of externally imposed leaders.

26. As with the results for regime change and irregular removal, the survivor curves generated by the leader-year dataset look similar but the confidence intervals overlap to a greater degree.

27. The curves produced by the leader-year data look quite similar but the difference between them is only intermittently significant.

28. The survivor curve based on the leader-year data diverges slightly from the one in figure 4.6c: in these data, for a little over two years, no leader brought to power in an institutional regime change lost office in a regular manner. Once the first such leader experienced a regular removal, however, the difference between the regime change and nonregime change curves is rendered insignificant.

29. In the leader-year data, the crossover point comes later, after slightly more than four years. In this dataset the difference between the two survival rates is never significant.

30. It is significant at the 90 percent level, however.

31. The difference between these effects across the two datasets previously manifested itself in the Kaplan-Meier survivor curves and suggests that leaders brought to power in institutional regime changes after 1918 have a better life expectancy in office than those empowered in this way from 1875 to 1918.

32. For this analysis, I classify the Dominican Republic, Nicaragua, Costa Rica, Panama, Iraq, and Afghanistan as less developed states, and West Germany, East Germany, Hungary, Czechoslovakia, Bulgaria, Romania, and Japan as more developed states.

33. This calculation excludes the irregular removals of leaders in the Baltic states in 1940 that followed Soviet institutional regime changes because the goal of these interventions from the beginning was annexation.

34. This allegation is made in the documentary *Murder in Kinshasa* by Marlene Rabaud and Arnaud Zajtman (2011).

35. Shtromas 1986.

36. Downes 2018.

37. Quoted in Raun 2001, 144.

38. Smith 2002, 24.

39. Raun 2001, 144–45.

40. On Latvia, see Smith 2002, 23–27; Šneidere 2005. On Lithuania, see Misiunas and Taagepera 1993, 18–22; van Voren 2011, 24–26.

41. The only other such case of which I am aware is Austria's Arthur Seyss-Inquart in 1938. On March 11, Hitler demanded that the pro-Nazi Seyss-Inquart be appointed chancellor in place of Kurt Schuschnigg. Seyss-Inquart was appointed on March 12 and the *Anschluss* of Germany and Austria was announced the following day. I do not code this as a case of foreign-imposed regime change given the near simultaneity of regime change and annexation, but the *Archigos* project does.

42. Germany occupied 48 percent of Poland, with the remainder going to the Soviet Union, which annexed its portion. Germany annexed half of its Polish territories and administered the remainder, known as the General Government, separately. In Czechoslovakia, the Germans renamed the Czech portion of the country the Protectorate of Bohemia and Moravia and annexed it; the Slovak part became a German puppet state.

43. The exception is Alexander von Falkenhausen in Belgium, who was arrested by the Germans after the July 20, 1944, assassination attempt on Hitler.

44. One additional case of a regime change reversed by a foreign power is Italy's occupation of Ethiopia (1936–41), ended by the British. *Archigos* also codes the restoration of Sheikh Jabir Al Ahmad Al Jabir Al Sabah as ruler of Kuwait by the US-led coalition in 1991 as a regime change reversal (Goemans, Gleditsch, and Chiozza 2009). I coded Iraq's conquest of Kuwait as a case of annexation rather than regime change.

45. Polyviou 1980, 155; Dodd 2010, 103.

46. On fears of Turkish intervention, see Dodd 2010, 103. To the embarrassment of the Greek junta, Makarios escaped capture and was whisked away by the British, initially to Malta and then to London.

47. Shaw and Shaw 1977, 431.

48. Mazower 1993, 70–71.

49. Mazower 1993, 120.

50. The ouster of the Trujillos sparked a transition that culminated in the inauguration of Juan Bosch in February 1963 in the country's first democratic elections. Bosch was soon overthrown in a military coup, however. Ironically, the United States would intervene in 1965 to prevent the restoration of the democratically elected Bosch to power for fear of his Leftist proclivities.

51. Gleijeses 1991, 351. After securing Árbenz's resignation, Díaz had warned some leading communists that they should seek refuge in foreign embassies lest they be arrested or killed (351). Díaz also permitted Árbenz to broadcast a resignation speech, in which the departing president attacked both Castillo Armas and the United States.

52. CIA officer Enno Hobbing, quoted in Schlesinger and Kinzer 1999, 206.

53. The Ambassador in Guatemala (Peurifoy) to the Department of State, July 7, 1954 (USDS 1983, doc. 498). The agreement established a five-man junta that added Castillo Armas and one of his supporters, Major Enrique Trinidad Oliva, to the existing trio. Monzón continued as president for the moment, but the deal called for a new president of the junta to be selected within two weeks. Unbeknown to Monzón, Peurifoy had paid the other two original junta members to resign, thereby ensuring that Monzón would be outvoted.

54. Baker 1965.

55. Edelman and Kenen 1989, 69–70.

56. Nelson 1983, 31–32.

57. Baker 1965, 21.

58. On Rivarola and the Paraguayan case, see Warren 1978; Lewis 1993. On Dacko and the Central African Republic, see Titley 1997; Baxter 2011.

59. Miller 2013, 266.

60. Some accounts blame the deaths on government troops who fired into the crowd, threw grenades, and crushed two children under their vehicles. Kahin 1987, 149; Kaiser 2000, 213; Jacobs 2006, 143. Other accounts blame the fatalities on a mysterious explosion and note that no one has ever been able to explain its origin. Hammer 1987, 114; Winters 1997, 29. The US ambassador, Frederick Nolting, eventually persuaded Diem to provide payments of $7,000 to the families of those killed in Hue. Jacobs 2006, 144.

61. Quoted in Karnow 1983, 281.

62. Kahin 1987, 149; Kaiser 2000, 214–18. For the US ultimatum to Diem, delivered by Nolting shortly before he left Saigon in August, see Winters 1997, 50–51.

63. Hammer 1987, 168.

64. Jacobs 2006, 153.

65. Kahin 1987, 152. The number of deaths is disputed, ranging from zero (Hammer 1987, 168) to several (Kahin 1987, 152) to several hundred (Jacobs 2006, 153).

66. Jacobs 2006, 153.

67. Telegram from the Embassy in Vietnam to the Department of State, August 24, 1963, 6:00 p.m. (USDS 1991a, doc. 274). Colonel Tung was commander of the Special Forces and closely allied with Nhu. All Vietnam documents cited herein are located in the *Foreign Relations of the United States* series.

68. See the conversation between General Tran Van Don, the recently appointed commander of the ARVN, and CIA officer Lucien Conein, related in Telegram from the Central Intelligence Agency Station in Saigon to the Agency, August 24, 1963, 6:45 p.m. (USDS 1991a, doc. 275). This was also the judgment of Diem's secretary of state and minister of defense, Nguyen Dinh Thuan. See Telegram from the Embassy in Vietnam to the Department of State, August 24, 1963, 11:00 a.m. (USDS 1991a, doc. 273).

69. Telegram from the Embassy in Vietnam to the Department of State, August 24, 1963, 11:00 p.m. (USDS 1991a, doc. 276).

70. Telegram from the Department of State to the Embassy in Vietnam, August 24, 1963, 9:36 p.m. (USDS 1991a, doc. 281).

71. This was the view of chairman of the Joint Chiefs of Staff General Maxwell Taylor, quoted in Jacobs 2006, 162.

72. The debate is well summarized in Kaiser 2000, 234–45. Key proponents of a coup were Lodge, Hilsman, Harriman, and Forrestal; opponents included Taylor, secretary of defense Robert McNamara, CIA director John McCone, and MACV commander General Paul Harkins.

73. According to the National Security Archive (2009), tapes of key meetings in the White House in late August show that even those officials who opposed an immediate coup were "united in the judgment that Vietnam would be lost if Ngo Dinh Nhu remained in the Saigon government."

74. Telegram from the Embassy in Vietnam to the Department of State, August 29, 1963, 4:00 p.m. (USDS 1991b, doc. 11).

75. Kaiser (2000, 246–47) argues that Kennedy chose a tougher line because he differed from his key advisers and "had concluded that Diem could not win the war on his present course."

76. Quoted in Kaiser 2000, 246 (italics in original).

77. Quoted in Office of the Secretary of Defense Vietnam Task Force (hereafter, Pentagon Papers) 2011a, 33. It would later emerge that this assessment of the military situation was quite overoptimistic. McNamara and Taylor ignored evidence that contradicted their positive message. Miller 2013, 300–301.

78. Pentagon Papers 2011a, 34.

79. Kahin 1987, 171. The generals further interpreted the recall on October 5 of CIA station chief John Richardson, whom they viewed as a supporter of the Ngo brothers, as encouragement for them to act (172–73).

80. Pentagon Papers 2011a, 41.

81. Kahin 1987, 168; Logevall 1999, 48–51, 63–64.

82. Quoted in Kahin 1987, 168.

83. Sullivan memo to Hilsman, October 3, 1963, quoted in Logevall 1999, 63. For Cooper's views, see Kahin 1987, 168–69.

84. Logevall 1999, 64.

85. Logevall 1999, 51.

86. Indeed, by the end, Kennedy did not fear a coup so much as a coup that failed. See Kaiser 2000, 265, 271–73.

87. For good accounts of the coup itself, see Hammer 1987, 284–301; Jacobs 2006, 173–81.

88. Minh sent General Mai Huu Xuan to pick up the Ngo brothers. As Seth Jacobs (2006, 179) recounts the story, "Minh turned to Captain Nguyen Van Nhung, who would accompany Xuan on this mission, and raised two fingers of his right hand. It was a signal to kill Diem and Nhu." See also Hammer 1987, 298; Winters 1997, 104.

89. Jacobs 2006, 180.

90. Moyar 2007, 277.

91. Logevall 1999, 64–65.

92. Logevall 1999, 80; Kaiser 2000, 290. On the disarray, confusion, and disintegration in the South after Diem's overthrow and their contribution to North Vietnam's decision to escalate the war in late 1963, see Elliott 2003, 194–96.

93. On the negative effects of this measure, see Catton 2002, 204.

94. Kaiser 2000, 259. On these reports, see 259–60, 268. According to the Pentagon Papers, "The overall statistical indicators had now begun to show deterioration dating back to the summer." Pentagon Papers 2011a, 63.

95. Karnow 1983, 324.

96. Quotes are from Winters 1997, 32, 66, and 244n3. The regime's energy was also sapped by infighting; many top military officers were replaced within a few weeks of the coup. Moyar 2007, 281.

97. It is not possible, however, to claim that Washington did not get what it wanted because the United States did not remove and replace Diem itself. US officials had known of the generals' plot for months and green-lighted it with the knowledge that Minh was its leader and probable successor to Diem.

98. Kahin 1987, 182.

99. As Kaiser (2000, 295) shows, there was some truth to Minh's assessment: Kaiser attributes the decrease in VC attacks starting in December 1963 in part to the removal of Diem. He writes: "In preceding months the Viet Cong had managed to take advantage of the Buddhist crisis to rally thousands of non-communist South Vietnamese to their cause. . . . Much of this support had evaporated after the coup, creating a possible political opportunity for the new government."

100. Kahin 1987, 185.

101. On the dire straits of the program in late 1963, see Catton 2002, 207.

102. Logevall 1999, 80.

103. Kahin 1987, 187.

104. Kahin 1987, 187.

105. Kahin 1987, 188; Kaiser 2000, 291–93.

106. Kaiser 2000, 293–94. The internal quote is from Pentagon Papers 2011c, 3.

107. Kahin 1987, 188.

108. Kahin 1987, 188–89; Logevall 1999, 81.

109. Kahin 1987, 189.

110. Quoted in Kahin 1987, 189. See also Winters 1997, 117.

111. Logevall 1999, 81.

112. Tho, quoted in Kahin 1987, 185.

113. Logevall 1999, 82–83.

114. Logevall 1999, 81.

115. Kaiser 2000, 290.

116. For Bundy's and Rostow's views, expressed in January 1964, see Kahin 1987, 191–92. For examples of McNamara's views, see Kaiser 2000, 291–92, 296.

117. Memorandum from the Secretary of Defense (McNamara) to President Johnson, December 21, 1963 (USDS 1991b, doc. 374). Ironically, after a brief onslaught following the coup, VC armed attacks declined precipitously in December and continued to decrease in the first three months of 1964. The total number of incidents, however, increased, as the VC changed tactics to rely more heavily on propaganda, sabotage, and terrorism. Kaiser 2000, 294–95.

118. Letter from the Director of Central Intelligence (McCone) to President Johnson, December 23, 1963 (USDS 1991b, doc. 375).

119. Quoted in Moyar 2007, 282.

120. Kahin 1987, 193–94.

121. Logevall 1999, 89.

122. Quoted in Logevall 1999, 89.

123. Logevall 1999, 90.

124. Kahin 1987, 183.

125. Kahin 1987, 190.

126. Memorandum from the Chairman of the Policy Planning Council (Rostow) to the Secretary of State, January 10, 1964 (USDS 1992, doc. 9).

127. Kahin 1987, 191.

128. Khanh initially retained Minh as a figurehead, but Minh went into exile in Thailand by the end of the year. Minh later returned to South Vietnam and briefly served as its last president as the country was overrun by the North Vietnamese.

129. Kahin 1987, 198.

130. Pentagon Papers 2011b, 27–28.

131. Kahin 1987, 197.

132. These three quotes appear in Kahin 1987, 201.

133. Kahin 1987, 199.

134. Pentagon Papers 2011b, 27.

135. Kahin 1987, 202. See also Logevall 1999, 101. According to the Pentagon Papers (2011b, 28), "Lodge sensed the intent of a coup, but evidently did not appreciate its imminence; for although he said he expected that there would be more to report later, he decided not to alter [sic] the government of Vietnam and had confided the news from Wilson only to Harkins and [CIA station chief] DeSilva."

136. Logevall 1999, 99.

137. Logevall 1999, 105.

138. Sater 1986; Farcau 2000.

139. Maximilian's execution was the subject of the famous painting by Édouard Manet in 1868 that appears on the cover of this book.

140. Although the Mexican emperor presided over a cabinet of ministers, there was no legislature, making Maximilian's regime an absolute rather than a constitutional monarchy.

141. Mexico, not having a regular system of taxation, relied on customs duties to fund the government. Much of the country's debt had been racked up by the Conservative government during the War of the Reform (1858–60) against the Liberals. McAllen 2014, 45, 54. Upon winning the war, Juárez at first agreed to repay Mexico's debt but later changed his mind because his government had played no part in accumulating it. In June, the Mexican Congress voted to stop paying interest on its foreign loans. Ridley 1992, 63.

142. Hanna and Hanna 1971, 38.

143. Quoted in Cunningham 2001, 215.

144. The European powers, notes Cunningham (2001, 58), "were not indifferent to the restoration of a strong and lasting political regime in Mexico."

145. Spain sent the largest contingent (6,000); France contributed 2,000 troops and 500 Zouaves, while England sent 700 Marines. Hanna and Hanna 1971, 40.

146. Quoted in Cunningham 2001, 78.

147. Cunningham 2001, 78. This episode illustrates the principal-agent problem that governments experience in controlling their diplomats abroad. The PA problem was exacerbated in the era before modern communications when it took weeks or months for policymakers'

instructions to reach local agents, giving the latter plenty of slack to follow their own initiative, which sometimes did not match the objectives of their political masters back home.

148. Cunningham 2001, 79.

149. More accurately, the prime minister, Lord Palmerston, and the foreign minister, Lord Russell, were not averse to seeing Maximilian on the Mexican throne but did not want to achieve that object with British troops since they doubted such a regime could be sustained. Cunningham 2001, 70–71.

150. Perhaps influencing his judgment was the fact that Prim's uncle by marriage was a member of Juárez's cabinet. Jurien complained that while he was prepared "to walk in agreement with Spain, I could not suspect that Spain would not be in agreement with herself." Quoted in Cunningham 2001, 80.

151. Instructions to Jurien, dated November 11, 1861, quoted in Robertson 1940, 181. The coastal region around Veracruz was also an unhealthy area so advancing inland to higher elevations made sense for the good of the troops.

152. The loans in question came from a Swiss banker named Jecker. Miramón borrowed a large sum from Jecker in 1859 but had received only a small fraction of the money by the time the war ended. Juárez had announced at the time the loans were made that his government would not honor them, given that the money was being used to fight against him. When Jecker's bank collapsed in 1860, bondholders demanded repayment, and their cause was taken up by the French. On this episode, see Hanna and Hanna 1971, 36; Cunningham 2001, 81–82; McAllen 2014, 45. Napoleon's half-brother, the Duc de Morny, was one of Jecker's investors; some speculate that the reason the French included the Jecker loans among their demands was to create a pretext for intervention in Mexico. Cunningham 2001, 81–82.

153. Quoted in Ridley 1992, 82.

154. Hanna and Hanna 1971, xiii–xiv.

155. Napoleon to Forey, July 3, 1862, quoted in Hanna and Hanna 1971, 80. British leaders shared this view. For Palmerston's concurrence, see Cunningham 2001, 70.

156. Bresler 1999, 309.

157. Black 1974.

158. McAllen 2014, 50, 51.

159. Hanna and Hanna 1971, 42.

160. Ridley 1992, 94.

161. General Lorencez to minister of war Randon, April 25, 1862, quoted in Ridley 1992, 95. The fact that the American Civil War would prevent US counterintervention further contributed to the perception that conquering Mexico would a simple task.

162. Willard-Foster 2018, 6.

163. Palmerston speech in the House of Commons, February 6, 1862, quoted in Cunningham 2001, 72.

164. Ridley 1992, 63–64.

165. Ridley 1992, 67. See also Corti 1928; Bock 1966; McAllen 2014.

166. Cunningham 2001, 52. British prime minister Palmerston also thought that "a monarchy was probably the best and most stable form of government for Mexico, and that Maximilian would be a good candidate"; he simply doubted its feasibility (53).

167. Napoleon to Lorencez, June 1862, quoted in Cunningham 2001, 116.

168. Napoleon to Maximilian, June 7, 1862, quoted in Cunningham 2001, 116.

169. McAllen 2014, 50.

170. Cunningham 2001, 52; McAllen 2014, 56–57.

171. Ridley 1992, 68; McAllen 2014, 58.

172. Ridley 1992, 68–69.

173. On British views of Napoleon's policy, see Russell to Lord Crampton (British minister to Spain), February 2, 1862, quoted in Cunningham 2001, 72. The British, however, changed their views once the French revealed their demands upon arriving in Mexico. Ridley 1992, 83.

174. Lorencez, letter to Randon, April 26, 1862, quoted in Cunningham 2001, 115. For evidence that other French officers believed that the goal of the intervention was to install Maximilian on the Mexican throne, see Cunningham 2001, 71–72.

175. Cunningham 2001, 148. Saligny also had personal reasons for remaining in Mexico that would obviously be facilitated by a French occupation (149).

176. Of course, the type of regime change that is implemented is important for my theory but is secondary to the question of whether or not regime change occurred.

177. Cunningham 2001, 51.

178. Cunningham 2001, 52.

179. Cunningham 2001, 87. Napoleon recalled his first military commander in Mexico, Admiral Jurien, two months later for agreeing to further negotiations with Juárez rather than moving directly on Mexico City (109–10).

180. Saligny's ultimatum was so outrageous that it convinced the British it had been designed to be rejected, which, in Lord Russell's words, would "afford thereby a *casus belli* for the allies." Ridley 1992, 83.

181. Ridley 1992, 90. See also McAllen 2014, 65.

182. Quoted in Cunningham 2001, 128.

183. Napoleon to Forey, July 3, 1862, quoted in Hanna and Hanna 1971, 78.

184. Dabbs 1963, 134.

185. Maximilian to Rechberg (Austrian foreign minister), quoted in Ridley 1992, 79.

186. Cowley to Russell, January 17, 1862, quoted in Cunningham 2001, 70.

187. Russell to Cowley, January 18, 1862, quoted in Cunningham 2001, 70.

188. Russell to Bloomfield, February 13, 1862, quoted in Cunningham 2001, 75.

189. Crampton to Russell, January 30, 1862, quoted in Hanna and Hanna 1971, 101.

190. Wyke to Russell, December 29, 1861, quoted in Cunningham 2001, 66–67.

191. Hanna and Hanna 1971, 42.

192. Jurien to Thouvenel, February 1, 1862, quoted in Hanna and Hanna 1971, 45.

193. Prim to Napoleon, March 17, 1862, quoted in Ridley 1992, 89–90.

194. Hanna and Hanna 1971, 45.

195. Hanna and Hanna 1971, 69.

196. McAllen 2014, 74.

197. Lorencez to Randon, July 22, 1862, quoted in Cunningham 2001, 123.

198. Lorencez to Randon, July 22, 1862, quoted in Hanna and Hanna 1971, 70.

199. As Napoleon wrote to Forey on August 3, 1862, "Wherever our flag waves you must be absolute master." Quoted in Ridley 1992, 134.

200. On these episodes, see Ridley 1992, 146–47; McAllen 2014, 104–5.

201. Cunningham 2001, 165.

202. Memoirs of French General du Barail, quoted in Cunningham 2001, 165.

203. According to McAllen (2014, 118) French troops peaked at 38,000, but figures in Dabbs (1963, 86, 112) indicate a peak size of closer to 30,000.

204. The views of the paymaster of French forces in Mexico, Ernest Louet, summarized in Cunningham 2001, 131.

205. Dabbs 1963, 104. At its height, the empire controlled twenty of twenty-four Mexican provinces and 93 percent of the population. Ridley 1992, 186.

206. Hanna and Hanna 1971, 108, 109.

207. Hanna and Hanna 1971, 143; Ridley 1992, 179; McAllen 2014, 150.

208. McAllen 2014, 153.

209. The Liberals' opposition to foreign rule might make it sound like nationalism was the key driver of resistance to Maximilian. There is no doubt that Mexican Liberals were intensely nationalistic, yet the Mexican Conservatives who supported the monarchy were equally nationalistic. Nationalism thus does not uniquely predict opposition to Maximilian in this case.

210. Cunningham 2001, 182.

211. Cunningham 2001, 182.

212. Hanna and Hanna 1971, 126.

213. Dabbs 1963, 182.

214. Dabbs 1963, 119.

215. Dabbs 1963, 126.

216. McAllen 2014, 157.

217. On these measures, see Dabbs 1963, 114, 122–23; Ridley 1992, 211–12.

218. Ridley 1992, 212. There is no doubt that Maximilian was a poor choice to lead Mexico and thus that adverse selection plays a role in this case. It is unclear, however, whether a more skilled leader could have overcome the difficult conditions he faced.

219. Ridley 1992, 189; Cunningham 2001, 184–85.

220. McAllen 2014, 232. The United States also threatened Austria to prevent Franz-Josef from sending Austrian volunteers to Mexico.

221. Dabbs 1963, 158. Cunningham argues that Napoleon was genuinely interested in regenerating Mexico rather than imperial expansion. She also contends that Napoleon's repeated claims that he backed a monarchy only if that was the expressed desire of the Mexican nation were sincere. In her account, the French commitment to Mexico was always limited and would be withdrawn when the Mexican Empire could stand on its own. As Napoleon learned that the monarchy was not nearly as popular as Saligny had led him to believe, he became "determined that his commitment would not be increased," stressed building an indigenous army, and eventually accelerated a withdrawal that was going to occur quite independently of rising tensions in Europe or US pressure. Cunningham 2001, 154 (quote), 164, 181, 197–99.

222. McAllen 2014, 260.

223. Ridley 1992, 228–29.

224. General François Castelnau, an emissary sent by Napoleon to Mexico in 1866 to assess the situation, recommended that Maximilian abdicate, but he ultimately refused.

225. McAllen 2014, 320, 328.

226. In a blistering denunciation sent to Paris the previous September, Bazaine predicted accurately that the "continued existence of the Mexican Empire was not a question of years but of 'days and hours.' The temper of Mexicans was not monarchist; temporarily inactive Liberals would at French withdrawal rise 'as one man against the Emperor who has no prestige.'" Bazaine to Randon, September 27, 1866, quoted in Hanna and Hanna 1971, 283.

227. German aircraft also ferried 13,500 men of the Army of Africa to Spain in the war's opening months.

228. Beevor 2006, 427–28.

229. Ruiz 2007, 97.

230. Ruiz 2005, 171; 2007, 97.

231. Ruiz 2005, 184, 171. According to the historian Paul Preston, even Heinrich Himmler was shocked by the scale of Francoist repression during a visit in October 1940. Preston 1993, 392.

232. Ruiz 2005, 190.

233. One study estimates that no more than 8,000 guerrillas were active in Spain from 1939 to 1952. Marco 2015, 179.

234. Richards 2012, 41.

235. Marco 2015, 186, 187.

236. This estimate is based on the following accounts. Official government figures released in 1968 put the number of "bandits" killed at 2,166, with 258 deaths among the Spanish civil guard (Téllez 1996). Téllez, however, estimates that 1,000 civil guards died during the conflict. Finally, Marco (2015, 148) argues that the guerrillas committed "less than 1,000" murders of civilians from 1939 to 1952. This case should thus arguably be coded as a civil war.

237. Goemans, Gleditsch, and Chiozza 2009.

238. On the coup in Iran and the CIA's role in it, see Wilber 1954; Kinzer 2003; Gasiorowski and Byrne 2004.

239. Zahedi, a retired general, led the coup that ousted Mossadegh, after which the shah named him prime minister.

240. Gasiorowski 1991, 86–87.

241. Kinzer 2003, 194–95.

242. Gasiorowski and Byrne 2004, 257.

243. Gasiorowski and Byrne 2004, 257.

244. Gasiorowski 1991, 86–89.

245. The group was allowed to hold a rally in 1962, but after 100,000 people showed up, the shah reinstated the ban on it (Kinzer 2003, 195).

246. Behrooz 2001, 364.

247. Gasiorowski and Byrne 2004, 257–58.

248. These countries also funded the organization.

249. Gasiorowski 1991, 153.

250. Gasiorowski 1991, 153.

251. Quoted in Faroughy 1974, 18. See also Keddie 2003, 136–37. In an investigation of trials of political prisoners carried out in the 1970s, Amnesty International did not identify a single case in which a defendant was acquitted. Amnesty International 1976, 4–5; Gasiorowski 1991, 156.

252. Keddie 2003, 136.

253. Gasiorowski 1991, 152.

254. In addition to SAVAK, three other components of the Iranian repression apparatus included the national police (which operated exclusively in urban areas and served to break up opposition rallies), the gendarmerie (which operated in rural areas and served to suppress tribal uprisings), and the armed forces. A fifth arm, the Imperial Inspectorate, was created to monitor the other security organizations and put down plots against the shah by top officials. Gasiorowski 1991, 151–55.

255. Gasiorowski and Byrne 2004, 257.

256. Bill 1988, 151.

257. Klement Gottwald (Czechoslovakia), Josip Tito (Yugoslavia), Georgi Dimitrov (Bulgaria), Mátyás Rákosi (Hungary), Walter Ulbricht (East Germany), and Bolesław Bierut (Poland) were all trained in the Soviet Union, as were the heads of the communist parties in France (Maurice Thorez) and Italy (Palmiro Togliatti).

258. Applebaum 2012, 65–66.

259. Applebaum 2012, 49.

260. Applebaum 2012, xxvii, 61.

261. Applebaum 2012, 194.

262. This is the combined vote and number of seats for the Czechoslovak and Slovak communist parties.

263. Applebaum 2012, xxviii.

264. Applebaum 2012, 115.

265. Applebaum 2012, 110, 111.

266. Goemans, Gleditsch, and Chiozza 2009.

267. Goemans 2008.

268. Box-Steffensmeier and Jones 2004.

269. On the use of competing risks models in this area, see Goemans 2008; Chiozza and Goemans 2011.

270. Goemans 2008.

271. Goemans 2008.

272. The sources for Goemans's data are described in Chiozza and Goemans 2004, 608, 617–18, and Chiozza and Goemans 2011, 206–13.

273. I modified the entry variable, however, so that it does not include foreign entry into office.

274. Tables with the complete results may be viewed in the Supplemental Materials.

275. The effect of institutional regime change appears to be particularly sensitive to the inclusion of regime type and especially economic and trade variables in models 4 and 5.

276. Roeder 2001; Colgan 2010.

277. Ross 2012.

278. It also includes several US officials who temporarily administered some of these countries, such as General Matthew Ridgway (Douglas MacArthur's successor as commander of US forces occupying Japan) and General Tommy Franks, Jay Garner, and Paul Bremer, each of whom led US occupation forces in Iraq.

279. This group consisted of Léon Mba (Gabon, 1964), restored by France; Ntsu Mokhehle (Lesotho, 1994), restored by South Africa; Caabi El-Yachroutu (Comoros, 1995), restored by France (El-Yachroutu was the interim president until Said Mohamed Djohar, overthrown by Bob Denard in September, returned to office); Denis Sassou-Nguesso (Republic of Congo, 1997),

restored by Angola; and Ahmad Tejan Kabbah (Sierra Leone, 1998), restored by Nigeria, Ghana, and Guinea.

280. More variables in this analysis violate the nonproportional hazards assumption, including regime change, institutional regime change, and restoration regime change. These variables are interacted with the log of time and included in the models. For complete tables, see the Supplemental Materials.

281. These results may be viewed in the Supplemental Materials.

282. These results are available in the Supplemental Materials.

283. Tables with balance statistics are available in the Supplemental Materials.

284. The combined regime change variable significantly reduces time to irregular removal and increases time to regular removal (significant at the 90 percent level of confidence).

5. Foreign-Imposed Regime Change and Interstate Relations

1. This chapter draws on material previously published in Downes and O'Rourke 2016. I acknowledge Lindsey O'Rourke's contribution to this joint work and thank her for our fruitful collaboration on this and related projects, which has greatly influenced my thinking on the consequences of regime change.

2. Su 2017–18.

3. Because there is such a well-developed literature on the origins of interstate conflict, I omit a discussion of the literature from the main body of the chapter. In the chapter appendix I highlight some of the prominent variables I will need to control for in my quantitative analysis.

4. On these alternatives, see Lo, Hashimoto, and Reiter 2008.

5. Lo, Hashimoto, and Reiter 2008. Indeed, regime changes by democracies that forcibly democratize a defeated belligerent are a near-sufficient condition for peace (732). For a related study on the effect of imposed democracy on regional conflict, see Enterline and Greig 2005.

6. Fortna 2004.

7. Lo, Hashimoto, and Reiter 2008, 720–21.

8. Lo, Hashimoto, and Reiter 2008, 727.

9. Lo, Hashimoto, and Reiter (2008) omit Luxembourg and Denmark, governments that were overthrown by Germany in 1940 and 1943, respectively, and restored by the Allies in 1945. Other cases of regime change and occupation from the World War II era that are left out because they did not occur in an interstate war between the intervener and target include Italy-Albania (1939) and Germany-Hungary (1944).

10. Lo, Hashimoto, and Reiter 2008, 725.

11. Three of these six cases (50 percent) experienced civil wars during the period of occupation.

12. Full restoration of Selassie's authority proceeded slowly, however, as the British—despite recognizing Ethiopia's sovereignty in January 1942—continued to play a major role in governing the country. See Sbacchi 1979, 35–36.

13. Sarkees and Wayman 2010.

14. Koulischer 1946, 175; Vanover 2009.

15. The *New York Times* estimated in 2019 that the cost of training the Afghan army and police forces was $87 billion. See Almukhtar and Nordland 2019.

16. In some cases, this interest divergence is compounded because interveners also ask the target leader to take actions that make the target more vulnerable to other external threats.

17. Byrne 2004, xv. Some might argue that although the 1953 coup in Iran contributed to anti-American sentiments during the 1979 revolution, from the US perspective, the coup may still be considered a foreign policy success because it achieved other national security goals—namely, preventing the pro-Soviet Tudeh Party from gaining power and facilitating twenty-six years of cooperative relations with the shah's regime. See Fearon 2011. This interpretation overestimates the benefits of intervention by inflating the threat posed by the Tudeh Party and underestimates its costs by minimizing the long-term negative effects of the coup on US-Iranian

relations. For accounts that reach similar conclusions, see Bill 1988; Kinzer 2003; Abrahamian 2013.

18. Some would argue, however, that such regime changes fail to produce governments in the target that share the interveners' interests. This may be true, but shared regime type could still prevent any disputes from escalating to armed hostilities. Compare Bueno de Mesquita and Downs 2006 and Willard-Foster 2018.

19. Peceny, Beer, and Sanchez-Terry 2002, 23–24.

20. O'Rourke 2018, 11. O'Rourke found that over 70 percent of US covert regime change attempts during the Cold War were publicly revealed by the target during the operation.

21. These types of pairs are known in the quantitative IR literature as "politically relevant" dyads.

22. Moreover, one of the data sources that Lo, Hashimoto, and Reiter (2008) use in their study includes only thirty-three regime changes that ended wars during this period, while the other includes thirty-seven. See, respectively, Werner 1996 and Goemans, Gleditsch, and Chiozza, 2009. Including regime changes that occurred outside of interstate wars substantially increases the total. For instance, Downes and Monten count seventy regime changes in the twentieth century, or roughly double the number in Lo, Hashimoto, and Reiter's study. See Downes and Monten 2013, 111. In this book I count eighty-four individual leader changes in the twentieth century.

23. The initial regime change occurred in 1912 and was followed by additional interventions in 1914 and 1916.

24. Hungary, however, fought the Soviet Union eleven years after the Soviets imposed communist rule in the country.

25. Maria was the daughter of Pedro IV, who abdicated the Portuguese throne in 1826 to remain emperor of Brazil shortly after the death of his father, King João VI. Pedro arranged for his brother Miguel to become regent in Maria's name despite his absolutist sympathies. Miguel seized power only a few months later and proclaimed himself king. Pedro eventually abdicated the Brazilian crown and returned to help restore his daughter. In this task he was aided by Britain, France, and Spain, which formed the Quadruple Alliance in 1834. British and Spanish military forces made crucial contributions to the defeat of the Miguelist forces and the restoration of Maria to the throne.

26. The term enduring rivals connotes states involved in a prolonged competition over a scarce resource in which the use of force is likely. There is obviously a good deal of overlap between enduring rivalries and territorial disputes. France and Germany in the nineteenth century, for example, were both enduring rivals and had an active territorial dispute (over Alsace-Lorraine). On enduring rivalries, see Goertz and Diehl 1992; on territorial disputes, see Huth 1996.

27. This result is consistent with O'Rourke's finding that failed US covert regime changes during the Cold War significantly increased the chance of a MID between the United States and its target. See O'Rourke 2018, 85–88.

28. Estimates were generated using CLARIFY (Tomz, Wittenberg, and King 2003). All other variables in the models are held constant at their means or modes. See the chapter appendix for details on additional variables in these models.

29. Careful readers may note that the 95 percent confidence intervals for the presence and absence of leadership regime change overlap, but this does not mean that the effect is not significant. Model 2 in table 5.3 (in the chapter appendix) shows that leadership regime change is significant at $p < 0.05$, and the 95 percent confidence intervals of the change in predicted probability calculated by CLARIFY (shown in the Supplemental Materials) are strictly positive.

30. The former are taken from Bailey, Strezhnev and Voeten 2017, the latter from Signorino and Ritter 1999.

31. Bailey, Strezhnev, and Voeten 2017, 431.

32. Bailey, Strezhnev, and Voeten 2017, 432.

33. The figure depicts marginal effects from a random effects ordinary least squares (OLS) regression with a lagged dependent variable and control variables. Using fixed effects changes

the sign of some types of regime change but all remain insignificant. Full regression results are available in the chapter appendix.

34. Voting data, for example, are missing for most of the Eastern European states in the decade after they experienced Soviet regime changes at the end of World War II. It is likely, therefore, that the effect of institutional regime change is an underestimate.

35. As in figure 5.4, this figure depicts results from a random effects OLS regression with a lagged dependent variable and controls.

36. It is worth noting, however, that after matching, the positive effect of institutional regime change on alliance portfolio similarity between interveners and targets falls by more than half and loses statistical significance.

37. Using fixed effects, the size of this negative effect increases and becomes significant at the 95 percent level of confidence. See the chapter appendix.

38. Although it is clear in retrospect that this is a case of foreign-imposed regime change, at the time the Rwandan leadership went to great lengths to conceal its military involvement. As I demonstrate below, however, the regime change plot was essentially hatched in Kigali, and Rwandan military forces participated extensively from beginning to end. This Rwandan presence was thus impossible to hide and was widely reported as it unfolded. For examples of this reporting, see Pottier 2002, 88.

39. Stearns 2011, 55. On state weakness in Zaire, in general, see Atzili 2006–07, 156–61.

40. The literature on the Rwandan genocide is substantial. For exemplars, see Prunier 1995; Des Forges 1999; Power 2002, 329–89; Straus 2006.

41. See the figures in Terry 2002, 158; Lischer 2005, 78–79; Prunier 2009, 25; Reyntjens 2009, 45. Most of the remaining Hutu refugees (about half a million) fled to Tanzania, with a smaller number ending up in Burundi.

42. On October 31, 1994, for instance, ex-FAR soldiers killed thirty-six people in Gisenyi in northwest Rwanda. See Prunier 2009, 26; Stearns 2011, 29.

43. Mobutu frequently hosted high-ranking leaders of the *génocidaire* regime. As Gérard Prunier (2009, 28) reports, "The former Rwandese leadership had free run of the country." Zairian military forces also made little attempt to disarm the FAR and other Hutu militants as they entered the country (Human Rights Watch 1995, 11; Terry 2002, 160–61; Lischer 2005, 85). Zairian authorities, moreover, looked the other way as the Hutu leadership imported arms from abroad, and in some cases facilitated these shipments (Human Rights Watch 1995, 6–15; Terry 2002, 161–63; Winter 2004, 111–12).

44. Human Rights Watch 1995, 5. See also Prunier 2009, 28.

45. Reyntjens 1999, 242. See also International Crisis Group 1998, 4; Thom 1999, 95; Longman 2002, 133–34; Nzongola-Ntalaja 2002, 225; Prunier 2009, 67; Reyntjens 2009, 46–47, 51.

46. On the conflicts in the Kivus that endangered ethnic Tutsis, see Prunier 2009, 46–58; Reyntjens 2009, 13–23.

47. The RPA and the rebels pursued the refugees who fled west, intent on wiping them out. On this murderous pursuit, see Prunier 2009, 143–48; Reyntjens 2009, 80–101. Prunier (2009, 148) estimates that some 300,000 Hutu refugees died.

48. The four groups were the Parti de la Révolution du Peuple (Party of the People's Revolution, headed by Kabila), Conseil National de Résistance pour la Démocratie (National Council of Resistance for Democracy), Mouvement Révolutionnaire pour la Libération du Zaïre (Revolutionary Movement for the Liberation of Zaire), and Alliance Démocratique des Peuples (Democratic Alliance of the People).

49. Reyntjens 2009, 104. On Kabila as a "Zairian face" for the Rwandan invasion, see also Rosenblum 1998, 194; Dunn 2002, 56; Turner 2007, 5; Stearns 2011, 87; Turner 2013, 16; Roessler 2016, 247. Kabila became president of the AFDL in January 1997 after the death in "mysterious circumstances" of the group's initial military commander, André Kisase Ngandu (Nzongola-Ntalaja 2002, 226). Before Kabila became the figurehead of the Rwandan invasion, his main claim to fame was hosting Che Guevara when the Cuban revolutionary came to fight in Congo in 1965 (Prunier 2009, 114).

50. Reyntjens 2009, 107.

51. Prunier 2009, 115.

52. Kabila was a member of the Luba tribe from Katanga.

53. Pomfret 1997. For articles in the Rwandan press that support the interpretation that regime change was premeditated, see Prunier 2009, 68; Reyntjens 2009, 45. One author claims that Rwanda intended from the outset to "push on all the way to the capital" and oust Mobutu (Van Reybrouck 2014, 419). Prunier (2009, 67) also mentions various discussions among African leaders about toppling Mobutu.

54. International Crisis Group 1998, 6; Thom 1999, 116. Reyntjens (2009, 51) also finds no direct evidence from before the war that Rwanda intended to eliminate Mobutu.

55. The principal reason that each of these countries supported or participated in military operations against Mobutu was to eliminate rebel groups that found safe haven (and in some cases material support) in Zaire: União Nacional para a Independência Total de Angola (National Union for the Total Independence of Angola) for Angola, Conseil National pour la Défense de la Démocratie—Forces pour la Défense de la Démocratie (National Council for the Defense of Democracy—Forces for the Defense of Democracy) for Burundi, and Allied Democratic Forces for Uganda. Other countries that supported the anti-Mobutu coalition included Zambia, Zimbabwe, Ethiopia, and Eritrea. See Reyntjens 1999, 242; 2009, 58–66; Stearns 2011, 51–54, 285–86.

56. See International Crisis Group 1998, 7.

57. Prunier 2009, 152, 151, 152, respectively. On the lack of regime institutionalization and the personalization of Kabila's rule, see also Reyntjens 2009, 156; Ngolet 2011, 6–7; Van Reybrouck 2014, 434–35.

58. Reyntjens 2009, 161.

59. Van Reybrouck 2014, 435. See also Reyntjens 2009, 158–59.

60. Turner 2007, 38. Some might contend that Kabila's incompetence or authoritarian nature was to blame for his domestic opposition. I argue below, however, that his poor governing choices and repressive responses to challenges were largely a product of his weak position, which in turn was a consequence of how he came to power. See Stearns 2011, 170–71.

61. Prunier 2009, 172.

62. Prunier 2009, 173; Reyntjens 2009, 174.

63. The Army for the Liberation of Rwanda was itself a further iteration of the Rassemblement pour la Rétour des Réfugiés et la Démocratie au Rwanda (Rally for the Return of the Refugees and Democracy in Rwanda), which was founded in April 1995, and would later evolve into the Forces Démocratiques pour la Libération du Rwanda (Democratic Forces for the Liberation of Rwanda). On the relationships among these groups, see Romkema 2007, 32–33.

64. Reyntjens 2009, 146.

65. Stearns 2011, 181.

66. Kisangani 2012, 134.

67. As Van Reybrouck (2014, 438) summarizes, "Every Tutsi was seen as Rwandan and every Rwandan as an occupier."

68. Kisangani 2012, 133–34.

69. Reyntjens 2009, 148. François Ngolet (2011, 12) agrees: "Tutsi hegemony was not well received by the rest of the Zairians. They felt humiliated and frequently accused the Tutsi of a triumphalist and arrogant attitude."

70. Kisangani 2012, 135. "Mai Mai" is a generic term that refers to local self-defense militias in Congo.

71. Osita Afoaku (2002, 113) notes that "Kabila maintained a narrow base of domestic support" that included only two non-Tutsi elements: the so-called *kadogos*—the child soldiers recruited by the AFDL during its drive to Kinshasa—and natives of Kabila's home province of Katanga.

72. Salehyan 2009, 152; Ngolet 2011, 12.

73. See Rosenblum 1998, 194.

74. Ngolet 2011, 12. Kabila's resistance to the attempts by the United Nations to investigate reports of human rights violations by the RPA in the campaign to overthrow Mobutu also constitutes powerful evidence of his reliance on Rwanda. On this episode, see Dunn 2002, 58; Ngolet 2011, 4–8; Van Reybrouck 2014, 437.

75. Reyntjens 2009, 167.
76. Cited in Reyntjens 2009, 167n87.
77. Van Reybrouck 2014, 439. For similar assessments, see Afoaku 2002, 113; Dunn 2002, 61; Longman 2002, 138; Prunier 2009, 177–78; Ngolet 2011, 12.
78. Prunier 2009, 177.
79. Kisangani 2012, 139.
80. Prunier 2009, 176.
81. Ngolet 2011, 11–17.
82. Roessler 2016, 254.
83. Roessler 2016, 254.
84. Roessler 2016, 256–58.
85. This move, however, sparked a mutiny, forcing a reversal of the decision. See Prunier 2009, 176; Ngolet 2011, 16.
86. Dunn 2002, 62.
87. Roessler 2016, 258, 259.
88. Roessler 2016, 261.
89. Stearns 2011, 183.
90. Roessler 2016, 261.
91. Kisangani 2012, 142. See also Roessler 2016, 262.
92. Roessler 2016, 261.
93. Roessler 2016, 262.
94. Roessler 2016, 262.
95. Kabila expelled more than 10,000 Rwandans and Banyamulenge from the armed forces. See Salehyan 2009, 152.
96. Longman 2002, 138.
97. Turner 2013, 17, 54.
98. Analysts prioritizing security concerns include International Crisis Group 1998, 2, 21; Afoaku 2002, 114. Of course, factors other than security fears contributed to the attack, such as ethnic solidarity with Congolese Tutsi, the domestic unifying effects of a foreign war, economic interests in the DRC, and high levels of confidence among RPF leaders. See Longman 2002, 130–33, 134–38.
99. Nzongola-Ntalaja 2002, 227. See also Dunn 2002, 62.
100. Prunier 2009, 183–84. Confirming the Rally's lack of independence, Jason Stearns (2011, 209) writes, "Major leadership changes were imposed by Kigali, and all military operations were led by Rwandan commanders in the field."
101. For an eyewitness account from one of the pilots of the hijacked jets, see French 1998.
102. Prunier 2009, 186.
103. Prunier 2009, 186. Burundi also again contributed to the anti-Kabila cause.
104. Prunier 2009, 187–93.
105. Prunier 2009, 210–11.
106. Rabaud and Zajtman 2011. Prunier (2011, 249–55), by contrast, attributes Kabila's murder to despair and anguish among his child soldiers, the *kadogo*, who, after much mistreatment, turned against their master. Angola was complicit since it knew of the plot but did nothing to stop it.
107. In Roessler's (2016) terms, Kabila accepted a war in the periphery of the country to escape an even more dangerous coup at the center.
108. For mortality estimates, see Roberts et al. 2003; Coghlan et al. 2006.
109. Sater 2007, 306.
110. Farcau 2000, 181.
111. On this case, see Warren 1978; Lewis 1993.
112. On the mismatched preferences in this case between Minh and his American patrons, see Kahin 1987, 182–94.
113. Titley 1997, 159.
114. Baxter 2011, 30.
115. Titley 1997, 159–60.

116. Kerevel 2006.
117. Munro 1964, 441–44.
118. Gleijeses 1991, 351–57.
119. O'Rourke 2018, 199–210.
120. Downes and O'Rourke 2019, 40.
121. Gall 2006; Glanz and Rohde 2006; Rosenberg 2013. What the Americans did not understand was that Karzai needed to distribute patronage to various warlords and power brokers to secure his hold on power domestically, which both caused aid money to disappear and hindered his ability to control the country. On patronage networks in Afghanistan, see Biddle 2012.
122. Human Rights Watch 2008, 3.
123. Associated Press 2007; Human Rights Watch 2008, 18, 21; Lakshman 2011; Rosenberg and Cooper 2012; Al Jazeera America 2013.
124. Sieff 2014b.
125. Quoted in Downes and O'Rourke 2019, 49.
126. Sieff 2014a, quoted in Downes and O'Rourke 2019, 49.
127. Biddle, Friedman, and Shapiro 2012.
128. Petit 2020, 213. See also Robinson 2008, 259; Gerges 2016, 105.
129. Brigadier General Nasser al-Hiti, commander of the Second ("Muthanna") Brigade of the Sixth Division of the Iraqi Army, quoted in Oppel 2008.
130. Oppel 2008; Nordland and Rubin 2009.
131. Petit 2020, 167. The SOIs in Abu Ghraib had a similar experience (273).
132. Sky 2015, 250. See also Gordon and Trainor 2012, 592–93; Gerges 2016, 106.
133. Gordon and Trainor 2012, 593. See also Fadel 2008. For the 40 percent figure, see Harari 2010, 2. There are disputes about the numbers involved. For example, contrary to a claim by the US military in September 2008 that 15,000 SOIs had been hired into the Iraqi security forces, others report that only 600 had received training. Wing 2008. For a different set of numbers for fall 2007, see Robinson 2008, 320.
134. Morse 2012.
135. Petit 2020, 173.
136. Petit 2020, 221–22. On payment irregularities, see also Gordon and Trainor 2012, 592.
137. Oppel 2008.
138. Rasheed and Susman 2008; Petit 2020, 275.
139. Petit 2020, 169, 154.
140. Gordon and Trainor 2012, 591; Petit 2020, 169.
141. Sky 2015, 283; Petit 2020, 218–19.
142. Gerges 2016, 111.
143. Quoted in Gordon and Trainor 2012, 592.
144. Gerges 2016, 114–15.
145. Chulov 2010; Garcia-Navarro 2010; Morse 2012.
146. Warrick 2015, 296–98; Gerges 2016, 119.
147. This case draws heavily on material originally prepared for Downes and O'Rourke 2017–18 and eventually posted online as Supplemental Material.
148. Matsusaka 2001, 258.
149. Boorman, Cheng, and Howard 1967, 117.
150. Sheridan 1983, 305.
151. It turned out that Feng had been bribed by the Japanese to switch sides, both to preserve Chang Tso-lin and return Duan Qirui to power.
152. Sheridan 1983, 316.
153. Sheridan 1983, 317. For a similar description of Chang's ascension to power, see Nathan 1983, 282–83.
154. It might even be possible to code Chang Tso-lin as the *effective* leader of China from December 1926. On December 1, Chang accepted the title of commander-in-chief of the combined and reorganized northern armies, now known as the Ankuochün, or "Pacify the Country Army." On December 27, Chang "made his ceremonial entry into Peking, over roads sprin-

kled with yellow earth in the manner of the Ch'ing emperors." McCormack 1977, 209. See also Itoh 2016, 56.

155. Ross and Spuler 1977, 129; Lentz 1999, 84–85; Cahoon n.d.; Schemmel n.d.

156. McCormack 1977, 212, 234. See also Suleski 2002, 177.

157. Advocate of Peace through Justice 1927, 473; Moore 1927.

158. Nathan 1983, 256.

159. Nathan 1983, 257.

160. Fenby 2008, 145.

161. Paine 2012, 19.

162. Su (2017–18, 173, emphasis added) implies as much when she writes that *"when he was killed*, Chang was not a state leader, but a Manchurian warlord."

163. Dull 1952, 454. See also Jansen 1975, 375; McCormack 1977, 215; Ienaga 1978, 59; Sheridan 1983, 317; Eto 1986, 113; Dreyer 1995, 150; Itoh 2016, 63; Kwong 2017, 135.

164. Abend 1928.

165. Wilbur 1983, 710.

166. Wilbur 1983, 710.

167. Bonavia 1995, 84.

168. Abend 1928.

169. Furuya 1981, 252.

170. Chang the younger officially switched the flags in what is referred to as the Northeastern Flag Replacement. Itoh 2016, 71, 73.

171. Ross and Spuler 1977, 2: 129; Lentz 1999, 84–85. Interestingly, the Lentz volume erroneously states that Chang's train was bombed on *October 4* rather than *June 4*, and thus codes his tenure as ending when he eventually died on October 10. It seems obvious that Lentz meant June when he wrote October, especially since Lentz also states that "Chang abandoned Peking to go to Mukden in early June 1928" (85).

172. Multiple sources also show that a new premier (Tan Yankai) did not take office until October. Ross and Spuler 1977, 2: 131; Cahoon n.d.; Schemmel n.d.

173. Goemans, Gleditsch, and Chiozza 2009; Ellis, Horowitz, and Stam 2015. Interestingly, the *Archigos* collection, which relies heavily on Lentz, reproduces his error regarding the timing of Chang's departure from office, dating it as October 10, 1928. See Goemans, Gleditsch, and Chiozza 2016.

174. It is also worth noting that my definition of regime change does not specify that regime change must be ordered by civilian leaders. To be considered an act of state policy, regime change must be authorized by the effective leadership of the country. I show that owing to pathologies of Japanese civil-military relations, the military was the effective leader of Japan.

175. Drea 2009, 164.

176. Dull 1952; Jansen 1975, 306; McCormack 1977, 247–48; Ienaga 1978, 59; Wilbur 1983, 710; Drea 2009, 164–65; Itoh 2016, 64.

177. McCormack 1977, 246; Wilbur 1983, 709.

178. McCormack 1977, 247.

179. McCormack 1977, 248.

180. For a detailed account of this event, see Dull 1952.

181. Ienaga 1978, 36. Ienaga also notes that the "service ministries remained the special preserve of professional military men. No civilian control was ever allowed. . . . Even a party cabinet—that is, a cabinet formed by the majority party in the Diet, the pattern from the 1920s on—had to name military men to the service posts. There could be no civilian or Diet-member cabinets" (35–36).

182. The following account is based on Dull 1952; Drea 2009, 165–66; Itoh 2016, 64–66. These accounts are not always consistent with one another. I have done my best to represent the key events accurately.

183. Drea 2009, 166.

184. Itoh 2016, 65.

185. Itoh 2016, 65–66.

186. Boorman, Cheng, and Howard 1967, 117; Matsusaka 2001, 258.
187. Shai 2012, 10.
188. Eto 1986, 113.
189. Quoted in Dull 1952, 455.
190. Eto 1986, 114.
191. Dull 1952, 457.
192. Jansen 1975, 376; Kristof 2001; Itoh 2016, 73. Chang Hsüeh-liang ultimately fell out of favor with Chiang Kai-shek as a result of the Xian incident in 1936, in which Chang kidnapped Chiang and held him hostage until he agreed to form a united front with the communists to resist Japanese aggression. Chiang's previous policy had been to fight the communists first and the Japanese second.
193. McCormack 1977, 248.
194. Jansen 1975, 306.
195. Wilson 1991, 28.
196. Jordan 1976, 168.
197. Ienaga 1978, 59.
198. Barnhart 1987, 31. For other, similar, assessments beyond those already cited, see Dreyer 1995, 151; Shai 2012, 17.
199. Iriye 1960, 34; Boorman, Cheng, and Howard 1967, 62; Wang 1969, 84.
200. Iriye 1960, 35.
201. Iriye 1960, 35–36; Wang 1969, 92.
202. Boorman, Cheng, and Howard 1967, 63.
203. Boorman, Cheng, and Howard 1967, 63.
204. Iriye 1960, 36.
205. Iriye 1960, 36. See also Wang 1969, 97.
206. Boorman, Cheng, and Howard 1967, 63. See also Iriye 1960, 37–38.
207. Iriye 1960, 39. See also Wang 1969, 101–4.
208. Iriye 1960, 41.
209. Both quotations are from Iriye 1960, 39–40 and 40, respectively.
210. Iriye 1960, 42.
211. Shai 2012, 24.
212. On this episode, see Castillo and Downes forthcoming; Gerzhoy 2015.
213. On how the nuclear and territorial control issues were linked, see Volpe 2017, 534–37.
214. The dataset was constructed using the EUGene program (Bennett and Stam 2000).
215. If the dependent variable has no chance—or virtually no chance—of occurring in a case, then that case does not belong in the analysis. See Goertz and Mahoney 2004. To be clear, the politically relevant criteria do exclude some instances of conflict, such as Cuba's participation in wars in Angola and Ethiopia in the mid-1970s.
216. On these rules and their flaws, see Fazal 2007, 243–58.
217. The two exceptions are the removal of Salvadoran president Andrés del Valle by Guatemala during the First Central American War in 1876 (Scheina 2003, 256–57), and the death of Guatemala's president Justo Rufino Barrios in another war against El Salvador in 1885 (257).
218. A good example is Honduras, which suffered regime changes by Guatemala in 1855, 1863, 1872, 1874, and 1876—and fought multiple conflicts against its tormentor, at least two of which qualify as interstate wars.
219. Specifically, I use the Dyadic MID Dataset v.3.1.
220. The MID dataset also has many disadvantages, particularly when used to test theories about phenomena it was not designed for, such as threat effectiveness. See Downes and Sechser 2012.
221. War is defined according to the Correlates of War criteria as a militarized conflict that exceeds 1,000 battle deaths. Sarkees and Wayman 2010.
222. Because some MIDs involve only the threat or display of force, I also tested my models on only those MIDs that escalated to the use of force or war. See the section on robustness tests below and the online Supplemental Materials.

223. Methodologists have recently questioned the assumption of statistical independence across dyads. See, for example, Neumayer and Plümper 2010b; Erikson, Pinto, and Rader 2014; Aranow, Samii, and Assenova 2015; Cranmer and Desmarais 2016. For a measured defense of dyads, see Poast 2016. I implement some suggested remedies for this potential problem below in the section on robustness checks.

224. Bailey, Strezhnev, and Voeten 2017.

225. Signorino and Ritter 1999.

226. Weeks 2014, 42.

227. Unless otherwise noted, these variables were generated by EUGene (Bennett and Stam 2000). My indicator for democracy is drawn from Boix, Miller, and Rosato 2012. A correlation matrix of the independent variables, available in the Supplemental Materials, indicates that multicollinearity is not a problem. Importantly, none of the regime change variables is highly correlated with any of the control variables.

228. King and Zeng 2001.

229. See Neumayer and Plümper 2010a; and Aranow, Samii, and Assenova 2015. I thank Peter Aranow and Cyrus Samii for assistance implementing their method.

230. In this case, the coefficients for the three types of regime change are identical to those shown in model 2 for all types of aggregate source and aggregate target contagion. These results can be found in the Supplemental Materials.

231. Using fixed effects, the coefficient for leadership regime change is reduced by half and loses significance ($p = 0.39$). Shortening the treatment effect of leadership regime change to five years produces statistically significant results at the 95 percent level using both random and fixed effects. See the Supplemental Materials.

232. On matching, see Ho et al. 2007; Diamond and Sekhon 2013.

233. Different matched analyses produced different results. Several runs of genetic matching generated treatment effects for leadership regime change from zero to 0.10. Rosenbaum sensitivity analysis performed after genetic matching, moreover, suggests that the effect of leadership regime change is not robust to the possibility of unobserved covariates. Numerous runs of nearest neighbor matching, however, which also produced extremely good improvement in balance (greater than 99 percent), consistently returned significant treatment effects of between 0.11 and 0.13, roughly doubling the likelihood of militarized disputes. All of these results are available in the Supplemental Materials.

234. Bailey, Strezhnev and Voeten 2017. The dyadic affinity score is calculated using Signorino and Ritter's (1999) S indicator. Results using three category vote data (yes, no, abstain) produce similar results, as does a dependent variable that measures change in these scores from year-to-year. See the Supplemental Materials.

235. Balance statistics are available in the Supplemental Materials.

Conclusion

1. Morgan, Bapat, and Kobayashi 2014, 542-43.

2. Art 2003b, 6.

3. Coercive violence during war is intended to compel target concessions without having to defeat its military forces in detail. It often takes the form of siege, blockade, or strategic bombing. Pape 1996; Downes 2008a.

4. Lo, Hashimoto, and Reiter 2008.

5. Democratic patrons also meddle overtly and covertly in their protégés' elections to ensure that acceptable leaders retain power. See Levin 2016; O'Rourke 2018.

6. Pei and Kasper 2003; Bellin 2004-05; Brownlee 2007; Downes and Monten 2013.

7. Biddle and Zirkle 1996; Quinlivan 1999; Biddle 2004; Castillo 2014; Talmadge 2015; Lyall 2020. For examples of quantitative work in this area, see Narang and Talmadge 2017; Lyall 2020.

8. Edelstein 2004, 2008.

9. Pei and Kasper 2003; Bellin 2004-05; Brownlee 2007; Enterline and Greig 2008a; Downes and Monten 2013.

10. Lake 2016, 1. In practice, nation building and state building appear to be closely related, if not identical, phenomena.

11. Enterline and Greig 2008b. Most imposed polities are states emerging from colonialism; less than 20 percent consist of regime changes in existing states (893–95).

12. Enterline and Greig 2008b, 895.

13. Downes 2008b; Peic and Reiter 2011; Downes and Monten 2013; Downes and O'Rourke 2016, 2019; Zachary, Deloughery, and Downes 2017; O'Rourke 2018. The exception is Lo, Hashimoto, and Reiter 2008.

14. Owen 2010.

15. Panama (1990) also successfully democratized after the United States ousted and apprehended Manuel Noriega.

16. According to *Archigos* v.2.9, 2,433 leaders took office via regular procedures and 549 gained power via (domestic) irregular methods. In this study I code roughly one hundred foreign-imposed leaders, some of which were coded as taking power through domestic irregular means by *Archigos*. In contrast, *Archigos* codes only forty-one leaders as foreign imposed. See Goemans, Gleditsch, and Chiozza 2009, 275.

17. Downes and O'Rourke 2016, 2019; O'Rourke 2018.

18. Willard-Foster 2018.

19. It should be noted that the United States did pursue covert regime change in Syria by arming the Free Syrian Army (O'Rourke 2018, 2, 233).

20. Gent 2008; Sullivan and Karreth 2015; Jones 2017.

21. Behrooz 2004, 106.

22. Behrooz 2004, 104.

23. On Arévalo's admiration for Roosevelt, see Schlesinger and Kinzer 1999, 34. For the CIA's assessment that Árbenz's policies were "patterned after New Deal reforms," see Central Intelligence Agency 1952.

24. It is an interesting thought experiment, however, to imagine a scenario in which the United States intervened militarily in Afghanistan to destroy Al Qaeda and apprehend Osama Bin Laden without overthrowing the Taliban.

25. Suskind 2006.

26. Summarized from MacDonald 2014, 72–84.

27. MacDonald 2014, 87.

28. MacDonald 2014, 88.

29. The light footprint approach was itself a reaction to the perceived failure of the Soviets' heavy footprint approach in Afghanistan in the 1980s.

30. Democracies, of course, did support brutal dictators during the Cold War. Were the international environment ever to return to a situation of bipolar competition—say, with China—democracies may once again feel compelled to resort to such measures.

31. The major exceptions are O'Rourke 2018 and Willard-Foster 2018.

32. O'Rourke 2018.

33. Willard-Foster 2018.

34. O'Rourke 2018; Willard-Foster 2018.

35. Saunders 2011.

36. Indeed, US democracy promotion has been so varied that it has spawned books on both its global mission to spread democracy and its proclivity for supporting right-wing dictators. Compare Smith 1994 and Schmitz 1999 and 2006.

37. For the former estimate, see Pape 1997, 93; for the latter, see Morgan, Bapat, and Kobayashi 2014, 546. See also Hufbauer, Schott, and Elliott 2007, who estimate a 34 percent success rate.

38. Biersteker, Tourinho, and Eckert 2016, 236.

39. Blechman and Kaplan 1978; Petersen 1986; George and Simons 1994; Art 2003a; Sechser 2011.

40. Sechser 2010, 2018; Haun 2015; Pfundstein-Chamberlain 2016.

41. Willard-Foster 2018. I say "especially" because power, as just noted, is negatively correlated with compellence success.

Works Cited

Abbas, Hassan. 2014. *The Taliban Revival: Violence and Extremism on the Pakistan-Afghanistan Frontier*. New Haven, CT: Yale University Press.

Abend, Hallett. 1928. "Peking Unharmed as Northern Hosts Pour Out of City." *New York Times*, June 4, 1928. https://www.nytimes.com/1928/06/04/archives/peking-unharmed-as-northern-hosts-pour-out-of-city-iron-discipline.html.

Abrahamian, Ervand. 2013. *The Coup: 1953, The CIA, and the Roots of Modern U.S.-Iranian Relations*. New York: New Press.

Advocate of Peace through Justice. 1927. "Chang Tso-lin's New Position." *Advocate of Peace through Justice* 89 (8): 473–74.

Afoaku, Osita. 2002. "Congo's Rebels: Their Origins, Motivations, and Strategies." In *The African Stakes of the Congo War*, edited by John F. Clark, 109–28. New York: Palgrave Macmillan.

Alexander, Don W. 1974. "Repercussions of the Breda Variant." *French Historical Studies* 8 (3): 459–88.

Al Jazeera America. 2013. "Karzai Blasts NATO on 12th Anniversary of Afghan War." October 7, 2013. http://america.aljazeera.com/articles/2013/10/7/karzai-pessimisticaboutprospectsfordealwithnato.html.

Almukhtar, Sarah, and Rod Nordland. 2019. "What Did the U.S. Get for $2 Trillion in Afghanistan?" *New York Times*, December 9, 2019. https://www.nytimes.com/interactive/2019/12/09/world/middleeast/afghanistan-war-cost.html.

Amnesty International. 1976. *Amnesty International Briefing: Iran*. November 1, 1976. https://www.amnesty.org/en/documents/mde13/001/1976/en/.

Applebaum, Anne. 2012. *Iron Curtain: The Crushing of Eastern Europe, 1944–1956*. New York: Doubleday.

Aranow, Peter M., Cyrus Samii, and Valentina A. Assenova. 2015. "Cluster-Robust Variance Estimation for Dyadic Data." *Political Analysis* 23 (4): 564–77.

Armstrong, Anne. 1961. *Unconditional Surrender: The Impact of the Casablanca Policy upon World War II*. New Brunswick, NJ: Rutgers University Press.

Art, Robert J. 2003a. "Coercive Diplomacy: What Do We Know?" In *The United States and Coercive Diplomacy*, edited by Robert J. Art and Patrick M. Cronin, 359–420. Washington, DC: United States Institute of Peace.

——. 2003b. "Introduction." In *The United States and Coercive Diplomacy*, edited by Robert J. Art and Patrick M. Cronin, 3–20. Washington, DC: United States Institute of Peace.

Associated Press. 2007. "Karzai Blasts U.S. on Civilian Deaths." June 23, 2007. https://www.presstelegram.com/2007/06/23/karzai-blasts-us-on-civilian-deaths/.

Atzili, Boaz. 2006–07. "When Good Fences Make Bad Neighbors: Fixed Borders, State Weakness, and International Conflict." *International Security* 31 (3): 139–73.

Avant, Deborah D. 1994. *Political Institutions and Military Change: Lessons from Peripheral Wars*. Ithaca, NY: Cornell University Press.

Avilés, William. 2005. "The Democratic-Peace Thesis and U.S. Relations with Colombia and Venezuela." *Latin American Perspectives* 32 (3): 33–59.

Avirgan, Tony, and Martha Honey. 1982. *War in Uganda: The Legacy of Idi Amin*. Westport, CT: Lawrence Hill.

Axelrod, Robert. 1967. "Conflict of Interest: An Axiomatic Approach." *Journal of Conflict Resolution* 11 (1): 87–99.

Axelrod, Robert, and Robert O. Keohane. 1985. "Achieving Cooperation under Anarchy: Strategies and Institutions." *World Politics* 38 (1): 226–54.

Azimi, Fakhreddin. 2008. *The Quest for Democracy in Iran: A Century of Struggle against Authoritarian Rule*. Cambridge, MA: Harvard University Press.

Bailey, Michael A., Anton Strezhnev, and Erik Voeten. 2017. "Estimating Dynamic State Preferences from United Nations Voting Data." *Journal of Conflict Resolution* 61 (2): 430–56.

Baker, George W., Jr. 1965. "Woodrow Wilson's Use of the Non-recognition Policy in Costa Rica." *The Americas* 22 (1): 3–21.

Ballard, John R. 1998. *Upholding Democracy: The United States Military Campaign in Haiti, 1994–1997*. Westport, CT: Praeger.

Banks, Arthur S., and Kenneth A. Wilson. 2020. *Cross-National Time-Series Data Archive*. https://www.cntsdata.com/.

Barfield, Thomas. 2010. *Afghanistan: A Cultural and Political History*. Princeton, NJ: Princeton University Press.

Barnhart, Michael A. 1987. *Japan Prepares for Total War: The Search for Economic Security, 1919–1941*. Ithaca, NY: Cornell University Press.

Bar-Siman-Tov, Yaacov. 1980. *The Israeli-Egyptian War of Attrition, 1969–1970*. New York: Columbia University Press.

Baxter, Peter. 2011. *France in Centrafrique: From Bokassa and Operation Barracuda to the Days of EUFOR*. Solihull: Helion.

Bayram, A. Burcu. 2017. "Due Deference: Cosmopolitan Social Identity and the Psychology of Legal Obligation in International Politics." *International Organization* 71 (S1): S137–63.

Beach, Derek, and Rasmus Brun Pedersen. 2019. *Process-Tracing Methods: Foundations and Guidelines*. 2nd ed. Ann Arbor: University of Michigan Press.

Beck, Neil, Jonathan N. Katz, and Richard Tucker. 1998. "Taking Time Seriously: Time-Series-Cross-Section Analysis with a Binary Dependent Variable." *American Journal of Political Science* 42 (4): 1260–88.

Becker, Elizabeth. 1998. *When the War Was Over: Cambodia and the Khmer Rouge Revolution*. New York: PublicAffairs.

Becker, Jo, and Scott Shane. 2016. "Hillary Clinton, 'Smart Power' and a Dictator's Fall." *New York Times*, February 27, 2016. https://www.nytimes.com/2016/02/28/us/politics/hillary-clinton-libya.html.

Beevor, Antony. 2006. *The Battle for Spain: The Spanish Civil War, 1936–1939*. New York: Penguin.

Behrooz, Maziar. 2001. "Tudeh Factionalism and the 1953 Coup in Iran." *International Journal of Middle East Studies* 33 (3): 363–82.

——. 2004. "The 1953 Coup in Iran and the Legacy of the Tudeh." In *Mohammad Mossadeq and the 1953 Coup in Iran*, edited by Mark J. Gasiorowski and Malcolm Byrne, 102–25. Syracuse, NY: Syracuse University Press.

Belasco, Amy. 2014. *The Cost of Iraq, Afghanistan, and other Global War on Terror Operations since 9/11*. Washington, DC: Congressional Research Service.

Bellin, Eva. 2004–05. "The Iraq Intervention and Democracy in Comparative Perspective." *Political Science Quarterly* 119 (4): 595–608.

Bennett, Andrew, and Jeffrey T. Checkel, eds. 2015. *Process Tracing: From Metaphor to Analytic Tool*. Cambridge: Cambridge University Press.

Bennett, D. Scott, and Allan C. Stam. 2000. "EUGene: A Conceptual Manual." *International Interactions* 26 (2): 179–204.

Bensahel, Nora, Olga Oliker, Keith Crane, Richard R. Brennan Jr., Heather S. Gregg, Thomas Sullivan, and Andrew Rathmell. 2008. *After Saddam: Prewar Planning and the Occupation of Iraq*. Santa Monica, CA: RAND Corporation.

Bergen, Peter L. 2011. *The Longest War: The Enduring Conflict between American and Al-Qaeda*. New York: Free Press.

Berger, Daniel, William Easterly, Nathan Nunn, and Shanker Satyanath. 2013. "Commercial Imperialism? Political Influence and Trade during the Cold War." *American Economic Review* 103 (2): 863–96.

Berman, Eli, and David A. Lake. 2019. *Proxy Wars: Suppressing Violence through Local Agents*. Ithaca, NY: Cornell University Press.

Berman, Eli, David A. Lake, Gerard Padró i Miquel, and Pierre Yared. 2019. "Principals, Agents, and Indirect Foreign Policies." In *Proxy Wars: Suppressing Violence through Local Agents*, edited by Eli Berman and David A. Lake, 1–27. Ithaca, NY: Cornell University Press.

Bermeo, Nancy. 2016. "On Democratic Backsliding." *Journal of Democracy* 27 (1): 5–19.

Betts, Richard K. 1977. *Soldiers, Statesmen, and Cold War Crises*. Cambridge, MA: Harvard University Press.

Biddle, Stephen. 2002. *Afghanistan and the Future of Warfare: Implications for Army and Defense Policy*. Carlisle, PA: US Army War College.

——. 2004. *Military Power: Explaining Victory and Defeat in Modern Battle*. Princeton, NJ: Princeton University Press.

——. 2012. "Salvaging Governance Reform in Afghanistan." Washington, DC: Council on Foreign Relations Policy Innovation Memorandum No. 16.

Biddle, Stephen, Jeffrey A. Friedman, and Jacob N. Shapiro. 2012. "Testing the Surge: Why Did Violence Decline in Iraq in 2007?" *International Security* 37 (1): 7–40.

Biddle, Stephen, Julia Macdonald, and Ryan Baker. 2018. "Small Footprint, Small Payoff: The Military Effectiveness of Security Force Assistance." *Journal of Strategic Studies* 41 (1–2): 89–142.

Biddle, Stephen, and Robert Zirkle. 1996. "Technology, Civil-Military Relations, and Warfare in the Developing World." *Journal of Strategic Studies* 19 (2): 171–212.

Biersteker, Thomas, Marcos Tourinho, and Sue Eckert. 2016. "The Effectiveness of United Nations Targeted Sanctions." In *Targeted Sanctions: The Impacts and Effectiveness of United Nations Action*, edited by Thomas J. Biersteker, Sue E. Eckert, and Marcos Tourinho, 220–47. Cambridge: Cambridge University Press.

Bill, James A. 1988. *The Eagle and the Lion: The Tragedy of American-Iranian Relations.* New Haven, CT: Yale University Press.

Black, Shirley. 1974. "Napoleon III and the French Intervention in Mexico: A Quest for Silver." PhD diss., University of Oklahoma.

Blechman, Barry M., and Stephen S. Kaplan. 1978. *Force without War: U.S. Armed Forces as a Political Instrument.* Washington, DC: Brookings Institution.

Bloch, Marc. 1968. *Strange Defeat: A Statement of Evidence Written in 1940.* New York: Octagon.

Bock, Carl H. 1966. *Prelude to Tragedy: The Negotiation and Breakdown of the Tripartite Convention of London, October 31, 1861.* Philadelphia: University of Pennsylvania Press.

Boix, Carles. 2008. "Economic Roots of Civil Wars and Revolutions in the Contemporary World." *World Politics* 60 (3): 390–437.

Boix, Carles, Michael Miller, and Sebastian Rosato. 2012. "A Complete Data Set of Political Regimes, 1800–2007." *Comparative Political Studies* 46 (12): 1523–54.

Bolton, John. 2019. "We Must Avoid a 'Diplomatic Waterloo' with Iran." *Washington Times*, July 10, 2019. https://www.washingtontimes.com/news/2015/jun/17/regime-change-in-iran-we-must-avoid-a-diplomatic-w/.

Bonavia, David. 1995. *China's Warlords.* New York: Oxford University Press.

Boorman, Howard L., Joseph K. H. Cheng, and Richard C. Howard, eds. 1967. *Biographical Dictionary of Republican China.* Vol. 1. New York: Columbia University Press.

Box-Steffensmeier, Janet M., and Bradford S. Jones. 2004. *Event History Modeling: A Guide for Social Scientists.* Cambridge: Cambridge University Press.

Brambor, Thomas, William Robert Clark, and Matt Golder. 2006. "Understanding Interaction Models: Improving Empirical Analysis." *Political Analysis* 14 (1): 63–82.

Braumoeller, Bear F. 2004. "Hypothesis Testing and Multiplicative Interaction Terms." *International Organization* 58 (4): 807–20.

Bresler, Fenton. 1999. *Napoleon III: A Life.* London: HarperCollins.

Brockett, Charles D. 2005. *Political Movements and Violence in Central America.* Cambridge: Cambridge University Press.

Brooks, Risa A. 2008. *Shaping Strategy: The Civil-Military Politics of Strategic Assessment.* Princeton, NJ: Princeton University Press.

Brown, Michael E. 1996. "The Causes and Regional Dimensions of Internal Conflict." In *The International Dimensions of Ethnic Conflict*, edited by Michael E. Brown, 571–601. Cambridge, MA: MIT Press.

Brownlee, Jason. 2007. "Can America Nation-Build?" *World Politics* 59 (2): 314–40.

Bueno de Mesquita, Bruce, and George W. Downs. 2006. "Intervention and Democracy." *International Organization* 60 (3): 627–49.

Bueno de Mesquita, Bruce, James D. Morrow, Randolph M. Siverson, and Alastair Smith. 1999. "An Institutional Explanation of the Democratic Peace." *American Political Science Review* 93 (4): 791–807.

Bueno de Mesquita, Bruce, Alastair Smith, Randolph M. Siverson, and James D. Morrow. 2003. *The Logic of Political Survival.* Cambridge, MA: MIT Press.

Bush, George W. 2002. "President Bush Outlines Iraqi Threat." October 7, 2002. https://georgewbush-whitehouse.archives.gov/news/releases/2002/10/20021007-8.html.

——. 2005. "Address to the Nation on the War on Terror from Fort Bragg, North Carolina." June 28, 2005. https://www.presidency.ucsb.edu/documents/address-the-nation-the-war-terror-from-fort-bragg-north-carolina.

Byman, Daniel, and Sarah E. Kreps. 2010. "Agents of Destruction? Applying Principal-Agent Analysis to State-Sponsored Terrorism." *International Studies Perspectives* 11 (1): 1–18.

Byrne, Malcolm. 2004. "Introduction." In *Mohammad Mossadeq and the 1953 Coup in Iran,* edited by Malcolm Byrne and Mark. J. Gasiorowski, xiii–xxiv. Syracuse, NY: Syracuse University Press.

Cahoon, Ben M. n.d. *WorldStatesmen.org.* http://www.worldstatesmen.org.

Calder, Bruce J. 1984. *The Impact of Intervention: The Dominican Republic during the U.S. Occupation of 1916–1924.* Austin: University of Texas Press.

Caprioli, Mary. 2000. "Gendered Conflict." *Journal of Peace Research* 37 (1): 51–68.

Castillo, Jasen J. 2014. *Endurance and War: The National Sources of Military Cohesion.* Stanford, CA: Stanford University Press.

Castillo, Jasen J., and Alexander B. Downes. Forthcoming. "Loyalty, Hedging, or Exit: How Weaker Alliance Partners Respond to the Rise of New Threats." *Journal of Strategic Studies.* DOI: 10.1080/01402390.2020.1797690, published online, June 30, 2020.

Catton, Philip E. 2002. *Diem's Final Failure: Prelude to America's War in Vietnam.* Lawrence: University Press of Kansas.

Cederman, Lars-Erik, Kristian Skrede Gleditsch, and Halvard Buhaug. 2013. *Inequality, Grievance, and Civil War.* Cambridge: Cambridge University Press.

Cederman, Lars-Erik, Nils B. Weidmann, and Kristian Skrede Gleditsch. 2011. "Horizontal Inequalities and Ethnonationalist Civil War." *American Political Science Review* 105 (3): 478–95.

Cederman, Lars-Erik, Andreas Wimmer, and Brian Min. 2010. "Why Do Ethnic Groups Rebel? New Data and Analysis." *World Politics* 62 (1): 87–119.

Central Intelligence Agency. 1952. "Personal Political Orientation of President Arbenz/Possibility of a Left-Wing Coup." Information Report 00-B-57327, October 10, 1952.

Chan, Sewell. 2015. "Ahmad Chalabi, Iraqi Politician Who Pushed for U.S. Invasion, Dies at 71." *New York Times,* November 3, 2015. https://www.nytimes.com/2015/11/04/world/middleeast/ahmad-chalabi-iraq-dead.html?_r=0.

Chanda, Nayan. 1986. *Brother Enemy: The War after the War.* New York: Macmillan.

Chandler, David. 1992. *A History of Cambodia.* Boulder, CO: Westview.

Chandrasekaran, Rajiv. 2006. *Imperial Life in the Emerald City: Inside Iraq's Green Zone.* New York: Alfred A. Knopf.

Chang, Pao-Min. 1985. *Kampuchea between China and Vietnam.* Singapore: Singapore University Press.

Chen, King C. 1987. *China's War with Vietnam, 1979: Issues, Decisions, and Implications*. Stanford, CA: Hoover Institution Press.

Cheney, Dick. 2002. "Vice President Speaks at VFW 103rd National Convention." White House, August 28, 2002. https://georgewbush-whitehouse.archives.gov/news/releases/2002/08/20020826.html.

Chiozza, Giacomo. 2013. "Managing Difficult Allies: Successor Leaders and the Domestic Sources of Patron Influence." Unpublished manuscript, Vanderbilt University.

Chiozza, Giacomo, and H. E. Goemans. 2004. "International Conflict and the Tenure of Leaders: Is War Still *Ex Post* Inefficient?" *American Journal of Political Science* 48 (3): 604–19.

———. 2011. *Leaders and International Conflict*. Cambridge: Cambridge University Press.

Chulov, Martin. 2010. "Sons of Iraq Turned the Tide for the US: Now They Pay the Price." *The Guardian*, May 13, 2010. https://www.theguardian.com/world/2010/may/13/sons-of-iraq-withdrawal-rebels.

Clark, George B. 2001. *With the Old Corps in Nicaragua*. Novato, CA: Presidio.

Clark, John F. 1998. "Democracy Dismantled in Congo." *Current History* 97 (619): 234–37.

Clarke, Richard A. 2004. *Against All Enemies: Inside America's War on Terror*. New York: Free Press.

Clausewitz, Carl von. 1976. *On War*. Translated and edited by Michael Howard and Peter Paret. Princeton, NJ: Princeton University Press.

Clement, Christopher I. 2005. "Confronting Hugo Chavez: United States 'Democracy Promotion' in Latin America." *Latin American Perspectives* 32 (3): 60–78.

Clodfelter, Micheal. 2008. *Warfare and Armed Conflicts: A Statistical Encyclopedia of Casualty and other Figures, 1494–2007*. 3rd ed. Jefferson, NC: McFarland.

CNN. 2002. "Top Bush Officials Push Case against Saddam." cnn.com. September 8, 2002. https://www.cnn.com/2002/ALLPOLITICS/09/08/iraq.debate/.

Cockburn, Andrew, and Patrick Cockburn. 1999. *Out of the Ashes: The Resurrection of Saddam Hussein*. New York: HarperCollins.

Coghlan, Benjamin, Richard J. Brennan, Pascal Ngoy, David Dofara, Brad Otto, Mark Clements, and Tony Stewart. 2006. "Mortality in the Democratic Republic of Congo: A Nationwide Survey." *The Lancet* 367 (9504): 44–51.

Cohen, Dara Kay. 2016. *Rape during Civil War*. Ithaca, NY: Cornell University Press.

Colgan, Jeff D. 2010. "Oil and Revolutionary Governments: Fuel for International Conflict." *International Organization* 64 (4): 661–94.

———. 2013. *Petro-aggression: When Oil Causes War*. Cambridge: Cambridge University Press.

Coll, Steve. 2018. *Directorate S: The C.I.A. and America's Secret Wars in Afghanistan and Pakistan*. New York: Penguin.

Collard-Wexler, Simon. 2013. "Understanding Resistance to Foreign Occupation." Paper presented at the Annual Meeting of the American Political Science Association, Chicago, IL.

Collard-Wexler, Simon, Constantino Pischedda, and Michael G. Smith. 2014. "Does Foreign Occupation Cause Suicide Attacks?" *Journal of Conflict Resolution* 58 (4): 625–57.

Collier, Paul. 2000. "Doing Well Out of War." In *Greed and Grievance: Economic Agendas in Civil War*, edited by Mats Berdal and David M. Malone, 91–111. Boulder, CO: Lynne Rienner.

Collier, Paul, and Anke Hoeffler. 1998. "On Economic Causes of Civil War." *Oxford Economic Papers* 50 (4): 563–73.

———. 2004. "Greed and Grievance in Civil War." *Oxford Economic Papers* 56 (4): 563–95.

Collier, Paul, Anke Hoeffler, and Dominic Rohner. 2009. "Beyond Greed and Grievance: Feasibility and Civil War." *Oxford Economic Papers* 61 (1): 1–27.

Conboy, Kenneth. 2013. *The Cambodian Wars: Clashing Armies and CIA Covert Operations*. Lawrence: University Press of Kansas.

Cook, Theodore Failor, and Haruko Taya Cook. 1992. *Japan at War: An Oral History*. New York: New Press.

Cooper, Matthew. 1979. *The Nazi War against Soviet Partisans, 1941–1944*. New York: Stein and Day.

Correlates of War Project. 2017. "National Material Capabilities (NMC) Data Documentation: Version 5.0." https://correlatesofwar.org/data-sets/national-material-capabilities.

Corti, Egon Caesar, Count. 1928. *Maximilian and Charlotte of Mexico*. Translated by Catherine Alison Phillips. New York: Alfred A. Knopf.

Cranmer, Skyler J., and Bruce A. Desmarais. 2016. "A Critique of Dyadic Design." *International Studies Quarterly* 60 (2): 355–62.

Crawford, Neta C. 2016. *Update on the Human Costs of War in Afghanistan and Pakistan, 2001 to mid-2016*. Providence, RI: Watson Institute for International and Public Affairs.

Crowley, Michael. 2017. "Trump Allies Push White House to Consider Regime Change in Tehran." *politico.com*, June 25, 2017. http://www.politico.com/story/2017/06/25/trump-iran-foreign-policy-regime-change-239930.

Cullather, Nick. 2006. *Secret History: The CIA's Classified Account of Its Operations in Guatemala, 1952–1954*. 2nd ed. Stanford, CA: Stanford University Press.

Cunningham, Michele. 2001. *Mexico and the Foreign Policy of Napoleon III*. Houndmills: Palgrave.

Dabbs, Jack A. 1963. *The French Army in Mexico, 1861–1867: A Study in Military Government*. The Hague: Mouton.

Dalrymple, William. 2013. *Return of a King: The Battle for Afghanistan, 1839–42*. New York: Alfred A. Knopf.

Davies, James C. 1962. "Toward a Theory of Revolution." *American Sociological Review* 6 (1): 5–19.

deGrandpre, Andrew, and Andrew Tilghman. 2015. "Iran Linked to Deaths of 500 U.S. Troops in Iraq, Afghanistan." *Military Times*, July 14, 2015. https://www.militarytimes.com/news/pentagon-congress/2015/07/14/iran-linked-to-deaths-of-500-u-s-troops-in-iraq-afghanistan/.

Denison, Benjamin. 2020. "The More Things Change, the More They Stay the Same: The Failure of Regime-Change Operations." Cato Institute Policy Analysis No. 883.

Department of the Army. 2006. *FM 3–24: Counterinsurgency*. Washington, DC: Department of the Army.

Des Forges, Alison. 1999. *"Leave None to Tell the Story": Genocide in Rwanda*. New York: Human Rights Watch.

De Witte, Ludo. 2001. *The Assassination of Lumumba*. Translated by Ann Wright and Renée Fenby. London: Verso.

Diamond, Alexis, and Jasjeet S. Sekhon. 2013. "Genetic Matching for Estimating Causal Effects: A General Multivariate Matching Method for Achieving Balance in Observational Studies." *Review of Economic and Statistics* 95 (3): 932–45.

Dixon, William J. 1994. "Democracy and the Peaceful Settlement of International Conflict." *American Political Science Review* 88 (1): 14–32.

Dobbins, James, John G. McGinn, Keith Crane, Seth G. Jones, Rollie Lal, Andrew Rathmell, Rachel M. Swanger, and Anga R. Timilsina. 2003. *America's Role in Nation-Building: From Germany to Iraq*. Washington, DC: RAND.

Dodd, Clement. 2010. *The History and Politics of the Cyprus Conflict*. New York: Palgrave Macmillan.

Dodge, Toby. 2006. "War and Resistance in Iraq: From Regime Change to Collapsed State." In *The Iraq War: Causes and Consequences*, edited by Rick Fawn and Raymond Hinnebusch, 211–24. Boulder, CO: Lynne Rienner.

——. 2012. "From Regime Change to Civil War: Violence in Post-Invasion Iraq." In *The Peace in Between: Post-war Violence and Peacebuilding*, edited by Astri Suhrke and Mats Berdal, 132–50. London: Routledge.

Downes, Alexander B. 2008a. *Targeting Civilians in War*. Ithaca, NY: Cornell University Press.

——. 2008b. "Review of Tanisha M. Fazal, *State Death: The Politics and Geography of Conquest, Occupation, and Annexation*." *International History Review* 30 (4): 845–47.

——. 2011. "Regime Change Doesn't Work." *Boston Review* 36 (5): 16–22.

——. 2018. "Step Aside or Face the Consequences: Explaining the Success and Failure of Compellent Threats to Remove Leaders." In *Coercion: The Power to Hurt in International Politics*, edited by Kelly M. Greenhill and Peter Krause, 93–114. New York: Oxford University Press.

——. 2020. "The Causes of Foreign-Imposed Regime Change: A Review Essay." Unpublished manuscript, George Washington University.

Downes, Alexander B., and Jonathan Monten. 2013. "Forced to Be Free: Why Foreign-Imposed Regime Change Rarely Leads to Democratization." *International Security* 37 (4): 90–131.

Downes, Alexander B., and Lindsey O'Rourke. 2016. "You Can't Always Get What You Want: Why Foreign-Imposed Regime Change Seldom Improves Interstate Relations." *International Security* 41 (2): 43–89.

——. 2017–18. "Correspondence: Reconsidering the Effects of Foreign-Imposed Regime Change." *International Security* 42 (3): 172–77.

——. 2018. "The Trump Administration Wants Regime Change in Iran. But Regime Change Usually Doesn't Work." *Washington Post Monkey Cage*, May 23, 2018. https://www.washingtonpost.com/news/monkey-cage/wp/2017/07/31/some-in-d-c-want-regime-change-in-iran-good-luck-with-that/.

——. 2019. "Picking Your Friends: Foreign-Imposed Regime Change and the Quality of Interstate Relations." Paper prepared for the 115th Annual Meeting of the American Political Science Association, Washington, DC, August 29–September 1, 2019.

Downes, Alexander B., and Todd S. Sechser. 2012. "The Illusion of Democratic Credibility." *International Organization* 66 (3): 457–89.

Downs, George W., and David M. Rocke. 1994. "Conflict, Agency, and Gambling for Resurrection: The Principal-Agent Problem Goes to War." *American Journal of Political Science* 38 (2): 362–80.

Doyle, Michael W. 1983a. "Kant, Liberal Legacies, and Foreign Affairs." *Philosophy and Public Affairs* 12 (3): 205–35.

———. 1983b. "Kant, Liberal Legacies, and Foreign Affairs, Part 2." *Philosophy and Public Affairs* 12 (4): 323–53.

Doyle, Michael W., and Nicholas Sambanis. 2000. "International Peacebuilding: A Theoretical and Quantitative Analysis." *American Political Science Review* 94 (4): 779–801.

———. 2006. *Making War and Building Peace: United Nations Peace Operations.* Princeton, NJ: Princeton University Press.

Drea, Edward J. 2009. *Japan's Imperial Army: Its Rise and Fall, 1853–1945.* Lawrence: University Press of Kansas.

Dreyer, Edward L. 1995. *China at War, 1901–1949.* London: Longman.

Drezner, Daniel W. 2003. "The Hidden Hand of Economic Coercion." *International Organization* 57 (3): 643–59.

———. 2011. "Sanctions Sometimes Smart: Targeting Sanctions in Theory and Practice." *International Studies Review* 13 (1): 96–108.

Dube, Arindrajit, Ethan Kaplan, and Suresh Naidu. 2011. "Coups, Corporations, and Classified Information." *Quarterly Journal of Economics* 126 (3): 1375–1409.

Dull, Paul S. 1952. "The Assassination of Chang Tso-lin." *Far Eastern Quarterly* 11 (4): 453–63.

Dunn, Kevin C. 2002. "A Survival Guide to Kinshasa: Lessons of the Father, Passed Down to the Son." In *The African Stakes of the Congo War,* edited by John F. Clark, 53–74. New York: Palgrave Macmillan.

Dupree, Louis. 1973. *Afghanistan.* Princeton, NJ: Princeton University Press.

Durand, Henry Marion. (1879) 2000. *The First Afghan War and Its Causes.* New Delhi: Bhavana Books and Prints.

Easterly, William, Shanker Satyanath, and Daniel Berger. 2008. *Superpower Interventions and their Consequences for Democracy: An Empirical Inquiry.* Washington, DC: Brookings Institution.

The Economist. 2001. "Laurent Kabila." *The Economist,* January 18, 2001. http://www.economist.com/node/481974#print.

Edelman, Marc, and Joanne Kenan, eds. 1989. *The Costa Rica Reader.* New York: Grove Weidenfeld.

Edelstein, David M. 2004. "Occupational Hazards: Why Military Occupations Succeed or Fail." *International Security* 29 (1): 49–91.

———. 2008. *Occupational Hazards: Success and Failure in Military Occupation.* Ithaca, NY: Cornell University Press.

Ellis, Cali Mortenson, Michael C. Horowitz, and Allan C. Stam. 2015. "Introducing the LEAD Data Set." *International Interactions* 41 (4): 718–41.

Elliott, David W. P. 2003. *The Vietnamese War: Revolution and Social Change in the Mekong Delta, 1930–1975.* Concise edition. Armonk, NY: M. E. Sharpe.

Enterline, Andrew J., and J. Michael Greig. 2005. "Beacons of Hope? The Impact of Imposed Democracy on Regional Peace, Democracy, and Prosperity." *Journal of Politics* 67 (4): 1075–98.

———. 2008a. "Against All Odds? The History of Imposed Democracy and the Future of Iraq and Afghanistan." *Foreign Policy Analysis* 4 (4): 321–47.

———. 2008b. "Perfect Storms? Political Instability in Imposed Regimes and the Future of Iraq and Afghanistan?" *Journal of Conflict Resolution* 52 (6): 880–915.

Enterline, Andrew J., J. Michael Greig, and Dawn Miller. 2006. "The Birth of Nations? The Durability of Imposed Polities and the Future of Iraq and Afghanistan." Unpublished manuscript, University of North Texas.

Erikson, Robert S., Pablo M. Pinto, and Kelly T. Rader. 2014. "Dyadic Analysis in International Relations: A Cautionary Tale." *Political Analysis* 22 (4): 457–63.

Esterbrook, John. 2002. "Rumsfeld: It Would Be a Short War." *cbsnews.com*, November 15, 2002. https://www.cbsnews.com/news/rumsfeld-it-would-be-a-short-war/.

Etcheson, Craig. 1984. *The Rise and Demise of Democratic Kampuchea*. Boulder, CO: Westview.

Eto, Shinkichi. 1986. "China's International Relations, 1911–1931." In *The Cambridge History of China*. Vol. 13, *Republican China, 1912–1949, Part 2*, edited by John K. Fairbank and Albert Feuerwerker, 74–115. Cambridge: Cambridge University Press.

Evans, George de Lacey. 1829. *On the Practicability of an Invasion of British India*. London: J. M. Robertson.

Evans, Grant, and Kelvin Rowley. 1990. *Red Brotherhood at War: Vietnam, Cambodia, and Laos since 1975*. Rev. ed. London: Verso.

Ewans, Martin. 2002. *Afghanistan: A Short History of Its People and Politics*. New York: HarperCollins.

Fadel, Leila. 2008. "Key U.S. Strategy in Danger of Collapse." *McClatchy Newspapers*, August 20, 2008. https://www.mcclatchydc.com/news/nation-world/world/article24496414.html.

Fairweather, Jack. 2014. *The Good War: Why We Couldn't Win the War or the Peace in Afghanistan*. New York: Basic Books.

Fallows, James. 2006. *Blind into Baghdad: America's War in Iraq*. New York: Vintage.

Farber, Henry S., and Joanne Gowa. 1997. "Common Interests or Common Polities? Reinterpreting the Democratic Peace." *Journal of Politics* 59 (2): 393–417.

Farcau, Bruce. 2000. *The Ten Cents War: Chile, Peru, and Bolivia in the War of the Pacific, 1879–1884*. Westport, CT: Praeger.

Farmer, Paul. 2004. "Who Removed Aristide?" *London Review of Books* 26 (8). https://www.lrb.co.uk/the-paper/v26/n08/paul-farmer/who-removed-aristide.

Farnham, Barbara, ed. 1995. *Avoiding Losses/Taking Risks: Prospect Theory and International Conflict*. Ann Arbor: University of Michigan Press.

Faroughy, Ahmed. 1974. "Repression in Iran." *Index on Censorship* 3 (4): 9–18.

Fazal, Tanisha M. 2007. *State Death: The Politics and Geography of Conquest, Occupation, and Annexation*. Princeton, NJ: Princeton University Press.

Fearon, James D. 1994. "Domestic Political Audiences and the Escalation of International Disputes." *American Political Science Review* 88 (3): 577–92.

———. 1998. "Commitment Problems and the Spread of Ethnic Conflict." In *The International Spread of Ethnic Conflict: Fear, Diffusion, and Escalation*, edited by David A. Lake and Donald Rothchild, 107–26. Princeton, NJ: Princeton University Press.

———. 2011. "Regime Change Doesn't Work." *Boston Review* 36 (5). http://bostonreview.net/fearon-taking-the-gamble.

Fearon, James D., and David D. Laitin. 2003. "Ethnicity, Insurgency, and Civil War." *American Political Science Review* 97 (1): 75–90.

———. 2011. "Sons of the Soil, Migrants, and Civil War." *World Development* 39 (2): 199–211.

Feaver, Peter D. 2003. *Armed Servants: Agency, Oversight, and Civil-Military Relations.* Cambridge, MA: Harvard University Press.

Feaver, Peter D., and Christopher Gelpi. 2002. "Speak Softly and Carry a Big Stick? Veterans in the Political Elite and the American Use of Force." *American Political Science Review* 96 (4): 779–93.

Felten, Peter. 1995. "The 1965–1966 United States Intervention in the Dominican Republic." PhD diss., University of Texas, Austin.

Fenby, Jonathan. 2008. *Modern China: The Fall and Rise of a Great Power, 1850 to the Present.* New York: HarperCollins.

Ferguson, Charles. H. 2008. *No End in Sight: Iraq's Descent into Chaos.* New York: PublicAffairs.

Ferwerda, Jeremy, and Nicholas L. Miller. 2014. "Political Devolution and Resistance to Foreign Rule: A Natural Experiment." *American Political Science Review* 108 (3): 642–60.

Filkins, Dexter. 2004. "The Reach of War: New Government; A Worn Road for U.N. Aide." *New York Times,* May 31, 2004. https://www.nytimes.com/2004/05/31/world/the-reach-of-war-new-government-a-worn-road-for-un-aide.html.

———. 2014. "What We Left Behind." *The New Yorker,* April 21, 2014. https://www.newyorker.com/magazine/2014/04/28/what-we-left-behind.

Findling, John. 1987. *Close Neighbors, Distant Friends: United States-Central American Relations.* New York: Greenwood.

Finn, Peter. 2009. "Detainee Who Gave False Iraq Data Dies in Prison in Libya." *Washington Post,* May 12, 2009. http://www.washingtonpost.com/wp-dyn/content/article/2009/05/11/AR2009051103412_pf.html.

Fletcher, Arnold. 1965. *Afghanistan: Highway of Conquest.* Ithaca, NY: Cornell University Press.

Foot, Rosemary. 1985. *The Wrong War: American Policy and the Dimensions of the Korean Conflict, 1950–1953.* Ithaca, NY: Cornell University Press.

Forero, Juan. 2004. "Documents Show C.I.A. Knew of a Coup Plot in Venezuela." *New York Times,* December 3, 2004. https://www.nytimes.com/2004/12/03/washington/world/documents-show-cia-knew-of-a-coup-plot-in-venezuela.html.

Fortna, Virginia Page. 2004. *Peace Time: Cease-Fire Agreements and the Durability of Peace.* Princeton, NJ: Princeton University Press.

———. 2008. *Does Peacekeeping Work? Shaping Belligerents' Choices after Civil War.* Princeton, NJ: Princeton University Press.

———. 2015. "Do Terrorists Win? Rebels' Use of Terrorism and Civil War Outcomes." *International Organization* 69 (3): 519–56.

Frank, Richard B. 1999. *Downfall: The End of the Imperial Japanese Empire.* New York: Random House.

Franks, Tommy. 2004. *American Soldier.* New York: Regan.

French, Howard W. 1998. "Pilot's Account Seems to Confirm Rwanda Role in Congo Strife." *New York Times,* August 10, 1998. https://www.nytimes.com/1998/08/10/world/pilot-s-account-seems-to-confirm-rwanda-role-in-congo-strife.html.

Friedman, Jeffrey A. 2011. "Manpower and Counterinsurgency: Empirical Foundations for Theory and Doctrine." *Security Studies* 20 (4): 556–91.

Friedman, Uri. 2019. "How an Elaborate Plan to Topple Venezuela's President Went Wrong." *The Atlantic*, May 1, 2019. https://www.theatlantic.com/politics/archive/2019/05/white-house-venezuela-maduro-failed/588454/.

Furuya, Keiji. 1981. *Chiang Kai-shek, His Life and Times*. Abridged English ed. Translated by Chun-Ming Chang. New York: St. John's University.

Gagnon, V. P. 1994–95. "Ethnic Nationalism and International Conflict: The Case of Serbia." *International Security* 19 (3): 130–66.

Gailmard, Sean. 2009. "Multiple Principals and Oversight of Bureaucratic Policy-Making." *Journal of Theoretical Politics* 21 (2): 161–86.

Galbraith, Peter. 2006. *The End of Iraq: How American Incompetence Created a War without End*. New York: Simon and Schuster.

Gall, Carlotta. 2006. "Opium Harvest at Record Level in Afghanistan." *New York Times*, September 3, 2006. https://www.nytimes.com/2006/09/03/world/asia/03afghan.html.

———. 2014. *The Wrong Enemy: America in Afghanistan, 2001–2014*. Boston: Houghton Mifflin Harcourt.

Garcia-Navarro, Lulu. 2010. "Bitterness Grows Amid U.S.-Backed Sons of Iraq." *National Public Radio*, June 24, 2010. https://www.npr.org/templates/story/story.php?storyId=128084675.

Gasiorowski, Mark J. 1991. *U.S. Foreign Policy and the Shah: Building a Client State in Iran*. Ithaca, NY: Cornell University Press.

Gasiorowski, Mark J., and Malcolm Byrne, eds. 2004. *Mohammad Mosaddeq and the 1953 Coup in Iran*. Syracuse, NY: Syracuse University Press.

Gellner, Ernest. 1983. *Nations and Nationalism*. Ithaca, NY: Cornell University Press.

Gent, Stephen. 2008. "Going in When It Counts: Military Intervention and the Outcome of Civil Conflicts." *International Studies Quarterly* 52 (4): 713–35.

George, Alexander L., and William E. Simons, eds. 1994. *The Limits of Coercive Diplomacy*. 2nd ed. Boulder, CO: Westview.

Gerges, Fawaz A. 2016. *ISIS: A History*. Princeton, NJ: Princeton University Press.

Gerzoy, Gene. 2015. "Alliance Coercion and Nuclear Restraint: How the United States Thwarted West Germany's Nuclear Ambitions." *International Security* 39 (4): 91–129.

Gift, Thomas, and Daniel Krcmaric. 2017. "Who Democratizes? Western-educated Leaders and Regime Transitions." *Journal of Conflict Resolution* 61 (3): 671–701.

Gilligan, Michael J., and Ernest J. Sergenti. 2008. "Do UN Interventions Cause Peace? Using Matching to Improve Causal Inference." *Quarterly Journal of Political Science* 3 (2): 89–122.

Giniger, Henry. 1964. "Gabon Insurgents Yield as France Rushes in Troops." *New York Times*, February 20, 1964.

Glanz, James, and David Rohde. 2006. "U.S. Report Finds Fault in Training of Afghan Police." *New York Times*, December 3, 2006. https://www.nytimes.com/2006/12/03/world/asia/04policecnd.html.

Gleditsch, Kristian Skrede. 2004. "A Revised List of Wars between and within Independent States, 1816–2002." *International Interactions* 30 (3): 231–62.

Gleijeses, Piero. 1991. *Shattered Hope: The Guatemalan Revolution and the United States, 1944–1954*. Princeton, NJ: Princeton University Press.

Gobat, Michel. 2005. *Confronting the American Dream: Nicaragua under U.S. Imperial Rule*. Durham, NC: Duke University Press.

Goemans, H. E. 2000. *War and Punishment: The Causes of War Termination and the First World War*. Princeton, NJ: Princeton University Press.

———. 2008. "Which Way Out? The Manner and Consequences of Losing Office." *Journal of Conflict Resolution* 52 (6): 771–94.

Goemans, H. E., Kristian Skrede Gleditsch, and Giacomo Chiozza. 2009. "Introducing Archigos: A Dataset of Political Leaders." *Journal of Peace Research* 46 (2): 269–83.

———. 2016. *Archigos: A Data Set on Leaders, 1875–2015: Case Descriptions*. http://www.rochester.edu/college/faculty/hgoemans/Archigos_4.1.pdf.

Goertz, Gary, and Paul F. Diehl. 1992. "The Empirical Importance of Enduring Rivalries." *International Interactions* 18 (2): 151–63.

Goertz, Gary, and James Mahoney. 2004. "The Possibility Principle: Choosing Negative Cases in Comparative Research." *American Political Science Review* 98 (4): 653–69.

Gordon, Bernard K. 1986. "The Third Indochina Conflict." *Foreign Affairs* 65 (1): 66–85.

Gordon, Michael R. 2004. "The Conflict in Iraq: Road to War; The Strategy to Secure Iraq Did Not Foresee a 2nd War." *New York Times*, October 19, 2004. https://www.nytimes.com/2004/10/19/washington/the-conflict-in-iraq-road-to-war-the-strategy-to-secure-iraq-did.html.

———. 2018. "U.S. Lays Out Demands for New Iran Deal." *Wall Street Journal*, May 21, 2018. https://www.wsj.com/articles/mike-pompeo-lays-out-next-steps-on-iran-1526909126.

Gordon, Michael R., and Andrew W. Lehren. 2010. "Leaked Reports Detail Iran's Aid for Iraqi Militias." *New York Times*, October 22, 2010. http://www.nytimes.com/2010/10/23/world/middleeast/23iran.html?pagewanted=print.

Gordon, Michael R., and Bernard E. Trainor. 2006. *Cobra II: The Inside Story of the Invasion and Occupation of Iraq*. New York: Pantheon.

———. 2012. *The Endgame: The Inside Story of the Struggle for Iraq, from George W. Bush to Barack Obama*. New York: Pantheon.

Gordon, Philip H. 2020. *Losing the Long Game: The False Promise of Regime Change in the Middle East*. New York: St. Martin's Press.

Gorst, Anthony, and Lewis Johnman. 1997. *The Suez Crisis*. London: Routledge.

Gourevitch, Peter. 1978. "The Second Image Reversed: The International Sources of Domestic Politics." *International Organization* 32 (4): 881–912.

Grandin, Greg. 2004. *The Last Colonial Massacre: Latin America in the Cold War*. Chicago: University of Chicago Press.

Greitens, Sheena Chestnut. 2016. *Dictators and their Secret Police: Coercive Institutions and State Violence*. Cambridge: Cambridge University Press.

Grow, Michael. 2008. *U.S. Presidents and Latin American Interventions: Pursuing Regime Change in the Cold War*. Lawrence: University Press of Kansas.

Gurr, Ted Robert. 1970. *Why Men Rebel*. Princeton, NJ: Princeton University Press.

———. 1993. *Minorities at Risk: A Global View of Ethnopolitical Conflicts*. Washington, DC: United States Institute of Peace.

———. 2000. *Peoples Versus States: Minorities at Risk in the New Century*. Washington, DC: United States Institute of Peace.

Haass, Richard N. 2005. "Regime Change and Its Limits." *Foreign Affairs* 84 (4): 66–78.

——. 2010. "Regime Change Is the Only Way to Stop Iran." *Newsweek*, January 21, 2010. http://www.newsweek.com/haass-regime-change-only-way-stop-iran -71005.

Hammer, Ellen J. 1987. *A Death in November: America in Vietnam, 1963*. New York: E. P. Dutton.

Hammond, Thomas H., and Jack H. Knott. 1996. "Who Controls the Bureaucracy? Presidential Power, Congressional Dominance, Legal Constraints, and Bureaucratic Autonomy in a Model of Multi-Institutional Policy-Making." *Journal of Law, Economics, and Organization* 12 (1): 119–66.

Hanna, Alfred Jackson, and Kathryn Abbey Hanna. 1971. *Napoleon III and Mexico: American Triumph over Monarchy*. Chapel Hill: University of North Carolina Press.

Harari, Michal. 2010. *Uncertain Future for the Sons of Iraq*. Washington, DC: Institute for the Study of War.

Harbom, Lotta, Stina Högbladh, and Peter Wallensteen. 2006. "Armed Conflict and Peace Agreements." *Journal of Peace Research* 43 (5): 617–31.

Harff, Barbara. 2003. "No Lessons Learned from the Holocaust? Assessing Risks of Genocide and Political Mass Murder since 1955." *American Political Science Review* 97 (1): 57–73.

Harrison, Benjamin. 1995. "The United States and the 1909 Nicaragua Revolution." *Caribbean Quarterly* 41 (3–4): 45–63.

Hasegawa, Tsuyoshi. 2005. *Racing the Enemy: Stalin, Truman, and the Surrender of Japan*. Cambridge, MA: Belknap Press.

Hashim, Ahmed S. 2006. *Insurgency and Counter-Insurgency in Iraq*. Ithaca, NY: Cornell University Press.

Haun, Phil. 2015. *Coercion, Survival, and War: Why Weak States Resist the United States*. Stanford, CA: Stanford University Press.

Hawkins, Darren G., David A. Lake, Daniel L. Nelson, and Michael J. Tierney, eds. 2006. *Delegation and Agency in International Organizations*. Cambridge: Cambridge University Press.

Hazelton, Jaqueline L. 2017. "The 'Hearts and Minds' Fallacy: Violence, Coercion, and Success in Counterinsurgency Warfare." *International Security* 42 (1): 80–113.

Healy, David. 1988. *Drive to Hegemony: The United States in the Caribbean, 1898–1917*. Madison: University of Wisconsin Press.

Hechter, Michael, Ioana Emy Matesan, and Chris Hale. 2009. "Resistance to Alien Rule in Taiwan and Korea." *Nations and Nationalism* 15 (1): 36–59.

Heder, Stephen P. 1981. "The Kampuchean-Vietnamese Conflict. In *The Third Indochina Conflict*, edited by David W. P. Elliott, 21–67. Boulder, CO: Westview.

Hegre, Håvard, and Nicholas Sambanis. 2006. "Sensitivity Analysis of Empirical Results on Civil War Onset." *Journal of Conflict Resolution* 50 (4): 508–35.

Heilbrunn, Jacob. 2015. "The Neocons—They're Back, and on Iran, They're Uncompromising as Ever." *Los Angeles Times*, April 2, 2015. http://www.latimes.com /nation/la-oe-heilbrunn-iran-framework-republican-neocon-response -20150403-story.html.

Heller, Joseph. 1961. *Catch-22*. New York: Simon and Schuster.

Herrmann, Richard K. 2017. "How Attachments to the Nation Shape Beliefs about the World: A Theory of Motivated Reasoning." *International Organization* 71 (S1): S61–S84.

Hitchins, Keith. 1994. *Rumania, 1866–1947*. Oxford: Clarendon Press.

Ho, Daniel E., Kosuke Imai, Gary King, and Elizabeth A. Stuart. 2007. "Matching as Nonparametric Preprocessing for Reducing Model Dependence in Parametric Causal Inference." *Political Analysis* 15 (3): 199–236.

Hobbes, Thomas. (1651) 1982. *Leviathan*. London: Penguin.

Hood, Steven J. 1992. *Dragons Entangled: Indochina and the China-Vietnam War*. Armonk, NY: M. E. Sharpe.

Horowitz, Donald L. 1985. *Ethnic Groups in Conflict*. Berkeley: University of California Press.

Horowitz, Michael C., and Allan C. Stam. 2014. "How Prior Military Experience Influences the Future Militarized Behavior of Leaders." *International Organization* 68 (3): 527–59.

Horowitz, Michael C., Allan C. Stam, and Cali M. Ellis. 2015. *Why Leaders Fight*. Cambridge: Cambridge University Press.

Hudson, Valerie M., Bonnie Ballif-Spanvill, Mary Caprioli, and Chad F. Emmett. 2012. *Sex and World Peace*. New York: Columbia University Press.

Hudson, Valerie M., Mary Caprioli, Bonnie Ballif-Spanvill, Rose McDermott, and Chad F. Emmett. 2008–09. "The Heart of the Matter: The Security of Women and the Security of States." *International Security* 33 (3): 7–45.

Hufbauer, Gary Clyde, Jeffrey J. Schott, and Kimberly Ann Elliott. 2007. *Economic Sanctions Reconsidered*. 3rd expanded ed. Washington, DC: Petersen Institute for International Economics.

Human Rights Watch. 1995. *Rwanda/Zaire: Rearming with Impunity—International Support for the Perpetrators of the Rwandan Genocide*. New York: Human Rights Watch.

——. 2008. *"Troops in Contact": Airstrikes and Civilian Deaths in Afghanistan*. New York: Human Rights Watch.

Huth, Paul. 1996. *Standing Your Ground: Territorial Disputes and International Conflict*. Ann Arbor: University of Michigan Press.

Ienaga, Saburō. 1978. *The Pacific War, 1931–1945: A Critical Perspective on Japan's Role in World War II*. New York: Pantheon.

Immerman, Richard H. 1982. *The CIA in Guatemala: The Foreign Policy of Intervention*. Austin: University of Texas Press.

International Crisis Group. 1998. *How Kabila Lost His Way: The Performance of Laurent Désiré Kabila's Government*. Brussels: International Crisis Group.

Iqbal, Zaryab, and Christopher Zorn. 2008. "The Political Consequences of Assassination." *Journal of Conflict Resolution* 52 (3): 385–400.

Iraq Coalition Casualty Count. 2020. http://icasualties.org/.

Iriye, Akira. 1960. "Chang Hsueh-liang and the Japanese." *Journal of Asian Studies* 20 (1): 33–43.

Isby, David. 2010. *Afghanistan: Graveyard of Empires: A New History of the Borderlands*. New York: Pegasus.

Itoh, Mayumi. 2016. *The Making of China's War with Japan: Zhou Enlai and Zhang Xueliang*. Singapore: Palgrave Macmillan.

Jacobs, Seth. 2006. *Cold War Mandarin: Ngo Dinh Diem and the Origins of America's War in Vietnam, 1950–1963.* Lanham, MD: Rowman and Littlefield.

Jaffe, Lorna S. 1985. *The Decision to Disarm Germany: British Policy towards Postwar German Disarmament, 1914–1919.* Boston: Allen and Unwin.

Jansen, Marius B. 1975. *Japan and China: From War to Peace, 1894–1972.* Chicago: Rand McNally.

Jeffrey, James F. 2017. "How to Get Regime Change Right." Washington Institute for Near East Policy, October 3, 2017. https://www.washingtoninstitute.org/policy-analysis/view/how-to-get-regime-change-right.

Jehl, Douglas. 2005. "Qaeda-Iraq Link U.S. Cited Is Tied to Coercion Claim." *New York Times*, December 9, 2005. https://www.nytimes.com/2005/12/09/politics/qaedairaq-link-us-cited-is-tied-to-coercion-claim.html.

Johnson, Rob. 2011. *The Afghan Way of War: How and Why They Fight.* Oxford: Oxford University Press.

Johnston, Patrick B. 2012. "Does Decapitation Work? Assessing the Effectiveness of Leadership Targeting in Counterinsurgency Campaigns." *International Security* 36 (4): 47–79.

Johnston, Patrick B., and Anoop Sarbahi. 2016. "The Impact of U.S. Drone Strikes on Terrorism in Pakistan." *International Studies Quarterly* 60 (2): 203–19.

Jonas, Suzanne. 1991. *The Battle for Guatemala: Rebels, Death Squads, and U.S. Power.* Boulder, CO: Westview.

Jones, Benjamin T. 2017. "Altering Capabilities or Imposing Costs? Intervention Strategy and Civil War Outcomes." *International Studies Quarterly* 61 (1): 52–63.

Jones, Seth G. 2009. *In the Graveyard of Empires: America's War in Afghanistan.* New York: Norton.

Jordan, Donald A. 1976. *The Northern Expedition: China's National Revolution of 1926–1928.* Honolulu: University of Hawai'i Press.

Jordan, Jenna. 2009. "When Heads Roll: Assessing the Effectiveness of Leadership Decapitation." *Security Studies* 18 (4): 719–55.

———. 2014. "Attacking the Leader, Missing the Mark: Why Terrorist Groups Survive Decapitation Strikes." *International Security* 38 (4): 7–38.

———. 2019. *Leadership Decapitation: Strategic Targeting of Terrorist Organizations.* Stanford, CA: Stanford University Press.

Joseph, Michael F. 2018. "Explaining Peace in a Complex and Uncertain World: Multi-Dimensional Preferences, Great Power Rivalry, Diplomacy, and Peace." PhD diss., George Washington University.

Kahin, George McT. 1987. *Intervention: How America Became Involved in Vietnam.* Garden City, NY: Anchor.

Kaiser, David. 2000. *American Tragedy: Kennedy, Johnson, and the Origins of the Vietnam War.* Cambridge, MA: Belknap Press.

Karlin, Mara E. 2018. *Building Militaries in Fragile States: Challenges for the United States.* Philadelphia: University of Pennsylvania Press.

Karnow, Stanley. 1983. *Vietnam: A History.* New York: Penguin.

Kaufmann, Chaim. 1996. "Possible and Impossible Solutions to Ethnic Civil Wars." *International Security* 20 (4): 136–75.

———. 2004. "Threat Inflation and the Failure of the Marketplace of Ideas: The Selling of the Iraq War." *International Security* 29 (1): 5–48.

Keddie, Nikkie R. 2003. *Modern Iran: Roots and Results of Revolution*. New Haven, CT: Yale University Press.

Keele, Luke J. 2010. "An Overview of Rbounds: An R Package for Rosenbaum Bounds Sensitivity Analysis with Matched Data." Unpublished manuscript.

Kerevel, Yann. 2006. "Re-examining the Politics of U.S. Intervention in Early 20th Century Nicaragua: Jose Madriz and the Conservative Restoration." Research Paper Series No. 43. Latin American Institute. Albuquerque: University of New Mexico.

Khalilzad, Zalmay. 2016. "How Regime Change Can Work." *CNN*, January 13, 2016. https://www.cnn.com/2016/01/13/opinions/khalilzad-regime-change/index.html.

Kim, Woosang, and James D. Morrow. 2002. "When Do Power Shifts Lead to War?" *American Journal of Political Science* 36 (4): 896–922.

King, Gary, and Langche Zeng. 2001. "Logistic Regression in Rare Events Data." *Political Analysis* 9 (2): 137–63.

Kinzer, Stephen. 2003. *All the Shah's Men: An American Coup and the Roots of Middle East Terror*. Hoboken, NJ: John Wiley and Sons.

———. 2006. *Overthrow: America's Century of Regime Change from Hawaii to Iraq*. New York: Times Books.

Kisangani, Emizet François. 2012. *Civil Wars in the Democratic Republic of Congo, 1960–2010*. Boulder, CO: Lynne Rienner.

Kocher, Matthew A., Adria K. Lawrence, and Nuno P. Monteiro. 2018. "Nationalism, Collaboration, and Resistance: France under Nazi Occupation." *International Security* 43 (2): 117–50.

Kocher, Matthew A., and Nuno P. Monteiro. 2016. "Lines of Demarcation: Causation, Design-Based Inference, and Historical Research." *Perspectives on Politics* 14 (4): 952–75.

Kohn, George C. 1999. *Dictionary of Wars*. New York: Checkmark.

Kornbluh, Peter. 2003. *The Pinochet File: A Declassified Dossier on Atrocity and Accountability*. New York: New Press.

Koulischer, Grégoire. 1946. "Belgian-American Relations, 1944–45." *Annals of the American Academy of Political and Social Science* 247 (1): 171–78.

Krahmann, Elke. 2016. "NATO Contracting in Afghanistan: The Problem of Principal-Agent Networks." *International Affairs* 92 (6): 1401–26.

Kristof, Nicholas D. 2001. "Zhang Xueliang, 100, Dies; Warlord and Hero of China." *New York Times*, October 19, 2001. https://www.nytimes.com/2001/10/19/world/zhang-xueliang-100-dies-warlord-and-hero-of-china.html.

Kuperman, Alan. 2008. "The Moral Hazard of Humanitarian Intervention: Lessons from the Balkans." *International Studies Quarterly* 52 (1): 49–80.

———. 2013. "A Model Humanitarian Intervention? Reassessing NATO's Libya Campaign." *International Security* 38 (1): 105–36.

Kwong, Chi Man. 2017. *War and Geopolitics in Interwar Manchuria: Zhang Zuolin and the Fengtian Clique during the Northern Expedition*. Leiden: Brill.

Kyle, Keith. 1991. *Suez: Britain's End of Empire in the Middle East*. London: I. B. Tauris.

Labs, Eric. 1997. "Beyond Victory: Offensive Realism and the Expansion of War Aims." *Security Studies* 6 (4): 1–49.

Ladwig, Walter C., III. 2016. "Influencing Clients in Counterinsurgency: U.S. Involvement in El Salvador's Civil War, 1979–92." *International Security* 41 (1): 99–146.

———. 2017. *The Forgotten Front: Patron-Client Relationships in Counterinsurgency*. Cambridge: Cambridge University Press.

Lafeber, Walter. 1984. *Inevitable Revolutions: The United States in Central America*. New York: Norton.

Lake, David A. 2010–11. "Two Cheers for Bargaining Theory: Assessing Rationalist Explanations for the Iraq War." *International Security* 35 (3): 7–52.

———. 2016. *The Statebuilder's Dilemma: On the Limits of Foreign Intervention*. Ithaca, NY: Cornell University Press.

Lakshman, Narayan. 2011. "Karzai Lashes Out at NATO on Civilian Casualties." *The Hindu*, June 1, 2011. https://www.thehindu.com/news/international/karzai -lashes-out-at-nato-on-civilian-casualties/article2068721.ece.

Lambeth, Benjamin S. 2005. *Air Power against Terror: America's Conduct of Operation Enduring Freedom*. Santa Monica, CA: RAND Corporation.

Landler, Mark. 2011. "Obama Tells Qaddafi to Quit and Authorizes Refugee Airlifts." *New York Times*, March 3, 2011. http://www.nytimes.com/2011/03/04 /world/africa/04president.html?pagewanted=print.

Lando, Barry. 2007. *Web of Deceit: The History of Western Complicity in Iraq, from Churchill to Kennedy to George W. Bush*. New York: Other.

Langley, Lester D. 1989. *The United States and the Caribbean in the Twentieth Century*. 4th ed. Athens: University of Georgia Press.

Langley, Lester D., and Schoonover, Thomas. 1995. *The Banana Men: American Mercenaries and Entrepreneurs in Central America, 1880–1930*. Lexington: University Press of Kentucky.

Lawrence, Adria K. 2010. "Triggering Nationalist Violence: Competition and Conflict in Uprisings against Colonial Rule." *International Security* 35 (2): 88–122.

———. 2013. *Imperial Rule and the Politics of Nationalism: Anti-Colonial Protest in the French Empire*. Cambridge: Cambridge University Press.

Leifer, Michael. 1980. "Kampuchea 1979: From Dry Season to Dry Season." *Asian Survey* 20 (1): 33–41.

Lemke, Douglas, and Suzanne Werner. 1996. "Power Parity, Commitment to Change, and War." *International Studies Quarterly* 40 (2): 235–60.

Lentz, Harris M., III. 1999. *Encyclopedia of Heads of State and Governments, 1900 through 1945*. Jefferson, NC: McFarland.

Leuchars, Christopher. 2002. *To the Bitter End: Paraguay and the War of the Triple Alliance*. Westport, CT: Greenwood.

Leurdijk, J. H. 1986. *Intervention in International Politics*. Leeuwarden, The Netherlands: Eisma, B.V.

Levin, Dov H. 2016. "When the Great Power Gets a Vote: The Effects of Great Power Electoral Interventions on Election Results." *International Studies Quarterly* 60 (2): 189–202.

Lewis, Paul H. 1993. *Political Parties and Generations in Paraguay's Liberal Era, 1869–1940*. Chapel Hill: University of North Carolina Press.

Liberman, Peter. 1996. *Does Conquest Pay? The Exploitation of Occupied Industrial Societies*. Princeton, NJ: Princeton University Press.

Lischer, Sarah Kenyon. 2005. *Dangerous Sanctuaries: Refugee Camps, Civil War, and the Dilemmas of Humanitarian Aid*. Ithaca, NY: Cornell University Press.

Littlefield, Frank C. 1988. *Germany and Yugoslavia, 1933–1941: The German Conquest of Yugoslavia*. Boulder, CO: East European Monographs.

Litwak, Robert S. 2007. *Regime Change: U.S. Strategy Through the Prism of 9/11*. Washington, DC: Woodrow Wilson Center Press.

Lo, Nigel, Barry Hashimoto, and Dan Reiter. 2008. "Ensuring Peace: Foreign-Imposed Regime Change and Post-War Peace Duration, 1914–2001." *International Organization* 62 (4): 717–36.

Logevall, Fredrik. 1999. *Choosing War: The Lost Chance for Peace and the Escalation of the War in Vietnam*. Berkeley: University of California Press.

Londregan, John B., and Keith T. Poole. 1990. "Poverty, the Coup Trap, and the Seizure of Executive Power." *World Politics* 42 (2): 151–83.

Long, Austin. 2014. "Whack-a-Mole or Coup de Grace? Institutionalization and Leadership Targeting in Iraq and Afghanistan." *Security Studies* 23 (3): 471–512.

Longman, Timothy. 2002. "The Complex Reasons for Rwanda's Entanglement in Congo." In *The African Stakes of the Congo War*, edited by John F. Clark, 129–44. New York: Palgrave Macmillan.

Lundahl, Mats, Colin L. McCarthy, and Lennart Petersson. 2003. *In the Shadow of South Africa: Lesotho's Economic Future*. Aldershot: Ashgate.

Lyall, Jason. 2009. "Does Indiscriminate Violence Incite Insurgent Attacks? Evidence from Chechnya." *Journal of Conflict Resolution* 53 (3): 331–62.

———. 2010. "Are Coethnics More Effective Counterinsurgents? Evidence from the Second Chechen War." *American Political Science Review* 104 (1): 1–20.

———. 2020. *Divided Armies: Inequality and Battlefield Performance in Modern War*. Princeton, NJ: Princeton University Press.

Lyall, Jason, and Isaiah Wilson III. 2009. "Rage against the Machines: Explaining Outcomes in Counterinsurgency Wars." *International Organization* 63 (1): 67–106.

MacDonald, Michael. 2014. *Overreach: Delusions of Regime Change in Iraq*. Cambridge, MA: Harvard University Press.

MacFarquhar, Neil. 2006. "Saddam Hussein, Defiant Dictator Who Ruled Iraq with Violence and Fear, Dies." *New York Times*, December 30, 2006. https://www.nytimes.com/2006/12/30/world/middleeast/30saddam.html.

Machiavelli, Niccolò. (1532) 1998. *The Prince*. Translated by Harvey C. Mansfield. 2nd ed. Chicago: University of Chicago Press.

Maddison Project Database. 2018. https://www.rug.nl/ggdc/historicaldevelopment/maddison/releases/maddison-project-database-2018.

Maltzman, Forrest. 1997. *Competing Principals: Committees, Parties, and the Organization of Congress*. Ann Arbor: University of Michigan Press.

Mansoor, Peter. 2013. *Surge: My Journey with General David Petraeus and the Remaking of the Iraq War*. New Haven, CT: Yale University Press.

Marco, Jorge. 2015. "The Long Nocturnal March: The Spanish Guerilla Movement in the European Narrative of Antifascist Resistance, 1936–1952." In *Mass Killings and Violence in Spain, 1936–1952: Grappling with the Past*, edited by Peter Anderson and Miguel Angel del Arco Blanco, 173–92. New York: Routledge.

———. 2016. *Guerrilleros and Neighbours in Arms: Identities and Cultures of Anti-fascist Resistance in Spain*. Brighton: Sussex Academic Press.

Matsusaka, Yoshihisa Tak. 2001. *The Making of Japanese Manchuria, 1904–1932*. Cambridge, MA: Harvard University Asia Center.

Maxwell, Neville. 1970. *India's China War*. New York: Pantheon.

May, Ernest R. 2000. *Strange Victory: Hitler's Conquest of France*. New York: Hill and Wang.

Mazower, Mark. 1993. *Inside Hitler's Greece: The Experience of Occupation, 1941–1944*. New Haven, CT: Yale University Press.

McAdam, Doug. 1982. *Political Process and the Development of Black Insurgency, 1930–1970*. Chicago: University of Chicago Press.

McAllen, M. M. 2014. *Maximilian and Carlota: Europe's Last Empire in Mexico*. San Antonio, TX: Trinity University Press.

McCormack, Gavan. 1977. *Chang Tso-lin in Northeast China, 1911–1928: China, Japan, and the Manchurian Idea*. Stanford, CA: Stanford University Press.

McCreedy, Kenneth O. 2001. "Planning the Peace: Operation Eclipse and the Occupation of Germany." *Journal of Military History* 65 (3): 713–39.

McCubbins, Mathew D., Roger G. Noll, and Barry R. Weingast. 1987. "Administrative Procedures as Instruments of Political Control." *Journal of Law, Economics, and Organization* 3 (2): 243–77.

McDermott, Rose. 1998. *Risk-taking in International Politics: Prospect Theory in American Foreign Policy*. Ann Arbor: University of Michigan Press.

Mearsheimer, John J. 1983. *Conventional Deterrence*. Ithaca, NY: Cornell University Press.

——. 2001. "Guns Won't Win the Afghan War." *New York Times*, November 4, 2001. https://www.nytimes.com/2001/11/04/opinion/guns-won-t-win-the-afghan-war.html.

——. 2018. *The Great Delusion: Liberal Dreams and International Realities*. New Haven, CT: Yale University Press.

Meldrum, Andrew. 2003. "David Dacko: Well Meaning, but Ineffectual, African Independence Leader." *The Guardian*, November 24. https://www.theguardian.com/news/2003/nov/25/guardianobituaries.andrewmeldrum.

Mendelsohn, Barak. 2016. *The Al-Qaeda Franchise: The Expansion of al-Qaeda and Its Consequences*. New York: Oxford University Press.

Merom, Gil. 2003. *How Democracies Lose Small Wars: State, Society, and the Failures of France in Algeria, Israel in Lebanon, and the United States in Vietnam*. Cambridge: Cambridge University Press.

Middle East Eye. 2020. "France's Sarkozy Charged with Criminal Conspiracy over Libya Money." October 16, 2020. https://www.middleeasteye.net/news/france-libya-sarkozy-charged-gaddafi-money.

Miller, Edward. 2013. *Misalliance: Ngo Dinh Diem, the United States, and the Fate of South Vietnam*. Cambridge, MA: Harvard University Press.

Miller, Gary J. 2005. "The Political Evolution of Principal-Agent Models." *Annual Review of Political Science* no. 8: 203–25.

Miller, Michael. n.d. "The Uses and Abuses of Matching in Political Science." Unpublished manuscript. Department of Political Science, George Washington University.

Misiunas, Romauld J., and Rein Taagepera. 1993. *The Baltic States: Years of Dependence, 1940–1990*. Expanded and updated ed. Berkeley: University of California Press.

Mitchell, Neil J., Sabine C. Carey, and Christopher K. Butler. 2014. "The Impact of Pro-Government Militias on Human Rights Violations." *International Interactions* 40 (5): 812–36.

Moe, Terry M. 1984. "The New Economics of Organization." *American Journal of Political Science* 28 (4): 739–77.

——. 1985. "Control and Feedback in Economic Regulation: The Case of the NLRB." *American Political Science Review* 79 (4): 1094–1116.

Moore, Frederick. 1927. "Chang Tso-lin Made Dictator in Move to Beat Back South." *New York Times*, June 18, 1927.

Morgan, T. Clifton, Navin Bapat, and Yoshiharu Kobayashi. 2014. "Threat and Imposition of Economic Sanctions, 1945–2005: Updating the TIES Dataset." *Conflict Management and Peace Science* 31 (5): 541–58.

Morgenthau, Hans. 1948. *Politics Among Nations: The Struggle for Power and Peace.* New York: Alfred A. Knopf.

Morris, Benny. 1999. *Righteous Victims: A History of the Zionist-Arab Conflict, 1881–1999.* New York: Alfred A. Knopf.

Morris, Stephen J. 1999. *Why Vietnam Invaded Cambodia: Political Culture and the Causes of War.* Stanford, CA: Stanford University Press.

Morrow, James D., Bruce Bueno de Mesquita, Randolph M. Siverson, and Alastair Smith. 2006. "Selection Institutions and War Aims." *Economics of Governance* 7 (1): 31–52.

Morse, Dan. 2012. "Former 'Sons of Iraq' Targeted by Insurgents after U.S. Pullout." *Washington Post*, January 28, 2012. https://www.washingtonpost.com/world/middle_east/former-sons-of-iraq-targeted-by-sunni-insurgents-after-us-pullout/2012/01/14/gIQAjf49VQ_story.html.

Moyar, Mark. 2007. *Triumph Forsaken: The Vietnam War, 1954–1965.* Cambridge: Cambridge University Press.

Muller, Edward N. 1985. "Income Inequality, Regime Repressiveness, and Political Violence." *American Sociological Review* 50 (1): 47–61.

Muller, Edward N., and Mitchell A. Seligson. 1987. "Inequality and Insurgency." *American Political Science Review* 81 (2): 425–52.

Munro, Dana G. 1964. *Intervention and Dollar Diplomacy in the Caribbean, 1900–1921.* Princeton, NJ: Princeton University Press.

Murray, Williamson, and Allan R. Millett. 2001. *A War to Be Won: Fighting the Second World War.* Cambridge, MA: Belknap Press.

Napoleoni, Loretta. 2005. *Insurgent Iraq: Al Zarqawi and the New Generation.* New York: Seven Stories.

Nathan, Andrew J. 1983. "A Constitutional Republic: The Peking Government, 1916–1928." In *The Cambridge History of Modern China.* Vol. 12, *Republican China, 1912–1949, Part 1,* edited by John K. Fairbank, 259–83. Cambridge: Cambridge University Press.

National Security Archive. 2009. "Kennedy Considered Supporting Coup in South Vietnam, August 1963." https://nsarchive2.gwu.edu/NSAEBB/NSAEBB302/index.htm.

Nelson, Harold D., ed. 1983. *Costa Rica: A Country Study.* Washington, DC: Department of the Army.

Neumayer, Eric, and Thomas Plümper. 2010a. "Making Spatial Analysis Operational: Commands for Generating Spatial-Effect Variables in Monadic and Dyadic Data." *Stata Journal* 10 (4): 585–605.

——. 2010b. "Spatial Effects in Dyadic Data." *International Organization* 64 (1): 145–66.

Ngolet, François. 2011. *Crisis in the Congo: The Rise and Fall of Laurent Kabila*. New York: Palgrave Macmillan.

Nguyen-Vo, Thu-Hong. 1992. *Khmer-Viet Relations and the Third Indochina Conflict*. Jefferson, NC: McFarland.

Nielsen, Daniel L., and Michael J. Tierney. 2003. "Delegation to International Organizations: Agency Theory and World Bank Environmental Reform." *International Organization* 57 (2): 241–76.

Nordland, Rod, and Alissa J. Rubin. 2009. "Sunni Fighters Say Iraq Didn't Keep Job Promises." *New York Times*, March 23, 2009. https://www.nytimes.com/2009/03/24/world/middleeast/24sunni.html.

Norris, J. A. 1967. *The First Afghan War, 1838–1842*. Cambridge: Cambridge University Press.

Nzongola-Ntalaja, Georges. 2002. *The Congo from Leopold to Kabila: A People's History*. London: Zed.

O'Dowd, Edward C. 2007. *Chinese Military Strategy in the Third Indochina War: The Last Maoist War*. London: Routledge.

O'Rourke, Lindsey. 2018. *Covert Regime Change: America's Secret Cold War*. Ithaca, NY: Cornell University Press.

Obama, Barack, David Cameron, and Nicolas Sarkozy. 2011. "Libya's Pathway to Peace." *New York Times*, April 14, 2011. http://www.nytimes.com/2011/04/15/opinion/15iht-edlibya15.html.

Office of the Secretary of Defense Vietnam Task Force. (1969) 2011a. *Pentagon Papers*. Part IV. B. 5, *Evolution of the War: The Overthrow of Ngo Dinh Diem, May–November, 1963*. Washington, DC: National Archives and Records Administration. https://nara-media-001.s3.amazonaws.com/arcmedia/research/pentagon-papers/Pentagon-Papers-Part-IV-B-5.pdf.

——. (1969) 2011b. *Pentagon Papers*. Part IV. C. 1, *Evolution of the War: U.S. Programs in South Vietnam, November 1963–April 1965*. Washington, DC: National Archives and Records Administration. https://nara-media-001.s3.amazonaws.com/arcmedia/research/pentagon-papers/Pentagon-Papers-Part-IV-C-1.pdf.

——. (1969) 2011b. *Pentagon Papers*. Part IV. C. 2.a, *Evolution of the War: Military Pressures Against NVN, February–June 1964*. Washington, DC: National Archives and Records Administration. https://nara-media-001.s3.amazonaws.com/arcmedia/research/pentagon-papers/Pentagon-Papers-Part-IV-C-2a.pdf.

Ollivant, Douglas A. 2011. *Countering the New Orthodoxy: Reinterpreting Counterinsurgency in Iraq*. Washington, DC: National Security Studies Program Policy Paper, New America Foundation.

Oppel, Richard A., Jr. 2008. "Iraq Takes Aim at U.S.-Tied Sunni Groups' Leaders." *New York Times*, August 21, 2008. https://www.nytimes.com/2008/08/22/world/middleeast/22sunni.html.

Owen, John M., IV. 2002. "The Foreign Imposition of Domestic Institutions." *International Organization* 56 (2): 375–409.

——. 2010. *The Clash of Ideas in World Politics: Transnational Networks, States, and Regime Change, 1510–2010*. Princeton, NJ: Princeton University Press.

Packer, George. 2005. *The Assassins' Gate: America in Iraq*. New York: Farrar, Straus and Giroux.

Paine, S. C. M. 2012. *The Wars for Asia, 1911–1949*. Cambridge: Cambridge University Press.

Palmerston, Henry John Temple. 1848. "Remarks in the House of Commons." March 1.

Pao-Min, Chang. 1985. *Kampuchea between China and Vietnam*. Singapore: Singapore University Press.

Pape, Robert A. 1996. *Bombing to Win: Air Power and Coercion in War*. Ithaca, NY: Cornell University Press.

——. 1997. "Why Economic Sanctions Do Not Work." *International Security* 22 (2): 90–136.

——. 2003. "The Strategic Logic of Suicide Terrorism." *American Political Science Review* 97 (3): 343–61.

——. 2004. "The True Worth of Air Power." *Foreign Affairs* 83 (2): 116–30.

——. 2005. *Dying to Win: The Strategic Logic of Suicide Terrorism*. New York: Random House.

Pape, Robert A., Kevin Ruby, and Vincent Bauer. 2015. "Hammer and Anvil: How to Defeat ISIS." *Foreign Affairs*, January 2, 2015. https://www.foreignaffairs.com/articles/iraq/2015-01-02/hammer-and-anvil.

Peceny, Mark, Caroline C. Beer, and Shannon Sanchez-Terry. 2002. "Dictatorial Peace?" *American Political Science Review* 96 (1): 15–26.

Pei, Minxin, and Sara Kasper, S. 2003. "Lessons from the Past: The American Record on Nation Building." Policy Brief 24, Carnegie Endowment for International Peace, Washington, DC.

Peic, Goran, and Dan Reiter. 2011. "Foreign-Imposed Regime Change, State Power, and Civil War Onset, 1920–2004." *British Journal of Political Science* 41 (3): 453–75.

Pelofsky, Eric. 2017. "Tillerson Lets Slip He Wants Regime Change in Iran." *Newsweek*, June 27, 2017. https://www.newsweek.com/tillerson-lets-slip-he-wants-regime-change-iran-629096.

Penney, Joe. 2018. "Why Did the U.S. and Its Allies Bomb Libya? Corruption Case against Sarkozy Sheds New Light on Ousting of Gaddafi." theintercept.com, April 28, 2018. https://theintercept.com/2018/04/28/sarkozy-gaddafi-libya-bombing/.

Perry, Mark. 2016. "James Mattis' 33-Year Grudge against Iran." *Politico*, December 4, 2016. http://www.politico.com/magazine/story/2016/12/james-mattis-iran-secretary-of-defense-214500.

Petersen, Roger D. 2001. *Resistance and Rebellion: Lessons from Eastern Europe*. Cambridge: Cambridge University Press.

——. 2002. *Understanding Ethnic Violence: Fear, Hatred, and Resentment in Twentieth-Century Eastern Europe*. Cambridge: Cambridge University Press.

Petersen, Walter J. 1986. "Deterrence and Compellence: A Critical Assessment of Conventional Wisdom." *International Studies Quarterly* 30 (3): 269–94.

Petit, Kevin S. 2020. "The Crying Game: The Logic of Armed Group Alliance in Civil War." PhD diss., George Washington University.

Petraeus, David H. 2007. "Charts to Accompany the Testimony of Gen. David H. Petraeus." United States Congress. House Armed Services and Foreign Affairs Committees. September 10–11, 2007.

Pfundstein-Chamberlain, Dianne. 2016. *Cheap Threats: Why the United States Struggles to Coerce Weak States*. Washington, DC: Georgetown University Press.

Phillips, Charles, and Alan Axelrod. 2005. *Encyclopedia of Wars*. New York: Facts on File.

Phillips, David L. 2005. *Losing Iraq: Inside the Postwar Reconstruction Fiasco*. Boulder, CO: Westview.

Piazza, James A. 2008. "A Supply-Side View of Suicide Terrorism: A Cross-National Study." *Journal of Politics* 70 (1): 28–39.

Pletka, Danielle. 2016. "'Regime Change' Has Often Succeeded." *New York Times*, July 25. https://www.nytimes.com/roomfordebate/2016/02/28/pursuing-regime-change-in-the-middle-east/regime-change-has-often-succeeded.

Poast, Paul. 2016. "Dyads Are Dead, Long Live Dyads! The Limits but Not Rejection of Dyadic Designs in International Relations Research." *International Studies Quarterly* 60 (2): 369–74.

Polk, William R. 2013. *Humpty Dumpty: The Fate of Regime Change*. United States: Panda Press.

Polyviou, Polyvios G. 1980. *Cyprus: Conflict and Negotiation, 1960–1980*. New York: Holmes and Meier.

Pomfret, John. 1997. "Rwandans Led Revolt in Congo." *Washington Post*, July 9. https://www.washingtonpost.com/archive/politics/1997/07/09/rwandans-led-revolt-in-congo/7d210372-e307-4222-a04b-a65cd816be5f/.

Posen, Barry R. 1984. *The Sources of Military Doctrine: France, Britain, and Germany between the World Wars*. Ithaca, NY: Cornell University Press.

———. 1993. "The Security Dilemma and Ethnic Conflict." *Survival* 35 (1): 27–47.

Pottier, Johan. 2002. *Re-imagining Rwanda: Conflict, Survival and Disinformation in the Late Twentieth Century*. Cambridge: Cambridge University Press.

Power, Samantha. 2002. *"A Problem from Hell": America and the Age of Genocide*. New York: Basic Books.

Prados, John. 2006. *Safe for Democracy: The Secret Wars of the CIA*. Chicago: Ivan R. Dee.

Preston, Diana. 2012. *The Dark Defile: Britain's Catastrophic Invasion of Afghanistan, 1838–1842*. New York: Walker.

Preston, Paul. 1993. *Franco: A Biography*. London: HarperCollins.

Price, Bryan C. 2012. "Targeting Top Terrorists: How Leadership Decapitation Contributes to Counterterrorism." *International Security* 36 (4): 9–46.

Prunier, Gérard. 1995. *The Rwanda Crisis: History of a Genocide*. New York: Columbia University Press.

———. 2009. *Africa's World War: Congo, the Rwandan Genocide, and the Making of a Continental Catastrophe*. Oxford: Oxford University Press.

Purs, Aidis. 1998. "Creating the State from Above and Below: Local Government in Inter-War Latvia." PhD diss., University of Toronto.

Quinlivan, James T. 1995. "Force Requirements in Stability Operations." *Parameters* 25 (4): 59–69.

———. 1999. "Coup-Proofing: Its Practice and Consequences in the Middle East." *International Security* 24 (2): 131–65.

Quinn, Andrew. 2011. "Clinton Says Gaddafi Must Go." *Reuters*, February 27, 2011. http://www.reuters.com/article/us-libya-usa-clinton/clinton-says-gaddafi-must-go-idUSTRE71Q1JA20110228.

Quinn-Judge, Sophie. 2006. "Victory on the Battlefield; Isolation in Asia: Vietnam's Cambodia Decade, 1979–1989." In *The Third Indochina War: Conflict between China, Vietnam and Cambodia, 1972–79*, edited by Odd Arne Westad and Sophie Quinn-Judge, 207–30. London: Routledge.

Qureshi, Lubna Z. 2009. *Nixon, Kissinger, and Allende: U.S. Involvement in the 1973 Coup in Chile*. Lanham, MD: Lexington.

Rabaud, Marlene, and Arnaud Zajtman, dir. 2011. *Murder in Kinshasa*. Al Jazeera, October 28, 2011. https://www.aljazeera.com/videos/2011/10/27/murder-in -kinshasa-2.

Rabe, Stephen G. 2016. *The Killing Zone: The United States Wages Cold War in Latin America*. 2nd ed. Oxford: Oxford University Press.

Randers-Pehrson, Justine Davis. 1999. *Germans and the Revolution of 1848–1849*. New York: Peter Lang.

Rasheed, Saif, and Tina Susman. 2008. "Iraq, U.S.-funded Militia at Loggerheads." *Los Angeles Times*, September 28, 2008. https://www.latimes.com/world/la-fg -sons12-2008sep12-story.html.

Rashid, Ahmed. 2008. *Descent into Chaos: The U.S. and the Disaster in Pakistan, Afghanistan, and Central Asia*. New York: Penguin.

Raun, Toivo U. 2001. *Estonia and the Estonians*. 2nd ed. Stanford, CA: Hoover Institution Press.

Recovery of Historical Memory Project. 1999. *Guatemala: Never Again!* Maryknoll, NY: Orbis.

Reisman, W. Michael. 2004. "The Manley O. Hudson Lecture: Why Regime Change is Almost Always a Bad Idea." *American Journal of International Law* 98 (3): 516–25.

Reiter, Dan. 2009. *How Wars End*. Princeton, NJ: Princeton University Press.

Reyntjens, Filip. 1999. "Briefing: The Second Congo War: More than a Remake." *African Affairs* 98 (391): 241–50.

——. 2009. *The Great African War: Congo and Regional Geopolitics, 1996–2006*. Cambridge: Cambridge University Press.

Richards, D. S. 1990. *The Savage Frontier: A History of the Anglo-Afghan Wars*. London: Macmillan.

Richards, Michael. 2012. "Violence and the Post-Conflict State in Historical Perspective: Spain, 1936–48." In *The Peace in Between: Post-war Violence and Peacebuilding*, edited by Astri Suhrke and Mats Berdal, 27–48. London: Routledge.

Richardson, Michael. 2000. "Singaporean Tells of Khmer Rouge Aid." *New York Times*, September 29, 2000. https://www.nytimes.com/2000/09/29/news /singaporean-tells-of-khmer-rouge-aid.html.

Ricks, Thomas E. 2006. *Fiasco: The American Military Adventure in Iraq*. New York: Penguin.

Ridley, Jasper. 1992. *Maximilian and Juárez*. New York: Ticknor and Fields.

Riedel, Bruce. 2008. *The Search for Al Qaida: Its Leadership, Ideology, and Future*. Washington, DC: Brookings Institution Press.

Roberts, Jeffrey J. 2003. *The Origins of Conflict in Afghanistan*. Westport, CT: Praeger.

Roberts, Les, Pascal Ngoy, Colleen Mone, Charles Lubula, Luc Mwezse, Mariana Zantop, and Michael Despines. 2003. *Mortality in the Democratic Republic of Congo: Results from a Nationwide Survey*. New York: International Rescue Committee.

Robertson, William Spence. 1940. "The Tripartite Treaty of London." *Hispanic American Historical Review* 20 (2): 167–89.

Robinson, Linda. 2008. *Tell Me How This Ends: General David Petraeus and the Search for a Way Out of Iraq*. New York: PublicAffairs.

Roeder, Philip G. 2001. "Ethnolinguistic Fractionalization (ELF) Indices, 1961 and 1985." http://pages.ucsd.edu/~proeder/elf.htm.

Roessler, Philip. 2016. *Ethnic Politics and State Power in Africa: The Logic of the Coup-Civil War Trap.* Cambridge: Cambridge University Press.

Romkema, Hans. 2007. *Opportunities and Constraints for the Disarmament and Repatriation of Foreign Armed Groups in the Democratic Republic of Congo: The Cases of the FDLR, FNL and ADF/NALU.* Washington, DC: World Bank.

Rosenberg, Matthew. 2013. "With Bags of Cash, C.I.A. Seeks Influence in Afghanistan." *New York Times*, April 28, 2013. https://www.nytimes.com/2013/04/29/world/asia/cia-delivers-cash-to-afghan-leaders-office.html.

Rosenberg, Matthew, and Helene Cooper. 2012. "Karzai Lashes Out at NATO over Deaths." *New York Times*, March 16, 2012. https://www.nytimes.com/2012/03/17/world/asia/karzai-lashes-out-at-united-states-over-inquiry-on-massacre.html.

Rosenblum, Peter. 1998. "Kabila's Congo." *Current History* 97 (619): 193–99.

Ross, Martha, and Bertold Spuler. 1977. *Rulers and Governments of the World: 1492–1929.* Vol. 2. London: Bowker.

Ross, Michael. 2004. "How Do Natural Resources Influence Civil War? Evidence from Thirteen Cases." *International Organization* 58 (1): 35–67.

———. 2006. "A Closer Look at Oil, Diamonds, and Civil War." *Annual Review of Political Science* no. 9: 265–300.

———. 2012. *The Oil Curse: How Petroleum Wealth Shapes the Development of Nations.* Princeton, NJ: Princeton University Press.

Rowley, Kelvin. 2006. "Second Life, Second Death: The Khmer Rouge after 1978." In *Genocide in Cambodia and Rwanda*, edited by S. E. Cook, 191–214. New Brunswick, NJ: Transaction.

Rubin, Alissa J., and Thom Shanker. 2013. "Afghan Leader Says U.S. Abets Taliban's Goal." *New York Times*, March 10, 2013. https://www.nytimes.com/2013/03/11/world/asia/karzai-accuses-us-and-taliban-of-colluding-in-afghanistan.html.

Rubin, James P. 2012. "The Real Reason to Intervene in Syria." Foreign Policy, June 4. https://foreignpolicy.com/2012/06/04/the-real-reason-to-intervene-in-syria/.

Ruiz, Julius. 2005. "A Spanish Genocide? Reflections on the Francoist Repression after the Spanish Civil War." *Contemporary European History* 14 (2): 171–91.

———. 2007. "Defending the Republic: The García Atadell Brigade in Madrid, 1936." *Journal of Contemporary History* 42 (1): 97–115.

Rungswasdisab, Puangthong. 2004. *Thailand's Response to the Cambodian Genocide.* New Haven, CT: Macmillan Center for International and Area Studies, Yale University.

Russett, Bruce. 1964. "Inequality and Instability: The Relation of Land Tenure to Politics." *World Politics* 16 (3): 442–54.

———. 1993. *Grasping the Democratic Peace: Principles for a Post-Cold War World.* Princeton, NJ: Princeton University Press.

Salehyan, Idean. 2009. *Rebels without Borders: Transnational Insurgencies in World Politics.* Ithaca, NY: Cornell University Press.

———. 2010. "The Delegation of War to Rebel Organizations." *Journal of Conflict Resolution* 54 (3): 493–515.

Salehyan, Idean, and Kristian Skrede Gleditsch. 2006. "Refugees and the Spread of Civil War." *International Organization* 60 (2): 335–66.

Salehyan, Idean, David Siroky, and Reed M. Wood. 2014. "External Rebel Sponsorship and Civilian Abuse: A Principal-Agent Analysis of Wartime Atrocities." *International Organization* 68 (3): 633–61.

Sambanis, Nicholas. 2004. "What Is Civil War? Conceptual and Empirical Complexities of an Operational Definition." *Journal of Conflict Resolution* 48 (6): 814–58.

———. 2006. "It's Official: There Is Now a Civil War in Iraq." *New York Times*, July 23, 2006. https://www.nytimes.com/2006/07/23/opinion/23sambanis.html.

Sanger, David E. 2003. "Aftereffects: Nuclear Standoff; Administration Divided over North Korea." *New York Times*, April 21, 2003. https://www.nytimes.com/2003/04/21/world/aftereffects-nuclear-standoff-administration-divided-over-north-korea.html.

Sarkees, Meredith, and Frank Wayman. 2010. *Resort to War: 1816–2007*. Washington, DC: CQ.

Sater, William F. 1986. *Chile and the War of the Pacific*. Lincoln: University of Nebraska Press.

———. 2007. *Andean Tragedy: Fighting the War of the Pacific, 1879–1884*. Lincoln: University of Nebraska Press.

Saunders, Elizabeth N. 2011. *Leaders at War: How Presidents Shape Military Interventions*. Ithaca, NY: Cornell University Press.

———. 2017. "No Substitute for Experience: Presidents, Advisers, and Information in Group Decision Making." *International Organization* 71 (S1): S219–S247.

Sbacchi, Alberto. 1979. "Haile Selassie and the Italians, 1941–1943." *African Studies Review* 22 (1): 25–42.

Scheina, Robert L. 2003. *Latin America's Wars*. Vol. 1, *The Age of the Caudillo, 1791–1899*. Washington, DC: Brassey's.

Schemmel, B. n.d. *Rulers*. http://rulers.org.

Schirmer, Jennifer. 1998. *The Guatemalan Military Project: A Violence Called Democracy*. Philadelphia: University of Pennsylvania Press.

Schlesinger, Stephen, and Stephen Kinzer. 1999. *Bitter Fruit: The Story of the American Coup in Guatemala*. Expanded ed. Cambridge, MA: Harvard University Press.

Schmidt, Hans. 1971. *The United States Occupation of Haiti, 1915–1934*. New Brunswick, NJ: Rutgers University Press.

Schmitt, Eric. 2003. "Threats and Responses: Military Spending; Pentagon Contradicts General on Iraq Occupation Force's Size." *New York Times*, February 28, 2003. https://www.nytimes.com/2003/02/28/us/threats-responses-military-spending-pentagon-contradicts-general-iraq-occupation.html.

Schmitz, David F. 1999. *Thank God They're on Our Side: The United States and Right-Wing Dictatorships, 1921–1965*. Chapel Hill: University of North Carolina Press.

———. 2006. *The United States and Right-Wing Dictatorships, 1965–1989*. Cambridge: Cambridge University Press.

Schoonover, Thomas D. 1991. *The United States in Central America, 1860–1911: Episodes of Social Imperialism and Imperial Rivalry in the World System*. Durham, NC: Duke University Press.

Schramm, Madison, and Ariane M. Tabatabai. 2017. "Why Regime Change in Iran Wouldn't Work." *Foreign Affairs*, July 20, 2017. https://www.foreignaffairs.com/articles/persian-gulf/2017-07-20/why-regime-change-iran-wouldnt-work?cid=nlc-fa_twofa-20170720.

Schroeder, Paul W. 1962. *Metternich's Diplomacy at Its Zenith, 1820–1823*. Austin: University of Texas Press.

———. 1994. *The Transformation of European Politics, 1763–1848*. New York: Oxford University Press.

Schultz, Kenneth A. 1998. "Domestic Opposition and Signaling in International Crises." *American Political Science Review* 92 (4): 829–44.

Scott, James C. 1976. *The Moral Economy of the Peasant: Rebellion and Subsistence in Southeast Asia*. New Haven, CT: Yale University Press.

Sechser, Todd S. 2010. "Goliath's Curse: Coercive Threats and Asymmetric Power." *International Organization* 64 (4): 627–60.

———. 2011. "Militarized Compellent Threats, 1918–2001." *Conflict Management and Peace Science* 28 (4): 377–401.

———. 2018. "Reputations and Signaling in Coercive Bargaining." *Journal of Conflict Resolution* 62 (2): 318–45.

Sekhon, Jasjeet S. 2011. "Multivariate and Propensity Score Matching Software with Automated Balance Optimization: The Matching Package for R." *Journal of Statistical Software* 42 (7): 1–52.

Shai, Aron. 2012. *Zhang Zueliang: The General Who Never Fought*. Houndmills: Palgrave Macmillan.

Shaw, Stanford, and Ezel Shaw. 1977. *History of the Ottoman Empire and Modern Turkey*. Cambridge: Cambridge University Press.

Sheridan, James. 1983. "The Warlord Era: Politics and Militarism under the Peking Government, 1916–28." In *The Cambridge History of China*. Vol. 12, *Republican China, 1912–1949, Part 1*, edited by John K. Fairbank, 284–321. Cambridge: Cambridge University Press.

Shipan, Charles R. 2004. "Regulatory Regimes, Agency Actions, and the Conditional Nature of Congressional Influence." *American Political Science Review* 98 (3): 467–80.

Shlaim, Avi. 1988. *Collusion across the Jordan: King Abdullah, the Zionist Movement, and the Partition of Palestine*. New York: Columbia University Press.

———. 1997. "The Protocol of Sèvres, 1956: Anatomy of a War Plot." *International Affairs* 73 (3): 509–30.

Showalter, Dennis E. 2004. *The Wars of German Unification*. London: Arnold.

Shtromas, Alexander. 1986. *The Soviet Method of Conquest of the Baltic States: Lessons for the West*. Washington, DC: Washington Institute for Values in Public Policy.

Sieff, Kevin. 2014a. "Interview: Karzai Says 12-year Afghanistan War Has Left Him Angry at U.S. Government." *Washington Post*, March 2, 2014. https://www.washingtonpost.com/world/interview-karzai-says-12-year-afghanistan-war-has-left-him-angry-at-us-government/2014/03/02/b831671c-a21a-11e3-b865-38b254d92063_story.html.

———. 2014b. "Karzai Suspects U.S. is Behind Insurgent-Style Attacks, Afghan Officials Say." *Washington Post*, January 27, 2014. https://www.washingtonpost.com/world/karzai-suspects-us-is-behind-insurgent-style-attacks-afghan-officials-say/2014/01/27/a70d7568-8779-11e3-a760-a86415d0944d_story.html.

Sigmund, Paul E. 1977. *The Overthrow of Allende and the Politics of Chile, 1964–1976*. Pittsburgh: University of Pittsburgh Press.

Signorino, Curtis S., and Jeffrey M. Ritter. 1999. "Tau-b or Not Tau-b: Measuring the Similarity of Foreign Policy Positions." *International Studies Quarterly* 43 (1): 115–44.

Simons, Marlise. 1995. "1,000 French Troops Invade Comoros to Put Down Coup." *New York Times*, October 5. https://www.nytimes.com/1995/10/05/world/1000 -french-troops-invade-comoros-to-put-down-coup.html.

Sky, Emma. 2015. *The Unraveling: High Hopes and Missed Opportunities in Iraq*. New York: PublicAffairs.

Smith, David J. 2002. *The Baltic States: Estonia, Latvia and Lithuania*. London: Routledge.

Smith, Tony. 1994. *America's Mission: The United States and the Worldwide Struggle for Democracy in the Twentieth Century*. Princeton, NJ: Princeton University Press.

Šneidere, Irēne. 2005. "The Occupation of Latvia in June 1940: A Few Aspects of the Technology of Soviet Aggression." In *The Hidden and Forbidden History of Latvia under Soviet and Nazi Occupations, 1940–1991*, edited by Valters Nollendorfs and Erwin Oberländer, 43–52. Riga: Institute of the History of Latvia.

Snyder, David, and Charles Tilly. 1972. "Hardship and Collective Violence in France, 1830 to 1960." *American Sociological Review* 37 (5): 520–32.

Snyder, Jack, and Erica D. Borghard. 2011. "The Cost of Empty Threats: A Penny, Not a Pound." *American Political Science Review* 105 (3): 437–56.

Stearns, Jason. 2011. *Dancing in the Glory of Monsters: The Collapse of the Congo and the Great War of Africa*. New York: PublicAffairs.

Stevenson, David. 2004. *Cataclysm: The First World War as Political Tragedy*. New York: Basic Books.

Stewart, Frances, ed. 2008. *Horizontal Inequalities and Conflict: Understanding Group Violence in Multiethnic Societies*. Houndmills: Palgrave Macmillan.

Straus, Scott. 2006. *The Order of Genocide: Race, Power, and War in Rwanda*. Ithaca, NY: Cornell University Press.

Streeter, Stephen M. 2000. *Managing the Counterrevolution: The United States and Guatemala, 1954–1961*. Athens: Ohio University Center for International Studies.

Su, Ruolin. 2017–18. "Correspondence: Reconsidering the Effects of Foreign-Imposed Regime Change." *International Security* 42 (3): 172–77.

Suleski, Ronald. 2002. *Civil Government in Warlord China: Tradition, Modernization and Manchuria*. New York: Peter Lang.

Sullivan, Michael J., III. 2008. *American Adventurism Abroad: Invasions, Interventions, and Regime Changes since World War II*. Revised and expanded ed. Malden, MA: Blackwell.

Sullivan, Patricia L., and Johannes Karreth. 2015. "The Conditional Impact of Military Intervention on Internal Armed Conflict Outcomes." *Conflict Management and Peace Science* 32 (3): 269–88.

Sullivan, Patricia L., and Michael T. Koch. 2009. "Military Intervention by Powerful States, 1945–2003." *Journal of Peace Research* 46 (5): 707–18.

Suskind, Ron. 2006. *The One Percent Doctrine: Deep Inside America's Pursuit of Its Enemies since 9/11*. New York: Simon and Schuster.

Taliaferro, Jeffrey W. 2004. *Balancing Risks: Great Power Intervention in the Periphery*. Ithaca, NY: Cornell University Press.

Talmadge, Caitlin. 2015. *The Dictator's Army: Battlefield Effectiveness in Authoritarian Regimes*. Ithaca, NY: Cornell University Press.

Talmadge, Caitlin, and Vipin Narang. 2018. "Civil-Military Pathologies and Defeat in War: Tests Using New Data." *Journal of Conflict Resolution* 62 (7): 1379–1405.

Taylor, Adam. 2014. "Karzai Joins a Long List of Leaders Ungrateful for U.S. Support." *Washington Post*, September 25, 2014. https://www.washingtonpost.com /news/worldviews/wp/2014/09/25/karzai-joins-a-long-list-of-leaders-ungrateful -for-u-s-support/.

Téllez, Antonio. 1996. "Armed Resistance to Franco, 1939–1965." libcom.org, September 25, 1996. https://libcom.org/history/articles/armed-resistance-to-franco.

Terry, Fiona. 2002. *Condemned to Repeat? The Paradox of Humanitarian Action*. Ithaca, NY: Cornell University Press.

Thom, William G. 1999. "Congo-Zaire's 1996–97 Civil War in the Context of Evolving Patterns of Military Conflict in Africa in the Era of Independence." *Journal of Conflict Studies* 19 (2): 93–123.

Thrall, A. Trevor, and Jane K. Cramer. 2009. *American Foreign Policy and the Politics of Fear: Threat Inflation since 9/11*. Abingdon: Routledge.

Thucydides. 1954. *History of the Peloponnesian War*. Translated by Rex Warner. New York: Penguin.

Thyne, Clayton L., and Jonathan M. Powell. 2016. "Coup d'état or Coup d'Autocracy? How Coups Impact Democratization, 1950–2008." *Foreign Policy Analysis* 12 (2): 192–213.

Tilly, Charles. 1978. *From Mobilization to Revolution*. Reading, MA: Addison-Wesley.

Titley, Brian. 1997. *Dark Age: The Political Odyssey of Emperor Bokassa*. Montreal: McGill-Queen's University Press.

Toft, Monica D. 2003. *The Geography of Ethnic Violence: Identity, Interests, and the Indivisibility of Territory*. Princeton, NJ: Princeton University Press.

Tomz, Michael. 2007. "Domestic Audience Costs in International Relations: An Experimental Approach." *International Organization* 61 (4): 821–40.

Tomz, Michael, Jason Wittenberg, and Gary King. 2003. "Clarify: Software for Interpreting and Presenting Statistical Results." *Journal of Statistical Software* 8 (1): 1–30.

Trachtenberg, Marc. 2011. "Audience Costs: A Historical Analysis." *Security Studies* 21 (1): 3–42.

Turner, Thomas. 2007. *The Congo Wars: Conflict, Myth, and Reality*. London: Zed.

——. 2013. *Congo*. Cambridge: Polity.

United Nations. 2005. "Sierra Leone—UNAMSIL—Background." UNAMSIL: United Nations Mission in Sierra Leone. https://peacekeeping.un.org/mission /past/unamsil/background.html.

US Department of State (USDS). 1954a. "Mass Arrests of 'Communist' Peasant Leaders." Dispatch 75 from William L. Krieg, American Embassy, Guatemala, July 29, 1954. Record Group 59, 714.00/7–2954.

——. 1954b. "Political Arrests in Guatemala." Dispatch 75 from American Embassy, Guatemala, September 21, 1954. Record Group 59, 714.00/9–2154.

——. 1983. *Foreign Relations of the United States, 1952–1954: The American Republics*. Vol. 4. Edited by N. Stephen Kane and William F. Sanford Jr. Washington, DC: Government Printing Office.

——. 1991a. *Foreign Relations of the United States, 1961–1963*. Vol. 3, *Vietnam, January–August 1963*. Edited by Edward C. Keefer and Louis J. Smith. Washington, DC: Government Printing Office. https://history.state.gov/historicaldocuments/frus1961-63v03.

——. 1991b. *Foreign Relations of the United States, 1961–1963*. Vol. 4, *Vietnam, August–December 1963*. Edited by Edward C. Keefer. Washington, DC: Government Printing Office. https://history.state.gov/historicaldocuments/frus1961-63v04.

——. 1992. *Foreign Relations of the United States, 1964*. Vol. 1, *Vietnam, 1964*. Edited by Edward C. Keefer and Charles S. Sampson. Washington, DC: Government Printing Office. https://history.state.gov/historicaldocuments/frus1964-68v01.

Valentin, Veit. 1965. *1848: Chapters of German History*. Translated by Ethel Talbott Scheffauer. Hamden, CT: Archon.

van der Kroef, Justus M. 1983. "Refugees and Rebels: Dimensions of the Thai-Kampuchean Border Conflict." *Asian Affairs* 10 (1): 19–36.

Vanhanen, Tatu. 2000. "A New Dataset for Measuring Democracy, 1810–1998." *Journal of Peace Research* 37 (2): 251–65.

Vanover, Christie. 2009. "Belgians Recall Battle of the Bulge." *DOD News*, US Department of Defense, December 3, 2009. https://www.dvidshub.net/news/42302/belgians-recall-battle-bulge.

Van Reybrouck, David. 2014. *Congo: The Epic History of a People*. Translated by Sam Garrett. New York: HarperCollins.

van Voren, Robert. 2011. *Undigested Past: The Holocaust in Lithuania*. Amsterdam: Rodopi.

Vaulerin, Arnaud, Hélène Despic-Popovic, and Thomas Hofnung. 2011. "Côte d'Ivoire: Gbagbo Capitule." *Liberation*, April 12, 2011. https://www.liberation.fr/planete/2011/04/12/cote-d-ivoire-gbagbo-capitule_728451.

Vlahos, Kelley Beaucar. 2013. "Neocons Are Back—But Not in the GOP." *American Conservative*, September 5, 2013. http://www.theamericanconservative.com/articles/neocons-are-back-but-not-in-the-gop/?print=1.

Volpe, Tristan A. 2017. "Atomic Leverage: Compellence with Nuclear Latency." *Security Studies* 26 (3): 517–44.

Vreeland, James R. 2008. "The Effect of Political Regime on Civil War: Unpacking Anocracy." *Journal of Conflict Resolution* 52 (3): 401–25.

Vulliamy, Ed. 2002. "Venezuela Coup Linked to Bush Team." *The Guardian*, April 21, 2002. https://www.theguardian.com/world/2002/apr/21/usa.venezuela.

Waller, John H. 1990. *Beyond the Khyber Pass: The Road to British Disaster in the First Afghan War*. New York: Random House.

Walter, Barbara F. 1997. "The Critical Barrier to Civil War Settlement." *International Organization* 51 (3): 335–64.

——. 2002. *Committing to Peace: The Successful Settlement of Civil Wars*. Princeton, NJ: Princeton University Press.

Waltz, Kenneth N. 1959. *Man, The State, and War: A Theoretical Analysis*. New York: Columbia University Press.

Wang, Chi. 1969. "Young Marshal Chang Hsueh-liang and Manchuria: 1928–1931." PhD diss., Georgetown University.

Warren, Harris Gaylord. 1978. *Paraguay and the Triple Alliance: The Postwar Decade, 1869–1878*. Austin: University of Texas Press.

Warrick, Joby. 2015. *Black Flags: The Rise of ISIS*. New York: Anchor.

Watkins, Eli. 2017. "CIA Chief Signals Desire for Regime Change in North Korea." *cnn.com*, July 21, 2017. https://www.cnn.com/2017/07/20/politics/cia-mike-pompeo-north-korea/index.html.

Weber, Max. 2009. "Politics as a Vocation." In *From Max Weber: Essays in Sociology*, translated and edited by H. H. Gerth and C. Wright Mills, 77–128. Abingdon: Routledge.

Weeks, Jessica L. 2008. "Autocratic Audience Costs: Regime Type and Signaling Resolve." *International Organization* 62 (1): 35–64.

———. 2014. *Dictators at War and Peace*. Ithaca, NY: Cornell University Press.

Weinberg, Gerhard L. 1994. *A World at Arms: A Global History of World War II*. Cambridge: Cambridge University Press.

Weiner, Tim. 2007. *Legacy of Ashes: The History of the CIA*. New York: Doubleday.

Weisiger, Alex. 2013. *Logics of War: Explanations for Limited and Unlimited Conflicts*. Ithaca, NY: Cornell University Press.

Weissman, Stephen R. 2014. "What Really Happened in Congo: The CIA, the Murder of Lumumba, and the Rise of Mobutu." *Foreign Affairs* 93 (4): 14–24.

Werner, Suzanne. 1996. "Absolute and Limited War: The Possibility of Foreign-Imposed Regime Change." *International Interactions* 22 (1): 67–88.

Whigham, Thomas. 2002. *The Paraguayan War*. Lincoln: University of Nebraska Press.

Wickham-Crowley, Timothy P. 1990. "Terror and Guerrilla Warfare in Latin America, 1956–1970." *Comparative Studies in Society and History* 32 (2): 201–37.

Wilber, Donald N. 1954. *Clandestine Service History: Overthrow of Premier Mossadeq of Iran, November 1952–August 1953*. Washington, DC: Central Intelligence Agency.

Wilbur, C. Martin. 1983. "The Nationalist Revolution: From Canton to Nanking, 1923–28." In *The Cambridge History of Modern China*. Vol. 12, *Republican China, 1912–1949, Part 1*, edited by John K. Fairbank, 527–721. Cambridge: Cambridge University Press.

Willard-Foster, Melissa. 2018. *Toppling Foreign Governments: The Logic of Regime Change*. Philadelphia: University of Pennsylvania Press.

Williams, William Appleman. 1959. *The Tragedy of American Diplomacy*. Cleveland, OH: World.

Wilson, Dick. 1991. *China's Revolutionary War*. New York: St. Martin's.

Wilson, Scott, and Joby Warrick. 2011. "Assad Must Go, Obama Says." *Washington Post*, August 18, 2011. https://www.washingtonpost.com/politics/assad-must-go-obama-says/2011/08/18/gIQAelheOJ_story.html.

Wimmer, Andreas, Lars-Erik Cederman, and Brian Min. 2009. "Ethnic Politics and Armed Conflict: A Configurational Analysis of a New Global Dataset." *American Sociological Review* 74 (3): 316–37.

Wing, Joel. 2008. "The End of the Diyala Sons of Iraq?" *Musings on Iraq*, September 15, 2008. http://musingsoniraq.blogspot.com/2008/09/end-of-diyala-sons-of-iraq.html.

Winter, Roger. 2004. "Lancing the Boil: Rwanda's Agenda in Zaire." In *War and Peace in Zaire-Congo: Analyzing and Evaluating Intervention, 1996–1997*, edited by Howard Adelman and Govind C. Rao, 109–36. Trenton, NJ: Africa World Press.

Winters, Francis X. 1997. *The Year of the Hare: America in Vietnam, January 25, 1963–February 15, 1964*. Athens: University of Georgia Press.

Wolford, Scott, Dan Reiter, and Clifford J. Carrubba. 2011. "Information, Commitment, and War." *Journal of Conflict Resolution* 55 (4): 556–79.

Woods, Kevin M. 2006. *The Iraqi Perspectives Report: Saddam's Senior Leadership on Operation Iraqi Freedom from the Official U.S. Joint Forces Command Report*. Annapolis, MD: Naval Institute Press.

Woodward, Bob. 2002. *Bush at War*. New York: Simon and Schuster.

Zachary, Paul, Alexander B. Downes, and Kathleen Deloughery. 2017. "No Business Like FIRC Business: Foreign-Imposed Regime Change and Bilateral Trade." *British Journal of Political Science* 47 (4): 749–82.

Index

Note: Tables are indicated by t, figures by f.

CPSIA information can be obtained
at www.ICGtesting.com
Printed in the USA
LVHW110926221022
731322LV00016B/199/J